ADMINISTRATIVE LAW
IN SCOTLAND

GREENS CONCISE SCOTS LAW

ADMINISTRATIVE LAW IN SCOTLAND

By

Christine Ashton, LL.B. (Hons.), M.A.,
Lecturer in Law, Napier University

and

Valerie Finch, LL.B. (Hons.), M.Sc.,
Senior Lecturer in Law, Napier University

W. GREEN/Sweet & Maxwell
EDINBURGH
1997

First published 1997

© 1997
W. GREEN & SON LTD

No natural forests were destroyed to make this product;
only farmed timber was used and replanted

ISBN 0 414 01144 9

A CIP catalogue reference of this book is available from the British Library

Typeset by Trinity Typesetting, Edinburgh
Printed in Great Britain by Redwood Books, Trowbridge, Wiltshire

PREFACE

Writing a book is a bit like painting the Forth Bridge; no sooner are you finished one bit, than you find that it has to be repainted, or in our case, rewritten. This book has certainly been our Forth Bridge; during the closing stages of writing, there was a General Election and the new Labour Government took office. This has heralded a number of changes, the effects of which will be become clearer in the coming months. These include the devolution proposals for Scotland, the moratorium on competitive tendering in the public sector while the Government's "best value" proposals are finalised, the future introduction of a Freedom of Information Bill to Parliament and the incorporation of the European Convention on Human Rights into the law of the United Kingdom. These will impact upon some of the sections of this book and so the reader should bear these in mind.

We have been greatly assisted by a number of friends and colleagues during the preparation of the book. In particular, we thank Alison Scott who worked as our research assistant at a crucial point in the book and whose meticulous attention to detail was much appreciated. We also acknowledge the assistance of the Law University, Francis McManus and Eleanor Russell, read various chapters of the book and made detailed and helpful comments. Our grateful thanks go to them, with the acknowledgment that any errors in the book are entirely our responsibility. We have tried to ensure that the law is accurately stated as at March 31, 1997.

Finally, we could not have written this book without the love, support and encouragement of our families and so we dedicate it to them — to Ted, Ben, Simon and Fiona, and to Ron, Ronnie and Caroline.

Val Finch
Chris Ashton

CONTENTS

TABLE OF CASES

TABLE OF STATUTES

Administration of Justice
(Scotland) Act (c. 59)
s. 1(1), (4) 16–03
s. 3(1) 9–21
(3) 9–21
European Communities Act
(c. 68) ... 2–35, 9–04, 15–25
s. 2 .... 2–39, 2–42, 15–44
(1) 2–35, 2–37, 2–39
(2) 2–36, 4–73,
5–07, 5–30
(4) 2–36, 2–39,
2–41, 5–07,
5–30
s. 3(1) 2–36
Sched. 2 .... 2–36, 5–30
Local Government Act (c. 70)
ss. 100A–100K 6–03
s. 122 10–31
1973 National Health Service
Reorganisation Act
(c. 32) 7–03
Northern Ireland Constitution
Act (c. 36) 8–13
Fair Trading Act (c. 41) 4–78
s. 64(4)(b) 11–57
Local Government (Scotland) Act
(c. 65) 5–57, 9–08,
10–51, 11–12
ss. 50A–50K 6–03
s. 51(2) 13–04
s. 103(3) 11–61
Sched. 7A 6–03
1974 Local Government Act
(c. 7) 7–03
Health and Safety at Work etc.
Act (c. 37) 5–50
1975 District Courts (Scotland) Act
(c. 20)
s. 8(1) 9–16
Criminal Procedure (Scotland)
Act (c. 21)
Pt. II 15–38
s. 456 15–38
House of Commons
Disqualification Act
(c. 24) 2–05
Ministers of the Crown Act
(c. 26) 4–56
Local Government (Scotland)
Act (c. 30) 7–03, 7–27
s. 21 7–27
(3) 7–27
s. 24(6) 7–28
s. 25 7–28

s. 29 7–29
Sched. 5 7–28
1976 Fatal Accidents and Sudden
Deaths Inquiry (Scotland)
Act (c. 14) 8–39
s. 6 14–12
Restrictive Trade Practices Act
(c. 34) 4–78
Licensing (Scotland) Act
(c. 66) ... 10–71, 11–06, 14–23
s. 13(2) 10–29, 13–03
s. 18 11–62
s. 33 13–14
(1) 13–14
s. 39(4) 9–12
(c) 11–43
(d) 10–71
Supplementary Benefits Act
(c. 71) 5–40
Race Relations Act (c. 74) .. 11–35
s. 71 10–49
Fishery Limits Act (c. 86)
s. 3 12–05
s. 4(5) 12–05
(6) 12–05
1977 Aircraft and Shipbuilding
Industries Act (c. 3) 15–57
Housing (Homeless Persons)
Act (c. 48) 14–22
s. 12 5–54
s. 17 12–10
National Health Service Act
(c. 49)
s. 84 8–40
1978 National Health Service
(Scotland) Act (c. 29)
s. 2(8) 15–44
Interpretation Act (c. 30) 5–31
Employment Protection
(Consolidation) Act
(c. 44) 2–40
s. 85(3) 9–23
Sched. 11, para. 12.......... 8–06
1979 Legal Aid Act (c. 26)........... 8–18
Ancient Monuments and
Archaeological Areas Act
(c. 46)
s. 1 .... 10–27, 13–22
1980 Education Act (c. 20)
s. 27 6–06
s. 54 13–16
Competition Act (c. 21)....... 4–78
Social Security Act (c. 30)
s. 14 .... 9–12, 10–43
Employment Act (c. 42) 5–49

STATUTORY INSTRUMENTS

Chapter 1

INTRODUCTION

DEFINITION OF ADMINISTRATIVE LAW

There is no authoritative definition of administrative law. It has often been 1–01
defined as the law relating to the administration of government. That
definition is, however, too wide for the scope of this book as it encompasses
all of the functional aspects of government. It is impossible to study, as one
subject, such diverse matters as taxation, planning, social security, education,
housing and immigration. This book concentrates on the general principles
of administrative law which are common to all functional aspects of
government administration. The general definition which we favour,
therefore, is Garner's definition: "Administrative law is the study of the
rules and procedures that on the one hand serve to promote good
administrative practice in Governmental agencies, and on the other hand
provide mechanisms of redress, judicial or otherwise, when grievances have
arisen as a result of decisions or actions of government."[1]

A more comprehensive definition was penned by Cane in 1993[1a]:

> "Administrative law is, by common agreement, at the interface between
> law and politics. Judicial control of governmental action in general, and
> judicial applications in particular, often raise fundamental issues about the
> distribution of decision-making power between the courts and the Execu-
> tive, between central and local government, between the UK and the EC,
> and so on. They also confront us with important questions about the forms
> of accountability in a democratic system, about the functions and powers
> of the Legislature, about the processes of appointment and training of judges,
> about the nature of the judicial process, about the role of tribunals and
> complaints commissioners, and so on."

Administrative law therefore has two main aspects. It is the law which
provides processes for the checking and control of the activities of
government departments, public authorities, public officials and other
organisations which have devolved powers and whose activities may infringe
individual rights. It also provides for redress of grievances against such

---

[1] Jones and Thompson, *Garner's Administrative Law* (8th ed., 1996), p. 4.
[1a] Cane, "The Law Commission on Judicial Review", M.L.R. Vol. 56, no. 6, p. 887.

organisations and officials when an infringement of rights has occurred. This may include the enforcement of duties which have been imposed on public authorities and officials by statute.

DEVELOPMENT OF ADMINISTRATIVE LAW

1–02 The identification of administrative law as a separate field of study is relatively recent. The study of constitutional law has always been seen as being of fundamental importance but the need to distinguish, within the field of constitutional law, the law which regulates the relationship between the State and its individual citizens was not recognised until the time of the development of the Welfare State in the twentieth century. Even then administrative law was usually linked to constitutional law and was not recognised as a sufficiently important or complex area to merit study as a separate subject. Reference was, however, made to administrative law in 1930 when it was defined in *Green's Encyclopaedia of the Laws of Scotland* in the following terms: "Administrative Law is a term used by the Scottish University Commissioners and borrowed from Continental usage. It may be held to include the great body of statutory law, dealing with police, burgh, county, and local government, poor, public health, education and similar subjects. Perhaps the details of taxation, stamps, excise and customs fall under this head."[2] This is a very functional definition concentrating on the areas of activity to which administrative law applies rather than defining its principles or purposes, but it does indicate that it relates to those areas of government which have immediate and direct effect on the citizen.

1–03   The development of the Welfare State reflected a philosophy that one of the most important functions of government was to provide services to create improved standards of health, education, housing, employment, safety and transport. The changes were achieved by an increasing amount of legislation but relatively little could be achieved simply by passing Acts of Parliament and leaving it to the courts to enforce them. There were far too many problems of detail and there were also many matters which could not be decided until a policy was in the course of being implemented. It was necessary, therefore, to give powers to government Ministers to work out the detailed procedures for the implementation of policies and to provide for the development of various types of administrative and regulatory authorities with discretionary powers to oversee the operation of the policies. Administrative law emerged as a separate subject due to necessity rather than conscious design. The development of the complex rules required for the operation of the Welfare State necessitated the development of a body of rules and principles to regulate the way in which the administrative

---

[2] *Green's Encyclopaedia of the Laws of Scotland* (2nd ed., 1930) *sub nom.* "Law", col. IX, p. 17.

agencies involved in the implementation of government policies perform their functions. Lord Denning said:

> "In the present century the Government has concerned itself with every aspect of life. We have the Welfare State and the Planned State. The Government departments have been given much power in many directions. They set up tribunals and inquiries. They exercise unfettered discretion. They regulate housing, employment, planning, social security and a host of other activities. The philosophy of the day is socialism or collectivism.
>
> But whatever philosophy predominates, there is always a danger to the ordinary man. It lies in the fact that all power is capable of misuse or abuse. The great problem before the courts in the 20th century has been: In an age of increasing power, how is the law to cope with the abuse or misuse of it?"[3]

Since Lord Denning made those comments there has been a radical   1–04 change in the philosophy of government. Many of the functions which were carried out by government departments have now been delegated to independent agencies and the majority of nationalised industries have been privatised. Administrative law has had to develop rapidly to keep pace with these changes and to provide a means of ensuring that there are adequate controls in place to prevent abuse or misuse of power by autonomous organisations as well as government departments and public authorities.

PURPOSES OF ADMINISTRATIVE LAW

Decisions made by the Government and public authorities affect the lives of   1–05 individual citizens in many ways. Parents, for example, may wish to prevent a local education authority closing the school which their children attend. Prisoners may wish to challenge policy guidelines which extend the terms which they have to serve in prison. Applicants for liquor and entertainment licences may wish to challenge a decision to restrict the hours for which their premises may open for business. Members of a local community may wish to prevent the building of a motorway close to their homes. Public interest groups may wish to challenge decisions which will have a detrimental impact on the natural environment. In addition to those specific matters which have a direct effect on the everyday life of citizens, everyone in the United Kingdom has an interest in ensuring that the Government does not exceed its legal authority. It is important that there should be access to information so that members of the public are aware of the decisions which are being taken by the Government and by public authorities and the effect that the decisions will have on their rights and interests.

The purposes of administrative law can therefore be summarised as being: 1–06

    1. To ensure that the powers of government are kept within their legal bounds.

---

[3]   *Breen v. Amalgamated Engineering Union* [1971] 2 Q.B. 175 at 189.

2. To protect the citizen from infringement of his fundamental rights and to provide redress where his rights have been infringed.
3. To ensure that public authorities fulfil the duties which have been imposed on them.
4. To ensure that there is provision for access to information so that members of the public are aware of government policies and actions and are able to access their own personal records held by government agencies.
5. To ensure that there is adequate accountability so that democratic procedures can operate to facilitate political control.

SCOPE OF ADMINISTRATIVE LAW

1–07   Administrative law is primarily concerned with the control of power. This may be control through democratic accountability or through procedures for redress of grievances by the individual citizen. Administrative law is now a complex field of study and, although it has developed rapidly over the last 30 years, it cannot yet be described as a coherent set of legal principles. In the absence of a distinct body of law which allows for both the needs of government and the rights of citizens, sometimes there has been a tendency for the needs of government to be recognised without an adequate protection for the citizen. At other times rigorous safeguards have impeded government agencies unreasonably without giving any benefit to the citizen. Administrative law needs to strike a careful balance between the rights of the individual and the need to have efficient and effective government which is not unduly impeded in its operations by a complicated system of checks and balances.

1–08   Administrative law is concerned mainly with the formal procedures for controlling government and redressing grievances. The formal processes do not, however, reflect the full range of interaction between the individual and the government departments, public authorities and officials. Many complaints are dealt with by direct informal complaint to a department, an authority or to an individual official. A complaint may be made by an individual citizen on his own behalf or by his member of Parliament, a local councillor, a trade union, or a political pressure group. The complaints which are dealt with by formal procedures are relatively few in number. They are, nevertheless, the most important complaints, even though they are not all concerned with issues of major importance. They are important because they illustrate the deficiencies in the informal procedures which have failed to provide a solution. They are also significant because they may influence the way in which administrative decisions may be made in similar circumstances in the future.

Administrative law is constantly changing and evolving. Changes in government policy involve the conferring of new powers and duties on government agencies and public authorities. Uncertainty about the extent of these powers may lead to decisions being made which are in excess of the powers delegated by Parliament. It is increasingly common to see reports in the press of investigations by ombudsmen into complaints of maladministration in central or local government or reports of public inquiry or judicial review hearings. The publicity which all of these attract, and the fact that the subject-matter may be politically controversial, increases public awareness of the potential courses of action available to an individual and this increased awareness leads to an increased use of the procedures available.

Academic writers on administrative law are not all in agreement about the best approach to the study of the subject. Some people think that the study of administrative law should be set against specific functions of administrative activity, such as local government, housing, planning, licensing and immigration. Administrative law is only one aspect of the law which applies to public authorities and to the specific functions which they carry out. There is also detailed law about their composition and structure which lies beyond the scope of administrative law. It is beyond the scope of a book on administrative law to deal with matters such as the composition and powers of local authorities and the details of their specific functions such as planning controls or licensing. Administrative law is concerned with the legality of decisions and the manner in which functions are carried out and the procedures by which functions are regulated. The approach taken in this book is to examine the general principles of administrative law in their own right. Authorities and examples are drawn from a broad range of administrative activities so that the student should have some awareness of the impact of the principles of administrative law in several different contexts. 1–09

This book concentrates on administrative law in Scotland. It is not, however, possible to study administrative law in Scotland without an appreciation of the wider United Kingdom and European context. In constitutional and governmental terms the United Kingdom is for many, but not, of course, for all, purposes a single unit. There is one Parliament, and, although some administrative functions are delegated to the Scottish Office, the administration of government is centrally controlled. The law relating to the controls over central government departments and officials and the procedures for accountability within central government applies throughout the United Kingdom. The treatment of those matters in this book reflects this. However, there is an emphasis on the Scottish context and in this respect there is, where appropriate, detailed discussion of recent Scottish judgments. 1–10

Scotland is, of course, a separate jurisdiction. Scotland has its own legal system and well-established principles of Scots law. The historical development of the law and the cultural context differs from the rest of the United Kingdom. Even though substantive administrative law in Scotland has a great deal in common with administrative law in England and Wales, the procedures which are followed and the remedies which may be awarded are strikingly different. The chapters on judicial control of administrative decision-making, the liability of public authorities and the Crown and public interest immunity are focused on Scots law. Comparisons are drawn with English substantive law and the procedures in Scotland are contrasted with 1–11 those in England and Wales. The sections on aspects of English administrative law are included only in order to assist understanding of the law in Scotland and to enable the student to refer to English administrative law textbooks without becoming confused about which topics are useful and relevant and which are applicable only in England and Wales. This book does not aim to provide a comprehensive comparative study of administrative law in Scotland with administrative law in England and Wales.

1–12　　It is impossible to give a full account of administrative law in Scotland without taking into account European Community law and certain international treaty obligations in areas such as human rights and the treatment of refugees. The impact of European Community law receives attention at various points throughout the book. The roles of the European Court and the European Court of Justice are considered with regard to the growing importance of the European Convention on Human Rights.[4] A number of scholars have recently suggested that the European Community should move, and to a certain extent is already moving, towards some sort of convergence in administrative law.[5] The most important and influential advocate of a harmonisation or convergence is Professor Jurgen Schwarze who has consistently argued that a reappraisal of domestic systems of administrative law in a European context should be undertaken. He wants to see a harmonisation between domestic procedures and procedures under E.C. law followed by a greater convergence between the domestic laws of Member States.[6] Schwarze emphasises the increasing practical need for harmonisation: "If one takes into consideration all the instances of interaction between national and European principles, then the thesis ... of a *ius commune* in the field of administrative law would seem to be fully confirmed. Community Law has now started to exercise an influence upon national legal systems and, as a medium and a catalyst, it is beginning to contribute to a convergence and approximation of administrative laws of Europe."[7] He suggests that harmonisation should develop by gradual, cautious and pragmatic development of case law in the community. This book takes account of the increasing European influence on substantive matters such as proportionality and equality before the law and on procedural matters such as the duty to give reasons, legitimate expectations and the need for fairness in decision-making. The liabilities of public authorities and the State itself under European Community law are also considered.

[4]　European Convention on Human Rights and Fundamental Freedoms, Cmd. 8969 (1950); (T.S. 71 of 1953) (effective November 4, 1950).
[5]　Ward, "The Anomalous, The Wrong and the Unhappy: UK Administrative Law in a European Perspective" (1994) 45 N.I. L.Q. 46–52.
[6]　Schwarze, "Tendencies Towards a Common Administrative Law in Europe" (1991) 16 ELR 17–190.
[7]　Schwarze, *European Administrative Law* (1992).

CHAPTER 2

THE DOCTRINES OF THE CONSTITUTION

The United Kingdom does not have a written constitution in the sense that 2–01
there is no one document to which we can point and say "that is the United
Kingdom constitution". However, it is nonsense to say that our constitution
is "unwritten". It comprises many statutes and legislative documents, legal
decisions, habits and practices which, taken together, create a democratic,
sophisticated system of government with many safeguards for the rights
and freedoms of the individual citizen. Its "unwritten" nature allows it to
be changed relatively easily to meet changing circumstances. This, of course,
can be a two-edged sword; a flexible constitution such as that of the United
Kingdom can be changed for the worse as well as the better and there needs,
therefore, to be a strong system of government which can check any abuses
of power. This strong system of government needs to be accountable to the
electorate to ensure that what it does is broadly accepted and follows what
the majority of the electorate want. If the majority of the electorate do not
want what the government is providing, there has to be a method of showing
this displeasure and this is done through the holding of democratic elections
at set intervals. In the United Kingdom elections are held at intervals not
exceeding five years[1] unless Parliament has voted to extend its life for a
particular reason, for instance war. Most constitutions have a system of
checks and balances, and the U.K. constitution is no different.

Constitutional law and administrative law are closely related and it would 2–02
be impossible to discuss the latter fully without reference to and knowledge
of the former. This chapter will briefly remind the reader of the three
doctrines of the constitution applicable in the United Kingdom: separation
of powers, rule of law and supremacy of Parliament. These topics are
complex and cannot be discussed in detail in this book; for a detailed
discussion the reader is therefore referred to one of the many excellent
constitutional law books now available.[2]

---

[1] Parliament Act 1911.
[2] For instance, Deans, *Scots Public Law* (1995); Bradley and Ewing, *Constitutional and
Administrative Law* (11th ed., 1993); Turpin, *British Government and the Constitution*
(3rd ed., 1995).

SEPARATION OF POWERS

2–03   A system of government is normally divided into three branches: the
Legislature, the Executive and the Judiciary. In the United Kingdom, these
are represented by Parliament, the political government and civil service,
and the courts. The doctrine of separation of powers states that the functions
carried out by each of the branches should be separate and there should be
no overlapping or mixing of these functions. The doctrine was stated by the
French jurist Montesquieu in 1748 as follows:

> "When the legislative and executive powers are united in the same person,
> or in the same body of magistrates, there can be no liberty... Again, there is
> no liberty, if the judicial power be not separated from the legislative and
> executive. Were it joined with the legislative, the life and liberty of the sub-
> ject would be exposed to arbitrary control; for the judge would then be the
> legislator. Were it joined in the executive however, the judge might behave
> with violence and oppression. There would be an end to everything, were the
> same man, or the same body, whether of the nobles or of the people, to exer-
> cise the three powers, that of enacting laws, that of executing the public
> resolutions, and of trying the causes of individuals."[3]

In common with other writers such as Locke, Montesquieu was convinced
that there should be a separation of the powers of government to ensure
that one branch would not become so powerful that it could override the
other two. It was, therefore, a device to control and prevent the abuse of
power.

2–04   The doctrine expounded by Montesquieu saw its greatest expression in
the constitution of the United States of 1789 where it was embraced to
great and lasting effect. In the constitution of the United States, the three
branches of government are dealt with separately. The Legislature is set up
in Article 1, with Article 2 providing for the Executive in the form of a
President. Article 3 gives judicial power to a Supreme Court and other
federal courts. Each article gives the powers, duties and responsibilities of
each branch in outline. The independence of the Judiciary is emphasised
and its powers to declare acts of the Executive or Legislature as
unconstitutional were established early.[4] The powers of each branch are
not, of course, exercised in isolation from each other. They can influence
each other and thus exert a measure of control to ensure that no one branch
becomes too powerful. The resignation of President Richard Nixon in 1974
over the Watergate affair showed that a powerful President elected by popular
vote could still be controlled by the combined powers of the Congress and
the Supreme Court.

---

[3]   Montesquieu, *De L'Esprit des Lois* (1748), Book XI, Chap. 6, quoted in Bradley and Ewing,
op. cit., n. 2, above, p. 56.

[4]   *Marbury v. Madison* (1803) 5 U.S. (1 Cranch) 137.

In the United Kingdom, the doctrine has not been developed to give 2–05
such defined boundaries. Indeed, there is not really a separation of powers
between the Legislature and the Executive; it is only in the judicial branch
that we see the doctrine at work. The concept of separation of powers
states that each branch of government should be separate and have
independent status, and no individual should serve in more than one branch.
It is obvious that in the United Kingdom the Legislature and the Executive
are closely related and that they have common members. For instance, by
convention, all members of the Government are also members of either the
House of Commons or the House of Lords, so that they may be questioned
on their policies and actions. However, civil servants, members of the non-
departmental public bodies, members of the armed forces and other
government agencies are prevented from sitting in the House of Commons
by means of the House of Commons Disqualification Act 1975. This is a
recognition of the importance of keeping the law-makers separate from
those who implement the law. The Lord Chancellor is a prominent member
of all three branches. In the Legislature he acts as the Speaker of the House
of Lords. In the Executive, he is a member of the Cabinet and has his own
government department. He is also head of the Judiciary in England and
Wales, being the titular head of the Chancery Division of the High Court of
Justice as well as a Lord of Appeal in Ordinary in the House of Lords. By
convention, however, he does not hear cases in the High Court and does
not normally sit to hear appeals in the House of Lords, particularly where a
government department is a party. He is thus able to maintain the doctrine
with regard to the independence of the Judiciary.

One of the functions of Parliament is to pass legislation but this function 2–06
is shared with the Executive where government departments may pass
subordinate legislation.[5] The Legislature and Executive are dependent on
each other. The Executive needs the Legislature to pass laws so that it can
implement them; similarly, the Legislature needs the work so that it has
something meaningful to do. The Executive controls the Legislature by
controlling the work and how it is carried out; but the Legislature also
controls the Executive by exerting its power to prevent legislation being
passed and ultimately it can bring about the downfall of a Government by
passing a vote of no confidence in it.

The independence of the Judiciary is arguably the most important part 2–07
of the doctrine. Judges in the superior courts cannot be removed easily; the
Act of Settlement 1700 gives judges security of tenure of office *ad vitam
aut culpam* (during good behaviour). The Supreme Court Act 1981, s. 11(3)
provides that judges of the superior courts in England and Wales may be
removed only by Her Majesty on an address presented to her by both Houses

---

[5]   This is discussed further in Chap. 5.

of Parliament. In Scotland there is no similar statutory provision of removal and it is therefore uncertain as to how a judge might be removed. In addition, the salaries of judges cannot be reduced because they have displeased either the Legislature or the Executive. Judges' salaries are a charge on the Consolidated Fund and do not require the annual authorisation of Parliament; they are not therefore debated in the House. Both of these contribute to the judges' independence and their ability to find against the Executive in cases brought before them. The judges fulfil an important role in ensuring that the rights of the individual citizen are not infringed by an Executive exceeding its powers. The independence of the Judiciary is thus a check on the power of the Executive.

The functions of the Executive and Judiciary do, however, mingle in some respects. For instance, the Executive does make decisions which have a judicial element. The reporter in a public inquiry is essentially a civil servant but his role is that of a judge in that he has to weigh the competing arguments and come to a decision. The Social Security Commissioner is another example of a civil servant exercising a judicial function. Tribunals are administrative authorities but again they fulfil a judicial function and are regarded as part of the machinery of justice. In Scotland, the sheriff has administrative duties as well as extensive judicial functions.

2–08   The Judiciary and the Legislature are less intermingled. Members of the Judiciary are disqualified from membership of the House of Commons, although there are, of course, judges who sit in the House of Lords to hear appeals from the lower courts. These Lords of Appeal in Ordinary may participate in debates on legislation but they are careful not to intervene in matters which are political in nature. By convention, lay peers do not participate in the work of the Appellate Committee.

A judge of the superior courts may be removed from office only by the Crown on an address from both Houses, an event which has occurred only once since 1707.[6] There have been a number of calls by M.P.s for the removal of judges but these are generally more of an expression of criticism about a judge's conduct rather than a serious attempt to remove him.[7] Members of the lower judiciary and members of tribunals are protected by statute from arbitrary removal by the Executive or Legislature.

2–09   Judges may not review the validity of an Act of Parliament although this convention has now been modified by the United Kingdom's membership of the European Community where it is now possible for a British court to declare that an Act of the U.K. Parliament is incompatible with E.C. law. This aspect of the doctrine of parliamentary supremacy is discussed below.

[6]   1830 — Jonah Barrington who had misappropriated money from litigants.
[7]   For instance Lane C.J. was heavily criticised by 100 M.P.s after the Birmingham Six miscarriage of justice — *R v. McIlkenny* [1991] 93 Cr.App.Rep.287.

The final aspect of the doctrine of the separation of powers to be 2–10 considered here is whether the Judiciary exercises the functions of the Legislature in making law. In Scotland, the Court of Session and the High Court of Justiciary have certain equitable powers which enable them to declare certain actions to be unlawful or to give a remedy where none is otherwise available. The exercise of the *nobile officium* (equitable power) of the Court of Session is important for the law of trusts where the court can relieve a trust of a condition which makes the trust unworkable.[8] The power may also be used, albeit very sparingly, to insert a provision into a statute or document where this provision was accidentally omitted or was unforeseen. For instance, in *Wan Ping Nam v. German Federal Republic Minister of Justice*[9] a member of a ship's crew was accused of a murder which had been committed while the ship was at sea. When the ship docked at Greenock, the crewman was taken into custody and held pending extradition to Germany where the ship was registered. The relevant extradition statute gave relief to persons so imprisoned by stating that they could apply to the sheriff court for a writ of *habeas corpus*. This writ, however, is unknown in Scots law and the court therefore invoked the *nobile officium* to give effect to the rights Parliament obviously intended to give.[10] The High Court of Justiciary has a similar equitable power whereby it can declare acts to be criminal. Again, the power is used sparingly, although it was seen in *Khaliq v. H.M. Advocate*[11] where a shopkeeper was found guilty of selling "glue-sniffing kits" to children; this offence had not been previously recognised in Scots law but the High Court of Justiciary decided that it was the type of behaviour considered by the common law to be harmful.

THE RULE OF LAW

The two doctrines, separation of powers and rule of law, are closely 2–11 connected. Since the United Kingdom does not have a "written" constitution, the rule of law and the independence of the Judiciary become most important in ensuring that the Government does not exceed its powers. The rule of law is not easy to define but it could be said to mean that the Executive and its officials must obey the law and should not act beyond its powers or without lawful authority. Lawful authority normally means authority derived from a statute and such authority will, in most circumstances, be subject to the control of the courts. Rule of law has a secondary meaning, however; often Parliament will legislate in such a way that the Executive is given

---

[8] *Gibsons's Trustees,* 1933 S.C. 190.
[9] 1972 J.C. 43; 1972 S.L.T. 220.
[10] See also *Roberts, Petr.* (1901) 3 F. 799; *The Law Society of Scotland, Petrs.,* 1974 S.L.T. (Notes) 66.
[11] 1984 J.C. 23; see also *Ulhaq v. H.M. Advocate,* 1991 S.L.T. 614.

12 *Administrative Law*

very wide discretionary powers so that virtually any exercise of the power is capable of being considered within the law. The rule of law therefore states that such discretionary powers need to be controlled by ensuring that government business is carried on using rules and principles which restrict the use of such power. An example of where the Executive abused its powers occurred in *Congreve v. Home Office* where Lord Denning stated that if the Minister revoked the licence

> "without giving reasons, or for no good reason, the courts can set aside his revocation and restore the licence. It would be a misuse of the power conferred on him by Parliament: and these courts have the authority — and, I would add, the duty — to correct a misuse of power by a minister of his department, no matter how much he may resent it or warn us of the consequences if we do".[12]

As with separation of powers, the rule of law acts to limit the powers of the Government. It is therefore important that the Government, that is the Executive, does not make the law itself but that this is entrusted to another institution, the Legislature. It can thus be seen how the two doctrines interrelate and depend on each other for their validity.

2–12　　The rule of law has a long history in the United Kingdom[13] and the courts, particularly in England, have upheld the rule against the King and the Executive.[14] The principle was under discussion at an early date in both Scotland and England; Mitchell quotes from George Buchanan, a sixteenth-century writer, who wrote of the rule of law: "They [the people] were taught by many experiences that it was better to trust their liberty to laws than to Kings."[15]

The classic case on rule of law is, of course, the English case of *Entick v. Carrington*[16] where the King's messengers executed a warrant from the Secretary of State to arrest Entick and to seize his books and papers. However, to do so, they broke and entered his house and took away papers. Entick sued for trespass to his house and goods. The defendants said that the warrant was commonly used and had been executed before without challenge and that the power of seizure was essential to the government. The court held that since there was no statute or judicial precedent upholding the legality of the warrant, the practice was illegal. Lord Camden said: "And with respect to the argument of State necessity, or a distinction that has been aimed at between State offences and others, the common law does not understand that kind of reasoning, nor do our books take notice of any

---

[12] [1976] Q.B. 629 at 651.
[13] See Bradley and Ewing, *op. cit.,* n. 2, above, p. 99; for discussion of the rule of law as a broad political doctrine see Raz, "The Rule of Law and its Virtue" (1977) 93 L.Q.R. 195.
[14] *Prohibitions del Roy* (1607) 12 Co. Rep. 63, 77 E.R. 1342.
[15] Mitchell, *Constitutional Law* (2nd ed., 1968) at p. 53.
[16] (1765) 19 State Tr. 1030 (Court of Common Pleas).

such distinction".[17] The principle was thus affirmed that a public official must show legal authority for interfering with a citizen or his property. However, there are now many statutes authorising such interference by the State. The broad powers of entry and seizure given to officers of the Inland Revenue under the Taxes Management Act 1970 and other statutes show how the principle in *Entick* can be overcome by the use of general wording and by the Executive following the provisions of the statute.[18] The powers given by statute must, however, be implemented strictly and any discretionary powers may be limited by the purposes of the Act.[19]

The act of a public authority may be upheld if it was in accordance with 2–13 the law in the sense that it did not infringe any law.[20] This was seen in *Malone v. Metropolitan Police Commissioner*[21] where the tapping of a suspect's telephone was held to be lawful since it was carried out on the authority of the Home Secretary using the normal procedure. Malone subsequently successfully complained to the European Court of Human Rights that the telephone tapping was a violation of Article 8 of the European Convention on Human Rights, the right to respect for private life and correspondence.[22]

Those who enforce the law must abide by it; there should be no "cutting 2–14 of corners" or "the end justifies the means". For instance, in *R. v. Horseferry Road Magistrates' Court, ex parte Bennett*[23] Bennett, a citizen of New Zealand, was wanted in the United Kingdom for a number of offences. He was arrested in South Africa but could not be extradited to the United Kingdom because there was no extradition treaty between the United Kingdom and South Africa. The South African authorities tried to deport Bennett to New Zealand by way of Taiwan but he was returned by the Taiwanese officials because he had destroyed his passport. The South African authorities again deported him, this time by way of London, where he was arrested. Bennett alleged that he had been returned to the United Kingdom against his will as a result of kidnapping and that this had been done at the request of the English police and that the South African authorities had colluded in his return to the United Kingdom. He argued in judicial review proceedings that this was an abuse of process and the prosecution could not proceed. The House of Lords upheld his appeal, saying that the prosecution had commenced once the extradition process was set in motion. In this case, the prosecution began when the abduction instead of extradition proceedings had occurred. The effect of this case is to uphold the rule of law over the public interest in

---

[17] (1765) 19 State Tr. 1030 at 1073.
[18] *R. v. Inland Revenue Commissioners, ex p. Rossminster Ltd* [1980] A.C. 952.
[19] *Commissioners of Customs and Excise v. Cure and Deeley Ltd* [1962] 1 Q.B. 340.
[20] Turpin, *op.cit.*, n. 2, above, p. 53.
[21] [1979] Ch. 344.
[22] *Malone v. U.K.* (1984) 7 E.H.R.R. 14.
[23] [1994] A.C. 42.

the prosecution of crime. However, the High Court of Justiciary came to a different conclusion in *Bennett, Petitioner*[24] where the same applicant made a petition to the *nobile officium* to have a Scottish warrant for his arrest set aside. The High Court of Justiciary said that the English courts had been too ready to believe that collusion between the English and South African authorities had occurred. The Scottish court said that it would be unreasonable to insist that the police must refrain from arresting a fugitive simply because he was in transit to another country from where he could be extradited. If there was no collusion, the Scottish warrant should be enforced.[25]

2–15   The rule of law will, of course, be undermined if the Government indulges in breaches of the law. The Matrix Churchill Affair in 1992 is an example of a Government, if not breaching the rule of law, coming very close to doing so. There have also been questions raised over the British Government's policies in Northern Ireland in the 1970s and 1980s where there were suspicions that the security forces were operating a "shoot to kill" policy and the Government was acceding to this. These suspicions have never been properly allayed since the Stalker Inquiry into the shooting of seven people by the RUC was not completed, since Stalker himself was suspended from duty.

An earlier breach of the doctrine occurred where it appeared that the ill-treatment of terrorist suspects was officially but unlawfully authorised. A Committee of Privy Councillors was set up to investigate the interrogation procedures used but the three were unable to agree and Lord Gardiner produced a minority report which was in fact accepted by the Government in preference to the majority report.[26] The issue was raised in the European Court of Human Rights which held that the procedures contravened Article 3 in that they amounted to inhuman and degrading treatment but they did not amount to torture.[27]

2–16   The idea of the rule of law was formulated by Dicey in *The Law of the Constitution* in 1885.[28] He defined it as the "absolute supremacy or predominance of regular law as opposed to the influence of arbitrary power". He went on to say that it meant "equality before the law, or the equal subjection of all classes to the ordinary law of the land administered by the ordinary law courts". His idea was that officials should not be exempt from obedience to the law and should comply with the decisions of the courts.

---

[24] 1994 S.C.C.R. 902.
[25] For general discussion of the *Bennett* case see Choo, "International Kidnapping, Disguised Extradition and Abuse of Process" (1994) 57 M.L.R. 626.
[26] Report of the Committee of Privy Councillors appointed to consider authorised procedures for the interrogation of persons suspected of terrorism (Lord Parker, Chairman), Cmnd. 4901 (1972).
[27] *Ireland v. U.K.* (1978) 1 E.H.R.R. 25.
[28] See p. 202.

The Doctrines of the Constitution   15

Dicey's ideas have been criticised as lacking foresight and, indeed, accuracy. Even at the time he was writing, certain people had immunity from suit and prosecution, for instance the monarch, diplomats, M.P.s and judges. The immunity of the Crown, as opposed to the monarch in her personal capacity, has been changed by the Crown Proceedings Act 1947 and the Crown is now in normal circumstances liable to suit for contract or delict as any ordinary citizen. However, some immunities still exist. Section 10 of the 1947 Act prevents an action of delict where a member of the armed forces has been killed or injured by another and the Secretary of State has certified that the injury was one attributable to service for the purposes of pension entitlement. This section threw up many injustices and it was put into suspense by the Crown Proceedings (Armed Forces) Act 1987, but it can be revived by the Secretary of State if he thinks it expedient to do so where there are warlike conditions.[29]

The immunities of the Crown have largely disappeared, including in 2–17 England and Wales the immunity of a Minister from the effects of an injunction. In *M. v. Home Office*[30] the Home Secretary was found to be in contempt of court by ignoring an injunction preventing the deportation of a Zairean national who had claimed political asylum. This case, however, has not been followed in Scotland where the Court of Session considered that interdicts against the Crown were prohibited by the Crown Proceedings Act 1947, s. 21.[31]

In his book, Turpin maintains that a state can "only claim to uphold the rule of law if it provides effective means for the prevention and redress of illegal action by those who wield public powers ... There should be courts or other agencies which will check and control the actions of public authorities to ensure their compliance with the law."[32] This means *inter alia* that there must be open access to the courts or tribunals so that a citizen may obtain redress of his grievance. In a civilised society, this also means that access to this redress should not depend on one's wealth; a state will assist a complainant who has only modest, or less than modest, wealth to bring his action to court. If this does not happen, then only those with financial resources will have access to justice.

It is also important that the Government should comply with judgments 2–18 of the courts and, in this regard, it is contrary to the principle of the rule of law that the Government should introduce retrospective legislation to mitigate the effects of a decision made against it. In *Burmah Oil Co. Ltd v.*

---

[29] *Adams v. War Office* [1955] 3 All E.R. 245; *Bell v. Secretary of State for Defence* [1986] 1 Q.B. 322; *Pearce v. Secretary of State for Defence* [1988] A.C. 755.
[30] [1994] 1 A.C. 377.
[31] *McDonald v. Secretary of State for Scotland*, 1994 S.L.T. 692; see Dickinson, "Still no interdicts against the Crown", 1994 S.L.T. (News) 217.
[32] Turpin, *op. cit.*, n. 2, above, p. 62.

Lord Advocate[33] the House of Lords found that the use of the Royal
Prerogative in the prevailing circumstances had imported an obligation to
pay compensation for property destroyed by the British military authorities
to prevent the company's installations falling into enemy hands. The
company's success in this case meant that others in a similar position would
have a claim against the Government; these claims would have amounted
to many millions of pounds which the Government was reluctant to pay.
The War Damages Act 1965 was passed to prevent such compensation being
payable. The Act was retrospective in that actions instituted before the Act
was passed were to be dismissed by the courts.

The Government has used its legislative powers to pass other statutes
which have retrospective effect, perhaps most notoriously the War Crimes
Act 1991. This Act allows charges to be brought for murder, manslaughter
or culpable homicide, against a person in the United Kingdom, who was
not necessarily a U.K. citizen at the time of the alleged offence, that offence
having been committed during the Second World War in Germany or in
territory occupied by Germany and where the offence constituted a violation
of the laws and customs of war. This Act was passed only after substantial
opposition in the House of Lords, and indeed it became the first statute to
be passed by a Conservative Government using the Parliament Acts 1911
and 1949 to bypass a Conservative-dominated House of Lords. To date
there have been no successful prosecutions under the Act. It is also notable
that retrospective penal legislation of this type may contravene Article 7 of
the European Convention on Human Rights.

2–19   On many occasions, the Government has used its legislative powers to
overturn judicial decisions it did not like. In 1995, the Home Secretary
proposed legislation to mitigate the effects of the decision in *R. v. Home
Secretary, ex parte Fire Brigades Union*[34] so that he could introduce his
tariff scheme for criminal injuries compensation.

The rule of law generally requires that laws should be prospective, open,
clear and stable.[35] There is a general presumption of law that statutes will
not be construed as retrospective unless there is a specific provision in the
statute to that effect.[36] In *Secretary of State for Social Services v. Tunnicliffe*[37]
Staughton L.J. defined the presumption thus:

> "In my judgment the true principle is that Parliament is presumed not to
> have intended to alter the law applicable to past events and transactions in a
> manner which is unfair to those concerned in them, unless a contrary intention
> appears. It is not simply a question of classifying an enactment as retrospective

[33] [1965] A.C. 75.
[34] [1995] 2 All E.R. 245.
[35] See Raz, *op. cit.*, n. 13, above.
[36] See Dickinson, "Retrospective Legislation and the British Constitution", 1974 S.L.T. 25.
[37] [1991] 2 All E.R. 712.

or not retrospective. Rather it may well be a matter of degree — the greater the unfairness, the more it is to be expected that Parliament will make it clear if that is intended."[38]

Laws should be open and made known by proper and sufficient 2–20 publication and publicity. In the United Kingdom it is generally held that "ignorance of the law is no excuse" and that everyone has access to the law. This, of course, is somewhat unreasonable; there are so many laws, rules and regulations being created by the Executive that it is impossible for the ordinary citizen to know them all. It should also be remembered that many guidelines and rules are not published at all and so the citizen cannot find out to which rules he is subject.[39] The problem of publicity has been recognised by the courts, for instance in *Fothergill v. Monarch Airlines Ltd*[40] Lord Diplock said that justice demanded that the rules binding a citizen should be publicly accessible and ascertainable.

Laws should be clear and plain and easily understood by those who have to apply it. In *Merkur Island Shipping Corp. v. Laughton*[41] Lord Diplock remarked: "Absence of clarity is destructive of the rule of law; it is unfair to those who wish to preserve the rule of law; it encourages those who wish to undermine it."[42]

The independence of the Judiciary has been discussed above but other 2–21 points may be made here. The courts must be free to interpret and apply the law as they see fit and various Lords Chancellor have agreed this proposition. Lord Mackay of Clashfern, for instance, in a House of Lords debate stated: "I personally believe very strongly and fundamentally in the independence of the Judiciary. I also believe that it is vitally important for the Lord Chancellor to do all he can to preserve the independence of the Judiciary."[43] This statement must, however, be viewed in its context; the debate was initiated to discuss concerns that the Lord Chancellor had interfered with the way in which the President of the Employment Appeals Tribunal implemented procedures for dealing with notices of appeal to the tribunal. In a series of letters, the Lord Chancellor insisted that a particular rule be applied in full and that if the judge was unable to give an assurance on that, the judge should "consider his position". The judge, Wood J., refused to comply with the Lord Chancellor's request. In the House of Lords debate, the Lord Chancellor denied that he was telling the judge how to do his work but said that he had merely requested an assurance that the rules enacted

---

[38] At 724. See also *L'Office Cherifien des Phosphates v. Yamashura-Shinnikon Steamship Co. Ltd* [1994] 1 A.C. 486; *In Re Barretto* [1994] Q.B. 392.
[39] See Chap. 5 on Subordinate Legislation.
[40] [1981] A.C. 251.
[41] [1983] 2 A.C. 570.
[42] *ibid.* at 612.
[43] *Hansard*, H.L., Vol. 554, cols. 751–804, April 27, 1994, at col. 791.

under the authority of Parliament would be applied. However, the implication in the exchange of letters was clear; the judge should comply with the instructions of the Lord Chancellor, acting in his Executive capacity, or resign. Such an implication does not, of course, accord with Lord Mackay's statement.

SUPREMACY OF PARLIAMENT

2–22   Although the doctrines of separation of powers and rule of law are important in their own right, there is no doubt that the doctrine of the supremacy of Parliament is crucial to our understanding of administrative law and the places of Government and Parliament within the law. The traditional doctrine has a number of elements: Parliament is the supreme law-maker in the United Kingdom; an Act of Parliament is the highest source of law in the United Kingdom; and no Parliament can bind its successors. Mitchell defined the doctrine as "the absence of any legal restraint upon the legislative power of the UK Parliament".[44] The doctrine, of course, has been modified by the effect of the United Kingdom's membership of the European Community and this will be considered later in this chapter. In Scotland, the courts have questioned the validity of the doctrine in Scots law, although it has never been tested beyond the Scots courts.[45] The challenges have centred mainly around the status of the Act of Union 1707 and whether it was a founding document of the U.K. Parliament.[46] This is discussed further below.

2–23   An Act of Parliament has to be passed by the House of Lords and the House of Commons and receive the Royal Assent. Although an Act may be passed without the consent of the House of Lords, the power to do so derives from the Parliament Acts 1911 and 1949. The House of Commons and the House of Lords acting alone may not pass statutes; the three elements of "the Queen in Parliament" are required for a statute to claim its legitimacy.

(a) Parliament can make or unmake any law it pleases

2–24   This aspect of the doctrine states that Parliament is the supreme law-maker and that there is no matter which cannot be legislated for.[47] However, the proposition is limited by the realities of what Parliament can and cannot do. It is, for instance, possible for Parliament to legislate to ban smoking on the streets of Paris; the reality is that such a law would be neither practicable nor possible.[48] Such a law would be absurd and could not be enforced. Parliament is thus restricted by its territorial jurisdiction, in that it can make

---

[44]   Mitchell, *op. cit.,* n. 15, above, p. 64.
[45]   See *MacCormick v. Lord Advocate,* 1953 S.C. 396; *Stewart v. Henry,* 1989 S.L.T. (Sh.Ct.) 34; *Fraser v. MacCorquodale,* 1989 S.L.T. (Sh.Ct.) 39; *Pringle, Petr.,* 1991 S.L.T. 330.
[46]   Deans, *op. cit.,* n. 2, above, p. 24; Bradley and Ewing, *op. cit.,* n. 2, above, p. 89.
[47]   *R. v. Jordan* [1967] Crim.L.R. 483.
[48]   Jennings, *The Laws of the Constitution* (5th ed., 1959), p. 170.

laws only for those areas it controls. It is, however, able to extend those areas by extending the boundaries of the State by legislation.[49]

Parliament may legislate to extend its own life; for instance the Parliament Act 1911 decreased the length of a Parliament from seven to five years. During both of the World Wars, Parliament extended its life so as to prevent the holding of a General Election during the war. Parliament has altered the succession to the throne by the Act of Settlement 1700 and again by His Majesty's Declaration of Abdication Act 1936. The composition of the House of Lords has been altered by the Life Peerages Act 1958 which allowed the creation of non-hereditary peerages. The composition of the House of Commons has been altered on many occasions by extending the franchise to both men and women.[50] Parliament may alter local democracy by abolishing authorities[51] and by reorganising them.[52]

(b) No other body may question the validity of an Act of Parliament

This has been interpreted as meaning that the courts may not question an 2–25 Act's validity and the courts have indeed shown considerable reluctance to interfere in how a statute has been passed. In *British Railways Board v. Pickin*[53] it was alleged that there had been procedural errors made during the passage of a private Act of Parliament. The courts, however, would not challenge the Act on the basis that it was *prima facie* valid.[54] The House of Lords held that the respondent was not entitled to examine proceedings in Parliament to show that fraud had occurred and that any question as to the validity of the statute would require to be investigated by "the High Court of Parliament", in other words by the internal procedures of the two Houses.

The courts will, however, now look at the proceedings in Parliament where they are considering the interpretation of a statute and there is some ambiguity in the terms of the statute and the intention of its proposers. The courts will then look at the official record of proceedings in the House, *Hansard*, to determine the words used and their meaning. However, only the words of the proposer of the Bill, whether Minister or private member, may be considered.[55]

---

[49] Continental Shelf Act 1964; Island of Rockall Act 1972.
[50] For instance, the Representation of the People Acts 1867 to 1990; Representation of the People (Equal Franchise) Act 1928 which gave the vote to all adults over 21.
[51] For instance, the Local Government Act 1985 abolished the Greater London Council and five other large authorities.
[52] For instance the Local Government etc. (Scotland) Act 1994 reorganised local authorities in Scotland.
[53] [1974] A.C. 765.
[54] See also *Edinburgh and Dalkeith Railway Co. v. Wauchope* (1842) 8 Cl. & F. 710.
[55] *Pepper v. Hart* [1992] 3 W.L.R. 1032.

(c) No Parliament can bind its successors

2–26   This element of the doctrine has a number of aspects.

First, a later Act of Parliament will repeal an earlier contradictory statute by implication. This is an extension of the "Parliament can make or unmake any law it pleases" aspect in that if a later statute were to be read subject to an earlier one, then the later Parliament is in effect bound by its predecessor. The courts recognised the principle of implied repeal in *Ellen Street Estates Ltd v. Minister of Health*,[56] where the wording of the Acquisition of Land (Assessment of Compensation) Act 1919, s. 7, said that the provisions of any Act authorising compulsory acquisition "shall ... have effect subject to this Act, and so far as inconsistent with this Act those provisions shall cease to have or shall not have effect". It was argued that this Act applied to later Acts, in particular to the Housing Act 1925. The Court of Appeal, however, rejected this argument and held that the 1919 Act had been overridden by the provisions of the later Act since the terms of the 1919 Act could not control future Parliaments.[57]

2–27   Secondly, there must be some limitations to the exercise of this element of the doctrine. For instance, during the 1940s to 1960s, Parliament granted many previous colonies their independence by passing a statute for that purpose. It would be ludicrous to suppose that Parliament now could repeal any of those independence statutes. Parliament had itself acknowledged the reality of this situation. The Statute of Westminster 1931, s. 4, enacted that Parliament would not legislate for a dominion[58] unless the dominion so requested and then consented to the legislation. This request and consent would be included in the preamble to any such statute. Parliament's power to legislate for Canada was challenged in *Manuel v. Attorney General*[59] where Manuel argued that the consent required by the 1931 Act had not been given properly and the Canada Act 1982 was invalid. The preamble of the Canada Act 1982 stated that the Act had been requested by the Canadian Parliament who had consented to the passing of the Act by the Westminster Parliament. The court held that *prima facie* the Act was valid and could not be questioned.

2–28   The ability of Parliament to legislate for a self-governing colony was seen during the Southern Rhodesian crisis where the white minority population sought to make a unilateral declaration of independence. Parliament passed the Southern Rhodesia Act 1965 to return the power to legislate to Parliament itself. The courts recognised Parliament's power to do so in

---

[56] [1934] 1 K.B. 590.
[57] See also *Vauxhall Estates Ltd v. Liverpool Corporation* [1932] 1 K.B. 733.
[58] An autonomous colony, *e.g.* Canada, Australia, New Zealand, Irish Free State, Newfoundland and South Africa.
[59] [1982] 3 All E.R. 786.

Madzimbamuto v. Lardner-Burke[60] where Lord Reid remarked: "That does not mean that it is beyond the power of Parliament to do such things. If Parliament chose to do any of them, the courts could not hold the Act of Parliament invalid." The courts have nonetheless recognised the reality of the doctrine with respect to independence statutes. Lord Denning declared it thus:

> "We have all been brought up to believe that, in legal theory, one Parliament cannot bind another and that no Act is irreversible. But legal theory does not always march alongside political reality. Take the Statute of Westminster 1931, which takes away the power of Parliament to legislate for the Dominions. Can anyone imagine that Parliament could or would reverse that statute? ... Freedom once given cannot be taken away. Legal theory must give way to practical politics."[61]

Thirdly, do any statutes have a special status and can they be considered to be irreversible, or, as constitutional law would term it, are they entrenched in the constitution? In the past, the Union Acts have apparently attempted to prevent their repeal by their wording. The Act of Union with Ireland 1801 established the United Kingdom of Great Britain and Ireland and its wording implied that the union was intended to be permanent. However, after a century of conflict, the Government of Ireland Act 1920 was passed to establish two Parliaments for Ireland, one for Northern Ireland and one for the South. The Irish Free State was subsequently established in 1922, thus finally breaking the terms of the Act of Union 1801. 2–29

Unlike the Irish union, the union between Scotland and England subsists and, in Scotland at least, is the subject of a belief that the Act of Union 1707 has a special status not found in other statutes. The Treaty of Union set up a new Parliament of Great Britain and appears to state that this Parliament could freely legislate in most areas of law, but acknowledged there would be some areas which were declared to be fundamental and unalterable. The question of special status is a difficult one. The Treaty was ratified by an Act of each Parliament, first in Scotland, then in England; the English Parliament recognised and agreed the terms of the Treaty and the contents of the Scottish Act. It could therefore be said that it agreed that certain parts of the Treaty were accepted as being unalterable. However, one of the unalterable provisions was repealed by the Universities (Scotland) Act 1853, which abolished the requirement that university professors should be Presbyterians. Article 19 of the Treaty retained the Court of Session and the High Court of Justiciary as the supreme courts of Scotland "subject nevertheless to such regulations for the better administration of justice as shall be made by the Parliament of Great Britain". The courts in Scotland 2–30

---

[60] [1969] 1 A.C. 645 at 723.
[61] *Blackburn v. Att.-Gen.* [1971] 1 W.L.R. 1037 at 1040.

have reserved their judgment on the hypothetical case of Parliament trying to pass legislation which would seek to abolish the Scottish supreme courts. Lord President Cooper said: "The principle of unlimited sovereignty of Parliament is a distinctively English principle which has no counterpart in Scottish constitutional law."[62]

2–31   In *Gibson v. Lord Advocate*[63] the provisions of Article 18 came under scrutiny. Article 18 had acknowledged that laws regarding trade and customs and excise duties should be uniform throughout Great Britain but that laws concerning "private right" should not be altered "except for evident utility of the subjects within Scotland". Gibson argued that membership of the European Economic Community would harm "private rights" by granting other EEC nationals access to the Scottish fishing grounds. The court held, however, that fishing rights in territorial waters were part of public law and were not protected by Article 18.

The Scottish courts have therefore shown a reluctance to be drawn into the debate regarding the status of the Union Treaty; they have tended to treat it as a political problem rather than a justiciable one.[64] The comment of De Smith is useful:

> " the position of the Established Church in Scotland and the Scottish system of judicature, entrenched as fundamental and unalterable in the Acts of Union, remains largely intact. Although the immunity of the surviving fundamental principles of the Union from legislative encroachment by the UK Parliament without Scottish consent is probably to be regarded now as a matter of convention rather than of strict law, one cannot be certain that Scottish courts would take this view".[65]

2–32   Finally, we consider the position of international law. British courts do not recognise international law as limiting the supremacy of Parliament. International law and domestic law are two separate systems and international law has no status within the United Kingdom unless and until it is incorporated into U.K. law by means of legislation. This is called a dualist approach and is contrasted with the monist approach whereby international law is automatically incorporated into domestic law, with no requirements for domestic legislation to be passed. Such international law then takes precedence over the domestic legislation.[66] The dualist approach of U.K. law was acknowledged in *Attorney-General for Canada v. Attorney-General for Ontario*[67] where Lord Atkin remarked: " If the government of the day decide to incur the obligations of a Treaty which involve the

---

[62]   *MacCormick v. Lord Advocate,* 1953 S.C. 396.

[63]   1975 S.L.T. 134.

[64]   *Pringle, Petr.,* 1991 S.L.T. 330.

[65]   De Smith and Brazier, *Constitutional and Administrative Law* (7th ed., 1994) at p. 79.

[66]   The monist approach can be seen in France and Italy.

[67]   [1937] A.C. 326.

alteration of the law they have to run the risk of obtaining the assent of Parliament to the necessary statute or statutes." Ratification by the Government is not sufficient; many treaties have been ratified by the British Government but not enacted by statute. The European Convention on Human Rights is a good example of this.[68] Persons claiming a breach of the Convention in the British courts will have no case because the Convention is not part of U.K. law. However, the British Government ratified the Convention and British citizens are free to take a complaint to the European Court of Human Rights and if the court finds in their favour, the British Government is bound to abide by the decision and change the law to give effect to it. If a treaty is to be ratified by the Government, the text of it is laid before Parliament before the ratification takes place.[69]

The courts will not interfere in the ratification process. In *Blackburn v. Attorney-General*[70] the court did not recognise the contents of the EEC Treaty which was about to be ratified by the Crown, that is the British Government. Lord Denning remarked, famously, that the treaty could not be looked at by the courts until it was embodied in a statute.[71]   2–33

The rights of individuals under international law are not protected in the United Kingdom unless they are incorporated in a legislative act. In *Civilian War Claimants Association v. R.*[72] the German Government had agreed in the Treaty of Versailles to pay sums in compensation to British victims of war damage. The claimants did not receive any sums and sued the Crown for the payments. The House of Lords said that the negotiation of the Treaty was a prerogative of the Crown and the Crown was not acting as an agent or trustee for any claimant, unless it declared itself expressly to be doing so. The claim failed when the claimants were unable to show that the Crown had acted as trustee or agent for its nationals.

Where domestic law conflicts with international law, the courts will always implement the domestic law. In *Mortensen v. Peters*[73] the Scandinavian captain of a fishing vessel was caught fishing in the Moray Firth and charged with and convicted of fishing illegally contrary to byelaws made under the Herring Fishery (Scotland) Act 1889. At the time of the offence, the boat was outside the three-mile limit, in international waters. However, the byelaw prohibited fishing in the whole of the Moray Firth, most of which was in international waters. On appeal, the High Court of Justiciary upheld the conviction; the terms of the legislation were   2–34

---

[68] Although the new Labour Government elected on May 1, 1997 have said they will bring forward legislation during the course of the first parliamentary session.
[69] H.C. Vol. 171, ser. 5, col. 2001, April 1, 1921.
[70] [1971] 1 W.L.R. 1037.
[71] See also *R. v. Secretary of State for Foreign and Commonwealth Office, ex p. Rees-Mogg* [1994] A.C. 14.
[72] [1932] A.C. 14.
[73] (1906) 8 F.(J.) 93; (1906) 14 S.L.T. 227.

unambiguous and affected everyone including foreigners. This decision has been upheld in other cases, including *Croft v. Dunphy PC*[74] where Lord MacMillan said: "Legislation of Parliament, even in contravention of generally acknowledged principles of international law, is binding upon, and must be enforced by, the courts of this country." Although the courts try to interpret domestic law as not being in conflict with international law[75] if there is a conflict the court will uphold the domestic law even if this results in the United Kingdom breaching a Treaty obligation.[76]

PARLIAMENTARY SUPREMACY AND E.C. LAW

2–35   The principles detailed in the previous section have to be read in conjunction with the principles of this section.

The United Kingdom became a member of the European Economic Community on January 1, 1973, having ratified the Accession Treaty in 1972 and having implemented it by means of the European Communities Act 1972. Parliament had to recognise the special status of the E.C. Treaties in the Act and in particular recognise the common requirements and objectives of E.C. law.

The European Communities Act 1972, s. 2(1), incorporates all existing E.C. law into U.K. law and states:

> "(1) All such rights, powers, liabilities, obligations and restrictions from time to time created or arising by or under the Treaties, and all such remedies and procedures from time to time provided for by or under the Treaties, as in accordance with the Treaties are without further enactment to be given legal effect or used in the United Kingdom shall be recognised and available in law, and be enforced, allowed and followed accordingly; and the expression 'enforceable Community right' and similar expressions shall be read as referring to one to which this subsection applies."

2–36   Future E.C. law is given effect by virtue of section 2(4): "The provision that may be made under subsection (2) above includes, subject to Schedule 2 to this Act, any such provision (of any such extent) as might be made by Act of Parliament, and any enactment passed or to be passed, other than one contained in this Part of this Act, shall be construed and have effect subject to the foregoing provisions of this section".

The Act gives power to the Government to amend existing legislation or create new legislation by means of statutory instruments (section 2(2)). This has the beneficial effect of allowing changes to be made quickly. However, some matters may require to be enacted by a statute rather than

---

[74] [1933] A.C. 156 at 164.
[75] *R v. Secretary of State for the Home Department, ex p. Brind* [1991] 1 A.C. 696.
[76] *Cheney v. Conn* [1968] 1 All E.R. 779.

subordinate legislation; for instance, where an E.C. directive had to be implemented with retrospective effect, this could only be achieved by passing a statute.[77] Section 3(1) of the Act states that questions of the interpretation of E.C. law are to be determined "in accordance with the principles laid down by any relevant decision of the European Court". Thus, the primacy of the European Court of Justice is recognised.

Section 2(1) clearly provides that E.C. law in existence on January 1,   2–37
1973 is to be given effect; this therefore provides that if a rule of E.C. law conflicts with a domestic law which was made before January 1, 1973, the E.C. law will prevail.[78] There is no difficulty with this; the principle in fact accords with the traditional doctrine of implied repeal that a later Act (here an E.C. Act) will prevail over a conflicting earlier one.

The problem occurs when a provision of E.C. law is inconsistent with a post-1972 Act. The European Court of Justice has always made it clear that it views E.C. law as supreme over domestic law. In *Costa v. ENEL*[79] the court remarked that Member States had limited their sovereign rights and created a body of law which bound their nationals and themselves: "The transfer by the states from their domestic legal system to the Community legal system of the rights and obligations arising under the Treaty carried with it a permanent limitation of their sovereign rights."[80] In *Walt Wilhelm v. Bundeskartellamt*[81] the court said: "The Treaty has established its own system of law, integrated into the legal systems of the member states, and which must be applied by their courts. It would be contrary to the nature of such a system to allow member states to introduce or to retain measures capable of prejudicing the practical effectiveness of the Treaty."

The European Court of Justice also decided that E.C. law prevails over   2–38
even the constitutional provisions of Member States.[82] The *Simmenthal* case[83] ruled that where there was a conflict between domestic law and a directly applicable E.C. law, the domestic law was rendered inapplicable.

With this background, it was inevitable that the British courts would have difficulty in reconciling the doctrine of supremacy of Parliament with the idea of supremacy of E.C. law.

Where a statute is passed after January 1, 1973 and conflicts with E.C. law, the British courts have tried to interpret the statute so as to conform with

---

[77] Case 150/85, *Drake v. Chief Adjudication Officer:* [1987] E.C.R. 1995.

[78] *R. v. Henn* [1981] 2 All E.R. 166; *R v. Goldstein* [1982] 1 W.L.R. 804.

[79] Case 6/64: [1964] E.C.R. 585.

[80] At 586; see also Case 26/62, *Van Gend en Loos v. Nederlandse Administratie der Belastigen:* [1963] E.C.R. 1.

[81] [1969] E.C.R. 1.

[82] Case 44/79, *Hauer v. Land Rheinland-Pfalz*: [1980] 3 C.M.L.R. 42; Case 11/70, *Internationale Handelsgesellschaft:* [1972] C.M.L.R. 255.

[83] Case 106/77, *Amministrazione delle Finanze dello Stato v. Simmenthal SpA*: [1978] E.C.R. 629.

the E.C. law. For instance, in *Garland v. British Rail Engineering Ltd*[84] Lord Diplock referred to the general presumption that Parliament does not intend to legislate contrary to an international treaty obligation and said that: "the words of a statute passed after the Treaty has been signed and dealing with the subject-matter of the international obligation of the United Kingdom, are to be construed, if they are reasonably capable of bearing such a meaning, as intended to carry out the obligation, and not to be inconsistent with it".

2–39   Thus, the Uniited Kingdom courts have interpreted the words in U.K. enactments as widely as possible to achieve consistency. This was seen in *Pickstone v. Freemans plc*[85] where the House of Lords interpreted the Equal Pay Amendment Regulations so that they did not conflict with Article 119 of the EEC Treaty; this was done by supplying words by implication into the regulations.[86] Where a U.K. statute cannot be construed as in conformity with E.C. law, then E.C. law must be applied in preference to the U.K. statute. This ruling was based by the House of Lords on section 2(4) of the 1972 Act in *R. v. Secretary of State for Transport, ex parte Factortame.*[87] This concerned a conflict between E.C. law and the Merchant Shipping Act 1988 and associated regulations governing the registration of fishing vessels. The House of Lords held unanimously that: "By virtue of section 2(4) of the European Communities Act 1972, Part II of the Act of 1988 is to be construed and take effect subject to directly enforceable Community rights and those rights are, by section 2(1) of the Act of 1972 to be 'recognised and available in law'." The case then went to the European Court of Justice for a preliminary ruling and on its return to the House of Lords, Lord Bridge declared: "Whatever limitation of its sovereignty Parliament accepted when it enacted the European Communities Act 1972 was entirely voluntary. Under the terms of the Act of 1972 it has always been clear that it was the duty of a United Kingdom court, when delivering final judgment, to override any rule of national law found to be in conflict with any directly enforceable rule of Community law".[88]

2–40   In a related action, the European Commission brought an action in the European Court of Justice against the United Kingdom seeking a declaration that the United Kingdom had failed in its obligations under the E.C. Treaty by imposing nationality requirements in the 1988 Merchant Shipping Act.[89] The European Court of Justice made an interim order that the United Kingdom suspend the application of the nationality requirements. The House of Lords granted an injunction against the Secretary of State requiring him

---

[84] [1983] 2 A.C. 751 at 771.
[85] [1988] 2 All E.R. 803.
[86] See also *Litster v. Forth Dry Dock Co. Ltd* [1989] 1 All E.R. 1134.
[87] Case C-213/89: [1990] 2 A.C. 85; [1989] 2 All E.R. 692.
[88] *Factortame Ltd v. Secretary of State for Transport (No. 2)* [1991] 1 A.C. 603 at 658–659.
[89] Case 246/89R, *Commission v. U.K. (Re Nationality of Fishermen)*: [1989] E.C.R. 3125; [1991] 3 C.M.L.R. 106.

to suspend the nationality requirements, although this had already been done by an Order in Council.[90] The *Factortame* case has continued to proceed through the courts, with a finding by the European Court of Justice in 1996 that the applicants were entitled to reparation for the loss they sustained.[91]

The principle of the supremacy of E.C. law was further reinforced in *R. v. Secretary of State for Employment, ex parte Equal Opportunities Commission*[92] where the provisions of the Employment Protection (Consolidation) Act 1978 were held to be incompatible with Article 119 of the EEC Treaty and with Council directives.[93] In this case, there was no reference to the European Court of Justice; the British courts decided for the first time without prompting from the European Court of Justice that British statutory provisions were unenforceable.

These cases have had a marked impact on the traditional doctrine of the   2–41
supremacy of Parliament. This is expressed by Bradley thus: "Dicey asserted that 'no person or body is recognised by the law of England as having a right to override or set aside the legislation of Parliament' (Law of the Constitution, page 40). In fact, U.K. law now recognises that Community organs have the right to make decisions and issue regulations, which may have the effect of overriding legislation by Parliament."[94] The doctrine of supremacy of Parliament has at its heart the principle that no Parliament can bind its successors. Yet there can be no doubt that the Parliament of 1972 attempted to do just that and apparently succeeded. The wording of section 2(4) of the 1972 Act includes the phrase "any enactment passed *or to be passed*".[95] These words bind future Parliaments and subordinate all future legislation to E.C. law. The judgments in the *Factortame* cases are evidence that the European Communities Act 1972 may be entrenched in U.K. law.[96] It should be remembered that the 1972 Act does not use any wording attempting to entrench its provisions; it is a statute like any other, and, like any other, may be amended or repealed. Its "entrenchment" lies in its political importance, not in its legal form.

However, an interesting question still arises: what would happen if   2–42
Parliament deliberately legislated contrary to E.C. law, using words which were express and unambiguous? The United Kingdom would, of course, then be in default of its Treaty obligations and there would be political repercussions, but would the courts then apply the U.K. statute or the E.C. law? The basis of all of the cases above is that Parliament gave authority by

---

[90] Merchant Shipping Act 1988 (Amendment) Order 1989 (S.I. 1989 No. 2006).
[91] *R. v. Secretary of State for Transport, ex p. Factortame (No. 4)* [1996] 2 W.L.R. 506.
[92] [1995] 1 A.C. 1.
[93] See also *Marshall v. Southampton Health Authority (No. 2)* [1993] 4 All E.R. 586.
[94] Bradley, "The Sovereignty of Parliament: In Perpetuity?" in Jowell and Oliver, *The Changing Constitution* (3rd ed., 1994), at p. 91.
[95] Emphasis added.
[96] Wade and Forsyth, *Administrative Law* (7th ed., 1994) at p. 31.

means of the European Communities Act 1972 for the implementation of
E.C. law in the United Kingdom and authorised the U.K. courts to refer
questions of E.C. law to the European Court of Justice for interpretation of
that law. If Parliament then chooses to override the 1972 Act by the specific
and express enactment of a statute which is contrary to E.C. law, it could be
argued that the U.K. courts would have no alternative but to implement the
later statute.[97] Lord Bingham thought this would be unlikely: "any rule of
domestic law which prevented the court from giving effect to directly
enforceable rights established in Community law would be bad".[98]

2–43   The court's generally pragmatic approach is shown in this quotation by
Hoffman J., who said:

> "The [E.C.] Treaty is the supreme law of this country, taking precedence
> over Acts of Parliament. Our entry into the European Economic Community
> meant that (subject to our undoubted but probably theoretical right to with-
> draw from the Community altogether) Parliament surrendered its sovereign
> rights to legislation contrary to the provisions of the Treaty on matters of
> social and economic policy which it regulated. The entry into the Commu-
> nity was in itself a high act of social and economic policy, by which the
> partial surrender of sovereignty was seen as more than compensated by the
> advantages of membership."[99]

Bradley also accepted this pragmatic viewpoint: "so long as the UK
wishes to remain in the EC, the supremacy of the law made by Parliament
must if necessary give way to the greater supremacy of Community law".[1]

SUPREMACY AND THE DIRECT EFFECT OF E.C. LEGISLATION

2–44 So far our discussions have been concerned with the supremacy of E.C.
law and its effect on U.K. statutes. However, the E.C. principle of "direct
effect" of Community legislation has the potential for greater impact. The
principle states that if a Community Treaty provision, or a regulation, or a
directive, is held to have direct effect, then individuals may claim that rights
or obligations have been created directly by that Community legislation
without the need for implementation by legislation of a Member State. The
individual may then rely on such Community legislation in the U.K. courts
in the same way as a British statute.[2]

   Not all Treaty provisions are directly enforceable and it has been left to
the European Court of Justice to define these. However, examples are: Article

---

[97] See dicta of Lord Denning in *Macarthys Ltd v. Smith* [1979] 3 All E.R. 325.
[98] *Factortame (No. 2)* [1991] 1 A.C. 603.
[99] *Stoke-on-Trent City Council v. B&Q plc* [1991] Ch. 48 at 56.
[1]   Bradley *op. cit.*, n. 94, above, p. 97.
[2]   Case 26/62, *Van Gend en Loos*, above.

48 on freedom of movement[3]; Article 52, conferring the right of freedom of establishment[4]; and Article 119, conferring the right of equal pay for equal work for men and women.[5]

These rights can have either vertical or horizontal effect. "Vertical effect" 2–45 means that an individual may rely on the provision against the Government whereas "horizontal effect" means that the provision can be relied on against another citizen or company.

An E.C. regulation has special status within the legal systems of the Member States. Article 189 states that: "A regulation shall have general application. It shall be binding in its entirety, and directly applicable in all member states." The concept of direct applicability is different from direct effect. Direct applicability means that the regulation automatically becomes law in the Member State with no legislation from the Member State's legislature required to implement it. A regulation will always be directly applicable; it does not necessarily have direct effect. For a regulation to have direct effect, it must be clear and precise, unconditional and leave no room for discretion in its implementation.

An E.C. directive is binding as to its effect, but it is left to the Member 2–46 State to decide how it is to be implemented. In the United Kingdom, directives are implemented either by Act of Parliament or by subordinate legislation. The European Court of Justice has indicated that a directive may have vertical direct effect, but not horizontal.[6] This can create anomalies; for instance an employee working for a public body can claim rights contained in a directive, but a person working in the same kind of job in the private sector may not. It is left to the national legislatures to correct such anomalies and injustices by implementing legislation to bring the private and public sectors into line.

---

[3] Case 41/74, *Van Duyn v. Home Office* [1975] Ch. 358.
[4] *Factortame* cases.
[5] Case 149/77, *Defrenne v. Sabena (No. 2)* [1978] E.C.R. 1365.
[6] Case C-188/89, *Foster v. British Gas*: [1990] E.C.R. I–3313.

CHAPTER 3

MINISTERIAL RESPONSIBILITY

3–01   The doctrine of Ministerial responsibility has a long and changeable history. In 1879, Gladstone described the doctrine thus: "In every free state, for every public act, someone must be responsible; and the question is, who shall it be? The British Constitution answers: 'the Minister and the Minister exclusively.'"[1] Traditionally, the doctrine has two elements: collective responsibility and individual Ministerial responsibility. The doctrine is crucial to the British system of government in that it is a central part of parliamentary scrutiny of Executive action, which is discussed in Chapter 4. Some of the difficulty arising with the doctrine is the use of the word "responsibility". The Government has tried to distinguish between responsibility and accountability but the terms can be, and are, used interchangeably. In evidence to the Treasury and Civil Service Committee, the Cabinet Office offered the distinction as between "the constitutional fact of ministerial accountability for all that a department does, and the limits to the direct personal responsibility (in the sense of personal involvement) of ministers for all the actions of their departments and agencies, given the realities of delegation and dispersed responsibility for much business".[2]

3–02   The term "accountability" basically means that a Minister is answerable to Parliament, or gives an account to Parliament, of the activities of his department and the policies implemented by his department. The Minister will, as part of this accountability, make statements to Parliament, answer questions, participate in debates on the policies and appear before Select Committees to answer questions from backbench M.P.s. The term "responsibility", on the other hand, implies an element of "taking the blame". It is this element of the doctrine which has caused most disquiet over the last few years. If an error is made by a civil servant in formulating a policy or carrying it out, the Minister has to make amends by making a statement to Parliament or, in the most extreme measure, resign. Resignation is, however, a rare occurrence; in December 1994 the Foreign Secretary,

---

[1]   Quoted in Public Service Committee, Second Report, *Ministerial Accountability and Responsibility*, (1995–96 H.C. 313–I) (1996), para. 1.
[2]   1993–94 H.C. 27–II, para. 189.

Douglas Hurd, made a statement to the House of Commons regarding the unlawful grant of funds to the Pergau Dam project in Malaysia after his department had been criticised in court.[3] He was called upon by the Opposition spokesman to resign or "at least offer his apologies". Hurd did neither.

This chapter will seek to define the two types of responsibilities, collective and individual, and in particular will try to guide the reader through the problems associated with individual Ministerial responsibility.

COLLECTIVE RESPONSIBILITY

It is not appropriate in this book to consider collective responsibility in any 3–03 great detail; that is best left to the major constitutional law texts.[4] However, in brief, it is the mechanism by which governments show a united front to Parliament and to the country at large. In Cabinet, discussions are held in secret so that the arguments put forward by various members remain undisclosed.[5] A vote is rarely taken in Cabinet; rather a consensus is reached and a common position is agreed. A similar approach is seen with decisions taken by the European Commission. Once the decision is made, all of the members agree to accept it and that decision becomes the policy of the Government. Each member of the Cabinet accepts responsibility for the decision and the Government thus shows a united front. If a Minister is unable to accept the decision of the majority, he must resign, as did Michael Heseltine in 1986 over the Westland Affair and Geoffrey Howe in 1990 over disagreements with the Prime Minister regarding the Government's position on the European Community. The doctrine applies to all Ministers of the Government and their parliamentary private secretaries and even extends to the members of the Shadow Cabinet.

Collective responsibility is rigidly adhered to by governments for a 3–04 number of reasons. First, the government must be seen to be strong and united, so that other Governments, friends or foes, will know that it is going to carry out its policies and also so that the Stock Market and money markets will be reassured. Secondly, if a Minister is under pressure in Parliament for his policies and a motion of censure is put down, the rest of the Government will rally round since his policy is their policy. The doctrine thus protects and defends Ministers who are unpopular, or even incompetent. Finally, the doctrine reinforces the belief that the Executive is one body and that all government departments are part of that body. During the annual

---

[3] *R v. Secretary of State for Foreign and Commonwealth Affairs, ex p. WDM* [1995] 1 W.L.R. 386.
[4] For instance, Wade and Ewing, *Constitutional and Administrative Law* (11th ed., 1993); Barnett, *Constitutional and Administrative Law* (1995).
[5] *Att.-Gen. v. Jonathan Cape Ltd* [1976] Q.B. 752.

financial discussions between departments, it could be harmful if one department is seen to be benefiting at the expense of another, thus communications between departments are secret as are the final expenditure discussions made by the Cabinet.

On rare occasions, it may be impossible for the Cabinet to show a united front. In recent years this has occurred twice, in 1975 and in 1977, and on both occasions the disputes related to matters concerning the European Community. In 1975, a referendum was to be held in the United Kingdom to decide whether the country would remain as a member of the European Economic Community. The Cabinet was split 16–7 in favour of retaining membership and it was agreed that Cabinet Ministers could campaign for a "no" vote so long as they did so outside Parliament. In 1977, a free vote was allowed to all members of the Parliamentary Labour Party on the European Assembly Elections Bill. In answer to a question on collective responsibility, the Prime Minister, James Callaghan, told the Commons: "I think the doctrine should apply except in cases where I announce that it does not."[6]

INDIVIDUAL MINISTERIAL RESPONSIBILITY

3–05   The second strand of the doctrine, individual Ministerial responsibility, is much more difficult to define. The original doctrine was developed in the mid-nineteenth century with the change from unanswerable boards to departments staffed by civil servants. Ministers became responsible to Parliament for the work of their civil servants, who became anonymous and held permanent posts. At this point, government was still relatively small and Ministers were able to supervise their civil servants personally. However, during the twentieth century, the scale of government work mushroomed but still civil servants are expected to carry out their work in the Minister's name, although there is no doubt that he can no longer know what that work is.

3–06   The doctrine states that the Minister answers to Parliament for the work of his department. The classic case illustrating individual Ministerial responsibility occurred in 1954 with the Crichel Down Affair. The facts of the affair are as follows. The Air Ministry acquired farming land in 1938 by compulsory purchase. When it no longer required the land for a bombing range, the Minister transferred it to the Ministry of Agriculture who then transferred it to the Commissioners for Crown Lands, who let it to a tenant. The original owner of the land was prevented from buying the land back or indeed leasing it. Other landowners were similarly affected. An inquiry into the affair concluded that civil servants in the Ministry of Agriculture

---

[6]   *Hansard*, H.C. Vol. 993, col. 552, June 16, 1977.

had acted in a high-handed and deceitful manner.[7] There was widespread criticism in Parliament and outside and the Minister, Sir Thomas Dugdale, resigned, taking full responsibility before Parliament for the mistakes and inefficiency of his officials. Although this may seem the ultimate exercise of the doctrine of Ministerial responsibility, in fact, it was not; the Minister had been involved personally in the decisions and the civil servants concerned were publicly named in the inquiry report.

The Public Service Committee investigated the doctrine in 1996 and 3–07 quoted extensively from a memorandum of the Permanent Secretary to the Treasury in 1954, at the time of the Crichel Down Affair. His interpretation of the doctrine includes the statement: "It follows that a civil servant, having no power conferred on him by Parliament, has no direct responsibility to Parliament and cannot be called to account by Parliament. His acts, indeed, are not his own. All that he does is done on behalf of the Minister, with the Minister's authority express or implied: the civil servant's responsibility is solely to the Minister for what he may do as the Minister's servant."[8] He went on to say that none of the Minister's officials should be named either to praise or to blame them. The Minister will take responsibility for the errors of his department, although he is not liable for conduct he has forbidden or has disapproved of. After the Crichel Down Affair, the Home Secretary gave his interpretation of how the responsibility should work. He said that a Minister must protect a civil servant who has carried out his explicit order or has acted in accordance with the Minister's policy. The Minister will accept responsibility for an error where there is no important issue of policy involved. If, however, the civil servant has acted contrary to the Minister's orders and without his knowledge, the Minister need not defend the civil servant, although he will remain "constitutionally responsible to Parliament for the fact that something has gone wrong".[9] There appears to be no obligation on the Minister to resign even if the Minister is personally at fault or his policy is shown to be defective. Oliver observes that a Minister now only resigns if they have lost the support of the Prime Minister or the party, or if they have lost credibility, or if they are an embarrassment.[10] Events of the mid-1990s appear to confirm this view.[11]

Generally, however, Ministers do not blame their civil servants when 3–08 things go wrong. The cases of civil servants being publicly blamed are rare; the Vehicle and General Insurance Company collapse and the blame attributed to a named official from the Department of Trade and Industry is

---

[7] Report of Inquiry into Disposal of Land at Crichel Down, Cmd. 9176 (1954).
[8] (1995–96 H.C. 313–I), para. 8.
[9] H.C. Vol. 21, cols. 1286–1287 (July 20, 1954).
[10] Oliver, "Parliament, Ministers and the Law" (1994) 47(4) *Parliamentary Affairs,* 630.
[11] For instance, the Home Secretary, Michael Howard, refused to resign after the escape of prisoners from Parkhurst prison — see below for discussion.

an exceptional case. While Ministers do not blame their officials publicly, they themselves do not necessarily take responsibility and resign. The examples of such resignations are almost as rare as those where officials are blamed. The example which appeared to uphold the doctrine is that of Lord Carrington, who, in 1982, resigned with two of his junior Ministers over the Argentinian invasion of the Falkland Islands. While there is no doubt that there were errors made by the Foreign and Commonwealth Office, and Lord Carrington resigned in response to the doctrine, his reasons were not all based on a recognition of the doctrine; his memoirs show that he resigned partly for political reasons and to provide a scapegoat to take pressure off the Prime Minister and the Government.[12]

3–09   The doctrine has been restated in recent years by the Government and this restatement appears largely to have been accepted by Parliament. The Treasury and Civil Service Committee referred to the government position which was stated to be: "It has never been the case that ministers were required or expected to resign in respect of any and every mistake made by the departments, though they are clearly responsible to Parliament for ensuring that action is taken to put matters right and prevent a recurrence."[13]

The Public Service Committee, however, has recognised the difficulties posed by the doctrine where it is found that Ministers are not to blame because they did not knowingly mislead Parliament and civil servants are not to blame because they carried out the Minister's policy. The unsatisfactory outcome is that no one is to blame and the Committee were concerned that the doctrine could reach such a conclusion.[14]

POLICY v. OPERATION

3–10   The doctrine as thus stated is that Ministers are accountable to Parliament for the actions or omissions of their department but they are not responsible for the administration or operation of the policy by the department. This view was expressed after the mass breakout by IRA prisoners from the Maze prison in 1983. The Hennessy Report[15] inquired into the circumstances of the escape and found that the prison governor had to be held accountable for the failure in the prison's security arrangements. The Secretary of State for Northern Ireland, James Prior, had intimated to the inquiry that if it was found that the escape was a result of his policy or that he had failed to do something he should have done, he would resign. In the House of Commons debate on the Report, he said that his policy was not at fault and

---

[12] Lord Carrington, *Reflect on Things Past* (1988), p. 371.
[13] Treasury and Civil Service Committee, Fifth Report, 1993–94, H.C. 27, para. 121 (1994).
[14] (1995–96, H.C. 313–I), para. 20.
[15] (1983–84, H.C. 203).

accordingly he would not resign.[16] Prior differentiated between responsibility for policy and responsibility for administration and stated that he did not accept that there was "any constitutional or other principle that requires ministerial resignations in the face of failure, either by others to carry out orders or procedures or by their supervisors to ensure that staff carried out those orders".[17] There was considerable criticism of this interpretation at the time, not least from Enoch Powell, a long-serving and respected Parliamentarian, who said:

> "the responsibility for the administration of a department remains irrevocably with the Minister in charge. It is impossible for him to say to the House or to the country 'The policy was excellent and that was mine, but the execution was defective or disastrous and that has nothing to do with me'... If the responsibility for administration so central to a department can be abjured by a Minister, a great deal of our proceedings in the House is a beating of the air because we are talking to people who, in the last resort, disclaim the responsibility for the administration".[18]

However, some years later the Home Secretary put forward the same view as Prior's after a similar incident and no criticism was heard. Lord Justice Scott in his Inquiry Report also appears to have accepted the new view that it is unrealistic to attach "blame to a minister simply because something has gone wrong in the department of which he is in charge".[19]

The new doctrine thus separates the policy of the Minister from the 3–11 administration or operation of it, and this would seem to be appropriate since the administration of a policy is carried out by many civil servants at various levels of responsibility and it is inconceivable that the Minister would be aware of every activity within his department. "The further the minister is, geographically or hierarchically, from the people or events complained of, the less he will generally be expected to take the blame for mistakes and resign."[20]

The separation of policy and administration has, of course, become important in the context of the relationship between Ministers and the agency chief executives of executive agencies and this is discussed further in Chapter 4.

The divide between operational matters and policy is difficult to define 3–12 and it would appear that Ministers prefer that no definition be found. If the division of responsibility is kept vague, then Ministers will have more room

---

[16] *Hansard* (H.C. Vol. 53, col. 1042), February 9, 1984.
[17] *ibid.* Note also that the question of Prior's resignation was one of public relations; if he had resigned, the IRA would have had a Ministerial "scalp" and considerable publicity for their cause. Politically, this would have been unacceptable to the Government.
[18] *ibid.* cols. 1060–1061.
[19] (1995–96 H.C. 115–I), para. K8.15.
[20] Brazier, *Constitutional Practice* (1994), p. 150.

to manoeuvre if problems arise. The minutes of evidence of the Treasury
and Civil Service Committee Report show how Ministers have tried to
avoid clarifying and defining the concept.[21] By failing to do so, Ministers
are able to argue that a failure has occurred in the operation of the policy,
not in the policy itself. However, Hennessy pointed out to the TCSC that:
"There is not actually a proper division between the two ... If operationally
you hit real trouble, it is usually because the policy is flawed."[22] Where
both policy and the operation are at fault, the Minister may be able to
divert attention away from his policy failure and place blame on the
operational failure, thus blaming his officials. The civil servants, of course,
are unable to defend themselves or respond by revealing for instance that
the policy was flawed because the Minister did not take their advice, or
that the policy could not be implemented because of a lack of resources.
Only Ministers may speak for their departments and, as the Public Service
Committee pointed out, there is no way of checking whether the Minister's
interpretation of the facts is accurate.[23] The problem is that many matters
of operation or administration of a policy are inextricably linked with the
policy itself. If officials are asked to implement a policy but are only
given £x, when in reality it requires £y, then there will be a shortfall in
the implementation. In other words, the policy will have to be modified
to take account of the reduced resources. Yet, the Minister will still say
that his policy is the original one and if it fails he will blame those who
implemented it, saying that they did not carry out his instructions. The
civil servant will be powerless to tell the true situation to Parliament.
The doctrine of Ministerial responsibility thus operates to protect the
Minister in this instance, not his officials.

3–13   The question of Ministerial responsibility was raised during the Scott
Inquiry[24] where the Head of the Home Civil Service, Sir Robin Butler, was
questioned on his interpretation of the doctrine. He made a distinction
between accountability and responsibility along the lines argued above.
Scott, in accepting this distinction, nonetheless said that Ministers needed
to be more forthcoming about an incident to show that they did not have
personal knowledge or involvement in the matter, and thus should escape
blame and personal criticism. This was necessary so that Parliament and
the public had all the facts to judge whether the Minister's position was
accurately stated.[25] In his report, Scott suggested that on a number of
occasions statements made by Ministers had "failed to discharge the

[21] See, for instance, the evidence of William Waldegrave, April 26, 1994 (1993–94, H.C. 27)
   QQ 1894–97.
[22] *ibid.* Q 93.
[23] (1995–96 H.C. 313–I), para. 27.
[24] (1995–96 H.C. 115–I).
[25] *ibid.* para. K8.16.

obligations imposed by the constitutional principle of ministerial accountability."[26]

The operational/policy divide as defended by the Conservative 3–14 Government allowed Ministers to have the best of both worlds, and this was illustrated in the dismissal of the Director General of the Prison Service, Derek Lewis, in 1995. The prison service became an executive agency in 1994 and its framework agreement stated that day-to-day operational decisions were to be entrusted to the Director General and a board of 10 directors. The Home Secretary was said to be "accountable to Parliament for the prison service"; he was not, however, to be involved in the day-to-day management but would be "consulted ... on the handling of operational matters which could give rise to grave public or Parliamentary concern". The Home Secretary and the Director General were to meet fortnightly and the Home Secretary was to be informed of anything which might give rise to grave public or Parliamentary concern. In late 1994, there was an attempted break-out from Whitemoor prison of a number of prisoners who had been convicted of terrorist offences. In January 1995, the alleged serial murderer Fred West hanged himself in prison while awaiting trial and a few days later three convicts escaped from Parkhurst prison. This sequence of events led to an inquiry, and in October 1995 the Learmont Report on the state of Britain's prisons was released. It was highly critical of the prison service. The report, however, referred to the high degree of political interference endured by the agency and recommended that there should be a change in the relationship between the Home Office and the agency to give the agency greater operational independence. The Home Secretary, Michael Howard, interpreted the report as identifying that all of the problems were related to the way in which his policies had been carried out, and he asked Lewis to resign. Lewis declined to do so, and was then dismissed, but later successfully negotiated substantial compensation for that dismissal. He has since maintained that there was persistent political interference with the way in which the agency operated to the extent that he indicated that he could not carry out his job properly. When the Learmont Report was debated in Parliament, Howard was able to resist Opposition calls for his resignation by calling on the support of the Prime Minister and his party and by claiming that operational matters were the sole concern of the agency chief executive.[27]

The fact that party colleagues will invariably rally to a Minister's support 3–15 was crucial in the above case, and generally if a Minister can gain this support he will be able to survive calls for his resignation. The Scott Inquiry

---

[26] (1995–96 H.C. 115–I), para. D4.63.

[27] November 18, 1995, *Hansard*, H.C. Vol. 264, cols. 502–520. A sequel to this occurred on May 19, 1997 when former junior Home Office Minister Ann Widdecombe made a statement to the House of Commons in which she doubted the veracity of Howard's version of the affair.

Report severely criticised the Attorney-General, Sir Nicholas Lyell, and another Minister, William Waldegrave, but it was found that neither had acted in bad faith and thus escaped. It is ironic that the language of the report ensured that there were sufficient doubts about their actions and their intentions to allow colleagues to give them the benefit of at least one of these doubts. The Government's arguments in refusing to allow the Ministers to resign referred to two facts, first that there was no intention to mislead Parliament (probably the most heinous crime an M.P. can commit) and second, that the advice of the Attorney-General on the signing of a public interest immunity certificate was a matter of legal opinion and dispute.

3–16   The accusation that a Minister may have misled Parliament is a serious one. The original "Questions of Procedure for Ministers" states that Ministers have a duty to give as full information as possible about the policies, decisions and actions of the Government and must not deceive or mislead either Parliament or the public. The TCSC in 1993 refers to concerns regarding this guidance.[28] It cited examples of its concern, the evidence of civil servants in the Scott Inquiry, the Foreign Affairs Committee Report on the Pergau Dam project, and statements made in 1994 by the Minister for Disabled People and by William Waldegrave, both of which were admitted to be somewhat economical with the truth. The committee believed that civil servants had a responsibility to advise Ministers so that their statements were not misleading. Ministers also have to show integrity in formulating their statements so that they are able to release part of the information without misleading the House. The committee found that a Minister who had knowingly misled the House should resign.[29] Following this criticism and proposals from the Nolan Committee[30] the Government issued a new version of "Questions of Procedure for Ministers".[31] This states:

> " (iii) Ministers must not knowingly mislead Parliament and the public and should correct any inadvertent errors at the earliest opportunity. They must be as open as possible with Parliament and the public, withholding information only when disclosure would not be in the public interest, which should be decided in accordance with established Parliamentary convention, the law, and any relevant Government Code of Practice".

Thus, a resignation is more likely to occur if the Minister has made "a grievous and foreseeable error in very high policy".[32] There must be no one else to take the blame and the Prime Minister must be content to lose the Minister. In addition, there must be uproar in the press and the Minister

---

[28] (1993–94 H.C. 27), para. 124.
[29] *ibid.* para. 134.
[30] Cm. 2850–I, 48–49.
[31] November 2, 1995, *Hansard*, H.C col. 456.
[32] Woodhouse, "Ministerial Responsibility in the 1990s: When Do Ministers Resign ?" (1993) 46 *Parliamentary Affairs,* 277 at 292.

must have a "sense of constitutional propriety". Although this is a fairly cynical view of the circumstances required for resignation, the instances referred to above seem to bear out its accuracy.

RESPONSIBILITY AND CIVIL SERVANTS

As we have seen, the doctrine protects both Ministers and civil servants, 3–17 and while Ministers may occasionally face public opprobrium, civil servants invariably do not. The previous guidance for civil servants was stated in the "Osmotherly Rules" or the "Departmental Evidence and Response to Select Committees" guidance document which was revised in 1994. This interpreted the doctrine so that civil servants were held to give evidence to Select Committees on behalf of their Ministers and under their directions. "Officials are accountable to Ministers and are subject to their instruction; but they are not directly accountable to Parliament in the same way."[33] Until the Civil Service Code was revised in 1996, civil servants did not have any general duty to Parliament or the public concerning the information being disclosed and whether that information was misleading.[34] The Code now states at paragraph 5 that civil servants "must not knowingly mislead Parliament or the public". If a civil servant believes he is being asked to act in an illegal, improper or unethical manner or is being asked to breach a constitutional convention or professional code, then he should report this to senior officials using the specified procedure.[35] An appeal from the decision of senior officials lies to the Civil Service Commissioners. The civil servant must at no time disclose the information to the public or to an unauthorised person, as Clive Ponting did in the Belgrano incident. The civil servant who conceals information which should be disclosed or gives misleading information is not therefore exposed to public scrutiny. Parliament is unable to insist upon a civil servant attending a Select Committee hearing if a Minister does not wish it. Parliament is unable to punish a civil servant; only a Minister can do so. It therefore makes it difficult, if not impossible, to ascertain the true facts of a situation if one of the key players is unable to give evidence or gives evidence which is misleading. This occurred during the hearings by Select Committees into the Westland Affair when the civil servants involved in releasing information to the press were forbidden to attend the Defence Committee's hearings. The Government and the committee eventually reached a compromise and the Head of the Civil Service appeared before the committee to give evidence about his internal inquiry into the affair. However, the Public Service Committee noted in its report that the Government has not generally refused

---

[33] para. 39.
[34] January 9, 1996, *Hansard*, H.L., WA 21.
[35] *ibid.* para. 11.

to allow civil servants to give evidence before Select Committees except in a few cases where the civil servant was a member of the Security Services.[36] It notes however that the Treasury is particularly reluctant to allow its officials to give evidence to other Select Committees.[37] Civil servants see their loyalties as lying with the government of the day, not directly with Parliament, and this was clearly indicated by those civil servants who gave evidence to the Scott Inquiry. One civil servant said: "It was simply a matter of us not telling the truth, of knowingly not telling the truth to the public and Parliament. The policy was bent and we concealed that policy."[38]

3–18   The accounting officers for departments are in a different situation from ordinary civil servants. They are appointed by the Treasury and are personally responsible for "the propriety and regularity of the public finances for which he or she is answerable".[39] Although they are still expected to serve their Ministers and follow the same rules as regards evidence to Select Committees on the advice given to Ministers, accounting officers have a duty to advise Ministers against taking any action which would breach the requirements of the rules regarding propriety and regularity. If their advice is ignored,[40] the accounting officer should seek written instructions from the Minister before the Minister's decision is carried out. The advice of the accounting officer and the fact that the Minister overruled it is then reported to the Public Accounts Committee. The accounting officer may then be called to answer questions on the advice he tendered to the Minister, thus going against the general principle of Ministerial responsibility.

3–19   However, the Government still maintains that civil servants appearing before a Select Committee, except in the instance of accounting officers, are appearing as the spokesmen of the Minister. The purpose of civil servants appearing is to "contribute to the central process of ministerial accountability, not to offer personal views or judgements on matters that may be of political controversy. To ask civil servants to do so would undermine their professional political impartiality".[41] In the Scott Inquiry, civil servants were able to give evidence on their own behalf, not on behalf of Ministers, and Scott recommended that this should be extended to appearances before Select Committees. The Government has resisted this idea.[42]

---

[36] (1995–96 H.C. 313–I), para. 75.
[37] *ibid.* para. 81.
[38] Mark Higson, quoted in Fenwick and Phillipson, *Source Book on Public Law* (1996), at p. 599.
[39] (1995–96 H.C. 313–I), para. 77.
[40] See *R. v. Secretary of State for Foreign and Commonwealth Affairs, ex p. WDM* [1995] 1 All E.R. 611.
[41] Public Service Committee, First Special Report: Government Response to the Second Report from the Committee (Session 1995–96) on Ministerial Accountability and Responsibility (1996–97 H.C. 67), p. ix.
[42] *ibid.* p. x.

RESIGNATIONS AFTER INDISCRETIONS

Many Ministerial resignations occur, not because a Minister has taken 3–20
responsibility for some action or omission of his department, but because
of a private indiscretion which has become known publicly and which
threatens to embarrass the Government. The resignation of David Mellor
in 1992 is an example of this. Initially, the details of Mellor's extra-marital
affair threatened him but he retained the support of the Prime Minister and
the party. Subsequently, other revelations about a family holiday allegedly
paid for by the daughter of a PLO sympathiser and his own robust and
sometimes unwise defence of his actions led to a forced resignation. In
1993, Michael Mates resigned after press revelations of his involvement
with the fugitive businessman Asil Nadir. His letter of resignation referred
to the damage being done to the Government. Further embarrassment for
the Government came in 1994 with the "Cash for Questions" allegations
where two junior Ministers were accused of accepting money to ask
Ministerial questions. Tim Smith resigned immediately but Neil Hamilton
did not, being forced to resign a week later after it became apparent that he
could no longer carry out his Ministerial duties effectively because of the
allegations. In 1996, Hamilton was forced to abandon a defamation action
against *The Guardian* newspaper and he became the subject of an
investigation by the Parliamentary Standards Ombudsman. The
Ombudsman's report was due to be released in March but was postponed
because Parliament was prorogued for the General Election.

A Minister may be required to resign if he makes foolish or incautious 3–21
remarks which leave him in an impossible position. Two examples of this
are Edwina Currie and the salmonella in eggs food scare in 1989 and
Nicholas Ridley's comments on German influence in the European
Community in 1990. Leon Brittan had to resign after it was disclosed that
he allowed one of his officials to leak a critical letter from the Solicitor
General to Michael Heseltine at the height of the Westland Affair in 1986.

THE COURTS AND MINISTERIAL RESPONSIBILITY

Until relatively recently, the courts exercised a low level of regulation of 3–22
the Executive in respect of Ministerial responsibility, taking the view that
this was a matter which was exercised by use of the prerogative. The "low
point" was the case of *Liversidge v. Anderson*[43] where a detention order
was made in respect of a person whom the Minister had "reasonable cause"
to believe to be hostile. The detainee argued that the order could only be
made if the Minister had objective reasonable cause for this belief. The
order was, however, upheld by majority in the House of Lords, where Lord

---

[43] [1942] A.C. 206.

Atkin dissented, saying that the words "if a man has reasonable cause" did not mean "if a man thinks he has reasonable cause". The court found that some matters were so important that they had to be determined personally by the Minister, such as in this case the detention of an enemy alien in time of war.

The House of Lords had previously stressed the Minister's responsibility to Parliament in respect of his own actions and those of his officials.[44] In *Johnson & Co. (Builders) Ltd v. Minister of Health*[45] Lord Greene M.R. said: "In a nutshell, the decision of the minister is a thing for which he must be answerable in Parliament and his actions cannot be controlled by the courts." Such a conclusion, of course, is not sustainable if the meaning of Lord Greene's statement is that the courts cannot control a Minister's decision because he is answerable solely to Parliament. Indeed, Bradley and Ewing observe that judicial control and Ministerial responsibility are not mutually exclusive; they exist together and are complementary to each other.[46] The judiciary have generally taken the view that they will not become involved in political controversy but will act if the Executive act outwith their powers to review the decision. In *R. v. Inland Revenue Commissioners, ex parte National Federation of Self-Employed and Small Businesses Ltd*[47] Lord Diplock said:

> "It is not, in my view, a sufficient answer to say that judicial review of the actions of officers or departments of central government is unnecessary because they are accountable to Parliament for the way in which they carry out their functions. They are accountable to Parliament for what they do in so far as regards efficiency and policy, and of that Parliament is the only judge; they are responsible to a court of justice for the lawfulness of what they do, and of that the court is the only judge."

3–23   There is a general presumption that statutes do not bind the Crown, although most statutes now do in fact expressly bind the Crown thus raising the question as to what will happen if the Crown disobeys a court order. Until 1993, it was thought that Ministers in England and Wales could not be held to be in contempt of court. In *M. v. Home Office*[48] the Home Secretary was held to be in contempt after he ignored an order of the court to procure the return of a political asylum-seeker who was the subject of judicial review proceedings. The court held that an officer of the Crown, acting in his official capacity, was amenable to final injunctions, interlocutory injunctions and contempt. In Scotland, the Court of Session decided that section 21 of the Crown Proceedings Act 1947 applied to all forms of judicial proceedings,

---

[44] *Local Government Board v. Arlidge* [1915] A.C. 120.
[45] [1947] 2 All E.R. 395 at 400.
[46] Bradley and Ewing, *Constitutional and Administrative Law* (11th ed., 1993), p. 125.
[47] [1982] A.C. 617.
[48] [1993] 3 W.L.R. 433.

including judicial review, so that interdict is still unavailable against the Crown.[49]

The courts will not interfere on the merits of a decision, only on the way in which it was made. There is still an assumption that Ministerial responsibility is effective and more appropriate than judicial review. However the court has said: "Many in government are answerable to Parliament and yet answerable also to the supervisory jurisdiction of this court."[50] The courts will now, in certain circumstances, have regard to Parliamentary proceedings to interpret statutes which are ambiguous, obscure or absurd if the words are given their natural meaning.[51]

The major justification for the Government being formed exclusively 3–24 from members of the House of Commons and the House of Lords is that Ministers can be held accountable to Parliament for their own conduct and that of their officials. Many decisions are taken by officials in the name of the Minister and this is recognised by the courts. In *Carltona Ltd v. Commissioner of Works*[52] the decision of the official was said to be the act of the Minister since the Minister was responsible to Parliament for its consequences. Lord Greene M.R. remarked:

> "In the administration of government in this country the functions which are given to ministers (and constitutionally properly given to ministers because they are constitutionally responsible) are functions so multifarious that no minister could ever personally attend to them... The duties imposed upon ministers and the powers given to ministers are normally exercised under the authority of the ministers by responsible officials of the department. Public business could not be carried on if that were not the case."[53]

This principle was reaffirmed in *R. v. Secretary of State for Home Department, ex parte Doody*[54] where it was held that the function of the Secretary of State in deciding the length of sentence for a life prisoner could be delegated, in this case, to a junior Minister. In *R. v. Secretary of State for Trade, ex parte Anderson Strathclyde*[55] the Secretary of State had a personal interest in the decision and passed it to a junior Minister.

The Minister's powers may therefore be exercised by a junior Minister 3–25 or a civil servant but the courts have maintained that the Minister remains responsible to Parliament. However, in some instances this general principle of delegation does not apply and the Minister is required by statute to exercise the power personally, for instance with regard to some powers of

---

[49] See *McDonald v. Secretary of State for Scotland*, 1994 S.L.T. 692.
[50] *R. v. Parliamentary Commissioner for Administration, ex p. Dyer* [1994] 1 All E.R. 375.
[51] See *Pepper v. Hart* [1992] 3 W.L.R. 1031.
[52] [1943] 2 All E.R. 560.
[53] *ibid.* at 563.
[54] [1993] 1 All E.R. 151.
[55] [1983] 2 All E.R. 233.

exclusion or deportation orders.[56] If a certificate "purporting to be signed by the Secretary of State" is said to be conclusive of certain matters, then it is agreed that the certificate has to be signed by the Secretary of State personally.[57] The delegation to civil servants of some statutory Treasury functions was not possible hence the need for the Civil Service (Management Functions) Act 1992 which authorises the delegation and sub-delegation to any other Crown servant.

LEGISLATIVE CONTROL OF THE GOVERNMENT

3–26 The introduction of the Welfare State in the 1940s led to a massive increase in the number of disputes between individuals and the Crown or Executive. The traditional route for these disputes would have been for an aggrieved citizen to approach their M.P. who would raise the matter with the Minister. Parliament would quickly have been overcome with a huge number of appeals so other methods of dispute resolution had to be found such as tribunals and ombudsmen.[58] Parliament therefore became the "last resort".

3–27 Statutes may make provision for appeals against decisions to be made first to a tribunal and then to the courts. Ministers are required to follow a set procedure before making a decision and this procedure can be reviewed by the courts. The statutes give clear-cut limits to Ministerial powers and this is regarded by Oliver as better than prerogative powers in three respects. Statutory provisions give the criteria against which action is judged, they may impose liability to civil or criminal proceedings and they may provide the procedure to be followed before the powers are exercised.[59]

Ministerial responsibility is perceived as becoming increasingly ineffective and inappropriate as a means of redress and Parliament is turning more to statutory controls as a method of regulating the Executive. Some of the reasons given for this are: Parliament is unable to monitor the Government in the way specialists or experts can; the immense increase in government activity means that there is less time for Parliament to scrutinise the Government's work; and the breakdown in "comity" between the political parties means that there is no brake on government excess.[60]

3–28 The Parliamentary Commissioner Act 1967[61] put the redress of grievances on a statutory footing with Parliament recognising that an M.P. may not be

---

[56] For instance, Immigration Act 1971, ss. 13(5), 14(3) and 15(4), and see *R. v. Secretary of State for the Home Department, ex p. Oladehinde* [1991] 1 A.C. 254.

[57] *R v. Clerkenwell Metropolitan Stipendiary Magistrate, ex p. DPP* [1984] Q.B. 821; [1984] 2 All E.R. 193.

[58] See Chaps. 7 and 8.

[59] See Oliver, *op. cit.,* n. 10, above. Oliver gives examples of statutes such as Crown Proceedings Act 1947, Interception of Communications Act 1985, Security Service Act 1989.

[60] See Oliver, *op. cit.,* n. 10, above, for other reasons.

[61] See Chap. 7.

able to secure remedies for their constituents by themselves. The Act
maintained the link with Parliament in three ways, by requiring the
aggrieved person to approach the PCA through their M.P. first, by
setting up a dedicated Select Committee to review the work of the
PCA and by making the PCA an officer of the House and answerable
to Parliament.

MINISTERIAL RESPONSIBILITY AND THE EUROPEAN UNION

The effect of the United Kingdom's membership of the European 3–29
Community on the doctrine of Ministerial responsibility has been profound.
As more areas of government action have become subject to legal regulation,
the freedom of government to govern has been limited. For instance, after the
Conservative Government introduced VAT on domestic fuel supplies,
the Labour Party made a manifesto promise to reduce that tax. However,
they were prevented from abolishing it because of E.C. rules. The European
Community places duties on governments and gives rights to individuals.
The European Court of Justice may declare an Act of Parliament to be
unlawful.[62] The voting mechanisms[63] in the Council of Ministers mean that
British Ministers can no longer be held "responsible" by Parliament for
decisions made in Council where no veto is available. E.C. regulations
automatically become part of the law of the United Kingdom with no input
from Parliament or the Government. E.C. directives must be given effect
by means of either primary or secondary legislation; although the
Government can choose how such directives are implemented they have
no choice but to implement them and they have limited say in their contents.
All of these points indicate that the Government's ability to legislate in
certain fields is limited and therefore the responsibility of Ministers in these
fields is also curtailed.

---

[62] *Factortame (No. 2)* [1991] 1 A.C. 603.
[63] For instance, qualified majority voting.

CHAPTER 4

THE STRUCTURE OF GOVERNMENT

4–01 Over the last decade or so, there is no doubt that the pattern of government in the United Kingdom has changed. The Conservative Government comprehensively changed how the Executive functions by means of the privatisation of public utilities and amenities, the introduction of executive agencies and management practices to the civil service and indeed the contracting-out of activities where it was perceived that such would lead to more efficiency and economy. This new structure of government system has been called "the new public management".[1] It is not a peculiarly British phenomenon; the new style has been seen in other countries including Australia and New Zealand.[2] The components of this doctrine include professional management, goals and targets identified and set, greater competition and decentralisation of functions to smaller units.[3] These components can be identified in many of the new practices to be discussed below where we will consider the changing relationship of the Executive with the Legislature, the relationship between central government, the non-departmental bodies and the executive agencies and finally the ways in which contract and service provision are now handled. These developments, together with three more, have thrown into relief the problems associated with the private and public spheres and in particular we shall identify the problems when private institutions come to exercise a degree of public power.[4] The last three developments are the changes in local government administration, the changes required to enhance open government,[5] and the control exercised by the PCA.[6]

Before we discuss these issues, it may be helpful to consider the strategies used for the changes implemented in government and the regulation of industries in the past and today.

---

[1] Hood, "A Public Management for All Seasons?" (1991) 69 *Public Administration* 3.
[2] In the USA it has been referred to as "Reinventing Government" after a book by Osborne and Gaebler, *Reinventing Government* (1992).
[3] See Schick, "Budgeting for results: Adaptation to fiscal stress in industrial democracies" (1990) 50(1) *Public Administration Review* 26.
[4] Craig, *Administrative Law* (1995), p. 64.
[5] See Chap. 6.
[6] See Chap. 7.

(a) Nationalisation

This was seen from 1945 to the late 1970s and involved the transfer of 4–02 ownership of large and important industries from the private to the public sector by means of forming a public corporation[7] or by the Government buying a majority shareholding in the company.[8] The aim was to operate these industries for the benefit of the public, particularly the major utilities such as gas, electricity, telecommunications, coal and water services. The arguments for nationalisation included a recognition of the importance of certain vital functions for the public which should not be left in private hands, the provision of services which the private sector would not or could not provide, a belief that natural monopolies should not be left in private hands where they could accumulate excessive profits and a belief that the people should own the assets of the country.

Nationalisation statutes did differ, but there were a number of common features. The general theme was that the industry should be autonomous in its day-to-day administration but the Minister should have power to determine overall policy. The Minister appointed boards of management, issued general directions to the boards and had the final say in financial matters.[9]

There was confusion regarding the nature of the function of nationalised 4–03 industries. Some saw them as commercial operations which had to fulfil obligations to balance revenue and expenditure, whilst others saw them as an extended arm of government which could help prevent regional unemployment or help implement the Government's economic policies. The industries therefore found themselves in the unenviable position of being criticised for poor commercial returns and cajoled by government to achieve ends which an ordinary commercial organisation would reject. The set-up was not successful; most Governments used the nationalised industries to respond to short-term pressures, *e.g.* in the 1960s there was a "Buy British" campaign and there have been a number of wages restraint policies. Governments also failed to look long-term at the industries and issue broad policy directives.

From 1979 the principal forms of control became financial target setting, supplemented by performance indicators. In addition, constraints were placed on the industries by means of external financing limits which restricted the difference between revenue and expenditure. The Government sought to control the spending of these public corporations since they had an effect upon the public sector borrowing requirement. There was therefore a tension between the exercise of commercial freedom and the utilisation of public corporations as part of government strategy.

---

[7] *e.g.* the coal industry, railways, electricity.
[8] *e.g.* British Petroleum, British Leyland.
[9] For discussion, see Prosser, "Regulation, Markets and Legitimacy", in Jowell and Oliver, *The Changing Constitution* (1994), p. 237.

(b) Privatisation

4–04 This term has a wider meaning than simply "denationalisation"; it has come to be used to describe "all withdrawals from direct state involvement in the provision of goods and services".[10] It involves a nationalised industry being returned to the private sector, that is, a sale of assets, or a government service being sold to the private sector. The result of privatisation is to remove the industry or service from the scrutiny of Parliament, although there may be indirect Parliamentary scrutiny if a regulator is appointed to supervise the industry.

The privatisation of public services has been accomplished using four methods: charging, contracting out, liberalisation and withdrawal. Charging requires the user to pay for the service although the service may remain in the public sector. Contracting out involves the provision of a service by the private sector which has been contracted to do the work by the State. Liberalisation means a break-up of monopoly power by means of competition. In withdrawal, the State responsibility for a particular service is abolished; the service will either be abolished or be provided by private or voluntary bodies.[11]

4–05 The reasons for privatisation include improvements in efficiency, a reduction of the Government's involvement in industry, the widening of share ownership, the encouragement of employee share ownership, an end to many of the problems of public sector pay negotiations, a reduction in the public sector borrowing requirement, the enhancement of economic freedom and the raising of finance to fund other government spending.

There are many arguments which can support or challenge each of these assertions. For instance, "economic freedom" assumes that a private monopoly is less threatening to such freedom than a public one. It also defines freedom to mean the absence of government intervention in the market. Yet the Government has recognised that some forms of control are necessary for some privatised industries, for instance the gas industry and telecommunications.

4–06 The contention that privatisation would widen share ownership was only partially fulfilled. When the shares were first offered for sale, large numbers of citizens bought the shares because the offer price was usually lower than could be expected on the open market, most offers allowed purchasers to buy by instalments and many gave "loyalty" bonuses of extra shares or discounts on bills if the shares were retained for a specified time. However, when these benefits ran out, many shareholders sold, taking their profits, and the shares were then bought by large institutional shareholders.

---

[10] Gamble, "Privatisation, Thatcherism and the British State" (1989) 16(1) *Journal of Law and Society* 1 at 4.

[11] *ibid.* at 10.

The privatisation programme of the Conservative Government has been immense; by 1991, 50 per cent of the public sector and some 650,000 employees had been transferred into the private sector.

Privatisation has not resulted in litigation, with two exceptions. In 1986, the trustee savings banks were floated on the stock market. Depositors in the statutory banks brought actions in which they claimed that they were entitled to the surplus assets of the statutory banks when they were abolished by the Trustee Savings Bank Act 1985. The House of Lords held that the depositors' rights were limited to receiving their deposits plus interest and not to a share in the surplus funds.[12] During the privatisation of public water authorities in England and Wales, several local authorities claimed that the Water Act 1989 had infringed their valuable property rights. The courts however held that the councils had no legal or equitable interests in the assets of the privatised water authorities.[13]

(c) Deregulation

This means that government control over an industry is reduced by repealing statutory controls in order to allow ordinary market forces to operate fully. Examples of such deregulation involved the financial services markets, domestic air tariffs and the bus services industry. The Deregulation and Contracting Out Act 1994 gives powers to the Minister to remove statutory burdens on businesses. **4–07**

(d) Self-regulation

This form of regulation of business has been favoured by the Conservative Government as it places responsibility for the regulation on the industry itself. Graham defines this as "the delegation of public policy tasks to private actors in an institutionalised form".[14] The National Consumer Council defined it thus: "In essence, self-regulation means that rules which govern behaviour in the market are developed, administered and enforced by the people (or their representatives) whose behaviour is to be governed."[15] There is seldom any legislative foundation for the body which carries out the self-regulatory function. However, many of these bodies are incorporated as a company limited by guarantee and thus are registered in the Register of Companies. This, Graham argues, gives them a limited form of **4–08**

---

[12] *Ross v. Lord Advocate,* 1986 S.L.T. 391.
[13] *Sheffield City Council v. Yorkshire Water Services Ltd* [1991] 2 All E.R. 280.
[14] Graham, "Self-Regulation", in Richardson and Genn, *Administrative Law and Government Action* (1994), p. 190.
[15] National Consumer Council, *Self Regulation* (1986), p. 1.

accountability in that there is public scrutiny of their constitutional framework.[16]

THE POWER OF THE EXECUTIVE

4–09   In order to understand the power held by the Executive today, we have briefly to discuss some historical issues. The situation at the start of this century is neatly stated in this quotation from Josef Redlich in 1905:

> "In the British cabinet today is concentrated all political power, all initiative in legislation and administration, and finally all public authority for carrying out the laws in kingdom and empire ... (T)he second half of the last century saw the gradual transfer from Crown and Parliament into the hands of the Cabinet of one after another of the elements of authority and political power. This process took place side by side and in organic connection with the passing of political sovereignty into the hands of the House of Commons, supported as it was now by an electorate comprising all sections of the population."[17]

In the early nineteenth century, the Government did not get involved in domestic policies; it was left to backbench M.P.s to implement the major reforms we now associate with that period in history, for instance the Factories Acts, anti-slavery Acts and prison reforms. The Government was expected to be involved in the maintenance of law and order, conduct foreign relations and ensure the defence of the country. The party system in the House of Commons was weak and any divisions were not along party lines.

4–10   The development of the suffrage was the catalyst for altering the constitutional balance of power; as more people became entitled to vote, the Government had to appeal to a wider cross-section of the public since it could no longer afford to buy the votes it needed to stay in power. The Liberal Government of 1906 to 1911 promised social reform but although there was a desire to help underprivileged people, the main motive for the Government was political, because such underprivileged people were also now voters. Political sovereignty passed to the House of Commons with the passage of the Parliament Act 1911 and the legitimacy of the Commons was strengthened by universal suffrage which finally came in 1928 with the extension of the franchise to all adults over the age of 21. This in turn led to a strengthening of the Executive who had to devise a programme of policies which would appeal to the electorate. The aspirations of voters were increasing as were their expectations.

The Government had to become increasingly involved in the control of the economy to ensure they had funds to carry out their policies. This

---

[16] Graham, *op. cit.*, n. 14, above, p. 196.
[17] Redlich, "The Procedure of the House of Commons", in Craig, *op. cit.*, n. 4, above, pp. 67–68.

necessitated a change in the political system; if the Government had to keep its promises it needed to be sure its M.P.s would support its legislative measures, so the party whip system was strengthened to ensure the maintenance of party discipline. In addition, the increased legislative programmes since 1945 have led to a need to ensure that no Parliamentary time is wasted. These have all led to the rigid party system which is now in place in British politics.

CHANGES IN THE LEGISLATIVE PROCESS

The centralisation of legislative initiative was encouraged by three 4–11 developments: the introduction of standing committees, the discussion of legislation in Cabinet committees, and the growth of delegated legislation.[18]

In the nineteenth century, standing committees were regarded as a device for the Government to escape criticism; it was generally accepted that the Government should defend its proposals in a Committee of the Whole House. As the Government's legislative proposals increased this led to an increased use of standing committees. In 1906 the Procedure Committee recommended that all Bills, except finance, consolidated fund and appropriation account Bills, be sent to a standing committee after second reading. It took four days of debate before the recommendations were accepted by the Commons.

In 1945 a Select Committee on Procedure was established to look at ways of speeding up the Parliamentary process since the Labour Government had a complex and technical legislative programme. The select committee reported that all Bills except those of a constitutional nature should be sent to a standing committee. In addition, it recommended that greater use of committees and the use of the guillotine or timetabling motion were necessary. For Scottish Bills, there are two Scottish Standing Committees which have the normal composition as other standing committees, that is they have a Government majority, and the other parties are represented according to their representation in the Commons. For the last few years, however, the Scottish Standing Committees have had to include M.P.s for non-Scottish constituencies to make up the numbers on the Government side. Bills applying exclusively to Scotland are passed using the normal procedure but their Second Reading debate and Report stage may be heard in the Scottish Grand Committee, which comprises all M.P.s from Scottish constituencies.[19] The votes at Second Reading and Report stage are taken on the floor of the House. Grand Committees have also been set up for Wales and Northern Ireland.

---

[18] See Craig, *op. cit.*, n. 4, above.
[19] See White Paper, *Scotland in the Union*, Cm. 2225 (1993); Winetrobe, "Governing Scotland" (1994) 39 J.L.S.S. 459.

4–12   Although Cabinet committees were used by the Liberal Government in 1911 to settle the details of their legislative proposals, it was the aftermath of the Second World War which saw an increase in the use of such committees. They allow discussion of proposed legislation to ensure that Bills which are presented to Parliament are well drafted and reflect the Government's policies. The Cabinet's involvement at early stages of the proposals will iron out or identify any areas of difficulty so that the passage of the Bill can be achieved with the minimum of problems. The volume of legislative proposals also means that the Cabinet cannot deal with every one in detail and the Cabinet committee is thus given the task of making proposals which the Cabinet can then agree. Until 1992, the existence of Cabinet committees was a badly-kept secret. Successive Governments refused to confirm their existence, citing as the reason that if their existence was acknowledged the doctrine of collective responsibility would be damaged. The Prime Minister announced the names, the composition and the terms of reference of some 26 committees and sub-committees in May 1992, as part of the Government's drive for more openness.[20]

4–13   Delegated legislation has centralised legislative initiative in the Executive. The increase in social legislation led to a corresponding increase in delegated legislation. The Government of course decides when and whether to initiate such legislation[21] and this has greatly increased the influence of the Executive. As Birkinshaw reflects: "The shell of power was in Parliamentary legislation, its substance was in statutory instruments, departmental rules, Codes of Practice, Ministerial circulars and letters, White papers, statements of intent, government contracts and all the informal deals struck between mighty departments and their client groups."[22]

THE SCRUTINY OF THE EXECUTIVE BY HOUSE OF COMMONS

4–14   If we believe that Parliament controls the Executive, then we are sadly mistaken — Parliament has two main roles, to pass legislation, including financial legislation, and to scrutinise the work of the Executive. In many ways, the latter is the more important but arguably it is also the one in which the Legislature is most ineffective. Ryle says: "Parliament is the forum where the exercise of Government is publicly displayed and is open to scrutiny and criticism. And the Commons does not control the executive

---

[20] *Hansard*, H.C., Written Answers, Vol. 208, cols. 110–118 (May 19, 1992).
[21] See Chap. 5.
[22] Birkinshaw, "Decision-making and its control" in McAuslan and McEldowney, *Law, Legitimacy and the Constitution* (1985), Chap. 7.

— not in any real sense; rather the executive control the Commons through the exercise of their party majority power."[23]

The traditional notion of Ministerial responsibility says that a Minister is answerable to Parliament for the work of his department — what the Minister controls, the Minister is accountable for.[24] Further, the doctrine infers that civil servants have "no constitutional personality or responsibility separate from that of the Government of the day".[25] This view is reinforced by the Civil Service Code issued in 1996 which states: "Civil servants are servants of the Crown. Constitutionally, the Crown acts on the advice of Ministers and, subject to the provisions of this Code, civil servants owe their loyalty to the duly constituted Government."

The Commons' role in controlling legislation is weak; the Government 4–15 of the day will almost certainly get its legislation passed as it wishes if it has a working majority. The role of the House of Lords has been reduced to that of a revising and questioning chamber since it is now possible for a Bill to be passed without the consent of the Lords. Although this is a rare occurrence, the use of the Parliament Acts 1911 and 1949 to bypass the Lords can be seen as a real threat to the existence of the Lords.[26] The last hurdle in the legislative process is the granting of the Royal Assent; this is now never refused. Thus, the power of the House of Commons could be said to be supreme and, indeed, it is possible to extrapolate from this that a Government with a working majority is supreme. However, it must be remembered that Governments can be overturned by losing a vote of confidence on an important matter in the Commons, and by a General Election defeat so, to that extent, the Government's power is limited.

The Commons' main function therefore will be to scrutinise what the Government is doing, but the effectiveness of its scrutiny will depend on the opportunities which may arise to raise matters and on the machinery for scrutiny.

NON-LEGISLATIVE DEBATES AND QUESTIONS

The effectiveness of these is limited; they can embarrass the Government 4–16 but not really explore an issue in any great depth. The Opposition has "supply" or opposition days where they choose the topic for debate.

---

[23] Ryle, "The Commons in the Seventies — A General Survey", in Walkland and Ryle, *The Commons in the Seventies* (1977), at p. 12.

[24] See Chap. 3.

[25] Bogdanor, "Ministers, Civil servants and the Constitution" (1993) 15 IALS Bulletin 10 at 17.

[26] The last time the procedure was used was to pass the War Crimes Act 1991; this was also the first time the procedure had been used by a Conservative Government against the Conservative-dominated Lords.

Individual members can table questions and have debates on motions for the adjournment. Only a few of the many questions tabled for a Minister will receive an oral reply at Question Time but in any case, the majority of M.P.s tabling questions require a written answer. The effectiveness of Ministerial Question Time as a method of scrutinising the Executive is debatable but there is no doubt as to the usefulness of the written answers. These require the Government to consider particular issues and to give out considerable information. "In Britain, the parliamentary question plays a peculiarly central role in arrangements for accountability, largely due to the lack of an effective system of administrative law or of a more sophisticated means of audit of Government."[27]

Debates on motions for the adjournment also have mixed effectiveness. If this motion is used by the M.P. to bring a particular matter to the attention of a Minister, then it can be most useful. The M.P. has the undivided attention of the Minister and the House for 15 minutes while he explains his motion; thereafter the Minister will reply for a similar time. The motion is tabled in advance so the Minister will be prepared using information compiled by his officials. The problem with this procedure is that it is held at the end of the Parliamentary day, is attended by very few M.P.s and receives little publicity.

MACHINERY FOR SCRUTINY

4–17 Since their reorganisation in 1979,[28] select committees have worked effectively in some instances, less so in others. They allow for a detailed scrutiny of the work of Government[29] and they prepare reports which are on occasions very critical. The membership of select committees is drawn from the ranks of backbench M.P.s. The members are nominated by the Committee of Selection, their appointments being confirmed by the House. The chairman of a select committee may come from either side of the House[30] and the membership will reflect the number of seats held by the parties in the House. There are some 33 select committees in total, with 17 of these being department-related. The Scottish Affairs Select Committee was reinstated in 1992 after a lapse of five years, caused by the fact that the number of Conservative M.P.s in Scotland was too small to both staff the Scottish Office and give a majority on the select committee.

---

[27] Prosser, *Nationalised Industries and Public Control: Legal, Constitutional and Political Issues* (1986).

[28] See Giddings, "Select Committees and Parliamentary scrutiny: plus ca change?" (1994) 47(4) *Parliamentary Affairs* 669.

[29] Procedure Select Committee in its Second Report (1989–90 H.C. 19–I) suggested at p. xxxii four ways in which select committees interact with government.

[30] Note that in practice chairmen are drawn from the Government party and the official Opposition party.

The committees' remit is to examine the "administration, policy and 4–18 expenditure" of the department.[31] They have had limited impact for a number of reasons. First, select committees do not have a role in the process of framing legislation or policy. They scrutinise policy after it is implemented and their comments may not affect future policy decisions. They can only make recommendations and are unable to force the Government to accept them — for instance, several committees made recommendations regarding the conduct of the Westland Affair, but all of these were firmly rejected by the Government. Secondly, they do not have adequate resources to carry out complex investigations; most select committees have only four or five civil servants assisting them in collecting information and compiling reports. In addition, there is insufficient time for the committees to hear evidence and discuss issues with interested parties. Thirdly, each committee decides its own agenda but the efficacy of the committee tends to depend on the style and enthusiasm of its chairman.[32] Further, the questions asked by members of the committee may be general in nature and based on the political needs of the member at the current moment. Fourthly, the Memorandum of Guidance[33] of officials means that civil servants are limited in the amount of information they can give to the committee. Fifthly, most of the committees give scant attention to the expenditure aspect of their remit. There may be two reasons for this: the PAC scrutinises the expenditure of departments (and the departmental committee may not wish to duplicate this), and most MPs are not interested in such detailed investigations.[34] Sixth, opportunities to debate the findings of the committee on the floor of the House are limited. Fewer than 25 per cent of the reports are debated in the House although the Government does now formally respond to reports.[35] Finally, the relationship between the select committee and the department may become too "cosy" in that the committee does not investigate controversial matters and fails to question the department closely. The Home Affairs Committee appeared in the late 1980s to have been in this situation.[36]

The position of civil servants appearing before select committees is 4–19 relatively straightforward; they appear on behalf of the Minister and are

---

[31] Standing Order 130.

[32] Rush, "Parliamentary Scrutiny", in Pyper and Robins, *Governing the UK in the 1990s* (1995), p. 122.

[33] Memorandum of Guidance of Officials Appearing before Select Committees, now re-drafted and entitled Departmental Evidence and Response to Select Committees (Cabinet Office, 1994).

[34] Giddings, *op. cit.,* n. 28, above, 682.

[35] Procedure Committee recommended that departments should respond to Select Committee reports within two months of publication. Second Report of select committee on Procedure, Working of Select Committee System (1989–90 H.C. 19–II, 217), para. 62.

[36] See Natzler and Silk "Departmental Select Committees and the Next Steps Programme" in Drewry and Giddings, *Parliament and Executive Agencies* (1994), at p. 76.

required to answer according to the policy of the Government.[37] The position of former civil servants is less straightforward. Two former civil servants were requested to give evidence to the Trade and Industry Select Committee but were prevented by the Government from doing so because they could no longer be said to be speaking on behalf of the Minister. Lord Justice Scott found this unsatisfactory since it was a failure "to comply with the obligations to assist a SC to obtain the best first hand evidence on the matters being investigated".[38] The problem for select committees trying to interview civil servants is that Ministerial responsibility gets in the way. The civil servant cannot express his own view because he speaks on behalf of the Minister and, according to the doctrine, the Minister alone is responsible. However, Ministers cannot be compelled to answer questions and so the select committee may be unable to investigate a particular issue effectively.[39] The situation therefore makes a mockery of the doctrine of Ministerial responsibility and shows that it has become a defence for the Government against accountability, preventing proper discussion and criticism, and perpetuating and protecting bad government and bad decision-making.[40]

4–20   Select committees are required to examine the associated public bodies of the department; these include the non-departmental public bodies (or quangos), nationalised industries and, more recently, executive agencies. The committees have tended to inquire into policy more than the administration or expenditure of a department, but in their inquiries into the associated public bodies, they are taking a broader view and looking at the administrative and financial arrangements of the body concerned.[41] However, with regard to executive agencies, there has been no systematic and sustained investigation of their work by the departmental committees. Most have referred in their reports to the introduction of agencies into the departments but as yet there have been relatively few inquiries. In this regard the committees may be following the previous pattern where select committees investigated nationalised industries once every two or three years; the select committees may therefore catch up in due course.

The very existence of select committees has, however, led to a number of benefits — for instance, departments are more careful in policy matters since the committee can probe them. There is also more evidence that select committees are willing to discuss issues which are controversial, for instance,

---

[37] Cabinet Office (1994), *op. cit.,* n. 33, above.

[38] Report of the Inquiry into the Export of Defence Equipment and Dual Use Goods to Iraq and Related Prosecutions (The Scott Report) (1995–96 H.C. 115) at para. F4.66.

[39] This was the position in 1986 when Ministers refused to allow civil servants to be questioned regarding the Westland Affair and themselves declined to do so. See discussion in Seventh Report of Treasury and Civil Service Committee (1986) Civil Servants and Ministers: Duties and Responsibilities (1985–86 H.C. 92).

[40] Oliver, "Parliament, Ministers and the Law" (1994) 47(4) *Parliamentary Affairs* 630.

[41] *ibid.*.

the NHS reforms, privatisation and so on. They have provided a forum for debate where interest groups can present their opinions and they are an important forum for debate on how government policies are being implemented and their impact.

In addition to select committees which "shadow" the departments, there 4–21 are other "single issue" select committees which monitor the workings of other Parliamentary bodies. The Public Accounts Committee is undoubtedly the most powerful and influential of all the committees. It was established in 1861 to examine department accounts and ensure authorised expenditure was properly spent. In this, its remit has not changed. However, the way in which it scrutinises departmental accounts has changed. The PAC receives the reports of the Comptroller and Auditor-General and his department, the National Audit Office (created by the National Audit Act 1983). The committee does not scrutinise the policy of the Government but is required to scrutinise the way in which these policies are implemented. The recommendations of the PAC are normally accepted by the Government since these recommendations are based on the detailed analyses of the department annual accounts prepared by the NAO. The committee also considers the value for money reports on government activities; these are carried out by the NAO.[42] The PAC/NAO relationship is close and this has considerable benefits for the scrutiny process. The NAO has a statutory foundation in the 1983 Act and it is relatively well-staffed to carry out its work.[43] The Comptroller and Auditor-General is an independent officer of Parliament; like the Parliamentary Commissioner for Administration, he cannot be removed from office on the whim of the Government. The membership of the PAC itself consists of experienced senior M.P.s who have the background knowledge to carry out the scrutiny process effectively and its chairman is by convention a member of the Opposition.

THE CHANGING FACE OF THE EXECUTIVE

The Executive consists of the Cabinet and Government Ministers, central 4–22 government departments, the civil service, local government and a myriad of agencies and public bodies carrying out executive or administrative functions. Central government departments are staffed by civil servants who work under the political direction of Ministers. Most departments are responsible for a particular function or group of functions, but three, the Scottish Office, the Welsh Office and the Northern Ireland Office, have

---

[42] National Audit Act 1983, s. 6(1) and (2); for a detailed account of a VFM scrutiny see Roberts and Pollitt "Audit or Evaluation? A National Audit Office VFM Study" (1994) 72(4) *Public Administration* 527.
[43] For a detailed account of the work of NAO, see Harden, White and Hollingsworth, "Value for Money and Administrative Law" (1996) P. L. 661.

territorial responsibilities which are multi-function. The central government departments are unable to carry out all of the functions assigned to them by Parliament; instead, the function may be carried out by an agency or public body outside the departmental hierarchy but funded by public funds. These types of bodies have been in existence for centuries, but their importance in recent times has grown, particularly because of the Conservative Government's drive for economy, efficiency and effectiveness. In addition, the Government has wanted to decrease the size of the civil service and has done so by various means, including the transfer of functions to non-elected, appointed boards and agencies.

4–23   Before the 1980s, there were many reasons for creating agencies. They included the theory that the agency protects certain activities from political interference; the theory that the creation of an agency allows that activity to escape from the known weaknesses of traditional government departments; the theory that it is desirable to spread power; the "back-double" theory[44] which means that if the Government cannot do what it wants to do in the current structure, then it creates a new organisation to make it possible; the "too many bureaucrats" view which says that if the public thinks there are too many civil servants, government relocates or "hides" some in quangos whose employees are not classified as civil servants; and the situation where the Government can direct criticism away from itself in politically sensitive areas, by creating an agency so that, in the public's mind, it is "X Commission" which gets the brunt of public criticism, not the Government.

The drive for lower public spending led to a number of reports and reviews of the civil service and how it works. The Fulton Committee[45] led to a number of major changes in the structure of the civil service and in particular how civil servants were recruited and promoted, recommending the formation of the Civil Service Department. The report recommended that departments should have a clearly defined authority and that some functions should be hived off to bodies which would exist outside the departmental framework although still being subject to Ministerial guidance. The latter recommendation led to the formation of some such bodies, for instance the Civil Aviation Authority in 1971 from the Department of Trade and Industry and the Health and Safety Commission in 1974 from the Department of Employment. The report's proposal for the creation of "semi-autonomous boards" was derived from the Swedish system of government which had a small core of civil servants making policy for boards and agencies to implement.[46] The Fulton Report also wanted to see greater

---

[44] So-called because of the practice of taxi drivers who use back streets, or back-doubles, when the main streets are too busy.

[45] Report of the Committee on the Civil Service, Cmnd. 3638 (1968).

[46] *ibid*. Chap. 5.

mobility of staff between the private sector and the civil service. The report was never fully implemented but it did provide a starting-point for the Thatcher reforms of the 1980s.[47]

In 1979, Margaret Thatcher set up a small unit of six civil servants under 4–24 Derek Rayner; this led to the formation later of the Efficiency Unit. Thatcher's intention was to reduce the size of the public sector by "deprivileging" civil servants and introducing privatisation so that reductions in the public sector borrowing requirement could be made. Rayner's chief task therefore was to investigate the workings of the civil service with a view to saving money. In 1982, the scrutiny programme was commenced with departments being required to question all of their activities, propose solutions and begin their implementation within 12 months. At each stage of the scrutiny process, there were strict time-limits which prevented civil servants from prevaricating and thus holding back the completion of the process. The scrutiny programme led to the introduction of MINIS — Management Information System for Ministers — into the Department of Environment. This led to a reorganisation of the department and a 29 per cent reduction in staff.[48] The objectives of MINIS were to ascertain departmental economic targets, how they were set and how they were being achieved. This information was given to the Minister so that he or she knew what was happening, when and who was responsible. It was in effect an information retrieval system[49] designed to strengthen top-down control within the department.

The Financial Management Initiative (FMI)[50] was introduced to give managers at all levels greater responsibility and control. It ensured that managers had a clear view of their objectives, had well-defined responsibilities and the training to ensure they could exercise those responsibilities. Departments were divided into "cost centres" with each centre having control over its own budget. In 1985, performance-related pay was introduced for civil servants on grades 3–7 and new productivity agreements were offered to higher-grade staff. In 1988, new running costs were imposed on departments with cash limits set on individual managers. As Dowding[51] comments, civil servants were asked to be innovative, with encouragement being given in the form of pay and promotion. However, such a "carrot" approach is not fully

---

[47] Dowding, *The Civil Service* (1995), pp. 20–21.
[48] *ibid.* p. 67.
[49] For discussion see McEldowney, *Public Law* (1994), pp. 283–286.
[50] For discussion of this and the other initiatives, see Drewry, "Revolution in Whitehall: The Next Steps and Beyond" in Jowell and Oliver, *op. cit.,* n. 9, above; Gray and Jenkins with Flynn and Rutherford, "The Management of Change in Whitehall: The Experience of the FMI" (1991) 69 *Public Administration* 41; Davies and Willman, *What Next? Agencies, Departments and the Civil Service* (1991).
[51] Dowding, *op. cit.,* n. 47, above, p. 71.

effective unless a stick is also involved, and this was introduced in the shape
of the removal of job security by the Next Steps Initiative and market testing.
4–25   The Ibbs Report in 1988[52] led to more radical reforms. This report ("the
Next Steps Initiative") recommended a split between service delivery and
the making of policy.

> "The aim should be to establish a quite different way of conducting the busi-
> ness of Government. The central civil service should consist of a relatively
> small core engaged in the function of servicing Ministers and managing de-
> partments, who will be the 'sponsors' of particular Government policies and
> services. Responding to these departments will be large numbers of agencies
> employing their own staff, who may or may not have the status of Crown
> servants, and concentrating on the delivery of their particular service, with
> clearly defined responsibilities between the Secretary of State and perma-
> nent Secretary on the one hand and the Chairman or Chief Executive of the
> agencies on the other."[53]

A further consequence of this split of function would be an end to the fiction
that the Minister was responsible for everything done in his name by
officials. The Next Steps Initiative was seen to be necessary because FMI
was not producing its expected results quickly enough. It had lost
momentum, having failed to convince civil servants in the middle ranks to
change their entrenched beliefs on the structure and culture of the civil
service.[54] The Treasury in particular seemed reluctant to lose its control
over expenditure, and the emphasis as noted above was on running costs,
not programme expenditure. Another problem identified was the lack of
management experience of top civil servants; the Ibbs Report implied that
the establishment of agencies to carry out the executive functions of
departments would release top civil servants from such management
functions and allow them to concentrate on policy formulation. The FMI
also showed that Ministers were not managers; this allowed the Next Steps
Initiative to proceed on the basis that Ministers would not be involved in
detailed management processes.[55]
4–26   The Ibbs Report, like the Fulton Report, also drew heavily on the Swedish
model of government, where a small core of civil servants are involved in
policy formulation and the service providers work in agencies which have
operational independence and responsibility. Resources and performance
targets are set by the core departments. However, the Swedish model
prevents Ministers from interfering in agency matters and there is also a

[52] Jenkins, Caines and Jackson, *Improving Management in Government: the Next Steps: Report to the Minister* (1988).
[53] *ibid.*.
[54] Zifcak, *New Managerialism: Administrative Reform in Whitehall and Canberra* (1994), p. 69.
[55] *ibid.* p. 81.

well-developed system of administrative courts and ombudsmen to offer mechanisms for redress.[56] None of these aspects were proposed by the report.

The Next Steps Initiative was soon to be overtaken by three others in 1991. The Fraser Report[57] recommended that departments adopt a more strategic role in their dealings with agencies, devolving finance and staffing matters to agency level, thus making savings in staffing costs in the departments. The Citizen's Charter[58] was also released in 1991 and introduced the idea of the citizen as a customer. This idea was necessary so that a distinction could be made between the citizen as the taxpayer and elector, and the citizen as customer who is the recipient of the services supplied by the State. If contracting out of services was to be legitimate, then this distinction would be required to separate service delivery from democracy.[59] Contracting out was the final initiative, introduced by the White Paper *Competing for Quality: Buying Better Public Services*[60] which proposed that competitive tendering for work would lead to lower costs and increased efficiency and would allow managers to innovate. Both of these initiatives are discussed later in this chapter.

These initiatives led to government departments being required by the Treasury to review all of their activities and consider the following possibilities for each activity: abolition, privatisation, contracting out, agency and the status quo. These possibilities are called "prior options" and a number of tests are considered.[61] Is the activity necessary, and if not, can it be abolished ? Does it need to be in the public sector; if not, should it be privatised or can the function be contracted out ? If an agency is finally set up, it will in fact have been rejected for privatisation and will have been considered to be better placed in the public sector, but almost at arm's length.[62] If the chosen option was status quo, this had to be specifically argued by the department. The option of abolition was preferred by the Treasury wherever possible, although usually one of the remaining three would be chosen. All agencies are subjected to a reconsideration of the prior options at five-year intervals.[63] This review can take place earlier particularly if it appears that privatisation has become a strong option.[64]

4–27

---

[56] Harden, *The Contracting State* (1992).
[57] The Efficiency Unit, *Making the Most of Next Steps: the Management of ministers' departments and their executive agencies* (1991).
[58] *The Citizen's Charter: Raising the Standard*, Cm. 599 (1991).
[59] Ridley, "Reinventing British Government" (1995) 48(3) *Parliamentary Affairs* 387.
[60] HM Treasury, Cm. 1730 (1991).
[61] The Efficiency Unit, *The Government's Guide to Market Testing* (1993).
[62] Note, though, that an agency can still be privatised; HMSO was set up first as a trading fund, then it became an executive agency and finally in 1996 it was sold off to The Stationery Office.
[63] Drewry, *op. cit.,* n. 50, above, p. 172.
[64] *Next Steps Agencies in Government Review 1996*, Cm. 3579 (1997), 27.

During 1996, seven agencies were transferred to the public sector as a result of this review.

4–28   Much of the civil service has now been hived off into agency status. On December 31, 1996, there were 129 executive agencies comprising some 365,000 civil servants.[65] The Department of Social Security has moved 97 per cent of its staff into five agencies, the largest being the Benefits Agency with 64,000 staff. Those departments which have not created executive agencies are nonetheless operating on Next Steps principles,[66] although their managerial freedom remains under careful central control.

Of course, the real impetus for these changes has been the Conservative Government's search for efficiency and economy. Once that started, it was logical to ask whether the service could be provided more cheaply in the private sector, or whether it should be provided at all, or whether it should be carried out in-house or contracted out. All of these options have been employed, making the administrative structure more complex, and posing problems for public law in terms of accountability and judicial review.

CENTRAL GOVERNMENT AND AGENCIES

4–29   The word "agency" is used to describe a number of institutions which carry out government functions outside the traditional departmental framework. The names given to these bodies vary, for instance, commission, directorate, agency, inspectorate, authority, service and office. They are sometimes also called quangos (quasi-autonomous non-governmental organisations) but this is misleading. They are non-departmental rather than non-governmental, and indeed the Government refers to them as NDPBs (non-departmental public bodies). The acronym "quango" is also translated as "quasi-autonomous national government organisation" but again this is a misleading term since it does not encompass a number of public bodies which are normally included, such as voluntary organisations.[67] Another, more recent, acronym is EGO (extra-governmental organisation).[68]

The term "agency" seems reasonably descriptive of those bodies which carry out government functions outside the normal departmental structure although they have to be distinguished from executive agencies created under the Next Steps Initiative, since the executive agencies are not non-departmental; they are created out of the department and have close links with the department.

---

[65]   *ibid*. p. (v).
[66]   Customs and Excise, Inland Revenue.
[67]   See Hogwood, "The Growth of Quangos: Evidence and Explanations" (1995) 48(2) *Parliamentary Affairs* 207.
[68]   See Weir, "Quangos: Questions of Democratic Accountability" in Ridley and Wilson, *The Quango Debate* (1995).

There is a further distinction to be made between regulatory agencies and service delivery agencies. Regulatory agencies are concerned with the regulation of, for instance, gaming, aviation, or race relations, whereas service delivery agencies are concerned with the provision of services such as social welfare. However, the distinction is not clear-cut: some service delivery agencies will have regulatory functions, and vice versa.

From the mid-nineteenth century until the 1970s, the civil service was a 4–30 unified and uniform service, carrying out government functions in departmental structures which could change to meet new needs. This contrasted with the previous structure where public functions were carried out by boards which operated outside the civil service. The board system fell into disuse because of the desire of Parliament to have one person directly answerable in the House for the board's activities. The current increase in agencies has led to the same problem, only now it is perhaps more acute because there is an expectation that someone will be accountable: "Those who perform a public duty should be fully responsible to an electorate — by way either of a Minister responsible to Parliament or of a locally elected council. The essence of the fringe body is that it is not so responsible for some or all of its actions."[69]

The organisational framework of agencies will differ according to whether they were created under the Next Steps Initiative or independent of it. We will first consider the difficulties and problems associated with independent agencies and then those associated with the Next Steps or executive agencies.

INDEPENDENT AGENCIES OR NDPBs

Independent agencies are created almost always by statute, for instance the 4–31 Civil Aviation Authority and the regulatory bodies for privatised industries. The statute will state the composition of the body, its powers, the role of the Minister and so on. Other agencies are set up by the operation of the prerogative or by an administrative act of the Minister. They have a "role in the processes of government but are not government departments or part of a government department".[70] They are set up to bring in expertise from bodies outside the civil service, for instance the Council on Tribunals and the Medical Research Council, or to perform functions which should be free from political interference such as the Advisory, Conciliation and Arbitration Service and the Health and Safety Commission. Legal action will be brought in the name of the agency unless a decision of a Minister is involved.

---

[69] Chester, "Fringe Bodies, Quangos and All That" (1979) 57 *Public Administration* 54.
[70] Report on Non-Departmental Public Bodies, Cmnd. 7797 (1980).

4–32   The appointment of people to run these agencies will depend on the type of organisation in question but normally it will be the Minister of the department concerned. It is this patronage by a Minister which has caused most of the concerns; the appointment is made by the person whose policy will be implemented and there are fears that this may lead to power being used inappropriately. The power to appoint does not, however, lie exclusively in the hands of the Minister; in 1995, the Commissioner for Public Appointments was appointed in response to a recommendation by the Nolan Committee.[71] His role is to "monitor, regulate and approve departmental appointment procedures for Ministerial appointments to executive non-departmental public bodies and NHS bodies".[72] The Minister is accountable to Parliament for appointments and he or she will consult with the Prime Minister on major posts. In addition, the names of appointees are published in various government publications. However, there was a perception that these posts were given to people of like mind to the Government and therefore were more likely to be given to party sympathisers,[73] hence the appointment of the Commissioner for Public Appointments. Such patronage has of course occurred in all Governments since it is a useful way of rewarding party political service while retaining control of the service being delivered. It does, however, beg the question, are the best qualified people being appointed?

4–33   The trend is towards a substitution of appointed boards for elected authorities; NDPBs are useful devices for bypassing local government which might be hostile to the Government's policy. In Scotland, for instance, the reorganisation of local government in 1996 saw the transfer of the responsibility for water and sewerage services from local authorities to three new water authorities, whose members were appointed by the Secretary of State for Scotland.[74] The transfer of functions from locally elected bodies to centrally appointed bodies has democratic consequences. Local authorities are required to keep a public register of members' interests, meetings are generally open to the public and there is public access to various council papers. Auditors' reports and criticisms and performance indicators are all published. However, NDPBs are under no such duties; many hold their meetings in private and their papers are not readily available, often because they contain "commercially sensitive information". This was criticised by the Nolan Committee which went on to recommend a Code of Best Practice

---

[71] Committee on Standards in Public Life, set up in October 1994 as a standing body, appointed for three years in the first instance, with the remit to examine concerns about standards of conduct of all holders of public office.

[72] See Office of Commissioner for Public Appointments leaflet at web site: http://www.open.gov.uk/ocpa/leaflet.htm (15.1.97)

[73] See Weir, *op. cit.*, n. 68, above, at 138.

[74] Local Government etc. (Scotland) Act 1994.

in Executive NDPBs and NHS Bodies.[75] The Code refers in particular to access to information, access to meetings and publication of accounts and performance targets.

There also appears to have been an increase in the number of these agencies; the Democratic Audit/Charter 88 Report identified 5,521 in the United Kingdom, with 443 at national level, 355 at regional level and 4,723 at local level.[76] This compares with the Government's figures in 1991 of 1,444 NDPBs, but this figure does not include NHS bodies or executive agencies.[77] Historically, it has been extremely difficult to calculate the numbers of NDPBs because of the problems in defining which organisations should be included, for instance the Democratic Audit Report included grant-maintained schools in England and Wales and housing associations which are run by unpaid volunteers. Neither of these types of organisation could be said to be NDPBs in the normal sense of the term. However, the 82 Training and Enterprise Councils in England and Wales were left out of the figures for the annual Public Bodies report, because they are viewed by the Government as "non-profit making private companies working under government contract". Yet these bodies are important for the delivery of the Government's policy and are set up and supervised by central government as well as receiving most of their funding from government.[78] The Government has maintained that the numbers have fallen by 38 per cent from 1979 and indeed there was a reduction in the number of executive NDPBs, brought about mainly by merging bodies rather than by abolition.[79] Of more concern perhaps than the numbers of NDPBs is the upward trend of the amount of expenditure and government funding now in the hands of these bodies. From 1979 to 1992, the government funding of NDPBs increased by 25 per cent or £2 billion.[80] Weir calculates that the NDPBs in 1992–93 were responsible for some 30 per cent of the total central government expenditure.[81]

It is possible to distinguish broad groupings of agencies; executive bodies, advisory bodies, tribunals and regulatory bodies. The first three groupings are used by the Cabinet Office when compiling the annual Public Bodies Report, but these groupings ignore the large number of local agencies such as F.E. colleges. Executive bodies are probably the most important category since they employ staff and have their own budgets. They are formed often

4–34

4–35

---

[75] First Report of Committee on Standards in Public Life, Cm. 2850 (1995).
[76] Hall and Weir, "EGO-Trip: Extra-governmental organisations in UK and their accountability" Democratic Audit Paper No. 2 (1994), University of Essex.
[77] *Public Bodies* (1991).
[78] Wilson, "Quangos in the Skeletal State" in Ridley and Wilson, *The Quango Debate* (1995), p. 3.
[79] Hunt, "Worthwhile Bodies" (1995) 48(2) *Parliamentary Affairs* 192.
[80] Hogwood, *op. cit.,* n. 67, above, 215.
[81] Weir, *op. cit.,* n. 68, above.

to distance a Minister from the day-to-day management of a particular function but they have the potential advantage that they can involve people from outside government in the management of the agency. Examples of these bodies are the Scottish Higher Education Funding Council and the Scottish Arts Council. Advisory bodies are unlikely to employ staff or incur expenditure on their own behalf. They are usually set up to advise Ministers and departments on specialist and technical matters. An example of this type is the Council on Tribunals and its Scottish Committee. Tribunals themselves are generally serviced by their sponsoring departments and are dealt with in Chapter 8.[82] Regulatory bodies fulfil a specific function in controlling an industry and examples include the Civil Aviation Authority, OFGAS and OFTEL. Other bodies will combine these functions, being regulatory in one respect and advisory in others, such as Scottish Natural Heritage.

Since 1990, the Next Steps principles have been applied to executive NDPBs and they have been encouraged to consider how they perform their services and whether these should be carried out in-house or contracted out.

4–36   Control and accountability are two concerns. By control, we mean how a parent department influences or directs an agency. Accountability, on the other hand, refers to the answerability of institution to the public, whether through Parliament, or by some direct means of public participation. The two concepts do not necessarily go hand in hand. For instance an agency may have been created so that it would have a large degree of independence in its decision-making but it does not follow that there will be little accountability.

Since most NDPBs are created by statute or by charter, the first form of control will follow from the degree of precision laid down in the enabling legislation or charter; what is to be done, how it is to be achieved, the relationship between the agency and the department. The agency may be given wide discretion in its duties or the Minister may set tight guidelines for the agency to follow. The second form of control is exercised by the way in which the decisions of the agency are monitored. Again, this will depend on the composition of the agency and what it deals with. The second Nolan Report referred to complaints about "excessively detailed central control" which had replaced detailed local control. The report recommended that bodies needed to be given "as much freedom of action as possible within clear policy guidelines and operating boundaries, supported by strong and well-understood sanctions".[83]

---

[82]   See discussion in Hogwood, *op. cit.,* n. 67, above.
[83]   Second Report of Committee on Standards in Public Life, Cm. 3270–1 (1995), Chap. 1, para. 4.

Accountability can assume three forms, accountability to the Minister, 4–37
direct Parliamentary supervision and accountability through the PCA. Where
the agency is accountable to the Minister, the Minister will then be
accountable to Parliament. The establishment of an agency means that the
decision-making, for whatever reason, has been located outside the
departmental framework. This is likely to be achieved through a statute
which will state the accountability route. Few agencies are directly
accountable to the public and where the agency's members are approved
by Ministers and the Public Appointments Unit, the members will be directly
accountable to him. The Minister will set out the strategy for the agency,
set performance indicators and strictly control the finances made available.
Such agencies will therefore find their independence circumscribed; they
will in effect act as dependent agencies of the Government.[84] The agency
may also be required to produce an Annual Report to the Minister, who
then lays it before Parliament. The Code of Practice on Access to
Government Information applies to these agencies as well as to departments.
Direct Parliamentary supervision through a select committee is problematic
in that the select committee is likely to consider the agency only once every
few years. Other problems include the expertise (or otherwise) of the M.P.s
on the select committee and the lack of resources to conduct a proper inquiry.
The accounts of the agency will be subject to the scrutiny of the NAO and
thus of the PAC, and the 1983 Act also empowers the Comptroller and
Auditor-General to carry out value-for-money audits. The PCA does exercise
oversight over many agencies[85] but it is difficult to see how he can have a
comprehensive oversight of an agency's activities. There is no systematic
scrutiny of the agency; it is only when a complaint of maladministration is
made that any inquiry is initiated.

The Legal Status of Agencies

In considering the legal status of an agency, we have to ask whether the 4–38
agency is an emanation of the Crown, what remedies may be available, and
who is to be sued, the agency or the department.

The answers depend on the way in which the particular agency was
established. Since most NDPBs are created by statute, this will set out the
agency's powers and responsibilities and the agency will be sued in its own
name, with judicial review being available in the usual way. The Minister
may also be a party if the applicant claims that Ministerial powers have
been exceeded. A decision of an agency may be struck down as *ultra vires*[86]

---

[84] Weir, *op. cit.*, n. 68, above, at 134.
[85] The Parliamentary and Health Service Commissioners Act 1987 extended the PCA's
jurisdiction to include many NDPBs.
[86] *e.g. Anisminic Ltd v. Foreign Compensation Commission* [1967] 2 A.C. 147.

or on the ground that the agency misapplied the rules under which it operates.[87]

4–39   The Civil Aviation Authority is a good example of how an agency operates and the problems which have occurred during its operation. The CAA evolved from the Air Transport Licensing Board which operated like a tribunal and was not considered to be very satisfactory. The Edwards Committee recommended that an agency be set up to look after economic and safety regulation, air traffic control and the negotiation of traffic rights. This agency should also be subject to guidance by the Minister by way of written policy statements.

The Civil Aviation Act 1971 followed most of the recommendations with the major exception that negotiation of traffic rights remained with the Minister. The Secretary of State for Trade was empowered to give guidance on policy while the CAA itself made reports which would have an impact on the policy guidance given by the Minister. The system of policy guidance was intended to achieve two objectives, maintain some political control over the agency and give it a clearer idea of how to exercise its broad discretion.

4–40   In a celebrated case, *Laker Airways Ltd v. Department of Trade*,[88] Laker sued the department, saying that the policy guidance which resulted in the withdrawal of their trans-Atlantic licence was *ultra vires*. The Court of Appeal agreed. The Secretary of State's power to give guidance was set out in section 3(2) of the 1971 Act; however, section 3(1) set out the four basic objectives of the CAA. The court held that the guidance given under section 3(2) could not reverse or contradict the objectives set out in section 3(1). The guidelines had attempted to do just that and so were *ultra vires*. Since this case, the Secretary of State has been limited in the policy guidelines he may make and this has resulted in the CAA structuring its discretionary powers.

The debates on the Civil Aviation Act 1980 show the difficulties of maintaining broad political control through the mechanisms of policy guidance. The Government wanted a "hands-off" approach with no policy guidance being issued. They argued that it was still possible to have political control by altering the statutory criteria. The Opposition parties disagreed, saying that legislative responsibility was being abdicated to an unaccountable body. It is arguable that the system of policy guidance in the 1971 Act preserved some accountability and gave clarification of vague statutory standards. Both of these are problems associated with agencies.

---

[87]   *e.g. R. v. Criminal Injuries Compensation Board, ex p. Schofield* [1971] 1 W.L.R. 926.
[88]   [1977] Q.B. 643.

Next Steps or Executive Agencies

The responsibility for ensuring that the Next Steps Initiative was 4–41 implemented was placed with the Office of the Minister for the Civil Service, a unit which was assimilated into the Office of Public Service and Science (OPSS) and is now called the Office of Public Service. These units ensured that departments identified activities for agency status, helped in setting up the agencies and ensured that they then had the necessary freedom to develop.[89]

In a Next Steps agency or executive agency, the powers are defined not by statute[90] but by a framework agreement made between the sponsoring department and agency and often also involving the Treasury. The framework agreement, similar to a corporate plan, will cover the present and future objectives for the agency, the financial arrangements, the personnel and staffing policy and the review procedures. A chief executive is responsible for the day-to-day running and he or she can be removed if the goals are not met. The framework agreement is subject to review every three to five years. The Ibbs Report said that an agency "should be left as free as possible to manage this framework ... to strengthen operational effectiveness, there must be freedom to recruit, pay, grade and structure in the most effective way".[91] However, Greer cites the approach of the DSS and its intention to remain as a single department: "While seeking to take maximum advantage of the freedoms offered by central initiatives such as Next Steps, the Department remains a single organisation with interlinked businesses and a shared set of management purposes and aims which underpin the wider aims and objectives of the social security programme".[92]

This quotation infers a degree of resistance to the loss of control over the service delivery work by senior civil servants in the core department, but it has to be noted that this reluctance has not prevented the Next Steps Initiative being implemented very quickly and across the whole civil service.

There are differences even among the executive agencies; some have 4–42 monopoly status, others do not; some are self-funding, others receive departmental funding; some perform regulatory roles, others do not. The Fraser Report identified four types of agency: those fundamental to mainstream policy, such as the Employment Service; those exercising statutory regulatory functions, such as the Scottish Fisheries Protection Agency and the Meat Hygiene Service; those providing services to departments and other agencies, such as the Buying Agency and the Royal

---

[89] Greer, *Transforming Central Government: The Next Steps Initiative* (1994), p. 46.
[90] Note, however, that there are a few exceptions to this, for instance the Child Support Agency.
[91] Jenkins, *et al, op. cit.*, n. 52, above, para. 21.
[92] DSS Annual Report 1993, Cm. 2213, quoted in Greer, *op. cit.*, n. 89, p. 51.

Mint; and agencies not linked to the main objectives of a department such as the Historic Royal Palaces.[93] There was a deliberate strategy employed to allow for these differences in agencies, to ensure flexibility and a better "fit" for the agency by moulding it to the task in hand, rather than the other way round.[94]

4–43   Executive agencies are staffed by civil servants but most of the chief executives have been recruited through open competition. In 1993, 63 out of the 94 chief executive appointments were made by open competition, with 34 being appointed from outside the civil service.[95] Their function has been described as being that of a "managing director of a distinct quasi-commercial or business enterprise operating as a wholly owned subsidiary of a parent department".[96] Agency chief executives are under contract to the department for a limited time, usually five years, and as with any other employed person with a contract of employment, the chief executive is able to sue for breach of contract or wrongful dismissal. The former Director General of the Prison Service Agency, Derek Lewis, raised an action against the Home Secretary for wrongful dismissal in 1996; the matter was settled out of court for an undisclosed sum, thus ensuring that the question of the alleged meddling of the Home Secretary in the day-to-day operations of the agency remained unresolved. The contracts of employment of senior civil servants in executive agencies now name the agency chief executive, not the Minister, as the person with whom the contract of employment is made on behalf of the Crown. The importance of the agency chief executive is thus emphasised.

EXECUTIVE AGENCIES AND CIVIL SERVANTS

4–44   Although those civil servants transferred to agencies remain, for the present, civil servants, there is a difficulty in maintaining an image of a uniform civil service. The Government now talks of a unified rather than a uniform civil service and says that the structural diversity of the changes will inevitably lead to differences in pay scales and conditions of service. The Head of the Efficiency Unit reflected that "the whole logic of the reforms in the civil service was leading us inexorably to the situation where ... a 'unified civil service' really is not compatible with the way we are going".[97] The

---

[93]   The Efficiency Unit (1991) *op. cit.,* n. 57, above, App. A.
[94]   Woodhouse, *Ministers and Parliament* (1994), p. 220.
[95]   Treasury and Civil Service Committee (1993) Sixth Report: The Role of the Civil Service, Interim Report (1992–93 H.C. 390), ii, 207. Note that the majority of the 34 were appointed from other public bodies; only six came from the private sector.
[96]   Freedland, "Rule against delegation and the Carltona doctrine in an agency context" (1996) 19 *Public Law* at 27.
[97]   Treasury and Civil Service Committee (1991) Seventh Report, The Next Steps Initiative (1990–91 H.C. 496), Q344.

Head of the Civil Service stated that the civil service was still bound together by "integrity, impartiality, objectivity, selection and promotion on merit and accountability through Ministers to Parliament."[98] However, a White Paper suggested that the only uniform conditions of service to remain would be a pension scheme and a code of conduct.[99] Another writer considers that the civil service is unified now only because it is a civil service and that ultimate accountability to Parliament rests with the Minister of the department.[1] Another writer states that civil servants working in executive agencies are encouraged to develop team spirit and loyalty to the agency, not the civil service.[2] There is competition between agencies, they contract with each other and charge a market rate for their services. These kinds of activities do not accord with the view that civil servants have a common unifying ethos. This ethos may have been undermined by other elements of the changes in the civil service, particularly the higher proportion of external appointments, the differences in pay scales and the introduction of agency chief executives.

If a civil servant is transferred from the mainstream civil service to an agency, will it be as easy for him to transfer back, or will his promotion prospects remain tied to the agency? If a civil servant is promoted to become an agency chief executive what will happen at the end of his appointment? Will the agency chief executive remain with the agency, in a lower post, or will he be transferred into the mainstream service ? The latter position might cause difficulties since finding a suitable post at the same or higher level may lead to a "career" civil servant not being promoted, thus causing concern and resentment. Flexibility in pay scales may also bring problems of transferability among civil servants in the agencies and in the mainstream service. **4–45**

In 1994, the Government published a White Paper called *The Civil Service: Continuity and Change*.[3] This paper announced the creation of a senior civil service employed under formal contracts of employment. The rationale for the introduction of contracts was "to remove any lack of clarity in terms and conditions of employment for members of the Senior Civil Service and would put them more on a par with their counterparts in other walks of life".[4] Later in 1994, the Treasury and Civil Service Committee published a report which included a draft Civil Service Code, including a **4–46**

---

[98] Minutes of evidence taken before Treasury and Civil Service Committee (1993–94 H.C. 27–vii), Q.2000.

[99] Cabinet Office, *The Civil Service, Continuity and Change*, Cmnd. 2627 (1994).

[1] Dowding, *op. cit.*, n. 47, above, p. 73.

[2] Chapman, "The End of the Civil Service?" (1992) 7(2) *Teaching Public Administration* 1–5.

[3] Cm. 2627.

[4] *ibid.* para. 4.32.

statement of the principles and standards by which the civil service should be run.[5] The Government's response to the report confirmed its intentions in *Continuity and Change* and committed the Government to producing a new Civil Service Code based on the select committee's draft.[6] A new code was subsequently published in 1996.[7]

ACCOUNTABILITY OF NEXT STEPS AGENCIES

4–47   The problems encountered in NDPBs have occurred here, but perhaps are more acute. The agencies are generally not created by statute, unlike most of the nationalised industries where responsibilities were set out in the statute or in a charter. The nationalised industries thus had an "underpinning" of duties and responsibilities and the degree of control by the Minister was more clearly defined. Executive agencies however, are created by a re-organisation of the administration of a department and the question of accountability thus becomes less clear. The Ibbs Report observed: "Clearly Ministers have to be wholly responsible for policy, but it is unrealistic to suppose that they can actually have knowledge in depth about every operational question. The convention that they do is in particular the cause of the overload we observed. We believe it is possible for Parliament, through Ministers, to regard managers as directly responsible for appropriate matters."[8] The Government, however, was unhappy with so radical a change in accountability and the Prime Minister made it clear that there would be no change in the doctrine of individual Ministerial responsibility. This has resulted in many criticisms of the Government's stance, not to mention difficulties for individual Ministers. For instance, Drewry and Butcher ask: "How can Ministers credibly cling to their virtual monopoly of accountability to Parliament, via traditional models of Ministerial responsibility that (according to Mrs Thatcher) were to remain unaltered by the *Next Steps*, in respect of agencies whose chief executives are expected to take managerial initiatives at arm's length from Ministerial control?"[9] Jordan comments: "There is a deliberate or accidental ambiguity. We are told Ministerial accountability remains. But in reality it is now accountability *to* the Minister by the chief executive rather than accountability *of* the Minister to the House of Commons that is now on offer: these are different."[10] Bogdanor muses: "Why, then, should it not be the chief executive who is

[5]   Fifth Report of Treasury and Civil Service Committee (1994 H.C. 27).
[6]   White Paper, *The Civil service: Taking Forward Continuity and Change*, Cm. 2748 (1995).
[7]   See http://www.open.gov.uk/co/cscode.htm (15.1.97).
[8]   Jenkins, *et al, op. cit.,* n. 52, above, para. 23.
[9]   Drewry and Butcher, *The Civil Service Today* (1991).
[10] Jordan, "Next Steps Agencies: From management by command to management by contract?", Aberdeen Papers in (1992) *Accountancy, Finance and Management*, W6.

held constitutionally responsible...for operational matters, so that if anything goes wrong in the agency, the chief executive takes the blame; just as it is the Board of British Rail which is responsible for ensuring the managerial efficiency of the railways."[11]

The Treasury and Civil Service Select Committee expressed similar 4–48 concerns: "The theoretical separation of accountability and responsibility is nowhere more untenable than in the operation of agencies; continued adherence to the theory behind such a separation might jeopardise the durability of the delegation at the heart of Next Steps. The delegation of responsibility should be accompanied by a commensurate delegation of accountability."[12] The Government, however, insisted that no change in the basic constitutional arrangements was required: "The government does not accept ... that delegation diminishes ministerial accountability to Parliament, or that it creates a new form of direct accountability to Parliament for civil servants. Delegation helps to make clear, however, the limits to ministers' personal involvement in the actions of their departments."[13] The Minister, William Waldegrave, claimed that the new forms of accountability created a "democratic gain" rather than a "democratic deficit": "We have not in any way altered or undermined the basic structure of public services accountable to Parliament and hence to individual citizens."[14] The argument used is that accountability "has been strengthened by making services more responsive to consumers, which is more meaningful than giving citizens a distant and diffuse voice over the make-up of services to be provided".[15]

Nonetheless, the concept of Ministerial responsibility or accountability 4–49 has changed. For instance, the Government suggested that M.P.s might wish to deal with chief executives instead of with the Minister on a matter which was within the remit of the executive agency. Many M.P.s were generally concerned that questions on "operational" matters were referred by the Minister to the agency chief executive. In the early days of the Next Steps Initiative, the reply to an M.P.'s question was not published; later they were placed in the House of Commons Library; now they are published in *Hansard* along with a standard form of reply from the Minister.[16] In its announcement of the change to this arrangement, the Government repeated its encouragement that members should write direct to the agency chief executive "wherever they judge it appropriate".[17] The chief executive will

---

[11] Bogdanor, *op. cit.,* n. 25, above, at 12.
[12] Fifth Report of Treasury and Civil Service Select Committee (1993–94 H.C. 27), para. 171.
[13] *ibid.* 189, para.10.
[14] Weir, *op. cit.,* n. 84, above, at 131.
[15] Wilson, *op. cit.,* n. 78, above, p. 6.
[16] See Leopold, "Letters to and from 'Next Steps' Agency Chief Executives" (1994) *Public Law* 214.
[17] *Hansard*, H.C. Vol. 212, col. 287–288w (1991–92).

give evidence to a select committee on behalf of the Minister but will answer questions on operational matters on their own account. The Minister will still be responsible for matters of principle or general policy. The chief executive is now visible, in other words, his or her name is known, and the agency objectives are published. However, this is not very satisfactory and various writers have commented on the confused picture these arrangements portray. Marshall says that they have set up "a new variety of quasi-responsibility for which we have no agreed constitutional label".[18] The relationship between the agency and the department now appears to be more one of employee/employer or agent/principal, both concepts of private law, not public law. When such relationships exist, it is normal, and expected, that the full extent of the relationship will remain known only to the parties and that reasons of commercial confidentiality will be used to exclude third parties from certain areas of the relationship. However, these areas of commercial confidentiality in the agency/department relationship may preclude full accountability to Parliament by the normal means of questions and select committee investigations.[19]

4–50   Central to the concerns about accountability is the extent to which the division between policy and service provision can be maintained. It was apparent with the nationalised industries that government did meddle in their day-to-day running while still maintaining that such matters were not their responsibility. Ministers had statutory powers to issue directions but often used informal means to give directions to the industries' boards. Such intervention by Ministers subverted the management of the industries but also allowed the Minister to avoid accepting public responsibility.[20] The Ibbs Report recognised that changes would be required: "Placing responsibility for performance squarely on the shoulders of the manager of the agency also has implications for the way in which Ministers answer to Parliament for operational issues."[21]

For a number of years, this distinction between policy matters and operational matters appears to have been used by Ministers to avoid taking responsibility when things go wrong. Since 1966, for instance, escapes from prisons have caused difficulties for Ministers but on each occasion they were able to blame the local prison management and thus avoid their own resignation.[22] In each case, there was evidence to suggest that the policies

---

[18]   Marshall, "The Evolving Practice of Parliamentary Accountability: Writing down the rules" (1991) 44 *Parliamentary Affairs* 460 at 469.

[19]   Winetrobe, "Next Steps and Parliamentary Scrutiny" in Drewry and Giddings, *op. cit.,* n. 36, above.

[20]   Harden, *op. cit.,* n. 56, above, p. 35.

[21]   Jenkins, *et al, op. cit.,* n. 52, above, para. 23.

[22]   1966, escape of spy George Blake;1983, mass breakout of IRA prisoners from Maze prison; 1991, escape of two IRA suspects from Brixton prison; 1995, attempted escape of IRA prisoners from Whitemoor and escape of prisoners from Parkhurst.

being pursued by Ministers had led to at least some of the operational failures. Ministers consistently indicate that the relationship between the parent departments and the agencies is at arm's length but the true position is not so clear. In evidence to the Treasury and Civil Service Committee, the Chief Executive of the Employment Service said:

> "the department look to us for information to enable policy formulation to proceed ... in our framework document there are two key sentences: one is that the Chief Executive is permitted to make proposals for policy changes to the Secretary of State, but equally as important, and perhaps some would argue more important, there is also a sentence which says no policy proposals regarding the work of the Employment Service can be made to the Secretary of State until we have actually been consulted".[23]

Such statements[24] suggest that the relationship is much closer and that 4–51 Ministers are involved in operational matters while chief executives are involved in policy matters. Hogwood refers to research which found that 50 per cent of the executive agencies had daily contact with their parent department, indicating that there did not appear to be a "hands-off" approach by the department.[25] He questions whether the line between policy and operational matters has in fact been defined clearly. While departments may continue to keep a close watch on operational matters, it follows that the agency chief executive will want to know what new policies are being developed and may indeed wish to contribute his ideas. As agency chief executives build up their expertise in their particular area, others will come to see them as the experts and they will increasingly become the source of factual information and thus be able to influence future policy decisions.[26] The dividing line between policy and operational matters is thus undoubtedly blurred.[27]

Many of the day-to-day activities of agencies have political impact, for 4–52 instance, in the Benefits Agency, taking away bullet-proof screens made the offices more "user-friendly" but led to accusations that staff were being put at risk. Delegation to agencies will be accepted by Ministers until a political problem occurs; if there is an adverse report or an administrative error is publicised, the Minister will inevitably become involved. The core department may thus intervene at an earlier stage to prevent such political

---

[23] Treasury and Civil Service Committee (1991 H.C. 496), *op. cit.,* n. 97, above, p. 3.
[24] See also the evidence of Sir Angus Fraser, the P.M.'s Adviser on Efficiency, (1990–91 H.C. 496), p. 55.
[25] Hogwood, "The Uneven Staircase: Measuring up to Next Steps", *Strathclyde Papers on Government and Politics*, No.92, (1993) University of Strathclyde, p. 13.
[26] See Barker, "Myth versus Management: Individual Ministerial responsibility in the new Whitehall", *Essex Papers in Politics and Government,* No. 5, (1996) University of Essex, p. 5.
[27] See Greer *op. cit.,* n. 89, above, p. 64.

difficulties for the Minister.[28] The Fraser Report in 1991[29] recognised that departments were still interfering in operational matters and recommended that the department's level of involvement should be reduced. The Ibbs Report had said: "A crucial element in the relationship would be a formal understanding about the handling of sensitive issues and the lines of accountability in a crisis."[30] It is difficult to believe that a Minister will not intervene in a "crisis", allowing his civil servants to deal with it. Indeed, it could be said that "crisis-handling" is the Minister's job.[31] After all, the Minister will be the person who is blamed by the public if something goes wrong and he may therefore wish to pre-empt criticism by "leaning" on the agency.[32]

4–53   Executive agencies may be formally supervised by a committee of senior civil servants from the core department; this is known as the "ownership board". The position of the core department has not, however, changed very much although the implications of the Next Steps Initiative for core departments are substantial. The core departments were supposed to re-organise to take account of the changing emphasis in their work. However, the departments have largely been overshadowed by the executive agencies because of their higher profile, the domination of the debate by operational rather than policy issues, and the secondary focus of attention being on public accountability and Ministerial responsibility.[33] If the changes are implemented to the extent envisaged by the Ibbs Report, then the agencies could become detached from the departments, thus allowing both the department and the agency to sell and buy services from any source. "Core departments would lose their sense of ownership. Instead they may cease, so to speak, even to be majority shareholders in the agencies they nominally sponsor."[34] The idea of supervision of executive agencies by departments thus became problematic. In addition, there is the difficulty in relation to executive agencies where the agency chief executive may have, in effect, a direct line to the Minister, by-passing the traditional route of making policy suggestions through the Permanent Secretary. This could have a two-fold effect; first, the Permanent Secretary's position would be downgraded, diminishing his authority with the Minister, the core department and the other executive agencies, and second, the agency chief executive may

---

[28]   Zifcak, *op. cit.,* n. 54, above, p. 76.
[29]   The Efficiency Unit, *op. cit.,* n. 57, above.
[30]   Jenkins, *et al, op. cit.*, n. 52, above, para. 21.
[31]   O'Toole and Chapman, "Parliamentary Accountability" in O'Toole and Jordan, *Next Steps: Improving Management in Government* (1994), p. 123.
[32]   Bogdanor, "Ministers, Civil servants and the Constitution" (Special Issue 1994) 29(5) *Government and Opposition* 676 at 680.
[33]   Barberis, "Next Steps: Consequences for the Core and Central Departments" in O'Toole and Jordan, *op. cit.,* n. 31, above, p. 99.
[34]   *ibid.* p. 102.

become part of the policy-making process while the role of the senior officials in the department becomes concentrated on managing the framework agreements and setting targets.

As the executive agency takes on more responsibility for itself, for 4–54 instance in personnel matters, this will lead to a reduction in the personnel staff at the core department. This was suggested by the Fraser Report at para. 2.14 and wholeheartedly embraced by the Conservative Government. [35]

Of course, accountability has another aspect, that of accountability to the public or the citizen. In this the Government has maintained that executive agencies are more transparent and accountable than are traditional departments. Public services depend on market mechanisms and on treating citizens as customers. They do not depend on elected bodies ensuring public accountability, particularly since these bodies can be distant and thus unable to offer a truly democratic solution. Instead public bodies "can be made more responsive by instituting mechanisms which build in publicly approved standards and redress when they are not attained".[36] It is this principle which is the foundation of the Citizen's Charter programme discussed later in this chapter.

THE FRAMEWORK AGREEMENT

Agencies owe their existence to administrative reorganisation and the basis 4–55 of their power is set out in the framework agreement; they are intended to operate as independent bodies. The agreement is not laid before Parliament nor does Parliament have any input into its provisions. Indeed an attempt by the Home Affairs Select Committee to comment on the draft framework documents for the Passport Office and the Forensic Science Service was rejected by the Government on the basis that the internal relationships within a department are not exposed to parliamentary scrutiny.[37] There is now a general presumption that the framework agreements will be published and that if one needs to remain secret then the Minister will justify this decision.[38] Select committees may inquire into how the framework document works and so can comment on the content, but there is no input from the House itself. The framework agreement varies from agency to agency, being drawn up to take into consideration the particular needs of the agency and the

---

[35] Barberis, in O'Toole and Jordan, *op. cit.*, n. 31, above, p. 103.
[36] Waldegrave, *The reality of reform and accountability in today's public service* (1993), p. 13.
[37] Home Affairs Select Committee (1991) Third Report: Next Steps (1990–91 H.C. 177).
[38] Government reply to Eighth Report of Treasury and Civil Service Committee (H.C. 494–I), Cm. 524 (1988), 9.

service it is to provide. They will, however, contain some common provisions, including the agency's aims and objectives, the relationship between the agency and its parent department, the arrangements for planning, finance, staffing and for reviewing the agreement.[39]

The framework agreement is not a contract in the sense of a legally enforceable agreement where there is redress to the courts in the event of a breach by one of the parties. The Treasury and Civil Service Committee said that the agreement should be "regarded as a contract ... If this principle is not adopted there is a danger that informal contracts of the type which characterised relations between departments and nationalised industries would make it very difficult to establish the precise responsibility for decisions."[40] It is thus clear that the agreement is to be treated as if it were a binding document and it is meant to separate the responsibility for deciding what functions are to be performed by the agency from the responsibility for the agency's performance in delivering the service.[41]

4–56   As well as the framework agreement, agencies are expected to prepare annual business plans and corporate plans for three or five years. The business plan sets out the agency's performance indicators and targets for the coming year and are published. The unpublished corporate plan combines the annual business plan with predictions of the future development of the agency and expenditure estimates.[42]

A number of statutory changes have enhanced the independence of the agencies. The Government Trading Act 1990 allows certain activities to be run through moneys obtained from the provision of goods and services.[43] This method of financing increases the autonomy of the agency.

The Ibbs Report had recommended that the management of an agency would need to be left as free as possible to manage and this would therefore require a freedom to pay, recruit, grade and structure in the most effective way.[44] The Civil Service (Management Functions) Act 1992 increased the autonomy of an agency in relation to the discharge of its functions and allowed separate appointment and management practices by agencies. The Act was required to allow executive agencies the power to manage their own employment affairs. These functions were generally non-statutory in nature, exercised under the prerogative and were shared between the Treasury and the Office of the Minister for the Civil Service. They were non-delegable under the principle of *delegatus non potest delegare*. The

[39] Butcher, "A New Civil Service? The Next Steps Agencies" in Pyper and Robins, *op. cit.*, n. 32, above, 71.
[40] Treasury and Civil Service Committee (1989), *The Civil Service Management Reforms: the Next Steps* (1988–89 H.C. 494–II), para. 38.
[41] Harden, *op. cit.*, n. 56, above, p. 27.
[42] See Greer, *op. cit.*, n. 89, above, p. 68 for detailed examination of these plans.
[43] Examples: Companies House, Patent Office.
[44] Jenkins, *et al*, *op. cit.*, n. 52, above, para. 21.

Ministers of the Crown Act 1975 allowed for the transfer of functions between different Ministers. The transfers were effected by a Transfer of Functions Order. If such an Order has been made the Minister in whom the function was vested may delegate it to any other Crown servant. The delegatee may in turn authorise other Crown servants to carry out the functions.

Section 2 of the 1992 Act states that the Minister may waive the need   4–57 for his approval of the exercise of statutory powers concerning appointments and management. Prior to this Act, pay awards had to be approved by the Treasury; now agencies may settle pay conditions themselves. Before the 1992 Act, it had been considered necessary to authorise such transfers of functions between Ministers by means of primary legislation, with subordinate legislation then used for each particular transfer. The Act allows this downward delegation without the need for subordinate legislation. The Government argued that the Act was concerned with the internal delegation of powers, rather than the contracting-out of functions. However, the Government also said that further legal powers to engage in contracting out would not be necessary.[45] Note that the Act delegates to an individual Crown servant (the agency chief executive), not to the agency itself and it does not permit delegation of any functions directly to persons who are not Crown servants.

SCRUTINY OF EXECUTIVE AGENCIES BY NATIONAL AUDIT OFFICE AND PUBLIC ACCOUNTS COMMITTEE

The funding of executive agencies has largely been made by voted money,   4–58 in other words, money which has been allocated to the agency by Parliament through the annual estimates. The agency will therefore be accountable to Parliament for the expenditure of that money and will be subject to audit by the National Audit Office (NAO). The report of the annual audit and of any value-for-money (VFM) audit carried out under section 6 of the 1983 Act will be presented to the Public Accounts Committee (PAC). The PAC may in turn scrutinise these reports and question the Accounting Officer of the department or agency concerned. In the early stages of the Next Steps Initiative, the accounting officer for an agency was the parent department's senior civil servant, the Permanent Secretary, and he or she would accompany the agency chief executive to any select committee hearing and answer questions on financial matters. This was seen as unsatisfactory and the Treasury and Civil Service Committee sought clarification of the agency chief executive's role in financial matters. The Government then decided that the agency chief executive would also act as the agency's accounting officer. The role of the agency accounting officer was outlined in a Treasury

---

[45] Freedland, "Civil Service (Management Functions) Act 1992" (1994) 23(1) *Industrial Law Journal* 32 at 33.

Minute[46]: "Clarity of roles, managerial authority and accountability go hand in hand with the establishment of executive agencies. The strategic direction of an agency is a matter for the responsible Minister. This includes the setting of published key targets for the agency ... The agency accounting officer ... is accountable for the agency's performance against these key targets."[47] Where the expenditure by an agency is a separate expenditure "vote" by Parliament, the agency accounting officer will be the full accounting officer; if, however, the agency's budget is part of the department's budget, both the department's accounting officer and the agency's accounting officer will be required to answer questions. The odd situation may also arise that the agency chief executive is the full accounting officer for part of the agency's expenditure and the agency accounting officer for other parts. There appears to be little "clarity of roles" as demanded by the Treasury Minute.

4–59   Agencies are required to submit separate accounts annually and these are individually audited. Previously, the area of function carried out by the agency would have been included in the department's accounts and scrutiny of that function would have been carried out but at longer intervals. The number of agencies now in existence has of course led to a large increase in the work of the NAO. In particular the NAO reports on VFM audits now have to be agreed with the core department and the executive agency; this will have the effect of increasing the cost of making such audits and the length of time taken to report.

The NAO has been closely involved in advising agencies on their accounting systems and the form of their accounts. However, there is some concern that the NAO has been asked to "ease off" in its scrutiny of the executive agencies. Greer refers to an external review of the NAO where the report's recommendations included one that not all of the VFM audits should be reported to the PAC. The NAO appears to be adopting most of the recommendations. Greer suggests that the watchdog may be in danger of losing some of its teeth.[48]

SCRUTINY BY SELECT COMMITTEES

4–60 The Treasury and Civil Service Committee played an important role in scrutinising the Next Steps Initiative and the early years of the executive agencies. The committee showed some enthusiasm for the initiative but also some understandable caution as to its effects. From 1987 to 1992, the committee held hearings each year, publishing a report in July to which the

---

[46] HM Treasury, *Executive agencies: a guide to setting targets and measuring performance*, Cm. 2175 (1992).
[47] *ibid.* paras. 11 and 12.
[48] Greer, *op. cit.,* n. 89, above, p. 92.

Government responded in the autumn. The committee set up a sub-committee on the civil service and it was through this sub-committee that much of the work was done. Evidence was taken from the Next Steps Project Manager, the Minister in charge of the initiative, the Treasury and from agency chief executives, as well as other interested bodies such as the civil service trade unions. The TCSC has been reorganised into two select committees, the Treasury Committee and the Public Service Committee, and it is the latter which now has responsibility for the civil service.

Over the years, the committee examined a number of issues including its own role (in 1990), accountability, the roles of the Treasury and of the civil servant, the relationship between agencies and departments and privatisation. The existence of the select committee system has allowed scrutiny of the Next Steps Initiative which could not otherwise have taken place. The initiative was three years old before a debate on its implications was held in the House of Commons in 1991. Such matters involving the administration and the executive are not normally the subject of debate in the House since they are matters controlled by prerogative powers.

Although most departmental select committees have now investigated 4–61 agencies, there has not been a systematic programme of inquiry. Natzler and Silk[49] suggest three reasons for this. First, Parliamentary scrutiny of agencies may undermine their *raison d'être*; agencies were set up to create a distance between the policy management and the operational function. Replacing close supervision by Parliament would not be conducive to encouraging initiative on the part of the agency management. Secondly, the committees may not have been convinced of the permanency of the new structure and so did not want to waste time on such investigations. Thirdly, the close involvement of the Treasury and Civil Service Committee may have discouraged other select committees from scrutinising the agencies. The work of the PAC may have had a similar discouraging effect.

SCRUTINY BY THE PARLIAMENTARY COMMISSIONER FOR ADMINISTRATION

On the face of it, executive agencies are definitely within the jurisdiction 4–62 of the PCA; they are a part of a department or exercise functions on behalf of a department and indeed the framework documents of many agencies declare them to be subject to the jurisdiction of the PCA. However, it has already been noted that M.P.s have been encouraged by the Government to contact agency chief executives direct, rather than asking a parliamentary question. The M.P. will then get a response, but he will not know whether any maladministration or injustice has occurred. Only an investigation by the PCA can reveal such to an M.P. and his or her constituent. The PCA, of course, may not initiate an investigation; he may conduct inquiries only if

[49] Natzler and Silk, *op. cit.*, n. 36, above, at 78.

he receives a complaint via an M.P.. There is therefore a possibility that cases of maladministration may not be brought into the open if M.P.s go direct to agency chief executives and not to the PCA. The advantage of doing this is, of course, a speedier answer for the M.P. and his constituent since it is well known that an investigation by the PCA can take an inordinate length of time. However, this may not be in the best interests of the administrative service, since maladministration may not be properly identified and resolved.

The PCA, however, continues to investigate complaints made regarding the actions or inactions of departments and executive agencies and indeed many of his cases are concerned with agencies. His reports do not show any difficulties in dealing with the agencies or with the departments and certainly his decisions have not lessened in the strength of their condemnation where this is applicable.

LEGAL STATUS OF EXECUTIVE AGENCIES

4–63   The relationship between executive agencies and departments is not a legal contract based on private law principles because the parties do not have separate legal identity. Parties to a contract must have legal personality before they can contract; the legal personality does not derive from the contractual relationship. Thus legal actions will have to be brought against the relevant Minister. Three issues arise from this.

First, is judicial review available against an agency ? The answer appears to be no; the agency will be regarded as part of the department and the Minister will appear in any action. In *R. v. Secretary of State for Social Security, ex parte Sherwin*[50] the court had to consider whether the decision of the Benefits Agency was a decision of the Secretary of State in law. The court considered that the operation of the *Carltona* principle[51] was not affected by the creation of the Benefits Agency and that the decision taken by the official was made on behalf of the Secretary of State. The principle of legitimate expectation is one which has been developed over the last decade or so, but it is not yet certain whether this will be available to the third party who claims legitimate expectation based on the framework agreement. Harden argues that there is a possible remedy based on the authority of *R. v. Panel on Takeovers and Mergers, ex parte Datafin.*[52]

Secondly, if an executive agency makes a contract, then who is contracting? The logic of the principal/agency relationship would indicate that the contract is with the department. The agency is not legally separate from the department and since the department makes contracts in the name

---

[50]   [1996] CO/1724/95, February 16, 1996.
[51]   *Carltona Ltd v. Commissioners of Works* [1943] 2 All E.R. 560.
[52]   [1987] Q.B. 815; Harden, *op. cit.,* n. 56, above, p. 45.

of the Secretary of State who acts on behalf of the Crown, it then follows that a contract made by an agency is in fact made by the Crown. If agencies were made statutory corporations this problem would not exist and the private law of contract would apply. However, the general thrust of the initiative suggests that the agency has contractual authority within its own areas.

Thirdly, does the parent department have delictual liability, or does the agency? The answer to this is similar to the previous discussion; the department will have delictual liability. However, in the case of vicarious liability, the agency chief executive may be named if he or she is named in a civil servant's contract of employment.

These are questions which have yet to be answered by the courts. They 4–64 highlight the difficulties of the Next Steps regime. There is on the one hand a desire to foster institutional autonomy and responsibility with performance being measured and evaluated. On the other hand there is the legal responsibility which appears to continue with the department; this follows from the lack of legal status afforded the agencies. The advantage for the department, is that the framework document can be revised easily without the need for legislation but the disadvantage is that legal liability remains with the department, meaning that the agencies do not necessarily bear the legal consequences of their actions.

CONTRACT AND SERVICE PROVISION

The Government has to make contracts to purchase goods and services. 4–65 The Crown has a common law right to contract, and indeed to put services out to tender, as was found in *R. v. Lord Chancellor, ex parte Hibbit and Sanders*.[53] In recent years extended use of contractual language has been made to denote relationships other than those between buyers and sellers. For instance, the term "contract" has been used to identify a particular relationship and the duties and responsibilities incumbent upon the parties in that relationship. The Government referred to the relationship between the universities and the State as one of "contract".[54] The idea of contract has influenced the relationship between executive agencies and their sponsoring departments although of course there is no contract because the agency has no legal personality of its own. There is also the misuse of contractual terms in the NHS reforms, where the term "NHS contract" is used to denote the relationship between an acquiring body and a provider body within the internal market created by the reforms. The "NHS contract", however, is specifically stated not to be a legally binding contract or to give rise to contractual rights or liabilities.[55]

---

[53] [1993] C.O.D. 326, D.C.
[54] Review of University Grants Committee, Cm. 81 (1987), para. 2.21.
[55] National Health Service and Community Care Act 1990, s. 4.

CONTRACTING OUT

4–66   We discussed earlier that when a department reviews its existing activities, it considers five options: abolition, privatisation, contracting out, agency or the status quo.

Contracting out can apply to both activities carried out in-house and those devolved to an agency. The options apply to a sphere of activity and may apply to a particular activity irrespective of whether it is done in-house or by an agency. When a function or activity is contracted out, the responsibility for the provision of the function remains with the department or public body but the function itself is carried out through a contract with a third party, which may be an in-house group, an executive agency or an independent contractor. The method has been used extensively in local authorities, NHS and parts of central government, such as the Ministry of Defence where examples are the refitting of warships, aircraft and vehicle repair, air transport and security guarding.[56]

4–67   Contracting out has benefits and disadvantages. The benefits include: an end to inefficient public sector in-house monopolies which often had low productivity; the "open-ended" financial commitment to public sector in-house units is ended and the units are required to take account of costs; competition generates new ideas, techniques and so on; and contractors can be penalised for defective performance and late delivery. The disadvantages of contracting out are: the unreliability of private contractors who may default; the use of low bids by contractors to eliminate in-house bids and so make the public body dependent on a private monopoly; competitive tendering incurs monitoring costs; and private contractors achieve cost savings by cutting jobs and reducing wages and conditions of service.

Market testing or competitive tendering

4–68   "The aim of market testing ... is to promote fair and open competition so that departments and agencies can achieve the best value for money for the customer and for the taxpayer."[57] The advantages are given as competition, quality of service, explicit customer/supplier relationships, innovation, and a focus on outputs, objectives and targets to improve efficiency and effectiveness.[58] It is the first step in deciding whether an activity is to be carried out in-house or contracted out. It may be a little less radical than contracting out because an in-house team does have an opportunity to tender for the work. This will not be the case with contracting out where the

---

[56] For definitions of contracting out and market testing see H.M. Treasury, Cm. 1730 (1991).
[57] The Efficiency Unit (1993), *op. cit.,* n. 61, para. 1.3.
[58] *ibid.* para. 1.4.

Government has decided that the activity need no longer be carried out in the public sector. The Government maintained that market testing was a logical extension of the Next Steps programme. Commentators, however, do not necessarily share this view. Market testing is seen as a solution to a failure of the Next Steps programme to bring about the changes expected. The department/agency relationship was too cosy, the framework documents "not worth the paper they [were] written on" and there was a need for a legally binding document.[59] "Market testing" was not the phrase initially used by the Government; the scheme was announced by the Treasury in the White Paper *Competing for Quality: Buying Better Public Services*,[60] and was abbreviated to CfQ.

Market testing effectively requires civil servants to bid for their own 4–69 jobs. The concept is to price or cost services supplied by a civil service unit to a department or agency; previously, these services were supplied 'free'. Now the unit has to fix a price and the department or agency will choose whether to purchase the service from the unit or from another provider. Market testing therefore introduces competition to the in-house provider. The process is relatively straightforward; first the department sets up a special project team to initiate the market testing process. The team decides which areas are to be market tested and the way in which they can be best packaged to stimulate competitive bids. A detailed specification of the service required is prepared and bids are invited from in-house groups and external contractors. The tenders are evaluated in terms of cost and quality and the contract is awarded. If an external contractor is successful, the in-house unit is closed down or transferred to a new contractor. In-house bids have won around 55 per cent of the competitive bids.

Nonetheless, the market testing programme caused a reduction of 20,200 civil servants between 1992 and 1995.[61]

The market testing process has aroused similar concerns to those made with executive agencies. However, there are particular concerns that the process will destroy the public sector ethics of impartiality and incorruptibility and that the private sector ethos of commercial considerations will become paramount.[62] The process also encountered legal problems in its early stages; in particular the position of workers being transferred to the successful external contractor caused confusion since it was not clear how far the Transfer of Undertakings (Protection of Employment) Regulations 1981 and the E.C. Acquired Rights Directive 77/187 protected them. The principle of the regulations was to protect the

---

[59] Richards and Rodrigues, "Strategies for Management in the Civil Service: Change of Direction" (1993) *Public Money and Management* 33.

[60] H.M. Treasury, Cm. 1730 (1991).

[61] The Efficiency Unit, *Competing for Quality Policy Review* (1996).

[62] Bogdanor, "Going private is the Next Step to Oblivion", *The Guardian,* August 29, 1992.

employment rights of an employee where his employer's business has been taken over. The employee's contract of employment must remain the same or he will have a claim for unfair dismissal.

4–70   Originally the U.K. regulations were held not to apply. In *Expro Services Ltd v. Smith*[63] catering services were contracted out to a private company by the Ministry of Defence. The court held that the regulations did not apply because the catering venture had not been a commercial one when it was carried out in-house. The courts took the view that awarding a contract was not a 'transfer of undertakings' because it fell short of being a going business.[64] These restrictions were removed by the Trade Union Reform and Employment Rights Act 1993, although the Government continued to insist that the regulations did not apply to contracting out because no undertaking was transferred. The ECJ decision in *Rask v. ISS Kantineservice A/S,*[65] however, caused a change of mind. In *Kenny v. South Manchester College*[66] prison education had been contracted out to a local authority, but on retendering was contracted out to a college. Staff previously employed by the local authority on that work had to be taken on by the college on the same terms and conditions.[67] Where a council had contracted out a service and subsequently took the service back in-house, this constituted a transfer of undertaking.[68] It is apparent that this area of law is not yet fully settled.

Problems in contracting out

4–71   The first question to be asked is whether there are any types of activity which should not be contracted out. Most people would say that the police, court process and prisons are three examples of such activities; but contracting out has occurred in all of these. Statutory authority to contract out custodial functions was sought in the Criminal Justice Act 1991, although normally no such statutory authority is sought or apparently required.[69] The 1991 Act allows the Secretary of State to enter into contracts with another person for the running of a prison. That prison is subject to the same legislative regime as others and the contract will state the number of prisoners and facilities as well as matters such as the number of assaults permitted in a year. The prison does not have a governor; it has a director appointed by the company with the Minister's approval, but he has no power to impose or mitigate any penalty. If there is a loss of control in the prison, the Secretary

---

[63] [1991] I.R.L.R. 156.
[64] *Curling v. Securicor Ltd* [1992] I.R.L.R. 549.
[65] Case C-209/91 [1993] I.R.L.R. 133, ECJ.
[66] [1993] I.C.R. 934, [1993] I.R.L.R. 265.
[67] See also *Wren v. Eastbourne Borough Council* [1993] 3 C.M.L.R. 166; [1993] I.C.R. 955; *Dines v. Initial Health Care Services* [1995] I.C.R. 11; [1994] I.R.L.R. 366.
[68] *Isles of Scilly Council v. Brintel Helicopters Ltd* [1995] I.C.R. 249; [1995] I.R.L.R. 6.
[69] Freedland, "Government by Contract and Public Law" (1994) *Public Law* 86 at 94.

of State can appoint a civil servant to act as governor and take over management of the prison. Each contracted-out prison has a controller, a Crown servant, whose duties include reviewing and reporting on the running of the prison and investigating and reporting on any allegations made against a prison officer.

Problems of accountability have to be addressed. The fact that the service has been contracted out, not privatised, means that the State still has responsibility for it and thus a Minister is still politically accountable. However, there is a danger that the contractor who has been employed to "execute" a policy may come to have real influence over the policy and future policy decisions. The contract has to be clear as to what is expected of the contractor, so the Government is required to set up control methods and have skilled personnel who can assess the work and performance criteria to use in that assessment.

In addition, there is the question of scrutiny by the PCA, whose remit does not allow him to scrutinise commercial or contractual matters. If a service activity is contracted out, then the PCA may not be able to take on any case of alleged maladministration against the contractor, only against the client department or agency. The PCA will be unable, however, to scrutinise the contract itself. This leaves a large gap in the system of non-judicial redress available to ordinary citizens.

So far as organisational questions are concerned, there needs to be enough 4–72 flexibility in the contract to allow for the fluctuations which sometimes occur in government business; for instance, in a recession, there is an increase in the numbers of people unemployed, and so any contracted-out benefits system would need to take account of that. Government policy may also change or even the Government itself, thus requiring a flexible approach to the contract to take account of this. Questions regarding the provision of a coherent integrated service may be raised where some parts of the service are in-house and some are contracted out.

The problems regarding the transfer of personnel are more complex than other areas of concern particularly because of the implications of the Transfer of Undertakings Regulations discussed above. The question of morale during and after the market testing exercise is also an issue. A final question to consider is the loss of the public sector ethos — if work is contracted out to a private firm, that firm's first duty is to its owners or shareholders, not to the public at large.

Contract formation and legal principle

The contracts are legal documents (unlike the agency framework 4–73 agreements or NHS contracts) and thus there are legal principles to be considered.

First, the creation of the contract. While this will be done using normal contractual procedures, market testing and competitive tendering are now subject to the E.C. laws on public procurement which cover services as well as goods. The holding of the competitive process and the criteria for choosing the successful contractor is subject to rules on publicity and reasoned decision-making. The Treasury implemented the Community directives by means of statutory instruments made under section 2(2) of the European Communities Act 1972. The first regulation applies to the supply of goods[70] while the second applies to the supply of works.[71] They apply to Government departments, local authorities and certain other public bodies when they are inviting tenders in relation to goods and building and engineering works. Some contracts are excluded from the process, for instance, defence, transport and any contract involving sums under the specified threshold. They deal with the treatment to be accorded to potential contractors who are nationals of and are established in a Member State. The public body must have separate legal personality and be financed in the main by the State or regional or local authorities, or have a managerial board of which at least 50 per cent of the members are appointed by the State or other authorities. There is no provision for bodies such as executive agencies where there is budgetary independence but no separate legal capacity to contract. However, there is some difficulty here. The directives will apply where there is a series of legally separate contracts entered into by a department, and the aggregate of these contracts reaches the specified threshold. The Treasury drafted the statutory instruments on the basis that independent contracts by separate parts of the department could be treated as separate and independent of the department. The statutory instruments therefore refer to the devolution of the decision to procure goods and services and the independent making of that decision by an operational unit.

4–74   The public body is required to use one of three methods of requesting tenders. These are: the open procedure, where anyone may tender; the restricted procedure, where only those invited to tender may do so; and the negotiated procedure, where the contract is negotiated by the public body and one or more selected contractors. This last procedure may be used only in limited circumstances.[72] The contracting body must publicise its intention to seek tenders in the *Official Journal* of the E.C., although this requirement is dispensed with if the negotiated tender procedure is used. The form of the advertisement and the information to be given are specified in the rules, together with the time-limits, selection of suppliers and matters which the public body may take into account in accepting or rejecting a tender. The public body must award the contract on the basis of the lowest price or the tender offering economic advantage.[73] Where a contract does not fall under the E.C. rules, the Government may choose whichever contractor it pleases,

---

[70] The Public Supply Contracts Regulations 1991 (S.I. 1991 No. 2679).
[71] The Public Works Contracts Regulations 1991 (S.I. 1991 No. 2680).
[72] For discussion of procedure, see Foulkes, *Administrative Law* (1995), p. 448.
[73] See *General Building Maintenance v. Greenwich LBC*, 92 L.G.R. 21.

taking into consideration its policies, for instance giving preference to U.K. firms, or to small firms. Local authorities, however, are required to exercise their contracting function without reference to "non-commercial" matters, including the political or industrial interests of the contractor.[74] The two 1991 regulations implemented a number of E.C. directives including the Compliance Directive[75] which had to be implemented by December 1991. This required national remedies to be made available where interested parties are harmed by an infringement of the directives or the national implementing measures. The remedies include suspending contract awards, setting aside unlawful decisions and damages.

The second principle to be considered is whether public law principles are to be applied to contracted-out activities. The contract will set out the legal rights and duties of the parties. The question then to be asked is how far these contractual obligations should be supplemented by principles which have traditionally been applied to public bodies, such as accountability to Parliament and reasoned decision-making. The general approach seems to be that if a department or agency is fulfilling a statutory function either as a duty or as a discretion, then it is subject to public law principles. If the department or agency then contracts out that function it would be contrary to principle for the protection to be reduced simply because of a change in the organisational framework. The alternatives are that the department keeps a residual public law responsibility for the contracted-out functions or that the private contracting party becomes subject to the rigours of public law controls. The latter approach seems to be the one which operates. The courts are willing to apply public law principles to private undertakings where they are performing a regulatory role with the backing of the state. It is not difficult to extrapolate this to firms which are performing a contract under the contracting-out system.

The third principle concerns the legal responsibility for services which have been contracted out. What will happen if a prison officer commits a delictual act against a person on the prison premises? The Scottish Prison Service is liable vicariously. What if the prison officer is working in a prison which is run by a private firm under contract? The prison officer and the private firm will of course be liable, but will the Scottish Prison Service also be liable? If the firm is not secure financially the implications of this answer will be considerable for the injured person. The statute may be interpreted as imposing a duty, the legal responsibility for which could not be delegated. The department or agency might find itself contracting out the administration but retaining legal responsibility.

4–75

---

[74] Local Government Act 1988.
[75] 89/665.

Deregulation and Contracting Out Act 1994

4–76 During the late 1980s, the Government considered methods of removing unnecessary burdens on business, the so-called "red tape". Business task forces were set up to advise departments which regulations should be removed to allow for greater competition; by 1992, these task forces had made more than 600 suggestions, the majority of which would require primary legislation to implement them. The Deregulation and Contracting Out Act 1994 aims to assist in this process. The first part of the Act gives power to a Minister to repeal, by subordinate legislation, primary legislation which imposes an unnecessary burden on business. The second aim of the Act is to empower a Minister to make an Order specifying which functions of Ministers and office-holders may be contracted out.[76] The functions of office-holders such as the Comptroller and Auditor-General, officers of Parliament, PCA and the courts are not included. The effect of the Order is to authorise a Minister or office-holder to contract out but does not compel him to do so. Before making an Order to specify the functions of an office-holder the Minister must consult him. The function concerned must have been conferred on the Minister by statute (so the exercise of prerogative powers is excluded) and the function must not be one which must be exercised by the Minister or office-holder personally.[77]

Section 72 provides that for all purposes, except those relating to criminal proceedings or contractual relations between Minister, office-holder, local authority and the contractor, the acts of the contractor are the acts of the Minister, etc. The contracting-out of functions does not diminish the accountability or legal liability of the Minister, etc., for the exercise or non-exercise of the functions.

4–77 The object of the Act is of course to facilitate the contracting-out of public services and to extend the principle in *Carltona Ltd v. Commissioner of Works*.[78] The principle is that civil servants are able to exercise the functions which have been conferred on Ministers. This means that acts which are properly done by an official on the Minister's behalf will be considered to be acts of the Minister. Widgery L.J. defined it thus: "It is not strictly a matter of delegation; it is that the official acts as the Minister himself and the official's decision is the Minister's decision."[79] In *H.M. Advocate v. Copeland*[80] a direction was signed by an official extending the period of detention under the Prevention of Terrorism (Temporary Provisions) Act 1984. The official signed on behalf of the Minister but

---

[76] s. 69.
[77] s. 70 applies to local authorities which will be enabled to contract out but not compelled to do so. The provisions are similar to those of s. 69.
[78] [1943] 2 All E.R. 560.
[79] *R. v. Skinner* [1968] 2 Q.B. 700 at 707 F-G.
[80] 1988 S.L.T. 249.

there was no evidence to suggest that the Minister had personally considered the matter or made the decision. The High Court of Justiciary said that this made no difference: "there is no obligation on the Minister to exercise his powers personally even when those powers involve a serious invasion of freedom or the property rights of a subject".[81] The *Carltona* principle is based on the realistic premise that Ministers cannot carry out every function personally and therefore civil servants must assist.[82] The 1994 Act extends that principle to allow private firms to act on behalf of Ministers and certain office-holders.

PRIVATISATION AND REGULATORY CONTROL

There are two situations which require to be discussed with regard to 4–78 privatisation and whether regulatory control is required. First, the privatisation of companies which do not possess undue market influence does not cause any problems as regards public law. Such companies[83] operate in competitive markets and do not require a regulatory regime to control prices and so on. They may have special features such as government directors, government shareholding and articles of association which prevent undesirable takeovers but these are more to address the political situation than to regulate them properly.

The second situation involves companies which possess significant market power and so require a regulatory regime: "The general purpose of the Government's extensive regulation is to protect the public from harm caused by the activities of private enterprise."[84] Regulation was seen as necessary to promote competition, protect customers and promote social and national objectives.[85] If competition is likely to be limited, then new controls will be needed to prevent abuse of the monopoly position. The legislative framework for the regulation of a privatised industry will include the enabling statute, the Competition and Service (Utilities) Act 1992, the Fair Trading Act 1973, the Restrictive Trade Practices Act 1976 and the Competition Act 1980. The laws of the European Community will also apply, particularly with regard to competition and environmental regulation. The privatised companies apply for licences under the enabling Act and the licence will detail the duration, the geographic area of operation, the

---

[81] See also *Re Golden Chemicals Ltd* [1976] Ch. 300.
[82] *R. v. Skinner* [1968] 2 Q.B. 700; *R. v. Secretary of State for Home Department, ex p. Oladehinde* [1991] A.C. 254.
[83] For instance, British Aerospace, British Airways.
[84] Austin, "Freedom of Information: the Constitutional Impact" in Jowell and Oliver, *op. cit.*, n. 9, above, p. 402.
[85] Price Waterhouse, "Regulated Industries: UK Framework" (Regulatory Brief 2, Centre for Study of Regulated Industries).

authorised activity, economic regulations, codes and standards, terms of revocation and payments to the Secretary of State to fund the regulator's office. The licence is issued by the Secretary of State and enforced by the regulator.

4–79   Where a privatised firm has significant market power, this can be addressed through its structure or through some regulatory scheme. The former requires the breaking-up of the large firm, the latter requires monitoring of the large firm together with the introduction of new competitors. The latter approach has been adopted in the United Kingdom and it depends for its effectiveness upon the criteria for regulation and the attitude of the regulator.[86]

The telecommunications industry is a good example of how regulation was implemented. The Telecommunications Act 1984 privatised the first major utility. The British Telecommunications Act in 1981 had separated the telecommunications section from the Post Office and established British Telecom as a public corporation. The 1981 Act also allowed the Minister to license other firms to run telecommunications systems. The 1984 Act privatised BT and set up a regulatory framework. A Director General of Telecommunications (DGT)[87] was created with powers to issue licences,[88] modify them[89] and enforce licence conditions.[90] BT's exclusive privilege of running telecommunications systems was abolished.[91] Section 3(1)(a) requires the DGT and the Minister to ensure the provision of telecommunications in the United Kingdom, including the provision of emergency services, public call boxes, maritime services and services in rural areas. This duty can be seen as a social one, since the provision of these services is not inexpensive. Section 3(1)(b) requires the DGT and the Minister to ensure that the providers of the services are able to finance them. In section 3(2), they are required to promote effective competition, efficiency and economy, research and development and international competitiveness. The social duties of the DGT and Minister are given first in the Act before the duties to promote competition; as Prosser points out, the principle of universal service is a major regulatory goal and is reflected in later privatisation statutes.[92] The DGT may investigate complaints, publish information to consumers and exercise the powers of the Director General of Fair Trading to investigate anti-competitive practices.

4–80   The success of the telecommunications scheme depends on the DGT; he runs OFTEL, an agency which has to follow various guidelines. The

---

[86] See Price Waterhouse, *op. cit.,* n. 85, above, for detailed discussion of the regulation of the main utilities.
[87] s. 1.
[88] s. 7.
[89] s. 12.
[90] s. 16.
[91] s. 2.
[92] Prosser, "Privatisation, Regulation and Public Services" (1994) 1 J. R. 3.

regulation of BT was originally to be a temporary measure, in place until competition caught up[93]; indeed the regulation was for an initial period of seven years and the evidence suggests that the DGT and OFTEL have pursued a pro-competitive strategy, although their performance is constrained by a number of factors, including a lack of resources, a lack of information received from BT, the decisions of the Monopolies and Mergers Commission which allowed BT to acquire companies subject to conditions which were difficult to enforce, and the choice of pricing formulae set by the Government which favoured BT. The regulatory powers of OFTEL were increased by the Competition and Service (Utilities) Act 1992 which by modifying section 27 of the 1984 Act gave power to the DGT to make regulations regarding the standard of performance and awards of compensation if these are not met.[94] The DGT must also be given information on the levels of performance.[95]

This information will be sent to the regulator and where there is non-compliance with the standards set, then presumably the regulator will take action, although both the non-performance and the action may not necessarily be made public. The implications of such secrecy could be significant; if the citizen is unaware that risks exist, he cannot make an informed choice about his own safety and welfare. A true assessment of the performance of the industry will not be possible if relevant information is withheld by either the regulator or the industry involved. The justification for such secrecy is given as commercial confidentiality. It is argued that the regulator cannot operate effectively unless he receives the required information in full from the regulated industry. However, there is a danger in providing this information in that it "provides opportunities for the utility to manipulate it (the information) to gain favourable outcomes — i.e. to capture the regulator".[96] The utility wishes to ensure that profits are maximised and controls minimised; there may therefore be a temptation to present the information selectively. However, it would be unusual for a regulator to be completely dependent on one source of information; he will obtain comparative information from competitors and from utilities abroad.

Although it might have been thought that regulation would be a temporary measure for a privatised industry, as in the telecommunications industry, it is argued that it is necessary to ensure that competition is developed and maintained. An open market may have to be created where none previously 4–81

[93] Littlechild, "Regulation of British Telecommunications' Profitability" (1984) Department of Industry.
[94] For discussion of Act, see McHarg, "The Competition and Service (Utilities) Act 1992: Utility regulation and the Charter" (1992) P. L. 385.
[95] 1984 Act, s. 27C.
[96] Helm, "British Utility regulation: Theory, Practice and Reform" in Helm (ed.), *British Utility Regulation: Principles, Experience and Reform* (1995), p. 45.

existed.[97] For instance, BT had such a huge share of the telecommunications market in the United Kingdom that its very size would have ensured that it kept out competitors. The regulator's job was to create a climate where competitors were encouraged to enter the market knowing that BT could not take protective measures.

The regulators find their authority in the statutes which privatised the major utilities. Some discussion has already been made above of one regulator, the DGT, and his office OFTEL. This section will consider the regulators generally and their accountability.

The agencies, like OFTEL, OFGAS, OFFER and so on, are headed by a Director General in whom the powers of regulation are vested personally. The agencies are "non-Ministerial government departments"; in other words, they are bodies at arm's length from central government and Ministers and their staff are seconded from the civil service. Although it therefore appears that the agencies are distanced from departments in their day-to-day operations, the Government appoints the Director General and issues the licences to operate and the conditions in the licences. The agency's task is to enforce these conditions. However, the agency also has a role in negotiating any amendments to the conditions and it could be argued that this allows the potential for a conflict of interest for the agencies; they are involved in setting the rules and in ensuring that the rules are implemented.[98]

The accountability of the Director General is to the Minister by means of an annual report which is then laid before Parliament. The regulators are often called before select committees to explain their policies and decisions, and in these circumstances they are little different from other public bodies and executive agencies.

4–82   All of the regulators are required by statute to protect the interests of consumers and the statute may also establish an advisory body to represent these interests. The Competition and Service (Utilities) Act 1992 requires the privatised companies to establish complaints procedures approved by the regulator. An aggrieved customer may complain to the regulator and in this sense, the regulator is taking on the role of an ombudsman. The 1992 Act, ss. 5–7, give the Director General an adjudicatory function in disputes on billing, fixing charges and deposits. There is potential for conflict of interest here; the agency is first and foremost concerned with the provision of services and the viability of the companies providing them.[99] The pricing structures, which are probably of greatest interest to consumers, are developed to ensure the continuation of those services and the viability of the companies. When British Telecom was privatised, the prices for business

---

[97] Prosser, *op. cit.,* n. 92, above.
[98] *ibid.* p. 240.
[99] See Lewis, "The Citizen's Charter and Next Steps: A New Way of Governing?" (1993) *Political Quarterly* 316.

users were brought down fairly quickly, but it was some years before domestic users saw a similar fall in their telephone bills. Competition increased with the entry of new service providers and the pricing structure was adjusted accordingly. The DGT did encourage the entry of new providers by ensuring that they could interconnect with the BT systems, but prices could not be brought down substantially until that competition had materialised. It could be said that the regulator's effect on prices is a by-product, albeit a welcome one, of his effect on competition. However, it should be noted that the regulator has the power to control the price increases sought by the privatised industry, by capping the maximum amount of increase possible.

Most of the privatised utilities were required by their enabling statutes 4–83 or, in the case of BT, by its licence provisions, to pay compensation to customers when the performance targets set by the regulator were not met. These ideas of the publication of standards and compensation for any failure to meet them were incorporated into the Citizen's Charter[1] and were, as mentioned above, enshrined in the 1992 Act.

Prosser reflects that regulators lack democratic legitimacy but he goes on to say that they are more open in their decision-making than other bodies.[2] The regulatory process does not, however, include public hearings or consideration of comments from members of the public, and as such is hardly transparent. Nevertheless, such openness as exists can improve the scrutiny of the decisions of the regulators by Parliament. In addition, where a company has refused to accept licence amendments proposed by the regulator, there is a kind of appeal mechanism of a reference to the Monopolies and Mergers Commission. This procedure is however not 'open'; the discussions are held in private. The commission is here being used to check the regulator's decisions and it is really the only check apart from judicial review. Cases against regulators are rare. In the first case, *R. v. Director General of Gas Supply, ex parte Smith*[3] the applicant was able to prove procedural impropriety but the court stressed that the Director General had broad discretion in the way he carried out his duties. This was reiterated in *R. v. Director General of Telecommunications, ex parte Let's Talk (UK) Ltd*[4] where the discretion of the DGT to revoke a code of practice permitting the operation of a chatline was upheld. The courts have shown a willingness to examine a substantive decision of a utility regulator, although the case was based on the seeking of a declaration of the interpretation of a contractual term, and thus was based on private law rather than public law principles.[5]

---

[1]   Cm. 1599 (1991).
[2]   Prosser, *op. cit.,* n. 9, above, p. 254.
[3]   CRO/1398/88, QBD (31.7.89).
[4]   CO/77/92, QBD (6.4.92).
[5]   *Mercury Communications Ltd v. Director of Telecommunications, The Times,* February 10, 1995. See also *R. v. Director General of Electricity Supply, ex p. Redrow Homes, The Times,* February 21, 1995

THE CITIZEN'S CHARTER

4–84   The Citizen's Charter[6] was announced by the Prime Minister in 1991 and was due to run for ten years; the concepts are rather vague, being about setting standards for public service organisations and redress mechanisms to assist the customers of the organisation when the standards are not met. The charter established a number of principles for service delivery: higher standards and assessment of performance against standards, openness as to how services are run, information on performance targets, non-discrimination in the services available, responsiveness to consumer needs and consultation with service users, value for money and remedies when things go wrong, including compensation.[7]

The Citizen's Charter has been said to be the "culmination of the movement to output measurement".[8] To measure the effectiveness of any organisation you need statistical evidence and criteria for using it. The Citizen's Charter requires government bodies to measure their outputs by setting themselves performance targets and reporting whether they achieve these targets. The Government has thus seen a link between executive agencies and the attainment of the objectives of the Citizen's Charter. "The Charter has become a prominent feature of the agendas of the Next Steps agencies and of the framework agreements that define their performance targets."[9] The Next Steps Initiative is the "vehicle for the delivery of the Citizen's Charter within central government via those Agencies which serve the public."[10] The two initiatives together can supply more information on the performance of government departments and executive agencies. This is of benefit in the parliamentary scrutiny process where select committees have more information to assist them in their inquiries; previously most select committees had to base their inquiries on the departmental annual reports which were not as detailed as the agency business plans now available.[11]

4–85   Public bodies are encouraged to publish their own "charters" which set out their standards, targets and the rights of consumers. There have been many of these charters published, including the Patient's Charter, the Parent's Charter, the Tenant's Charter and so on. The technique has also been employed by private sector firms and by public bodies which are not covered

---

[6]   Cm. 1599 (1991).
[7]   *ibid.* p. 251.
[8]   Butler, "The Evolution of the Civil Service — a Progress Report" (1993) 71 *Public Administration* 402.
[9]   Drewry, "Mr Major's Charter — Empowering the Consumer" (1993) P.L. 248 at 250.
[10]   Office for Public Service and Science,Next Steps Briefing Note (1992), para. 29.
[11]   Greer, *op. cit.*, n. 89, above, p. 83.

by the programme, for instance the universities. The charters have no legal status; they are aspirational. However, when a body does not meet its charter targets, the resulting bad publicity may adversely affect its business. The body will therefore attempt to reach its targets and accordingly the charter standards will take on a degree of importance, approaching a service guarantee for the customer.[12]

The charter gives the citizen more opportunity to hold these bodies accountable at a local level. "[The charter] enhances [accountability] by building in addition a pull downwards and outwards — to the local provider, the user and the local community… it empowers through greater openness and the ending of anonymity and it empowers through public accountability with the publication of both standards and results."[13]

The Government has attached importance to attaining charter goals 4–86 because executive agencies are at the forefront of service delivery. As part of this, the charter requires consultation to ascertain the views of customers on the existing service and what future services should be provided. An organisation will require to show evidence of this consultation if they seek the "Chartermark" award, which is given if an organisation meets the standard set by implementing the charter principles. It is a certification system which shows the customer that the organisation has met high standards and which operates as "a market asset" to the organisation.[14] The charter has provided the impetus for legislation designed to measure standards of performance in the utilities[15] and local government,[16] where the Accounts Commission (Audit Commission in England and Wales) was given additional powers, particularly to require local authorities to collect and publish information on performance standards which the commission can publish in league tables of performance. The charter has also led to the extension of compulsory competitive tendering in local authorities and market testing in central government, executive agencies and the NHS.[17]

Some problems with the Citizen's Charter have been identified. First, the standards set are not legally binding and so the legal rights of customers are not increased. Secondly, it is questionable whether the quality of information supplied is of a high standard; information on the time taken to answer the telephone is not of any practical significance. Thirdly, there is a possibility that when a particular area of a service is targeted and

---

[12] Barron and Scott, "The Citizen's Charter Programme" (1992) 55(4) M.L.R. 526 at 529.

[13] Waldegrave, Speech to the Institute of Directors, Office of Public Service and Science Press Release 18/92.

[14] Harden, *op. cit.*, n. 56, above, p. 72. Note that the loss of the Chartermark for British Gas in 1995 was a severe blow to its status.

[15] Competition and Service (Utilities) Act 1992.

[16] Local Government Act 1992.

[17] H.M. Treasury, Cm. 1730 (1991).

performance indicators set, administrators may concentrate on trying to achieve these targets, ignoring other areas of the service. Fourthly, there may be extra expenditure involved in implementing the Citizen's Charter; if the standards are not met, compensation may be payable. The Chartermark scheme, however, requires innovation without extra cost.[18] It has been seen as somewhat cynical in its approach; the giving of small sums of money, for instance, to a rail-user who has been inconvenienced by poor service is a cheaper option than pumping in the very considerable funds needed to improve the rail infrastructure which would provide the better service required by the rail-user.[19] Finally, the Citizen's Charter programme has been associated with the Conservative Government's other public sector initiatives such as privatisation and competitive tendering. In its report on the Citizen's Charter, the Public Service Committee indicated that the Charter Programme needed to be clarified to show that the programme was about quality of service to the citizen, not the means by which the service is delivered.[20]

4–87   The PCA Select Committee had felt that his work might decrease with the introduction of the internal adjudication and complaints procedures advocated by the charter.[21] However, in his 1992 Report, the PCA noted that the public's expectations of standards had been raised and this had led to more complaints to his office. The internal adjudication and complaints procedures announced by the charter seem largely to have been quietly shelved. In particular, the charter proposed that departments should have lay adjudicators who would adjudicate on grievances, but this seems to have been too costly to contemplate. The Inland Revenue, however, appointed a Revenue Adjudicator to investigate complaints from taxpayers. This scheme came into effect in May 1993. The adjudicator will look at complaints of "excessive delays, errors, discourtesy or the way in which the Revenue has exercised a discretion". Matters of a legal nature, such as the interpretation of the rules and tax liability, are not within his remit; these remain with the Tax Commissioners and the courts.[22]

[18] See Connolly, McKeown and Milligan-Byrne, "Making the Public Sector more user-friendly? A Critical Examination of the Citizen's Charter" (1994) 47(1) *Parliamentary Affairs* 23.
[19] Drewry, (1993) *op. cit.,* n. 9, above, at 251.
[20] Third Report of Public Service Committee, *The Citizen's Charter* (1996–97 H.C. 78-I) at p. x.
[21] Second Report of Select Committee on PCA: *The Implications of the Citizen's Charter for the Work of the PCA* (1991–92 H.C. 158).
[22] For discussion of the Revenue Adjudicator, see Morris, "The Revenue Adjudicator — the First Two Years" (1996) *Public Law* 309.

CHAPTER 5

SUBORDINATE LEGISLATION

Parliament is the law-making body of the United Kingdom and the validity 5–01
of any Act of Parliament is beyond question. However, Parliament found it
increasingly difficult during the later part of the nineteenth century to
legislate for every eventuality. Hence Parliament delegated power to the
Executive in the form of Ministers and Government departments. The use
of subordinate legislation increased during the First World War to regulate
the progress of the war and control essential supplies. This trend continued
after 1918, leading to criticism of its use by writers such as Lord Hewart.[1]
In 1932, the Donoughmore Committee[2] reported its findings, saying that it
did "not agree with those critics who found the practice ... wholly bad".
The committee's remit had been to report on:

> "the powers exercised by or under the direction of (or by persons or bodies
> appointed specially by) Ministers of the Crown by way of
>
> a) delegated legislation, and
>
> b) judicial or quasi-judicial decisions,
>
> and to report what safeguards are desirable or necessary to secure the consti-
> tutional principles of the sovereignty of Parliament and the supremacy of the
> law".[3]

The committee found many advantages in the use of subordinate 5–02
legislation but warned that safeguards were necessary to ensure that abuse
was minimised. It recommended that a new standing committee be set up
in the House of Commons "to consider and report on ... every regulation
and rule made in the exercise of delegated legislative power, and laid before
the House in pursuance of statutory requirements".[4]

---

[1] *The New Despotism* (1929).
[2] Committee on Ministers' Powers, Cmd. 4060 (1932).
[3] For a discussion of the findings of the committee, see Miers and Page, *Legislation* (1990),
    pp. 106–109.
[4] Cmd. 4060 (1932), Recommendation XIV(B).

The Second World War saw a further strengthening of the power of the Executive through the use of delegated powers.[5] The election of a Labour Government in 1945 heralded the beginning of the Welfare State and an increase in the involvement of government in all areas of life. The Government was in a hurry to change the social structure of the country and had a large legislative programme; it was obvious that the primary legislation thus proposed could not be so detailed as perhaps it had been in the past and powers of delegation to Ministers were sought. The criticisms of the past had not been completely forgotten, however, and the Statutory Instruments Act 1946 reaffirmed the importance of parliamentary scrutiny of subordinate legislation and laid down rules to ensure this. Unfortunately the provisions of the Rules Publication Act 1893, with its safeguards of consultation of affected interests, were repealed and no equivalent safeguards inserted.

5–03   Subordinate legislation is "a feature of all modern states now that Governments expect, and are expected, to intervene actively in economic, social and welfare matters".[6] It is obvious that Parliament is not able to pass all legislation itself but it has become even less able to scrutinise the large number of statutory instruments which are placed before it. The number of statutory instruments published each year has grown steadily, reaching more than 3,000 a year. This chapter will consider what subordinate legislation is and how it is made, the safeguards afforded by parliamentary scrutiny and the controls exercised by the courts.

THE PURPOSES OF SUBORDINATE LEGISLATION — ADVANTAGES AND DISADVANTAGES

5–04   Reference has already been made above to one of the main purposes of subordinate legislation, that is the saving of parliamentary time. The increase in the numbers of government measures presented to Parliament has led to a marked decrease in the amount of time available for the detailed scrutiny of both primary and secondary legislation. It is general practice now to enact policy within the statute and leave the details to be worked out in rules and regulations made by the Executive. This has major advantages in that the rule-makers are able to draw upon the knowledge and expertise of people outside Parliament to advise on the precise content of the rules.[7] This kind of expertise is not found within Parliament and, it is argued,

---

[5]   *e.g.* see the Emergency Powers (Defence) Act 1939, s. 1(3), and the express power to sub-delegate to officials and local bodies.

[6]   Jones and Thompson, *Garner's Administrative Law* (1996), p. 72.

[7]   *e.g.,* the Road Traffic Act empowers the Secretary of State to make rules as to the use of vehicles and their construction. He will consult with experts in this field to draw up detailed rules.

drawing up such detailed rules should not be the work of the Legislature whose priorities should be general policy.

Subordinate legislation is very useful in times of emergency when there may be no time to pass primary legislation. Powers stated in the Emergency Powers Act 1920 allow the Government to declare a state of emergency and take steps to safeguard essential supplies.[8] Subordinate legislation was used to deal with the effects of the Chernobyl disaster when radioactive fallout affected animals on upland pastures.

One of the most common uses of subordinate legislation is to give power 5–05 to bring a statute, or part of it, into operation. The parent Act will state whether it is to come into force on a particular date or whether the Secretary of State is to make a commencement order. The Secretary of State may have to consult with various bodies before making regulations to bring part of the Act into operation; this may take time and so the timing of the commencement is left to the Minister. However, this power can be used to defeat the purposes of an Act, as was seen in *R. v. Home Secretary, ex parte Fire Brigades Union.*[9] The case concerned the Criminal Injuries Compensation Scheme, set up under prerogative powers and not therefore subject to parliamentary approval, except as regards the moneys allocated to fund the scheme. In 1988, Parliament approved a new statutory scheme[10] which was to be brought into force by the Home Secretary. In 1993, a Government White Paper[11] indicated that a new non-statutory scheme would be introduced and in 1994 the Home Secretary announced that he would introduce legislation to repeal the 1988 provisions at a convenient opportunity. The case raised the issue of whether the Secretary of State is required to lay a commencement order but has discretion as to the timing of this, or whether he has a discretion which is wide enough to include non-implementation of the statutory provision. The House of Lords did not specifically rule on this, saying that there was a need for flexibility over the implementation of legislation by the Government in the light of changing circumstances. They further recognised that the implementation of the statutory scheme was a political and administrative act and not subject to judicial review. They did, however, find that the Home Secretary was under a duty to keep the implementation of the Act under consideration and the announcement in the White Paper and the introduction of the new scheme amounted to an unlawful renunciation of that power.[12]

---

[8] This Act has been used on a handful of occasions such as the General Strike in 1926, the Seamen's Strike in 1966 and the Coal Strike in 1973.

[9] [1995] 2 All E.R. 245.

[10] Criminal Justice Act 1988, ss. 108–117 and Scheds. 6 and 7.

[11] *Compensating Victims of Violent Crime: Changes to the Criminal Injuries Compensation Scheme*, Cm. 2434 (1993).

[12] For a discussion of this case, see Leigh, "The Prerogative, Legislative Power and the Democratic Deficit: the Fire Brigade Union Case" (1995) 3 Web Journal of Current Legal Issues http://webjcli.ncl.ac.uk.

Other advantages attached to the use of subordinate legislation include equal and consistent treatment, the enhancement of the legitimacy of decisions and the encouragement of broad public participation.[13] The area under consideration may be technically complex and difficult to set out in a statute, for instance additives in food or the composition of drugs, or the area may be novel and time may be required to experiment and see how the legislation operates in practice, for instance in road traffic measures.

5–06   There are, of course, disadvantages associated with the extensive use of subordinate legislation rather than primary legislation. The problems of two of these, lack of consultation and lack of publicity, are discussed below but the other two main disadvantages are the use of skeleton statutes and the "Henry VIII" clauses.

The use of skeleton statutes has been frowned upon by commentators over the years, for instance, Ganz suggests that such Acts alter the balance of power between Parliament and the Executive.[14] A skeleton statute is one which states the briefest detail of the policy and leaves the Minister to fill in the details by means of regulations. Recent examples include the Child Support Act 1991[15] and the Education (Student Loans) Act 1990. The House of Lords Select Committee on the Scrutiny of Delegated Powers pointed out the dangers of such statutes and stated their intention to call the attention of the House to Bills "which are little more than authority for Ministers to determine the policy and to legislate to give effect to it".[16] They did so with the Education Bill in 1994, where clauses were considered to be inappropriate because they would interfere with the freedom of association of students; the clauses were dropped. The Joint Committee has also highlighted the problem of "skeleton instruments" where departments seek to bypass Parliament "by omitting necessary detail from instruments (or alternatively by qualifying detailed provisions) and thus confer wide discretion on the Minister to vary provisions without making a further instrument".[17]

5–07   "Henry VIII" clauses are used to delegate a power to amend a statute.[18] The Donoughmore Committee criticised such clauses and said they should

---

[13] See Baldwin, "Governing with Rules: the Developing Agenda", in Richardson and Genn, *Administrative Law and Government Action* (1994), pp. 158–159.

[14] Ganz, *Understanding Public Law* (2nd ed., 1994), p. 50.

[15] This Act has more than 100 regulation-making powers.

[16] First Report of the House of Lords Select Committee on the Scrutiny of Delegated Powers, (1992–93 H.L. 57), paras. 15 and 28.

[17] First Special Report of Joint Committee on Delegated Legislation (1977–78 H.L. 51, H.C. 169), paras. 9–12.

[18] "Henry VIII" clauses are so called because of the autocratic nature of that monarch and also referring to the Statute of Proclamations 1539 whereby Henry was given power by the English Parliament to legislate by proclamation.

be used only where there were compelling reasons for doing so.[19] A recent example of the clause is found at section 1 of the Deregulation and Contracting Out Act 1994, but the most extensive use is seen at sections 2(2) and (4) of the European Communities Act 1972 which is considered below. The House of Lords Select Committee on Delegated Powers expressed its concern at the use of such devices, saying that "the government should be expected to justify the use of such clauses as being necessary: they should not be used simply for convenience".[20] The courts have construed such clauses strictly.[21]

DEFINITIONS

As Puttick[22] points out, there is no definition of subordinate legislation either 5–08
in statute or in case law. Indeed there are a number of terms used, such as, administrative legislation, secondary legislation, rule-making and delegated legislation. This latter term is commonly used and is indicative of the source and type of legislation being described. Subordinate legislation, or delegated legislation, is legislation made by a person or body lower than Parliament, according to powers delegated and recoverable by Parliament. It is thus "every exercise of a power to legislate conferred by or under an Act of Parliament".[23] It follows that subordinate legislation will be subject to the scrutiny of the courts to ensure that the powers thus conferred are exercised validly.[24]

Subordinate legislation divides into two main categories: those instruments or rules which require to be scrutinised by Parliament, and those which do not. The latter category can then subdivide into two types: those instruments or rules which are expressed to be statutory instruments and are within the terms of the Statutory Instruments Act 1946, and those which are more administrative in nature because of their lack of generality, for instance, orders, directions and so on.

Statutory instruments are defined by the Statutory Instruments Act 1946, 5–09
s. 1(1), as documents where legislative powers are conferred on the Queen in Council and exercised by Order in Council, or those where legislative powers are conferred on a Minister and are required to be exercised by statutory instrument.

---

[19] Cmd. 4060 (1932), p. 61. The committee listed all of the existing legislation with Henry VIII clauses — all nine of them.
[20] (1992–93 H.L. 57), para. 14.
[21] *e.g. Britnell v. Secretary of State for Social Security* [1991] 2 All E.R. 726.
[22] Puttick, *Challenging Delegated Legislation* (1988), para. 1.05.
[23] Report of Joint Committee on Delegated Legislation (1971–72 H.L. 184, H.C. 475).
[24] Although the statute may state that there should be no judicial scrutiny, *e.g.* Intelligence Services Act 1994, s. 9(4); Interception of Communications Act 1985, s. 7(8).

If properly made, subordinate legislation will have the same force of law as a statute. If it is not made properly, then it may be subject to challenge in the courts. Judges have not been slow to criticise subordinate legislation which is defective although they are cautious in their approach. The reasons for their caution will be discussed below but it may be noted here that the Government is not often thwarted if it wants particular rules to be implemented. If the courts find an instrument to be invalid or *ultra vires*, primary legislation will often reinstate the provision with retrospective effect.[25]

Orders in Council fall into two categories: those made under prerogative powers and those which are subject to the 1946 Act. Prerogative Orders in Council are used for matters such as the establishment of the civil service and non-statutory governmental bodies. Such Orders in Council are not made under statutory authority; however, they may take the form of a statutory instrument and be numbered and published as such.[26] Statutory Orders in Council are used when the powers will be exercised by more than one department or when the matter under consideration requires greater formality.[27]

5–10   Most subordinate legislation is made by Ministers, using instruments under various names, such as regulations, rules, orders, directions and so on. Although there is no hard and fast rule, the word "regulation" tends to be used for matters of general importance such as social security regulations. "Rule" on the other hand is used to indicate procedures for a particular body, for instance, Rules of the Supreme Court are used in England to regulate the procedures in those courts. In Scotland, the supreme courts are regulated by Acts of Adjournal for the High Court of Justiciary and Acts of Sederunt for the Court of Session. Those instruments which fall within the terms of the 1946 Act are assured of uniformity of style but there is no such uniformity for those instruments which are outwith the Act. These take different forms depending on their purpose, for instance, interpretative guides which are official statements of the department's policy, or evidential rules such as the Highway Code.[28]

Some types of rules made by the Government under statutory authority do not have full legal force but may have some of the qualities of legislation. For instance, the Immigration Rules made under the Immigration Act 1971,

---

[25]   See *Malloch v. Aberdeen Corporation,* 1974 S.L.T. 253; *McKeirnon v. Secretary of State for Social Security, The Times,* November 1, 1989.

[26]   An example is the Order in Council which authorised the requisitioning of ships for the Falklands war in 1982 — S.I. 1982 No. 1693.

[27]   For instance, the fixing of the date for the referendum on U.K. membership of the EEC in 1975, and the dates for the referendum on devolution for Scotland and Wales held in 1979.

[28]   See Baldwin & Houghton, "Circular Arguments: the Status and Legitimacy of Administrative Rules" (1986) *Public Law* 239.

s. 3, are not published in the form of law but as House of Commons Papers.[29]
The rules are applied in court but may be overridden at the discretion of a
Minister.[30]

Rules such as these are criticised heavily by various commentators. Ganz   5–11
observes that the use of rules and codes is increasingly popular with
government: "hardly a statute is passed without a provision for a code of
practice or guidance".[31] Baldwin and Houghton[32] observe: "one view of
such 'rules' is that they offer a useful structuring of discretion; another is
that they are often used cynically so as to make law without resort to
Parliament".

Other types of subordinate legislation which are used are orders of local
authorities such as compulsory purchase orders, which after confirmation
by a Minister have legal effect, and byelaws made by local authorities and
other public bodies (again the Minister's confirmation is required). Although
there is a presumption against sub-delegation,[33] express authority to sub-
delegate will overcome the presumption.[34]

CREATING STATUTORY INSTRUMENTS

The terms of the enabling legislation will state whether the instrument is to   5–12
take the form of a statutory instrument or not and whether it requires to be
laid before Parliament.

1. MAKING A STATUTORY INSTRUMENT

The department concerned will consider what is required to implement the
policy laid out in the parent Act. This may involve consultation with
interested parties. A draft instrument will then be submitted to the Minister
for approval after which it will be printed and submitted to the Minister for
signature. The instrument is "made" when it has been signed. If necessary
the instrument will then be sent to the Queens' Printer where it is numbered,
printed and published[35] and laid before Parliament.[36] An instrument is proved

---

[29] The current rules are found in (1993–94 H.C. 395).
[30] 1971 Act, s. 19(2).
[31] Ganz, *Quasi-Legislation: Recent Developments in Secondary Legislation* (1987), p. 3.
[32] Baldwin and Houghton, *op. cit.,* n. 28, above, at 241.
[33] The Latin maxim *delegatus non potest delegare* (a delegate may not delegate) applies normally.
[34] *e.g.* Emergency Powers (Defence) Act 1939, s. 1(3).
[35] 1946 Act, ss. 2 and 3. Note the provisions of the Statutory Instruments (Production and Sale) Act 1996 which allows the publication by the privatised Stationery Office.
[36] 1946 Act, s. 4.

by the production by the government department of a copy printed or issued by the Stationery Office.[37]

2. Laying Statutory Instruments

5–13 For those instruments which are required to be laid before Parliament, the 1946 Act, s. 4(1), states that they must be laid before they come into operation, except in exceptional circumstances, for instance if changes are being to made to licence fees. In these cases, the Lord Chancellor and the Speaker of the House of Commons must be informed and an explanation given. The wording of the 1946 Act is that "a copy of the instrument ... shall be laid before the instrument comes into operation". The judicial view in *R. v. Sheer Metalcraft Ltd* [38] was that these words should be read in their literal sense.[39] The courts have long been concerned not to impinge upon the sovereignty of Parliament by inquiring too closely into its procedures. In *R. v. Secretary of State for Social Services, ex parte Camden LBC*[40] the Court of Appeal accepted that a legislative command to lay an instrument did not amount to a mandatory requirement. However, the duty to lay an instrument before Parliament is said to be "a constitutional safeguard of some value and an omission to carry out this duty ought not to be lightly regarded".[41]

The Laying of Documents before Parliament (Interpretation) Act 1948, s. 1, provides that, except where the contrary intention appears, a document is "laid" if it is laid in accordance with the internal procedures of each House and, again, unless there is a contrary intention, the document must be laid before both Houses.[42] The reason for imposing laying requirements is "to bring important rules and documents to Parliament's notice and thereby to facilitate Parliamentary control over the rule-making process".[43] The statutory instrument will be "laid" when a copy is delivered to the Votes and Proceedings Office of the House of Commons and the Printed Paper Office of the House of Lords. At the same time as the instrument is laid, a copy is sent to the Joint Committee on Delegated Legislation with an explanatory memorandum.

There are a number of different "laying" procedures.

---

[37] See *Scott v. Baker* [1969] 1 Q.B. 659, where a circular was held not to be admissible as evidence of the Minister's approval of a breath test device. The Minister then made an order signifying his approval and this was published by HMSO.

[38] [1954] 1 Q.B. 586.

[39] See De Smith, Woolf and Jowell, *Judicial Review of Administrative Action* (5th ed., 1995), para. 5–075.

[40] [1987] 1 W.L.R. 819.

[41] De Smith *et al, op. cit.,* n. 39, above, para. 5–075.

[42] See also *R. v. Immigration Appeal Tribunal, ex p. Joyles* [1972] 3 All E.R. 213.

[43] Puttick, *op. cit.,* n. 22, above, para. 7.03.

(a) Simple laying

The parent Act may simply state that the statutory instrument is to be laid 5–14
before Parliament after being made. The statutory instrument must be
laid before coming into operation (section 4) and it will then come into
operation on the date specified in the instrument itself. This is a relatively
uncommon procedure.

(b) Negative resolution

This is the most common procedure and consists of the instrument being
made, then laid with a view to coming into operation on the specified date
unless there is a resolution by either House within 40 days that it be
annulled.[44] The laying procedure requires that the instrument be registered
with the Statutory Publications Office and authenticated copies of the
instrument be supplied to the Votes Office of the House of Commons and
the Printed Paper Office of the House of Lords; it is the supply of the
authenticated copies which starts the 40-day period. Any member can seek
annulment by moving that an address be presented to Her Majesty praying[45]
that the instrument be annulled. If the resolution is approved, the Government
has to revoke the statutory instrument, but anything done in the meantime
will not be prejudiced by the later revocation of the instrument.[46] The 1946
Act does not deal with the consequences of a successful prayer against an
instrument which has already come into force.

(c) Affirmative resolution

In this procedure, the order is made, then laid, but it then requires the 5–15
approval of Parliament before it comes into operation. There is no special
procedure for the affirmative resolution and the Government must set aside
time for the instrument to be debated. This debate will be limited to 90
minutes, unless the instrument is a Northern Ireland measure, when it will
be debated for up to two-and-a-half hours.

The Joint Committee on Delegated Legislation[47] indicated the
circumstances in which it believed that the affirmative procedure was
appropriate:

  • where the powers substantially affected the provisions of a statute, *i.e.* they
    were not "trivial, tidying up or consequential" provisions;

  • where the powers sought to impose a tax or financial burden; and

---

[44] 1946 Act, s. 5.
[45] A "prayer" is an address to the Queen in Council to issue an Order revoking the instrument
under the powers conferred by the Statutory Instruments Act 1946, ss. 5 and 6.
[46] 1946 Act, s. 5(1).
[47] Second Report (1972–73 H.L. 304).

• where the powers were used in a novel area, for instance to create new varieties of criminal offences.

In both the negative and affirmative resolution procedures, the debate need not take place on the floor of the House. It is open to the Minister to move that the instrument be referred to a standing committee; in this event, there will be no debate unless the reference to the committee is discharged. The motion by the Minister can be blocked by 20 M.P.s rising in their places.[48]

(d) Draft instrument requiring affirmative procedure

5–16 The parent Act may state that a draft instrument must be laid before Parliament to receive an affirmative resolution. This particular method gives an opportunity to members to comment on the draft and perhaps seek changes which the Government may be more amenable to making because they are less committed to a draft than to an instrument which has already been made.[49]

(e) Draft instrument to be laid according to the negative procedure

The draft instrument may have to be laid and not be the subject of a negative resolution in order for it to come into operation. Section 6 of the 1946 Act states that the draft has to be laid for 40 days and if a resolution is passed within that time that the instrument be not approved, then the draft must be withdrawn.

(f) No laying procedure

5–17 The instrument may not be required to be laid. This is the second most common type of instrument and is used particularly for commencement orders.

The general rule regarding the scrutiny of statutory instruments is that Parliament cannot amend an instrument; it can only approve or reject it.[50] The scrutiny of subordinate legislation in the House of Commons is generally thought to be inadequate. The machinery for voting out a defective regulation by means of a 'prayer' is inadequate, given that the Minister can in effect side-step a debate by proposing that the prayer be debated not in the House but in a standing committee.

In the House of Lords, the scrutiny of statutory instruments is carried out as part of the normal business of the House but there are few instances of the House disagreeing with the terms of an instrument to the extent that

---

[48] For a discussion of this and other laying procedures see Hayhurst and Wallington, "Parliamentary Scrutiny of Delegated Legislation", 1988 P. L. 547.
[49] Foulkes, *Administrative Law* (8th ed., 1995).
[50] There are a few exceptions to this rule, *e.g.* Emergency Powers Act 1920, s. 2(4).

a division is called. A notable example of this, however, occurred during the Rhodesian crisis when a number of divisions were called on various instruments and one, the Southern Rhodesia (UN Sanctions) Order 1968 was defeated in the Lords. This led to a government proposal to remove the power of veto from the House of Lords[51] although in the end it was not proceeded with.

PUBLICATION OF RULES

The publication of subordinate legislation is an important issue; if an 5–18 instrument is not published how then can those affected by it know of its existence? The 1946 Act, s. 2, lays down the procedure for numbering, printing, publishing and citing statutory instruments, but there is no such procedure for the many administrative rules, guidelines and suchlike which are made by government officials. These are of great importance to individuals since they often set out how the official will exercise a discretion conferred by statute. The government recently promised, on a voluntary basis, to publish codes and rules which affect individuals.[52]

The rules in the 1946 Act for the publication of statutory instruments exempt certain instruments from the requirements of printing and sale.[53] These include instruments which are classified as local or general by their subject-matter; those where the Minister considers printing and sale to be unnecessary because the statutory instrument will have a short "life"; where the printing and sale of a schedule to the statutory instrument is certified as unnecessary by the Minister because of the nature or bulk of the schedule; and where the Minister certifies that the printing and sale before the instrument comes into force would be contrary to the public interest.

Section 3 of the Act requires that the Stationery Office publish lists of the dates on which every statutory instrument printed and sold by it was first issued.[54] If someone is prosecuted for contravening an instrument, section 3(2) provides a defence if he can show that the instrument, although made, was not issued at the date of the contravention. This defence can be overcome by the prosecution if it can be shown that reasonable steps were taken to inform the public of the contents of the instrument.

---

[51] The power under the Parliament Acts 1911 and 1949 to pass legislation without the consent of the House of Lords does not apply to subordinate legislation.

[52] Cabinet Office, *Open Government Code of Practice on Access to Government Information* (1994).

[53] 1946 Act, ss. 3 and 8(1) and S.I. 1948 No. 1.

[54] Note that the Statutory Instruments (Production and Sale) Act 1996 allows lists of statutory instruments to be received in evidence even although they do not "bear the imprint of the Queen's printer". This provision allowed the privatisation of HMSO.

5–19   Two cases are of interest here. In *Simmonds v. Newell*[55] a Ministerial order was issued giving, in a schedule, the maximum prices for steel. The schedule was not printed and sold by HMSO. S was convicted summarily of selling steel at prices higher than those permitted, but he argued that there had been no valid Ministerial certificate. No certificate was in fact produced in the magistrates' court and no evidence was led that sufficient steps had been taken to inform those affected of the contents of the schedule. His conviction was quashed on appeal because the prosecution had not discharged the burden of proof that sufficient notification had taken place. In the *Sheer Metalcraft* case[56] it was argued that since there was no Ministerial certificate exempting the schedules of an order, the order had not been validly made. Streatfeild J. regarded the printing and issuing requirements of the Act as "matters of procedure" and went on: "It seems to follow from the wording of this subsection [3(2)] that the making of an instrument is one thing and the issue of it is another. If it is made it can be contravened; if it has not been issued then that provides a defence to a person charged with its contravention." In a more recent case,[57] the court held that where a statutory instrument is required to be laid before Parliament and the instrument refers to information in other documents which are not part of the instrument, failure to lay the referred document does not, as a general rule, negate the effectiveness of the instrument.

The parent Act of subordinate legislation which does not fall within the 1946 Act may state specific requirements for publication of the instrument. Failure to follow these requirements may cause the instrument to be declared invalid.[58] Many other administrative orders are subject to complex publicity rules, for instance, compulsory purchase orders, or applications for planning permission.

The courts have recognised that there is no statutory or common law duty to publish sub-delegated legislation but have indicated that the maxim "ignorance of the law is no excuse" depends for its validity on the whole of the law being accessible to the public.[59]

The Select Committee of the Parliamentary Commissioner for Administration has also noted that publication of changes in rules is just as necessary as publication of the rules themselves.[60] They observed that where significant changes in administrative rules occurred there should be immediate publicity.

---

[55] [1953] 2 All E.R. 38.
[56] *R. v. Sheer Metalcraft Ltd* [1954] 1 Q.B. 586.
[57] *R. v. Secretary of State for Social Services, ex p. Camden LBC* [1987] 1 W.L.R. 819.
[58] For an example of this see *Vale of Glamorgan Borough Council v. Palmer and Bowles* (1982) 81 L.G.R. 678.
[59] *Blackpool Corporation v. Locker* [1948] 1 All E.R. 85.
[60] Select Committee of Parliamentary Commissioner for Administration, First Report (1970–71 H.C. 240), paras. 12–21.

CONSULTATION

Before a statutory instrument is made, the department concerned will often 5–20
consult with interested bodies[61] as to the most effective means of
implementing the policy stated in the Act. The department may be required
by the statute to consult or there may be, more rarely, a duty at common
law to consult. In the absence of these however there is no general duty to
consult; officials may do so in order to seek consensus and to ensure the
rule will operate with the least amount of opposition. The situation in
the United Kingdom can be contrasted, rather unfavourably, with that of the
USA where the Administrative Procedure Act 1946 imposes a duty on federal
bodies to afford "interested persons the opportunity to participate in the
rulemaking through submission of written data, views or arguments with
or without opportunity to present the same orally in any manner". This is
referred to as the "notice-and-comment" procedure.[62] In the United
Kingdom, the courts have been generally unwilling to correct any deficiency
in consultation, although in *R. v. Liverpool Corporation ex parte Liverpool
Taxi Fleet Operators' Association*[63] the court granted an order of prohibition
to enforce an informal undertaking by the corporation that there would be
no increase in the number of taxi licences without prior consultation with
the taxi owners' association.

(a) Statutory duty to consult

The duty to consult may be mandatory or directory. If it is mandatory, then 5–21
a failure to consult before the instrument is made may render the instrument
invalid. A directory requirement, however, will not necessarily invalidate
the instrument.

The problem which often occurs regarding statutory consultation is not
whether consultation should take place but who should be consulted. In
Rollo v. Minister of Town and Country Planning[64] the New Towns Act 1946
gave the Minister power to make an order designating an area as a site for
a New Town, after consulting with any local authorities "who appear(ed)
to him to be concerned". Objectors to an order claimed that the Minister
had not consulted all local authorities concerned but the court held that
since the Minister had concluded that some local authorities were not
concerned then this was all that was required to fulfil the provisions on
consultation. In *R. v. Post Office, ex parte ASTMS*[65] there was a requirement

---

[61] Such as trade associations, trade unions, parents' associations, pressure groups.
[62] See discussion in Harlow and Rawlings, *Law and Administration* (1984), Chap. 5; Baldwin, *op. cit.*, n. 13, above, pp. 169–170.
[63] [1972] 2 W.L.R. 1262.
[64] [1947] 2 All E.R. 488.
[65] [1981] 1 All E.R. 139.

on the Post Office to "seek consultation with any organisation appearing to it to be appropriate." On the facts, the court held that the Post Office had considered the appropriateness of the ASTMS "fairly and reasonably". This decision appears to indicate that rule-makers have to apply the *Wednesbury* principle of reasonableness when they are selecting with whom to consult.

5–22   Two further cases illustrate the importance of consultation and the effect of not consulting properly. In *Agricultural, Horticultural and Forestry Industry Training Board v. Aylesbury Mushrooms Ltd*[66] the statute indicated that consultation with affected bodies was most important because the regulations would be setting a levy on organisations covered by the board. The court said that this, coupled with the fact that an unsuccessful attempt had been made to contact the Mushroom Growers Association, clearly indicated that there was a right of consultation. Since a form of taxation was being proposed, the requirement to consult had to be construed strictly. The effect of the decision was to invalidate the regulations so far as they purported to apply to the Mushroom Growers Association.

In *R. v. Secretary of State for Social Services, ex parte Association of Metropolitan Authorities*[67] an obligation to consult organisations which were representative of local authorities was held to be mandatory in a situation where the regulations proposed to change the housing benefit scheme, the administration of which was undertaken by the local authorities who also bore 10 per cent of the costs. The Secretary of State could require a quick response to his proposals but he had in this case failed to carry out sufficient consultation. The regulations were, however, not quashed because they were already in force and being operated by local authorities.

5–23   Consultation must be properly carried out with the rule-maker on the one hand supplying "sufficient information" to those being consulted "to enable them to tender advice and on the other hand a sufficient opportunity must be given ... to tender that advice".[68] The time-limit for consultation will depend upon the circumstances, but it is appropriate that a longer time for consultation should be given to bodies such as the AMA where a committee structure is in place.

If the duty to consult is mandatory and there is a failure to consult, the order may be declared void.[69]

(b) Common Law duty

5–24 There is no general duty to consult at common law. However, recent case law appears to have increased the scope of consultation rights where an individual

---

[66] [1972] 1 All E.R. 280.
[67] [1986] 1 All E.R. 164.
[68] *Rollo v. Minister of Town and Country Planning* [1948] 1 All E.R. 13, *per* Bucknill L. J. at 17.
[69] *R. v. Warwickshire District Council, ex p. Bailey* [1991] C.O.D. 284; *R. v. British Coal Corporation and Secretary of State for Trade and Industry, ex p. Price* [1993] C.O.D. 482.

is able to argue that an established policy should be applied. Where a public body has informed an individual or group that it will be following a particular policy, or has said that it will inform the individual or group before changes are made, then the individual or group is, at least, entitled to be consulted before changes are made and may even be able to insist that the original policy continues.[70] In *R. v. Secretary of State for the Home Department, ex parte Khan*[71] K obtained from the DHSS a Home Office circular which contained the criteria for adoption of children born outside the United Kingdom. K then proceeded to try to adopt a child using these criteria but the Secretary of State rejected his application, using different criteria to decide the case. The Secretary of State contended in court that he had unfettered discretion and was entitled to take into consideration other matters not in the circular. The Court of Appeal, however, decided that where an individual, affected by a decision of a public authority, has legitimate expectation based on a statement or undertaking by the authority that certain criteria or procedures would be used, then the authority was under a duty to follow these provided they did not conflict with any statutory duty. The criteria in the circular amounted to rules made by the Secretary of State for deciding an application for entry and the Secretary of State had acted unfairly and unreasonably by applying different criteria from those set out in the circular. In *Re Findlay*[72] a change in parole policy was held not to infringe legitimate expectations of prisoners even although they would have been released earlier under a previous policy. The legitimate expectation of the prisoners was that their case be considered individually under whatever policy the Minister adopted.

The duty to consult may be wider than only allowing consultation before changes occur; the duty may allow an individual to contest a new policy. In *R. v. Birmingham City Council, ex parte Dredger*[73] stallholders were held to have a legitimate expectation of being consulted about changes in the council's rent policy. This meant that the council had to give details of proposals to the applicants, give them time to respond and take these into account when making a final decision.

PARLIAMENTARY SCRUTINY OF SUBORDINATE LEGISLATION

"There is now general agreement about the necessity for delegated 5–25 legislation; the real problem is how this legislation can be reconciled with the processes of democratic consultation, scrutiny and control."[74]

---

[70] *R. v. Liverpool Corporation, ex p. Liverpool Taxi Fleet Operators' Association*, above.
[71] [1985] 1 All E.R. 40.
[72] [1985] A.C. 318.
[73] [1993] C.O.D. 340.
[74] Aneurin Bevan speaking in 1953 and quoted in Stewart, "Reformation of American Administrative Law" (1975) 88 Harvard L. R. 1669.

Subordinate legislation is made as a result of the delegation of legislative power by Parliament to a public authority. It follows that in a democracy parliament must oversee this legislative activity and ensure that subordinate legislation is being used in the way Parliament intended. The main problem associated with this scrutiny by Parliament is the same one which gave rise to the increased use of subordinate legislation in the first place — lack of Parliamentary time. It could also be said that there is a lack of political will to ensure proper scrutiny of subordinate legislation, most of which appears to be passed with no more than a cursory glance. The scrutiny of subordinate legislation is not exactly a high profile job which will bring an M.P. to the attention of either his party or the electorate at large. There is accordingly little interest in scrutinising such measures. In addition, the process in the House of Commons makes proper scrutiny difficult. The 40-day time-limit for prayers to be made is strictly observed with no extra time being allowed if an instrument is reported by the Joint Committee on Delegated Legislation. Further, if an instrument does attract controversy on party lines, the debate thus generated tends to concentrate not on the procedural defects of the instrument but on the merits of the policy.[75] Indeed, there are few government defeats in the House of Commons on subordinate legislation.[76]

5–26   The problem of lack of proper scrutiny was highlighted by the Joint Committee in 1986 when it reported that the volume and complexity of instruments had increased markedly in the period 1981–86. They observed that "instead of simply implementing the 'nuts and bolts' of Government policy, statutory instruments have increasingly been used to change policy, sometimes in ways that were not envisaged when the enabling legislation was passed".[77] The initial scrutiny of subordinate legislation when instruments are laid before both Houses was discussed above.[78] Instruments which are subject to either the affirmative or negative resolution procedure receive some scrutiny although there is insufficient time allocated for debate on instruments which members consider problematic.

The Joint Committee on Delegated Legislation carries out most of the scrutiny of subordinate legislation laid before Parliament. The joint committee was created in 1973 from the House of Commons Select committee on Statutory Instruments which existed from 1944 to 1972.[79] The committee is strictly speaking two select committees of each House

---

[75] Hayhurst and Wallington, *op. cit.,* n. 48, above, 557.

[76] *ibid.* 558 — from 1970–1988, there were three Government defeats on subordinate legislation — none of them were reported by the joint committee.

[77] Report of Joint Committee on Delegated Legislation (1986 H.C. 31), p. xxxvii, p. 2.

[78] See paras. 5–14 to 5–17.

[79] See Hayhurst and Wallington, *op. cit.,* n. 48, above, at 549–551 for historical background to the creation of these committees.

with each House having equal membership on the joint committee. The Donoughmore Committee[80] made specific recommendations that both Houses should have a standing committee on delegated legislation. That Committee envisaged that these would "supply the private member with knowledge he lacks at present, and thus enable him to exercise an informed discretion whether to object or criticise". The two select committees meet together to consider instruments laid before both Houses. The House of Commons Select Committee meets alone to consider instruments which are laid before the Commons alone, such as fiscal measures.

The joint committee considers the technical form of the instrument; it 5–27 may not consider its merits. Before it reports on an instrument, the joint committee must give the department concerned an opportunity to explain why the instrument was made in that form. If the instrument is then reported to Parliament, the joint committee must give their reasons for doing so. Unfortunately, there is no procedure in the House of Commons for ensuring that the views of the joint committee are taken into account before the instrument comes into force. The instrument can be discussed by a House of Commons Merits Committee with up to 90 minutes' debate but there is no vote taken in the committee and no debate on the floor of the House. Further, there is no amending procedure for defective instruments; they can only be withdrawn by the department, corrected and relaid.

The terms of reference of the joint committee require it to examine every statutory instrument, rule, order, or scheme laid or laid in draft before Parliament in order to determine whether the attention of the House needs to be drawn to it for one of nine reasons[81]:

1. The instrument imposes a tax or charge.

2. The instrument is excluded from challenge in the courts by virtue of its enabling Act.

3. The instrument purports to have retrospective effect where there is no express power in the enabling Act.

4. There appears to have been an unjustifiable delay in the publication or laying of the instrument.

5. The instrument has come into operation prior to laying and the Lord Chancellor and the Speaker have not been informed under section 4(1) of the 1946 Act.

6. There is doubt whether the instrument is *intra vires* or there appears to be an unusual or unexpected use of the delegated power.

---

[80] Cmd. 4060 (1932).
[81] House of Commons Standing Order 124.

7.   The instrument requires elucidation.

8.   The drafting appears defective.

9.   Any other ground which does not impinge on the merits or the policy behind the instrument.

5–28   In the House of Lords, a new committee was set up in 1992 to consider the contents of Bills in which it was proposed to delegate legislative powers. The Delegated Powers Scrutiny Committee "reports whether the provisions of any bill inappropriately delegate legislative power; or whether they subject the exercise of legislative power to an inappropriate degree of Parliamentary scrutiny".[82] This committee considers the powers being given to Ministers and departments particularly where the proposed legislation takes the form of a skeleton Bill or "Henry VIII" clause. The Government agreed to provide the committee with a memorandum on each Bill identifying subordinate legislation provisions in the bill, explaining the purpose of the Bill and the reasons for selecting the procedure.

5–29   A specialist committee was set up in the House of Commons as a result of concern expressed by the Delegated Powers Scrutiny Committee at the wide powers given to Ministers by the Deregulation and Contracting Out Act 1994. The Act states that deregulation orders must be laid in draft before, and approved by, both Houses. The Minister is required to consult with appropriate organisations before making the draft. The draft orders are laid but are not made before the expiry of 60 days to allow for longer consideration by Parliament. The Minister is also required to consult with appropriate organisations before the draft is laid. The Deregulation Orders Committee of the House of Commons comprises 16 senior M.P.s who are concerned with both the *vires* of the draft orders and their merits. This committee can allow those affected by an order to express their concern and it has the power to propose amendments to the order. The Delegated Powers Scrutiny Committee of the House of Lords undertakes the scrutiny of deregulation orders.

SCRUTINY OF EUROPEAN COMMUNITY LEGISLATION

5–30   The European Communities Act 1972 was identified above as an example of a statute containing "Henry VIII" sections. Section 2(2) empowers the Government to legislate by way of statutory instrument for the purposes of "implementing any Community obligation of the United Kingdom or enabling any such obligation to be implemented, or of enabling any rights enjoyed by the United Kingdom under or by virtue of the Treaties to be

---

[82]   See discussion of this Committee in Himsworth, "Delegated Powers Scrutiny Committee", (1995) P. L. 34.

exercised". Section 2(4) provides that such legislation made under section 2(2) may include "any provision as might be made by Act of Parliament, and any enactment passed or to be passed ... and shall be construed and have effect subject to the foregoing provisions of this section". Schedule 2 to the Act states that the powers conferred by section 2(2) will not include power to make provisions to impose or create taxation, provisions to have retrospective effect, provisions to allow sub-delegation except to make rules of procedure for a court or tribunal, and provisions which create new criminal offences punishable by imprisonment of more than two years or summary offences with imprisonment of more than three months or a fine of more than the statutory maximum.

Both Houses of Parliament have committees looking at European legislation. These have two functions: first, they consider U.K. subordinate legislation made to implement the provisions of a Community directive or regulation and, secondly, they scrutinise proposals from the Council of Ministers in order to inform Parliament about the likely effect of European legislation. The House of Commons Select Committee on European Legislation was formed in 1991 with a remit to refer legislation which it deems to merit further debate, to one of the two standing committees of the House of Commons. This committee can question Ministers and officials, consider the merits of proposed legislation and refer the issue, with the consent of the Leader of the House, to the floor of the House for debate. The select committee in its first year of operation considered over 600 documents and sent around 10 per cent to the standing committee for discussion.

PRESUMPTIONS OF LEGISLATIVE INTENT

Before we consider the scrutiny of subordinate legislation by the judiciary, 5–31 it is as well to consider briefly the rules or presumptions recognised by the courts when they consider the intention of Parliament in construing primary or subordinate legislation. Note that subordinate legislation is also subject to the provisions of the Interpretation Act 1978, although the court's attitude to interpretation may be different given that it is subordinate legislation which is being interpreted, not primary legislation.[83] The initial presumption of the courts is that "Parliament means what it says"; in other words, the courts use the plain or literal meaning of a word in the context of the whole statute except where it is clearly indicated by the statute that a different meaning should be taken. The importance of the context of the words was shown in *Padfield v. Minister of Agriculture, Fisheries and Food*[84] where a

---

[83] *e.g.* see *Pickstone v. Freemans plc* [1989] A.C. 66.
[84] [1968] A.C. 997; [1968] 1 All E.R. 694.

phrase, taken in isolation, appeared to confer a power on the Minister but, when taken in the context of the Act as a whole, was seen to have imposed a duty on him.

In normal circumstances, words in a statute are construed without reference to the debates in Parliament or other extraneous sources. However, the case of *Pepper v. Hart*[85] established the principle that judges may have recourse to parliamentary debates, reported in *Hansard*, to aid the "construction of legislation which is ambiguous or obscure or the literal meaning of which leads to an absurdity".[86] Only the words of the Minister or promoter of the Bill may be examined to ascertain the meaning. The principal objections to the use of *Hansard* in court proceedings relate to parliamentary privilege and the practical inconvenience of consulting *Hansard*.[87]

5–32   In addition to the above, the courts also use presumptions of legislative intent which are used to resolve ambiguities, provide answers to problems not foreseen by the legislative draftsman or modify the meaning of the words used to give a meaning which appears to conform more to the intention of Parliament.

Note that all of the presumptions can be rebutted by clear and precise words in the statute. The presumptions include:

1. Parliament does not intend to exclude access to the courts.This presumption has been used in a number of cases. In *Chester v. Bateson*[88] a Minister was given wide statutory power "to issue regulations for securing the safety and the defence of the realm ... and to prevent ... successful prosecution of the war being endangered". This power was used to make a regulation preventing the eviction of munitions workers from their homes. The regulation made it an offence to take court proceedings for the recovery of such property. The court held that the regulation was *ultra vires*; access to the courts could not be taken away except with the express authority of Parliament.[89]

5–33   More recently, in *R. v. Secretary of State for the Home Department, ex parte Leech*[90] rules made by the Home Secretary under the Prison Act 1952, s. 47, to regulate and manage prisons, were held to be *ultra vires* in so far as they could not be used to stop correspondence between a prisoner and his solicitor.

2. Parliament does not intend to regulate to take away the vested rights of a class of individuals without the authority of a statute.[91]

---

[85] [1993] A.C. 593; [1993] 1 All E.R. 42.
[86] *ibid., per* Lord Browne-Wilkinson at 64.
[87] For discussion of the difficulties associated with this decision, see Baker, "Statutory Interpretation and Parliamentary Intention" (1993) 52 C.L.J. at 353.
[88] [1920] 1 K.B. 829.
[89] See also *Kerr v. Hood*, 1907 S.C. 895; *R. v. Housing Appeal Tribunal* [1920] 3 K.B. 334.
[90] [1994] Q.B. 198.
[91] See *Malloch v. Aberdeen Corporation*, 1974 S.L.T. 253.

3. Parliament does not intend legislation to apply retrospectively. In *Secretary of State for Social Services v. Tunnicliffe*[92] the Court of Appeal decided that section 53 of the Social Security Act 1986 could allow the Secretary of State to recover overpayments of non-means tested benefits where the overpayment had been made prior to the commencement of the section. The presumption against retrospective legislation was inapplicable here. This decision was overruled by the House of Lords in *Plewa (Executrix of Estate of Jozif Plewa, dec'd) v. Chief Adjudication Officer*[93] where it was held that the presumption against retrospective legislation applied where a new liability had been created under a statutory regime.[94] In cases where the courts have found against the Government, legislation may be passed swiftly to remedy the situation, as occurred after the decision in *Burmah Oil (Burma Trading) Ltd v. Lord Advocate*[95] when the War Damage Act 1965 was passed retrospectively to remove governmental liability to compensation for certain types of war damage.

4. Parliament does not intend to impose a tax or charge unless by clear 5–34 express statements. In *Att.-General v. Wiltshire Dairies Ltd*[96] there was an attempt by the Food Controller to impose a charge on milk as a condition of issuing licences for the supply of milk. This was held to be invalid on the ground that the Food Controller's power under the Defence Regulations to regulate the supply of milk did not confer power to impose charges on the subject. In *Daymond v. South West Water Authority*[97] the water authority had power to fix and recover "such charges for the services … performed by them" as they thought fit. Daymond objected to paying a sewerage charge, arguing that since his house was not connected to the public sewer he was not in receipt of any service. The House of Lords held that in the absence of an express power stating who could be charged, only those who received the service were subject to such charges.[98]

5. A statute does not bind the Crown unless such an intention is clear. This rule of interpretation is expressly saved by the Crown Proceedings Act 1947, s. 40(2)(f).

6. There is a presumption against a regulation or a byelaw having a 5–35 wider territorial effect than is authorised by the enabling Act. In *Dunkley v. Evans*[99] a prosecution against Evans failed because the Order classifying

---

[92] [1991] 2 All E.R. 712.

[93] [1994] 3 W.L.R. 317.

[94] See discussion of these cases in Feldman, "Presumption against Retrospective Legislation" (1995) L.Q.R. 33.

[95] [1965] A.C. 75.

[96] (1921) 37 T.L.R. 884.

[97] [1976] A.C. 609.

[98] See also *Commissioners of Customs and Excise v. Cure and Deeley Ltd* [1962] 1 Q.B. 340; *Congreve v. Home Office* [1976] Q.B. 629.

[99] [1981] 1 W.L.R. 1522.

area as a prohibited fishing area included a small part over which the Minister had no power to make the Order. The prosecution appealed and this was upheld on the basis that the court could sever the invalid part of the Order. The test then was whether the severance would make a radical or substantial difference in the Order.

7. Subordinate legislation may not add to restrictions authorised by the parent Act. In *Rossi v. Magistrates of Edinburgh*[1] it was held that the magistrates might not insert conditions into a licence where the conditions were not authorised by the parent Act.

8. Subordinate legislation may not seek to sub-delegate a discretion without authority or authorise increases in statutory charges without complying with the statutory procedure.[2]

9. There is a presumption against the use of a power to regulate activity in order to ban it.[3]

CONTROL BY THE COURTS

5–36 The essential difference between a statute and a statutory instrument is that the Minister or official who makes the statutory instrument does not have the unlimited powers of Parliament. Accordingly, statutory instruments are subject to control by Parliament itself and, once they have come into operation, by the courts. However, it should be noted that the courts will on occasions look at subordinate legislation which is passing through its preliminary or parliamentary process. The courts are careful not to interfere with the political process and so persons seeking a review of proposed subordinate legislation will have difficulty in placing the matter before the courts. The decisions of the Boundary Commission for England were held to be reviewable although the courts in this case found that there was no irrationality or material misdirection by the commission.[4] The court further stated that if the case had succeeded on its merits, it would have granted a declaration although such would not have prevented the commission from presenting its report to the Home Secretary.

When it appears that the subordinate legislative process has not followed the authority conferred by the parent Act, it may be in the public interest to intervene.[5] The courts may be asked to intervene in the period between making the statutory instrument and its coming into effect; this is more problematic particularly if the statutory instrument also has the effect of

---

[1] (1904) 7 F. (H.L.) 85.

[2] See *Freight Transport Association v. Lothian Regional Council,* 1978 S.L.T. 14.

[3] See *Scottish General Transport Co. Ltd v. Glasgow Corporation,* 1928 S.C. 248.

[4] *R. v. Boundary Commission for England, ex p. Foot* [1983] Q.B. 600.

[5] *R. v. Electricity Commissioners, ex p. London Electricity Joint Committee Co.* [1924] 1 K.B. 171.

excluding judicial review.[6] In *R. v. H.M. Treasury, ex parte Smedley*[7] a draft Order in Council was held to be reviewable and the application for judicial review was not premature.

Judicial control is not excluded where a statutory instrument is laid before Parliament subject to the negative resolution procedure and no prayer is made. Similarly, it is not excluded where the statutory instrument is subject to the affirmative resolution and is approved by such a resolution.[8] "The two Houses are not 'the Queen in Parliament' which alone has legislative supremacy." However, it is likely that judicial review on the grounds of irrationality or unreasonableness would be excluded where a statutory instrument subject to the affirmative procedure was approved by the resolution of the House of Commons.[9]   5–37

During the two World Wars, the Government had powers which appeared limitless and the courts were loathe to countenance challenges to these powers. In the now largely discredited case of *Liversidge v. Anderson*[10] the courts found it impossible to challenge the grounds on which the Home Secretary claimed to have "reasonable cause to believe" a person to be of hostile origin or association. Any challenge of the Minister's powers was limited to demonstrating that the Minister had acted in bad faith.   5–38

The ground of challenge usually used in cases involving subordinate legislation is that it is *ultra vires*; the subordinate legislation goes beyond the powers conferred by the enabling statute on the Minister or other rule-maker. The principle is that the Minister has no power to legislate other than that conferred on him by the enabling Act. The doctrine of *ultra vires* falls into two categories: procedural *ultra vires* and substantive *ultra vires*.

1. Procedural *Ultra Vires*

When a statute authorises subordinate legislation to be made, it will state the person or body on whom the power is conferred and also the procedure for making the legislation. Procedural *ultra vires* will occur when there is a non-compliance with the procedural requirements for making the instrument. It should be noted, however, that not every procedural error will lead to the instrument being declared invalid. The courts distinguish between a mandatory requirement, that is, an important procedural requirement, and a directory requirement, which is less serious. Non-compliance with a   5–39

---

[6]   See *ex p. Foot,* above.
[7]   [1985] Q.B. 657.
[8]   See *F. Hoffman-La Roche & Co. AG v. Secretary of State for Trade and Industry* [1975] A.C. 295.
[9]   *Nottinghamshire County Council v. Secretary of State for Environment* [1986] A.C. 240.
[10]   [1942] A.C. 206.

mandatory requirement will vitiate the exercise of power[11] while non-compliance with a directory requirement will not necessarily have such a drastic effect. Indeed, substantial compliance may be sufficient. An example of this is a failure by the Minister to consult interested parties before the legislation is made[12]; the failure may be caused by inadequate consultation or a complete failure to consult.[13]

The instrument may not comply with the requirements of the Statutory Instruments Act 1946. Some of the requirements of the Act, for instance with regard to numbering and printing specifications, are thought to be directory in nature. In *R. v. Sheer Metalcraft Ltd* [14] a company prosecuted under an Order challenged the validity of the Order for non-compliance with the printing requirements of the 1946 Act, s. 3(2). The company was convicted since the Order was held to be valid when it was "issued" prior to printing, in other words when it was laid before Parliament.

5–40　　It has been argued that failure to lay a statutory instrument, which is required to be laid before Parliament before it comes into operation, will invalidate it.[15] Some commentators state that a requirement to lay draft regulations before Parliament and have them approved by affirmative resolution amounts to a mandatory requirement.[16] However, in *R. v. Secretary of State for Social Services, ex parte Camden LBC*[17] the question of the validity of a statutory instrument not laid before Parliament arose. The Supplementary Benefits Act 1976 provided that regulations which may be made under the Act "shall not be made" unless a draft is laid before Parliament and approved by a resolution of each House. The regulations, duly laid in draft form and approved, fixed an amount for an item of expenditure by reference to a booklet which was not laid before Parliament. The Court of Appeal accepted that a legislative command to lay did not amount to a mandatory requirement and failure to lay the booklet did not make the regulations invalid.

What will give rise to strict compliance? Consideration of case law gives an indication of what the courts have considered to be important. Where a statute imposes a duty to consult prior to taking a decision, then failure to

---

[11] *F. Hoffman-La Roche & Co. AG v. Secretary of State for Trade and Industry* [1975] A.C. 295.

[12] *Agricultural, Horticultural and Forestry Industry Training Board v. Aylesbury Mushrooms Ltd* [1972] 1 W.L.R. 190; [1972] 1 All E.R. 280.

[13] *R. v. Secretary of State for Social Services, ex p. Association of Metropolitan Authorities* [1986] 1 W.L.R. 1; [1986] 1 All E.R. 164, where there was insufficient consultation and the duty to consult was mandatory.

[14] [1954] 1 Q.B. 586.

[15] *Stair Memorial Encyclopaedia*, Vol. 1, "Administrative Law", para. 300.

[16] Campbell, "Statutory Instruments — Laying Legislation by Reference", 1987 P.L. 328.

[17] [1987] 2 All E.R. 560.

do so is likely to invalidate the decision.[18] Similarly, where there is a duty to give notice to the public of matters so that those who wish may make representations or take appropriate action, the courts will look for strict compliance.[19] In particular, requirements to give citizens notice of their rights of appeal are considered to be important.[20] The courts appear to be fairly strict on the appeal mechanism and any failure on the part of the public body but are less strict when the appellant fails to state the grounds of appeal in good time.

The courts will take a number of factors into account as follows: 5–41

(i) The context of the procedure — what was the importance of the procedure in the context of what it was intended to achieve and in relation to the statute ?

Lord Penzance gave the classic statement on this:

> "I believe, as far as any rule is concerned, you cannot safely go further than that in each case you must look to the subject matter; consider the importance of the provision that has been disregarded, and the relation of that provision to the general object intended to be secured by the Act; and upon a review of the case in that aspect decide whether the matter is what is called imperative or only directory."[21]

In *Cullimore v. Lyme Regis Corporation*[22] the court looked at the whole "scope and object" of the legislation under consideration. The case concerned a statutory scheme for carrying out coastal protection works under the Coast Protection Act 1949. The council set itself a timescale for assessing charges to be imposed on interested parties but then failed to carry out the assessment within the timescale. The court held that this was a condition with which the council had to comply; the notification requirements in the Act had an important purpose, to prevent the effects of delay on those who were to be levied.

(ii) The statutory language used is also considered by the courts. The   5–42
procedural provision may state that the rule-maker "shall" do something. The courts have held that this does not necessarily mean that the procedure is mandatory. Lord Salmon in *Grunwick Processing Laboratories v. ACAS*[23] said thus: "The result of this appeal turns solely on whether the part of s. 14(1) which I have cited is mandatory or directory. Prima facie the word 'shall' suggests that it is mandatory but that word has often been rightly

---

[18] See *Aylesbury Mushrooms* case above; *Lee v. Secretary of State for Education and Science* (1967) 66 L.G.R. 211 where two or three days' notice of proposals was held to be "wholly unreasonable" and denied objectors their important procedural rights.

[19] See *Steeples v. Derbyshire County Council* [1984] 3 All E.R. 468; *R. v. Chief Constable of Merseyside Police, ex p. Calveley* [1986] Q.B. 424.

[20] See *Rayner v. Stepney Corporation* [1911] 2 Ch. 312; *Johnston v. Secretary of State for Scotland,* 1992 S.L.T. 387.

[21] *Howard v. Bodington* (1877) 2 P.D. 203 at 211.

[22] [1962] 1 Q.B. 718.

[23] [1978] A.C. 655.

construed as being directory. Everything turns upon the context in which it is used: the subject-matter, the purpose and effect of the section in which it appears." The company was able to challenge a formal report which recommended union recognition; the statutory provision stated that ACAS "shall" ascertain the opinions of workers involved in the dispute before making a recognition recommendation.

(iii) Prejudice to the complainant is a third factor. The statute will usually require "substantial" prejudice, although the requirements may be couched in such strong language or be construed as so important that non-compliance will result in invalidity of the subordinate legislation whether other parties have been prejudiced or not. The courts must be clearly persuaded that prejudice has occurred and they may find that the prejudice to the applicant is not sufficient to invalidate the rule in its general application. For instance, in the *Aylesbury Mushrooms* case,[24] a failure to consult mushroom growers about the proposed levy order was dealt with by ordering that the levy could not be charged on them while leaving the order intact as regards other parties.

In *Wilson v. Secretary of State for the Environment*[25] a misdescription in a notice was held to have "substantially prejudiced" parties who had thereby been deprived of the right to make representations and objections. In *R. v. Secretary of State for Social Services, ex parte Association of Metropolitan Authorities*[26] the fact that local authorities were responsible for administering and partly financing housing benefits was a factor in finding that proper consultation with them before the making of the regulations should have taken place.

5–43   (iv) The argument that invalidating a rule would cause public inconvenience or affect third parties has been used successfully in a number of cases. This argument is particularly relevant when the court is deciding what to do about the particular failure. In the *ex parte AMA* case[27] the regulations were already implemented and this was an important factor in the court's decision not to invalidate them. In *Coney v. Choyce*[28] the prejudice to the education of a number of children and the educational machine in the area was a factor in the court's decision not to grant an order which would have delayed school reorganisation.

(v) Where strict compliance is not required by the statute, the question of "substantial" compliance may be raised. In *Bates v. Lord Hailsham*[29] Megarry J. said "If the consultation procedure laid down by Parliament is

---

[24] [1972] 1 All E.R. 280.
[25] [1973] 1 W.L.R. 1083.
[26] [1986] 1 All E.R. 164.
[27] *ibid.*
[28] [1975] 1 W.L.R. 422.
[29] [1972] 1 W.L.R. 1373.

fairly and substantially followed, I cannot see that the committee need do more".[30] On the other hand, in the *Cullimore*[31] case it was held that strict compliance was required and, even if that were not so, there had been "nothing approaching substantial compliance".

2. SUBSTANTIVE *ULTRA VIRES*

This may occur when a subordinate law-making body has acted properly 5–44 regarding the procedure for making the subordinate legislation but has purported to act beyond the substantive scope of the powers conferred by the enabling statute. The courts have tended to interpret the terms of the enabling legislation strictly[32] and it is in this context that the rules of legislative intent discussed above are important.[33]

The subordinate legislation may infringe the parent Act or another statute and will accordingly be held to be *ultra vires*.[34] The powers are granted for a particular purpose and if the subordinate legislation is used for a different purpose, which is not what Parliament intended, then it will be void.[35]

The courts will also intervene if the exercise of the power is unreasonable. 5–45 If the instrument is too vague it may be unreasonable but the courts may place a generous construction on the wording in certain circumstances. In *McEldowey v. Forde*[36] the Northern Ireland Minister was empowered to make regulations "for the preservation of peace and maintenance of order" under the Civil Authorities (Special Powers) Acts (Northern Ireland) 1922–43. Regulations made in 1922 proscribed membership of certain stated organisations. In 1967, the list was amended to include organisations describing themselves as "Republican Clubs" and "any like organisation however described". The House of Lords, by majority, held that the regulations proscribing membership of clubs and organisations were in principle capable of being related to the purposes of the enabling legislation. The use of the power was to be determined according to established principles relating to the review of the exercise of the discretionary powers. In another case, the court struck down a byelaw which purported to restrict access to a military base on the grounds that the area covered by the byelaw was not delineated clearly enough. The byelaw also included areas which

---

[30] [1972] 1 W.L.R. 1373 at 1378.
[31] [1962] 1 Q.B. 718.
[32] See *Utah Construction & Engineering Pty Ltd v. Pataky* [1966] A.C. 629.
[33] See paras. 5–32 to 5–35.
[34] See *Att.-Gen. v. Wiltshire United Dairies* (1921) 39 T.L.R. 781; *Bromley London Borough Council v. Greater London Council* [1983] 1 A.C. 768; *R. v. Secretary of State for Home Department, ex p. Leech* [1993] 4 All E.R. 539.
[35] See *R. v. H M Treasury, ex p. Smedley* [1985] Q.B. 657.
[36] [1971] A.C. 632.

were common land, although this was specifically prohibited by the statute.[37] The courts have also held that if a statutory instrument has been laid in Parliament and has received some consideration from the House of Commons, it may not be reviewed by the courts on the ground of unreasonableness.[38]

5–46   There is a notable paucity of successful challenges to statutory instruments on the grounds of either substantive or procedural *ultra vires*. Several reasons have been put forward for this: the quality of the drafting of subordinate legislation leaves little room for dispute; the enabling powers are so wide as to encompass most uses of the power; the infrequency of challenges has precluded other challenges; and judicial reticence.[39] Hayhurst and Wallington cite only 16 cases between 1914 and 1986 where there was a successful challenge on substantive grounds. It is notable also that of the 16, 12 of them concerned subordinate legislation which had been considered by the Joint Committee on Delegated Legislation or its predecessor, only three of those had a report or discussion and in none of them was the question of *vires* raised.[40]

QUASI-LEGISLATION

5–47   We have seen that in addition to the large number of statutory instruments which fall within the terms of the Statutory Instruments Act 1946, there is a large body of subordinate legislation which does not come under the 1946 Act but has the authority of an enabling statute. However, an even greater volume of rule-making is carried out by the Executive in the form of rules, guides and statements of general applicability which are made without express statutory authority. The legitimacy of such rules has been discussed in a number of cases and by various commentators. The courts tend to look for an indication from Parliament that rules are to have legal effect.

> "The courts will look to the quality of delegation in assessing a rule and will relate this to the stated rule; also they will look for ancillary provisions, for example, a duty to abide by the rules ... All too often, however, such statutory guidance offers little help. In that event, the courts must look to the nature of the ensuing rule itself."[41]

These rules can be classified in a number of ways. Baldwin and Houghton[42] identified eight models which make useful starting points.

---

[37] *Bugg v. DPP* [1993] 2 All E.R. 815.
[38] See *Edinburgh District Council v. Secretary of State for Scotland,* 1985 S.L.T. 551.
[39] Hayhurst and Wallington, *op. cit.,* n. 48, above, 572.
[40] *ibid.* 568–569.
[41] Baldwin and Houghton, *op. cit.,* n. 28, above, 248.
[42] *ibid.* 241–245.

1. Procedural rules

This type of rule will regulate the way in which policy is to be implemented, 5–48
such as the Prison Rules and Rules made under the Police and Criminal
Evidence Act 1984 or regulate bodies which distribute licences or moneys,
such as the Gaming Board.

2. Interpretative guides

These are defined as official statements of departmental or agency policy
which explain how terms and rules will be interpreted by the department or
agency.

3. Instructions to officials

Such rules are mainly for internal consumption and will not normally be
published outside the department or agency. They are aimed at controlling
the exercise of powers within the department, so encouraging consistency
in decision-making. Examples would include Prison Department Circulars,
Standing Orders and Regulations and Home Office Circulars to Chief
Constables and magistrates.

Baldwin and Houghton[43] refer to the problem that these rules are secret
and may in fact conflict with published law.

4. Prescriptive and evidential rules

These rules go further than describing policies or instructing officials; they 5–49
will state what affected parties are required to do and will also state some
sort of indirect sanction for non-compliance. A breach of the rule will not
normally lead to legal liability but may have strong evidential value. Some
examples will illustrate this.

Breach of the Highway Code will not of itself be a criminal offence but
the code may be taken into account in any criminal or civil proceedings.
For instance, before the wearing of seat belts in vehicles became compulsory,
the practice was recommended in the 1968 version of the Highway Code.
Lord Denning used this provision to find an element of contributory
negligence in an accident case where the injured party had not used a seat
belt.[44]

The Secretary of State's Code of Practice on Picketing published in 1980[45]
stated that no more than six trade union members should picket a place of
work during an industrial dispute. The code was authorised by the

---

[43] *op. cit.*, n. 28, above, 241.
[44] *Froom v. Butcher* [1976] Q.B. 286.
[45] Employment Code of Practice (Picketing) Order 1980 (S.I. 1980 No. 1757).

Employment Act 1980 which stated that the code could be taken into account in proceedings before a court or tribunal. This provision gave tacit legal force to the contents of the code and the restriction on the number of pickets was used to great effect during the miners' strike in 1984–85.[46]

A code of practice issued by the Secretary of State under section 66 of the Police and Criminal Evidence Act 1984 is admissible in all criminal or civil proceedings and any provision in the code which appears to the court to be relevant to any question arising in the proceedings shall be taken into account in determining that question. For instance, the court may decide on the admissibility of a confession by reference to the code's provisions on the questioning of suspects by the police.

5. Commendatory rules

5–50 The principal function of these rules is to recommend a course of action, but some form of sanction may be included.

The Health and Safety at Work etc. Act 1974 gives a hierarchy of rules, starting with statutory duties, then giving powers to the Secretary of State to make regulations, where a breach will incur criminal liability. Next are codes of practice which offer "practical advice" and which have evidential status. At the lowest level are guidance notes issued by the Health and Safety Commission and Health and Safety Executive; these give advice on how health and safety objectives can be achieved although they lack legal force.

6. Voluntary codes

These codes are made by bodies outside the public sector to stave off statutory regulation. Although voluntary, they may carry considerable force. One of the best-known examples is the City Code on Take-overs and Mergers which is issued by the Council for the Securities Industry to ensure good standards of commercial behaviour. A breach of this code may be investigated by the Department of Trade and Industry.

7. Rules of practice, management or operation

5–51 These are arrangements made by administrative bodies which affect the operation of the law between one subject and another. They are the department's understanding of the law and the practical way in which the department proposes to give effect to the law. This category also includes the extra-statutory concessions listed in a booklet published by the Commissioners for Inland Revenue. Examples of concessions include allowances to employees who have to maintain their own tools or the non-taxation of cash payments to miners which were made in lieu of free coal.

---

[46] *e.g. Thomas v. NUM* [1983] 2 W.L.R. 1081.

The courts have shown a dislike for these, however. In *Absalom v. Talbot*[47] Scott L.J. remarked: "No judicial countenance can or ought to be given in matters of taxation to any system of extra-legal concessions ... The fact that such extra-legal concessions have to be made to avoid unjust hardships is conclusive that there is something wrong with the legislation."[48] The concessions were held to have no real statutory foundation in *Vestey v. Inland Revenue Commissioners.*[49]

Stair Memorial Encyclopedia[50] distinguishes between statements of practice and extra-statutory concessions. The former "gloss the statutory text" whereas the latter "derogate from the text of the statute, supposedly to give effect to its spirit."[51] Further, the interpretation of a statement of practice may be challenged in court while the extra-statutory concessions may not be justiciable.

8. Consultative devices and administrative pronouncements

Baldwin and Houghton use this category as a "safety net" for administrative 5–52 documents which do not fit into the other groups but which have general significance. They include consultative documents which invite comments from interested parties on draft outlines or departmental policy.

CODES OF PRACTICE

Codes of practice are now regarded as major administrative tools, but their status is difficult to define. Indeed, some codes appear to have the status of subordinate legislation, for instance, the Food Safety Act 1990 allows the minister to issue codes of recommended practice for the guidance of food authorities. The minister may give specific directions to the authorities on how they are to comply with the code and the Minister may apply to the court to enforce these directions. A code can be authorised by a parent Act and be subject to laying before Parliament, or it can be made by a department but not subject to parliamentary scrutiny or it may be contained in a circular or notes of guidance from the department.

Compliance with a code may constitute a defence in criminal proceedings. For instance, the Building Act 1984 provides that failure to comply with an "approved document" may be relied on as tending to establish liability. Proof of compliance with the document may be relied on as tending to negate the liability.[52]

The courts have taken the view that if a code or set of rules is meant to 5–53 create a legal effect, then precise language should be used. The use of

---

[47] [1943] 1 All E.R. 589.
[48] *ibid.* at 598.
[49] [1980] A.C. 1148; [1979] 3 All E.R. 976.
[50] *Stair Memorial Encyclopaedia,* Vol. 22, "Sources of Law", para. 243.
[51] *ibid.* para. 243.
[52] s. 7(1).

colloquial language in such documents has been heavily criticised.[53] In some rules, the duties imposed on the administrative body by the rules may also confer rights on the persons against whom they are enforced. In *Payne v. Lord Harris*[54] the Local Review Committee Rules 1967 were held to form a comprehensive code with the relevant statute, the Criminal Justice Act 1967, and thus conferred rights on prisoners who were entitled to complain if the duties imposed on the committee were not carried out.

Codes of practice do, however, have a number of benefits although they have almost as many disadvantages. Their use may be beneficial where the material is technical and detailed, or the language to be used is inappropriate for ordinary usage, or to allow wider consultation. They can also have the benefit of being flexible and easily amended. The criticisms of such codes are neatly summed up by Streatfeild J. in *Patchett v. Leathem*[55]:

> "Whereas ordinary legislation, by passing through both Houses of Parliament or, at least, lying on the table of both Houses, is thus twice blessed, this type of so-called legislation is at least four times cursed. First, it has seen neither House of Parliament; secondly, it is unpublished and is inaccessible even to those whose valuable rights of property may be affected; thirdly, it is a jumble of provisions, legislative, administrative, or directive in character, and sometimes difficult to disentangle one from the other; and fourthly, it is expressed not in the precise language of an Act of Parliament or an Order in Council but in the more colloquial language of correspondence, which is not always susceptible of the ordinary canons of construction."

5–54   The two types of code of practice which are most commonly encountered are those which state that an administrative body "shall have regard to" the code or which state that the code "shall be admissible in evidence".[56] The first type is often used in planning, housing and so on[57] and the second type has been used in, for instance, the code of practice issued under the Police and Criminal Evidence Act 1984 where failure to comply with the code renders a police officer liable to disciplinary proceedings at which the code will be used in evidence if it appears relevant. While there may be no legal duty to follow a code, the courts recognise that administrative authorities should take account of any code although they may then disregard it if it appears to, for instance, fetter their discretion.[58]

---

[53] See, for instance, *Patchett v. Leathem* (1949) 65 T.L.R. 69.
[54] [1981] 1 W.L.R. 754.
[55] (1949) 65 T.L.R. 69.
[56] See discussion in Samuels, "Codes of Practice and Legislation" (1986) Stat.L.R., 29.
[57] For instance, Code of Guidance issued under Housing (Homeless Persons) Act 1977, s. 12, where the housing authority "shall have regard in the exercise of their functions to such guidance".
[58] In *Simpson v. Edinburgh Corporation,* 1960 S.C. 313, the court held that a planning authority "should have regard to" a development plan but might disregard it.

The Immigration Rules have caused many problems over the years. These are made under the Immigration Act 1971, s. 3(2) and are required to be laid before Parliament although they are not contained in or given effect to by a statutory instrument. They are published as House of Commons papers and are binding on officials.[59] Their status in judicial proceedings is conferred by section 19(1) of the 1971 Act although they may be overruled at the discretion of a Government Minister.[60] The courts have had difficulty in establishing the legal status of the rules. Roskill L.J. said: "These rules are just as much delegated legislation as any other form of rule-making which is empowered by Parliament."[61] This view was disputed by Geoffrey Lane L.J. in *R. v. Secretary of State for Home Affairs, ex parte Hosenball*[62] where he referred to the rules as "a practical guide for the immigration officers ... little more than explanatory notes in the Act itself." Lord Denning said "they are not rules in the nature of delegated legislation so as to amount to strict rules of law." The difficulty of ascertaining the legal status of the rules is summed up by Bridge L.J. in *Singh v. Immigration Appeals Tribunal*[63]: "The Immigration Rules ... are quite unlike ordinary delegated legislation ... the rules do not purport to enact a precise code having statutory force. They are discursive in style, in part merely explanatory, and on their face frequently offer no more than broad guidance as to how discretion is to be exercised in different typical situations."[64]

The Executive also makes extensive use of circulars to inform other 5–55 bodies, to instruct them in new policy matters, to interpret legislation and policy and to indicate how the Government proposes to exercise its discretion. The general legal principle is that such circulars have no legal effect.[65] However, a statute may authorise the issue of directions and these may be embodied in a circular.[66]

A circular may also gain legal recognition because it sets out the criteria by which a Minister proposes to use his discretion thus giving rise to a legitimate expectation by persons relying on the criteria that these will be used.[67]

---

[59] The current rules are contained in (1993–94 H.C. 395) and were effective from October 1, 1994.

[60] 1971 Act, s. 19(2).

[61] *R v. Chief Immigration Officer Heathrow Airport, ex p. Bibi* [1976] 1 W.L.R. 979.

[62] [1977] 1 W.L.R. 766.

[63] [1986] 2 All E.R. 721.

[64] See also *Alexander v. Immigration Appeal Tribunal* [1982] 2 All E.R. 766; *Re Amin* [1983] 2 A.C. 818.

[65] See *Inglis v. British Airports Authority*, 1978 S.L.T. (Lands Tr.) 30; *Newbury District Council v. Secretary of State for Environment* [1981] A.C. 578.

[66] See *Palmer v. Inverness Hospitals Board of Management*, 1963 S.C. 311; 1963 S.L.T. 124.

[67] *e.g.* see *R v. Secretary of State for Home Department, ex p. Khan* [1985] 1 All E.R. 40 discussed above at para. 5–24.

The guidance given in a circular is the view of the Minister or department regarding the law; it is not the law itself.[68] It may confer powers or impose duties on the recipients, for instance, in *Palmer v. Inverness Hospitals Board*[69] the Scottish Office issued a circular to hospital authorities in which the procedures to be followed in disciplinary cases were set out. The court held that the circular was incorporated into P's contract of employment with the board.

5–56   Administrative bodies are expected to follow the guidance given in circulars and other advisory documents, but they may find that the advice is illegal. In *Daymond v. South West Water Authority*[70] the water authority acted on the advice of a circular, later finding that the advice was incorrect. In *R. v. Police Complaints Board, ex parte Madden*[71] not only did the board rely on Home Office guidance relating to disciplinary proceedings but in so doing they fettered their discretion by allowing themselves to be bound by the guidance. The question of whether such guidance is susceptible to judicial review proceedings was raised in *Gillick v. West Norfolk and Wisbech Area Health Authority*.[72] The general rule was held to be that the reasonableness of advice contained within non-statutory guidance could not be subject to judicial review except where the department promulgated advice in a public document and that advice was erroneous in law. The courts in these circumstances could correct the error.[73]

BYELAWS

5–57   The power to make subordinate legislation is not confined to government departments; local authorities and public authorities may also be granted power to make subordinate legislation in the form of byelaws. The parent Act will stipulate how the byelaw is to be made. The usual practice is for the parent Act to state that the byelaw will not come into effect until a "confirming authority" has confirmed the order. The confirming authority is normally the Minister and he will also be able to consider the policy of the byelaws submitted to him.[74]

The parent Act will stipulate the procedure for making the byelaw, setting out requirements of publicity and commencement. Normally the authority making the order will have to give public notice of its intention to apply for confirmation and allow interested parties an opportunity to inspect the draft

---

[68] *e.g.* see *Bristol District Council v. Clark* [1975] 3 All E.R. 976; *Annison v. District Auditor for Metropolitan Borough of St Pancras Borough Council* [1962] 1 Q.B. 489.
[69] 1963 S.C. 311.
[70] [1976] A.C. 609.
[71] [1983] 2 All E.R. 353.
[72] [1986] A.C. 112.
[73] See also *Royal College of Nursing v. DHSS* [1981] A.C. 800.
[74] *Glasgow Corporation v. Glasgow Churches' Council,* 1944 S.C. 97.

order. Interested parties then have one month to object and the authority must take into account any objections which are received. The confirming authority may fix the date on which the byelaw is to come into force, failing which the byelaw will come into force one month from the date of confirmation. The fact that a byelaw has been confirmed does not bar challenge on the ground of *ultra vires*. However, challenge on the ground of unreasonableness is difficult. Byelaws made by a local authority must be reviewed every 10 years.[75]

[75] Local Government (Scotland) Act 1973, s. 202A added by the Civic Government (Scotland) Act 1982, s. 110(3).

CHAPTER 6

ACCESS TO INFORMATION

6–01   "Freedom of information is a fundamental human right and is the touchstone for all the freedoms to which the United Nations is consecrated."[1] In the United Kingdom, there is no freedom of information legislation along the lines of those in the United States of America, Canada, Australia and the Scandinavian countries. Indeed, although the British Government has introduced measures to assist citizens in obtaining information, the position is still difficult and there is no automatic right to obtain information from government departments. "The right to receive and impart information is subject to legal and operational limitations which mean that the system falls far short of internationally recognised standards."[2]

The Fulton Committee[3] observed that the administrative process was too secret and "the public interest would be better served if there was a greater amount of openness". Four years later the Franks Committee went further: "A government which pursues secret aims, or which operates in greater secrecy than the effective conduct of its proper functions requires, or which turns information services into propaganda services, will lose the trust of the people."[4] In their reply to the Franks Committee, the Government said: "there is an inescapable tension between the need to keep some information secret and the requirements of openness if people are to participate in government as they should. A balance must be struck and it has to be reviewed from time to time to see that it is in keeping with current perceptions of the threat to our security and the needs of democracy".[5]

In 1976 the Prime Minister announced that more background information on major policies would be made available and the Head of the Home Civil Service issued instructions to implement this.[6] These instructions had a

---

[1]   United Nations General Assembly Resolution 59(2), December 14, 1946.
[2]   Oliver, *Government in the UK: The Search for Accountability, Efficiency and Citizenship* (1991), p. 170.
[3]   Report of Committee on Civil Service (Fulton Committee), Cmnd. 3638 (1968), para. 278.
[4]   Report of Committee on Section 2 of the Official Secrets Act 1911 (Franks Committee), Cmnd. 5104 (1972), para. 12.
[5]   Home Office, Reform of Section 2 of the Official Secrets Act 1911, Cmnd. 7285 (1978), Introduction.
[6]   Civil Service Department Directive on Disclosure of Official Information (Croham Directive) (1977) issued by Sir Douglas Allan, later Lord Croham.

modest effect on the disclosure of information but quickly fell into disuse with the change of government in 1979.

This chapter discusses the access to central and local government information, and compares the U.K. situation with that of other countries which do have freedom of information legislation.

STATUTORY RIGHTS TO INFORMATION IN THE UNITED KINGDOM

A number of statutes have led to rights being granted to individuals regarding 6–02 information held about them. These include the Data Protection Act 1984, the Local Government (Access to Information) Act 1985, the Access to Personal Files Act 1987 and the Access to Health Records Act 1990.

Data Protection Act 1984

This Act is concerned only with computerised records of personal information or data. It incorporated into U.K. law the provisions of the European Convention on Data Protection 1981; the Act was necessary to ensure the flow of information from other signatory states and thus secure information handling businesses in the United Kingdom. Section 1 defines the terms used in the Act. "Data" is defined as information recorded in a form in which it can be processed by equipment operating automatically in response to instructions given for that purpose. "Personal data" is data relating to a living individual, while a "data subject" is the individual who is the subject of the personal data. Section 2 refers to the Data Protection Principles which are set out in Schedule 1, Part I . The seven principles include statements that personal data is to be obtained lawfully and fairly, it is to be held for specified lawful purposes, it will be accurate and kept up-to-date, and the individual will be entitled to access the data and if necessary have it corrected or erased. Section 3 sets up the Data Protection Tribunal and appoints a Data Protection Registrar. The tribunal's chairman is appointed by the Lord Chancellor after consultation with the Lord Advocate and will be a barrister or advocate or solicitor of at least seven years' standing. The deputy chairman will be similarly qualified. Exemptions from the Act are stated towards the end of the Act and include exemption on national security grounds,[7] crime or taxation grounds,[8] and health and social work grounds where there is exemption on the grounds of the physical or mental health of the data subject.[9] Information should be made available within 40 days of the request[10] and there is a maximum fee chargeable of £10.

---

[7] s. 27 — only a Cabinet Minister, the Attorney-General or the Lord Advocate may sign the certificate of exemption.
[8] s. 28.
[9] s. 29.
[10] Overseas legislation is usually 20–30 days.

6–03   The Criminal Justice and Public Order Act 1994 amended the 1984 Act
by creating new offences. Over the 10 years of the operation of the 1984
Act, it had been found that there was a growing, and highly lucrative, trade
in personal information obtained from data users. Sometimes the information
was obtained by bribery, sometimes by deceit; in neither case was there a
criminal sanction against the person obtaining the information. The 1994
Act made it an offence to procure the disclosure of personal information by
a person who knows or has reason to believe that he is a person to whom
the data user is not registered to disclose the information. The sale or offering
for sale of personal data so procured is also an offence.

The trade in information may also be affected by an E.U. Directive
adopted in July 1995[11] which seeks to harmonise the laws on personal data
throughout the European Union. The directive applies to both manual and
computerised records and is required to be implemented within three years.[12]
The main difficulty associated with the 1984 Act appears to be its limited
scope; it does not cover manual or paper records. Birkinshaw[13] recounts
that the National Computing Centre advised its members to transfer sensitive
personal information to manual files, beyond the reach of the Data Protection
Act. The E.U. Directive will have an impact on this.

The Local Government (Access to Information) Act 1985

This Act added new sections to the existing legislation[14] thus allowing
members of the public access to meetings of local authorities, including
meetings of committees and sub-committees, and access to agendas and
papers. Access to these materials includes access by the press and other
elected members. There is also a right of access to inspect minutes and
background papers. There are 15 categories of exemptions given in Schedule
7A[15]; the categories include information on employees or tenants,
applications for financial assistance, information on the care of children,
the instructions to and opinions of counsel and the contractual interests
of the authority so long as required to protect the interests of the authority.
The "proper officer" (usually the Chief Executive) and chairperson of the
meeting have powers to select information which may be divulged but there
is no specific means of challenging such a decision.[16]

---

[11] Directive of European Parliament and Council 95/46: O.J. 1281/31.
[12] For discussion, see Birkinshaw, *Freedom of Information: the Law, the Practice and the Ideal* (2nd ed., 1996), p. 249.
[13] *ibid.* p. 258.
[14] Local Government (Scotland) Act 1973, new ss. 50A – 50K; Local Government Act 1972, new sections 100A –100K.
[15] Local Government (Scotland) Act 1973.
[16] The working of the 1985 Act in England and Wales was investigated by Steele, "Public Access to Information" (1995), London Policy Studies Institute/Dept of Environment.

The Local Government Act 1986 as amended prohibits and restricts 6–04 publicity exercises of local authorities by preventing the publication of materials designed to support the policies of one political party. The Government may also issue codes of practice which guide local authorities on the content, style and so on of publications and to which local authorities "shall have regard".[17] The Local Government and Housing Act 1989 introduced measures to control staff appointments, the political balance of committees and controls on councillors' allowances and interests. The Local Government Act 1992 requires the publication of information relating to standards of services offered by authorities; this is published under the direction of the Accounts Commission in Scotland and the Audit Commission in England and Wales. The information (called 'league tables' by its critics) gives details of such items as the time taken for housing repairs and time taken for complaints about environmental health matters to be resolved.

The opening-up of local government decision-making has been criticised 6–05 as encouraging an increased involvement by politicians in that process, leading to poorer decision-making. "The quality of decision-making falls as rational input from professional officials declines and politicians engage increasingly in point-scoring and being seen to be effective by the sectional interests whom they represent, rather than by the community as a whole."[18]

The Access to Personal Files Act 1987

This Act applies to Scotland, England and Wales but not to Northern Ireland. The Act allows citizens access to the housing and social work records of a local authority where those manual records contain personal information.[19] The right of access only applies to records made by the local authority after the date of commencement of the Act.

The provisions of the Act are to be implemented by regulations made by 6–06 the Secretary of State[20] who is required to consult with appropriate bodies or authorities.[21] The Act is a very watered-down version of a private member's Bill which was wide-ranging in the type of information it included; however, many organisations opposed the Bill and it was in danger of failing to reach the statute book before the General Election in 1987. The proposers of the Bill thus accepted government amendments to ensure some useful legislation was passed. The Act has little in common with freedom of information legislation, which the Bill's proposers intended it to be.[22]

---

[17] s. 2.

[18] Birkinshaw, *op. cit.*, n. 12, above, p. 240.

[19] s. 1.

[20] s. 3(1).

[21] s. 3(4).

[22] For discussion of the debates, see Birkinshaw's annotations to the Act in *Current Law Statutes Annotated, 1987* (c. 37).

In the debates on the Bill, the Government agreed to make regulations under the Education Act 1980, s. 27, to allow access to education records. The regulations were made in 1989 and apply to records made after September 1989. Information received from third parties regarding allegations of child abuse and the teacher's personal notes are not covered by the regulations.

The Access to Health Records Act 1990

Similar to the 1987 Act, this Act allows access by individuals to their health records held by doctors. It was implemented by the Access to Health Records (Control of Access) Regulations in 1993.[23] The term "record" is defined as information relating to the health, physical or mental, of an individual made by or on behalf of a health professional. An exemption is allowed where disclosure of the records would be detrimental to the health of the applicant.[24] Information collected before the Act came into operation in November 1991 is also exempted unless it is required to make sense of the information which is available.

ACCESS TO PUBLIC RECORDS IN THE UNITED KINGDOM

6–07　The rights given in the statutes discussed above are important for the individual and they are extensive, with safeguards for privacy incorporated into them. The right of the individual to information held in the public records is less extensive although some rights are found in statutes.

The Public Records Acts 1958 and 1967

The main purposes of legislation in this area are to ensure the selection of public records which should be preserved, to safeguard these for posterity and to make them available for public inspection.[25] Most departmental records are destroyed at the first review held after five years because they are regarded as unimportant; only about one per cent of records are kept to the next review at 25 years and it is at this time that their historical context will be considered. Some records may be disclosed earlier than the norm because they are part of a government inquiry, for instance, material on the Falklands War became available very quickly because of the Franks Inquiry.[26]

---

[23]　S.I. 1993 No.746.

[24]　*R. v. Mid-Glamorgan Family Health Services, ex p. Martin,* unreported, *The Times,* August 16, 1994.

[25]　Roper, "Access to Public Records" in Chapman and Hunt, *Open Government* (1987).

[26]　Franks Inquiry on the Falklands War, Cmnd. 8787 (1983).

The Public Records Act 1958[27] provided that the records of courts, government departments and some non-governmental public bodies are to be transferred to the Public Records Office before they become 30 years old and they then become available for public inspection when they are 50 years old. The Public Records Act 1967 reduced the closed period to 30 years.[28] There are different time periods for certain types of document. Those which are highly sensitive may be kept in departments for 30 years or more, if the Lord Chancellor approves.[29] The documents must be reviewed at 30 years and periodically thereafter. Examples of such documents are Cabinet Office records, Ministry of Defence records and the records of the United Kingdom Atomic Energy Authority. Other sensitive documents may be transferred to the Public Records Office but withheld beyond the 30 years with the approval of the Lord Chancellor. Three types of document were covered by this provision: exceptionally sensitive papers, information received in confidence, and documents about individuals where disclosure would cause distress or endanger them. The period of closure varied although 50 years was the most common length of time. Documents about individuals could be closed for 75 years and documents on the affairs of the Royal family may be closed for 100 years.

Two reviews of the criteria for closure have been undertaken in recent 6–08 years. In 1981, the Wilson Committee[30] recommended disclosure beyond the 30 years if documents were exceptionally sensitive and disclosure was likely to harm the public interest; contained information supplied in confidence; or contained information about individuals, disclosure of which would distress them or endanger lives. In 1992, another review of the criteria was ordered by the Lord Chancellor, Lord Mackay of Clashfern. The three criteria for closure recommended by the Wilson Committee were retained.

More recently, documents have been released earlier than expected as a result of the White Paper on Open Government.[31] The White Paper lays down one basic principle regarding the publication of information; this says that information should be released after 30 years unless: (a) it is possible to establish that actual damage will be caused by the release; and (b) the damage would fall within the listed criteria in Annex C of the White Paper "Guidelines on Extended Disclosure". The White Paper also brings the closure time down to 40 years for most documents but retains longer times for information such as that given in confidence, or concerning tax data (75 years) or population census records (100 years). The release of

---

[27] This Act, and the 1967 Act, do not apply to Scotland although the provisions of the Acts are adopted procedure for public records in Scotland. Scottish legislation is the Public Records (Scotland) Act 1937.

[28] 1958 Act, s. 5(1), as amended by the 1967 Act.

[29] 1958 Act, s. 3(4).

[30] *Modern Public Records*, Report of the Wilson Committee, Cmnd. 8204 (1981).

[31] Cm. 2290 (1993).

Joint Intelligence Committee records is now possible and many wartime records are being reviewed to allow their release.[32]

OFFICIAL SECRETS ACTS

6–09   The secrecy of the British Government is well documented[33] and is perhaps typified by the Official Secrets Act 1911, s. 2, which made it an offence for a Crown servant or agent to disclose, without authority, any information which had been acquired in the course of employment or contractual duties. It was also an offence willingly to receive such information. This provision was a "catch-all" and effectively meant that, unless disclosure was authorised, all official information was secret regardless of its content. The section was heavily criticised over the years. "The leading characteristic [is] its catch-all quality. It catches all official documents and information. It makes no distinction of kind, and no distinction of degree. All information which a Crown servant learns in the course of his duty is 'official' for the purposes of section two, whatever its nature, whatever its importance, whatever its original source. A blanket is thrown over everything: nothing escapes."[34]

6–10   The House of Commons Treasury and Civil Service Committee[35] reported that section 2 was unenforceable after the fiasco of the Ponting trial.[36] The Spycatcher saga forced the Government finally to take action and a White Paper was issued in 1988.[37] The Spycatcher cases showed the problems of enforcing section 2. The cases involved the publication of the memoirs of Peter Wright, a retired MI6 officer. The Government first tried to prevent publication of the book in Australia, where Wright lived, and then when this was unsuccessful, the Attorney-General sought injunctions against British newspapers to prevent them from publishing confidential information about the security services. Interim injunctions were allowed[38] but final injunctions were refused because, as the court acknowledged, the material was already in the public domain and it was futile to attempt to restrain further publication.[39] A further case, *Lord Advocate v. Scotsman Publications Ltd* [40] concerned the publication of a

[32] Cm. 2290, Annex D.
[33] See Ponting, *Secrecy in Britain* (1990) for a readable account of the history of secrecy laws in Britain; Birkinshaw, *op. cit.*, n. 12, above.
[34] Cmnd. 5104 (1972).
[35] Seventh Report, H.C. 92–1 (1985–86).
[36] *R v. Ponting* [1985] Crim. L.R. 318.
[37] Reform of s. 2 of the Official Secrets Act 1911, Cm. 408 (1988). See Birkinshaw, *op. cit.*, n. 12, above, p. 106.
[38] *Att.-Gen. v. Guardian Newspapers Ltd* [1987] 1 W.L.R. 1248.
[39] *Att.-Gen. v. Guardian Newspapers Ltd* (No.2) [1990] 1 A.C. 109.
[40] [1989] 2 All E.R. 852, H.L.

book by another former member of the intelligence and security services. The Lord Advocate attempted to say that the memoirs contained information which was covered by the Official Secrets Act 1989 and thus the author, Cavendish, was prohibited from disclosing it. The Crown had already conceded that the information was harmless. The court held that Cavendish was in breach of the Act but that when he circulated the memoirs to third parties, they did not commit an offence by disclosing harmless information. A third party would only be guilty of the offence if the information was damaging in the sense defined by the Act.

The civil courts have generally been more amenable to assisting the 6–11 Government in preventing the disclosure of information. In *Attorney-General v. Jonathan Cape* [41] the duty of confidentiality was effectively extended to "public" secrets and the Lord Chief Justice stated that the courts had jurisdiction to restrain publication of official information if it could be shown that the public interest demanded it. The civil law has proved to be more attractive than criminal prosecutions for a number of reasons: the standard of proof is lower — balance of probabilities instead of the criminal standard which is beyond reasonable doubt; there is no jury to sympathise with a public interest defence; and civil actions can be brought to prevent publication whereas criminal prosecution can only be brought after the offence has been committed and the harm done. [42]

The Official Secrets Act 1989 [43] was duly passed, repealing section 2 of the 1911 Act and replacing it with a list of categories of information which are protected. The categories on the list are security and intelligence, defence, international relations and law enforcement. If information in the first three categories is released without lawful authority, no offence will be committed unless the information is "damaging". This defence does not apply with regard to information on law enforcement. A third party coming into possession of information obtained without authority will no longer commit an offence unless the information is used to make a further damaging disclosure and that party had reasonable cause to believe the disclosure would be damaging. It is no defence that disclosure is made in the public interest; indeed it could be said that the Act is set up to make it easier to obtain a conviction rather than to allow access by the citizen to Government information. [44] A member of the security or intelligence services, or a GCHQ officer, is prohibited for his whole life to disclose information obtained by virtue of his position. [45] Criticism has been levelled at this provision since it

---

[41] [1976] Q.B. 752.

[42] Oliver, *op. cit.*, n. 2, above, p. 173.

[43] See Birkinshaw, *op. cit.*, n. 12 above, p. 114 for detailed critique of the Act; also Feldman, *Civil Liberties and Human Rights* (1993), Chap. 14.

[44] Tant, "The Campaign for Freedom of Information: A Participatory Challenge to Elitist British Government" (1990) 68(4) *Public Administration* 477.

[45] s. 1(1) and (2).

would have prevented information being disclosed about several high profile cases, including the spying activities of Anthony Blunt.

6–12   The Act offers no protection to a civil servant who "blows the whistle" in the public interest.[46] The defence of "prior publication" was not included either although it may be that the Spycatcher cases have assisted in formulating such a defence. This means therefore that civil servants who find themselves in a similar position to Clive Ponting could still be prosecuted under the 1989 Act. Alternative methods have been provided for a civil servant to pursue a grievance within their own department. The Armstrong Memorandum[47] states that a civil servant may use the Head of the Home Civil Service as a final appeal after departmental routes for redress have been exhausted. "Any civil servant whose loyalty is put under strain is advised to refer his complaint to his superiors, even up to his Permanent Secretary ... but in no circumstances to seek by his actions to frustrate the Minister's policies or decisions."[48] This memorandum was criticised by the Treasury and Civil Service Committee since it appeared to equate the Crown with the Government and implied that civil servants had to show loyalty to Ministers first and foremost. As a result of this criticism in 1994, the Government produced a further draft code on Ministers and civil servants; this draws mainly on the Armstrong Memorandum but gives an appeal to the Civil Service Commissioners, not the Head of the Home Civil Service. The Civil Service Code states that where the civil servant is unable to accept the decision of the Civil Service Commissioners he or she should either "carry out his or her instructions, or resign from the civil service".[49]

6–13   Security and intelligence personnel have access to a staff counsellor; this officer has access to all documents and reports at least annually to the Prime Minister, the Home Secretary and the Foreign Secretary.[50] In the USA, the US Civil Reform Acts 1978 and 1989 protect civil servants who report violations of the law or regulations, mismanagement, gross waste of public funds, or danger to public health and safety. Reports of investigations carried out by the public authority are submitted to the Congress, the President and the complainant.

There is no general legal right to information and the Government may withhold information without any good cause. In *R. v. Secretary of State for*

---

[46] In 1987, a Private Member's Bill was proposed which would have made a public interest defence available; the Bill was killed off by the Government using a three-line whip in January 1988. The Government subsequently refused to countenance the defence in the 1989 Act.

[47] Armstrong, "The Duties and Responsibilities of Civil Servants in Relation to Ministers: Note by Head of Home Civil Service" H.C. Official Report, Vol. 74 (1984–85).

[48] *ibid.* pp. 7–9.

[49] Civil Service Code 1996, para. 13; *Hansard*, H.L., January 9, 1996, WA 21; http://www.open.gov.uk/co/cscode.htm (15.1.97).

[50] Palmer, "Tightening Secrecy Law: Official Secrets Act 1989" (1990) P.L., Summer, p. 243. The Security Service Act 1989 established a tribunal to decide such matters of conflict.

Defence, ex p. Sancto[51] the parents of a dead soldier were refused access to the report of the board of inquiry into the fatal accident and there was held to be no legal duty to disclose the information. The court however said that the refusal to disclose the report was "outrageous".

THE WHITE PAPER — OPEN GOVERNMENT

Governments throughout the post-war period have been heavily criticised 6–14 for their lack of openness. Successive Conservative Governments from 1979 to date have expected other bodies such as local authorities to open their proceedings to public scrutiny but until 1993 resisted all calls for central government proceedings to be more open. In 1993, the Government published a White Paper called "Open Government". The paper was issued as a development of the Citizen's Charter programme: "the provision of full, accurate information in plain language about public services, what they cost, who is in charge and what standards they offer is a fundamental principle of the Citizen's Charter … public services appeared for too long to be shrouded in unnecessary secrecy. The government is now giving the public — often for the first time — the information they need".[52] The proposals were a welcome development but there are some problems associated with the procedures which have since evolved. In particular, the access is to government information, not to government papers, and such access is dependent on the discretion of officials who are guided by a Code of Practice which was updated in 1997.[53] The White Paper incorporated some of the recommendations of the 1978 Justice Report,[54] in particular the provisions regarding the Code of Practice and the involvement of the PCA.

The code sets out the circumstances in which government will volunteer information and where it will produce information on request. The revised Code of Practice came into operation in February 1997 and covers all those bodies which are under the jurisdiction of the PCA, who will investigate complaints. The code cannot override existing statutory restrictions on disclosure; some 250 of these are listed in the White Paper.[55]

The intentions of the Government are: 6–15

* to handle information to promote informed policy-making and debate and efficient delivery of service;
* to provide "timely and accessible" information to explain the Government's policies, actions and decisions; and
* to restrict access only where there are good reasons for doing so.

---

[51] (1992) 5 Admin. L.R. 673.
[52] Cm. 2290 (1993), para. 2.3.
[53] The original Code is found at Cm. 2290, Annex A; the revised Code is available on the Internet at http://www.open.gov.uk/m-of-g/code.htm.
[54] Justice Report, "Freedom of Information" (1978).
[55] Cm. 2290, Annex B, Parts I and II.

The White Paper sets out the Government's efforts to provide greater information, but these are mainly non-legal and thus are unenforceable. The Office of Public Service (OPS) in evidence to the PCA Select Committee[56] said that while the code "provides a powerful impetus towards increased transparency, and a check to unnecessary or unjustifiable secrecy, it does not put either departments or applicants to the expense of more legalistic procedures". The Government felt that using a code of practice instead of legislation would allow for greater flexibility. Legislation, they maintained, would be too cumbersome; of course it would also be subject to judicial scrutiny, which the Government wanted to avoid. Examples of the kind of information which has been released are the details of Cabinet committees and their remit,[57] information on the security services, including details of senior personnel, and Questions of Procedure for Ministers. The White Paper however does not open the process of decision-making to public scrutiny; in other words there is no opening of the network of government advisory committees and processes of tendering advice. This can be compared to the more open situation in the USA where the "Sunshine Laws" open the meetings of most major federal agencies to the public. The U.S. Federal Advisory Committee Act 1972 which covers drug testing, food production and so on gives access to the public to the advice which is tendered.

6–16   There is no definition of a "code request" given in the White Paper. Departments were first allowed to devise their own criteria and decide which requests should be classified as requests made under the code. However, departments were encouraged not to introduce new forms or new bureaucracy. This led to differences in the classification of requests among the departments and thus to difficulties in determining the true number of code requests made by citizens. In 1995, the OPS asked departments to register as code requests those which mentioned the code, those where a charge was made, and those where information was refused on the basis of a code exemption.

All Freedom of Information Acts will exclude or exempt certain information and the White Paper is no exception. There are three main categories of exemption.

- Those requiring a "harm test" to justify exemption such as documents relating to defence and national security, international relations and proceedings of Cabinet and Cabinet committees. The PCA has indicated[58] that he expects departments to persuade him that harm or prejudice will result from the disclosure of information; he is, in other words, putting the onus of proof on the department, not on the complainant.

---

[56] Open Government Minutes of Evidence (1994–95, H.C. 290), i–iii, p. 15, para. 7.
[57] *Hansard*, H.C., Vol. 208, cols. 110–118, May 19, 1992.
[58] Report of Select Committee on PCA, Open Government, Minutes of Evidence, p. 2.

- Those which do not require the "harm test", for instance information regarding immigration and nationality. The Government[59] indicated that these records should be exempt because of the nature of the information contained in them, for instance sensitive information provided by third parties. The exemptions apply only to individual cases, not to information on Government policy on immigration and nationality.
- Other grounds for refusing access include personal privacy, information given in confidence, unreasonable requests and premature disclosure. In their evidence to the Select Committee for the PCA, OPS stated that the exemption extended to information provided in confidence either under statutory guarantee of confidentiality or voluntarily given but where the supplier of the information has not waived his right of confidentiality.[60] They pointed out that such disclosure could jeopardise the Government's ability to obtain such information in future.

The White Paper also exempts internal discussions and advice, whether   6–17
given by experts or by civil servants. The policy seeks to protect civil servants in their role as neutral advisers to the Government. However, the White Paper indicates that facts and the analysis of facts "which government considered important and relevant" in framing major policy proposals and decisions will be released. The amended code also gives an undertaking that departments will publish or make available explanatory material on the department's dealings with the public except where publication will prejudice any matter which should be kept confidential. The material will include rules, procedures, internal guidance and administrative manuals. The Government published *Guidance on the Interpretation of the Code* in March 1994; this gives further information on the reasons for the Government's approach and in particular more detailed explanations of the reasoning behind the decision to exempt certain information. In cases where the harm test is used, the code states that: "In such cases it should be considered whether any harm or prejudice arising from the disclosure is outweighed by the public interest in making information available. The exemptions will not be interpreted in a way which causes injustice to individuals."[61]

The White Paper does not give a commitment to access to pre-existing   6–18
specific documents; the commitment is to information. This contrasts with the attitude of the Hong Kong Government which published its own Code of Access to Information in 1995; it is identical to the U.K. Code except that it says: "So far as possible, information will be provided in the form it exists." The proposals for a statutory right of access to personal records outlined in the U.K. White Paper also suggests that access is given to the

---

[59] Cm. 2290., para. 5.16.
[60] H.C. 290 i–iii, p. 21, para. 14.
[61] Cm. 2290, Preamble to Exemptions.

documents. In the USA, there is a presumptive right to the documents and assistance is given to locate them. The White Paper, on the other hand, states: "People will ... find it easier to describe the information they seek, rather than the documents they wish to see."[62] This, of course, will allow officials to exercise their discretion and decide what is or is not to be in the information given. It is likely that this will be unpopular with information seekers. Most people will want to see the document itself, not a sanitised précis of its contents drafted by a civil servant. "Experience overseas suggests that many requesters will not be satisfied until they see the documents."[63] The White Paper envisages a safeguard regarding the accuracy of information; the PCA will have access to departmental working papers and "can check that the information is consistent with them and constitutes a proper response to the application".[64] However, an information seeker may be concerned that the "proper response" is not detailed enough or that the information is misleading; it is likely therefore that they will not be satisfied with the information but will press to see the documents. The *Guidance on Interpretation of the Code* justifies withholding the documents by saying that there is an increasing number of different ways in which information is held, for instance, paper or computer records, and so it is more appropriate that information is released rather than documents.[65] The PCA has recommended that documents be revealed since this may be the easiest way to deal with a request.

6–19   Where a request for information is refused, the code states that an appeal should first be made through the department's internal resolution procedure; should the complainant still be dissatisfied, a further complaint can be made to the PCA using the M.P. filter.[66] In normal complaints to the PCA, the complainant has to show that he has suffered injury or injustice because of maladministration by the department. In complaints under the code, it is enough that he has not been given the information he should have received.[67] The PCA has wide investigatory powers although it is not clear whether he will have the power to override a departmental decision and recommend the release of a document considered confidential. If the decision to refuse access shows maladministration, then conceivably the PCA has the power to override the decision and disclose the information. However, the Minister

---

[62] Cm. 2290, para. 4.8.
[63] Hazell, "Freedom of Information: Implications for the Ombudsman", 1995 *Public Administration* 264.
[64] Cm. 2290.
[65] Guidance on Interpretation (1994), paras. 50–52.
[66] H.C. 290, i–iii, p. 55 where Maurice Frankel asked whether it was appropriate that Code complaints be made through the M.P. filter; he asked whether this right should be enjoyed by every citizen without restriction.
[67] Second Report of PCA (1994–95, H.C. 91), *Access to Official Information: the First Eight Months*, para. 3.

does have the power to certify that the PCA should not make the information public.[68] It is unlikely that the courts will become involved very often in disputes, given that the PCA has been designated as the avenue of redress, although it will still be possible to argue on the basis of abuse of discretion or legitimate expectation and so on. The PCA has in fact observed that it is the code, not he, who will say what information is and is not to be made available. "I regard it as very much my task to see that access to official information which is in principle supported by the Code is not narrowed in practice. More than that, if … I conclude that the line has been drawn too restrictively in places I shall make my views known."[69]

As previously mentioned, the PCA has no enforcement powers. The   6–20
White Paper states why enforcement powers were considered unnecessary.[70] "The Ombudsman approach has shown to be effective in the U.K.; although the Parliamentary Ombudsman has no power to enforce his decisions, there is a very high level of compliance with his recommendations." In evidence to the select committee, a witness[71] pointed out that in early 1995 two departments had refused to comply with the PCA's recommendations, thus implying that it would be "entirely possible that the Government may reject some of the Ombudsman's disclosure recommendations". The Government maintains that if a department refuses to comply with a recommendation, then the PCA may bring the matter to the select committee for investigation; the Government felt that this would make departments more reluctant to reject recommendations. However, it has been suggested that cases under the code are likely to be more difficult than ordinary maladministration cases, since they are more likely to have a political dimension and requests will be made by a different group, for instance, journalists, lobby groups and so on.[72] Government departments may therefore be more resistant to pressure by the PCA and the select committee. Certainly this was the case in New Zealand before their Official Information Act was passed; Ministers preferred to have a rough ride in Parliament than release information which might be contentious or embarrassing. Defying a select committee is also easier than defying a court or tribunal. It should also be noted that the lack of enforcement powers of the PCA is in direct contrast with the powers of the Data Protection Registrar who receives complaints regarding access to information and who has power to enforce her decisions.

The amended code does not allow citizens access to public records held   6–21
under the 1958 and 1967 Acts. The merits of decisions of the Lord

---

[68]   Parliamentary Commissioner Act 1967, s. 11(3).
[69]   Annual Report of PCA for 1993 (1993–94, H.C. 290), para. 3.
[70]   Cm. 2290, para. 4.21.
[71]   H.C. 290, i–iii (1994–95), p. 46, evidence of Maurice Frankel, Campaign for Freedom of Information.
[72]   Hazell, *op. cit.*, n. 63, at 265.

Chancellor, Secretary of State for Scotland and the Secretary of State for Northern Ireland are not reviewable by the PCA if the decision is taken without maladministration.[73] The code does not apply to information held by the courts or contained in court documents.

The operation of the code falls within the traditional conventions of British government: a Minister is responsible to Parliament for the decisions of officials made under the code.[74] Further, it has been suggested that parliamentary oversight was retained because of the political nature of the judgments which may have to be made and Parliament is more appropriate than the courts for resolving such matters.[75] The code does not require departments to acquire information they do not have, or provide information which has already been published, or provide information the Government does not consider reliable, or provide information for which an existing service is available at a cost. The target response rate from a department for a simple request is 20 working days. Departments may charge for providing the information; the White Paper envisaged two categories of charge, a standard charge for simple requests and an additional charge for a complex request.[76] The U.S. Freedom of Information Act provides that fees may be waived where disclosure is in the public interest and not primarily for the requester's commercial interests. In the United Kingdom, a number of departments offer a few hours' free time, then charge per hour thereafter. It has been suggested that the charging rate could differ between requests for personal files and general information, where the majority of requests come from businesses and the media.[77] The OPS produces an annual report on the operation of the code in which the figures for code requests are published. In 1994, a total of 2,600 requests were made to all departments with 110 requests rejected either in full or in part; in 1995, there were 1,353 requests with 114 refusals.[78] The most common reasons for the rejection of requests were: internal discussion and advice; effective management and operation of public service; commercial confidentiality of third parties; and information given in confidence.

6–22   The PCA in evidence to his select committee[79] said that there was an insufficient level of awareness of the code by citizens. In 1996, he reported

---

[73] Parliamentary Commissioner Act 1967, s. 12(3).

[74] Birkinshaw, *op. cit.,* n. 12, above, p. 203.

[75] *ibid.*, p. 204.

[76] The charges appear to range from no charge to £50 per A4 page (National Rivers Authority). The PCA has said that he will investigate charges only if someone makes a complaint to him. See Code of Practice on Access to Government Information, 1995 Report, pp. 33–34.

[77] The Constitution Unit, *Introducing Freedom of Information* (1996).

[78] Code of Practice on Access to Government Information, 1995 Report. The reduction in the number of code requests in 1995 is due to a change in the definition of "code request" implemented in 1995.

[79] (1994–95 H.C. 290), i–iii, p. 1.

that "I continue to find a degree of confusion amongst those responsible for operating the Code, particularly in relation to the application of the exemptions in Part II".[80] A witness[81] to the select committee pointed out that the small number of complaints might be explained by the lack of publicity of the code by the Government. He observed that the total expenditure on publicising the code was £51,000, whereas £311,000 were spent publicising the 1993 Chartermark winners under the Citizen's Charter, and £2 million were spent distributing the Parent's Charter in 1991. The low number of code complaints to the PCA[82] is compared by Hazell to the numbers received in New Zealand where 1,000 Official Information Act complaints are received annually by the New Zealand Ombudsman.[83]

As well as a code of practice for Government departments, a code of practice was issued in 1995 to cover NHS bodies.[84] The code covered the NHS organisations in England and aimed to ensure that people have access to information on services, costs, quality standards and performance targets; have explanations of proposed service changes and an opportunity to influence decisions on changes; are aware of reasons for decisions and actions affecting their own treatment; and know what information is available and how to get it. The code requires an acknowledgement of a request for information to be sent within four working days, with the information following within 20 working days. As with the central government code, there is no requirement to make documents available although the NHS code recognises that this may be the best way of answering the inquiry. The code recommends that charging for information should be "exceptional" and requires that no charge is made for individuals inquiring about services or their own treatment, media inquiries, and those from local authorities, M.P.s, citizen's advice bureaux and community health councils. A maximum charge of £20 per hour is stated for other applicants. The exemptions are similar to those in the central government code, covering personal information, unreasonable requests, internal discussion and advice, legal matters, personnel matters, commercial or contractual matters and information given in confidence.

The practices outlined in this code of practice are in some respects 6–23 superior to the central government code. In particular, the specific provisions on charging give certainty to any applicant of the amount they may have to pay and the majority of applicants will not have to pay anything. The recognition that providing actual documents may be the best way of fulfilling

---

[80] *Sixth Report of PCA, Access to Official Information* (1995–96, H.C. 593), Introduction.
[81] (1994–95 H.C. 290), i–iii, p. 39, evidence of Maurice Frankel.
[82] 44 in 1995.
[83] Hazell, *op. cit.,* n. 63, above, at 265. See also Constitution Unit, *op. cit.,* n. 77, above, which cites 37,000 freedom of information requests in 1994–95 in Australia and 13,000 in 1995–96 in Canada.
[84] NHS Executive, *Code of Practice on Openness in the NHS* (1995).

a request is an acknowledgment not made by central government which still insists on providing information, not documents.

A possible benefit of the NHS code appears to be to allow access to information held in pre-1991 medical records. The Access to Health Records Act 1990 restricts such access but the code appears to acknowledge a patient's right to see these.

ACCESS TO PERSONAL RECORDS AND HEALTH AND SAFETY INFORMATION

6–24　The White Paper also promises new statutory rights of access to two types of information. To date, neither promise of legislation has been met.[85]

First, the White Paper envisages a statutory right of access by individuals only to personal information held by public bodies, including universities, on paper documents. The access will be to copies of the documents, "with exempted material edited out as necessary".[86] The right to access will apply to records created on or after the date on which the legislation comes into effect. Enforcement of the statutory right would be through an extension of the functions of the Data Protection Registrar with the right to take court action as a last resort. Employment records, whether in the private or public sector, are not included; employees are considered to be "servants", not "consumers".

Secondly, the right to health and safety information is proposed to help citizens "make decisions to help themselves". The White Paper gives an example of the kind of information to which it is difficult to get an answer. The Government stated that an individual would want to know the answer to an immediate problem, for instance "is this building safe?". The citizen would not want to know the answer to the question, "is the U.K.'s fire safety regime effective?".

6–25　　The Government proposes a statutory right of access to information concerning human health and safety held by public authorities subject to exemption protecting confidentiality. The White Paper envisages that the legislation will follow the model of, and be complementary to, the Environmental Information Regulations 1992 and will extend to information on the safety of public places, transport systems, food, consumer goods and environmental health risks. The legislation would not have retrospective effect to allow access to existing materials; the reason given is one of confidentiality. The Government says that information currently held was given on the basis that it would not be disclosed; once the legislation is in place, organisations will know that information could be disclosed and will

---

[85]　According to the Constitution Unit, *op. cit.*, n. 77, above, the Home Office is preparing for limited legislation on access to personal files by October 1998.

[86]　Cm. 2290, para. 5.11(vi).

act accordingly. The issue of information on medicines is dealt with separately[87]; the White Paper promises a reconsideration of the existing restrictions on disclosure of information in the Medicines Act 1968, s.118 to try to make more information available while still protecting the trade secrets of the pharmaceutical industry. The Government also refers to the proposed European legislation which may have an effect on the U.K. legislation.

ACCESS TO INFORMATION AND INFORMATION TECHNOLOGY

In late 1996, the Government published a Green Paper, *Government direct* — *A prospectus for the electronic delivery of Government services*.[88] This set out the Government's ideas regarding the use of information technology to deliver government services to the customer. It details the principles under which the electronic services should operate including choice, confidence, accessibility, efficiency, rationalisation, fraud prevention and open information. "The strategy should rest on a clear commitment to make information of all kinds available electronically. This should cover the whole range of government information, barring that which needs to be withheld to protect personal or commercial confidentiality or in the public interest."[89]

6–26

The Green Paper envisages terminals being made available in libraries, post offices and shopping centres and further access being available through Internet services. The paper clearly states that the Government does not intend to merge all personal or sensitive information into one database; instead the existing systems will retain their separate identities but a new infrastructure, privately owned, will provide a link between the various systems and the individual citizen or business. The Government acknowledges that there are some legal restrictions on the sharing of information between departments and legislation may be required to allow sharing to take place.

The Government also refers to benefits to open government: "By making more accessible the information which is used in the development of government policy, the information service would allow the citizen to be more fully involved in the democratic process."[90] A series of pilot projects is envisaged, to test customer reaction and measure efficiency and service quality. Although the results of the consultation exercise and the pilot schemes are not expected before mid-1998, a Ministerial statement on the Government's response to comments on the Green Paper has been made.[91] This reported some 300 responses to the paper.

6–27

---

[87] Cm. 2290, paras. 6.18–6.22.
[88] Cm. 3438 (1996).
[89] *ibid.* Chap. 5.
[90] *ibid.* para 6.17.
[91] See at http://www.open.gov.uk/citu/gdirect/govresp.htm (5.3.97).

THE CASE FOR FREEDOM OF INFORMATION LEGISLATION

6–28 The right to have information about government and its work is recognised in many countries and there are a number of good reasons for freedom of information legislation being implemented.

1. Access to information regarding the decision-making process is central to a democratic society. Government and its agencies must be accountable and this cannot occur if they have all the information. "Without openness and a 'right to know' Ministerial responsibility to Parliament is enfeebled, opposition to Governments disarmed and democracy undermined."[92]
2. Individuals should know what information is held by government relating to them and there should be procedures for the correction of errors. Access to such information will also assist individuals in making more informed decisions for themselves and their families.
3. If the process of decision-making is known, then it can be improved because it will be visible and open to scrutiny.
4. Much of the information held by government relates to matters of great interest to consumers, for instance, housing, education, transport, and so on. The information is paid for by the taxpayer/consumer and so arguably they have a right to see such information unless there are good reasons for not disclosing it.[93]

6–29 The U.K. Government has resisted calls for freedom of information legislation by saying that it would undermine the accountability of Ministers to Parliament. This is an absurd argument; where there is a right to obtain information, Ministers have to give full answers and so are genuinely accountable to the Legislature.

> "Ministerial accountability may be strengthened because Parliamentary scrutiny is increased. But what the Minister is accountable for is the action (or inaction) revealed by the information, and not the provision of the information itself. Under freedom of information, Ministers lose some of their discretion in relation to the provision of information; but their accountability for the underlying activity or decision remains unchanged."[94]

The availability of information would mean that Ministers would be unable to manipulate the information or give half-truths.[95] Indeed the evidence given to Sir Richard Scott in his inquiry has indicated that Ministers do not wish Parliament, and therefore the public, to know what is happening since this would give away the political advantage they presently enjoy.[96] The

---

[92] Turpin, *British Government and the Constitution* (3rd ed., 1995), p. 468.
[93] Oliver, *op. cit.,* n. 2, above, p. 169.
[94] Hazell, "Freedom of information in Australia, Canada and New Zealand" (1989) 67 *Public Administration* 189 at 198.
[95] Wass, "Scott and Whitehall", 1996 P.L. 467.
[96] *ibid.* at 467.

argument that civil servants and other government advisers will not speak candidly if they think that their opinions might eventually be made public has little merit; a civil servant who proffers advice which is based on sound reasoning and research will not fear disclosure of that advice at a later date. Safeguards could be built in to any freedom of information legislation to ensure that civil servants were not discriminated against for advice given to a previous Government. In any case, the argument does beg the question: what happened to civil servants in other countries which have freedom of information legislation?[97] Do their civil servants refrain from giving proper advice? It does seem unlikely that this is the case. The assumption must therefore be that Ministers and the Government do not wish the disclosure of information for another reason, perhaps the risk that the Government will be embarrassed by the information, for instance where the information shows that the Minister based his policy not on facts but on political expediency. Where information has been released which shows dissent between a Minister and an adviser, such as disclosed by the minutes of meetings between the Chancellor of the Exchequer and the Governor of the Bank of England in 1996 and 1997, there has been no real impact on the credibility of either participant. The money markets have not been de-stabilised nor have the reputations of the officials been harmed; indeed it could be said that the openness of their discussions has shown the strength of both points of view and has enhanced the operation of government. If "leaks" of information had occurred, these would have had the potential to be very damaging since the uncertainty of the veracity of the information would have unsettled the markets and public opinion. The leaking of information or the telling of half-truths in Parliament both foster a climate of uncertainty and distrust.[98]

The creation of executive agencies affects the principle of Ministerial 6–30 accountability since Ministers are no longer responsible for the day-to-day operations of the agencies. Birkinshaw comments: "In several respects this constitutes a subversion of the major shibboleths of the British constitution: Ministerial responsibility and the anonymity of civil servants."[99] The fact that Ministers do not accept full accountability means that a large tranche of the public service is now effectively beyond parliamentary control. Further, information regarding the services provided by the agencies may not be fully available because of "commercial confidentiality" since the agencies may be required to work in the commercial world to ensure they

---

[97] Fifteen Commonwealth Governments have introduced freedom of information, all by use of legislation. The majority have a parliamentary system which is based on the Westminster model.

[98] See the comments of Sir Richard Scott on the evidence of Robin Butler who said that telling half-truths was sometimes necessary and Lord Howe who spoke of "packaging information" to Parliament (1995–96 H.C. 115), para. D.4.52.

[99] Birkinshaw, *op. cit.*, n. 12, above, p. 148.

provide services more efficiently and effectively. Of course they prepare annual reports and their accounts are subject to scrutiny by the National Audit Office; but increased reliance on commercial practices may lead to the abuse or misuse of power.

It is not only the public and Parliament who are "kept in the dark" about Government policy. The system of Cabinet committees has the effect of keeping policy discussions within a narrow range of Ministers. No Minister can insist on knowing what another Minister is doing unless it touches upon his own area of responsibility. This means that in the Government itself, there are few people who know the full range of Government policies and proposals.

6–31   The Government uses a number of ways to release information including selective "leaking", non-attributable briefings to Lobby journalists and the manipulation of statistics.[1]

The U.K. Government has insisted that other bodies such as local authorities and NHS bodies open their meetings to public scrutiny. However, the Government has itself steadfastly refused to open up its own meetings and the decision-making process. The Code of Practice does not allow access to the advice tendered by civil servants and Government advisers. This is in direct contrast with other countries, particularly the USA where the Government in the Sunshine Act of 1976 (the Sunshine Act) allows access to meetings of certain agencies. There is no right to participate in the meetings and the meeting can be closed to the public if a majority of all members of the agency so agree. The Federal Advisory Committee Act 1972 opened federal advisory committees to the public, with hearings publicised in advance, minutes published and membership of the committee balanced. These requirements are enforceable in the courts.

PARLIAMENT AND INFORMATION

6–32   We have considered the statutory and non-statutory methods by which individuals may obtain information in the United Kingdom. The Government has resisted calls for freedom of information legislation and, by and large, Parliament has happily accorded with that view. Parliament is, however, entitled to obtain information and to scrutinise, both in general and in detail, the work of the Executive.

Parliament can ask questions of Ministers, can demand debates, summon witnesses and call for evidence. Parliamentary proceedings are protected by absolute privilege. The Public Accounts Committee receives written

---

[1]   For instance, unemployment statistics — in February 1997, there was a large and unexpected fall in unemployment figures. The Government hailed this as a triumph for their policies but a junior Minister was forced to admit that about 50 per cent of the reduction was due to the introduction of the new Job Seeker's Allowance.

minutes by the accounting officers of departments where they disagree with
Ministers on expenditure matters. This procedure was strengthened as a
result of the Pergau Dam Affair[2] where an accounting officer was overruled
by the Minister but because the civil servant did not consider there was any
irregularity in the conferral of the overseas aid, he did not report the matter
to the Comptroller and Auditor-General and the Treasury. The payment
was subsequently discovered by the NAO when conducting an audit and
the court held that the payment was *ultra vires*. The Government accepted
that if an accounting officer is overruled, the matter should be referred to
the Comptroller and Auditor-General immediately. As a result of the Nolan
Committee's deliberations, the Government has further modified this
procedure, now saying that if a Minister is "minded" to overrule the
accounting officer's opinion, the accounting officer may inform the
Chairman of the PAC.

One of the main methods of parliamentary scrutiny of the Executive is   6–33
the select committee. Since 1979, a select committee has existed for each
main government department and its associated bodies and agencies.[3] There
are currently 16 departmental committees, whose membership is drawn
from the ranks of backbench M.P.s, Government Ministers and
Parliamentary Private Secretaries and frontbench spokesmen by convention
do not sit. The membership of each committee broadly mirrors the party
membership in the Commons but the chairpersons are drawn from all of
the major parties. Select committees may request the presence of witnesses
and can call for evidence from departments. By and large, Ministers co-
operate by allowing civil servants to attend and give evidence. After the
Westland Affair in 1986, the Defence Select Committee wanted to question
the civil servants who were involved in the leak of the Attorney-General's
letter to the press. They had to settle for the Head of the Home Civil Service
and Cabinet Secretary, Sir Robert Armstrong.

Civil servants and agency chief executives are "subject to Ministerial
instructions as to how to answer questions". The OPS issued a revised set
of the Osmotherly Rules in 1994[4]; these give detailed instructions on how
information is to be treated. They state that information should be produced
except in certain circumstances, including where the terms of guidance say
it should not, where excessive costs will be incurred, where it involves
internal advice to Ministers and inter-departmental exchanges on policy
issues, where discussions were in Cabinet or Cabinet committee, information
supplied in confidence, or where the interests of national security are
involved.

---

[2]   *R. v. Secretary of State for Foreign Affairs, ex p. WDM* [1995] 1 All E.R. 611.
[3]   Note that a Scottish Affairs Select Committee was not formed between 1987 and 1992
      because of a lack of Conservative M.P.s to sit on it and a Select Committee for N. Ireland
      Affairs was not created until 1995.
[4]   Cabinet Office, Departmental Evidence and Response to Select Committees (1994).

The position of agency chief executives before select committees has caused difficulty. On the one hand, they speak with regard to policy on behalf of the Minister to whom they are accountable. On the other hand, agency chief executives are deemed to be responsible for the day-to-day operations of their agency and for this they are accountable, not the Minister. This policy/operational divide is not clear-cut and thus could be said to shelter both the Minister and the agency chief executive and allow them both to escape accountability.[5] The difficulties were shown in sharp relief in 1994–95 when, after escapes at Whitemoor and Parkhurst prisons, the agency chief executive of the Prison Services Agency was sacked by the Home Secretary for "operational defects". The former agency chief executive protested that the defects were as a result of the policy of the Government and alleged that the Home Office had interfered in the day-to-day operations of the agency thus preventing him and his staff from managing the agency properly. The Home Secretary was forced to pay compensation to Mr Lewis for the repudiation of his contract.

6–34   The scrutiny of administration of executive finances is an important task of the Legislature.[6] The Public Accounts Committee (PAC) is one of the oldest[7] and most powerful of the select committees of the House of Commons. The PAC receives reports from the Comptroller and Auditor-General, who is an officer of Parliament. He is charged with the duty under the National Audit Act 1983 of carrying out the audit and certification of all government departments and a large number of other public bodies. In addition, the Comptroller and Auditor-General's department, the National Audit Office, carries out a wide range of value-for-money (VFM) audits.[8] The reports of VFM audits are presented to Parliament and are designed to show any imprudent, uneconomic or extravagant expenditure or waste.[9]

The PAC tends to adopt a non-political stance. "The PAC — the doyen of the Parliamentary Committees — remains in my view superior to the others: its chairman is invariably a former senior Minister; its membership is of a very high calibre; it is not a 'political' committee; and it is genuinely concerned with the real stuff of Parliament."[10] It is also the only select committee with in effect its own department to assist it and carry out its research, namely the National Audit Office, which produces reports for the consideration of the PAC and Parliament. All other select committees are subject to the limitations in the Osmotherly Rules[11] as regards the evidence

---

[5]   Birkinshaw, *op. cit.,* n. 12, above, p. 161.
[6]   For detailed discussion, see, for instance, McEldowney, *Public Law* (1994), Chap. 11.
[7]   It dates from 1861.
[8]   National Audit Act 1983, s. 6.
[9]   Treasury, *Government Accounting* (1989), para. 7.1.20.
[10]   Cooper, "Select Committees — a view from a witness" (1987) 1(1) *Contemporary Record,* 16–17.
[11]   Cabinet Office, *op. cit.,* n. 4, above.

given by civil servants. The 1983 Act gives the NAO a statutory right to obtain information "reasonably required for the investigations in question."[12] The information thus obtained is made available to the PAC in NAO reports; this, of course, puts the PAC in a more powerful position than other select committees. While the PAC has the same power to call Ministers to give evidence, discussions usually involve the accounting officer of the department under investigation.

DIFFERENCES IN FREEDOM OF INFORMATION LEGISLATION

Open government is usually associated with freedom of information. It 6–35 assumes a greater openness by a Government in making documents, papers and records available and further assumes that a statute is necessary to bring this openness about. Freedom of information legislation will have an appeal mechanism, but administrative discretion will remain. Some questions however arise in considering the differences between the various legislative systems.

1. Do you need a Privacy Act with freedom of information ?

One of the difficulties associated with freedom of information legislation 6–36 is that personal information or commercial information may be too easily obtained by persons who should not have access. This problem has been resolved by different methods in different countries. In the USA, the Privacy Act 1974 allows access by individuals only to their personal information held by government agencies, although there is no access under this Act to the files of the FBI or CIA.[13] The Freedom of Information Act 1966 (amended in 1974, 1976 and 1986) does allow access to the files of these two agencies and also requires an answer to an inquiry within 10 working days. The 1976 Act was given the short title "The Government in the Sunshine Act". The U.S. Food and Drug Administration receives about 40,000 requests for information each year, with around 80 per cent of these coming from businesses seeking information about competitors. It has been argued that requests from competing businesses do not fall within the original spirit of the legislation since the requests are made to aid the applicant businesses at the expense of their competitors.[14]

In Canada, the Privacy Act 1982 created a Privacy Commissioner and tries to protect business privacy by requiring the government agency to

---

[12] s. 8.
[13] For detailed discussion see Birkinshaw, *op. cit.,* n. 12, above, p. 60.
[14] Gillis, "Information Law, Policy and Ethics: Canadian Federal Government Experience" in Thomas, *Teaching Ethics* (Cambridge Centre for Business and Public Sector Ethics) (1993).

notify a company if a competitor has requested information about them. The company may then argue why the information should not be released. New Zealand adopted a Privacy Act in 1993 and has a separate Privacy Commissioner. The Act covers both public and private sectors and codes are produced which are binding on the sector concerned.

2. Do you need a Secrecy Act with freedom of information ?

6–37　It is generally recognised that there are some matters which should not be released into the public domain. In Sweden, the Secrecy Act 1980 contains prohibitions against the divulgence of information by public servants and restricts access to some official documents. In the USA, there is no Secrecy Act but official information may be classified under Executive Orders. In 1982, an Executive Order "broadened the discretion to create official secrets".[15] The balancing test requiring the need for secrecy to be weighed against the right of public access was removed and the numbers of documents classified as secret increased. In 1995, the Clinton administration made a further Executive Order to ease the effects of the 1982 Order.[16] This order partially restored the balancing test, changed the classification system and required reasons to be given for the classification chosen. The U.S. Code contains an Espionage Act to prevent spying. However, it should be noted that some countries have managed to change to a statutory right of access to information without the repeal of their existing official secrecy legislation.[17]

3. Similarities in freedom of information legislation

6–38　Three principles crop up in most freedom of information legislation: disclosure of official information as of right; exemptions to protect secrets; and appeal machinery.

(a) Disclosure as of right

Generally, the onus is on the Government to justify withholding the information. There may be restrictions on the people who can request information, for instance, in Sweden, there is free access to all Swedish citizens, although in practice, foreigners are treated the same. In the USA, "any person" may request information; this openness has benefited more than the general public. Foreigners, criminals, businesses and the press have all been able to access information. New Zealand and Canada restrict access to citizens or permanent residents.

---

[15]　EO 12356 47 FR 14874, April 1982.
[16]　EO 12958.
[17]　For instance, Australia, Canada and New Zealand.

In Sweden there is a public right to inspect and publish documents held by government authority. This applies to "official documents". Under the Secrecy Act 1980, official documents have to be registered when they arrive and thereafter individuals are able to put in a request to see them; this can even be done by telephone. In the USA, federal agencies publish information about themselves in the Federal Register; this then confers a right on the public to see documents held by the agency. It is not necessary to request a specific document, since the information can be obtained if the citizen "reasonably describes" the document. The agency may only recover the "direct costs" of the search and duplication of the information. "The 'need to know' standard has been replaced by a 'right to know' doctrine. The Government now has to justify the need for secrecy."[18]

(b) Exemptions from disclosure

Most freedom of information legislation exempts certain types of information. Sometimes the legislation is mandatory and disclosure is always denied; there is no discretion afforded the official. If, however, the law is permissive, the official still has discretion and may release the document if no harm will result from its disclosure.   6–39

In Sweden, there is very little discretion as regards exempted material. The Secrecy Act 1980 gives seven grounds for exemption, including national security and foreign policy, central financial policies, prosecution and prevention of crime, and personal and economic privacy. The Swedish view on exempted material is: "If there is an important interest in free access, an exception should only be allowed if this is regarded as necessary in view of strong interests pointing in the opposite direction."[19]

In the USA, the exempted categories are mainly permissive and include national defence and foreign policy, commercial and financial information, personal medical and other files and information regarding oil wells. The Executive Order of 1982 referred to above reversed the trend which was towards a more permissive attitude to security classifications. Mandatory secrecy requirements are more common and the balancing test modified by the 1995 Executive Order is weighed more in favour of government secrecy.[20]

Australian legislation exempts 26 government agencies from the freedom of information, with a further 19 being exempted regarding certain classes of documents. The basic approach of the Freedom of Information Act 1982 is defined in terms of "public interest" and a harm or balancing test is used.   6–40

---

[18] House Report 102–146, 102nd Congress (1991), p. 2.
[19] Swedish Government, "Swedish Working Document concerning Access to documents in the European Institutions" (1996) 4 *European Access* 12.
[20] Birkinshaw, *op. cit.,* n. 12, above, pp. 51–66.

To prevent disclosure, the agency must show that the information falls under the exemption and it is contrary to the public interest to disclose. Ministers are, however, encouraged to disclose a document even though the document might have a claim to exemption. If, nonetheless, the Minister signs a certificate of exemption the certificate is conclusive evidence of the public interest and may not be reviewed by the Administrative Appeals Tribunal. The courts and the Administrative Appeals Tribunal have rejected "class" claims in all but Cabinet documents; each case is taken on its merits and the public interest related to it.

Excluded material in Canada includes Cabinet secrets, policy proposals, background papers and advice given to Ministers. However, discussion papers may be released if the decision has been made public, or if the decision was made more than four years prior to the request or if the papers have been in existence 20 years or more. The Act also provides for mandatory and discretionary exemptions. These are wide-ranging and include information from foreign Governments, personal information, international affairs, Canadian defence and so on.

(c) Appeal machinery

6–41   In the USA, appeal procedures are specified in each agency's Freedom of Information Act regulations. The exemption and the reason for refusal must be given to the applicant together with details of the right to appeal to the federal court where there is a rehearing with the onus of proof on the defending agency.

In New Zealand, complaints are made to the Ombudsman whose recommendations on disclosure are legally binding unless vetoed by Order in Council approved by the whole Cabinet within 21 days. The difficulty in New Zealand is that the Ombudsman has to carry out the judicial function; there is no tribunal to assist him and build up case law for future reference.

The Australian procedure requires an internal review first, then a complaint can be made to the Administrative Appeals Tribunal. If a Minister does not accept the finding of the AAT, he must notify the applicant of his reasons and place a copy of these before both Houses of Parliament. There is an appeal on a point of law from the AAT to the Federal Court.

The Information Commissioner in Canada deals with complaints that access has been refused. Although the Information Commissioner's decision cannot be enforced against a department, the Commissioner may send certain points for judicial interpretation.

Appeals in Sweden are readily available and, after internal review of a refusal of access, the applicant may appeal to the administrative courts.

IS THERE MORE OPENNESS IN A COUNTRY WITH FREEDOM OF INFORMATION ?

6–42   The extent of openness will depend upon how liberal the information law is. In the USA, there is a liberal system but this has had to be tightened because of the damage to national security caused by the 1974 amending Act. The National Security Act 1984 was passed in response to this. There is also a heavy price to be paid in terms of time and money; some agencies have a huge workload and were unable to claim back the true cost of making a document available. There are also abuses of the system; businesses are able to see what their competitors are doing and gain unfair commercial advantage. The 1986 Reform Act extended the exemptions available to law enforcement practices and exempted some categories of documents from the Freedom of Information Act. Requests for commercial purposes are now charged the actual cost of obtaining the information.

Openness depends on a clear definition of what an official document is, on balancing or harm tests and on a fair system of review where disclosure is refused.

EUROPEAN UNION AND FREEDOM OF INFORMATION

The European Union has been moving steadily towards more open 6–43 government. A sectoral right of access was established by the Directive on Freedom of Access to Information on the Environment.[21] The Final Act of the Treaty on European Union included Declaration No.17 which recommended that the Commission submit a report by 1993 to the Council on how to improve public access. The Commission reported that there should be greater access by the public and some administrative measures followed, including public access to some meetings of the Council, the publication of some records and more information published in the *Official Journal*.[22] Official discussion papers (Green Papers) were to be published in order to allow public participation and debate; these would be followed by White Papers giving the detailed proposals before submission to the Council and Parliament. The Parliament also agreed to open all its plenary sessions and Committee meetings.[23]

In 1993, three measures were implemented dealing with access to 6–44 information. These were the Code of Conduct on Public Access to Council and Commission Documents,[24] the Decision on Public Access to Council documents[25] and the Rules of Procedure adopted by the Council.[26] "Document" is given a wide definition; it means "any written text, whatever its medium, which contains existing data and is held by the Council or the

[21] [1990] O.J. L158/56.
[22] For discussion see Michael, *Freedom of Information comes to the EU* (1996), p. 31; Birkinshaw, *op. cit.*, n. 12, above, p. 128.
[23] Preston, "Openness and the European Union Institutions" (1996) 4 *European Access* 7.
[24] Decision 93/730/EEC; [1993] O.J. L340/41.
[25] Decision 93/731/EEC; [1993] O.J. L340/43.
[26] Decision 93/662/EEC; [1993] O.J. L340/1.

Commission".[27] This will include documents which have not been finalised but are still at the working document stage. The first two measures gave a general right of access subject to specific exemptions, a right to a reasoned examination of applications, and a right of appeal to the ECJ[28] or Ombudsman[29] if the application were refused. The Rules of Procedure, however, provided at Article 5 that the deliberations of the Council should be covered by "the obligation of professional secrecy". The profusion of measures caused confusion. In *Carvel v. Council of the E.U.*[30] the Court of First Instance observed that the Decision of the Council was the only legislative measure: "The Decision 93/731 is ... the only measure governing the citizen's rights of access to documents; the Council's Rules of Procedure ... regulate its own internal operating mechanisms." The CFI allowed the appeal by Carvel, a journalist on the *Guardian* newspaper, stating that the Council had not complied with its obligation to balance the interests involved: "the Council must, when exercising its discretion under art. 4 (2) [of the Decision 93/731] genuinely balance the interests of its citizens in gaining access to its documents against any interest of its own in maintaining the confidentiality of its deliberation". The Governments of Denmark and the Netherlands gave significant evidence in this case that the interest-balancing exercise had not been undertaken by the Council.

6–45   Decision 93/731, Article 4(1), gives the exemptions to the right of access. These include protection of the public interest, protection of the individual and of privacy, the protection of commercial and industrial secrecy and protection of confidentiality as required by the provider of the information or as required by the legislation of the Member State which supplied the information. The exemptions in Article 4(1) are mandatory, with refusal based on a determination that disclosure could undermine the various interests. Article 4(2) gives the Council discretion to refuse access to documents in order to protect the institution's interest in the confidentiality of its proceedings. Institutions of the European Union must inform an applicant within one month whether the request is to be approved or not; a failure to reply within one month is automatically a rejection and the applicant is then entitled to appeal through the internal procedures and then to the Ombudsman, under Article 138e E.C. or take legal proceedings under Article 173 E.C. The Ombudsman has wide powers of access to documents in the possession of Community institutions and documents originating in Member States. Documents classified by the Member State as secret may be withheld.[31] The Member State must be informed if a request has been

---

[27]   Decision 93/730/EEC.
[28]   Art. 173.
[29]   Art. 138c.
[30]   Case T–194/94, October 19, 1995.
[31]   Art. 223.

made. Where the Ombudsman has requested information from a Member State through its Permanent Representative, the Member State is obliged to provide it subject to its secrecy laws or other measures preventing its disclosure.[32]

The Maastricht Treaty had declared "the transparency of the decision- 6–46 making process strengthens the democratic nature of institutions and the public's confidence in the administration". The concept of "transparency" adopted in some areas instead of access to information is wider than simple access. It implies access to the methods of making decisions and the reasons for those decisions. The Council adopted a Code of Conduct on Transparency of Council Proceedings on October 2, 1995; the Code refers to access to minutes and statements in the minutes and states that the Council will try to incorporate statements of reasons from Member States in legislative Acts, although only a simple majority of the Council is required to keep the statements closed. The Council agrees also that a Member State's statement will not be made public without the consent of the Member State. The Code commits the Council to "systematically examine" its minutes, before their adoption, to ascertain whether to make public documents submitted to the Council, as well as the decisions and the conclusions of the Council. This amended Code was passed shortly before the *Carvel* case decision and it addresses in advance of the decision the question on which the Council was found wanting, namely the exercise of its discretion under Article 4(2). The Commission's Code on Access[33] was published in 1994 and provides that access will be allowed to any written text if the written application is sufficiently precise; no access will be allowed if the information is classified. Documents will be made available either by means of a copy of the document or by making it available for consultation at one of the Commission's offices. Appeals against refusal of access must be made within one month to the Secretary-General of the Commission; a decision on the appeal must be sent within one month to the applicant. Appeals thereafter will lie with the Ombudsman or the European Court of Justice.

Both the Council and Commission state that if a document was written 6–47 by someone other than them, the request for access has to be made to the author of the document.[34] This means that a Member State can seek to keep confidential information supplied by it to the institutions through the operation of Article 4(1) of Decision 93/731 and through the operation of its own national laws. So even if the information were liable to be made available by the institutions under E.C. procedures, the information might not be released because of the Member State's own laws. The refusal of

---

[32] Statute of European Ombudsman, O.J. L113, May 4, 1995, p. 15, Art. 3.
[33] Code on Access to Documents of Commission, 94/90/ECSC, EEC, Euratom O.J. 46/58.
[34] Decision 93/731, Art. 2(2).

information by the institutions is reviewable by the E.C. judicial process; the refusal by the Member State is not reviewable by this process and there is no treaty provision which guarantees access to documents and which "could be invoked to test the legality of national laws".[35]

6–48   The duty to disclose information is not incumbent only on Member States; Community institutions may be required to provide information to Member States and the European Court of Justice has held that Community institutions must actively assist national legal proceedings by providing documents or by giving evidence.[36]

In 1996, the European Parliament appointed a member to consider the issues of openness and transparency; he presented proposals to the Inter-Governmental Conference in 1996 suggesting more openness in the legislative process, in the administrative process and an extension of the powers of the European Ombudsman.[37]

EUROPEAN CONVENTION ON HUMAN RIGHTS

6–49   Article 10 of the Convention refers to the right to receive and impart information. The Committee of Members of the Council of Europe adopted a Recommendation in 1981 that Member States adopt freedom of information legislation.[38] It was hoped, certainly by those in favour of freedom of information legislation in the United Kingdom, that the European Court on Human Rights would interpret Article 10 as requiring legislation to implement the rights. However, two cases decided by the Court found that Article 10 was limited to the right of a willing provider of information to communicate it, and did not imply a public right of access to Government information.[39]

The Council has also passed Recommendation No. R(91) 10 which is concerned with the communication to third parties of data of a personal nature held by public institutions. This says that "data of a personal nature may not be communicated to third parties for goals incompatible with the reason for which it was collected".

---

[35] Armstrong, "Citizenship of the Union? Lessons from *Carvel and the Guardian*" (1996) M.L.R. 59 (4), at p. 585.
[36] *Zwartfeld case* [1990] I ECR 3365.
[37] See web site http://www.europarl.eu.int/dg7/bonde/en/bonden07.htm (February 5, 1997).
[38] Recommendation No. R 81(19) in Council of Europe DH–MM(91)1.
[39] *Leander v. Sweden* (1987) 9 E.H.H.R. 433; *Gaskin v. U.K.* (1989 11 E.H.H.R.) 402.

CHAPTER 7

OMBUDSMEN

INTRODUCTION

The word "ombudsman" comes from the Norse word "ombud" meaning 7–01
commissioner or charge. Nowadays, it is used to describe a public official
who investigates the grievances of ordinary people. The term is also used
in the private sector to describe an internal complaints adjudicator, a practice
deplored by the British Parliamentary Commissioner for Administration.[1]
An ombudsman exists to investigate the grievances of an individual but
also has a second important function — to raise the standards of service to
the public within the department or industry concerned.[2]

In the United Kingdom it has long been the situation that when a citizen
has a grievance against a decision made by a Minister or an official in a
government department, the citizen has the right to approach his Member
of Parliament to ask for help in resolving the dispute. The M.P. then has the
right to raise the matter with the Minister concerned. However, until 1967,
the M.P. had no access to officials in the government departments except
through the Minister. The Crichel Down Affair had exposed deficiencies in
the system and the need for a new, effective non-legal remedy.[3]

In 1961, the Justice Report, or Whyatt Report,[4] recommended the 7–02
appointment of a Commissioner for Complaints. The idea was not new; in
Sweden, for instance, a commissioner (the justicieombudsman) had been
in existence since 1809. Denmark adopted the mechanism in 1954 and in
1962, New Zealand introduced an ombudsman.[5]

In the United Kingdom, the Conservative Government of the early 1960s
did not like the Whyatt Report recommendations. They said an ombudsman
would erode the doctrine of individual Ministerial responsibility by

---

[1] First Report of Select Committee on Parliamentary Commissioner for Administration:
    Powers, Work and Jurisdiction, Vol. I (1993–94, H.C. 33).
[2] Wilkinson, "Complaining to the Ombudsman" (1992) 142 New L.J. 1348.
[3] For discussion, see Chap. 3.
[4] Justice, "The Citizen and the Administration: The Redress of Grievances" (1961).
[5] Other countries have also adopted the scheme, e.g. France has a "mediateur" (1973) and
    Spain a "defensor del pueblo" (1981). For a discussion of the development of ombudsmen
    see Seneviratne, *Ombudsmen in the Public Sector* (1994).

undermining the role of an M.P. as the channel of complaint by electors. However, the incoming Labour Government of 1964 accepted the need for a complaints commissioner and in 1967 the Parliamentary Commissioner for Administration Act was passed. In the debates on the Bill, it was said that the commissioner would provide "a new and powerful weapon with a sharp cutting edge to be added to the existing antiquated armoury of parliamentary questions and adjournment debates".[6]

7–03   There then followed a flurry of Acts setting up other commissioners. In 1969, the Parliamentary Commissioner (Northern Ireland) Act was passed. Health Service Commissioners were established by the National Health Reorganisation Acts 1972 (for Scotland) and 1973 (for England and Wales).[7] The Local Government Act 1974 established local commissioners for administration in England and Wales and a similar office was set up in Scotland by the Local Government (Scotland) Act 1975. The principle of complaints commissioners has been adopted by the private sector with various industries setting up their own schemes, for instance, banking, insurance and travel agents. The legal profession have also seen the establishment of ombudsmen in both Scotland[8] and England and Wales.[9] The Maastricht Treaty[10] made provision for the establishment of a European Parliament Ombudsman and an appointment to this position was eventually made in July 1995 after an 18-month search for a suitable candidate.

This chapter will deal with the office of the Parliamentary Commissioner for Administration and two other ombudsmen who have a particular Scottish dimension, the Local Government ombudsman and the Scottish Legal Services Ombudsman.

THE PARLIAMENTARY COMMISSIONER FOR ADMINISTRATION

7–04 The Parliamentary Commissioner for Administration (PCA) investigates complaints from members of the public who claim to have sustained "injustice in consequence of maladministration" from action taken by a government body or department "in exercise of the administrative functions of that department".[11]

The PCA is appointed by the monarch and holds office during good behaviour.[12] He enjoys the same security of tenure of office as a High Court judge and may be removed only by addresses of both Houses of Parliament except that if a PCA becomes incapable for medical reasons, he may be

---

6   *Hansard*, H.C. Vol. 734, col. 44.
7   The posts of Health Service Commissioners are all held by the PCA.
8   Law Reform (Miscellaneous Provisions)(Scotland) Act 1990.
9   Courts and Legal Services Act 1990.
10   Treaty on European Union 1992.
11   Parliamentary Commissioner for Administration Act 1967, s. 5(1)(a).
12   1967 Act, s.1(1) and (2).

removed without the need for the addresses from both Houses.[13] The PCA is answerable to the House of Commons, not to the Government of the day, thus giving him a high degree of independence.[14] He is also an *ex officio* member of the Council on Tribunals.[15]

His work is scrutinised by the Select Committee on the Parliamentary 7–05 Commissioner (now renamed the Select Committee on Public Administration), whose chairman is consulted on the appointment of the PCA. The select committee examines the PCA's reports and, like other select committees, hears evidence on matters of concern and produces its own reports. The PCA compiles an annual report, produces a quarterly report containing selected cases and from time to time issues special reports. These are presented to Parliament under section 10(4) of the 1967 Act.

It is important to note that the PCA is an independent adjudicator, not the citizen's lawyer or advocate: "He has a duty of objectivity which would be incompatible with such an approach ... he is not the citizen's lawyer for the simple reason that if his investigation vindicates the acts of civil servants, he must not hesitate to uphold them."[16] In 1994, the Government agreed that the PCA's name should be changed to "Parliamentary Ombudsman" and "Health Service Ombudsman" and that the relevant statutes should be amended as soon as possible.[17] There is no annual debate within the Commons on the work of the PCA, although this was suggested by the select committee in 1994 and later rejected by the Government who maintained there was no demand from M.P.s for an annual debate.

COMPLAINTS PROCEDURE AND THE M.P. FILTER

In 1967, it was argued that open access to the PCA by the public would 7–06 undermine the focal role of M.P.s as investigators for complaints as well as leading to a huge increase in the workload for the PCA, thus increasing the cost of the scheme. There was also a fear that it would conflict with the doctrine of Ministerial responsibility.

However, the PCA is undoubtedly a development of an existing system and does not supplant the role of an M.P.; instead the PCA adds an extra dimension. The M.P.'s role still exists because all complaints have to be

[13] Parliamentary and Health Service Commissioners Act 1987, s. 2.
[14] Legislation is likely to be introduced to provide that the Parliamentary Ombudsman and Health Service Ombudsman be appointed by the Crown, on an address of the House of Commons, with no motion for the address except by the Prime Minister with the agreement of the Chairman of the Select Committee and the Leader of the Opposition. See, further, First Report from Select Committee on Parliamentary Commissioner (1993–94, H.C. 33), p. xi.
[15] For more detail on the work of the council, see Chap. 8.
[16] Maloney, "The Ombudsman as Mediator, Reformer and Fighter" in Caidon (ed.) *International Handbook of the Ombudsman — Evolution and Present Function* (1983).
[17] (1993–94 H.C. 33), p. 10.

channelled, one way or another, through the M.P. to the PCA.[18] The 1967
Act at section 5(1) retains the investigative role of the M.P. by stating that
all complaints to the PCA must be made through an M.P.. There have been
a number of reports[19] recommending that the M.P. filter be dispensed with.
However, the Government has retained the principle, quoting a number of
reasons for its retention, for instance, the filter prevents the PCA's office
being flooded by complaints, and by becoming involved M.P.s are able to
establish whether changes in legislation are necessary.[20] In the early years,
the PCA often received complaints made directly to him but because of
section 5(1) he was unable to investigate. Instead he had to return the
complaint to the citizen with a note to the effect that the citizen had to send
the complaint to his or her M.P. first. The PCA expressed concern that this
was discouraging citizens who had valid complaints since they might think
that they had no good cause or think that their M.P. would not refer the
matter. Sir Alan Marre, who was PCA from 1973 to 1976, objected to the
use of the M.P. filter on the grounds that "six hundred and fifty people
cannot be expected to act in the same way. If they cannot do so, is it fair
that constituents in one part of the country should have less access to the
Parliamentary Commissioner than in other parts?".[21]

7–07   Fears at the outset of the scheme that the system would be swamped by
complaints have not materialised and indeed there is some evidence to
suggest that although the removal of the M.P. filter would increase the PCA's
workload this would be moderate.[22] The statutory M.P. filter is not used as
rigidly as before; since 1978, complaints which are made directly to the
PCA are referred to the M.P. if the PCA believes that a case of
maladministration is indicated. The M.P. will then refer the matter back to
the PCA who can begin his inquiries.[23] The M.P. decides whether or not
to refer the matter to the PCA and so is indirectly in a position to determine
the extent to which the scheme is utilised. M.P.s appear to prefer to handle
complaints themselves rather than use the PCA; in a study of the workload
of seven M.P.s, Rawlings found that only seven cases out of several thousand
were sent to the PCA. The main reasons for failure to invoke the ombudsman

---

[18] The M.P. does not have to be the complainant's constituency M.P.. Note that even peers
have to complain through an M.P. although peers do not vote in Parliamentary elections
and so do not have an M.P..
[19] For instance — Justice-All Souls Report, "Administrative Justice — some necessary
reforms" (1988).
[20] Drewry and Harlow, "A Cutting Edge? The Parliamentary Commissioner and MPs" (1990)
53(6) M.L.R. 745.
[21] *Hansard*, H.C. Vol. 615, p. 65.
[22] When the filter was removed from the Local Government Ombudsman the increase in his
workload was 44 per cent. Translated into the PCA workload, this would mean an increase
of around 500 cases each year.
[23] This is in direct contrast with other public sector ombudsmen who accept direct complaints.

procedure were the length of time taken to complete the investigations and the lack of involvement of the M.P.s in that investigation.[24]

It does appear that the PCA has enabled Parliament and Ministers to 7–08 correct faults in the administration which would otherwise not have come to light. Wade and Forsyth quote a Government Minister's evidence to the Select Committee as saying that the Parliamentary Commissioner system "works extremely well [but] not always comfortably for the Government".[25] The general view is that the Minister and PCA operate on different levels and therefore they are generally compatible.

A complaint can be made only by a person claiming to have suffered injustice as a result of maladministration. The complaint must be made by the aggrieved person or, if he is deceased, by his legal representative.[26] Although the complainant need not be a British citizen, there is a requirement under section 6(4) that the person aggrieved should be resident in the United Kingdom or have been present in the United Kingdom when the action complained of took place. Complaints can be made by individuals (including prisoners and immigrants) and corporate bodies but not by bodies such as local authorities or nationalised industries.

Screening a complaint takes up most of the time in an investigation and 7–09 in order to speed this up, the PCA has appointed a Director of Screening.[27] The Director decides what further information is needed from either the M.P. or the complainant before any decision is made as regards the commencement of an investigation. If the complaint lies outwith the jurisdiction of the PCA, the Director may advise the M.P. if redress is possible elsewhere. In any case the PCA is required to give the M.P. a statement of reasons for refusing to start an investigation.[28] The Director will now deal directly with the complainant thus speeding up the process.[29] The target time for the screening process is three weeks.[30]

Section 5(3) gives the PCA discretion on whether to pursue a complaint and which issues to investigate. This was recognised in one of the few cases involving the PCA to come to court. In *R. v. Parliamentary Commissioner for Administration, ex parte Dyer*[31] the court upheld the right of the PCA to decide which aspects of Ms Dyer's complaint to investigate.

---

[24] Rawlings, "The MPs Complaints Service" (1990) 53 M.L.R., 22 and 149.
[25] Wade and Forsyth, *Administrative Law* (1994), at p. 83.
[26] 1967 Act, s. 6(2).
[27] PCA Annual Report (1994 H.C. 307), para. 19.
[28] Contrast this with the Health Service Commissioner who sends a statement of reasons to the complainant and the body complained against.
[29] For a fuller account of how a complaint is handled, see PCA's Management Plan 1992/93–1994/5, paras. 1.6–9.
[30] Annual Report of PCA (1994 H.C. 307), App. B.
[31] [1994] 1 W.L.R. 621.

7–10   There are no legal means to compel the PCA to investigate if he declines to do so[32] and this was confirmed by the House of Lords in 1970.[33] However, the PCA may not act on his own initiative, a source of regret to previous Commissioners[34]; indeed, an M.P. cannot ask the PCA to investigate an issue if there has been no written complaint from a member of the public. The select committee recommended that the PCA be given the power to investigate a department where it appeared that it was not carrying out its administrative duties properly.[35] This proposal was rejected by the government on the grounds that it was unnecessary and would detract the PCA from considering the complaints of individuals.

There is a time-limit for complaints. According to section 6(3) a complaint has to be made to the M.P. within 12 months of the complainant having notice of the matter which is the subject of the complaint. However the PCA does have some discretion in allowing a complaint which is technically out of time.

7–11   When the PCA has decided to conduct an investigation, he has to inform the department or body concerned in the complaint and the person who is alleged to have committed the act complained of. He has to allow them to comment on any allegations in the complaint.[36] This can lead to delays in commencing the investigation although there is an expectation that departments will comment initially within six weeks.[37]

The PCA can be very effective in looking behind the scenes at the workings of the department under investigation. One important implication is that the PCA does not have to be satisfied with an answer from a Minister as an M.P. would have to be. The PCA has the authority to call for written and oral evidence from officials and even from Ministers and he may examine departmental files; he can in fact ask questions which individual M.P.s would be unable to ask. A Minister may not veto an investigation and officials cannot hide behind public interest immunity. The investigation is however conducted in private with no publicity. Section 8 of the Act gives the PCA the same authority as a superior court to obtain evidence and wilful obstruction of the PCA is punishable as in contempt proceedings.[38] His reports are protected by absolute privilege.

7–12   After an investigation is completed, a report is sent to the M.P. and to the head of the department or authority since they must be given an opportunity to comment on the findings.[39] There is no requirement for the

[32] 1967 Act, s. 5(5).
[33] *Re Fletcher's Application* [1970] 2 All E.R. 527.
[34] Annual Report 1983, para. 8.
[35] Select Committee Report (1978 H.C. 615).
[36] 1967 Act, s. 7(1).
[37] Seneviratne, *op. cit.*, n. 5, above, p. 36.
[38] 1967 Act, s. 9(1).
[39] *ibid.* s. 7(1).

complainant to see a copy of the report for comment; this was confirmed in
Dyer[40] where the applicant argued that she should have been given an
opportunity to comment on the draft report. The court, however, rejected
her arguments, saying that it was the department which had to point out
inaccuracies since they might have to justify their actions publicly before
the select committee. Another reason for non-disclosure to the complainant
is the possibility of the inclusion of secret material in the draft report which
would have to be removed before the final report. This appears to put the
Government in a stronger position regarding the secrecy of information in
their dealings with the PCA as compared to their position with the courts.[41]

Unlike some ombudsmen,[42] the PCA has no direct legal powers to enforce   7–13
his findings. He may recommend remedial action, including the award of
compensation. Any compensation awarded is invariably granted on an *ex
gratia* basis, with no legal right being accorded to the complainant. The
PCA's recommendations are not binding and the department may indeed
ignore them. He may lay a special report before both Houses of Parliament
and the select committee may then require the principal officer of the
department to explain why the recommendations have been ignored.
However, if the department still resists (albeit a most unusual occurrence)
nothing else can be done to enforce compliance. The select committee is
the body which is able to hold government to account by subjecting senior
civil servants to public questioning of the actions which led to the finding
of maladministration; this appears in most cases to have the effect of
encouraging the department to make some sort of compromise.

REMIT OF THE PCA

The PCA cannot investigate a case where there is still a remedy through   7–14
either the courts or a tribunal.[43] There is an exception, however, where the
PCA is satisfied that it is unreasonable to expect the complainant to resort
to the legal remedy.[44]

Sometimes there will be an overlap between the PCA and the courts. In
Congreve v. Home Office[45] the PCA investigated the complaint at the same
time as legal action was being taken. It appears that there was some doubt
in the PCA's mind as to whether the complainant had legal redress and so
the complaint was investigated until the matter became clearer. The PCA

---

[40] [1994] 1 W.L.R. 621.
[41] Marsh, "The Extent and Depth of Judicial Review decisions of PCA" 1994 P.L. 347.
[42] For instance the Commissioner for Complaints in N. Ireland.
[43] 1967 Act, s. 5(2)(a) and (b).
[44] *ibid.* proviso to s. 5(2).
[45] [1976] 1 All E.R. 697.

subsequently criticised the action of the Home Office in a special report[46] although he found no injustice caused by maladministration.[47]

7–15   The bodies now included in the jurisdiction of the PCA are set out in Schedule 1 to the 1987 Act, whilst specific exclusions of jurisdiction are stated in Schedule 3 to the 1967 Act. The list of included bodies may be amended by means of an Order in Council[48] and a newly created body must be specifically brought within the PCA's jurisdiction. His general jurisdiction is similar to that of an M.P. holding a body to account through Ministerial responsibility.

Schedule 2 to the 1967 Act included all the major government departments and some other bodies. The Parliamentary and Health Service Commissioners Act 1987, Schedule 1, extended the PCA's remit to over 100 departments and non-departmental bodies such as the Royal Mint, the Arts Council, the Horse Race Betting Levy Board, the British Library and the Equal Opportunities Commission. More recently, the Rail Regulator and the Director General of the National Lottery were added to the list. Broadly speaking, a body will be included if it acts on behalf of the Crown, or it is established by means of the Royal Prerogative, or it receives at least 50 per cent of its finances from Parliament. Advisory bodies and tribunals are not included, although the Parliamentary Commissioner Act 1994 extended jurisdiction to the administrative functions of tribunal staff.

7–16   Schedule 3 gives the exclusions from the jurisdiction of the PCA. He may not investigate matters such as actions involving foreign relations or actions taken outside the United Kingdom by an officer acting under the authority of the Crown; actions regarding the investigation of crime or the protection of the security of the State; commencement or conduct of civil or criminal proceedings; the exercise of the Royal Prerogative of mercy; contractual or commercial transactions by central government[49]; personnel matters in the civil service or armed forces[50]; or the grant of honours.

It can be difficult to know whether a body or department is excluded from or included in the PCA's remit. The Select Committee on the Parliamentary Commissioner commented "we believe that in principle all areas of government administration should be investigatable by him (the ombudsman) unless in particular cases a compelling argument can be made out for their exclusion".[51] The Government, however, felt that listing all the

---

[46] (1974–75 H.C. 680).

[47] For discussion, see Brown, "The Ombudsman" in Richardson and Genn, *Administrative Law and Government Action* (1994).

[48] 1967 Act, s. 4.

[49] This exclusion has caused much controversy — see Birkinshaw, *Grievances, Remedies and the State* (1994), at pp. 198–201.

[50] Note that personnel matters are not excluded from the jurisdiction of the PCA for N. Ireland or the Commissioner for Complaints.

[51] Fourth Report of Select Committee (1979–80 H.C. 593), para. 8.

excluded bodies would be more complex than listing only the included bodies. The PCA's jurisdiction now extends to the "Next Steps" agencies[52] although there is an anomalous position regarding court administration staff in Scotland. Such staff in England and Wales are now included in an executive agency and within the PCA's jurisdiction whereas in Scotland the agency staff are still excluded. The Government's reason for the exclusion is that these staff are accountable to the Scottish judiciary.[53] In his 1994 Report, the PCA criticised the Government's practice of establishing a charity to distribute government money since this has the effect of removing that area of administrative activity from his jurisdiction. "It sits oddly beside the government's assurances, referred to in my Annual Reports for 1992 and 1993, that the growth of executive agencies, 'market testing', 'contracting out' or 'competing for quality' would not affect my jurisdiction."[54]

The decisions of Ministers may also be investigated and ultimately 7–17 criticised by the PCA. Two examples of such criticism of Ministers were the *Sachsenhausen* case[55] where the Foreign Secretary was criticised and the *Court Line* case[56] where the Secretary of State for Industry was criticised for giving misleading information.

The PCA can investigate the procedures in setting up a public inquiry, how it was held and how the inspector compiled his report but the merits of the decision are outwith his jurisdiction.[57] In 1974, the PCA investigated the inquiry into the construction of a new runway at Edinburgh airport[58] and criticised aspects of the procedure in his report. However, while he was investigating the runway was constructed. This illustrates a problem associated with an investigation by the PCA; while he is investigating, the department or body under investigation may continue to act as it had previously decided.

DEFINITION OF MALADMINISTRATION

The term "maladministration" is found in sections 5(1)(a) and 10(3) of the 7–18 1967 Act but is nowhere defined. In the second reading debate on the Bill, Richard Crossman attempted to define the term; the "Crossman catalogue",

---

[52] Report of Select Committee (1993), p. xii.
[53] Fifth Report of the Select Committee (1993–94 H.C. 619), para. 19.
[54] Annual Report (1994 H.C. 307), para. 26, referring to the Independent Living Fund and DSS.
[55] PCA Special Report (1967 H.C. 54).
[56] Statements made by the Ministers misled travellers to suppose that a travel firm was sound financially; Special Report (1974–75, H.C. 498).
[57] Bradley, "Ombudsmen and the Protection of Citizens' Rights" in Caidon (ed.), *op. cit.*, n. 16, above.
[58] First Report of PCA (1974 H.C. 2), p. 140.

as it is often called, includes terms like bias, neglect, inattention, delay, incompetence, ineptitude, perversity, turpitude and arbitrariness. The Government deliberately did not define the term in the Act so that there would be no limitation on the term's potential development. In the debates, the view was expressed that the term would be "filled out by the practical processes of casework"[59] and this indeed appears to have occurred. The term implies an element of injustice to the extent that if there is a finding of maladministration without injustice, the department will not be required to take any further action. Maladministration has nothing to do with the nature, quality or reasonableness of a decision and generally the PCA will not examine the merits of a decision or the policies which underlie it, except in the circumstances discussed later.

Justice in their 1977 Report suggested a wider description of the term to include investigation of any "unreasonable, unjust or oppressive action".[60] The definition was not accepted but in 1993 the PCA updated and further defined maladministration to include rudeness, unwillingness to treat a complainant as a person with rights, refusal to answer reasonable questions, knowingly giving misleading or inaccurate advice, refusal to notify a person of a right of appeal, failure by the management to monitor compliance with adequate procedures and strict adherence to the letter of the law thus causing hardship.[61] The courts have also recognised the open-ended nature of the term as evidenced by Lord Denning's discussion in *R. v. Local Commissioner for Administration, ex parte Bradford MCC.*[62]

7–19	It was clearly the intention of Parliament that the PCA was to be confined to investigating procedural matters rather than substantive issues.[63] So if a discretionary decision is taken and errors are made in the administrative procedures leading to the decision, the PCA would be justified in finding maladministration. An example of this occurred in the *Sachsenhausen* case in 1967.[64] This concerned 12 victims of Nazi persecution who had been denied compensation by the Foreign Office in accordance with their rules of distribution. The PCA found there were many procedural defects which had led to the reputations of the claimants being damaged. The Foreign Secretary protested that the principle of Ministerial responsibility was being eroded by the investigation but the select committee stressed that Ministers were meant to be subjected to examination and criticism.[65]

[59] *Hansard*, H.C. Vol. 734, cols. 51–52 (1966–67).
[60] Justice, "Our Fettered Ombudsman" (1977).
[61] Report of Select Committee, Minutes of Evidence (1992–93 H.C. 650i), p. 4.
[62] [1979] Q.B. 287.
[63] 1967 Act, s. 12(3).
[64] PCA Special Report (1967 H.C. 54).
[65] (1967–68 H.C. 258), para. 13–16.

The first PCA declined to investigate matters which introduced questions 7–20
on the merits of a decision; he interpreted section 12(3) strictly by confining
his investigations to the procedures by which decisions are made. He felt
unable to question the quality of a decision. The select committee encouraged
him in their second report[66] to interpret his remit so as to include the so-
called "bad decision" and "bad rule". A bad decision was defined as one
"which, judged by its effect on the aggrieved person appears to be thoroughly
bad in quality, he might infer from the quality of the decision itself that
there had been an element of maladministration in the taking of it and ask
for its review".[67] Wade and Forsyth define it thus: "Bad decisions are bad
administration and bad administration is maladministration."[68] The select
committee considered that the bad rule occurred where injustice and hardship
are occasioned despite the fact that the administrative rules have been
properly applied.[69] Maladministration could be inferred from a failure to
consider the adequacy and appropriateness of the rule in question. Following
this report, the PCA accepted the recommendations but has continued to
treat them carefully to ensure that he does not undermine the terms of section
12(3) and so extend his discretionary powers. However as Bradley says:
"The British Ombudsman has developed principles, standards and rules
that he believes to constitute good administration, since otherwise, no notion
of maladministration could have emerged — it may not be pressing analogy
too far to conclude that the individual citizen thus acquires what may be
properly called new rights to the maintenance of a certain quality of
administration."[70]

WORKLOAD OF THE PCA

The PCA is ancillary to M.P.s and this has an effect on his workload. The 7–21
M.P. sees the complaint first and may be able to resolve it without recourse
to the PCA. The majority of complaints made to M.P.s are resolved by
means of parliamentary questions, letters and so on.

The PCA in fact receives only about 1,300 complaints each year[71]
although this is an increasing figure. In 1994, 60 per cent of the complaints
were rejected as falling outwith the jurisdiction of the PCA. About 38 per
cent of these did not concern administrative action and 25 per cent still had

---

[66] (1967–68 H.C. 350).
[67] (1967–68 H.C. 258), para. 14.
[68] Wade and Forsyth, *op. cit.*, n. 25, above, p. 90.
[69] (1967–68 H.C. 258), para. 17.
[70] Bradley, "Role of the Ombudsman in relation to the protection of the citizen's rights"
(1980) 39(2) C.L.J., pp. 304–332.
[71] It was originally thought that the PCA would receive between 6,000 and 7,000 complaints
each year. Compare this with the Swedish Ombudsman who receives around 4,000
complaints each year from a population of 8 million.

the right of appeal to a tribunal. This high proportion of cases falling outwith the PCA's jurisdiction suggests either that M.P.s do not fully understand the extent of that jurisdiction or, perhaps more cynically, that they refer "no-hope" cases to the PCA to get difficult constituents "off their backs".[72] There is also a problem in that many people do not understand the PCA's jurisdiction. The PCA is aware of this and recently published a leaflet explaining his role and functions.

However, of the small number of complaints investigated, around 90 per cent are found to be justified. Most complaints concern the DSS and Inland Revenue and their associated agencies; their combined share averages 47 per cent of the annual complaints.

7–22   According to his 1994 Annual Report, an investigation by the PCA takes on average 70 weeks to complete. This, of course, is one of the main reasons why M.P.s do not refer more cases to the PCA.[73] The PCA has responded to the issue of delay in completing his investigations by reporting in 1993 that where a department offers immediate redress to a complainant after the approach by the PCA, he will pass the information on immediately to the M.P.. Thus, the complainant may receive redress well in advance of the completion of the formal investigation.[74] The PCA has also set himself a target of nine months for completion of an investigation.[75]

7–23   The longest and most detailed report produced by the PCA concerned the so-called Barlow Clowes Affair in 1989. The Barlow Clowes companies collapsed in 1988, leaving many elderly people without their savings. Many had thought they were investing in government stocks which are normally a safe and tax-efficient method of investment. Around one-quarter of all M.P.s received complaints from some 18,000 savers who were affected by the collapse and 12 M.P.s referred the matter to the PCA. Barlow Clowes had been set up in the 1970s; at that time, the Department of Trade and Industry were required by the Prevention of Fraud (Investments) Act 1958 to perform a regulatory function by surveillance and the issuing of licences. Under its discretionary powers the DTI allowed the company to operate for 10 years without a licence. In 1984 the company applied for a licence and the DTI then tried to bring it within the regulatory framework. A licence was granted in 1985 and this was renewed for the next two years. The existence of a partnership operating in Jersey came to light and the licence was withdrawn. The Jersey firm was significantly involved in the fraud which was discovered

---

[72] For discussion of reasons, see Drewry and Harlow, *op. cit.*, n. 20, above.

[73] Mays, "Twenty-five Years of the Ombudsman" (1992) 195 SCOLAG 185; see also the results of the questionnaire survey by the select committee where 54.3% of M.P.s stated that they "never" or "hardly ever" read PCA reports ((1993–94, H.C. 33–I), para.25); Rawlings, *op. cit.*, n. 24, above.

[74] Select Committee Report on Powers, Functions and Jurisdiction of PCA, Vol. I (1993–94, H.C. 33–I), p. viii.

[75] Annual Report 1994, App. B.

shortly after. The PCA found substantial maladministration in five crucial areas.[76] The Government rejected most of the criticisms of the DTI but agreed to pay *ex gratia* payments of almost £150 million.[77]

As well as reporting on the outcomes of complaints made to him, the PCA also reports on examples of good administration and practice he has found in the course of his investigations and, of course, matters of concern to which he wishes attention to be drawn. The Government has agreed that it will circulate epitomes of the PCA's reports to all government departments so that civil servants are aware of his work.[78]

Recent Developments

The PCA is accountable to the House and in particular to the select 7–24 committee which considers his reports. However, the PCA has also been held to be accountable to the courts by way of judicial review. This was confirmed by the *Dyer* case[79] where Simon-Brown L.J. referred to the recognition of jurisdiction of the Local Ombudsman in the *Eastleigh* case[80] and said that the involvement of Parliament in the PCA scheme would not necessarily mean that the PCA was in a different position from the local commissioners.

Although the scheme is still used by only a relatively small number of citizens each year, the number of complaints made to the PCA is growing[81] and as the number of complaints increases so does the expertise of the office. One particular aspect which deserves mention is the development by the PCA of the right to official advice. The number of cases involving advice given by government departments now accounts for around 20 per cent of the studies published by the PCA in his selected case reports. The citizen has a right to advice and information,[82] including factual information (as in leaflets, etc.) and opinions given by officials. The citizen must have relied or acted upon the advice and suffered injustice as a result, injustice being equated with direct financial disadvantage. However, before relying on the

---

[76] For discussion see Wade and Forsyth, *op. cit.,* n. 25, above, p. 99.

[77] (1989–90 H.C. 76).

[78] Fifth Report from Select Committee (1993–94 H.C. 619), paras. 13–15. Note that the Government has published a pamphlet called "The Ombudsman in your files" to assist civil servants who may come under investigation by the PCA.

[79] [1994] 1 W.L.R. 621.

[80] *R. v. Local Commissioner for Administration for the South, the West, West Midlands, Leicestershire, Lincolnshire and Cambridgeshire, ex p. Eastleigh Borough Council* [1988] Q.B. 855.

[81] For instance, see figures quoted by the PCA in evidence to the select committee (1993–94 H.C. 33–II), at p. 27.

[82] For instance, the report of the complaint against DHSS C573/84 (1984–85 H.C. 150).

right to advice, the citizen must have stated all the facts relating to his inquiry and must have sought the advice at the earliest opportunity.[83]

7–25   Access to information is a further development of the PCA's role in grievance procedures. The PCA is responsible for investigating the complaints of breaches of the Code of Practice on Access to Government Information.[84] The code is discussed more fully in Chapter 6. The PCA has, of course, often investigated complaints made about the failure of departments to provide information.[85] Interestingly this major extension of the PCA's jurisdiction, which led to his staff complement being increased by 14, is wholly extra-statutory.

The Citizen's Charter[86] is another new development in which the PCA has involvement. In fact, if the charter succeeds in one of its main thrusts, namely to provide effective grievance remedies within the bodies covered by the charter, then it is conceivable that the PCA may become redundant.[87] The select committee examined the relationship between the PCA and the charter in 1992[88], concluding that the internal resolution of complaints was complementary to the external investigation provided by the PCA. The select committee was adamant that there should be no expectation of the internal mechanism being exhausted before the PCA can become involved.[89] However, the PCA has said that the "general strengthening of internal complaints procedures" has reinforced his view that the complainant should first complain to the department before approaching him. He feels that such internal inquiry would provide more evidence for him in his investigations.[90] The PCA has welcomed the charter as giving him further publicity to his office and in his 1993 Annual Report[91] he stated how he would approach a failure to meet charter targets. He distinguishes between a target as a promise and as an indicator of performance. A failure to meet the former may justify an award of compensation whereas a failure to meet the latter does not necessarily mean that compensation is justified.[92]

7–26   The Citizen's Charter also envisages the use of lay adjudicators to provide an external complaint mechanism for dissatisfied citizens.[93] The select

[83] Mowbray, "A Right to Official Advice: the Parliamentary Commissioner's Perspective" (1990) P.L. 68.
[84] Code came into operation in April 1994. The PCA's first report was (1994–95 H.C. 14).
[85] See, for instance, (1992–93 H.C. 947) where PCA found maladministration in the MAFF's "lack of frankness" regarding their explanation of the rights of farmers regarding salmonella in chicken flocks.
[86] *The Citizen's Charter: Raising the Standard*, Cm. 1599 (1991).
[87] Birkinshaw, *op. cit.,* n. 49, above, pp.191–2.
[88] Select Committee on PCA (1991–92 H.C. 158).
[89] Note, however, that the Local Government Ombudsmen insist that a complaint is made to the appropriate body first.
[90] Annual Report (1994 H.C. 307), para. 23.
[91] (1993–94, H.C. 290), para. 6.
[92] Birkinshaw, *op. cit.,* n. 49, above, p. 192.
[93] Seneviratne, *op. cit.*, n. 5, above, p. 55.

committee recommended that such adjudicators should be advisory only and where a speedy resolution was unlikely, the matter should be referred to the PCA.[94] The use of lay adjudicators has not at the date of writing been implemented.

LOCAL GOVERNMENT OMBUDSMAN

Correctly called the Commissioner for Local Administration in Scotland, 7–27 the office was created by the Local Government (Scotland) Act 1975 as amended by the Scottish Legal Services Ombudsman and Commissioner for Local Administration in Scotland Act 1997. The main role of the Local Government Ombudsman (LGO) is to consider complaints of injustice arising from maladministration by local authorities, licensing boards and various joint boards and committees. In addition, he may consider complaints on housing matters against Scottish Homes in their capacity as landlords. The 1997 Act extends the LGO's jurisdiction to enable him to investigate complaints against a member or officer of an authority.[95] The LGO is appointed by the Crown on the recommendation of the Secretary of State for Scotland[96] and can be removed from office only on the grounds of misbehaviour or incapacity or on reaching the age of 65.[97]

Originally, complaints had to be made through a local councillor — a filter system — but in 1988 this requirement was dropped.[98] However, the LGO does require that the local authority has had an opportunity to investigate the complaint before it is accepted for investigation. The abolition of the filter system has resulted in an increase in the number of complaints received by the LGO. There is, like the PCA scheme, a time-limit of 12 months but this can be waived in exceptional circumstances. The LGO also has the power to demand information from local authorities.[99] This power had to be given by Parliament after a decision of the Divisional Court of the Queen's Bench Division in England and Wales interpreted the LGO's powers restrictively.[1]

On receipt of a complaint the LGO decides whether he has jurisdiction. 7–28 The complaint must be made by the person aggrieved but no complaints may be made by a local authority or body which is funded wholly or mainly from moneys provided by Parliament.[2] This is to prevent one local authority from using the LGO to protest about action taken by another. As with the

---

[94] Select Committee Report (1992 H.C. 158).
[95] 1997 Act, s. 7(1).
[96] Local Government (Scotland) Act 1975, s. 21.
[97] *ibid*. s. 21(3).
[98] Local Government Act 1988, Sched. 3, para. 13.
[99] Local Government, Planning and Land Act 1980, s. 184.
[1] *Re a complaint against Liverpool C.C.* [1977] 2 All E.R. 650.
[2] 1975 Act, s. 25.

PCA, the LGO may not investigate a complaint if there is still a remedy available by means of an appeal to a tribunal, a Minister or official, or a court.[3] He may not investigate matters which involve most or all of the inhabitants of the local authority area or matters listed in Schedule 5 to the 1975 Act. These include matters regarding civil or criminal proceedings in court; matters of a contractual or commercial nature; and matters involving personnel issues. Once a complaint is judged to be within the LGO's jurisdiction it is then referred to the local authority so that they can respond to the allegations made against them. When a response is received the LGO will decide whether to proceed to a formal investigation.

The number of investigations which proceed past this point is very small; in 1994–95 there were 1,002 complaints, of which 556 were sent to the local authority but where only 13 became formal investigations.[4] Around 20 per cent of the cases sent to the local authorities for comment were settled by the authorities with no further action required by the LGO. In the rest of the cases sent to the local authorities the LGO found that the explanation of the local authorities disclosed no maladministration and he took no further action. The LGO is somewhat speedier than his parliamentary counterpart; the average length of time from commencing a formal investigation to issuing a report is less than six months.[5]

7–29   If the LGO finds injustice caused by maladministration, his ability to provide a remedy is no more effective than that of the PCA. He is unable to force the local authority to adopt his recommendations. He can only issue another report against the council[6] expressing dissatisfaction and calling upon them to remedy the complaint. If the local authority still fails to do so, the LGO may require the council to publish in the local press a statement detailing the circumstances of the complaint and the outcome.[7] The LGO may also require the full Council to consider an adverse report on which the local authority proposes to take no action. It appears that the local authorities are more resistant to the recommendations of the LGO than are government departments to those of the PCA.

The largest group of complaints relates to housing matters (33 per cent) of which 25 per cent of complaints now relate to anti-social behaviour.[8] Complaints on planning matters and land and property issues account for the majority of other cases.

---

[3]   1975 Act, s. 24(6).
[4]   Annual Report 1994–95, p. 14.
[5]   *ibid.* p. 15.
[6]   1975 Act, s. 29, as amended by the Local Government and Housing Act 1989, s. 27.
[7]   Local Government and Housing Act 1989, s. 27.
[8]   Annual Report 1994–95, pp. 12–15.

SCOTTISH LEGAL SERVICES OMBUDSMAN

The Scottish Legal Services Ombudsman (SLSO) was created by the Law   7–30
Reform (Miscellaneous Provisions)(Scotland) Act 1990 to replace the office
of Lay Observer, which had been in existence since 1976. The Lay Observer
had been created to examine allegations of mishandling, by the Law Society
of Scotland, of complaints made by the public regarding the conduct of
solicitors. The Lay Observer started his investigations only when the Law
Society had completed theirs. The Lay Observer had the power to require
production of files and would make observations on the handling of the
case by the Law Society; the Law Society, however, were not obliged to
follow any of the recommendations.

The 1990 Act extended the remit of the Lay Observer to encompass
complaints handled by the Faculty of Advocates and the Scottish
Conveyancing and Executry Services Board (also created by the 1990 Act).[9]
The title of the office was changed to Scottish Legal Services Ombudsman
to reflect the increased jurisdiction. The SLSO is an interesting example of
a "hybrid" ombudsman; the office was set up by statute to regulate the
operation of the private sector. The 1990 Act was amended by the Scottish
Legal Services Ombudsman and Commissioner for Local Administration
in Scotland Act 1997.

The SLSO is a lay person appointed by the Secretary of State for Scotland   7–31
in consultation with the Lord President of the Court of Session.[10] His remit is
to investigate complaints made to him about the way in which the professional
body has handled a complaint about one of its members. He does not
act as an appeal from the findings of the professional body and he does
not act as a conciliator between the complainant and the member of the
professional body. He reviews the actions of the professional body and
reports on whether they acted properly in handling the complaint. "The
ombudsman is concerned with the treatment by the professional body of
the complaint, ie whether the investigation by the professional body has
been fair and thorough, whether all the relevant heads of complaint have
been properly addressed and whether appropriate action has been taken."[11]
The report is made to the complainant and the professional body but the
SLSO has no powers of enforcement. He may take a case directly to
the Scottish Solicitors' Discipline Tribunal, but this is a significant power
he has not as yet exercised.

---

[9] The operation of the SCESB was suspended in 1992 because of the economic recession and before it had licensed any practitioners. It was reinstated in June 1996 and the first practitioners were licensed in 1997.
[10] 1990 Act, s. 34(1).
[11] Annual Report (1994 H.C. 377), p. iii.

7–32   An error in the 1990 legislation caused difficulties for the SLSO in the early years of office. There were no transitional arrangements in the Act and so all those complaints submitted before the office came into existence were excluded from his investigation.[12] This resulted in a substantial number of cases being dropped, to the consternation of the complainants.[13] The same mistake has not been made in the 1997 Act where transitional arrangements are in place.

The caseload of the SLSO is between 200–250 cases each year, a similar number to his predecessor, the Lay Observer. Around a third of the complaints are outside his jurisdiction. Most cases concern conveyancing matters; the complaints made are usually concerned with failure to communicate and delay.[14] Written complaints are made directly to the SLSO; there is no filter mechanism as in the PCA scheme. However, complaints about a solicitor or advocate must be made to the professional body first and the complaints made to the SLSO will concern how the professional body dealt with the complaint about their member; the SLSO does not consider the substance of the original complaint. The complaint to the SLSO must be made within six months of notification of the decision of the professional body. The SLSO may decide not to investigate a complaint or to discontinue an investigation; in these circumstances he must notify the complainant and the professional body concerned, giving his reasoned decision.[15] Although the SLSO cannot normally investigate a complaint until after the professional organisation has completed its investigation, there are occasions when he may intervene, for instance, if the professional body has failed to start its investigation, or has not completed its investigation in reasonable time, or the ombudsman considers that an investigation by him is justified even though the professional body is conducting an investigation. Once the SLSO has started an investigation, he may require the professional body "(a) to provide him with such information, being information which is within the knowledge of the professional organisation, as he considers relevant to his investigation; or (b) to produce to him such documents, being documents which are within the possession or control of the organisation, as he considers relevant to his investigation".[16]

7–33   Originally the SLSO had no power to compel production of material; this contrasted with the Legal Services Ombudsman in England and Wales who was given similar powers to the PCA to require production of documents. The reason for the original difference in powers lay in the different investigatory practices of the Law Society of Scotland and

---

[12] Scottish Legal Services Ombudsman General Directions 1993, para. 4.
[13] Discussed in the Second Annual Report (1992).
[14] Fourth Annual Report (1994–95 H.C. 377), App. 2.
[15] 1990 Act, s. 34(1C) and (1D).
[16] *ibid.* s. 34 (2A), as amended by the 1997 Act.

the Solicitors Complaints Bureau. The former had the solicitor's files whilst the latter did not always require the files to be produced. The 1997 Act resolved this anomaly.

Another major difference between the SLSO and the Legal Services Ombudsman was in respect of their powers to make recommendations. Any recommendation made by the SLSO, whether remedial in nature or procedural, could be disregarded by the professional body concerned. On the other hand, the Legal Services Ombudsman could make procedural recommendations which the professional body was under a duty to consider or he might make remedial recommendations requiring the professional body to reconsider the complaint, or requiring the body or the member complained of to pay compensation of up to £1,000, or requiring the body to take further action against the member. The 1997 Act again removed these differences between the two ombudsmen and the SLSO now has the same powers as the Legal Services Ombudsman.[17]

The SLSO now has formal enforcement powers; he has power to require   7–34 a professional body which has not complied with his recommendations within three months to publicise the failure and the reasons for it. He has no binding power of enforcement for this power but if it is not done, he may publicise the matter, charging the professional body for any expenses so incurred.[18]

Like most ombudsmen, the SLSO has some successes; for instance, in his Second Annual Report the SLSO recommended that the number of lay members on complaints committees should be increased from two to three.[19] The SLSO makes recommendations to professional bodies on improving their services, for instance he has recommended the establishment of a help line to assist and provide information.[20] The 1997 Act inserts a new section 34A into the 1990 Act; this concerns the recommendations which the SLSO may make to a professional body regarding its procedures for dealing with conduct complaints. The professional organisation is under a duty to consider the recommendation and inform the ombudsman of its considerations and actions taken. The SLSO may also report to the Secretary of State at any time on any matter relating to the discharge of his functions. The Law Society was criticised in the 1994 report in around one-third of the cases considered by the SLSO. His main criticisms concerned inadequate investigation or inadequate consideration. Of the 31 cases so criticised, the Law Society accepted or took further action in 25 cases, took no action in four and had not responded in the remaining two.[21]

---

[17]   1997 Act, s. 2.
[18]   *ibid.* s. 23(8)–(10).
[19]   Second Annual Report (1992).
[20]   Fourth Annual Report (1994), p. 1.
[21]   *ibid.* App. 2.

CHAPTER 8

TRIBUNALS AND INQUIRIES

8–01 Tribunals and inquiries are important features of the British administrative law system. They offer redress to individuals who have been aggrieved by government or administrative action but they are quite distinct from each other. Tribunals are concerned with ascertaining facts, applying legal rules to those facts and finally making a binding decision. Inquiries also ascertain facts but instead of making a decision, the inquiry makes recommendations to a Minister regarding a matter of policy. The tribunal is judicial in nature whereas the inquiry is administrative. The inquiry exists to allow citizens an opportunity to put forward their objections and give them a fair hearing before a decision is made. Tribunals are defined by statute and have a permanent existence, whereas inquiries are established or convened as needed or the law requires. This was summed up by the Council on Tribunals: "Tribunals, generally speaking, exercise an independent jurisdiction: they decide particular cases by applying rules and regulations and sometimes by using their own discretion. Inquiries, on the other hand, form part of a process by which a minister exercises his discretion — a discretion for which he is answerable to Parliament."[1]

TRIBUNALS

8–02 As the State becomes involved in more and more areas of our lives disputes inevitably arise from the application of the numerous rules and regulations made by the Executive. These disputes could be settled in the courts but they would clog up an already overcrowded legal system. Alternatively, they could be settled by the government departments or bodies which have responsibility for the regulations.

The problem here was that the bodies would in effect be "policing" themselves. Neither of these options was considered satisfactory, hence the creation of a new machinery to handle these disputes — tribunals. Tribunals are sometimes referred to as "administrative tribunals" but they deal with such a wide variety of disputes, not all of them administrative in nature, that now they are more properly and simply called "tribunals". "Very

---

[1] Council on Tribunals, Second Report, para. 12.

commonly [tribunals] are concerned with the merits of a decision and typically they will be given the task of deciding, as between citizen and state, whether an official has dealt correctly with a claim or application."[2]

There are a number of reasons why tribunals are necessary in modern society. First, the ordinary courts could not cope with the volume of cases likely to arise. For instance, in 1993, tribunals heard over a quarter of a million cases. Secondly, there is often no necessity for the formality encountered in a court, for instance, many tribunals are not bound by the rules of evidence and so may reach their decisions more quickly. However, minimum standards of evidence are maintained to ensure fairness. Thirdly, there may be a need for expert and specialised knowledge which a judge may not have. Members of the panel may therefore be doctors, or trade union officials, or lay persons with a relevant expertise. Fourthly, a tribunal is relatively cheap to set up and operate since it does not need the array of pomp and splendour associated with a court. Fifthly, judges are required to interpret legislation as it is written and are generally unable to take into account the social principles and policies behind the legislation. Tribunals on the other hand are uniquely placed to consider the wider implications of such legislation. Finally, the subject-matter of the dispute may be comparatively "trifling" and so not warrant the use of scarce court resources.[3]

Tribunals are independent adjudicatory bodies set up under statute and 8–03 occasionally by Prerogative, for instance the Criminal Injuries Compensation Board.[4] The term "tribunal" is not defined in legislation but it appears to cover any person or body of persons who have judicial or quasi-judicial functions.[5] Lord Denning described a tribunal hearing as "more in the nature of an inquiry before an investigating body charged with the task of finding out what happened".[6] Tribunals are the primary mechanism provided by Parliament for the resolution of certain grievances between the citizen and the State but a few tribunals also cover disputes between citizen and citizen, for instance, the industrial tribunal. There are around 2,000 different tribunals in the United Kingdom today covering a wide range of topics such as social security appeals, VAT tribunals, immigration adjudicators, disability appeals, child support appeals, special education needs and one found only in Scotland, the children's hearing. Many of the tribunals come under the supervisory control of the Council on Tribunals.

---

[2] Justice-All Souls Report, "Administrative Justice: some necessary reforms" (1988), p. 212.

[3] Genn, "Tribunal Review of Decision-making", in Richardson and Genn, *Administrative Law and Government Action* (1994).

[4] Note that the CICB is now subject to the provisions of the Criminal Injuries Compensation Act 1995.

[5] Jowett, "UK Tribunals — Observations of a Legal Chairman" in (1992) 17 *International Legal Practitioner* 106.

[6] *R. v. National Insurance Commissioner, ex p. Viscusi* [1974] 1 W.L.R. 646.

This section is concerned primarily with tribunals set up under statutory authority and working in the public field. However, it should be noted that there are also "domestic tribunals" which act as the disciplinary committees of private organisations such as trade unions, stewards of the Jockey Club and the General Medical Council.

DEVELOPMENT OF TRIBUNALS

8–04   There were very few tribunals before the twentieth century,[7] most disputes being settled in the courts.

The National Insurance Act 1911 created the Court of Referees which was a tribunal set up to hear appeals from an Umpire. More tribunals followed, but by 1932 there was sufficient disquiet to lead to the setting up of the Donoughmore Committee[8] which considered delegated legislation and the making of judicial or quasi-judicial decisions by Ministers or civil servants. The report made a few positive recommendations including that tribunals should remain.

From the end of the Second World War, tribunals proliferated mainly because of the setting up of the Welfare State. They were seen as necessary for the benefit of the public and to ensure fair treatment by officials. In more recent times, tribunals have also been used to "sanitise" unpopular government measures by providing a system of appeals for changes in benefits to which individuals had been entitled before the changes occurred.[9] Sometimes it seems that tribunals are set up just for the sake of it. For instance, in 1991, the Council on Tribunals criticised the setting up of two new tribunals, the child support tribunal and the disability appeal tribunal, both of which were concerned with social welfare benefits. The Council asked why the jurisdiction of existing tribunals was not extended to include these new ones.[10] However, some rationalisation does occur. In 1964, rent tribunals were set up to decide "reasonable rents" for furnished tenancies. In 1965, rent assessment tribunals were set up to decide "fair rents" for unfurnished tenancies. After continued criticism from the Council on Tribunals, the two were merged in 1980.

8–05   The outcome of the Crichel Down Affair[11] led to the setting up of the Franks Committee[12] to investigate the working of tribunals although it should be noted that Crichel Down was not concerned with either tribunals or

---

[7]   General and Special Commissioners of Income Tax trace their origins back to 1799–1805.
[8]   Report on Ministers' Powers, Cmd. 4060 (1932).
[9]   For discussion, see Prosser, "Poverty, Ideology and Legality: Supplementary Benefit Appeal Tribunals and their predecessors" in (1977) *British Journal of Law and Society* (4) at p. 44.
[10]   Annual Report of Council on Tribunals (1990–91 H.C. 97), para. 3.14.
[11]   See Chap. 3 for discussion.
[12]   Report of the Committee on Administrative Tribunals and Inquiries, Cmnd. 218 (1957).

inquiries. The Franks Committee was limited in its scope in two ways: first, it could not discuss decisions made in the ordinary courts, and secondly, it could discuss only those areas where a decision was reached after a formal statutory procedure. The importance of the report lies in its systematic consideration of tribunals to clarify their place in the system of justice. Franks stated that the tribunals were part of the machinery of justice, not of the administration. "Tribunals are not ordinary courts, but neither are they appendages of government departments."[13] The recommendations contained in the Franks Report were largely implemented by the Tribunals and Inquiries Act 1958, now consolidated into the Tribunals and Inquiries Act 1992. Other parts of the report were implemented by means of changes in administrative procedures.

A recurring theme in the Franks Report was that there were three characteristics of a tribunal — openness, fairness and impartiality.[14] The Council on Tribunals has added other standards — efficiency, expediency and economy.[15] Openness includes knowledge of the essential reasoning behind decisions and publicity of proceedings, while impartiality refers to the freedom of the tribunal from the influence of the government department with which it is associated. However, most tribunals are sponsored by specific government departments and this raises questions of their independence.[16] Fairness refers to the adoption of a clear procedure so that parties know their rights and the case they have to meet. "In short, the procedure should make the tribunals easily accessible to the public; it should be cheap, swift and free from technicality. The whole proceedings should be, and should be seen to be, independent and impartial, and fair to the powerful and the professional, but also to the vulnerable."[17]

WHAT CONSTITUTES A TRIBUNAL ?

The terminology used in describing what constitutes a tribunal can be 8–06
confusing; for instance, the Employment Appeal Tribunal is in fact a superior court of record[18] and in Scotland is presided over by a judge from the Court of Session.[19] Other tribunals are called authorities, commissions, committees and so on. "The label [tribunal] is given to many different kinds of bodies with widely differing functions, and covering a vast range of subject areas

---

[13] *op. cit.,* n. 12 above, para. 40.
[14] *op. cit.,* n. 12, above, para. 23.
[15] Annual Report of Council on Tribunals (1985–86 H.C. 42), para. 2.5.
[16] Partington, "The Future of Tribunals", 1993 *Legal Action* 9.
[17] (1986–87 H.C. 42), para. 2.9.
[18] Industrial Tribunals Act 1996, s. 20(3).
[19] In England and Wales, a judge from the High Court of Justice will preside.

including private as well as public issues."[20] The Government in recent years has increasingly opted to use internal review procedures rather than the traditional tribunals. The appointment of one-person tribunals is also a recent feature. The Pensions Ombudsman, appointed under the Social Security Act 1990, has full adjudicatory and enforcement powers and is subject to the supervision of the Council on Tribunals. The Government said that this ombudsman had the virtues of a tribunal in informality and expeditiousness while having the powers of investigation of an ombudsman. The Council on Tribunals in its 1989–90 Annual Report was unconvinced by this argument, stating that the office as proposed seemed to be dictated by financial considerations rather than good adjudication.[21] The Industrial Tribunals Act 1996 provides that the chairman of an industrial tribunal sitting alone may adjudicate certain categories of cases.[22] The types of cases may be varied by the Secretary of State by means of regulations.

8–07   The courts have ruled on some issues regarding the status of tribunals. In *Pickering v. Liverpool Daily Post and Echo Newspapers Ltd*[23] a mental health review tribunal was held to be exercising judicial powers of State and so the law of contempt applied to its proceedings. The Mental Health Act 1983 had made the tribunal a decision-making body. In a later case, the House of Lords held that the Social Security Commissioners could consider the issue of the legality of regulations made by the Secretary of State instead of having to refer regulations of disputed validity to the courts by way of judicial review.[24] The commissioners are designated a tribunal under the supervision of the Council on Tribunals and the House of Lords rejected an argument that only courts of law had jurisdiction in this kind of issue. Their Lordships stated that the expertise of the commissioners was a resource which should be utilised before a case reached the appellate courts.

The Council on Tribunals objected in its 1988 Report to the use of the word "court" in respect of bodies which were tribunals, for instance the Local Valuation Court was eventually renamed the Valuation Tribunal after its remit was altered.[25]

Most tribunals will have some but not all of the following properties: it will make final, legally enforceable decisions; it will be independent of any department; it will hold a public hearing which is judicial in nature; its members will possess relevant expertise; it will give reasoned decisions;

---

[20]   Genn, *op. cit.,* n. 3, above.
[21]   Annual Report of Council on Tribunals, 1989–90 (1990–91 H.C. 64), para. 2.51.
[22]   s. 4(3).
[23]   [1990] 1 All E.R. 335.
[24]   *Chief Adjudication Officer v. Foster* [1993] 1All E.R. 705.
[25]   The local Valuation Court was held not to be a court for the purposes of contempt proceedings — see *Att.-Gen. v. BBC* [1980] 3 All E.R. 161.

and it will allow an appeal to the Court of Session or High Court of Justice on a point of law.

Those tribunals which are under the direct supervision of the Council on Tribunals are specified in Schedule 1 to the Tribunals and Inquiries Act 1992. Tribunals can be added to the list in Schedule 1 by means of an Order made by the Lord Chancellor or the Lord Advocate.[26] Around 60 tribunals are named at present. Many more are not scheduled and so remain outside the jurisdiction of the Council, for instance the housing benefit review boards.

Attempting to catalogue the different types of tribunals is very difficult. They deal with such varying topics that it is difficult to get more than a few in each topic or category. There have been suggestions that tribunals are either "court-substitute", that is one which is constrained by its parent Act from exercising too much discretion, or "policy-oriented", one which is more flexible and able to take into consideration broader policy issues, such as the Monopolies and Mergers Commission.[27] A policy-oriented tribunal may be an independent administrative agency with the responsibility of making regulations or granting licences, such as the Civil Aviation Authority. A court-substitute tribunal will hear appeals against decisions on welfare benefits or assessments to tax; it will not have the responsibility for making regulations or devising policy but will act as an informal court. Jones[28] refers to "independent review tribunals" which make decisions on the placement of children in schools or the licensing of air services. Using any of these definitions, however, it can be seen that most tribunals will fall somewhere between the two extremes of court-substitute and independent review body. "The place which any particular tribunal may occupy on the spectrum is determined by various factors, deliberate choice, force of circumstances, accidents of history, Parliamentary pressures and, of course, the nature of the issue to be settled."[29]

As well as varying in type, the tribunals vary considerably in workload; for instance, the Social Security Appeal Tribunals deal with over 75,000 cases each year, while the Wireless Telegraphy Tribunal has never been convened.

Most tribunals are set up by statute and their powers and duties are regulated either in the statute itself or in regulations made under the statute. The Council on Tribunals has voiced concern about the growing trend of the Government to establish new tribunals or modify existing ones by subordinate legislation.[30] The Council felt that tribunals should be established

8–08

8–09

---

[26] 1992 Act, s. 13(1), allows Part 1 or Part 2 to be amended by adding tribunals.
[27] Abel-Smith and Stevens, *In Search of Justice: Society and the Legal System* (1968).
[28] Jones, *Garner's Administrative Law* (1989).
[29] Wraith and Hutcheson, *Administrative Tribunals* (1973).
[30] Annual Report of Council on Tribunals 1992–93 (1993–94, H.C. 78), para. 1.36.

by statute since that would be "a clear indication of the independent standing
of the tribunal concerned".[31]

THE FRANKS REPORT

8–10   As discussed above, the Franks Committee was set up as a direct result of
the Crichel Down Affair even though the type of administrative behaviour
criticised in that matter did not come within the committee's remit.
   The committee reported in 1957, clearly stating that tribunals were part
of the machinery for adjudication not of the administration: "Parliament
has deliberately provided for a decision outside and independent of the
Department concerned, either at first instance ... or on appeal from a decision
of a Minister or of an official in a special statutory position ... The intention of
Parliament to provide for the independence of tribunals is clear and
unmistakable."[32]
   The report was the first systematic examination of the work of tribunals
and is remarkable for its clarity. However, the report makes no mention of
an important paradox relating to tribunals. Social welfare matters are sent
before a tribunal because the ordinary courts are expensive, formal and
technical in their procedure. Cases involving planning matters are heard by
a tribunal because of the lack of expertise of the courts. So different
weaknesses in the courts give rise to different reasons for using tribunals.[33]
   The report made a number of recommendations, most of which were
either enacted in the 1958 Act or implemented by changing administrative
procedures. One of the main recommendations was that two Councils on
Tribunals be set up, one for England and Wales and one for Scotland. These
councils would have a general co-ordinating role regarding existing tribunals
and an advisory role in respect of new ones. In the event, one Council on
Tribunals was created with provision for a Scottish Committee to oversee
tribunals with a Scottish dimension.[34]

8–11   Some of the other important recommendations and the Government's
reactions are:
   (a) The chairmen of tribunals should be appointed by the Lord Chancellor
and wing members by the Council. The committee felt that the practice of
Ministers appointing the members could be open to claims of bias and
partiality, and so taking the appointment away from departments would
ensure the independence of the tribunal system.
   The 1992 Act, s. 5, provides that chairmen will be appointed by the
Lord Chancellor directly, or by the Minister concerned from a panel proposed

[31] (1993–94 H.C. 78), para.1.37.
[32] Cmnd. 218, para. 40.
[33] Abel-Smith and Stevens, *op. cit.*, n. 27, above, p. 220.
[34] 1992 Act, ss.1 and 2.

by the Lord Chancellor. Wing members are normally appointed by the Minister. The Council may make general recommendations to the Minister regarding the appointment of members of tribunals and the Minister "shall have regard" to these recommendations.[35] The Minister may not dismiss a member of a Schedule 1 tribunal except with the authority of the Lord President of the Court of Session for tribunals which sit only in Scotland, or the Lord President and Lord Chancellor for tribunals which sit throughout Great Britain.[36]

(b) Chairmen should normally have legal qualifications, particularly in appellate tribunals. This has become the norm for most tribunals.

(c) The procedure in tribunals should be formulated by the Council to ensure an orderly procedure in an informal atmosphere.

Although the Council must be consulted by departments, it has an advisory role only in the formulation of tribunal procedure.

(d) The citizen should be informed of any right to apply to a tribunal and be given information on the case he has to meet.

Generally, this recommendation is now followed by tribunals.

(e) Tribunal hearings should be public except where public security or 8–12 intimate personal or financial details are to be discussed.

Most tribunals are held in public although the public are unlikely to know of their existence. Industrial tribunals are often reported in the press. Some tribunals are always held in private, for instance children's hearings.

(f) Legal representation should normally be allowed.

One of the difficulties in allowing legal representation is that legal aid is not available except in a very few instances. This aspect is considered later in this chapter.

(g) Decisions should be fully reasoned and written notice of the decision sent to the parties as soon as possible.

Section 10 of the 1992 Act provides that a party has to request a reasoned decision when or before the decision is notified. The statement of reasons can be refused or restricted for reasons of national security. The reasons must be "proper, adequate reasons" which are intelligible and deal with the substantial points raised.[37]

(h) Appeals to the Court of Session or High Court of Justice should be allowed on questions of fact, or law, or merits.

Section 11 of the Act limits appeals to questions of law only but the appellant may require the tribunal to state a case to the Court of Session or High Court of Justice.

---

[35] 1992 Act, s. 5(1).
[36] *ibid.* s. 7(1).
[37] *Re Poyser and Mills' Arbitration* [1964] 2 Q.B. 467.

THE COUNCIL ON TRIBUNALS

8–13 The membership of the Council is no less than 10 and no more than 15; in addition, the Parliamentary Commissioner for Administration is an *ex officio* member of both the Council and the Scottish Committee. The members are appointed by the Lord Chancellor and the Lord Advocate. The Scottish Committee consists of two or three members of the Council designated by the Lord Advocate and three or four non-members of the Council appointed by the Lord Advocate.

The principal functions of the Council are detailed in section 1 of the 1992 Act.

The Council must be consulted before procedural rules for any Schedule 1 tribunal are made and before any procedural rules are made by the Lord Chancellor or Lord Advocate regarding a statutory inquiry.[38] The Council must also be consulted before exemption is granted from the requirement in section 12 of the Act to give reasons for decisions. In addition, the Council may make recommendations to Ministers regarding appointments to scheduled tribunals. While the Council's jurisdiction extends to the whole of Great Britain, it has no authority to deal with any matter in respect of which the Parliament of Northern Ireland would have had power to make laws had the Northern Ireland Constitution Act 1973 not been passed.[39]

One of the main functions of the Council is therefore its consultative function regarding primary legislation where new adjudicative bodies are being created or existing tribunals are being altered. A "Code of Practice on Consultation with the Council" was issued by the Council to government departments in 1981 and reissued in 1986.[40] This states that a period of at least four weeks should be given for consultation on routine proposals and six weeks for proposals which involve questions of principle.

8–14 The Council has no power to investigate complaints made in respect of tribunals and is unable to initiate investigations other than those regarding the constitution and working of tribunals. As regards statutory inquiries, the Council has the power to initiate investigations on matters it considers to be of special importance. This incongruous difference in the Council's powers as between tribunals and inquiries was discussed in a special report by the Council on its functions[41] and although the Government appeared generally to accept that changes were required, no legislation has yet been laid before Parliament. [42]

---

[38] 1992 Act s. 1.
[39] *ibid.* s. 1(2).
[40] Annual Report of Council on Tribunals, 1986–87 (1987–88 H.C. 234), App. C.
[41] The Functions of the Council on Tribunals: Special Report, Cmnd. 7805 (1980), para. 5.6.
[42] See Annual Report, 1990–91 (1991–92 H.C. 97), pp. 37–38.

Council members visit scheduled tribunals from time to time to observe and report on their operation.[43] The Council also visits some tribunals which are not within the jurisdiction of Schedule 1, for instance, by agreement members visit the Criminal Injuries Compensation Board and the Parole Board. Visits are not inspections although the Council has stated that if the visit showed that the tribunal was not working properly then the Council would take action to prevent a recurrence of the problem.[44] The Council members are able to visit only a few tribunals each year, usually the major ones and any newly created tribunals. It is open to a tribunal to invite the Council to visit. Members' reports are confidential and not made available to the tribunals.[45]

WHY CHOOSE A TRIBUNAL TO SETTLE A DISPUTE ?

An ordinary court is not always the most suitable forum for the resolution   8–15
of a conflict between private and public interests, particularly one emanating from the application of Ministerial policy. Instead Parliament will offer one of three methods of resolution of a dispute concerning a statutory scheme: a tribunal; a Ministerial decision after a statutory inquiry; or a Ministerial decision using the power of discretion afforded to a Minister. The Justice Report[46] stated that Parliament's choice of a tribunal in preference to a court was not just to prevent an overloading of the courts but also to ensure that tribunals would be "cheap and accessible". Others have commented that the reason for using tribunals rather than courts was based on political and cost considerations more than the belief that it would provide greater access to justice.[47]

The Franks Report stated: "As a matter of general principle, we are firmly of the opinion that a decision should be entrusted to a court rather than a tribunal in the absence of special considerations which make a tribunal more suitable."[48] The special considerations were situations where specialised or expert jurisdiction was appropriate; a more flexible approach was needed; an inquisitorial approach was required; and accessibility, speed, informality and cheapness were needed.

1. Informality

Most tribunals are not bound by complex rules of procedure or evidence.[49]   8–16

---

[43] 1992 Act, s. 1(a).
[44] Annual Report of Council on Tribunals, 1985–86 (1986–87 H.C. 42), para. 6.18.
[45] Foulkes, "The Council on Tribunals: visits policy and practice" (1994) P. L. 564.
[46] Justice-All Souls Report on Administrative Justice, *op. cit.*, n. 2, above, p. 212.
[47] For instance, see Genn, "Tribunals and Informal Justice" (1993) 56 M. L. R. 393.
[48] Cmnd. 218 (1957), para. 38.
[49] *R. v. Deputy Industrial Injuries Commissioner, ex p. Moore* [1965] 1 Q.B. 456.

They may admit hearsay evidence[50] but must adhere to the rules of natural justice. The members of tribunals may use their professional or industrial knowledge to assist them in deciding the case before them. This was acknowledged in *Metropolitan Properties v. Lannon*[51] where Edmund-Davies L.J. remarked that the tribunal members could rely on "their cumulative knowledge and experience of the matter in hand".[52] So a doctor was held able to advise other members of a tribunal of the weight to be given to evidence relating to medical matters.[53]

Tribunals have formal rules based on the Franks criteria of openness, fairness and impartiality. The Tribunals and Inquiries Act 1992, s. 8(1), states that the Council on Tribunals must be consulted wherever procedural rules are being drafted. The Council itself produced *Model Rules of Procedure for Tribunals*[54] in 1991 which were intended to "lead in due course to a degree of uniformity and simplification of the many differing rules governing tribunal procedure".[55]

If tribunals now have formal procedural rules, it may be asked what has happened to the notion of "informality". An analysis of cases disposed of by tribunals suggests that, whilst the procedure is less formal than in a court, the matters being decided by the tribunals are often very complex and require legal expertise. Genn argues that this informality is superficial and decisions have to be reached on "the basis of evidence of the applicant's factual situation within the framework of relevant statutes, regulations and case-law".[56]

2. Cheapness and speed

8–17   A court hearing is a costly affair; apart from the salaries of the judge and fees of legal counsel involved, the court requires premises, security provisions and administrative assistance. A tribunal can be set up relatively cheaply; the members of the tribunal are often unpaid, receiving only expenses and loss of earnings payments. There is less need for expensive court buildings; often a small suite of offices in an office block will suffice. The administrative assistance is usually provided by the relevant department.

The informality of the tribunal system contributes to the speed of the adjudication process. There is, of course, a need in many tribunals to deal speedily with applications; any delay could lead to hardship for the applicant.

---

[50]   The courts have held that hearsay evidence has to be heard with proper safeguards — see *R. v. Hull Prison Board of Visitors, ex p. St Germain (No. 2)* [1979] 1 W.L.R. 1401.

[51]   [1969] 1 Q.B. 577.

[52]   *ibid.* at 603.

[53]   *R. v. Medical Appeal Tribunals, ex p. Hubble* [1958] 2 Q.B. 228.

[54]   Council on Tribunals (1991).

[55]   *op. cit.*, n. 54, above, para. 2.7.

[56]   Genn, *op. cit.*, n. 3, above, p. 273.

For instance, review by a social security appeal tribunal takes an average of 19 weeks from lodging the application to a hearing being convened. While this timescale compares favourably with court proceedings, it is still a long time for an applicant who is living on a small income.

An appeal to a tribunal costs the applicant nothing. Costs are rarely awarded against the losing party and then only if the party has acted unreasonably.[57] The original idea was that the procedures in a tribunal would be so simple and informal that an applicant would be able to conduct their own case. However, it has not quite worked out like that. Research has shown that representation, whether legal or not, will enhance the chance of success of the party.[58] For instance, in the social security appeal tribunal, the research showed that an applicant's chances of success increased from 30 per cent to 48 per cent if he or she were represented. Legal aid is not generally available in tribunals.[59] The Legal Aid Act 1979 provided that the Lord Chancellor can designate a tribunal hearing so that the 'green form' scheme is available. So far only a few tribunals have been so designated, for instance the mental health review tribunals and hearings before Prison Boards of Governors. Assistance by way of representation (ABWOR) is available for hearings before the Parole Board panels considering parole for discretionary life prisoners.[60] The non-availability of legal aid continues to be a major problem, although a number of organisations have developed tribunal expertise to assist their clients (*e.g.* trade unions, CABs). Partington[61] suggests that the new Child Support Appeal Tribunal was created especially to ensure that disputes under the Child Support Act 1991 should not attract legal aid, a certainty if a court procedure had been adopted.

8–18

3. Accessibility

It has been mentioned that tribunals deal with hundreds of thousands of cases every year. If these cases were transferred to the courts, the work of the courts would grind to a halt. Tribunals therefore play an important part in making justice more accessible. This was recognised in the Justice Report: "Parliament's choice of a tribunal in preference to a court has been based on more than a desire to spare the courts from an unsupportable

8–19

---

[57] For instance, in industrial tribunals.

[58] See research described by Genn, *op. cit.*, n. 47, above, p. 393.

[59] There are exceptions such as the Lands Tribunal and Employment Appeals Tribunal but these are presided over by judges of the Supreme Courts and are therefore court-like in their procedure.

[60] This was implemented by the Criminal Justice Act 1991, s. 4, after criticism of the existing procedures by the European Court of Human Rights in *Thynne v. U.K.* [1991] 13 E.H.R.R. 616.

[61] Partington, *op. cit.*, n. 16, above, 9.

burden. The intention has been that tribunals should be cheap and accessible."[62]

Genn[63] argues that Parliament's choice of tribunals as opposed to courts is based on political and cost considerations, not a belief that tribunals will provide greater access to justice. She goes on to argue that the choice was not between an appeal to a court or to a tribunal, but rather a choice between an appeal to a tribunal or no appeal at all.

Accessibility will, however, depend on the type of tribunal. There are over 160 social security appeal tribunals but only 14 or so mental health review tribunals. An applicant is therefore more likely to live near an SSAT than an MHRT. However, because of the high workload of the SSATs, an applicant may have to wait longer to appear before an SSAT than before an MHRT with its fewer number of cases.

4. Flexibility

8–20 A court is formal in its proceedings, rules of evidence, statutory interpretation, use of precedent and so on. These may not be necessary or even desirable in a tribunal. Professor Harry Street said:

> "Flexibility is seen as a key attribute in a decision-maker. Yet the courts have long had a different approach: that once a decision has been reached in a case, it should be a binding precedent for other judges to follow in similar future cases. If the new class of cases has been tried by the courts, principles would have become rigid… it was thought that this judicial inflexibility was inappropriate for many of the new kinds of cases."[64]

Consistency is important and tribunals have to balance flexibility and consistency, while administering a clear set of rules. This appears to be contradictory but the courts have recognised that tribunals have to strike this balance. Indeed, if a tribunal blindly follows precedent without considering the merits of a case, the decision is likely to be overturned on appeal. For instance, in *Merchandise Transport Ltd v. British Transport Commission*[65] Lord Devlin said that "a tribunal must not pursue consistency at the expense of the merits of an individual case". In this case, the British Transport Commission was not considered to be a "true" tribunal, but the same principle was later applied in *R. v. Greater Birmingham Appeal Tribunal, ex parte Simper*.[66] In a later case, Lord Denning suggested that the problem of inflexibility in decisions was exacerbated by the reporting

---

[62] Justice-All Souls Report, *op. cit.,* n. 2, above, p. 212.
[63] Genn, *op. cit.,* n. 47, above, at p. 396.
[64] Street, *Justice in the Welfare State* (1975).
[65] [1961] 3 All E.R. 495 at 507.
[66] [1974] Q.B. 543.

of tribunal decisions and he recommended that reporting should be limited because each case turned on its own facts.[67]

There is, however, a growing practice for some tribunals to publish selected decisions. In many tribunals also the decisions of appellate bodies are binding. Social security appeal tribunals are bound by the decisions of commissioners and immigration adjudicators are bound by the immigration appeal tribunals and are greatly influenced by the decisions of the Court of Session and the High Court of Justice.[68]

5. Expert knowledge

A court has general jurisdiction whereas a tribunal will have a narrow 8–21 jurisdiction based on the statutory scheme which set it up. The jurisdiction will be specialised so it is likely that the tribunal will have experts among its members.

A lawyer will often be the chair of the tribunal. This may have the effect of making the procedure more court-like and therefore raises the question as to whether there is a real necessity for the lawyer to be present as an adjudicator. However, the answer will depend upon whether the legal content of the decision is paramount.

A tribunal is more suitable than a court when a decision involves a specialist topic like mental health or fair rents. The presence of a lawyer is important since the decision has to be made in accordance with the statutory scheme. Other experts are equally important, for instance at a mental health review board, the presence of a doctor is required.

The traditional tribunal consists of three members, a chairperson who is often legally qualified and two "wings". The "wings" will be either an expert and a layperson with relevant experience (as in mental health review tribunals) or persons who represent each side of the dispute (as in industrial tribunals).

Franks recommended that the chairpersons be appointed by the Lord Chancellor and other members by the Council on Tribunals to "enhance the independence of tribunals, both in appearance and fact". However, this was not accepted by the Government and appointments are made by the Lord Chancellor, although by the Tribunals and Inquiries Act 1992, s. 5(1) the Council may make recommendations to the Lord Chancellor.

6. Inquisitorial approach

Courts adopt an adversarial approach; in other words, there is a contest 8–22 between the parties as to whose arguments find favour with the court. This

---

[67] *Walls Meat Co. v. Khan* [1978] IRLR 499.
[68] Genn, *op. cit.*, n. 3, above.

raises the question as to whether tribunals should be places of contest. A contest may be appropriate in some cases, for instance in a mental health review tribunal where the citizen is claiming his or her rights against the State and a battle of arguments is appropriate. However, in most tribunals, their job is to inquire into a case to ensure that justice is done. The tribunal members may be involved, for instance when the appellant is unrepresented and may need the assistance of the panel in drawing out the facts. The tribunal must, of course, beware of becoming too involved in the investigation since they are required to remain impartial and independent.

7. Reasoned decisions

8–23   The reasons for decisions are now recorded in all tribunals. The Court of Appeal recently held that the recording of decisions needs to be improved. Kennedy L.J. observed: "Very soon after the decision has been made the persons affected are to receive, not simply notification of the decision, but a copy of the chairman's record."[69]

In some very busy tribunals, such detailed records may prove difficult to produce given that the chairperson is an unpaid volunteer. It may make it even more difficult to recruit legal chairpersons.[70]

APPEALS

8–24   The Franks Report recognised the necessity of the right of appeal from a tribunal decision: "The essence of a right of appeal is salutary and makes for right adjudication. Provision for appeal is also important if decisions are to show reasonable consistency. Finally, the system of adjudication can hardly fail to appear fair to the applicant if he knows that he will normally be allowed two attempts to convince independent bodies of the soundness of his case."[71]

Franks recommended that appeals be available on grounds of fact, law or merits of the case. Section 11 of the Tribunals and Inquiries Act 1992 gives the right of appeal to anyone who is dissatisfied in point of law with the decision of a tribunal specified in the section, for instance tribunals dealing with schools, mines, nurses and so on. The Court of Session, or High Court of Justice for England and Wales, is empowered to make a decision, or to order the tribunal to rehear the case or to give directions to the tribunal.[72]

---

[69] *R. v. Solihull MBC Housing Benefit Review Board, ex p. Simpson* [1994] C.O.D. 225; [1995] 1 F.L.R. 140.
[70] Buck, "Recording Tribunal Decisions" (1994) 144 New L.J. 1559.
[71] Cmnd. 218 (1957), para.104.
[72] 1992 Act, s.11(4).

The meaning of "point of law" has caused difficulties for the courts in   8–25
interpretation. Some case examples will help to illustrate the court's thinking
on the meaning of the phrase. In *O'Brien v. Associated Fire Alarms Ltd*,[73]
the question was whether there was an implied term in O'Brien's contract
of employment that he was required to work away from home. The court
held that the question of whether the term was implied was a question of
law, not of fact, and according to section 9 of the 1958 Act[74] was open to
reconsideration on appeal. In *Lord Advocate v. Reliant Tool Co.*[75] the House
of Lords held that deciding whether the design of a product was a separate
activity or was part of the activity of making a product was a pure question
of fact for the tribunal. There was no question of statutory interpretation. In
Woodhouse v. Peter Brotherhood Ltd[76] it was argued that the meaning of
"transfer of business assets" was a question of fact. The case involved the
calculation of continuity of employment for the purposes of redundancy
payments and questions regarding the transfer of business assets. Lord
Denning M.R. disagreed with the contention. He said the primary facts
were not in dispute and the question was one regarding the correct meaning
of a statutory term, in other words it was a question of law. He cited the
case of *Edwards v. Bairstow*[77] where Lord Radcliffe had stated that if a
tribunal reached a conclusion which could not reasonably be drawn then it
would be wrong in law. Lord Denning paraphrased this — if a tribunal
drew the wrong conclusion from the primary facts it would be wrong in
law.[78]

An appeal from a tribunal to an appellate tribunal or court of law is   8–26
made according to the provisions of the statute which set up the tribunal. If
no appeal to the court is provided by the parent Act or by section 11 of the
1992 Act, then challenge in the courts is by way of judicial review. In some
tribunals, the appeal is to a Minister rather than to a court or appellate
tribunal,[79] but it should be remembered that this is what Parliament intended.

The power of decision may be given to a Minister; this usually means
that a decision will be taken by an official in the Minister's name and the
persons affected may have an entitlement to be heard by the official before
a report is made.

In social security cases, the appeal route is first to an adjudication officer,
then to a social security appeal tribunal, then the social security
Commissioners and finally, on a point of law or by judicial review, into the
courts.

---

[73]   [1968] 1 W.L.R. 1916; [1969] 1 All E.R. 93.
[74]   Now s. 11 of 1992 Act.
[75]   [1968] 1W.L.R. 205; [1968] 1 All E.R. 162.
[76]   [1972] 2 Q.B. 520.
[77]   [1956] A.C. 14.
[78]   See discussion in Craig, *Administrative Law* (1994).
[79]   For instance, the appeal from a decision of the Civil Aviation Authority is to the Minister.

DISPUTE SETTLEMENT UNDER STATUTORY SCHEMES

8–27   When a new statutory scheme is being proposed, Parliament has three
choices as to who should settle the dispute. It can choose to allow resolution
by the courts, or by tribunals, or it can retain the dispute settlement within
the Executive. In this last case, the Government will want to retain dispute
settlement where it has an interest in the final outcome, for instance where
a major policy issue is at stake. There are a number of examples where the
Government retained the right to resolve disputes; two of these are national
security issues under immigration legislation and appeals from Social Fund
officers.

The Immigration Appeals Act 1969 gave deportees a statutory right of
appeal. However, if the deportation was ordered on grounds of national
security, there was an appeal to a special tribunal which used special rules
of procedure. These rules allowed evidence to be given without the presence
of the deportee or his legal adviser. This system was used only once and
attracted much unfavourable publicity because of its inherent unfairness.
The Immigration Act 1971 changed the law so that the right of appeal was
abolished and replaced with a right to make representations to a panel of
three advisers, the so-called "wise men". The deportee had no right to know
any details of the evidence against him or her, no right of legal representation
and no right to know what recommendations were made to the Home
Secretary.

8–28   Whilst judicial review is possible, the chances of success are minimal, as
was seen in *R. v. Secretary of State for the Home Department, ex parte.
Hosenball*[80] where an American journalist working in the United Kingdom
was informed that he was to be deported under section 3(5)(b) of the 1971
Act because he had received information for publication which was harmful
to the security of the United Kingdom. Hosenball requested details of the
allegations against him but the Home Secretary declined to give these in the
interests of national security. A hearing of the advisory panel heard
representations from him and made their report to the Home Secretary, who
considered the report but confirmed the deportation order. In an application
for an order of certiorari to quash the deportation order, Hosenball argued
that under the rules of natural justice the Home Secretary was obliged to
distinguish between allegations which might be revealed without disclosing
the sources of information and those which could not. The Home Secretary
merely made a general statement that it was not in the interests of national
security to give any particulars of the allegations. The Court of Appeal said
that where national security was involved, the rules of natural justice were
likely to be modified if the requirement of the public interest in keeping

---

[80]   [1977] 3 All E.R. 452.

information confidential outweighed the public interest in the administration of justice. The balance between these was for the Home Secretary to decide since he had been entrusted with the decision-making power by the 1971 Act.[81]

The Social Security Act 1986 introduced the Social Fund, a system of loans and grants made to persons receiving certain benefits. Each DSS office was given a Social Fund budget, thus limiting the amount available to applicants. If an applicant is unsuccessful in obtaining a loan or grant, he may appeal to a DSS officer for a review of the decision, and thence to the Social Fund Inspector. There is no appeal to an independent tribunal. The only opportunity for an independent review is by way of judicial review. This system replaced one where an appeal to an independent tribunal was possible. The right of appeal was removed by the Government because the Social Fund is cash-limited and an unrestricted and unlimited appeal system is pointless if there is no money to meet the claims. This system of internal review appears to be unfair; the usual arguments regarding the independence of those conducting the review can be made. However, research has shown that 25 per cent of decisions are changed by internal review whilst 19 per cent of cases at the SSAT are decided in favour of the appellant.[82]

8–29

INQUIRIES

Where there is a question of government policy affecting the rights of a citizen, such as the compulsory purchase of land for building a new road or the siting of a new power station, a statutory inquiry may be held before the final decision is taken because of the enormous impact the consequences of the decision may have upon the individual and indeed upon the whole community. Such projects can cause great disruption and even displacement of large numbers of people. The rights of those affected are protected by the statute under which the work is required to be authorised, by the principles of natural justice and by the provisions of the Tribunals and Inquiries Act 1992.[83]

8–30

Wade and Forsyth refer to the inquiry as a "hybrid legal-and-administrative process".[84] Lord Greene M.R. described the inquiry as "merely a stage in the process of arriving at an administrative decision".[85] The hearings often give a legal or judicial impression which can disappoint

---

[81] See also *R. v. Secretary of State for the Home Department, ex p. Cheblak* [1991] 2 All E.R. 319.

[82] Wikeley and Young, "The Administration of Benefits in Britain: Adjudication Officers and the influence of Social Security Appeal Tribunals" in (1992) P. L. 238.

[83] Note that in certain important areas, there is no provision for a public inquiry, for instance the award of TV franchises, siting of nuclear missile bases.

[84] Wade and Forsyth, *Administrative Law* (1994), p. 965. For note on evolution of inquiries see p. 971.

[85] *B. Johnston & Co. (Builders) Ltd v. Minister of Health* [1947] 2 All E.R. 395.

objectors when they realise that the inquiry does not make decisions, only recommendations, which may or may not be followed.[86] The Justice-All Souls Report observed this, stating that "the superficial resemblance of inquiries to judicial proceedings tends to encourage expectations of a judicial result that cannot be satisfied".[87]

8–31   The final decision does not have to be based on the evidence heard in the inquiry; other matters may take precedence. Objections heard at an inquiry may be only one factor to be weighed by the Minister; other factors such as national policy may also be taken into account. The decision will often have a political motive and such matters are properly for a Minister to decide since he is accountable to Parliament for the decision. This has long been recognised by the courts.[88] The most important aspects of an inquiry are that objectors are able to put their case, such objections are fairly taken into account and the public are seen to have a role to play in the decision-making process. Lord Justice Scott has said that the inquiry procedure has three objectives: the need to be fair and to be seen to be fair, the need to conduct the proceedings efficiently and expeditiously, and the need to keep costs to a reasonable level.[89]

CLASSIFICATION OF INQUIRIES

8–32   Classifying inquiries is almost as difficult as classifying tribunals. Wraith and Lamb[90] suggest seven ways to classify inquiries by their objectives. These are fairly lengthy and so they later give a "shorthand" version,[91] classifying inquiries as appeals, objections, investigations and post-mortems. Garner[92] classifies inquiries as mandatory or discretionary; inquiries into objections or investigative inquiries; and ordinary inquiries and "big" inquiries. For our purposes, Wraith and Lamb's shorthand classifications are probably the more convenient.

1. Appeals

8–33   These inquiries cover such matters as appeals against refusal of planning permission. In Scotland, these are regulated by the Town and Country Planning (Scotland) Act 1997, s. 29. An applicant may appeal to the Secretary

---

[86] Hutton quotes from research which states that the public sees an inquiry as a legal institution, as a kind of neutral mediator or arbiter between the individual and the State: Hutton, *Lay Participation in a public local inquiry* (1986).

[87] *op. cit.,* n. 2, above, p. 263.

[88] *General Poster and Publicity Co. Ltd v. Secretary of State for Scotland and East Lothian County Council,* 1960 S.C. 266; see opinion of L.J.C. Thomson at 275.

[89] Scott, "Procedures at Inquiries — the duty to be fair" (1995) 101 L.Q.R. 596.

[90] Wraith and Lamb, *Public Inquiries as an Instrument of Government* (1971) at p. 305.

[91] *ibid.* p. 306.

[92] Jones, *op. cit.,* n. 28, above, p. 322.

of State if a planning authority refuses planning permission, or if consent is granted subject to conditions, or if a planning authority has failed to come to a decision within two months of the application. The appeal will be decided either on the basis of written submissions or at a public local inquiry. Most appeals (around 90 per cent) are now heard using the former method but it is open to the appellant or the planning authority to request an inquiry. The advantages of using the former method are speed and cheapness but the main disadvantage is that there is no opportunity to test the evidence in cross-examination. The Justice-All Souls Report stated that about 38 per cent of appeals made by written representation were successful compared to 52 per cent of those which go to inquiry.[93]

The notice of appeal must be lodged in writing within six months of the decision of the planning authority and the grounds of appeal must be stated.

Appeals, whether by written submissions or by public local inquiry, take place before a Reporter,[94] so-called because originally he heard evidence and arguments and reported back to the Secretary of State to make the decision. Reporters now have delegated authority to make the decision.[95] The Secretary of State retains the power to recall any delegated case for his own decision, a power used rarely. In *London & Clydeside Properties Ltd v. Secretary of State for Scotland*[96] the Secretary of State made a direction that he would determine an appeal personally. This direction was challenged unsuccessfully by the company on the grounds that the proposed development was within the Secretary of State's own constituency and he had, some years before becoming Secretary of State, supported objections to development of the same site. The company maintained that the Secretary of State could not therefore bring an unbiased and independent mind to the consideration of the appeal.

The procedure for appeal by written submissions is governed by regulations.[97] The reporter, or the Secretary of State, in making his decision must take into account only written submissions made within the deadlines stated within the regulations. If any other matters are taken into consideration, the decision is open to challenge in the courts.[98] There is no

8–34

---

[93] *op. cit.*, n. 2, above, p. 290.

[94] In England and Wales, this official is called an inspector.

[95] Town and Country Planning (Determination of Appeals by Appointed Persons)(Prescribed Classes)(Scotland) Regulations 1987 (S.I. 1987 No. 1531), as amended by Town and Country Planning (Determination of Appeals by Appointed Persons)(Prescribed Classes)(Scotland) Amendment Regulations 1989 (S.I. 1989 No. 577).

[96] 1983 S.C. 145.

[97] Town and Country Planning (Appeals)(Written Submissions Procedure)(Scotland) Regulations 1990 (S.I. 1990 No. 507). For a description of the procedure for appeals by written submissions see McAllister and McMaster, *Scottish Planning Law* (1994), p. 143.

[98] See, for instance, *Wells v. Secretary of State for Environment* [1992] 1 P.L.R 51.

obligation on the reporter to seek out additional information where the written submissions do not cover all of the points in the appeal.[99]

8–35		A public local inquiry may be held if the appellant or planning authority so request, or where a large development is involved, or a complex issue is at stake, or there is significant interest by third parties. The procedure is again governed by regulations, two sets, depending on whether the appeal is heard by the reporter or the Secretary of State himself.[1] The Franks Report stressed the need for inquiries to show openness, fairness and impartiality in their procedures[2] and the regulations allow for the provision of preliminary information supplied to and by the planning authority, notification of the local planning inquiry to interested parties and the procedure to be followed. They also prescribe who may appear at the inquiry, in other words who is entitled to be heard. The procedure is less formal than a court, with no necessity for legal representation (although this is often advisable), no requirement for evidence to be given on oath and more flexibility regarding hearsay evidence.[3] The regulations are enforceable in court and so the objectors are not confined to relying on breach of natural justice if the rules are breached.

Where an appeal has been delegated to the reporter, he will draft and issue a decision letter. The reporter's decision must be supported by adequate evidence although it is for him to decide how much weight he will attach to the various pieces of evidence.[4] He may rely on his own knowledge as well as the evidence presented to him.[5] His reasons must be adequate, proper, clear and intelligible and his decision must deal with the substance of the submissions made to him.[6] If the reporter takes into account new evidence not heard at the inquiry, he must inform all the parties and give them an opportunity to make representations. Where the decision is to be taken by the Secretary of State, the reporter will make a report, which consists of his findings in fact and his recommendations, together with his reasoning. Any new evidence taken into account must again be intimated to the parties. A failure to allow this opportunity may lead to a breach of natural justice.[7]

---

[99]	*City of Glasgow District Council v. Secretary of State for Scotland and William Hill (Scotland) Ltd,* 1992 S.C.L.R. 453.
[1]	Regulations governing an inquiry by the reporter — Town and Country Planning (Determination by Appointed Persons)(Inquiries Procedure)(Scotland) Rules 1980 (S.I. 1980 No. 1677), as amended by Amendment Rules 1987 (S.I. 1987 No. 1522).
[2]	Cmnd. 218 (1957), para. 287.
[3]	See Hutton, *op. cit.,* n. 86, above, for a detailed account of the procedure at an inquiry.
[4]	*Banks Horticultural Products Ltd v. Secretary of State for Environment* [1980] J.P.L. 33.
[5]	*Ainley v. Secretary of State for Environment and Fylde Borough Council* [1987] J.P.L. 33.
[6]	*Re Poyser and Mill's Arbitration* [1964] 2 Q.B. 467.
[7]	See *Fairmount Investments Ltd v. Secretary of State for Environment* [1976] 2 All E.R. 865; *Wordie Property Co. Ltd v. Secretary of State for Scotland,* 1984 S.L.T. 345; *Anduff Holdings Ltd v. Secretary of State for Scotland,* 1992 S.L.T. 696: see also the Chalkpit case — *Buxton v. Minister for Housing and Local Government* [1961] 1 Q.B. 278.

The Minister has a greater discretion where matters of opinion or policy are involved.[8]

The Minister is usually required to give reasons for his decision. This is, 8–36 of course, important for appeals. The adequacy of the reasons given has caused some controversy. In *Save Britain's Heritage v. Number 1 Poultry Ltd*[9] the reasons advanced by a Minister in a planning matter were heavily criticised for lack of clarity and precision. However, the reasons were to be read in conjunction with the inspector's report which was incorporated into the Minister's Decision. The court did not set out what it considered to be adequate but said that if the alleged deficiency "substantially prejudiced" the interests of the applicants then the decision could be quashed. However, the burden of proof rested with the applicants to prove that the reasons were inadequate and that they had suffered prejudice as a result.

The Secretary of State has the power to award expenses[10] although usually the Secretary of State and the planning authority will meet their own expenses unless the appellant has acted unreasonably.

2. Objections

These are also mainly concerned with planning matters but instead of an 8–37 appeal against an adverse decision by a planning authority, objections are made by individuals or groups to proposals for planning permission by developers. The public inquiry thus generated is held on the same basis and on similar conditions to the appeal against planning permission. These inquiries may be held to inquire into major developments, such as the "super-quarry" inquiry held on the island of Harris in 1995. Indeed public oral hearings occur now more rarely and are usually reserved for cases involving considerable controversy and where the lengthy and expensive process can be justified. Here the issues are likely to include consideration of national policy.

The reporter has discretion to allow members of the public to appear at the inquiry and participate.[11] Usually community groups and interest groups are permitted to take part and as a result these bodies will acquire the right to enforce the rules of procedure through the courts.[12]

If a person "is aggrieved by any order" or "by any action on the part of 8–38 the Secretary of State"[13] he may apply to the Court of Session within six

---

[8] See *Lithgow v. Secretary of State for Scotland,* 1973 SC 1; *London & Clydeside Properties Ltd v. Secretary of State for Scotland,* above; *Wordie Property Co. Ltd v. Secretary of State for Scotland,* above.

[9] [1991] 1 W.L.R. 153.

[10] Town and Country Planning (Scotland) Act 1997, s. 265(9), (10), (11) and (12).

[11] *Bushell v. Secretary of State for the Environment* [1981] A.C. 75.

[12] *Turner v. Secretary of State for the Environment* (1973) 72 L.G.R. 380.

[13] 1997 Act, s. 239.

months of the order being given or the action being taken for reduction of the order or action. The types of orders which may be challenged are specified in section 237(2) and the actions of the Secretary of State are detailed in section 237(1). The Act does not specify who qualifies as an "aggrieved person". The planning authority and the appellant will qualify but the position of third parties is less clear and the courts have had to try to clarify this. Generally they have taken a liberal view and it appears that those included in the definition will be persons whose property or legal rights are affected and persons who made representations to the planning authority or local public inquiry or who have taken part in an appeal.[14]

If the objector does not qualify as an "aggrieved person" under section 239, they may apply for judicial review of the decision provided they have sufficient interest in the matter. Where the objectors want to appeal against the decision of a planning authority, they are on more difficult ground because there is no right of appeal against a planning authority's decision to grant planning permission. Judicial review may be the only course of action.[15]

3. Investigations and post-mortems

8–39 Inquiries may be set up either under statutory authority[16] or in rare cases on a non-statutory basis to investigate issues of public interest and concern. Examples of this latter type include the inquiry by Lord Justice Scott into the Arms to Iraq Affair,[17] the King's Cross Underground fire in 1987[18] and the Orkney Child Abuse Inquiry in 1991.[19] The importance of these inquiries should not be underestimated; their recommendations will often lead to changes in legislation or administrative procedures. They are essentially retrospective in nature, examining why something occurred or did not occur.

Formal versions of these inquiries may be held under the Tribunals of Inquiry (Evidence) Act 1921. These are held to investigate "a definite matter

---

[14] See *Strathclyde Regional Council v. Secretary of State for Scotland (No. 2)*, 1990 S.C.L.R. 11; 1990 S.L.T. 149; *North East Fife District Council v. Secretary of State for Scotland*, 1990 S.C.L.R. 647; 1991 S.L.T. 373; *Cumming v. Secretary of State for Scotland*, 1992 S.C.L.R. 831; 1993 S.L.T. 228.

[15] See *Inverness, Loch Ness and Nairn Tourist Board v. Highland Regional Council* (1988) S.P.L.P. 47; *Jas. Aitken & Sons (Meat Producers) Ltd v. City of Edinburgh District Council*, 1989 S.C.L.R. 674; 1990 S.L.T. 241.

[16] For instance, fatal accident inquiries under the Fatal Accidents and Sudden Deaths Inquiry (Scotland) Act 1976.

[17] Report of the Inquiry into the Export of Defence Equipment and Dual-Use Goods to Iraq and Related Prosecutions (1995–96 H.C. 115).

[18] (1987–88 H.C. 499).

[19] Report by Lord Clyde on the Inquiry into the removal of children from Orkney in February 1991 (1991–92 H.C. 195).

of urgent public importance"[20] such as national disasters like the Aberfan landslide disaster in 1967,[21] or political controversies such as the leaking of Budget secrets by the Chancellor of the Exchequer in 1936. One of the most recent of these was chaired by Lord Cullen and investigated the events at Dunblane primary school in March 1996 when 16 children and a teacher were killed by a gunman.[22]

An inquiry under the 1921 Act will be chaired by a senior judge since he 8–40 or she has the same powers as a judge of the superior courts to send for documents, administer oaths and summon witnesses. Two other members may sit to assist. The inquiry makes recommendations to the Minister. In the 1960s, there was disquiet over the inquisitorial procedure of the 1921 Act inquiry, particularly since it was felt that the process could make scapegoats out of people involved. This led to the setting-up of the Salmon Royal Commission in 1966 but many of its recommendations have never been implemented.[23] It is thought that this inquisitorial procedure is the reason why an inquiry under the 1921 Act was not used for the Scott Inquiry.[24] Nonetheless, some of the witnesses, for instance Lord Howe and Douglas Hurd, criticised the inquisitorial approach of Lord Justice Scott in conducting the inquiry.[25]

A Minister may set up an inquiry either because he is obliged to do so by statute or because he thinks it fit to do so regarding a matter connected with his statutory functions.[26] Some statutes may make the holding of an inquiry discretionary and many of these will fall within the ambit of the Tribunals and Inquiries Act 1992. Where a Minister is obliged to hold an inquiry before he makes an order, then the statutory procedure and the rules of natural justice must be properly followed, otherwise there is no valid inquiry and the order may be quashed.

Inquiries, the Franks Committee and the Council on Tribunals

The terms of reference for the Committee on Administrative Tribunals and 8–41 Inquiries[27] included a direction to consider and make recommendations on the working of inquiries or hearings by or on behalf of a Minister on an

---

[20] 1921 Act, s. 1(1).
[21] (1967–68 H.C. 33).
[22] The Public Inquiry into the Shootings at Dunblane Primary School on March 13, 1996 (Cullen Report), Cm. 3386 (1996).
[23] Report of the Royal Commission on Tribunals of Inquiry (Salmon report), Cmnd. 3121 (1966). Scott L. J. discusses the report and its findings in (1995) 111 L.Q.R. 596.
[24] *ibid.*
[25] Scott L. J. discusses the procedure he adopted in a speech to the Chancery Bar Association, printed in (1995) 111 L.Q.R. 596: "Procedures at Inquiries — the Duty to be Fair".
[26] Examples are National Health Service Act 1977, s. 84; Town and Country Planning Act 1990, s. 282.
[27] Cmnd. 218 (1957).

appeal. The report said that inquiries had a distinct role to play in situations where there were often conflicting interests. They help to protect the public most directly affected by proposals of government by giving them rights to be heard. Franks also maintained that inquiries were a way of ensuring that Ministers were better informed. Franks believed that inquiries were a necessary part of the process of adjudication but the report also recognised that in carrying out the will of Parliament, the Minister could not be impartial. "There is also the public interest which requires both that ministers should not be frustrated in carrying out their duties and also that their decisions should be subject to effective checks or controls, and these can no longer be applied by Parliament in the general run of cases."[28]

The Franks Report made a number of recommendations, the majority of which, unlike those made with regard to tribunals, were accepted by the Government. First, individuals should know in good time before the inquiry the case to be presented against them. Secondly, relevant lines of government policy should be revealed at the inquiry. Thirdly, the inspector's report should be published coincidentally with the letter from the minister. Fourthly, the decision letter should contain the reasons for the decision. Fifthly, it should be possible to challenge the decision in the Court of Session or High Court of Justice on the grounds of jurisdiction and procedure. Finally, inspectors should be under the control of the Lord Chancellor. This last recommendation was rejected by the Government.

8–42   The Tribunals and Inquiries Act 1992, s. 9, allows the Lord Chancellor, after consulting the Council on Tribunals, to make rules to regulate statutory inquiries. A statutory inquiry is defined in the 1992 Act, s. 16(1), as

> "(a) an inquiry or hearing held or to be held in pursuance of a duty imposed by any statutory provisions, or
>
> (b) an inquiry or hearing, or an inquiry or hearing of a class, designated for the purposes of this section by an order under subsection (2)".

The Lord Chancellor or Lord Advocate can designate any inquiry to be one under this subsection and around 100 inquiries have been so designated.

The 1992 Act at section 1(1)(c) gives the Council on Tribunals more power in respect of inquiries than it has in respect of tribunals. The Council on Tribunals may consider and report on matters referred to it and also it may itself instigate investigations on the administrative procedures of an inquiry if it considers these of special importance.

Franks stopped short of recommending allowing full-blown participation in the making of decisions. Objectors should not be able to cross-examine civil servants on matters of policy and there should not be an opportunity to air alternative schemes.

---

[28] Cmnd. 218 (1957),.paras. 262–277.

The role of the reporter

In Scotland, the reporters are qualified surveyors, architects and so on who 8–43
are employed by the Secretary of State for Scotland. In England, inspectors
are specially trained civil servants appointed by a Minister to hold a hearing
on his or her behalf. The Department of the Environment has around 400
inspectors who carry out 3,000 inquiries each year. The inspectors now
work in the executive agency, the Planning Inspectorate, which was
established in 1992.

In most planning appeals, the making of the final decision is now
delegated to the reporter. The Council on Tribunals has observed that this
has had the effect of converting the inquiry into a tribunal hearing.[29] The
Framework Document for the Planning Inspectorate reflects this assertion
by stating expressly that one of the objectives of the Inspectorate is to
"maintain the integrity of each Inspector as an independent tribunal, not
subject to any improper influence".

Reporters make a finding of fact which is reported to the Minister. The 8–44
reporter must therefore be impartial and independent but will always operate
under the umbrella of government policy. The level of impartiality wanted
by Franks is not met since reporters are not appointed by the Lord Chancellor
or Lord Advocate.

The reporter's findings are published at the same time as the Minister's
letter. Although the Minister may decide against the reporter's findings, he
has only a limited discretion to disagree in some circumstances. For instance,
in planning matters, if the Minister's decision differs from that of the reporter,
he must notify the parties and allow them 21 days to make representations
or alternatively reopen the inquiry.

Issues of natural justice and fairness

A balance has to be struck between the need to ensure fair procedures and 8–45
the important requirement that delays in procedure may impede the decision-
making process.[30]

Such matters are taken into account in the rules of procedure set for the
different types of inquiry. One objective is to ensure there is no "over-
judicialisation" of the procedure. In the Scott Inquiry[31] some of the parties
giving evidence were unhappy that they were unable to be legally
represented. It is likely, however, that if legal representation had been
allowed, the inquiry would have taken much longer and witnesses would

---

[29] Annual Report of Council on Tribunals, 1979–80 (1980 H.C. 246), para. 6.41: see also
Justice-All Souls Report, *op. cit.*, n. 2, above, pp. 228–229.
[30] See *R. v. Secretary of State for Environment, ex p. Fiedler Estates (Canvey) Ltd* (1989) 57
P.&C.R. 424.
[31] (1995–96 H.C. 115).

not have divulged some of the information which was in fact given. The existence of the rules of procedure has assisted ordinary citizens to some extent, by clarifying their role at the inquiry, but the ordinary citizen may be disadvantaged by his lack of knowledge of the rules and the formal procedures employed.[32]

8–46   In *Bushell v. Secretary of State for the Environment*[33] the House of Lords had to consider an inquiry into the scheme for the building of an extension to the M40 motorway. Lord Diplock emphasised that inquiries were distinct from courts of law and they had to conduct themselves in such a way as to guarantee fairness to those who would be affected by any decision made. Such an inquiry should be held in public and in the locality where the scheme is to take place. Lord Diplock said further that the purpose of an inquiry is to provide the Minister with as much information as is needed so that in making his decision he is able to weigh the harm caused to local residents against the public benefit of the scheme. The Minister was under a duty to take into account any matters which he ought to take into account.

The courts have also stressed that the inquiry process should be looked at as a whole and that some degree of procedural impropriety by the reporter or inspector could be remedied by the Minister when he considered the inspector's report.[34]

How should a Minister decide what constitutes the public interest? In *B Johnson & Co. (Builders) Ltd v. Minister of Health*[35] Lord Greene said that not only was the Minister entitled to be informed in a number of ways, he was also entitled to have his own policy and view of what the public interest demanded.

8–47   Where the Minister in considering the inspector's report has no judicial or quasi-judicial duty imposed on him, then considerations of bias in the execution of his duty are irrelevant, the sole question being whether or not he genuinely considered the report and the objections.[36] In reality, the Minister may have made up his mind before the inquiry starts but so long as the correct procedure is followed and objections are heard fairly, little can be done to challenge the final decision.

In planning inquiries, there is a requirement that the parties be given an opportunity to comment on all issues of fact relevant to the final decision.[37] If there is a failure to allow such comment this may constitute a breach of natural justice. However, the courts distinguish between a failure to allow

---

[32] Wraith and Lamb, *op. cit.,* n. 90, above, pp. 317–319.
[33] [1981] A.C. 75.
[34] *R. v. Secretary of State for Transport, ex p. Gwent County Council* [1987] 2 W.L.R. 961.
[35] [1947] 2 All E.R. 395.
[36] *Franklin v. Minister for Town and Country Planning* [1948] A.C. 87.
[37] See *Fairmount Investments Ltd v. Secretary of State for Environment* [1967] 2 All E.R. 865; *Wordie Property Co. Ltd v. Secretary of State for Scotland,*1984 S.L.T. 345; *Anduff Holdings Ltd v. Secretary of State for Scotland,* 1992 S.L.T. 696.

comment on matters of fact and comment on matters of opinion or policy. A failure to allow comment on the former will be a breach of natural justice, whilst a failure in respect of the latter will generally not be.[38]

The right to legal representation is expected as a matter of course in   8–48 planning inquiries, as is the right to call witnesses.[39] There are legislative restrictions on the questioning of witnesses, for instance, an official giving evidence for a government department may not be questioned on the merits of government policy. This is a matter for which the Minister is accountable to Parliament.[40] Members of the public not directly affected by the decision under consideration may still make representations or call witnesses but only at the discretion of the inspector or reporter. Generally this discretion is exercised generously.[41]

---

[38] See *Lithgow v. Secretary of State for Scotland*, 1973 S.C. 1; *London & Clydeside Properties Ltd v. Secretary of State for Scotland*, 1983 S.C. 145; *Wordie Property Co Ltd*, above.
[39] For instance, the Town and Country Planning (Determination by Appointed Persons) (Inquiries Procedure) (Scotland) Rules 1980 (S.I. 1980 No. 1677).
[40] Rule 9(4) (S.I. 1980 No. 1677); and see *Bushell v. Secretary of State for Environment*, above.
[41] See *Strathclyde Regional Council v. Secretary of State for Scotland (No. 2)*, 1990 S.L.T. 149; *North East Fife District Council v. Secretary of State for Scotland,* 1990 S.C.L.R. 647.

CHAPTER 9

JUDICIAL CONTROL OF ADMINISTRATIVE DECISION-MAKING: SCOPE OF JUDICIAL CONTROL OF ADMINISTRATIVE ACTION

INTRODUCTION

9–01 The twentieth century has been a period of growth in the scope and complexity of functions carried out by government. It has also been a period in which there has been increased incidence of State intervention in lives of citizens, particularly in areas such as health, housing, immigration, planning, education and, more recently, the environment. The scale of this intervention has increased dramatically in the period since 1945. Many of the tasks undertaken by public authorities in the course of providing public services do not fall within the categories of activity for which control by the courts is suitable. Political judgment, for example, is best controlled by political process but the political process is more concerned with democracy and accountability than with protecting individual rights. Nevertheless, it has been observed that no defect in the constitution of a state deserves greater reproach than the giving licence to wrong without affording redress.[1] The rule of law requires that public authorities must have lawful authority for their actions and that they must not exceed the scope of their powers. Where there is a dispute as to whether or not a public authority is acting within the terms of its powers recourse to the courts to determine the issue is entirely appropriate. The courts are careful to avoid interfering with political decisions by permitting the challenge of the merits or motivation for decisions but they have jurisdiction to ensure that decisions are made on the basis of legal authority and that there is compliance with certain standards of fair procedure.

NEED FOR JUDICIAL CONTROL OF ADMINISTRATIVE ACTION

9–02 As the extent to which the Government acts to regulate the affairs of individuals, and commercial and other organisations, has increased, there

---

[1] Lord Kames, *Historical Law Tracts* (4th ed., 1778) at pp. 228–229, as cited in *West v Secretary of State for Scotland*, 1992 S.L.T. 636 at p. 639.

has been a corresponding increase in the frequency with which the courts are asked to intervene on the ground that a public authority has exceeded its powers and has thereby infringed the rights and interests of a person or organisation.[2] There are, of course, political controls to keep the administration in check. The Government is democratically elected and a principle of Ministerial responsibility should ensure that the executive branch of government is answerable to the legislature for its decisions. Political controls ensure that a Government refrains from a course of action which is abhorrent to the majority of those who elected it to power. These political controls do not, however, give adequate protection against the infringement of individual rights, especially where there is a Government with an overall majority in the House of Commons. Political accountability may be effective in controlling the policy decisions made by Ministers but there is a need for redress for individuals whose rights have been infringed by the day-to-day operation of these policies and it is through the courts that this redress is obtained.

SOURCES OF ADMINISTRATIVE POWER

As there is no written constitution in the United Kingdom, administrative power is not derived from one single source. The power to make administrative decisions may be delegated by Parliament, or it may be based on the residual powers of the Crown. Increasingly, powers may be derived from the laws of the European Community, either through Parliamentary process or from directives and regulations having direct effect. The rights of the citizen may also be affected by the actions of organisations which are not part of the Government but who have power to make decisions which may impinge on the fundamental rights of an individual. 9–03

STATUTE

The majority of administrative decisions are made under statutory powers, conferred on public authorities by numerous Acts of Parliament. When a court has to decide whether a public official is acting lawfully or unlawfully, the nature and extent of his authority has to be found in most cases by defining the intention of Parliament as expressed or implied in the relevant Act. Often the powers are not expressly conferred by a section in a statute but are reasonably incidental to a power to achieve a particular purpose or a duty to provide a service.

---

[2] Deans, *Scots Public Law* (1995), p. 137.

CROWN PREROGATIVE

9–04 Where the power of a public authority has not been derived from an Act of Parliament it may be based on prerogative power. The prerogative powers are the ancient powers of the Crown which survived the constitutional upheavals of the seventeenth century. Although described as the prerogative powers of the Crown, they are now virtually all exercisable by Ministers of the Crown rather than by the sovereign in person. Dicey described the prerogative powers as "the residue of discretionary or arbitrary authority which at any given time is left in the hands of the Crown".[3] Prerogative powers are anomolous in many ways in a democratic society, being contrary to the fundamental doctrines of the rule of law and the supremacy of Parliament. In the case of *Laker Airways v. Department of Trade*,[4] Lord Denning described the prerogative as "a discretionary power exercisable by the executive government for the public good, in certain spheres of governmental activity for which the law has made no provision." Prerogative powers include the power to make treaties, the power to direct the armed forces,[5] the power to issue passports and to deny or permit entry into the United Kingdom,[6] the power to requisition property in order to secure the defence of the realm,[7] and the power to maintain the Queen's peace.[8] As the prerogative power is a residual power it is not expected that it will develop or increase in its scope. Rather, if the rule of law is to be valued as a fundamental precept in modern society, prerogative powers should be successively replaced by powers exercised under statutory authority. In the case of *British Broadcasting Corporation v. Johns*,[9] the court considered whether the BBC was entitled to Crown immunity from taxation. It was argued for the BBC, that, because wireless telegraphy and telephony were new inventions, the Crown had a prerogative right to a monopoly of their use and had chosen to exercise this monopoly as respects broadcasting solely before 1954 and partially thereafter through the instrumentality of the BBC. However, Lord Diplock said: "it is 350 years and a civil war too late for the Queen's Courts to broaden the prerogative. The limits within which the

---

[3] Dicey, *The Law of the Constitution* (Wade, ed.) (10th ed.,1959); Wolffe, "Crown and Prerogative in Scots Law", in Finnie, Himsworth and Walker (edd.), *Edinburgh Essays in Public Law* (1991).

[4] [1977] 2 All E.R. 182.

[5] *Chandler v. D.P.P.* [1964] A.C. 763.

[6] *R. v. Home Secretary, ex p. Hosenball* [1977] 1 W.L.R. 766; *R. v. Foreign Secretary, ex p. Everett* [1989] 1 All E.R. 655.

[7] *Burmah Oil Co. Ltd v. Lord Advocate*, 1964 S.C. (H.L.) 117; *Att.-Gen. v. de Keyser's Royal Hotel Ltd* [1920] A.C. 508.

[8] *R. v. Home Secretary, ex p. Northumbria Police Authority* [1989] Q.B. 26.

[9] [1965] Ch. 32.

executive government may impose obligations or restraints upon citizens of the United Kingdom without statutory authority are now well settled and incapable of extension".[10] It was held that the BBC was created as an independent legal entity, quite separate from the Crown. It was not an instrument of the Crown and therefore enjoyed none of the Crown's immunities.

European Community Law

The laws of the European community have overriding legal force where there is a conflict with national laws. Therefore, in the event of a conflict between an Act of Parliament and Community law having direct effect it is the Community law which will prevail. Much of the operation of implementing Community law in the United Kingdom has been achieved by Ministerial orders, rules and guidelines. Strictly speaking, all of these rules and regulations are issued under authority of the European Communities Act 1972 and therefore are made under national statutory authority but in reality, as much Community law now has direct effect, the citizen may have rights which are based directly on Community law.

Contract

Although most of the actions which may have impact on the rights of individual citizens are carried out under authority of a statute, a prerogative power or a European regulation or directive, some of the powers which are exercised in such a way as to affect individual rights may be derived from a contractual relationship or even a less formal consensual submission to a jurisdiction.[11] These sources of power may be derived from membership of an organisation rather than from the constitution of the State. Organisations such as the regulatory bodies which govern certain sports, religious organisations, or financial regulatory bodies are not part of the Government but they may exercise powers over their members which affect the members individual rights in the same way as actions by a government body. Some of the same legal principles which apply to administrative decision-making by public officials and organisations may also apply to non-governmental organisations, especially with regard to the requirements for procedural fairness in circumstances where the fundamental rights of individuals may be infringed.

9–05

---

[10]   [1965] Ch. 32 at 79.
[11]   Alder, "Hunting the Chimera — the End of O'Reilly v. Mackman" (1993) 13 L.S. 183.

THE NATURE OF ADMINISTRATIVE DECISION-MAKING

POWERS, DUTIES AND DISCRETIONS

9–06 An individual may be affected by a variety of decisions made in a variety of ways. The development of a policy by the Government will not be enough to put it into operation. An Act of Parliament will lay down the changes to the law which will effect the change of policy. The detailed provisions which are necessary to bring the change into effect may be made in the form of delegated legislation. In addition to delegated legislation, rules may be made by a Minister, a local authority, agency or other public body. Delegated legislation fills in the detailed provisions of the government policy but additional rules, procedural guidelines and operational decisions will be required to ensure that the policy can be implemented in practice. Statutory authority is the basis for most of the rules and policy guidelines developed by government departments but not every decision which is made is based on an express rule or regulation. Powers are delegated to officials or organisations so that they can implement policy decisions and they will have implied authority to make the decisions necessary to bring the policy into operation. The implementation of government policy may also involve the imposition of a duty on an official or an organisation. In the day-to-day management of public administration, decisions are frequently made which are based on the informal exercise of a discretion. Such a discretionary decision may be based on an official policy or may simply be the exercise of judgment by an individual official. Powers, duties and discretions may be very closely related and so, as in the case of *Padfield v. Minister of Agriculture*,[12] there may be a duty to exercise a discretion. If a public authority is to fulfil the duties imposed on it, it must be equipped with the necessary powers to enable it to act.

Powers

9–07 The fundamental ground on which a decision may be challenged by judicial review proceedings is that there has been an excess of power on the part of the authority which made the decision. The principle that government must be conducted according to law means that there must be legal authority for everything which is done or decided to be done by an official or public authority, that is to say, every act or decision must be *intra vires*. In administrative law the word "power" has two meanings. First, it means simply the capacity to act in a certain way and so there may be references to the power to provide a service. Secondly, it can mean the authority to confer, to infringe or to take away the rights of others. An example of this is

---

[12] [1968] A.C. 997.

the power to license premises or to vary or to revoke licences. All officials and agencies whose acts or decisions affect the rights and duties of private individuals must be able to show that:

> (a) the power originated from statute or common law;
> (b) the power has been entrusted to that office or agency;
> (c) the power is being exercised only in accordance with the statutory or common law rules as interpreted by the courts.

Duties

Statutes commonly impose duties on Government Ministers, departments or agencies to carry out a function. Duties are usually expressed in broad terms, such as the duty to provide a service, although there are examples of very specific duties; for instance the Local Government (Scotland) Act 1973 created an obligation on a council official to produce council minutes for inspection by an elector. Duties are more commonly expressed in broader terms. An Act which imposes a duty on a public authority to provide a service usually confers: 9–08

> (a) a broad duty to fulfil certain broad policy objectives;
> (b) narrower duties to act in specified situations; and
> (c) various powers to promote the purposes of the Act.

Many of the duties imposed by common law or statute create a reciprocal right in an individual to enforce the duty. If, for example, a person fails to maintain safe premises in accordance with the duty imposed by the Occupier's Liability (Scotland) Act 1960, a person who is injured because of that breach of duty has the right to claim compensation. Many of the duties imposed on public bodies, however, are not capable of being enforced by the assertion of individual rights, and it is in such cases that the jurisdiction of the courts to provide suitable remedies for redress for the infringement of individual rights and the protection of individual interests affected by administrative decision-making becomes important.

Discretions

The process of administration of government involves a great variety of decisions being made by a large and diverse population of administrators at all levels of government. Decisions are taken by central government on matters such as the amount of tax which a person must pay, whether a person will be allowed to enter into or remain in the country and whether a person is entitled to a social security benefit. At local level, decisions are made on matters such as the granting or refusing of planning permission, closure of schools, allocation of school places, entitlement to housing and granting or refusing licences for a broad range of commercial activities including licences for public houses and restaurants, betting and gaming licences and taxi operators' licences. These decisions all involve 9–09 the exercise of a discretion by the relevant body, *i.e.* a choice between more than one course of action, even if that choice is simply between granting and refusing a licence.

Lord Diplock defined administrative discretion in the case of *Secretary of State for Education v. Tameside Metropolitan Borough Council.*[13] That case involved the decision of a newly elected council to abandon an existing plan to move to comprehensive education and to continue to have selective entry to five grammar schools. The Secretary of State issued a direction that the council revert to the existing scheme. The House of Lords held that the direction would have been valid, under section 68 of the Education Act 1944, only if the Secretary of State was satisfied that the council was acting unreasonably. This would be the case if the Secretary of State considered that no reasonable authority could act as the council was proposing to do. There was no evidence of any basis on which the Secretary of State could have reached a conclusion that the authority was acting in a way in which no reasonable authority would act. In the course of reaching this decision, however, Lord Diplock observed that the courts are reluctant to interfere with the exercise of a discretion which Parliament has chosen to delegate to an individual official or to an organisation. He said: "The very concept of administrative discretion involves a right to choose between more than one possible course of action on which there is room for reasonable people to hold differing opinions as to which is to be preferred."[14]

9–10   Discretion therefore involves a choice as to how, (and sometimes whether or not) to act. However, even where a statute confers a very wide discretion on an official, administrative discretion is very rarely unlimited and a remedy may be sought on the ground that a particular decision is beyond legal authority. This could be the case if, for example, a decision was made in a way which sought to achieve policies which are not authorised by the relevant enabling instrument. There may also be scope for challenge if the proper procedures have not been followed.

Scope of Judicial Control

9–11 Although decision-making by public officials is controlled by political means such as Ministerial responsibility to Parliament and, of course, the need to satisfy the electorate, such controls do not provide redress for individual grievances and a system which provides redress through litigation in the courts is required. There are several routes for obtaining legal redress through judicial process. The appropriate action will depend on the source of the authority for the decision which is being challenged.

---

[13] [1977] A.C. 1014.
[14] *ibid.* at 1064.

Statutory appeals procedure

Where it is the exercise of a power derived from a statute which has caused   9–12
an infringement of rights there may be a specific right of recourse provided
by the statute which conferred the power to make the decision. There is, for
example, a statutory right of appeal on points of law from decisions of the
Social Security Commissioners.[15] It is increasingly common for statutes to
provide for a right of appeal from the decision of a public authority or a
tribunal. The nature of the right of appeal will depend on the provision in
the relevant statute. It may allow a further inquiry into the factual basis of
a decision, or it may be substantially comparable with the grounds for judicial
review at common law and be confined to reviewing the legality of the
decision. Even where the grounds are similar to the grounds for judicial
review at common law they may not be exactly co-extensive with the
common law grounds, for example, the Licensing (Scotland) Act 1976,
s. 39(4), provides that the sheriff may uphold an appeal from a licensing
board only on the grounds of an error in law, or if the decision is based on
an incorrect material fact, or a breach of natural justice in the procedures
followed, or that the decision was an unreasonable exercise of discretion.
The appeal may be to a court,[16] (often the sheriff court) or there may be a
right of appeal to a Government Minister or, occasionally, to a tribunal. As
a general rule, where there is a statutory right of appeal a litigant must
make use of that right rather than seeking judicial review at common law.

Recourse to the European Commission and Court of Human Rights

The two European courts, the Court of Justice of the European Communities   9–13
and the European Court of Human Rights, exist to protect individuals against
harm caused by the misuse of power by public officials and public authorities
within the states which are parties to European treaties and conventions on
human rights. The two European Courts have regard to the jurisprudence
of each other and use similar legal principles and techniques. The European
Convention on Human Rights,[17] unlike European Community law, has not
yet been incorporated into the law of the United Kingdom although the
United Kingdom is a party to the Convention.[18] The Convention covers
the right to life, liberty and a fair trial; the right to marry and have a family;
freedom of thought, conscience and religion; freedom of expression,

---

[15] Social Security Act 1980, s. 14.
[16] See *Glasgow Corporation v. Glasgow Churches' Council*, 1944 S.C. 97; 1944 S.L.T. 317;
Grant Committee, *Report of the Committee on the Sheriff Court*, Cmnd. 3248 (1967).
[17] European Convention for Human Rights and Fundamental Freedoms, 1950; T.S. 71 (1953);
Cmd. 8969.
[18] A Bill to incorporate the European Convention on Human Rights was proposed in the
Queen's Speech, May 14, 1997.

including freedom of the press; freedom of peaceful assembly and association; the right to have a sentence reviewed by a higher tribunal; the prohibition of torture and inhuman and degrading treatment. Adherence to the European Convention on Human Rights[19] creates an obligation on the Government of the United Kingdom to secure the rights and freedoms of the individual in the domestic law of the jurisdictions within the United Kingdom and to provide effective remedies before national authorities for breaches of the provisions of the Convention. The rights and freedoms which the Convention contains also provide protection for individuals, as a matter of international law, against the misuse of legislative, executive or judicial powers within the United Kingdom. Therefore, the European Court of Human Rights in Strasbourg has power to award compensation for breaches of the Convention by public authorities for which the U.K. Government is responsible. The court sits in chambers of seven judges or exceptionally as a grand chamber of 17 judges. Litigants must first have exhausted all available legal processes in their own countries. The Court of Justice in Luxembourg also takes account of the European Convention as a source of law so that, for example, decisions by the European Commission may be annulled if there has been a failure to follow procedures which secure fundamental human rights such as the right to be heard.

Action to enforce a statutory duty

9–14   Where there is a statutory duty on an official or body, such as a duty to provide a service, it may be possible for an individual to take action to enforce performance of that duty, although not all statutory duties can be enforced in this way. A general power to enforce a statutory duty is provided by the Court of Session Act 1988, s. 45(b),[20] which provides that the Court of Session may order the specific performance of any statutory duty under such conditions and penalties (including fines and imprisonment where consistent with the statute) in the event of the order not being implemented as to the court shall seem proper. This section applies where a clear, definite duty is laid by statute upon some definite body or individual on whom the court can lay its hand and order the specific performance of the duty. It must be clear that the statute is imposing a duty, not merely conferring a power.[21]

9–15   This power was little used until recent times. The attitude of the courts was evidenced by the comments of Lord Dundas, in the case of *Carlton Hotel v. Lord Advocate*,[22] that the remedy provided by section 91[23] was

---

[19]   The U.K. is also a party to the International Covenant on Civil and Political Rights, New York, December 19, 1966; T.S. 6 (1977); Cmnd. 6702.
[20]   Formerly by Court of Session Act 1868, s. 91.
[21]   Maxwell, *The Practice of the Court of Session* (1979), p. 649.
[22]   1921 S.C. 237.
[23]   s. 91 of the Court of Session Act 1868, now replaced by Court of Session Act 1988, s. 45(b).

"peculiar and drastic". It has been said that, "the jurisdiction to restrain is much more effective than the jurisdiction to compel actions".[24] However, in *Leishman v. Scott*,[25] a case concerning the enforcement of a statutory duty under the Friendly Societies Act 1896, Lord President Clyde described it as "a convenient suitable and practical method" of seeking redress through the courts. The case of *T. Docherty v. Burgh of Monifieth*,[26] showed that a remedy for the implement of duties of local authorities can be very useful and more frequent use of the power to enforce the statutory duties of local authorities has been made in recent years.[27] In that case the local authority was ordained to perform its statutory duty under the Burgh Police (Scotland) Act 1892 to construct sewers to the borders of land owned by Docherty. It had been contended that a remedy under the Court of Session Act[28] should not be available if there was an alternative remedy in a specific statute but Lord President Clyde could see nothing in the terms of the Court of Session Act that all other remedies had to be exhausted before a remedy under that Act was sought. In 1985 the general remedy under the Court of Session Act was expressly referred to as appropriate in judicial review procedure.[29]

Local authorities have duties which arise from a wide range of statutes. 9–16 The duty may be owed to members of the public or to other authorities. The case of *Strathclyde Regional Council v. City of Glasgow District Council*.[30] concerned the duty of every local authority to provide suitable and sufficient premises and facilities for the purposes of the district court by virtue of section 8(1) of the District Courts (Scotland) Act 1975. Glasgow District Council intended to build a new district court for the city of Glasgow. Plans were drawn up which did not include cells for prisoners in custody. Strathclyde Regional Council, as police authority, presented a petition for judicial review of the district council's decision and interdict against them constructing a district court without cell accommodation. The district council submitted that the duty of providing facilities to hold accused persons rested on the regional council as the police authority but it was held that the court staff were responsible for prisoners in custody within the court building and that accordingly the respondents had a duty to provide cells.[31]

Actions to enforce a statutory duty under section 45(b) are appropriate 9–17 only where the relevant duty is specific and unequivocal. In the case of

---

[24] Mitchell, *Constitutional Law* (2nd ed., 1968), p. 314.
[25] 1926 S.C. 418. See also *Langlands v. Mason,* 1962 S.C. 493.
[26] 1970 S.C. 200.
[27] See *Walker v. Strathclyde Regional Council (No. 1)*, 1986 S.L.T. 523.
[28] Now Court of Session Act 1988, s. 45(b).
[29] Act of Sederunt (Rules of Court Amendment No. 2) (Judicial Review) 1985, r.260B, para. 2.
[30] 1988 S.L.T. 144.
[31] This decision was affirmed on appeal: 1989 S.L.T. 235.

Re Tayside Regional Council,[32] the council sought judicial review of a decision of the British Railways Board to close a level crossing across a railway line in Broughty Ferry. The council sought declarator that the British Railways Board was under a duty to maintain the crossing and an order ordaining them to reopen it. The British Railways Board argued that an order should not be made as they were seeking authority through a private Act of Parliament to close the crossing permanently. They argued that the court should not grant the declarator and order, despite the existence of a statutory duty, on the ground that the jurisdiction of the court was supervisory and equitable, and that the power to order specific performance of statutory duties rested upon the word "may" in section 45 of the 1988 Act. Lord Prosser said: "Where a body subject to the Court's supervision has a discretion, the Court will only take it upon itself to make a specific order where that is seen as essential to the justice of the case. But where a body has a specific statutory duty, and the Court is being asked to ordain performance of that duty, the position seems to me to be very different." It was held that the declarator and the order should both be granted. The word "may" in section 45 of the 1988 Act was held to show that section 45 is an empowering section and does not give the court a discretion to tell a person that he need not do what Parliament has said must be done.

9–18   Duties may be derived from European law as well as the domestic law of a Member State. The enforcement of duties by the State and emanations of the State is an area where European law now provides a source of redress. Action may be taken against the Minister responsible for the relevant function. In the case of *R. v. Secretary of State for the Environment, ex p. Friends of the Earth*,[33] the obligation of the Secretary of State to take remedial action when the United Kingdom had been found to be in breach of European law in relation to water quality was considered and in *R. v. Secretary of State for the Environment, ex p. RSPB*,[34] the obligation of the Secretary of State in designating Special Protection Areas under the Birds Directive was considered.

Ordinary actions for breach of contract and delict

9–19   In certain circumstances actions may be brought against the Crown for breach of contract although there are limits on the remedies available. Contracts by local authorities and other public bodies are subject to the ordinary rules of contract. The Crown and other public bodies, unless acting within their powers, are liable like any ordinary person for delicts such as nuisance and negligence.[35]

---

[32] O. H. Cases, December 9, 1993.
[33] [1994] 2 C.M.L.R. 760.
[34] *The Times*, February 10, 1995, H.L.
[35] See Chap. 15.

Nobile officium

An important "safety net" in Scots law is the extraordinary jurisdiction of the Court of Session through the exercise of the *nobile officium*. Where there is a need for a remedy to be granted because of harm caused by the acts of public officials or authorities, the *nobile officium* of the court provides a means to grant a remedy where justice requires it, but none is otherwise available. In the case of *Ferguson, Petitioners*,[36] an electoral registration officer wrongly removed the names of certain voters from the draft electoral register. There was no statutory procedure for revising the list of voters, however, the court ordered the officer to reinstate the names on the register so that the petitioners could vote in an imminent election. In the case of *Maitland*,[37] the error of a licensing court was corrected by the exercise of the *nobile officium* in ordering a special meeting of the licensing court. Resort to the *nobile officium* is, however, a power which is exercised in limited circumstances where no remedy is available but there is a clear need for a justice to be done. In the case of *Bell's Executor*,[38] Lord President Clyde emphasised that the *nobile officium* was not to be used to cloak inefficiencies in the representation of clients by their lawyers nor to extend the provisions of Acts of Parliament. The court makes sparing use of this power.[39] It cannot be used against a statute even where an apparent legislative error has been made.[40] Historically, recourse to the supervisory jurisdiction of the Court of Session to challenge the actions of public authorities was an aspect of the *nobile officium*. The existence of a dedicated judicial review procedure has not completely replaced actions under the *nobile officium* and there may still be cases which fall outside the scope of existing procedures and which may be dealt with thereunder.

JUDICIAL REVIEW

Scope of judicial review

An application for judicial review is a common law remedy. Although it is 9–20 increasingly common for statutes to provide for a right of appeal from the decision of a public authority there are many instances where decisions are made which affect the rights of the citizen and no specific statutory right of appeal is provided. In these cases the court has a jurisdiction at common law to ensure that the decision-maker has acted within his powers. The procedure by which courts fulfil this function is known as judicial review.

---

[36] *Ferguson, Petrs.*, 1965 S.C. 16.
[37] 1961 S.C. 291.
[38] 1960 S.L.T. (Notes) 3.
[39] Scot. Law Com. Memorandum No. 14 (1971). "Remedies in Administrative Law", p. 39.
[40] *Hamilton v. Roxburgh C.C.*, 1971 S.L.T. 2.

The jurisdiction under which judicial review is carried out is referred to as the supervisory jurisdiction of the Court of Session. In Scotland, the subject matter of the supervisory jurisdiction extends, not only to the actings of central government and of local authorities but also to some extent to voluntary associations and private bodies.[41] Judicial review procedure provides an important safety net for the rights of the citizen as judicial review of administrative decision-making is available in circumstances when no other procedure is available.

Judicial review as a remedy of last resort

9–21 Many of the areas in which judicial review would provide an appropriate remedy, such as town and country planning, roads and licensing, are governed by statutes which provide extensive appeal procedures. An application for judicial review is a remedy of last resort and, unless there are exceptional circumstances, judicial review is incompetent where there is an alternative remedy which either has been used without success or where the remedy has not been made use of, as in the case of *O'Neill v. Scottish Joint Negotiating Committee for Teaching Staff.*[42] Angela O'Neill was employed as a teacher by Strathclyde Regional Council. She was granted maternity leave from January to June 1983 and was paid her full salary less a deduction of State maternity allowance. O'Neill claimed she was entitled to full salary without deduction of maternity allowance. The regional council rejected her claim. She appealed to the Scottish Joint Negotiating Committee, a committee established by an Act of Parliament for the purpose of considering pay and conditions of teachers. The joint committee also rejected her appeal, quoting an amendment to the 1971 scheme of conditions for Scottish teachers which stated that maternity allowance would be deducted. O'Neill brought a petition for judicial review seeking reduction of the decision. The regional council argued that the petition was incompetent since there were still other remedies available under the Administration of Justice (Scotland) Act 1972, s. 3(1), which allows for an opinion of the Court of Session in a case involving arbitration. O'Neill argued that under section 3(3) the scheme was a "collective agreement" which exempted it from the application of section 3(1), therefore judicial review was competent. It was held that O'Neill could indeed have proceeded by way of section 3(1) of the 1972 Act. Although the scheme was in itself a collective agreement, it had been incorporated in the teacher's contract of employment and since the dispute arose from the contract and not the agreement section 3(1) was applicable. Lord Jauncey, in considering the supervisory

---

[41] Lord Clyde, "The nature of the supervisory Jurisdiction and the Public/Private Distinction in Scots Administrative Law" (1991) in Finnie, Himsworth and Walker, *op. cit.,* n. 3, above.
[42] 1987 S.L.T. 648.

jurisdiction of the Court, said: "The supervisory jurisdiction of the Court of Session will continue to be exercised in only those cases in which it could have been exercised before the rule[43] was introduced. That jurisdiction is not available as a general mode of appeal against decisions of tribunals or other bodies but is rather available in limited circumstances where no other means of review exist."[44] Where a statutory remedy exists there is a concept of implied exclusion. The provision of the statutory remedy impliedly excludes the common law remedy of judicial review because it is presumed that where Parliament provides a remedy in a statute it must have intended to exclude common law remedies.[45] This argument is stronger where Parliament has created a new jurisdiction by statute, such as town and country planning. In such a situation it is easier to argue that the exercise of this new jurisdiction must be regulated entirely by the conditions of the statute under which it is conferred. A right or liability created by statute exists only to the extent that it can be enforced in accordance with that statute.[46] Use of the judicial review procedure would therefore extend the scope of the right or liability beyond its statutory limits.[47]

This approach was evident in the case of *Strathclyde Buses v. Strathclyde Regional Council*,[48] in which a bus company sought to interdict Strathclyde Regional Council from proceeding with a scheme for pedestrianisation of certain roads. Paragraph 35 of Schedule 9 to the Road Traffic Regulation Act 1984, provides that any person wishing to challenge an order made under the schedule on the grounds that it is outside "the relevant powers" may make an application to the Court of Session within six weeks of the making of the order. Paragraph 37 provides that an order, "to which this part of this Schedule applies shall not either before or after it is made be questioned in any legal proceedings whatever". The bus company sought judicial review of the proposed scheme before any order had been made on the grounds that there had been procedural improprieties. The bus company intimated that they would appeal under the terms of paragraph 35 but in the meantime they sought interim relief to prevent the local authority issuing and implementing an order with no time allowed for challenge. The judicial review proceedings were sisted (*i.e.* stopped) when the local authority undertook to give 14 days' notice of any implementation of an order. Some weeks later the local authority made the experimental traffic order but delayed its implementation for six weeks. The bus company appealed to

9–22

---

[43] Rules of the Court of Session 1994 (S.I. 1994 No. 1443), Chap. 53 (formerly 1985, rule 260B).

[44] 1987 S.L.T. 648 at 650.

[45] *Aberdeenshire Trustees v. Knowles* (1811) Hume 262.

[46] *Nahar v. Strathclyde Regional Council,* 1986 S.L.T. 570.

[47] Collar, "Judicial Review: The Significance of an Alternative Remedy" (1991) 36 J. L. S.S. 299–303.

[48] 1994 S.L.T. 724.

the Inner House, seeking interdict and quashing of the order. They also sought, by this case, to recall the sist in the action for judicial review on the grounds of unreasonableness (lack of consultation). It was held that judicial review procedure was not appropriate once the order had been made. The proper procedure was for statutory appeal under the 1984 Act. When competent statutory proceedings had already been raised the same question could not be litigated in separate legal proceedings.[49] In the case of *Bell v. Fiddes*,[50] it was held that judicial review procedure could not be used to challenge a decision by an inferior court. Individuals against whom decree had passed in an undefended action in the sheriff court sought reduction of the decree and suspension and interdict of diligence on it. They did so by petition for judicial review. It was held that it was incompetent to seek reduction of a decree of an inferior court by judicial review.[51]

9–23   In the case of *Dante v. Assessor for Ayr*,[52] a pursuer brought an action in the Court of Session seeking declarator that he was not the tenant or occupier, for the purposes of the Valuation Acts, of certain tracts of land and that he was not liable to be rated or assessed in respect of that land. He had appealed to the valuation committee but only against the value of the subjects and not against the entry of his name on the valuation roll as tenant or occupier. The action was held to be incompetent because he had failed to exhaust his available remedies and he had not proved that his failure to use the statutory remedy was due to any irregularity on the part of the authorities in making up the valuation roll or to any mistake of which he had no notice.[53] Similarly, in the case of *Nahar v. Strathclyde Regional Council*,[54] a teacher who had been dismissed on the ground of misconduct and who claimed that the disciplinary hearing procedures were marred by a failure to observe natural justice was refused a petition for judicial review as he had failed to exhaust the remedies available to him under section 85(3) of the Employment Protection (Consolidation) Act 1978. The duty is expressed as a duty to exhaust a statutory remedy before seeking judicial review. This appears to leave open the possibility of judicial review once the statutory remedies have been pursued but it is unlikely that an application for judicial review could be successfully pursued once the statutory remedies have been exhausted as the duty is based on the concept of judicial review as a remedy

---

[49] See also *Kirkwood v. City of Glasgow District Council*, 1988 S.L.T. 430; *Ingle v. Ingle's Tr.* 1996 G.W.D. 6–331.
[50] 1996 S.L.T. 51.
[51] Rules of the Court of Session 1994 (S.I. 1994 No. 1443), Chaps. 53, 58 and 60. (The general notes in *Greens Annotated Rules of the Court of Session 1994*, at rr. 53.2 and 60.6, were disapproved.)
[52] 1922 S.C. 109.
[53] See also *British Railways Board v. Glasgow Corporation*, 1976 S.C. 224.
[54] 1986 S.L.T. 570.

where none is otherwise available. An exception may, however, be made to the duty to exhaust available remedies in exceptional circumstances.[55] A determination of what amounts to exceptional circumstances is a matter to be decided on the consideration of each case.

In *British Railways Board v. Glasgow Corporation*,[56] Lord Wheatley 9–24 stated that examples of such special circumstances would be averments of *ultra vires* or fraud. If he was referring to *ultra vires* in its broad sense it would encompass all of the forms of conduct which amount to grounds for judicial review, in which case the duty to exhaust statutory remedies would have no substance. If he was referring to the narrower meaning of *ultra vires* as jurisdictional error then it would include only those instances when the body which made the decision was acting outside its statutory powers. In such circumstances the applicant should not be confined within those statutory powers in seeking redress. In the case of *Tarmac Econowaste v. Assessor for Lothian Region*,[57] Tarmac sought judicial review of the actions of the assessor with regard to a tip operated by them. The assessor argued that the petition for judicial review was incompetent because Tarmac had a statutory remedy consisting of an appeal to the Valuation Appeal Tribunal. Tarmac argued that the case should be regarded as an exception because it was based on the ground that the assessor's actions were *ultra vires*. Lord Clyde recognised that fraud and *ultra vires* could be recognised as exceptions and went on to identify two further exceptions, first where the complainer has been prevented from pursuing a statutory appeal through a procedural irregularity on the part of the authority,[58] and secondly, where a statutory remedy is available but provides an inadequate method of resolving the issue.[59] The statement that *ultra vires* actions would render the case exceptional should not, however, be taken to include all *ultra vires* actions. It was held in that case that the available statutory remedy was an effective one and the petition for judicial review was refused.[60]

In the case of *Shanks & McEwan (Contractors) v. Mifflin Construction*,[61] it was held that judicial review of an arbiter's decision was competent despite the existence of other remedies. The parties to an arbitration challenged the relevancy and specification of each other's pleadings. The respondent in the arbitration had presented a note to the Inner House seeking, *inter alia*, to have the arbiter ordained to state a case. The claimant challenged the

---

[55] *Cumming v. Inverness Magistrates*, 1953 S.C. 1; *McDaid v. Clydebank District Council*, 1984 S.L.T. 162; *Pollock v. Secretary of State for Scotland*, 1993 S.L.T. 1173; 1992 S.C.L.R. 972.
[56] 1976 S.C. 224 at 239.
[57] 1991 S.L.T. 77.
[58] *Moss Empires Ltd v. Glasgow Assessor*, 1917 S.C. (H.L.) 1.
[59] *City Cabs (Edinburgh) Ltd v. City of Edinburgh District Council*, 1988 S.L.T. 184.
[60] See also *Hope v. Edinburgh Magistrates* (1897) 5 S.L.T. 195.
[61] 1993 S.L.T. 1124.

competency of the note. A hearing on the note was pending before the Inner House. Thereafter, the respondent in the arbitration presented a petition for judicial review of the arbiter's interlocutor which had postponed consideration of the application for a stated case. A first hearing took place to consider the competency of the petition. It was argued for the claimant in the arbitration and for the arbiter that the petition was incompetent as there was an alternative statutory remedy which was being pursued before the Inner House. It was held that an alternative statutory remedy had to be an effective one and as the proceedings before the Inner House were being challenged by the first respondents as incompetent, the effectiveness of those proceedings was called into question and the existence of an alternative remedy could not found a challenge to the competency of the petition for judicial review.

9–25   The special circumstances which make judicial review procedure available even where a statutory remedy exists may arise because of the impact on fundamental human rights of failure to follow proper procedures. This was held to be so in the case of *Choi v. Secretary of State for the Home Department*.[62] The petitioner held a British passport as a citizen of Hong Kong where he lived with his mother until July 1992, when he came to the United Kingdom. Before travelling he had obtained an entry certificate as a student for single visit until October 31, 1993. In November 1992 Choi applied for indefinite leave to remain. This application was refused and he appealed. In July 1993 he returned to Hong Kong to visit his mother. He came back to the United Kingdom in September 1993 to resume his studies. On his return his passport was removed and he was given a notice of temporary admission and asked to attend for interview. Notice of refusal of leave to enter was given on October 5, along with directions for removal to Hong Kong on October 12. The reasons for refusal were that the petitioner was to be treated as a new entrant and that the immigration officer was not satisfied that the petitioner intended to leave the United Kingdom on completion of his studies. The decision made no reference to the outstanding appeal. Choi sought judicial review on the grounds that the decision to treat him as a new entrant was *ultra vires* and illegal, that the decision was not reasonable, and that the circumstances of the interview were oppressive and in breach of natural justice. It was argued that as there was an appeal procedure available in terms of the Immigration Act 1971, s. 13, the application for judicial review was incompetent. It was held that the immigration officer was not acting in excess or want of jurisdiction in refusing leave to re-enter in the absence of any current entry clearance. Choi's outstanding appeal against refusal of unlimited leave to remain could not give rise to a legitimate expectation that he could leave and return to the United Kingdom at any time but it was a material consideration which

---

[62]   1996 S.L.T. 590.

should have been taken into account. The accumulation of grounds of procedural impropriety and irrationality constituted a special circumstance such as to be an exception to the general rule that judicial review was not competent when a statutory remedy was available and had not been exhausted.

An alternative remedy which has not been used will only operate as a 9–26 bar to proceedings for judicial review when the other remedy is an effective one. In the case of *Brown v. Executive Committee of Edinburgh Labour Party*,[63] it was held that a petition for judicial review was competent despite the existence of an appeal procedure which was still available. The petition was bought for interim interdict and suspension with regard to disciplinary proceedings by the local labour party. The grounds of challenge included an allegation of bias amongst the panel members. It was held that the existence of an appeal procedure was not a bar to the court's exercise of its powers as no information had been brought before the court on the nature of such appeal procedures, therefore the court could not decide that the appeal procedure would provide an effective remedy. The balance of convenience also favoured the petitioners. This case was exceptional as it involved a breach of natural justice which amounted to an infringement of the rights of the councillors.

Judicial review as an exclusive procedure for challenging administrative decision-making

When judicial review procedure was introduced in England and Wales it 9–27 was not the only procedure which could be used for challenges to administrative decision-making. There would be some instances in England and Wales when judicial review procedure would be appropriate and others where alternative remedies could be used and even some circumstances where there would be a choice of procedure. In order to resolve any uncertainty it was decided that judicial review must be used for public law matters.[64] This principle has caused further difficulties and confusion and so, in order to avoid the difficulties in England and Wales caused by the distinction between public law matters, where use of judicial review was obligatory, and private law disputes, Lord Dunpark recommended that the new procedure for judicial review in Scotland should be exclusive. All applications for the exercise of the supervisory jurisdiction of the Court of Session must be made through judicial review procedure. This recommendation was implemented in the new procedure which specifies that "An application to the supervisory jurisdiction of the court which immediately before the coming into operation of this rule would have been made by way of summons or petition, shall be made by way of an application

---

[63] 1995 S.L.T. 985.
[64] *O'Reilly v. Mackman* [1983] 2 A.C. 237.

for judicial review." There are some exceptions in that, despite a proposal that applications for review under statutory provision should be under the same procedure (with different time-limits in some instances), they may be subject to different procedures. Applications for review of planning decisions made by or on behalf of Secretary of State for Scotland, for example, proceed directly as applications to the Inner House.[65] Summary petitions under the Court of Session Act 1988, s. 45(b), however, are subject to judicial review procedure.

In the case of *McDonald v. Secretary of State for Scotland (No. 2)*[66] it was made clear that an application for judicial review must be made by means of petition to the Court of Session. A prisoner raised an action in the sheriff court against the Secretary of State in which he alleged that he had been subjected to many illegal searches. He sought declarator that the orders under which the searches were carried out were *ultra vires*, and interdict to prevent any more illegal searches and damages. The prisoner contended that a standing order issued by the Scottish Home and Health Department to governors of prisons setting out the circumstances in which prisoners were to be searched had been issued without parliamentary approval and had no status other than that of guidelines. The sheriff dismissed the action on the basis that it was a case for judicial review, which process was incompetent in the sheriff court. The pursuer appealed to the sheriff principal who held it was properly a matter for inquiry by the sheriff court. The Secretary of State appealed to the Court of Session which held that the question of the validity of the standing orders could be challenged only by way of judicial review in the Court of Session.

Public law/Private law

9–28 In Scotland, unlike England, the different role played by the courts in matters of judicial review, as distinct from an ordinary action, does not appear to relate to whether the rights or duties which are under consideration are public or private or whether the bodies who are party to the case are public officials or private individuals or organisations. The difference in role when the court is exercising its supervisory jurisdiction is a difference of function. In an ordinary action, the court is required to find facts, apply the law, decide what is reasonable and apply its standards. Its jurisdiction encompasses the whole merits and substance of the issue before it and it has the competence to determine the whole matter in respect of both fact and the law. In contrast to this, in matters of judicial review the court is not exercising an original jurisdiction but a supervisory one. Usually, the court is concerned with a decision of some kind made by an individual or

---

[65] rule 58.3(2).
[66] 1996 S.L.T. 575.

organisation. It is not for the court to reconsider the facts or to impose its own views on the issue. It is concerned solely with procedure, to secure that a decision has been made fairly and properly.[67]

The approach of the English courts to the distinction between public law and private law jurisdiction caused some confusion in the Scottish courts. The practice of considering English precedents with regard to the substantive principles of administrative law as persuasive was established before the development of a separate judicial review procedure in Scotland. After the introduction of that distinct Scottish judicial review procedure, there was a series of judgments in the Court of Session which appeared to follow English case law in deciding whether or not proceedings for judicial review were competent. The distinction was made between cases involving matters of public law where judicial review was competent and those involving private law matters where judicial review was not competent. One of those cases was *Connor v. Strathclyde Regional Council*,[68] which was a petition for judicial review of a local authority appointment process. A regional council, as education authority, held a selection board for two assistant head teachers' posts. The head teacher of one school was present as an assessor during the interviews and the consideration thereafter. He was the uncle of the successful applicant for the post at the other school. Neither had disclosed their relationship. An unsuccessful applicant petitioned for judicial review. Regarding the competency of the petition, Lord Allanbridge said that he was satisfied it was appropriate to consider English case law and dismissing the petition he said: "In my view the Court of Session has no power in the exercise of its supervisory jurisdiction to intervene in a situation where there is no element of public law arising which is sufficient to attract public law remedies".[69] To describe judicial review as a "public law remedy" was inappropriate in Scotland, and was a consequence of the confusion which had arisen from the absorption of English law terminology relating to procedural matters into Scottish cases where English cases were cited to support arguments relating to the grounds for applications for judicial review.[70]

The case of *Tehrani v. Argyll and Clyde Health Board (No. 2)*[71] was 9–29 heard when the confusion was at its peak. The application for judicial review was made by a surgeon employed by the National Health Service in Glasgow. He had been suspended from duty following a complaint about his treatment of a patient. A committee of inquiry was set up by the local health board to investigate the allegations. The board then dismissed Tehrani and he sought

---

[67] Lord Clyde, *op. cit.,* n. 41, above, p. 286.
[68] 1986 S.L.T. 530.
[69] *ibid.* at 534.
[70] See also *Safeway Food Stores Ltd v. The Scottish Provident Institution,* 1989 S.L.T. 131.
[71] 1990 S.L.T. 118. See also *Kyle and Carrick District Council v. A.R. Kerr,* 1992 S.L.T. 629.

to challenge the decision by judicial review. At first instance it was held that the manner in which the dismissal had been carried out was unreasonable and a decree of reduction was granted. The board reclaimed on the basis that the application for judicial review was incompetent. Their plea was sustained. It was held the dispute was related to the contractual relationship between the board as an employer and Tehrani as an employee and must be dealt with as a matter of employment law under ordinary jurisdiction. The terminology used in the judgments, particularly references to "public administrative law" and "public law remedies" in that case contributed further to the confusion as to the scope of judicial review in Scotland. The outcome of the case was correct but it was the existence of unused remedies for breach of contract which rendered judicial review incompetent, not whether or not public law remedies were called for. At first instance Lord Weir had allowed the petition and found the decision of the board amenable to judicial review, stating that: "The supervisory jurisdiction of the Court of Session has not in the past been confined to matters of public law and the introduction of judicial review procedure has not affected the extent of this jurisdiction."[72] Lord Weir stated that he "respectfully disagreed" with the public and private distinction in Scots law as far as eligibility for judicial review was concerned. However his decision was overturned on appeal. Lord Justice-Clerk Ross stated: "Accordingly, in determining whether or not the present petition is competent, the question is whether a matter of public law is raised in the application."[73] He went on to say: "I am satisfied in the present case that there are no public law elements in the petitioner's case which could give rise to any entitlement to a public law remedy such as judicial review."[74] Lord Wylie noted that: "The fact that the employer is a public body does not *per se* inject an element of public law into the contract of service, nor does the fact the employee had the benefit of statutory provisions in relation to condition of service." He also said that: "the board was exercising rights arising out of a private contract of employment, and not withstanding the statutory background, it was not an exercise of powers conferred by statute".[75]

9–30   In the case of *Watt v. Strathclyde Regional Council*[76] Lord Clyde gave his opinion that in considering the competency of an application for judicial review it was inappropriate to ask whether there was a public law element, for, even if meaning could be given to the expression "public law," the distinction was not consistent with the development of Scots law. The Lord Ordinary held that the petition in *Watt* was incompetent since it related only

---

[72] 1990 S.L.T. 118 at 124.
[73] *ibid.* at 132.
[74] *ibid.* at 135.
[75] *ibid.* at 137 and 138.
[76] 1992 S.L.T. 324 at 330.

to alleged breaches of contracts between the individuals and their employers (the local council had decided unilaterally to amend teacher's contracts). The respondents' "private" interests did not call for protection by means of judicial review procedure and this case could not be distinguished from *Tehrani v. Argyll and Clyde Health Board*.[77] Lord President Hope, in the Inner House, said he would have found himself in full agreement with this view if he had been satisfied that the case only concerned the determination of issues relating to the petitioners under their contracts of employment with the council. He noted that when Lord Fraser made his comments, in the case of *Brown v. Hamilton District Council*, on the public law area and the public law field in relation to judicial review, what he had in mind was a change in procedure and not a change in the supervisory jurisdiction. In Scotland the public and private dichotomy is not an appropriate way of assessing eligibility for judicial review. Lord President Hope said: "No doubt the ordinary contractual remedies are available to the petitioners, including that of interim interdict, in regard to such breaches of contract as may result. But that does not, in my view, have the effect of excluding the decision itself from the remedy of judicial review at this stage."[78]

Lord Clyde agreed with Lord President Hope and pointed out that rule 260B[79] makes no reference to public or private bodies, but merely to applications to the "supervisory jurisdiction of the court".[80] He observed that there is a problem in defining the scope of judicial review in relation to cases which concern the legality of an employer's actings and the contractual rights of the employee, and that "resort" had on occasion been made to categories of matters of "public law" and "private law" but that the distinction had been disowned in this case. He went on to say: "The contractual element of the case does not seem to me fatal to the competency of the application ... The attack is directed essentially at an alleged excess of power."[81] The reclaiming motion against the Lord Ordinary's decision that the petition was incompetent was allowed.

Extensive clarification on the scope of judicial review is provided by the judgment of Lord Hope in the case of *West v. Secretary of State for Scotland*[82] wherein it was held that the supervisory jurisdiction does not depend on a distinction between public and private law but is dependent upon whether the court has jurisdiction over the person or body making the relevant decision. The test is whether a jurisdiction (meaning a power) has been delegated or entrusted to a person or body so as to create a tripartite 9–31

[77] 1990 S.L.T. 118.
[78] *ibid*. at 329.
[79] Now Rules of the Court of Session 1994 (S.I. 1994 No. 1443), Chap. 53.
[80] 1990 S.L.T. 118 at 330.
[81] *ibid*. at 331–332.
[82] 1992 S.L.T. 636; 1992 S.C.L.R. 385 (*sub nom West v. Scottish Prison Service*).

relationship which distinguishes the circumstances from ordinary contractual obligations. The facts of the case seem relatively unimportant for a decision of such moment but they are as follows: a serving prison officer was transferred from H.M. Young Offenders Institution in Polmont to H.M. Prison in Edinburgh. His contract of employment stated that he was liable to be transferred to any prison in Scotland. Reimbursement of removal expenses was at the discretion of the Scottish Prison Service. His application for expenses was refused and he brought an action for judicial review, seeking reduction of the decision and a declaration that he was entitled to expenses. He argued that the decision to refuse expenses was an unreasonable exercise of a discretion. At first instance the Lord Ordinary held that the petition was incompetent on the ground that the dispute was a pure matter of contract between the parties. This decision was upheld by the Inner House but the Lord President (Lord Hope) took the opportunity to deliver a judgment which would clarify the uncertainties which had arisen over the scope of judicial review in Scotland. He stated:

1. The Court of Session has power, in the exercise of its supervisory jurisdiction, to regulate the process by which decisions are taken by any person or body to whom a jurisdiction, power or authority has been delegated or entrusted by statute, agreement or any other instrument
2. The sole purpose for which supervisory jurisdiction might be exercised is to ensure that the person or body does not exceed or abuse that jurisdiction, power or authority or fail to do what the jurisdiction, power or authority requires.
3. The cases in which the exercise of the supervisory jurisdiction is appropriate involve a tripartite relationship constituted by the conferring (whether by statute or private contract) of a decision-making power or duty on a third party to whom the taking of the decision is entrusted, but whose manner of decision-making might be controlled by the court.[83]
4. To describe the supervisory jurisdiction as a public law remedy, and to look for an element of public law as the test of whether it was available, is to introduce concepts which had no part in the development of the supervisory jurisdiction in Scotland over the last two centuries.

9–32   The competency of the action therefore did not depend upon any distinction between public law and private law, nor was it confined to those cases which English law had accepted as amenable to judicial review, nor was it correct in regard to issues about competency to describe judicial review as a public law remedy. It was also observed that the delegated jurisdiction in the context of this judgment meant simply "power to decide". It was also observed that there was no difference of substance between the law of Scotland and the law of England as to the substantive grounds on which a decision might be challenged by an application to the supervisory jurisdiction. Another important point which was made is that the categories of what might amount

---

[83] 1992 S.L.T. 636 at 643–651.

to an excess or abuse of jurisdiction are not closed and are capable of being developed in accordance with the development of administrative law.[84]

Tripartite relationships

The rejection of the public law/private law distinction as the principle on 9–33 which the supervisory jurisdiction should be based has been welcomed by some as a means of escape from the misguided rigidity of the English rules.[85] Others have been more sceptical.[86] Whether or not the concept of a tripartite relationship as the basis for the supervisory jurisdiction of the Court of Session provides a definitive test of jurisdiction, it does have the advantage that it avoids the need to draw the distinction made by the English courts between private law and public law remedies. The principle that the supervisory jurisdiction of the Court of Session does not depend on distinctions between public bodies and those who exercise jurisdiction under a private contractual agreement was apparent in the judgment of Lord President Inglis in the nineteenth century case of *Forbes v. Underwood*.[87] That case concerned the power of the court to compel an arbiter to perform his duty and a comparison was made between the position of an arbiter and that of a judge. It was held that the public or private nature of the inferior body is not decisive, nor does jurisdiction depend entirely on whether the decision of the inferior body was administrative in character. The essential factor is that a decision-making function has been entrusted to that body or tribunal which it can be compelled by the court to perform. The tripartite relationship is significant as it involves the conferring, whether by statute or private contract, of a decision-making power or duty on a third party to whom the taking of the decision is entrusted but whose manner of decision-making may be controlled by the court.

Parties to a Tripartite Relationship

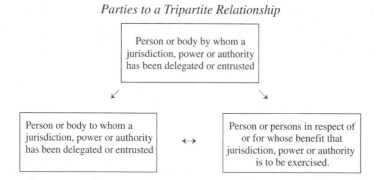

---

[84] 1992 S.L.T. 636 at 641 and 650–651.

[85] Wade and Forsyth, *Administrative Law* (7th ed., 1994), pp. 667 and 682.

[86] Himsworth, "Judicial Review in Scotland", in *Judicial Review: A Thematic Approach* (Hadfield ed., 1995), p. 291.

[87] (1886) 13 R. 465.

9–34   This approach was followed throughout the cases this century. Any inferior tribunal or administrative body which has had entrusted to it a decision-making power or duty which must be exercised within the jurisdiction conferred upon it is subject to the jurisdiction of the Court of Session. The tripartite relationship principle for jurisdiction also has the advantage that it provides for the continuation of the court's supervisory jurisdiction over "domestic tribunals", established by bodies such as voluntary associations, religious organisations or clubs, where the basis for the authority to act is derived from a contract rather than a statute.[88] These bodies exercise powers to make decisions which affect the rights and interests of members of the organisation and, although it might be argued that membership is voluntary and only a matter of contractual agreement, the decisions may affect such fundamentally important matters as a person's ability to work or trade.

9–35   In the case of *McDonald v. Burns,*[89] it was held that the court has jurisdiction to review the decisions of an ecclesiastical body if certain conditions are fulfilled. The court will have jurisdiction where that body has acted beyond its own constitution in a manner calculated to affect the civil rights and patrimonial interests of any of its members. The court will also have jurisdiction where, although acting within its own constitution, procedure of the body has been marked by gross irregularity such as would, in the case of an ordinary civil tribunal, be sufficient to vitiate the proceedings. The distinction between public and private law was been shown to be unhelpful in the case of *St Johnstone Football Club v. Scottish Football Association Ltd.*[90] The articles of the Scottish Football Association conferred power on the council of that organisation to discipline its members. A tripartite relationship was established by an internal delegation of the association's disciplinary powers to the council. The council had acted contrary to natural justice in the process by which it had taken a decision to fine St Johnstone Football Club. This case serves as an example to show that the tripartite principle can be applied to cases involving private organisations.

---

[88] *St Johnstone Football Club Ltd v. Scottish Football Association Ltd,* 1965 S.L.T. 171; *Brown v. Edinburgh District Labour Party,* O. H., January 10, 1994, unreported.
[89] 1940 S.L.T. 325; 1940 S.C. 376.
[90] 1965 S.L.T. 171.

Parties to the Tripartite Relationship in St Johnstone v. SFA

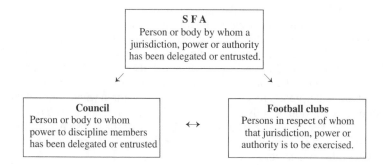

Presumably, if the association had acted directly against the club, rather than through a disciplinary council, there would have been no tripartite relationship and the action would not have been reviewable.[91] In the case of *Gunstone v. Scottish Women's Amateur Athletic Association*,[92] Lord Prosser affirmed that the two sets of circumstances in which the court would interfere in the internal affairs of voluntary organisations were, first, where an association, through its agencies had acted clearly and demonstrably beyond its own constitution and a manner which infringed the rights of its members and, secondly, where there has been a gross procedural irregularity."[93]

The courts in England have "with reluctance" refused to grant leave to apply for judicial review in cases where the decision has been made by an organisation which is not part of the Government or an organisation operating under statutory authority. In the case of *R. v. Disciplinary Committee of the Jockey Club, ex p. Aga Khan*,[94] the Aga Khan's horse won the Oaks but was disqualified by the disciplinary committee of the Jockey Club for failing a dope test. The Aga Khan sought judicial review of the committee's decision but it was held that the decision was not reviewable. The Jockey Club's powers derived from private agreement and could not be challenged by judicial review. In the case of *Law v. National Greyhound Racing Club Ltd*,[95] the licence of a trainer (Law) was suspended. He sought a declaration that the decision was *ultra vires*. It was held that the authority of the body derived wholly from contract and judicial review was not appropriate. Similarly in the case of *R. v. Disciplinary Committee of the*

9–36

---

[91] Himsworth, *op. cit.,* n. 86, above, p. 298.
[92] 1987 S.L.T. 611.
[93] *ibid.* at 613.
[94] [1993] 1 W.L.R. 909, C.A.
[95] [1983] 1 W.L.R. 1302.

Jockey Club, ex p. Massingberd-Mundy,[96] the decision of the Jockey Club withdrawing its approval of a steward chairman was challenged as unfair. It was held, with reluctance, that judicial review was not available.

9–37   The application of the tripartite relationship test in Scotland avoids such problems. In many of the circumstances which lead to petitions being brought before the Court of Session for judicial review, the "person or body by whom the jurisdiction, power or authority has been delegated or entrusted" will be Parliament itself. The majority of judicial review cases involve an interpretation of a statute in order to ascertain whether or not the actions of a person or body have been within the powers conferred on him by statute. The "person or persons in respect of or for whose benefit that jurisdiction, power or authority is to be exercised" will be persons or bodies having title or interest to sue

9–38   The test of the tripartite relationship is not without problems, particularly where a contractual relationship exists. In cases involving contractual relationships it is not always a straightforward matter to distinguish between those rights and obligations which arise from contract and those which arise from the conferring of a power upon a body or an official.[97] In the case of *R. v. East Berkshire Health Authority, ex p. Walsh,*[98] a distinction was drawn between the rights and remedies enjoyed by an employee arising out of a private contract of employment and the performance by a public body of the duties conferred on it as part of the statutory terms under which it exercises its powers. Walsh had been employed as a senior nursing officer at Wrexham Park Hospital. He was dismissed as a result of alleged misconduct. He applied for judicial review. It was held that the fact that Walsh was employed in a public service did not make his dismissal a matter suitable for consideration by way of judicial review. If the dispute had related to the national negotiations over conditions of service and the resulting agreement which was approved by the Secretary of State, for example, if Walsh's treatment had conflicted with the conditions of service, he would have had a remedy by way of judicial review. There will therefore, within the relationship of employee and an employer who is a public body, be some rights and obligations where contractual remedies are appropriate and other aspects of the relationship which are part of the tripartite relationship and which may be amenable to judicial review. The same situation arises in the case of other contracts, such as that between a university and its students. In the case of *Bank of Scotland, Petitioner,*[99] IMRO had refused to waive restrictions on a member's life policy business.

---

[96] [1993] 2 All E.R. 207.
[97] Himsworth, *op. cit.,* n. 86, above.
[98] [1985] Q.B. 152.
[99] *The Times*, November 21, 1988.

It was held that the decision was amenable to judicial review. The existence of contractual obligations was no bar to judicial review.

The case of *Naik v. University of Stirling*[1] concerned the decision to prevent a student who had failed to pay fees continuing with a course of study at Stirling University. She sought judicial review on the grounds of breach of natural justice and unreasonableness. The university challenged the competency of the application for judicial review on the basis that there was no tripartite relationship. Lord MacLean observed that if there was indeed a need to establish a tripartite relationship in every case in which application was made to the supervisory jurisdiction of the Court of Session "[t]hat seems to me to impose an inflexible and over formal restraint upon the court's jurisdiction".[2] He considered that there was, however, a tripartite relationship in the case. Powers were granted to the university by royal charter and those powers included the power to prescribe rules to discipline students.

The case of *Joobeen v. University of Stirling*[3] was related to the case of   9–39 *Naik v. University of Stirling*.[4] The petitioner, also a former student at Stirling University, sought declarator that the decision of the respondents to terminate his registration for, and participation in the course in Japanese Studies, and to exclude him from the university and its campus was contrary to natural justice, unreasonable, and contrary to his legitimate expectations. The university pleaded that the application was incompetent. Lord Prosser held that the university was entitled to rescind its contract with the student for non-payment of his fees, and accordingly refused the petition for judicial review. In relation to competency he went on to say:

> "the requirement of a 'tripartite' relationship, which appeared to be laid down in *West v. The Secretary of State for Scotland,* 1992 S.L.T. 636, must not be given too narrow a meaning ... a large number, and indeed the classic, examples of disputes subject to judicial review involved issues between the citizen and local or central Government, where the 'third' party must apparently be merely Parliament, as the body having conferred powers. In the present case, the University's Royal Charter produced a comparable tripartite background. The petitioner became a member of the University by contract, but the contract created a situation in which he was subject to University authority, and could question it by judicial review".[5]

It was held, however, that the real issues in the case were not of a kind suitable for judicial review, but were matters of simple rights and obligations under contract law, requiring the court's ordinary, and not its supervisory jurisdiction.

---

[1]   1994 S.L.T. 449.
[2]   *ibid.* at 451–452.
[3]   1995 S.L.T. 120 (Note).
[4]   1994 S.L.T. 449.
[5]   1995 S.L.T. 120 (Note) at 122.

In *Blair v. Lochaber District Council*,[6] the chief executive of the council sought judicial review of the decision to suspend him from duties on full pay pending an investigation into allegations made in internal audit reports. The council said that the petition for judicial review was incompetent as the *West* case had clearly shown that contractual matters were not open to judicial review. Despite pleadings by the petitioner over the scope and meaning of tripartite relationships which invoke the supervisory jurisdiction of the Court of Session it was held that no such relationship existed in this case. Although there may be cases concerning an employee, an employer and no third party which could be open to judicial review this case was not one of those cases. It was held that the matter was purely a contractual one concerning the contract of employment. It was also noted that the petitioner had, in any case, an alternative remedy under the ordinary law. Lord Clyde said:

> "If ... the tripartite test is conclusive in the context of employment contracts then the petitioner fails here on competency ... There is no third party in the present case to whom the council entrusted the making of the decision; they made it themselves ... The priority to be given to a contractual remedy should be recognised equally in relation to contracts by public bodies as well as private ones and the ordinary judicial processes may be expeditious enough to provide rapid remedies."[7]

9–40   Lord Clyde interpreted the purpose of the tripartite relationship approach as being to provide for similarity of treatment between the private and public sectors. The nature of the relationship itself and the effect on the rights of the individual should be seen as more important than whether or not the relationship is between parties in the private sector or parties in the public sector of society. Lord Clyde acknowledged that the tripartite test would not resolve every issue of competence in the field of employment and further clarification is still required to define the boundaries of the scope of judicial review. It is important, however, to remember that judicial review is a remedy of last resort and therefore all other remedies should be exhausted prior to applying for judicial review. Judicial review will not be available where there is an available statutory remedy. In employment law disputes there will usually be a provision for a remedy under employment law legislation. The position is less straightforward when the alternative remedy is a right of action based on contract at common law but the need to exhaust other remedies before seeking judicial review provides a practical solution to many of the situations in which there are difficulties in defining the scope of judicial review.

The supervisory nature of the jurisdiction presupposes the existence of some individual or body whose behaviour is subject to supervision.

---

[6]   1995 S.L.T. 407.
[7]   *ibid.* at 409 and 411.

However, it is not easy to see why any distinction should be drawn between the kinds of individual or body concerned or why it should make a difference if the functions which are exercised by the individual or body are based on the authority of a statute as opposed to a contract. What is important is that where certain remedies are sought, such as reduction of a decision, then the action is competent only in the Court of Session because it is the supervisory jurisdiction which is being invoked. According to Lord Clyde,[8] it is not any element of the public or private nature of the dispute which makes the difference but the nature of the jurisdiction which is being invoked and the kind of remedy which may be required.

In the case of *Importa Ltd, Petitioner*,[9] Importa Ltd argued that a 9–41 disposition, conveying rights in common over Tay Square in Dundee in favour of Dundee Repertory Theatre, had been prepared and executed by officers of the Tayside Regional Council who did not have the delegated authority to do so and had not sought specific authority from the council for the granting of the disposition. Importa sought judicial review for declarator that the council's decision to grant the disposition was invalid and ineffective, reduction of the decision and interdict to prevent the Dundee Repertory Theatre from exercising its purported rights under the disposition. The petition was challenged on the grounds of competency. It was held that *West*[10] now determined the competency of applications to the supervisory jurisdiction of the court and that this case did not fall within that determination as there was no tripartite relationship. Importa had also chosen the wrong remedy, the correct one being an ordinary action for production, reduction and declarator in which the theatre would be called as a defender. Lord Kirkwood said:

> "In my opinion the present case does not involve such a tripartite relation-ship ... the unauthorised grant of the Disposition does not, in the circum-stances of the case, raise any question regarding an excess or abuse of power or jurisdiction nor do I consider that the case involves the exercise of a deci-sion-making power which has been entrusted to the respondents. The issues sought to be raised in the petition are, in my view, of the nature of a private dispute concerning the heritable rights in Tay Square and are not amenable to judicial review."

The competence of judicial review procedure where there is also a contract 9–42 of employment was considered in the case *Matthew Rooney, Petitioner*,[11] which was a petition for judicial review raised by a former police constable who had submitted his resignation to his chief constable. He sought

---

[8] Lord Clyde, *op. cit.,* n. 41, above, p. 288.

[9] O. H., July 13, 1994; 1994 G.W.D. 26–1542.

[10] *West v. Secretary of State for Scotland; sub nom. West v. Scottish Prison Service,* 1992 S.C. 385; 1992 S.L.T. 636.

[11] O. H., November 15, 1995; 1996 G.W.D. 39–2235.

declarator that the chief constable had failed to follow proper procedures in accepting his resignation and refusing to accept his subsequent withdrawal of the resignation. Lady Cosgrove considered the issue of competency and found that the relationship between a police constable and a chief constable was not a relationship of employer and employee. The functions of a police constable are conferred by section 17 of the Police (Scotland) Act 1967. The chief constable has statutory powers to direct constables and is also given disciplinary powers in terms of section 26. There were also regulations and guidelines relating to matters such as procedures for resignation and dismissal. Lady Cosgrove said: "It is clear that while there is no room for judicial review where there are contractual rights or obligations which can be enforced, at least as a matter of general principle, the existence of a tripartite relationship explains the availability of judicial review to an employee in cases where the decision-making process has been entrusted to a body other than the employer." She found that jurisdiction had been entrusted to the chief constable as distinct from the police authority, "that is to say an individual with separate identity from that authority". The procedures in the procedures manual: "emanate from a higher authority and while they are not enshrined in statute or statutory instrument, it is clear from the terms ... that the chief constable is being entrusted with the responsibility for ensuring that they are applied in each and every case". Judicial review was therefore held to be competent in that case.

9–43   Whether it is the test of a tripartite relationship or a test based on whether a decision is a public law matter or an administrative matter, the most important consideration is that narrow and technical interpretations do not develop in a way which would limit rather than facilitate access to justice for those who have suffered a wrong or which would render the law even more complex by causing fine and artificial distinctions to be drawn between individual cases. Under the tripartite test the same access to justice is provided to those whose rights have been infringed whether or not the organisation which has exercised the authority conferred on it to infringe those rights has done so under authority derived from public law or private law. The scope of judicial review is therefore extended in accordance with the views of the Dunpark Committee that the purpose of judicial review procedure should be to facilitate access to justice. The reviewability of actions taken under prerogative powers is an issue which has not been resolved by the test of a tripartite relationship and ultimately, if the wish for relative certainty as to the competency of judicial review applications is to be secured, some further treatment of the issues would seem to be desirable.[12]

---

[12] Junor, "Judicial Review and the Intricacies of the Tripartite Relationship" (1995) 226 SCOLAG.

Reviewable acts

All decisions, acts and omissions by public authorities and officials are 9–44
potentially reviewable. However, where the decisions which are subject to
review are those of a domestic rather than a public body the scope of
amenability to judicial review is not easy to determine. In *McDonald v.
Burns*[13] Lord Justice-Clerk Aitchison said: "The internal discipline of any
such body is a matter of domestic concern, notwithstanding that status or
civil rights may be involved and it is only in extraordinary circumstances
that the courts will regard it as within their competence to intervene." The
Lord Justice-Clerk explained that the extraordinary circumstances might
arise in two situations:

> (i) where the association has acted beyond its constitution in a manner calcu-
> lated to affect the civil rights and patrimonial interests of its members;

> (ii) where, although acting within its constitution, the procedure of its judi-
> cial or quasi-judicial tribunals has been marked by gross irregularity, such as
> would, in the case of an ordinary civil tribunal be sufficient to vitiate the
> proceedings. It must be so fundamental an irregularity that it goes beyond a
> mere matter of procedure and becomes something so prejudicial to a fair and
> impartial investigation of the question to be decided as to amount to a denial
> of natural justice.[14]

It is not clear whether the requirement that the qualification that civil
rights and patrimonial interests should be affected applies to the second set
of circumstances as well as the first, but as a breach of natural justice is in
itself a serious erosion of a person's rights it would not be reasonable to
require any other infringement of rights or detrimental impact on patrimonial
interests where a breach of natural justice has been established. This was
discussed in *St Johnstone Football Club v. Scottish Football Association
Ltd.*[15] Lord Kilbrandon said, referring to the judgment of Lord Justice-Clerk
Aitchison in *McDonald*:

> "in the second of these situations the Lord Justice Clerk makes no mention
> of the civil rights and patrimonial interests of the members, and in my judge-
> ment this case is authority, by which I am bound, for the proposition that this
> court will entertain actions arising out of the 'judgements' of the governing
> bodies of private associations, whether or not the civil rights and patrimonial
> interests of members have been interfered with by the proceedings com-
> plained of, where a gross irregularity, such as a departure from the rules of
> natural justice has been demonstrated".[16]

---

[13] 1940 S.L.T. 325.
[14] *ibid.* at 331–332.
[15] 1965 S.L.T. 171.
[16] *ibid.* at 171.

(There was in fact a patrimonial loss in that case as a fine had been levied against the club in circumstances contrary to the principles of natural justice.)

9–45   Expressions of opinion or expressions of intention with regard to future actions are not subject to review. In the case of *Hands v. Kyle and Carrick District Council*,[17] Lord Prosser said: "The expression of views by planning authorities, when these views do not take the form of an actual decision with legal consequences, is not a matter open to review." Hands had been granted planning permission in 1978 for a hotel extension which consisted of 16 self-catering suites. Ten were built and foundations had been laid for the remaining six units. In 1983 planning permission was granted to change the use of the main hotel building and the suites so as to form 18 residential flats. Hands sought declarator, by way of an ordinary action, that he was entitled to build the remaining six suites. It was held that as no work had been carried out which could attract an enforcement notice or the appeal procedure for such notices, the parties rights could be restored only by a process such as the present, but that since the defenders had not as such made a decision on the matter judicial review was not appropriate. (It seemed therefore that the only way for Hands to resolve the dispute was to commence building operations and then challenge any enforcement notices issued by the planning authority.)

9–46   Judicial review procedure is not available in relation to criminal proceedings where the High Court of Justiciary has jurisdiction. In the case of *Reynolds v. Christie*[18] George Reynolds applied for legal aid to defend a charge of assault against him. The stipendiary magistrate refused the application. Under the Act of Adjournal rules governing legal aid in criminal proceedings, rule 5(4) stated that an application may be refused where it is not in the interests of justice to make legal aid available. Rule 9 provides that such a decision is final, except in certain circumstances. These circumstances did not apply to the petitioner and he sought to nullify the decision by way of a petition for judicial review. This could not be done since jurisdiction in criminal matters lies exclusively with the High Court of Justiciary. Lord Morison noted that Hume's *Commentaries,* ii, 59 state that the power of providing a remedy for extraordinary occurrences in the course of criminal business is: "the exclusive province of the Court of Justiciary, without exception of any other judicature, how eminent soever its degree".[19] The petitioner claimed that the proceedings were concerned with the civil right, not a criminal one, of all persons to be awarded legal aid if the qualifications are met. It was held that the power to refuse legal aid in this case was governed by statutory provisions which applied

---

[17]   1988 S.C.L.R. 470 at 473.
[18]   1988 S.L.T. 68.
[19]   *ibid.* at 69.

exclusively to criminal proceedings and enacting these falls naturally within the course of criminal business as described by Hume.

Judicial review is not available unless there is an issue to be resolved   9–47 which has real consequences for the parties. In the case of *Conway v. Secretary of State for Scotland*,[20] a prisoner sought judicial review of a decision by a deputy prison governor finding him guilty of disciplinary offences, and sentencing him to confinement in his cell, deprivation of mattress, forfeiture of remission, earnings and privileges, and exclusion from work for 14 days. The decision had been taken two years earlier and the punishments were mainly spent. It was argued that judicial review was not competent since there would be no practical consequences of any determination but it was held that it was inappropriate to deny a remedy simply because part of the consequences had been implemented and were incapable of being restored. The loss of earnings and loss of remission were still live issues and so judicial review was competent. It was inappropriate to deny a remedy where only part of the consequences of an unlawful decision had been implemented and were incapable of being restored or rectified. Judicial review was available to any person whose rights were affected by a decision so long as a successful challenge would have a practical consequence which would reflect in his patrimonial or human rights. The petitioner was accordingly entitled to seek judicial review.

Prerogative powers

One area of uncertainty is the reviewability of actions taken under   9–48 prerogative powers of the Crown. In the not too distant past the view was held that, since the Crown itself was not subject to review, actions taken under authority of prerogative power could not be subject to judicial review. However, this view has been eroded to a certain extent in recent years. In the case of *R. v. Home Secretary, ex parte Fire Brigades Union*,[21] it was held that the courts may review the way in which a prerogative power has been exercised, in proceedings similar to those in which judicial review may be sought of the exercise of a power based on statutory authority. In *Laker Airways v. Department of Trade*,[22] where it was held that where a person has acquired a right under statute (in this case an air transport licence to operate on an international route) that right could not be taken away by a prerogative act, carried out under a treaty, which purported to remove that person's designation as a scheduled air carrier on a transatlantic route, Lord Denning stated: "Seeing that the prerogative is a discretionary power to be exercised for the public good, it follows that its exercise can be examined

---

[20] 1996 S.L.T. 689.
[21] [1995] 2 All E.R. 244.
[22] [1977] Q.B. 643.

by the courts just as any other discretionary power which is vested in the executive ... the courts can examine the exercise of them so as to see that they are not used improperly or mistakenly."

Although there had previously been some doubt as to whether decisions taken under the authority of the prerogative were reviewable there had been instances of the courts considering the extent of the prerogative. In *Burmah Oil Co. v. Lord Advocate*,[23] the House of Lords set a limit to the war prerogative (of requisitioning property for the defence of the realm) when it declared that, even in time of war, the property of a British subject cannot be requisitioned or demolished without making compensation to the owner of it. In *Nissan v. Attorney-General*,[24] the treaty prerogative, the right to make treaties with foreign powers, was circumscribed by holding that it cannot be used to violate the legal rights of a British subject, except on being liable for any damage suffered.

9–49   The House of Lords considered the reviewability of the prerogative power again in *Council of Civil Service Unions v. Minister for the Civil Service*,[25] (the GCHQ case). The Government sought, under the prerogative power for the management of the civil service, to prohibit civil servants working at the Government Communications Headquarters (GCHQ) from belonging to trade unions. The instruction to the civil servants, prohibiting membership of trade unions, was challenged on the ground of procedural unfairness. The civil servants should have been consulted before the instruction was issued but there had been no such consultation. The majority of the House of Lords found that the government action was subject to judicial review despite the fact that the actions were taken under the authority of prerogative powers. (The challenge by the CCSU was, however, unsuccessful as the Government had shown that the reason for the failure to hold consultations was in the interests of national security which took priority over the civil servants' right to a judicial remedy.) It was indicated in the judgments that, although some decisions made under prerogative powers are reviewable, not every exercise of prerogative powers should be subject to challenge in the courts. Lord Fraser said:

> "the courts will enquire into whether a particular prerogative power exists or not and, if it does exist, as to its extent. But once the existence and the extent of a power are established to the satisfaction of the court, the court cannot inquire into the propriety of its exercise. That is ... plainly reasonable in relation to many of the most important prerogative powers which are concerned with control of the armed forces and with foreign policy and with other matters which are unsuitable for discussion or review in the law courts. In the present case the prerogative power involved is the power to regulate

---

[23] [1965] A.C. 75.
[24] [1970] A.C. 179.
[25] [1985] A.C. 374.

the Home Civil Service, and I recognise that there is no obvious reason why the mode of exercise of that power should be immune from review by the courts".

In the case of *R. v. Home Secretary, ex parte Bentley*,[26] the question under consideration was the reviewability of a refusal to exercise a prerogative power to issue a posthumous pardon. The applicant's brother, Derek Bentley, was convicted of the murder of a police officer in 1952. Despite the recommendation of the jury and the advice of Home Office officials to the effect that the death penalty should not be enforced in this case, Bentley was executed in 1953. In 1992 the Home Secretary, whilst indicating that he had sympathy for the view that Bentley should not have been hanged, refused to grant him a posthumous pardon, on the ground that it was not Home Office policy to do so unless the defendant concerned had been proved to be both technically and morally innocent of any crime. The Home Secretary was satisfied, following a review of Bentley's case, that Bentley's innocence had not been established. On an application for judicial review of the refusal by the Home Secretary the court declined to make any order, but invited the Home Secretary to look again at the range of options that might permit some formal recognition of the view that Bentley should not have been hanged. Salmon L.J. accepted the argument that, in principle, a failure to consider exercising the power to grant a pardon should be reviewable in appropriate circumstances, for example, where there had been a failure to consider relevant material or failure to act in accordance with guidelines, or if there was an error in law. He concluded that some aspects of the exercise of the royal prerogative are amenable to the judicial process. "The question is ... whether the nature and subject matter of the decision is amenable to the judicial process. Are the court qualified to deal with the matter or does the decision involve such questions of policy that they should not intrude because they are ill-equipped so to do?"

9–50

The principle that certain prerogative powers are subject to judicial review was confirmed in the case of *R. v. Secretary of State for Foreign and Commonwealth affairs, ex parte Everett*.[27] The applicant, whilst residing in Spain, had applied for the renewal of his passport. The power to issue passports derives from prerogative power. As there was a warrant for his arrest issued in England, the Foreign Office declined to renew his passport, but did offer to issue a one-way travel document to the United Kingdom. He was not informed of the reason for the refusal of the passport renewal. At first instance the decision not to renew the passport was quashed but the decision was overturned on appeal. It was held that the issue of a passport was a matter which was amenable to judicial review.

---

[26] [1994] 2 W.L.R. 101.
[27] [1989] 2 W.L.R. 224.

9–51   In the recent case of *R. v. Secretary of State for the Home Department, ex parte Fire Brigades Union*,[28] the House of Lords considered whether it was lawful to use the prerogative power in preference to a statutory scheme. A scheme existed for allocating funds by way of compensation for the victims of crime. The scheme was created under prerogative powers and was adMinistered by the Criminal Injuries Compensation Board. Sections 108–117 of the Criminal Justice Act 1988 sought to codify this scheme and give it statutory force. The amounts to be awarded to victims were to be determined by application of the common law principles. The Secretary of State, under section 17(1), had power to bring the scheme into effect on a day to be announced. In November 1993, the Secretary of State, acting under his prerogative powers, announced a new tariff scheme under which set amounts would be payable to the victims of crimes, according to fixed criteria. The effect of this new scheme was that much lower awards would be made in the future. The applicants applied for judicial review of the failure of the Secretary of State to implement the statutory scheme, and his exercise of prerogative powers in introducing the new tariffs. The application was dismissed at first instance but on appeal it was held that it was an abuse of his common law prerogative powers for the Secretary of State to introduce a compensation scheme other than that provided by the 1988 Act. The Secretary of State appealed to the House of Lords and the applicants cross-appealed. Both appeals were dismissed. Lord Browne-Wilkinson said that it would be most surprising if, at the present day, prerogative powers could be validly exercised by the executive so as to frustrate the will of Parliament expressed in a statute: "The constitutional history of this country is the history of the prerogative powers of the crown being made subject to the overriding powers of the democratically elected legislature as the sovereign body." Although the victim of a crime committed before the scheme came into force had no right to receive compensation in accordance with the old scheme, he certainly had a legitimate expectation that he would do so. Moreover, he had a legitimate expectation that, unless there were proper reasons for further delay in bringing sections 108–117 of the Criminal Justice Act 1988 into force, his expectations would be converted into a statutory right. If those legitimate expectations were defeated by the decision of the Secretary of State to discontinue the old scheme and not to bring the statutory scheme into force and those proceedings were unlawfully taken, he has *locus standi* in proceedings for judicial review to complain of such illegality.

9–52   Although prerogative powers cannot be used to override a statute they will still exist insofar as the scope of a statute permits. In the case of *R. v. Secretary of State for the Home Department, ex parte Northumbria Police Authority*,[29] a residual power was held to exist despite the existence of a

---

[28]   [1995] 2 W.L.R. 464.
[29]   [1988] 2 W.L.R. 590.

statute. The Home Secretary issued a circular to all chief constables informing them that the Home Office maintained a central store of riot equipment such as CS gas. It went on to state that, if chief constables experienced difficulties in persuading their respective police authorities to sanction the supply of such equipment, it would be made available directly from the Home Office on request. The Home Secretary claimed that the power to provide such equipment was provided either by section 41 of the Police Act 1964 or under the prerogative power to maintain law and order. The Police Authority claimed that it alone was responsible for providing such equipment under section 4(4) of the 1964 Act and any action to equip police forces under prerogative powers would be inconsistent with that section. It was held that the Home Secretary was empowered to supply such equipment under section 41. Even if this had not been the case, he could still do so acting under prerogative powers to maintain law and order. This power had not been replaced by statute because section 4(4) did not give the police authority exclusive control over the supply of equipment.

Although matters relating to defence of the realm are not subject to   9–53 judicial review it has been held that the decision to ban homosexual men and women from the armed services was a decision which was amenable to judicial review.[30] That the most important prerogative powers are still not subject to judicial review was confirmed in the case of *R. v. Secretary of State for Foreign and Commonwealth Affairs, ex parte Rees-Mogg*.[31] Lord Rees-Mogg sought judicial review of the decision to ratify the Maastricht Treaty. The grounds for the application included a claim that it would be an unlawful transfer of executive powers. The application failed.[32]

Where powers are exercised under the authority of Crown prerogative it is difficult to identify the parties who would be regarded as the three elements of a tripartite relationship. Prerogative powers are exercised by Government Ministers as part of the Crown, *i.e.* the Government, but there is no legally recognised conferring of power.[33] Judicial review of prerogative powers should be seen therefore as exception to the test of the tripartite relationship and as an additional area where the court can exercise a supervisory jurisdiction.

---

[30] *R. v. Ministry of Defence, ex p. Smith* [1996] 1 All E.R. 257.
[31] [1994] 1 All E.R. 457.
[32] See also *Blackburn v. Att.-Gen.* [1971] 1 W.L.R. 1037.
[33] Finnie, "Triangles as Touchstones of Review", 1993 S.L.T. (News) 51.

CHAPTER 10

GROUNDS FOR JUDICIAL CONTROL OF ADMINISTRATIVE DECISION-MAKING: ILLEGALITY AND IRRATIONALITY

INTRODUCTION

10–01 No administrative authority, whether it is a local authority, a government department, or any other public body, may lawfully take any action unless it has authority, either by statute or at common law. As the powers of public bodies are subject to legal limitation it is up to the courts, if the matter is referred to them, to decide whether or not the action is lawful. Acts of Parliament are the main source of law in the United Kingdom and so the powers conferred upon a public body are usually ascertained by examining the terms of the relevant statute. In *Moss Empires Ltd v. Glasgow Assessor,*[1] Lord Kinnear stated that: "Wherever any inferior tribunal or any administrative body has exceeded the powers conferred on it by statute to the prejudice of the subject, the jurisdiction of the Court (of Session) to set aside such exercise of power is not open to dispute." This supervisory jurisdiction is exclusive to the Court of Session although the sheriff court has powers relating to the local administration of public services. Unlike the jurisdiction of the Court of Session, the jurisdiction of the sheriff court is dependent on specific statutory powers.

THE CATEGORIES OF CHALLENGE ARE NEVER CLOSED

10–02 The law relating to the grounds for judicial control is constantly evolving and there continues to be scope for further development of the law. One reason for this is that it results mainly from judicial decisions, not from legislation. The lack of a systematic and coherent approach in the development of judicial review is not, however, without certain advantages. Two of the important precepts of judicial review are access to justice and flexibility. The lack of rigid rules and definitions may make the study of judicial review difficult. The absence of an inflexible system of rules does,

---

[1] 1917 S.C. (H.L.) 1 at 6.

however, have the advantage that individual cases can be dealt with as justice requires and the law can develop to meet changing circumstances. In the case of *London and Clydeside Estates Ltd v. Aberdeen District Council*,[2] Lord Hailsham warned against relying on rigid legal categories which required individual cases to be stretched or cramped "on a bed of Procrustes invented by lawyers for the purpose of convenient exposition".

In the exercise of its supervisory jurisdiction the court is required to consider detailed questions of statutory interpretation in cases of very diverse subject matter. At first sight the cases have little in common with each other, ranging from questions of planning to the rights of the inmates of prisons, from licensing of public houses to matters involving immigration, education or housing. In considering this diverse range of cases the court applies an established set of principles or grounds of review in order to test the legality of the decisions made by officials or public authorities. However, as many judicial review cases involve interpretation of statutory terms in order to determine the legality of individual actions, judges may disagree between cases, or even within cases as to where the boundary of legality should be drawn.

The principles of judicial review have been developed by the courts 10–03 over many years. With a few exceptions the principles do not have any statutory basis but are founded in the common law. Their purpose has been described as being, "to ensure that the bodies which make up the executive branch of government do not exceed the powers given to them by Parliament."[3] The courts do not, however, act upon their own initiative. Litigation depends upon a suitable litigant having both the motivation and the means (or perhaps a strategic lack of means[4]) to challenge the decision of an official or public authority. The litigant may be an individual, a company or a public authority. The courts will only consider cases where they are founded upon a real issue in dispute and will not consider hypothetical questions.[5] The purpose of judicial review may be described more realistically as protecting litigants against the infringement of their rights by an official or public body acting in excess of the powers conferred upon it. Consequently, an important factor in interpreting the extent of an authority's statutory powers is the effect of the proposed action upon the rights of affected individuals.

In the absence of a specific statutory authority there is a presumption that a public authority will exercise its powers in such a way as to avoid

---

[2] 1980 S.C. (H.L.) 1 at 30–31.
[3] Deans, *Scots Public Law* (1995).
[4] See *McColl v. Strathclyde Regional Council*, 1983 S.L.T. 616 where a legally aided pursuer raised an action in order to allow a pressure group to take an action which it could not otherwise afford.
[5] *Shaw v. Strathclyde Regional Council*, 1988 S.L.T. 313; *Marco's Leisure Ltd v. West Lothian District Licensing Board*, 1994 S.L.T. 129.

infringing individual property rights. Therefore, in the case of *Greenock Corporation v. Bennett,*[6] it was held that, although a local authority had power under the Burgh Police (Scotland) Act 1892 to require the owners of a private street to ensure that the road surface was maintained to a satisfactory standard, the power did not extend to an order to the owners of land to surface an area of ground so as to extend the surface of the street. The function of the courts in trying to protect rights which are derived from statute may involve reconciling apparently conflicting statutory provisions. In the case of *Hunter v. Ayr County Council,*[7] it was held that, although a person is barred by statute from holding office in a council of which he is a paid employee, it was *ultra vires* for Ayr County Council to impose disqualification from membership of the education sub-committee by reason of a potential member's employment as a teacher within the county. There is statutory authority to the effect that education sub-committees may have teacher representatives who are employed by the authority.

10–04   One important and developing role which the courts have is that of protecting rights derived from international treaties and conventions. Where obligations under a treaty or a convention, which has been ratified by the U.K. Government, have been incorporated into U.K. law the rights which arise under such treaties or conventions will be protected in the same way as any other rights arising from national law. However, when a treaty or convention has been ratified but has not been incorporated into national law the extent to which it needs to be taken into account is less certain. In the case of *R. v. Secretary of State for the Home Department, ex parte Kaur,*[8] it was held that domestic law prevailed over rights under the European Convention on Human Rights. Kaur, a citizen of India, had originally entered the United Kingdom as the spouse of a British citizen. She later remarried and was refused variation of leave and became an overstayer. The Secretary of State decided to deport her. In response, Kaur's husband and children lodged a petition with the European Court of Human Rights. They complained to the Commission that the European Convention on Human Rights 1950, Article 8, concerning family life and unity, had been breached by the Secretary of State's decision to deport. They applied for leave to move for judicial review of the Secretary of State's refusal to defer deportation until a decision came from Europe on the ground that it was unreasonable. They also applied for an injunction to prevent the Secretary of State from proceeding with deportation. It was held that the court had no power to prevent the Secretary of State deporting Kaur pending the decision from Europe. Since he was acting within domestic law and the Secretary of State's decision was not unreasonable given the time it would take to resolve

---

[6]   1938 S.C. 563.
[7]   1969 S.C. 45.
[8]   [1996] Imm. A.R. 359.

the matter in Europe. The incorporation of the European Convention on Human Rights into the domestic law of the United Kingdom will extend the grounds on which judicial review may be sought.

The fact that an invalid exercise of power by a public authority has lead 10–05 to the acquisition of contractual rights by an individual may not prevent the court from finding that the action or decision was invalid and has no legal effect. In the case of *Coull v. Fife Education Authority,*[9] the local authority had exceeded its powers in applying a revised scale of salaries for head teachers before it had received the approval of the Department of Education. The Department of Education had no power to sanction the scheme retrospectively so as to affect the pursuer's contractual rights to his salary. The question of the legality of the decision takes priority over the contractual rights of the individual.

GROUNDS FOR JUDICIAL REVIEW

There have been attempts from time to time to clarify and categorise the 10–06 grounds upon which the court may, in exercise of its supervisory jurisdiction, review the exercise of a power, jurisdiction or authority. The most widely recognised statement is that of Lord Diplock in the case of *Council of Civil Service Unions v. Minister for Civil Service,*[10] Lord Diplock stated that the grounds are:

(i)   illegality,
(ii) irrationality, and
(iii) procedural impropriety.

ILLEGALITY

A decision may be quashed on grounds of illegality where a decision-maker has not understood correctly the law that regulates his decision-making power and has not given effect to that law. Such a failure will render his decision unlawful. Illegality may arise where;

1.   A public authority has acted in excess of its statutory powers, or
2.   A decision has been made by taking into account irrelevant considerations, or
3.   A decision has been taken after failing to take relevant considerations into account, or
4.   A statutory power has been used for an improper purpose or a policy has been adopted which amounts to a fettering of a future discretion.

---

[9]   1925 S.C. 240.
[10] [1985] A.C. 374..

10–07   A decision may be quashed on the grounds of irrationality or unreasonableness. This applies to a decision which is so outrageous in its defiance of logic, or of accepted moral standards, that no sensible person who had applied his mind to the question to be decided could have arrived at it.

10–08   A decision may be quashed on grounds of procedural impropriety where there has been a failure to observe the basic rules of natural justice, or where there has been a failure to act with procedural fairness towards the person who will be affected by the decision or where there has been failure by an administrative tribunal to observe procedural rules that are expressly laid down in the legislative instrument by which its jurisdiction is conferred, even where such failure does not involve any denial of natural justice.

Lord Diplock expressed his opinion that further development on a case by case basis may, in the course of time, add further grounds. Lord Diplock's grounds of review provide an interesting summary and overview of the principles under which judicial review is conducted but they are too generalised to be of much practical assistance in determining whether or not a decision-maker has overstepped its powers. Lord Hope, in *West v. Secretary of State for Scotland*,[11] stated that:

> "an excess or abuse of jurisdiction may involve stepping outside it, or failing to observe its limits, or departing from the rules of natural justice, or a failure to understand the law, or taking into account of matters which ought not to be taken into account. The categories of what may amount to an excess or abuse of jurisdiction are not closed and they are capable of being adapted in accordance with the development of administrative law".

These grounds of review make it clear that the court is restricted to considering the formal limits of an authority's powers and the ways in which decisions have been made. The court may not consider the merits of decisions. In the case of *Edinburgh District Council v. Secretary of State for Scotland*,[12] Edinburgh District Council raised an action for reduction and suspension of an order restricting the use of the housing revenue account. The council claimed that the order of the Secretary of State should be reduced on grounds of illegality, irrationality and procedural impropriety. It was held that the statutory instrument was valid but the judgment of Lord

---

[11] 1992 S.L.T. 636.
[12] 1985 S.L.T. 551.

Dunpark[13] clarified that these three grounds as explained by Lord Diplock are also applicable to Scotland.

For the purpose of analysis in this chapter the grounds for judicial review have been further divided into categories. This further categorisation is only for the purpose of aiding study and it is important to remember that the grounds of judicial review are complex and are not amenable to straightforward or rigid classification.[14] A further complicating factor is that a case may be based on more than one ground of challenge and that the grounds for challenge are often overlapping and interrelated.

COMPARISON WITH SUBSTANTIVE LAW IN ENGLAND AND WALES

The substantive grounds for judicial control are broadly the same in Scotland   10–09
as they are in England and Wales. In the case of *Governors of Donaldson's Hospital v. Educational Endowments Commissioners*,[15] Lord President Clyde observed that all discretionary powers, without exception must be used both reasonably and according to law:

> "Were it otherwise, there would be no difference between a discretionary power and an arbitrary one; and, if those upon whom a discretion is conferred exercise it, not reasonably or according to law, but arbitrarily, they are not using, but abusing their discretion. Whenever this can be established as matter of fact, their acts become liable to be interfered with by a Court of law. The right and duty of the Court so to interfere — whenever, that is to say, discretionary powers are exercised either unreasonably or in a manner contrary to law — is illustrated by many cases, alike in the law of Scotland and in that of England."

The milestone judgment of Lord Hope, in *West v. Secretary of State for*   10–10
Scotland,[16] confirmed that although the procedures and the remedies are different the substantive grounds for judicial review are nevertheless substantially the same in Scotland as in England and Wales. It is therefore appropriate to consider the decisions in cases under English as well as Scots law when considering the development of legal principle in this area. The judgment also clarified that, although the substantive law relating to the grounds for judicial review is similar to that in England and Wales "the origins and development of judicial review in the two countries are indeed different... the English approach appears to be to fasten not upon principle but upon remedies, whereas the Scottish approach is based essentially on

---

[13] 1985 S.L.T. 551 at 562–564.
[14] Deans, *op. cit.*, n. 3, above, p. 140.
[15] 1932 S.C. 585 at 599; 1932 S.L.T. 417.
[16] 1992 S.C. 385; 1992 S.L.T. 636.

principle."[17] In addition to the differences that are due to the historical context, there is a further problem which is encountered when consulting English authorities. In the judgments from English judicial review proceedings discussion of questions which relate to substantive matters may be interspersed with consideration of questions which relate to procedural matters. There are significant differences between the jurisdictions as regards the procedures and remedies which are available. This means that care must be taken when reading English cases to concentrate only on those aspects which relate to the substantive grounds on which a judicial challenge to administrative action may be based.

10–11   English cases, particularly the leading cases of *Wednesbury*[18] and the *Council of Civil Service Unions*[19] have been referred to and followed in Scotland but there are few instances of Scottish cases being followed in England. In a climate of increasing harmonisation of laws within the United Kingdom and throughout the European Community it is important that care is taken that access to justice is comparable within each jurisdiction and that any divergence of substantive law or procedure is justifiable in terms of providing better access to justice in Scotland. The Scottish Law Commission[20] recognised the general advantage of convergence in administrative law, stating that: "where problems are common it is clearly desirable that they should be addressed in both jurisdictions and that our respective rules should produce solutions which are in harmony." Uniformity is not required but the approach in each jurisdiction should fulfil the same function and provide equivalent rights of redress for citizens. The European Union is an even stronger harmonising influence. Harmonisation of procedures and remedies between the domestic laws of European States is likely to develop as equivalence of treatment and non-discrimination are important principles of the laws of the European Community.

ULTRA VIRES DOCTRINE

10–12   An *ultra vires* act is an act carried out by a public or other body which it has no legal authority to perform. The person or body has acted in excess of its power. The term "*ultra vires*" means "outwith the powers". Where the act exceeds the substance of the conferred power it may be referred to as substantive *ultra vires*. Where a person or body has done something which it is legally empowered to do but has not adhered to a prescribed statutory procedure this may be referred to as procedural *ultra vires*.

---

[17] *West v. Secretary of State for Scotland,* 1992 S.L.T. 636, *per* Lord Hope at 648.
[18] *Associated Picture Houses v. Wednesbury Corporation* [1948] 1 K.B. 223.
[19] [1985] A.C. 374.
[20] Scottish Law Commission 27th Annual Report 1992, Scot. Law Com. No. 139, para. 2.5.

SCOPE OF *ULTRA VIRES* DOCTRINE

When a public authority stays within its powers it is said to be acting *intra* 10–13
vires. When its actions are not authorised by its powers they are *ultra vires*
and unlawful and may be challenged successfully in court by way of judicial
review procedure. The *ultra vires* doctrine, when used to describe the
challenge of administrative decision-making, may be used in a broad sense
as a term referring to the whole body of law on which an action or decision
of a public authority may be subject to judicial review. When used in this
sense the term "*ultra vires*" includes defects in procedure and breaches of
natural justice. The term "*ultra vires*" may also be used in a narrow sense to
mean no more than beyond legal capacity. It may be unclear whether a
term in a statute refers to the wider or the narrower meaning of the term. An
example of the narrower meaning being applied is the case of *Peter Holmes
& Son v. Secretary of State for Scotland*.[21] In a dispute about land acquired
by compulsory purchase, it was held that the Secretary of State had not
acted *ultra vires* in confirming the compulsory purchase order as he was
empowered so to do (by section 35(1) of the Town and Country Planning
(Scotland) Act 1947).

    Ultra vires, when used in its broad sense, means that an authority will be
regarded as acting unlawfully if, in the course of doing something that is
intra vires, in the strict or narrow sense it acts improperly or unreasonably
in various ways. These ways include such matters as disregard of the rules
of natural justice, unfairness, taking into account irrelevant considerations,
fettering discretion, attempting to raise taxation, and interfering with
the free exercise of liberties.[22] The basis of this wider interpretation of the
doctrine of *ultra vires* is that there is a presumption that Parliament, as
the authority conferring the power or jurisdiction to act, must have intended
that the recipients of such power would exercise them in accordance with
principles of good administration. An authority may be held to be acting
ultra vires if it uses its powers for a wrong purpose, or uses powers in bad
faith or when it abuses a discretion. In considering whether a body has
acted in excess of its power the court will consider not just whether there
has been action which is not authorised by an explicit statutory provision
but also whether the power may be reasonably implied or whether it is
reasonably incidental to a power which has in fact been conferred. In
Graham v. Glasgow Corporation,[23] a local authority wanted to establish a
printing works to meet its own printing, manufacturing and binding
requirements. Graham, a ratepayer, sought suspension of this resolution

---

[21] 1965 S.C. 1.
[22] Oliver, "Is the Ultra Vires Rule the Basis of Judicial Review?" (1987) P.L. 543–569.
[23] 1936 S.C. 108.

and interdict. The Inner House held that the proposals were *intra vires* as the production of printed material was reasonably incidental to the functions of the council. The English case of *Att.-General v. Smethwick Corporation*,[24] was cited with approval in the decision in *Graham v. Glasgow Corporation*. In the *Smethwick* case it had been decided that a local authority did not need to have explicit authority to set up a stationery, printing and binding works. Provided that the printing was for council documents and publications the work could be regarded as reasonably incidental to other statutory powers and the establishment of a printing works was therefore *intra vires*.[25] This can be compared with the case of *Attorney-General v. Fulham Corporation*[26] in which, although a local authority was empowered under the Baths and Washhouses Acts 1846 and 1847 to set up wash-houses where residents could wash their own clothes the establishment of a laundry where the work would be done by council employees on a commercial basis was held to be *ultra vires*.

10–14   The case of *D. and J. Nicol v. Dundee Harbour Trustees*,[27] was a challenge to a decision by the Dundee Harbour Trustees to use ferries for pleasure cruises. The trustees were authorised to operate ferry services on the river Tay. D. and J. Nicol, who were local shipowners, sought suspension and interdict with regard to the pleasure cruises. The House of Lords held that such usage was *ultra vires* since the use of the ships for pleasure cruises could not be interpreted as being reasonably incidental to the authorised purpose of running a ferry service. Lord Patmor said: "It is settled law that bodies such as the appellants constituted by statute have no authority except such as Parliament has conferred on them." Imposing a fee for an authorised function may not necessarily be *intra vires*. The legality of charging for a service was challenged in the case of *R. v. Richmond upon Thames Council, ex p. McCarthy and Stone Ltd.*[28] A local planning authority imposed a charge of £25 for informal consultations with developers intending to seek planning consent. It was not disputed that the council had a duty to determine all applications for planning consent and that it had the powers required to achieve this. There was no statutory requirement that informal preliminary consultations should take place. The House of Lords held that the holding of informal preliminary consultations was *intra vires*. The imposition of a fee was, however, *ultra vires* as it was not incidental to the planning functions of the council. No charge can be imposed on the public without clear statutory authority.

Local authorities must be careful to act within their powers when dealing with financial administration. The case of *Hazell v. Hammersmith and*

---

[24]   (1932) 1 Ch. 562.
[25]   See also *Piggins & Rix Ltd v. Montrose Port Authority,* 1995 S.L.T. 418.
[26]   (1921) 1 Ch. 440.
[27]   1915 S.C. (H.L.) 7.
[28]   [1992] 2 A.C. 48.

Fulham Council[29] was a challenge to the legality of a council's strategy to engage in speculative investments. The council set up a fund to invest so that profits could be made if interest rates fell; a type of investment known as "Swap deals". Interest rates rose, the council lost money and then made further swaps in order to try to limit the losses. The district auditor sought a declaration that such transactions were unlawful. The House of Lords held that a local council had no power to enter into interest rate swap transactions as they were inconsistent with the statutory borrowing powers of a local authority.

In the case of *Pirie v. City of Aberdeen District Council*[30] it was held that a local authority had acted *ultra vires* in taking into account behaviour of a tenant's wife in considering his application for housing. The Housing (Scotland) Act 1987 provides by section 19(1)(d) that a local authority, in considering whether an applicant for local authority housing is entitled to be admitted to a housing list, is to take no account of any outstanding liability for rent where the applicant was not the tenant. The applicant's wife had incurred rent arrears before eviction from a council flat of which she was the sole tenant. The refusal by the local authority to admit the applicant to the list was stated to be because of the arrears and because his wife's tenancy had been conducted unsatisfactorily. In the judicial review proceedings it was accepted by the local authority that reliance on the wife's rent arrears was not a valid reason for refusal of the applicant's application. 10–15

Challenges to *ultra vires* decisions which are raised promptly may be effective in preventing the implementation of those decisions. In the case of *Hughes v. Strathclyde Regional Council*[31] the closure of a school was prevented in this way. Strathclyde Regional Council planned to close a Roman Catholic school in Govan. The pupils from that school would be transferred to a secondary school in Renfrew. During the period when consultations were taking place, the parents of pupils attending the Renfrew school lodged a petition for implementation of the procedures leading to self-governing status. It was held that the order by the council to close the Govan school was *ultra vires* because, if that school was closed, the closure would result in the pupils being sent to the Renfrew school and, under the Self-Governing Schools, etc. (Scotland) Act 1989, s. 21(1), Strathclyde Regional Council would be acting *ultra vires* if they closed the Govan school before all the procedures in relation to the Renfrew school were complete.

The *ultra vires* rule applies to all bodies created by statute. It also applies to government departments but, as they are not created by statute, there is a presumption that, as they are part of the Crown, in addition to the powers conferred on them by statute, they have power to own property and to enter 10–16

---

[29] [1992] 2 A.C. 1.
[30] 1993 S.L.T. 1155.
[31] 1994 S.C.L.R. 49.

into contracts. Where they are exercising a specific statutory function they must act within the powers conferred by the relevant statute. In the case of *Laker Airways v. Department of Trade*[32] it was held that administrative actions may be *ultra vires* even where they have been subject to Parliamentary approval. The Civil Aviation Act 1971 gave the Civil Aviation Authority power to regulate air services to and from the United Kingdom. Section 3(1) imposed a duty on the Civil Aviation Authority to ensure that British Airways was not given a monopoly on any route. Section 3(2) stated that the Secretary of State could give written guidance to the Civil Aviation Authority on its functions. In 1975 the Secretary of State issued "guidance" that Laker Airway's licence should be revoked and that, except with the consent of British Airways, only one British airline should operate on each long distance route. The "guidance" was approved by a resolution of each of the Houses of Parliament. The Court of Appeal held that the guidance of the Secretary of State was *ultra vires* since it conflicted with the terms of the 1971 Act by creating a monopoly for British Airways. The power to issue guidance did not include power to alter the objectives set out in the Act itself.

DISTINCTION BETWEEN MERITS AND LEGALITY OF A DECISION

10–17   Where a discretion is given to an administrator no appeal can be made to the courts solely on the merits of the decision which he has chosen to take. If the discretion is used legitimately the court cannot substitute its discretion for that of the administrator. In the case of *Campbell v. Brown*,[33] it was held that the Court of Session had a *jus supereminens* (supereminent jurisdiction) which entitled it to review the decision of a presbytery to dismiss a schoolmaster. Lord Lyndhurst L.C. said: "But I apprehend that … a jurisdiction is given in this case to the Court of Session, not to review the argument on its merits, but to take care that the Court of Presbytery shall keep within the line of its duty, and conform to the provisions of the Act of Parliament."[34] Provided that a public authority stays within the limits of its powers it has discretion and so can choose between different courses of action and may exercise good or bad judgment in making those choices. It is only the legality of a decision which the courts may review and not the merits and so the courts will not interfere unless the powers have been exceeded.[35] Lord President Hope said:

---

[32] [1977] Q.B. 643.
[33] (1829) 3 W. & S. 441.
[34] *ibid.* at 448.
[35] *Stewart v. Monklands District Council,* 1987 S.L.T. 630; *Cashley v. Dundee District Council,* 1994 S.C.L.R. 6.

"On the one hand there is no jurisdiction to review the judgment of the inferior tribunal or jurisdiction on the merits of the question which has been entrusted to them alone. On the other hand the court has authority to see that the decision taking body — the inferior tribunal or jurisdiction — keep within the limits of their duty and do not exceed the authority which has been given to them by the enabling power."[36]

An exception to this is where there is an express right of appeal conferred by a statute. This may be a right of appeal to a Minister who may then consider the merits of the decision which is being challenged. Similarly, a statute may provide for a right of appeal to a court. This is not the same as a challenge to the legality of a decision by way of judicial review and the court may have been given express authority to consider the merits of the decision. One example is section 63 of the Civic Government (Scotland) Act which gives a local authority power to prohibit a public procession or to give permission for the procession to be held subject to conditions. There is a right of appeal to the sheriff court. In considering such an appeal the sheriff may consider the merits of the decision as well as its legality provided that he gives due regard to the opinions of the local authority.

The case of *Pryde v. Heritors and Kirk Session of Ceres*,[37] gives an example of the difficulties of distinguishing between the merits and the legality of a decision. The Court of Session was asked to review the amount of poor relief awarded to the widow of a weaver who had seven children to support. A majority of the court required the heritors and kirk session to reconsider the sum which had been awarded. As parish authorities they were under a statutory duty to provide for the "needful sustenation" of the family. They were in breach of that duty because they had made a provision which was grossly inadequate and was therefore reviewable. The Lord President referred to evidence about weavers' earnings and suggested that the poor relief should be increased from three shillings and sixpence per week to six shillings per week. Lord Cockburn, in a dissenting judgment, found that the heritors and kirk session had not acted unlawfully as they had made a decision which was within the limits of their powers to determine the amount of poor relief to be awarded. The court was not entitled to interfere with the merits of the decision by the parish authorities. He said: "Road trustees, police commissioners, managers of docks or harbours, etc. can be compelled to do their duty, and can be corrected if they err in law; but are nevertheless entrusted by the legislature with a discretion within a given range, as to amount and the application of assessments, with which discretion ... this court cannot interfere."[38] It is this dissenting judgment which is reflected in modern case law.

10–18

---

[36] *West v. Secretary of State for Scotland,* 1992 S.L.T. 636 at 641.
[37] (1843) 5 D. 552.
[38] *ibid.* at 559 and for a discussion of this case see Deans, *op. cit.,* n. 3, above, p. 136.

10–19   A similarly difficult decision for the judges arose in the recent English case of *R. v. Cambridge District Health Authority, ex parte B*.[39] The daughter of the applicant was a 10-year-old girl suffering from acute myeloid leukaemia. Doctors treating her determined that a further course of chemotherapy and a possible bone marrow transplant could not be justified. The course of treatment would cost in excess of £75,000 and carried only a small chance of success. Without receiving this treatment it was anticipated that the girl would have a life expectancy of only eight to 10 weeks. At first instance, the decision not to fund further treatment was quashed on the ground that where fundamental rights were at stake, such as the right to life, the authority had to be able to show a substantial public interest justification for its decision. The authority had failed to justify its refusal to offer treatment. The health authority appealed and the appeal was allowed. The comment was made that the courts, contrary to what is sometimes believed, are not arbiters as to the merits of cases of this kind. Courts have one function only, which is to rule upon the lawfulness of decisions. Difficult and agonising decisions have to be made by health authorities as to how a limited budget is best allocated to the maximum advantage of the maximum number of patients. This is not a judgment which the court can make.

In the case of *Stewart v. Monklands District Council*,[40] Lord Clyde stated: "I have no difficulty in affirming that the supervisory jurisdiction is distinct from an appellate jurisdiction and that it does not allow the court to interfere with the merits of a discretionary decision where that decision has been legally and properly reached. The court cannot simply substitute its own decision on the merits because it prefers a different construction of the facts." Lord Greene in the case of *Associated Provincial Picture Houses v. Wednesbury Corporation* said:

> "When an executive discretion is entrusted… by Parliament what appears to be an exercise of that discretion can only be challenged by the courts in a strictly limited class of case. When discretion of this kind is granted the law recognises certain principles upon which that discretion must be exercised, but within those four corners of those principles the discretion is an absolute one which cannot be questioned in any court of law."[41]

In the case of *Chief Constable of the North Wales Police v. Evans*,[42] Lord Brightman had observed that judicial review was concerned, not with the decision, but with the decision-making process. In *R. v. Entry Clearance Officer, Bombay, ex parte Amin*,[43] Lord Fraser stated that judicial review is

---

[39] [1995] 1 W.L.R. 898.
[40] 1987 S.L.T. 630.
[41] [1948] 1 K.B. 223.
[42] [1982] 1 W.L.R. 1155 at 1173.
[43] [1983] 2 A.C. 818.

concerned not with the merits of a decision but with the manner in which the decision was made.[44]

In a petition for judicial review to challenge the refusal by the Secretary of State for Scotland to refer a criminal conviction back to the High Court, it was held that the court could consider whether the Secretary of State had misconstrued the ambit of his power. Once it was established that he had not exceeded his powers the court could not review the substantive merits of his decision.[45] In the case of *R. v. Ministry of Defence, ex parte Smith*,[46] a challenge was raised to the ban on homosexual men and women in the armed services. Opinion was divided over whether the threshold for irrationality should be lowered in a case involving fundamental freedoms. It was held that the human rights context is important: "The more substantial the interference with human rights, the more the court will require by way of justification." The challenge to the ban on homosexuals was held to be valid on the grounds that there was implied statutory authority for the decision in section 146 of the Criminal Justice and Public Order Act 1994 and in the special report from the Select Committee on the Armed Forces Bill in 1991. The failure of the challenge in this case is a forceful reminder of the distinction between an appeal and a review.[47]

10–20

EXCESS OF POWER

The fundamental ground on which a decision may be challenged by judicial review proceedings is that there has been an excess of power. The principle that government must be conducted according to law means that every act performed in the course of government must have legal authority, that is to say, it must be *intra vires*. As the majority of powers which affect the rights of citizens are exercised under the authority of a statute, the problems arising for the judges are largely those of statutory interpretation. Decisions are not, however, based merely on the interpretation of the words in the statute. The courts also take into account the purpose which the relevant statute was intended to achieve. In the case of *Association of Optical Practitioners Ltd v. Secretary of State for Scotland*,[48] the petitioners sought reduction of a determination of the Secretary of State, under regulation 10(1) of the National Health Service (General Ophthalmic Services) Scotland Regulations 1974, to fix fees payable for ophthalmic services carried out on or after September 1985. The fees proposed were less than they otherwise

10–21

---

[44] See also *R. v. Secretary of State for the Home Department, ex p. Brind* [1991] 1 A.C. 696, *per* Lord Lowry at 764–765.
[45] *McDonald v. Secretary of State for Scotland,* 1996 S.L.T. 16.
[46] [1996] 1 All E.R. 257.
[47] Hare, "Military Bases and Military Biases" (1996) 55 C.L.J. 179–182.
[48] O. H., October 10, 1985.

would have been, because during preceding months manufacturers had supplied optical appliances at a discount. The overall remuneration of the optical practitioners had therefore been greater than the Secretary of State intended. It was held that that the Secretary of State's decision was *ultra vires*. The exclusive purpose of any determination under the regulations was to set a fair level of remuneration for the future and not to redress any unintended generosity in the past.

10–22   In addition to considering the purpose of the individual statute or regulation the circumstances giving rise to the decision or instrument must be taken into account. This will include the context of the legislation and, in particular, any overall objective to which the individual decision or document is intended to contribute. In the case of *Leech v. Secretary of State for Scotland*,[49] Leech, a prisoner, reclaimed against the Lord Ordinary's decision dismissing his petition for judicial review of rule 74(4) of the 1952 Rules and standing orders relating to scrutiny of correspondence with his legal advisers. Leech argued that the Lord Ordinary had failed to recognise that all rules referred to in section 39 of the Prisons (Scotland) Act 1989 had to be issued by statutory instrument and not as standing orders. He had also failed to recognise the right of privilege attaching to communications for the purpose of obtaining legal advice. It was held that rule 74(4) was not *ultra vires*. It had to be looked at in its whole context. It was clear that the 1952 Rules, read as a whole, did permit Leech to obtain confidential advice and contained no practical restriction which would deny access to such advice. Leech was not prevented by the regulations from having confidential communications with his lawyer because he could write to his lawyer and invite him to meet him at the prison.

In the case of *Adams v. Secretary of State for Scotland*,[50] the pursuers, who were both women living in Edinburgh, sought to interdict the Secretary of State and the area hospitals board from offering the post of consultant physician in two Edinburgh hospitals to men. The hospitals were both dedicated to the treatment of women and children and it was in accordance with the Founder's objects that the medical staff were exclusively female. The hospitals had been transferred to the Secretary of State under the National Health Service (Scotland) Act 1947, under which Act he was required to ensure, as far as practicable, that the hospitals continued to fulfil their former purposes. Interdict was granted to prevent the offering of the post to male consultants until it had been advertised as open to women doctors only.

10–23   In the case of *Ward v. Secretary of State for Social Security*,[51] Ward, a retired person on income support, sought judicial review of a decision of a

[49]   1993 S.L.T. 365.
[50]   *Adams v. Secretary of State for Scotland and South-Eastern Regional Hospital Board*, 1958 S.C. 279.
[51]   1995 S.C.L.R. 1134.

social security appeal tribunal to set aside a decision of another tribunal in his favour. Ward had submitted unsuccessful claims to the Department of Social Security for additional diet payments and laundry costs. Ward appealed and his appeal was heard by a tribunal. There was no representative of the Department of Social Security present as there was no one available on that day. The tribunal overturned the decision to refuse payment. The Department of Social Security then sought to set aside this decision under the Social Security (Adjudication) Regulations 1986, reg. 11, on the grounds that it was inappropriate to proceed with the hearing in the absence of a presenting officer. The application was granted by a further tribunal on the grounds that the Department of Social Security's representative was not present and it was in the interest of justice to set aside the decision for procedural irregularity. Ward sought judicial review of that decision, arguing that absence of a representative of the Department of Social Security from the hearing did not automatically invalidate the proceedings and did not amount to a procedural mishap. It was held that the reasons for setting aside the earlier decision were flawed. The power to set aside under regulation 11 was intended to provide a short, simple and speedy alternative to the appeal process where something had gone wrong with the procedure. It should be confined to cases where there was a readily identifiable error or mishap and should not be used as a substitute for an appeal. The petition was granted and the earlier decision reduced.

The case of *Malloch v. Aberdeen Corporation*[52] was a challenge to the 10–24 legality of a decision to dismiss teachers. The Teaching Council (Scotland) Act 1965 set up the General Teaching Council for Scotland with a duty to establish and maintain a register of qualified teachers. The Act did not take away the previous power of the Secretary of State, under the Education (Scotland) Act 1962 and its predecessors, to award certificates of competency to teach. The Secretary of State was empowered to "make regulations prescribing the standards and general requirements to which every education authority shall conform in exercising their function". The Schools (Scotland) Code 1956 stated that "every teacher employed by an education authority shall be a certified teacher holding the qualifications required by this code for the post in which he is employed" but subsequent regulations substituted the term "registered teacher" in place of "certified teacher." The effect of this was that the new regulations said that every teacher employed by a local authority must be a registered teacher. It was held that the amendment to the regulations by the Secretary of State was *ultra vires*.

Whether a decision is lawfully made depends on the legal basis for that decision, not the accuracy of the facts on which the decision was based. A

---

[52] 1973 S.C. 227.

factual error had occurred in the case of *Thomson v. City of Glasgow District Council*.[53] A licensing sub-committee granted taxi drivers' licences to a number of applicants and rejected other applications. As they had only a few licences available they granted them to the drivers with the longest period of driving experience. Later they discovered that the information which they had been given was incorrect and that two drivers had much less experience than the sub-committee believed. They decided to fix a new hearing to reconsider the applications. The recipients of the licences sought judicial review on the ground that the local authority did not have power under the Civic Government (Scotland) Act 1982 to make such a decision. It was held that the authority had no power to reverse its decision to grant a licence except in specific circumstances which had not arisen in this case.

10–25   The conditions under which a power is to be exercised are also an important consideration in deciding whether or not a decision is *intra* or *ultra vires*. In the case of *Ferguson v. Scottish Football Association*,[54] declarator was granted that a decision by the Scottish Football Association to discipline a player was *ultra vires*. Ferguson was involved in an incident during a football match as a result of which he was subsequently convicted of assault. Although no action was taken at the time by the match referee or the linesmen, and they did not submit any report in respect of the incident, the disciplinary committee imposed a 12-match suspension on Ferguson. It was held that the decision was *ultra vires* because the constitution of the Scottish Football Association only provided for disciplinary action of this kind when a report had been received from the match officials.

In the case of *Watt v. Secretary of State for Scotland*,[55] Watt challenged as *ultra vires*, illegal and void a decision by the British Government to reduce his licence to fish for various species including haddock. The E.C. Council decided that in order to preserve haddock stocks, fishing for haddock should be reduced by 30 per cent in 1990. It was held that the variation was compatible with section 4 of the Sea Fish (Conservation) Act 1967. It was not discriminatory on grounds of nationality under Article 7, since only United Kingdom vessels were covered by the licensing rules. There was nothing within the rules that indicated that there would be any variation of treatment on the grounds of nationality. A court in one member state cannot decide that a decision which conforms with E.C. law is *ultra vires* on the basis that other member states may not have imposed similar restrictions on the allocation of licences for their vessels. The licensing rules applied to all U.K. vessels and complied with Community law.

---

[53]   1992 S.L.T. 805.
[54]   1996 G.W.D. 11–601.
[55]   [1991] 3 C.M.L.R. 429.

REVIEW OF DISCRETIONARY DECISIONS

The review of discretionary decisions can be difficult because the conferring   10–26
of a discretion implies that an official is being given the power to choose
between two or more courses of action. The freedom within which that
choice of action is exercised varies in different situations. In certain fields
of activity such as taxation there is little scope for divergence in decision-
making. The legislation is prescriptive and there is a system of strictly applied
rules and procedures to be followed. In other fields of activity there may be
a wide discretion conferred on an administrator. In relation to immigration
matters, for example, the Minister has a wide discretion in relation to making
decisions with regard to leave to enter and leave to remain in the United
Kingdom. A wide discretion is also conferred on the Secretary of State for
Scotland in relation to the operation of prisons for security reasons. In the
case of *Thomson, Petitioner*,[56] a prisoner sought judicial review of
the Secretary of State for Scotland's decision to transfer him from Glenochil
prison to Peterhead prison and to remove his category C grading. The ground
on which he sought to challenge the decision was that no reasons, or no
proper reasons, were given for that decision. It was held that, as a matter of
principle, a decision of the Secretary of State for Scotland to transfer a prisoner,
under section 9 of the Prisons (Scotland) Act 1952, might be reviewable. The
policy of the statutory provision was, however, to confer an absolute discretion
within the law on the Secretary of State to make such executive decisions as
he thought fit for operational and security reasons. Such a decision was only
reviewable if it could be shown that in exercising that very wide discretion
the Secretary of State had misdirected himself in law. Furthermore, the prison
administration was under no duty to make known to prisoners the reasons for
its decision and the petition was dismissed.

The courts can review the legality of decisions by way of judicial review
but may not consider the merits of decisions which have been made. The
review of the legality of the decision will often amount to a question of
interpretation of the terms of a statute. Where the discretion is conferred by
an Act of Parliament, the provisions of the Act itself cannot be challenged,
but where a discretion is conferred by subordinate legislation it may be
possible to show that the term in the subordinate legislation exceeds the
powers conferred by the parent Act. Where an Act has conferred a very
broad discretion the ability of the court to review the decision will be
reduced. In the case of *R. v. Environment Secretary, ex parte Rose Theatre
Trust Company*,[57] developers of land in Southwark had found the remains
of the Rose Theatre, where some of Shakespeare's plays had been performed

---

[56] 1989 S.L.T. 343.
[57] [1990] 1 Q.B. 504.

for the first time. A trust company was set up to preserve the remains of the
theatre and to make them accessible to the public. Under the Ancient
Monuments and Archaeological Areas Act 1979, s. 1, the Secretary of State
may list any monument which appears to him to be of national importance.
A consultation procedure must be followed before this is done. The trust
company requested the Minister to list the site. He agreed that it was an
important historical site but declined to list it. The trust company applied
for judicial review on the grounds that there had been a misdirection in law
and that the decision was unreasonable. It was held that the Minister had a
broad discretion and had not acted unlawfully.

10–27   Exercise of a discretion for an improper purpose or without taking into
account all relevant considerations is regarded as a failure to exercise the
discretion lawfully but the court must be careful not to substitute its own
discretion for that of the administrator.[58] In the case of *Associated Picture
Houses v. Wednesbury Corporation*,[59] Associated Picture Houses challenged
the validity of the decision by Wednesbury Corporation to grant permission
for Sunday cinema performances only on condition that no children under
15 years of age should be admitted. The Sunday Entertainments Act 1932
gave a local authority power to permit cinemas to show films on Sundays
"subject to such conditions as they see fit to impose". It was held that the
local authority had not acted *ultra vires* as the decision was not so
unreasonable that no reasonable authority could ever have come to it. The
welfare of children was a consideration to which it was reasonable for the
corporation to have regard. Lord Greene said: "The court may consider
whether an authority has taken into account matters which it ought not to
take into account, or has refused to take into account matters which it ought
to take into account." A discretion must be exercised reasonably, for instance,
a person entrusted with a discretion must direct himself properly in law. He
must call his own attention to matters which he is bound to consider and
exclude from his consideration matters which are irrelevant to what he has
to consider. When the authority has kept to the matters which they ought to
consider they may even so have come to a conclusion so unreasonable that
no reasonable authority could ever come to it. In such a case the court can
interfere.

10–28   There are two aspects to this principle: irrelevancy and unreasonableness.
Irrelevancy occurs where an administrative body misdirects itself by taking
irrelevant matters into account. This can be by considering irrelevant matters,
or failing to consider relevant matters, or giving undue weight to one aspect,
or using a discretionary power for a wrong purpose. Unreasonableness may
be used in a broad sense as a general description of the things that must not

---

[58] Wade and Bradley, *Constitutional and Administrative Law* (1993), p. 675.
[59] [1948] 1 K.B. 223.

be done when making decisions. This would include, taking account of irrelevant considerations, failing to take relevant considerations into account, bad faith and dishonesty. The word unreasonableness may be used in a narrow sense to also refer to a decision which is so unreasonable that no reasonable authority could have come to it. It is this narrow meaning to which the term "Wednesbury unreasonableness" is applied.

Despite the *Wednesbury* judgment, prior to 1968 the courts were often 10–29
reluctant to inquire into the basis on which discretionary decisions were made. In the case of *Liversidge v. Anderson*,[60] the House of Lords held that the court could not inquire into the grounds for the belief which led to the making of a detention order. An objective test of reasonableness could be applied but not a subjective test. The case of *Padfield v. Minister of Agriculture*[61] was a milestone in the development of the law relating to the regulation of discretion. Under the Agricultural Marketing Act 1958, which put into effect a milk marketing scheme, there was provision for a committee of investigation to be set up to examine any complaint about the operation of the scheme "if the Minister in any case so directs." Padfield complained about prices paid to farmers in the South East Region. The Minister refused to refer the complaint to a committee of investigation, claiming that he had unfettered discretion in deciding whether or not to refer complaints. It was held that the Minister must deal with the complaint according to law. The reasons for refusing to refer the complaint to a committee must be good reasons in law. In this case there was no evidence of a decision based on good reasons in law and the Minister had not, therefore, exercised discretion in accordance with the intention and objects of the Act. Similarly, in the case of *Tait v. City of Glasgow District Licensing Board*,[62] an applicant for renewal of a public house licence had his application returned by the clerk to the licensing board on the ground that it was too late. The lateness of the application arose from confused circumstances in which the applicant believed that the licence had already been transferred into his name. The applicant sought judicial review of the clerk's decision to reject the application for renewal, arguing that the board had discretionary power to consider the late application under section 13(2) of the Licensing (Scotland) Act 1976. It was held that the clerk was exceeding his powers in rejecting the application without giving the applicant an opportunity to seek an exercise of the board's discretion. An order was pronounced requiring the board to consider the licence application.

European law is now having a significant impact on the review of 10–30
discretion. In several areas of administrative activity it is no longer simply

---

[60] [1942] A.C. 206.
[61] [1968] A.C. 997.
[62] 1987 S.L.T. 340.

a question of determining the extent of the discretion enjoyed by authorities under United Kingdom legislation. It is also necessary to ascertain whether there are any provisions in European law which impose further limitations on the way in which a discretion can be exercised.[63] In the case of *Kincardine and Deeside District Council v. Forestry Commissioners,*[64] the Court of Session considered whether or not European law required that an environmental impact assessment should have been considered before a forestry expansion project was granted permission to proceed.[65] When applying directly effective E. C. law, the jurisprudence of the European Court of Justice must be taken into account by the courts. The European Convention on Human Rights[66] in particular may need to be taken into account, although it was held in the case of *R. v. Secretary of State for the Home Department, ex parte Brind,*[67] that when the courts are considering national law rather than directly effective Community law, and a broad discretionary power has been conferred on an official and the scope of the power is not ambiguous, a failure to make reference to the European Convention will not always invalidate a decision.[68]

IRRELEVANT CONSIDERATIONS

10–31 In order for decisions to be made within the limits of the powers conferred it is essential that decision-makers should have regard to all relevant considerations, and only to those which are relevant. The courts have to exercise discretion in determining what considerations are relevant in the particular context so that they do not substitute their judgment for that of the person empowered to make the decision. The effect of the considerations which he has taken into account on the mind of the administrator is not a matter for review. The importance which he ascribes to each of the factors which he takes into account is a matter of judgment. Were the court to inquire into such matters of judgment it would be overstepping its role under the supervisory jurisdiction of considering only the legality and not the merits of the decision.[69] However, powers must be exercised in

---

[63] Jowell and Birkenshaw, "On the Convergence of the Administrative Laws of the EU Member States in Schwarze", *Administrative Law under European Influence* (Jowell ed., 1996).

[64] 1992 S.L.T. 1180.

[65] See also *Twyford Parish Council v. Secretary of State for the Environment* [1992] 1 C.M.L.R. 276.

[66] European Convention for Human Rights and Fundamental Freedoms, 1950; T.S. 71 (1953); Cmd. 8969.

[67] [1991] 1 A.C. 696.

[68] A Bill to incorporate the European Convention on Human Rights into U.K. law was proposed in the Queen's Speech on May 14, 1997.

[69] *McTear v. Scottish Legal Aid Board*, 1995 S.L.T. 108.

accordance with the intention of Parliament as may be inferred from statute by the courts, not as may have been inferred by the administrator when the decision was made. In *Padfield v. Minister of Agriculture,* Lord Reid said: "The policy and objects of the Act must be determined by construing the Act as a whole and construction is always a matter of law for court."[70] In the case of *R. v. Somerset County Council, ex parte Fewings,*[71] three members of the Quantock staghounds successfully obtained judicial review of a decision by the council to ban staghunting on its land. It was held that the council had only narrow, specific statutory powers and could not base decisions purely on moral or ethical considerations. These were irrelevant considerations and decisions made on such considerations were outside the powers conferred by the Local Government Act 1972, s. 122 to make decisions for the "benefit, improvement or development" of the area.

The requirement for decision-makers to base their decisions on relevant   10–32 considerations and to ignore irrelevant considerations is long established in Scots law. In the case of *The Heritors of Corstorphine v. Ramsay,*[72] the court considered the validity of a decision by a local presbytery. Ramsay, a schoolmaster in Corstorphine, had been indicted to stand trial before the High Court on charges including fraud and forgery. The trial had been postponed on several occasions and eventually, when the time-limits for trial under the Wrongous Imprisonment Act 1701 had expired, he was liberated. That Act provided that once a person had been so liberated: "he shall be for ever free from all question or process for the foresaid crime or offence." The heritors nevertheless sought to have the local presbyters declare that Ramsay was unfit to remain as a parish schoolmaster. They argued that the Wrongous Imprisonment Act only concerned criminal prosecutions and was irrelevant to the present complaint. The Court of Session, however, found it a relevant consideration and held that the presbytery had acted *intra vires* in their decision not to declare Ramsay unfit.

General principles of fairness will often require that where a power to take certain considerations into account exists there is also a corresponding duty to consider all relevant factors before making a decision. In *Young v. Milne,*[73] road trustees in Banff were empowered to take private land for road-making purposes under the authority of a local Act. A jury was to be appointed to set a value on any land which had been so taken. In estimating the amount of compensation, the jury was empowered, "to take under consideration all circumstances." When Milne and others had their land taken, the jury refused to receive evidence which they wished to have

---

[70] [1968] A.C. 997 at 1030.

[71] (1994) 6 Admin. L.R. 446.

[72] March 10, 1812, F.C..

[73] June 23, 1814, F.C..

considered regarding the value of their land. The jury awarded only nominal damages. The Inner House held that the jury had acted *ultra vires* and that the intention of the statute was that all evidence should be considered when valuing land.

10–33   Careful attention must be given to the intention of Parliament when deciding which matters must be considered and which will be classed as irrelevant. Sections of statutes should not be considered in isolation but all of the relevant legislation and its purpose and context should be considered. In the case of *Tayside R.C. v. Secretary of State for Scotland*,[74] a firm of builders who had been refused permission by Tayside R.C., as the water authority, for connection of a development to the public sewer in terms of section 12(3) of the Sewerage (Scotland) Act 1968 appealed against this refusal to the Secretary of State. The connection had been refused on the ground that the public sewer was already overloaded. The Secretary of State took the view that lack of capacity was not a valid ground for the refusal of permission. Tayside R.C. sought judicial review of the Secretary of State's decision on the grounds of material error in law. The council argued that he should have based his decision on section 12 of the Act relating to a lack of capacity, which was a valid ground of refusal, rather than an appeal under section 1 which related to the duty of a water authority to provide necessary public sewers. It was held that the Secretary of State was entitled to consider all relevant considerations in making his decision and a duty under section 1 of the same Act which had led to the reason given for refusal was relevant to consideration of the appeal. The fact that an existing public sewer was already overloaded was not necessarily a valid reason for refusing permission for connection and so the petition was rejected.

In the case of *City Cabs (Edinburgh) v. City of Edinburgh District Council*,[75] it was held that it is the person or body to whom the responsibility for making the decision has been delegated who should take the relevant considerations into account. A taxi operator's association applied for judicial review and reduction of a decision of a district council to increase the number of taxi licences. The district council had commissioned a company of transport consultants to report on whether there was a significant unmet demand for taxi services in Edinburgh. The company engaged a consultant. The consultant and the company disagreed about the number of licences which should be issued. The consultant proposed that only 50 licences were justified but the company considered that up to 350 licences could be issued. The consultant wrote to the district council's licensing committee setting out his views. His letter was considered by the district council officials, but was not brought to the notice of the licensing committee. At a meeting on April 9, 1987, at which the company's report, but not the consultant's letter,

---

[74] 1996 S.L.T. 473.
[75] 1988 S.L.T. 184, O.H.

was considered, the district council resolved to invite 85 persons on the waiting list to apply for taxi licences. They also agreed in principle that a further 200 licences should be issued. The petitioners argued that the failure to consider the terms of the consultant's criticisms invalidated the decision. The district council's argument was that, as their departmental officials had considered the consultant's letter and deemed it unnecessary to place it before the committee, it could not be said that the material had not been considered. It was held that relevant material which was only considered by a licensing committee's officials could not be said to have been considered by the authority in reaching their decision. The district council had therefore failed to consider all relevant material and the decision was reduced.

The courts are not always left completely free to determine which 10–34 considerations should have been taken into account. A statute may specify which matters should be taken into account when reaching a type of decision. The case of *Safeway Stores plc v. National Appeal Panel (No. 2)*[76] was an appeal against the dismissal of Safeway's petition for judicial review of a decision by the National Appeal Panel. The decision had overturned an earlier decision to place Safeway on a health board's pharmaceutical list. In terms of the National Health Service (General Medical and Pharmaceutical Services) (Scotland) Regulations 1974, regulation 28(4), Safeway was required to establish either that the provision of pharmaceutical services at Safeway's premises was necessary or that it was desirable to secure adequate provision of pharmaceutical services in the area. Safeway's application had originally been granted on the latter ground but the National Appeal Panel's decision had been based on the former and the panel had never considered whether provision was desirable. It was held that there was nothing to indicate that the National Appeal Panel had reached any conclusion that provision of services by Safeway was not desirable. The National Appeal Panel had therefore failed to consider a relevant consideration and the decision was reduced and the matter was referred back for a new hearing. [77]

Provided that all relevant considerations are taken into account, it is 10–35 left to the judgment of the person who is authorised to make a discretionary decision on the relative weight which may be ascribed to each of the considerations which he has to take into account. In the case of *London and Midland Developments v. Secretary of State for Scotland,*[78] London and Midland Developments appealed against the Secretary of State's decision refusing their application for outline planning permission for a development in Kilmarnock. As a result of a public local inquiry the reporter made recommendations to the Secretary of State. He stated that

---

[76] 1997 S.C. 189.
[77] See also *McKinstry v. The Law Society of Scotland,* 1996 S.C.L.R. 421.
[78] 1996 S.C.L.R. 465.

two significant considerations were the environmental impact and the
potential for environmental improvement, and the potential for economic
regeneration. The reporter preferred London and Midland's application,
rather than competing applications, because he considered that the potential
for economic regeneration was the most important factor. The Secretary of
State did not accept the reporter's recommendation and decided in favour
of a competing application. He concluded that the issue of environmental
benefits was more important than the potential for economic regeneration.
It was held that the Secretary of State had given an adequate reason for his
decision by stating that he attached more weight to environmental benefits
and less to the potential for economic regeneration. As long as he took all
material considerations into account, he was entitled to determine as a matter
of planning judgment what weight should be attached to each material
consideration. He was entitled to prefer his own views on the weight to be
given to planning considerations to those of the reporter.

In other fields of activity there may be legally approved circulars or
guidance notes which must be taken into account. Much of the guidance
which is produced to aid administrative decision-making has no express
statutory status and has not been preceded by any formal procedural stages.
Consequently there may have been no opportunity for public or ministerial
scrutiny. Therefore, although such guidance may amount to a relevant
consideration which an administrator should have taken into account when
making a decision it should not be regarded as a binding constraint on
decision-making. The importance of policy guidance in modern
administration is recognised by the willingness of courts to consider directly
the effect of a circular even though, by itself, it decides nothing and has no
immediate legal effect.[79] Although the courts may regard circulars and policy
guidelines as helpful aids when defining the scope of legal duties and the
extent of legal powers, it is on the legislation itself that decisions will be
based.

10–36   The matters which need to be taken into account as relevant
considerations may include European or international obligations. Where
international obligations have resulted in changes to the laws of the
jurisdictions within the United Kingdom these international obligations
automatically receive the same consideration as the rest of national law.
The position is less certain where an international obligation exists but the
protection of individual rights arising under it has not been incorporated
into United Kingdom laws. The usual method for incorporating protection
of international human rights, freedoms and privileges into a state is to
introduce legislation for the express purpose of ensuring that the standards
of the treaty or convention are met. In the United Kingdom successive

[79] *Scottish Old People's Welfare Council, Petrs.*, 1987 S.L.T. 179.

governments have failed to introduce legislation to protect the rights freedoms and privileges guaranteed to the individual by the European Convention on Human Rights[80] which has been ratified by the United Kingdom. The governments have claimed that United Kingdom law already meets the standard required by the Convention and any minor failings could be remedied as they become apparent. This view has not been born out in practice and, following the 1997 general election, a Bill to incorporate the convention into U.K. law was proposed in the Queen's speech on May 14, 1997. The Government is also proposing the creation of a Human Rights Commission with powers to advise and help law centres and specialist groups to bring test cases.

Although the courts are, as yet, unable to enforce the Convention directly   10–37 they have made some progress towards giving effect to it indirectly as a relevant consideration which must be taken into account in certain circumstances. Courts have regard to the provisions of the Convention where a statute is ambiguous[81] or where the law is uncertain.[82] However, the rights and freedoms guaranteed by the Convention cannot be invoked in the courts in the absence of any ambiguity or uncertainty in the legislation which is the source of the decision-maker's authority. In *R. v. Secretary of State for the Home Department, ex parte Brind*,[83] it was held that where a statute is clear and unambiguous international principles and standards may not be relevant. It has been held, however, that regard ought to be had to the Convention as an aid to interpretation, the presumption being applied that Parliament must have intended to legislate in accordance with the Convention.[84] In the case of *R. v. Secretary of State for the Home Department, ex parte Norney*,[85] it was held that, where legislation has been passed with the purpose of bringing domestic law into line with the Convention, the court should have regard to the relevant provisions of the Convention. The Criminal Justice Act 1991 provided that the Home Secretary should have a discretion to refer cases of discretionary life prisoners to the parole board. This provision was made in order to bring national law into line with the Convention. In considering the exercise of that discretion it would be perverse to ignore the relevant provisions of the Convention.

---

[80] European Convention for Human Rights and Fundamental Freedoms, 1950; T.S. 71 (1953); Cmd. 896.
[81] *R. v. Miah* [1974] 1 W.L.R. 683; *Garland v. British Rail* [1983] 2 A.C. 751; *R. v. Home Secretary, ex p. Brind* [1991] 1 A.C. 696.
[82] *Derbyshire County Council v. Times Newspapers* [1993] A.C. 534.
[83] [1991] A.C. 696.
[84] *R. v. Home Secretary, ex p. Bhajan Singh* [1976] Q.B. 198; *R. v. Home Secretary, ex p. Phansopkar* [1976] Q.B. 606; *R. v. Heathrow Airport Immigration Officer, ex p. Bibi* [1976] 1 W.L.R. 979.
[85] (1995) 7 Admin. L.R. 681.

10–38   The English courts have been increasingly willing to hold that the impact of a decision on the fundamental human rights of an individual is a relevant consideration which should be taken into account.[86] The obligation to take human rights under the Convention into account has been held to amount to more than paying lip service to a requirement to give consideration to the Convention. In the case of *Britton v. Secretary of State for the Environment*,[87] the court was asked to consider the legality and rationality of the decision by the Secretary of State to uphold a planning enforcement notice and a refusal of planning consent in the light of an obligation to take account of international obligations. The applicants were residents in a collective of 20 adults and six children, living in environmentally friendly homes called benders. They had been refused planning permission "for the establishment of an experimental, sustainable living system" and an enforcement notice had been served requiring them to demolish the homes. The Department of the Environment's *Planning Policy Guidance* advises that international obligations should be taken into account. These include respect for one's home under Article 8 of the European Convention on Human Rights. An inspector appointed by the Secretary of State to investigate found that there had been no violation of Article 8 as the interests of the residents had to be balanced against a wider public interest. The Secretary of State indicated that he had regard to Article 8 but he refused to determine whether or not the European Convention on Human Rights would be breached by enforcement action. The court quashed his decision because he had failed to have regard to a material consideration. In having regard to a policy in taking a particular decision it was necessary to make up one's mind as to whether the policy would, "admit or forbid or be neutral as to the proposal". The judge said that the Secretary of State must answer the question of the effect of the Convention. He need not decide as a matter of law whether a particular convention would be breached but failure by the Secretary of State to decide may be considered unlawful or irrational.

10–39   The same gradual acceptance of the importance of the European Convention on Human Rights was not apparent in Scotland. In the case of *Kaur v. Lord Advocate*,[88] it was contended as part of a petition for judicial review of a decision to deport a mother of three British-born children that the European Convention on Human Rights and the Fourth Protocol to European Convention of Human Rights 1963 were enforceable in the municipal law of Scotland. It was held that the Convention was not part of the municipal law of Scotland as Parliament had not passed legislation giving effect to the treaty provisions. A Scottish court was not therefore entitled to have regard to the European Convention on Human Rights either as an aid

---

[86] *R. v. Horseferry Road Magistrates' Court, ex p. Bennett* [1994] A.C. 42.
[87] CO/1348/96 and CO/1349/96, October 24, 1996.
[88] 1980 S.C. 319; 1981 S.L.T. 322.

to construction or otherwise.[89] This situation prevailed in the Scottish courts until the decision in the case of *AMT (known as AC), Petitioner*,[90] where Lord President Hope took the opportunity to clarify the extent to which regard should be given to the European Convention on Human Rights in Scots law. The case itself was not a petition for judicial review but was an appeal against a decision by the Lord Ordinary refusing to allow an adoption of a child by a homosexual man. The Lord President observed that the comments of Lord Ross, in *Kaur v. Lord Advocate*,[91] to the effect that the court is not entitled to have regard to international conventions such as the European Convention on Human Rights either as an aid to construction or otherwise, are no longer to be regarded as good law. When legislation is found to be ambiguous in the sense that it is capable of a meaning which either conforms to or conflicts with an international convention, Parliament is to be presumed to have legislated in conformity with the convention and not in conflict with it. In *Kaur v. Lord Advocate,* Lord Ross had reviewed the English authorities at the time. He shared the view of Lord Diplock that the Convention was irrelevant in legal proceedings unless and until its provisions had been incorporated or given effect to in legislation. Lord President Hope considers that what Lord Diplock was saying was that the terms of a statute could not be departed from if they were clear and unambiguous. In the light of subsequent developments Lord Hope said:

> "It is now clearly established as part of the law of England and Wales, as a result of decisions in the House of Lords, that in construing any provision in domestic legislation which is ambiguous in the sense that it is capable of a meaning which either conforms to or conflicts with the Convention, the Courts will presume that parliament intended to legislate in conformity with the Convention, not in conflict with it."[92]

In the case of *Anderson v. H.M. Advocate*,[93] reference was made to the Convention and to the observations of Lord Bridge in *Brind* but opinion was reserved as to whether these observations were part of the law of Scotland. In the *AMT* case Lord Hope observed: "It is now an integral part of the general principles of European Community Law that fundamental human rights must be protected and that one of the sources to which regard may be made for an expression of rights is international treaties for the protection of human rights on which member states have collaborated or of   10–40

---

[89] See also *Moore v. Secretary of State for Scotland,* 1984 S.L.T. 38; *Hamilton v. Secretary of State for Scotland*, 1991 G.W.D. 10–624.

[90] 1996 S.C.L.R. 897.

[91] 1980, S.C. 319; 1981 S.L.T. 322.

[92] See *R. v. Home Secretary, ex p. Brind* [1991]1 A.C. 696, *per* Lord Bridge at 747–748; *R. v. Miah* [1974] 1 W.L.R. 683; *Derbyshire County Council v. Times Newspapers Ltd* [1993] A.C. 534.

[93] 1996 S.C.L.R. 114 at 121.

which they are signatories."[94] Lord Hope also declared that the drawing of
a distinction between the law of Scotland and the rest of the United Kingdom
on this point can no longer be justified. The probable effect of incorporating
the European Convention on Human Rights into U.K. law will be that, in
addition to courts being required to construe statutes and common law as
being consistent with the convention, Ministers, civil servants and other
public authorities will be required to discharge the powers delegated to
them by Parliament in a manner consistent with the convention.

<h3 style="text-align:center">ERROR IN LAW</h3>

10–41 An authority which is entrusted with a discretion must direct itself properly
on the law or its decision may be invalid. In Scots law if an administrator
directs himself wrongly as to the law which must be applied and that error
is so fundamental that his acts are outside his jurisdiction the acts will be
invalid. English law treats errors differently. If the error in law was on the
face of the record; in other words if it appeared on the written determination
or decision, the decision will be reviewable. The effect of errors not on the
face of the record depends on the circumstances. In the case of *Anisminic v.
Foreign Compensation Commission*,[95] the consequence of such errors was
considered. It was decided that, where an administrator was mistaken about
the law applicable to the facts as he found them, he must have asked himself
the wrong question. This wrong question was one which he was not
empowered by Parliament to consider and was therefore outside his
jurisdiction. The Foreign Compensation Commission was a tribunal set up
by the Foreign Compensation Act 1950 to administer a scheme to
compensate British subjects who had lost property in Egypt during the Suez
crisis in 1956. Anisminic's claim for compensation had been rejected as the
assets of the company had been acquired by an Egyptian company. The
tribunal interpreted the relevant Order in Council to mean that only those
successors in title of British nationality could claim. The House of Lords
held that the Commissions had wrongly interpreted the Order in Council as
the Egyptian company was not a successor in title. The Commission had
therefore taken into consideration a matter which was irrelevant to
Anisminic's claim. The decision of the Commission was therefore *ultra
vires* and void.

10–42 In the case of *Perilly v. Tower Hamlet Borough Council*,[96] the council
believed that it was under a statutory duty to deal with licences granting

[94] 1996 S.C.L.R. 897 at 910. See also *Stair Memorial Encyclopaedia*, Vol. 10, "European
Community Law", para. 95.
[95] [1969] 2 A.C. 147.
[96] [1973] Q.B. 9.

permission to trade in Petticoat Lane market in the strict order in which they were received. Consequently, an application by Perilly for a licence was refused although his mother had held the licence for the pitch for 30 years until her death. The Council gave the licence to a newcomer but the court quashed that licence and ordered the council to issue a licence to Perilly. The council had erred in their opinion that they had no discretion to give priority to license applications where special circumstances applied. In *R. v. Patents Appeal Tribunal, ex parte Beecham Group Ltd,*[97] an error in law had been made in relation to patents. Beechams manufactured and marketed an antibiotic called ampicillin. They unwittingly produced and sold a variation on the formula, ampicillin trihydrate which had a better shelf-life. A competitor applied to patent ampicillin trihydrate. The Patents Act 1949 gave a right to object to a patent where the product had already been used in the United Kingdom, but this right did not arise if the previous use had been "secret use". Beechams opposed the patent application but the Patents Appeal tribunal rejected their opposition as the previous use had been secret use. Beechams sought judicial review of the decision and it was held that there had been an error in law. Beecham's use of the drug had not been secret use in the sense which Parliament had intended although they had not knowingly used the drug.

It was established in the Scottish case of *Watt v. Lord Advocate,*[98] that, 10–43 although the remedy of reduction could be used to set aside decisions of tribunals which are in excess of their jurisdiction, it is not available to review errors in law made by a tribunal acting within its jurisdiction. The case was challenge to a decision of a National Insurance Commissioner who had applied the wrong test in determining whether a person was subject to a statutory disqualification from receiving unemployment benefit. He was required to decide whether a person who was laid off from work because of industrial action was entitled to benefit. According to the legislation he would not be eligible for benefit if he was directly interested in the trade dispute which led to the stoppage of work. The Commissioner decided that he was not eligible without considering whether he was directly interested in the dispute. It was decided in the case that the error in law as to the meaning of the provisions of section 22(1) of the National Insurance Act 1965 was so fundamental that it had led the tribunal to exceed its jurisdiction, since it had caused a statutory entitlement to unemployment benefit to be wrongfully withheld.[99] Lord Emslie said: "This case is not one where the Commissioner misconstrued certain statutory provisions in the course of

---

[97] [1974] A.C. 646 (H.L.).

[98] 1979 S.C. 120.

[99] Note that there is now a stautory right of appeal on points of law from decisions of the Social Security Commissioners. Social Security Act 1980, s. 14.

attempting to answer the right question remitted to him. He misconstrued that very question and answered a very different question as a result of his error. For these reasons, I am persuaded that the Commissioner's decision was *ultra vires*." The effect of this decision is to apply in Scotland the principle which is illustrated in the English case of *Anisminic v. Foreign Compensation Commission*.[1]

10–44   In the case of *Shanks & McEwan (Contractors) v. Mifflin Construction*,[2] it was observed that an error of law by an arbiter was insufficient to found a challenge by judicial review unless that error resulted in an excess or abuse of jurisdiction. In the case *Re EK v. The Secretary of State for the Home Department*,[3] an appeal against a decision of an immigration tribunal to dismiss an appeal against deportation to Turkey by a Kurd, it was held that the tribunal had applied the wrong test in deciding whether or not a person was under fear of persecution in his own country. The tribunal had concluded that he was not personally marked out for persecution as an individual but they should also have considered whether he had a justifiable fear of persecution as a member of a Kurdish national minority group. The Immigration Rules provide that, where a person is a refugee, full account is to be taken of the provisions of the Convention and Protocol relating to the Status of Refugees.[4] Paragraph 165 of the Immigration Rules provides that: "a deportation order will not be made against a person if the only country to which he can be removed is one to which he is unwilling to go owing to a well-founded fear of being persecuted for reasons of race, religion, nationality, membership of a particular group or political opinion". It was held that the tribunal had, in effect, asked themselves the wrong question, namely, whether the petitioner was "personally marked out for persecution" and hence whether there was something special about him which would give rise to a well-founded fear of persecution.

In *Wilson v. Nithsdale District Council*,[5] it was held that a decision not to house a homeless person was invalid when the wrong test had been used to decide whether the person could be classed as vulnerable and so entitled to priority. An 18-year-old girl who had left her college course and was unable to return to the family home was sexually assaulted. After this she suffered an ectopic pregnancy and developed feelings of constant anxiety and distrust. A homeless persons' advisory officer decided that the girl was

---

[1]   [1969] 2 A.C. 147. See also *Cooper v. City of Edinburgh District Licensing Board*, 1990 S.L.T. 910 and *East Kilbride District Council v. Secretary of State for Scotland*, 1995 S.L.T. 1238.

[2]   1993 S.L.T. 1124. See also *Rae v. Criminal Injuries Compensation Board*, 1997 S.L.T. 291.

[3]   O. H. Cases, March 11, 1988.

[4]   (Cmnd. 9171 and Cmnd. 3096.)

[5]   1992 S.L.T. 1131.

not vulnerable in terms of section 25(1) of the Housing (Scotland) Act 1987 because she was not "at great risk". It was held that, in assessing vulnerability a comparison should have been made with some assumed average or normal or run-of-the-mill homeless person. If a person was less able to fend for herself then she should be classed as vulnerable for the purposes of the 1987 Act. Asking whether the petitioner was "at great risk" was the wrong question. The decision was reduced and district council ordered to secure that accommodation became available for the petitioner's occupation.[6]

The whole context of the legal authority for the decision will be 10–45 considered by the courts in deciding whether an administrator has asked himself the wrong question. Problems may arise where there are apparent conflicts between legislation which has been passed for different purposes. The case of *Mulvey v. Secretary of State of State for Social Security,*[7] involved such a conflict. The case was particularly important as it was a petition brought by one individual in circumstances which would be applicable to many others. The petitioner was sequestrated with effect from February 3, 1993. Prior to that date she had received loans from the Social Fund in terms of the Social Security Contributions and Benefits Act 1992. Some of these had not been repaid by the time of her sequestration. The Secretary of State for Social Security, acting in terms of section 78(2) of the Social Security Administration Act 1992, deducted sums in repayment of the loans from the income support paid to the petitioner. The petitioner sought declarator that in making the deductions after she has been sequestrated the respondent had acted *ultra vires* under the Bankruptcy (Scotland) Act 1985. Moneys due from a debtor prior to sequestration cannot be withheld from money due to the debtor after sequestration. (This prevents any one creditor gaining an unfair advantage over others.) Section 78 of the Social Security Administration Act gives the Secretary of State power to deduct sums due in repayment of loans from benefits paid. No provision is made, however, relating to the situation that arises when the debtor becomes bankrupt. It was held that as there was nothing in the social security legislation which related to bankruptcy, Parliament's intention must have been that section 78(2) of the Social Security Administration Act 1992 be read against the background of that law. At first instance it was held that the Secretary of State for Social Security was not entitled to recover the petitioner's pre-sequestration loans from the Social Fund by deduction from her post-sequestration income support. This decision was reversed on appeal to the Inner House. On a further appeal to the House of Lords (April 10, 1997) it was held that the Secretary of State had power to make the deductions.

---

[6] See also *Kelly v. Monklands District Council,* 1986 S.L.T. 169 and *R. v. Waveney District Council, ex p. Bowers* [1983] Q.B. 238.

[7] 1995 S.C.L.R. 102.

There was no conflict with bankruptcy law as it was not a case of one creditor obtaining an unfair advantage over others.

10–46   In the case of *Morgan Guaranty Trust Co. v. Lothian Regional Council*,[8] Lord Hope stressed the importance of ensuring that the Scottish and English courts adopt the same approach to the recovery of tax payments made under error in law, as a difference in approach between two jurisdictions in relation to the same statute could have unjust consequences. He said: "We will be achieving the same result by reference to the principles of Scots Law. I regard that as satisfactory because it would be inequitable that a remedy which is available in England in this important field of transactions between the citizen and a public authority should be denied here on the ground that it was not permitted by our law."[9]

Error as to a fact is not a separate ground of challenge but an erroneous impression of facts may amount to an irrelevant consideration. However in *Shetland Line v. Secretary of State for Scotland*,[10] it was held that an error which had only been discovered with the benefit of hindsight did not necessarily make the decision irrational. The case related to a discretionary scheme of subsidies paid to shippers of freight to the Northern Isles. Companies applied for subsidies on the basis of freight projections for each financial year. Two shipping companies submitted under-estimated projections for three financial years having relied on wrong information from the Scottish Office. Other companies had submitted projections which had been made on the correct basis, and this resulted in the two companies receiving a smaller share of the subsidies. The companies brought a petition for judicial review on the grounds that the decisions of the Secretary of State were irrational, unfair and based on errors of fact. The petition was dismissed because the error was only discovered at a later date and the decision was not irrational at the time when it was made.

IMPROPER PURPOSES

10–47   A decision may be challenged if it has been made for an improper purpose. Improper purposes may include malice or personal dishonesty on the part of individual officials, but it is more common to find that, rather than an intentional misuse of a power, there has been an incorrect interpretation of the statutory powers conferred on the authority, as in the case of *Association of Optical Practitioners v. Secretary of State for Scotland*,[11] where the Scottish Home and Health Department set low fees for sight testing and

---

[8]   1995 S.L.T. 299.
[9]   *ibid.* at 315.
[10] 1996 S.L.T. 653.
[11] *Association of Optical Practitioners v. Secretary of State for Scotland*, O. H., October 10, 1985.

dispensing by opticians. This was held to be an attempt to retrieve profits made by opticians in previous years and was therefore *ultra vires*. In the case of *Municipal Council of Sydney v. Campbell*,[12] it was held that the council had used its powers for an improper purpose. The council had used its powers of compulsory purchase of land, not for the statutory purpose of extending and improving the city, but to resell at a profit. This was held to be *ultra vires*. Similarly, in *Webb v. Minister of Housing and Local Government*,[13] Bognor Urban District Council used its compulsory purchase powers under the Coast Protection Act 1949 to acquire land for a promenade development. It was held that, as the intention of the Act was to empower local authorities to purchase land to build defences against encroachment by the sea, building a promenade as a recreational development was *ultra vires*. In the case of *R. v. Hillingdon London Borough Council, ex parte Royco Homes Ltd*[14] a local authority was held by the House of Lords to be using its planning powers for an improper purpose. It had granted planning permission for residential development subject to a condition requiring the developer to provide homes for persons on the council's housing waiting list.

The purpose for which a decision is made is deemed to be improper if it is a purpose which was not that intended by Parliament when the authority to make the decision was delegated. In *Macbeth v. Ashley*[15] it was held that a power had been used for the improper purpose of changing the national liquor licensing laws as they applied in the town of Rothesay. The Public Houses Amendment Act 1862 declared the opening times and closing times of public houses to be 8 a.m. and 11 p.m. respectively, with the qualification that the times could be reduced by up to two hours within any area by the local magistrates. The magistrates of Rothesay resolved to set a closing time of 10 p.m. for an area that included all public houses, inns and hotels in Rothesay. Ashley and other hotel-keepers raised an action seeking reduction, declarator and damages, together with the substitution of 11 p.m. for 10 p.m. in their licensing certificates. The House of Lords held that the magistrates had acted *ultra vires* because they had attempted, with regard to all the licensed premises in their district, to change the rule laid down by Parliament.

In the case of *Blair v. Smith*,[16] it was alleged that a statutory power had 10–48 been improperly used to compel Sunday observance. Blair was a boat-hirer in Saltcoats. He was convicted of hiring out a boat on a Sunday in contravention of his licence. He was fined £5 but appealed on the ground

---

[12] (1925) A.C. 338.
[13] [1965] 1 W.L.R. 755.
[14] [1974] Q.B. 720.
[15] (1874) I.R. (H.L.) 14.
[16] 1924 J.C. 24.

that the condition against Sunday hiring contained in the licence was *ultra vires* the Burgh Police Act (Scotland) Act 1892 in that its purpose was to promote Sabbath day observance. The High Court of Justiciary held, however, that the Sunday veto was *intra vires* as it was necessary for reasons of safety as fewer rescue facilities were available on Sundays. This case can be contrasted with the case of *Western Isles Islands Council v. Caledonian MacBrayne Ltd.*[17] The islands council introduced a byelaw prohibiting the shipping or unloading of goods or vehicles at Lochmaddy pier on Sundays. The byelaw was held to be *ultra vires* on the grounds that it was intended to fulfil an improper purpose of Sunday observance. There were no other grounds on which the decision could be justified.

In some instances where decisions of public authorities have been held to be invalid on the ground that the statutory powers were used for an improper purpose the intention behind the decision was to achieve a purpose which was desirable. It is not appropriate for a public authority to anticipate desirable changes in the law or to try to use a power which was conferred for one purpose to achieve a different purpose. It must wait for the democratic law-making procedures to be followed and then exercise its powers lawfully. A challenge to powers used in this way was made in the case of *McColl v. Strathclyde Regional Council.*[18] The Water (Scotland) Act imposed a duty on the council to provide wholesome supplies of piped water. The council decided to add fluoride to the water supply, not for the purpose of making the water more wholesome but to improve the dental health of the population. The Court of Session decided that there was no power under the Water (Scotland) Act 1980 to add fluoride to the water supply and so the decision of the council was *ultra vires*. (In 1985 Parliament passed the Water (Fluoridation) Act 1985 which authorised water authorities to add fluoride to the water supply with retrospective effect.)

10–49   In *Wheeler v. Leicester City Council,*[19] despite the duty of local councils under the Race Relations Act 1976, s. 71, to have due regard to the need to eliminate racial discrimination, it was held to be *ultra vires* for a council to use its power over the booking of playing fields to exercise pressure on officers of a rugby club to denounce players who were participating in a tour of South Africa at a time when sanctions against South Africa were in place. In the case of *R. v. Barnet Council, ex parte Johnson,*[20] it was held that powers under public health legislation could not be used for other purposes. The council owned a park called Cherry Tree Wood. Under the Public Health Act 1875, byelaws had been passed regulating the use of the park. Certain activities, such as the erection of stalls and tents, were

[17]   1990 S.L.T. (Sh.Ct.) 97.
[18]   1983 S.L.T. 616.
[19]   [1985] A.C. 1054.
[20]   (1981) 89 L.G.R. 581.

prohibited without the council's express permission. Each year the council gave consent for a local community festival in the park. In 1988 the council asked the organisers to guarantee that no political parties or groups likely to support political parties would take part in the festival. The organisers said that all they could do was to prevent political parties booking stalls. The council decided that this was not a sufficient undertaking and they refused consent for the festival. The Court of Appeal held that the power to regulate the park was for public health purposes and did not include a power to prevent people being in the park peacefully for political purposes. The withholding of consent was held to be *ultra vires*. Similarly in *Mixnam's Properties Ltd v. Chertsey Urban District Council*,[21] it was held that, although in granting a caravan site licence, the local authority had powers under public health legislation to impose conditions as to the operation of the site, Chertsey UDC had used their powers improperly to impose conditions regarding the rent charged and the security of tenure of the residents. This was held to be *ultra vires* as the purpose of the public health legislation was simply to enable the local authority to regulate the physical conditions of the site in order to ensure that the premises were safe. In *R. v. Lewisham Council, ex parte Shell UK Ltd*,[22] it was held that a local authority had acted *ultra vires* in boycotting a company's products in an attempt to induce the company to terminate its trading links with South Africa.

Not all instances of powers being used for an improper purpose arise from an excess of zeal in the public interest. A successful challenge to a decision by a government department on the ground that it had been made for an improper purpose was raised in the case of *Congreve v. Home Office*.[23] A number of holders of television licences renewed their licences early one year in order to avoid paying for the licence at an increased rate. The Home Office threatened that certain television licences would be revoked if their holders did not pay an extra £6. The Court of Appeal held that it was an improper exercise of the discretionary power of revocation by the Home Secretary to use it as a threat to obtain money which Parliament had given the executive no authority to demand. **10–50**

Recently, in *Highland Regional Council v. British Railways Board*,[24] the Highland Regional Council, in a petition for judicial review, sought declarator that the British Railway Board's proposal to withdraw the Fort William to London sleeper service constituted a proposal to discontinue all passenger services on three sections of a line. The council also sought reduction of the decision to discontinue the service; and interdict against

---

[21] [1965] A.C. 735.
[22] [1988] 1 All E.R. 938.
[23] [1976] Q.B. 629.
[24] 1996 S.L.T 274.

the board from withdrawing the service until the statutory closure procedure had been followed. British Railways Board had scheduled certain trains onto the three sections of line which were of no conceivable benefit to the travelling public so that they could not be deemed to have ceased to operate any service on the line. A complete withdrawal of a railway passenger service from a line would require statutory closure procedures to be followed. It was held that a "railway passenger service" had to be a genuine service which was intended for the carriage of passengers, and a late night service, for which there was not shown to be any need and which no passengers were using could not properly be regarded as such a service. The petition was granted. The effect of this decision was that the closure was prevented until the required consultations had taken place.

10–51   In the case of *R. v. Derbyshire Council, ex parte Times Supplements Ltd*[25] it was held to be unlawful for a council to cease to place its advertisements for teaching posts in the *Times* supplements because the leader of the council was suing the *Times* newspaper for damages for defamation of character. In *Sleigh v. City of Edinburgh District Council*[26] certain members of a local authority sought interdict to prevent the council negotiating a housing covenant scheme through the International Bank of Japan. Interim interdict was granted as the court held that the proposed scheme was illegal. It was a device to avoid the prohibition by the Secretary of State for Scotland of covenant schemes for general capital expenditure under the Local Government (Scotland) Act 1973. In the case of *Meek v. Lothian Regional Council*,[27] an interim interdict was granted against a local authority preventing it from supporting a publication known as the *Lothian Clarion* during a local election campaign as it would have been improper for the authority to give active support to a political publication.

MALICE AND BAD FAITH

10–52   Where a power has been exercised for reasons of malice or bad faith a decision made under that power may be reduced. If a decision has been motivated by malice, fraud, dishonesty or personal animosity it will amount to an unfair discrimination against the individual affected and would be contrary to the principle that everyone should be treated equally under the law. Instances of malice and bad faith are rare. In the case of *Pollok School Co. Ltd v. Glasgow Town Clerk*,[28] a house belonging to a private school was requisitioned as accommodation for homeless families under emergency powers during the war. The school challenged the requisition on the grounds

---

[25] *The Times*, July 19, 1990.
[26] 1987 S.C.L.R. 563.
[27] 1983 S.L.T. 494.
[28] 1946 S.C. 373.

that the house had been selected only because it belonged to a fee-paying school. The Inner House determined that if this could be proved the action of the town clerk would be open to review on the grounds of bad faith.[29]

The fact that a decision is unfair does not necessarily indicate that there has been malice or bad faith and unfairness alone is not a ground for review. In *Shetland Line v. Secretary of State for Scotland*,[30] where companies applying for subsidies had applied for too little because of incorrect information given by the Secretary of State. It was argued on behalf of the companies that the decisions were unlawful on the grounds that they were irrational, unfair and based on errors of fact. It was not suggested that the Secretary of State had acted in bad faith. It was held that, in the context of judicial review the concept of unfairness (other than procedural unfairness) was not a substantive ground of review on its own.

FETTERING OF DISCRETION

Where a discretion has been conferred on a body it may not limit the future   10–53
use of that discretion by laying down strict rules and policies. There is a need, however, to maintain a balance between official policy which is necessary to guide administrators and the needs of those affected by an individual decision. In *R. v. Police Complaints Board, ex parte Madden*,[31] it was held that it was *ultra vires* for the Police Complaints Board to adopt a rule of taking no action on complaints which the Director of Public Prosecutions had decided should not lead to criminal proceedings. Discretion should be exercised according to the circumstances of each individual case.

There are circumstances in which it has been held that an overall policy as to how a discretion is to be exercised will not invalidate the decisions made provided that it is evident that the official or body exercising the discretion is willing to depart from the policy where it is appropriate to do so. Such a policy was considered in the case of *British Oxygen Company v. Minister of Technology*.[32] The Board of Trade administered a scheme under the Industrial Development Act 1966 for the award of discretionary grants to industry. British Oxygen Company had been negotiating with the Board of Trade as to whether capital expenditure grants would be awarded for the purchase of equipment costing over £4 million. The equipment included a large number of oxygen cylinders and the Board of Trade declared that the purchase of these items would not attract a grant as they had decided to

---

[29] See also *Innes v. Royal Burgh of Kirkcaldy*, 1963 S.L.T. 325; *R. v. Secretary of State for the Environment, ex p. Ostler* [1977] Q.B. 122.
[30] 1996 S.L.T 653.
[31] [1983] 2 All E.R. 353.
[32] [1971] A.C. 610, H.L.

apply a rule that capital grants would not be awarded for items costing less than £25 each. British Oxygen sought a declaration that the board was not entitled to operate this rule. The House of Lords accepted that the rule was permissible provided that the board was "always willing to listen to anyone with something new to say".

10–54   In the case of *Cinderella's Rockafella's Ltd v. Glasgow District Licensing Board*[33] the petitioners sought judicial review on several grounds which included an argument that the board had adopted a policy which amounted to an unlawful fettering of discretion. The petitioner had applied to extend opening hours in their city centre entertainment premises from 11 p.m.– 3 a.m. from Monday to Saturday. The licensing board granted opening only until 2 a.m. This decision was made pursuant to a new policy recommended by the police to the Board in order to avoid public disorder and violence in the city centre. It was held that the board had acted within its statutory authority. There was no procedural unfairness in the acceptance of the police recommendations as, although the weight accorded to the policy could not be determined in advance, the great significance attached to the policy was made clear. There were no grounds to hold that the board had fettered their discretion since they had not excluded the possibility of individual exceptions being made to the general policy. The statement of reasons for the decision was sufficiently clear and there was no real reason to show that the petitioner's application merited a departure from the policy and the petition was duly dismissed.[34] An administrative authority is not, however, allowed to pursue consistency at the expense of the merits of individual cases. In *Stringer v. Minister of Housing and Local Government*[35] it was held that the existence of a policy did not necessarily amount to an unlawful fettering of a discretion but the decision-maker must be able to show that individual cases are considered and decided on their merits. The Minister had a policy of discouraging developments which might interfere with the Jodrell Bank telescope. The local planning authority entered into an agreement with the directors of the telescope that planning permission should not be granted for developments which would cause a risk of interference. Stringer applied for planning permission to build in the area and his application was refused. His appeal to the Minister was also unsuccessful. He then challenged the legality of the refusal of planning consent and the general policy. It was held that the decision of the planning authority was *ultra vires*. The agreement with the directors of the Jodrell Bank telescope had fettered its future discretion. However, the decision by the Minister was not unlawful. He was entitled to have a policy with regard

---

[33]   1994 S.C.L.R. 591.
[34]   See also *Centralbite v. Kincardine and Deeside District Licensing Board*, 1990 S.L.T. 231.
[35]   [1970] 1 W.L.R. 1281, D.C.

to the telescope provided that it did not prevent him from considering each appeal fairly on its merits.

The case of *Aitken v. City of Glasgow District Council*[36] concerned a   10–55 policy adopted by a licensing authority of limiting the taxi operators' licences in their area to a fixed number. An applicant for such a licence appealed against the authority's refusal to grant him a licence. That refusal had been the result of applying the limitation policy. It was held that, although the policy was not *per se ultra vires*, the licensing authority had fettered their discretion by applying a fixed maximum number of licences rather than a general guide number and had thereby erred in law and the appeal was allowed. The policy amounted to a fetter on the discretion of the authority because they applied it rigidly without taking the circumstances of individual applications into account.

The implications of this more restrictive approach are that, not only must   10–56 an authority direct itself as to whether in the light of the particular situation a predetermined policy ought to be altered but also it must refrain from regarding the policy as anything more than one factor amongst others to take into account. In other words, a policy may not become a norm which determines the outcome of particular decisions unless there is a very strong reason for departing from it. Standard rules and procedures may serve the purpose of clarifying vague legislation. There is a strongly held view amongst some jurists that it is better that policies be arrived at through rule-making rather than on a case-by-case basis because it allows more consultation and participation by interested parties. Where there are rules and guidelines there is less likelihood of inconsistencies in individual cases and less likelihood of error. There are also circumstances where the existence of a policy or a guideline may serve a positive purpose by indicating that a decision has not been made on arbitrary or biased grounds. In the case of *Kilmarnock Magistrates v. Secretary of State for Scotland*[37] the decision of the Secretary of State not to approve the appointment of a chief constable was challenged. The Secretary of State had refused to approve the appointment because the proposed chief constable came from within the local force. There was no regulation which said that the chief constable could not be appointed from within the local force but it was not disputed that the Secretary of State had a discretionary power to withhold his consent. The Court of Session rejected the argument that the Secretary of State should have declared his policy openly by incorporating it into regulations and upheld his decision. Where a Minister has both a power to exercise a discretion and a power to make regulations under the same statute it is reasonable to allow him to choose to exercise discretion in each case rather than making regulations.

---

[36] 1988 S.C.L.R. 287.
[37] 1961 S.C. 350.

A preponderance of rules can lead to a legalistic approach which is inflexible and does not give scope for the needs of justice to be served in individual cases.[38] It can also be argued that the existence of too many rules would not lead to certainty and consistency. Once the complexity of the rules reaches a certain level, the likelihood of error increases rather than diminishes. The optimum balance between rules and discretion will vary from area to area. In areas such as taxation a detailed system of rules and regulations is appropriate but in areas where individual rights may be infringed such as social welfare law, immigration and homelessness a wider discretion is important.

UNREASONABLENESS

10–57 Unreasonableness as a distinct ground for review will only arise where an authority has taken all proper considerations into account but has done something so absurd that no sensible person could ever suppose that it lay within the powers of the authority. In *Associated Provincial Picture Houses Ltd v. Wednesbury Corporation*[39] Lord Greene summarised the principle applicable as follows:

> "The court is entitled to investigate the action of the local authority with a view to seeing whether they have taken into account matters which they ought not to take into account, or, conversely, have refused to take into account or neglected to take into account matters which they ought to take into account. Once that question is answered in favour of the local authority, it may still be possible to say that, although the local authority have kept within the four corners of the matters which they ought to consider, they have nevertheless come to a conclusion so unreasonable that no reasonable authority could ever have come to it. In such a case, again, I think the court can interfere. The power of the court to interfere in each case is not as an appellate authority to override a decision of the local authority, but as a judicial authority which is concerned, and concerned only, to see whether the local authority have contravened the law by acting in excess of the powers which Parliament has confided in them."

The decision must be proved to be unreasonable in the sense that the court considers it to be a decision which no reasonable body would have reached, rather than being a decision which the court considers unreasonable *per se*. The court will not substitute its own judgment for that of the administrator, but it is very difficult when considering the reasonableness of a decision to draw the line between looking at the merits and the legality of a decision. Lord Greene said: "It is not what the court considers reasonable, a different thing altogether. If it is what the court

---

[38] 1961 S.C. 350 at 397.
[39] [1948] 1 K.B. 223.

considers unreasonable the court may well have different views to that of a local authority on matters of high public policy of this kind ... The effect of the legislation is not to set up the court as an arbiter of the correctness of one view over another."[40]

In *Council of Civil Service Unions v. Minister for the Civil Service*,[41]   10–58
Lord Diplock described an unreasonable decision as being one which is "so outrageous in its defiance of logic or of accepted moral standards that no sensible person who had applied his mind to the question to be decided could have arrived at it". In the context of an application for judicial review the test which requires to be satisfied to demonstrate unreasonableness is an exacting one. In the case of *McRae v. Parole Board for Scotland*,[42] having decided that the parole board had not acted unreasonably in revoking a licence and recalling a prisoner to prison when he was accused of a serious crime and had been apprehended under the influence of a drug, Lord Weir observed that, in challenging the reasonableness of a decision of a parole board, a very strong case would have to be made out before intervention by judicial review would be justified.

In *Ettrick and Lauderdale District Council v. Secretary of State*,[43] Ettrick and Lauderdale District Council sought judicial review of a direction issued by the Secretary of State on September 1, 1993 in terms of section 14 (2) (d) of the Local Government Act 1988 requiring the district council to repeat the process of putting out to tender ground maintenance works. The work was divided into 13 items in a bill of quantities which stated that "each item shall be priced independently of any other work scheduled". Condition 1.2 of the standard conditions of contract stated that the council "reserves the right to accept a tender, either in whole or in part". A contractor had tendered a price for the whole works which was less than the council's own district services organisation, but part of the work was offered to the district services organisation as their tender was lower for that part. The contractor withdrew and so the whole work was allocated to the district services organisation. He then complained to the Secretary of State who issued a directive that the council had awarded the work to the district services organisation without adequate reason. It was held that the direction of the Secretary of State should be reduced. It was clear from the tender document that each item was to be priced separately and the council had the right to accept in respect of some of the items only. The Secretary of State had misdirected himself in law in issuing the notice and his decision was therefore unreasonable. No one in the Secretary of State's position, acting reasonably, could have reached the view that the council was acting anti-competitively.

---

[40] *Associated Provincial Picture Houses v. Wednesbury Corporation* [1948] 1 K.B. 223 at 233–234.
[41] [1985] A.C. 374 at 410.
[42] 1996 G.W.D. 14–853.
[43] 1995 S.L.T. 996.

10–59   In the case of *Imperial Chemical Industries v. Central Region Valuation Appeal Committee*[44] a decision was quashed as being unreasonable because of the procedures followed. Section 12(1) of the Rating and Valuation (Amendment) (Scotland) Act 1984 gives the Lands Tribunal for Scotland power to determine valuation appeals when such appeals are referred to it by a valuation appeal committee. Ratepayer appellants sought to have an appeal in which the question of comparisons with equivalent English properties was raised referred by the valuation appeal committee to the Lands Tribunal. The Valuation Appeal Committee Procedure (Scotland) Regulations 1984 provide for the committee to decide whether to hear the appeal themselves or refer it to the Lands Tribunal. The decision is to be made without hearing the parties in person but regard must be given to any written representations. Regulation 4(3) provides that, if it appears to the committee that the case is highly technical or that the law applicable to the case is uncertain and the case is likely to create a precedent the committee is to refer the appeal for determination to the Lands Tribunal. The appellants asked the valuation appeal committee to refer the appeal to the Lands Tribunal on these grounds. The committee decided to refuse the application for referral. The applicants presented a petition for the judicial review of this decision on the ground that it was unreasonable to refuse to refer without asking the applicants to provide further representations. It was held that it was a defiance of logic for the committee to reach the conclusion which it had reached and that no reasonable tribunal faced with the representations by both parties as to the uncertainty of the law could have found it impossible to say that the law applicable to the case was uncertain. A reasonable committee would have called for more information. The decision of the committee not to refer the case to the Lands Tribunal was quashed.

10–60   In dealing with unreasonableness as a ground for review it can be difficult for the court to draw the boundary between reviewing the legality of a decision and interfering with the decision on the merits of the case. This difficulty was evident in the case of *McTear v. Scottish Legal Aid Board*.[45] Section 14(1) of the Legal Aid (Scotland) Act 1986 provides *inter alia* that:

> "(Civil) legal aid shall be available to a person if, on an application made to the Board
> (a) the Board is satisfied that he has a *probabilis causa litigandi*; and
> (b) it appears to the Board that it is reasonable in the particular circumstances of the case that he should receive legal aid."

Prior to his death from lung cancer, McTear raised an action of damages against the tobacco company which had manufactured the principal brand of cigarettes which he had smoked for many years. He claimed that the

---

[44] 1988 S.L.T. 106.
[45] 1995 S.C.L.R. 611.

company was aware of the dangers of smoking, that it had a duty to warn persons smoking its products of the fact that smoking could cause lung cancer, that it had failed in that duty and that as a result he had contracted the disease. The tobacco company denied liability. After McTear died his widow applied for legal aid to continue with the action in her own name. Her application was refused by the Scottish Legal Aid Board. In giving its reasons for the refusal, the board stated that in its view the case would raise difficult questions and that it was not persuaded that any or all of these questions would be resolved substantially in favour of the applicant. Further, the board took the view that the case could be anticipated to be long, complex, expensive and difficult and that it would be unreasonable to hazard a substantial amount of public money on a case with such limited prospects of a worthwhile return. The widow sought a judicial review of the decision to refuse legal aid. It was held that although the remedy of judicial review was open in this case, the court could not substitute its own view on the merits of the application for that reached by the board, unless the latter had arrived at a perverse or unreasonable decision. The board was, however, entitled to take the prospects of success and the costs of the action into account in assessing the reasonableness of the application. The decision of the board could not be characterised as perverse or unreasonable but, on the contrary, fell within the limits of its discretion; and the petition was refused.[46]

It was made clear in the judgment that the court was not dealing with the merits of the petitioner's claim against the tobacco company or considering whether or not that claim would be likely to succeed. Also, there was no question of the court deciding what it would have done in relation to the application if it had been in the position of the board or seeking to substitute its own decision for that of the board. It was not for the court to decide whether or not the petitioner should receive legal aid. It was agreed that the board's decision to refuse the petitioner legal aid was subject to the remedy of judicial review. However, as Lord Fraser observed in *R. v. Entry Clearance Officer, Bombay, ex parte Amin*[47]:

10–61

> "Judicial review is concerned not with the merits of a decision but with the manner in which the decision was made ... Judicial review is entirely different from an ordinary appeal. It is made effective by the court quashing an administrative decision without substituting its own decision, and is to be contrasted with an appeal where the appellate tribunal substitutes its own decision on the merits. In an application for judicial review the court cannot interfere with the decision of the Board merely because the court might have reached a different conclusion or exercised its discretion in a different way."

---

[46] See also *Banks v. Scottish Legal Aid Board*, 1996 G.W.D. 17–1008.
[47] [1983] 2 A.C 818 at 829.

The parties in the *McTear* case were agreed that the petitioner's case fell to be tested by reference to *Wednesbury* unreasonableness. The question then arose as to whether it would be reasonable to: "hazard what would certainly be a substantial amount of public money on a case with such limited prospects of a worthwhile return". This was a matter for the board to decide in the exercise of its discretion. The decision reached by the board could not be regarded as a decision which no board, acting reasonably, could have reached.

10–62　　The case of *Gerry Cottle's Circus v. City of Edinburgh District Council*[48] arose because a circus company had applied to a district council for a temporary public entertainment licence which was refused. The council stated that "there was no question of a blanket policy being imposed" but that "The District Council Policy which did not permit circuses featuring performing animals was based on the fact that the whole concept of animals performing in circuses is wrong". The circus petitioned for judicial review, on grounds which included an argument that such a policy was outwith the district council's powers under the Civic Government (Scotland) Act 1982, Sched. 1, para. 5(3)(d), and was irrational. The court brought to the attention of the parties the terms of the Performing Animals (Regulation) Act 1925 which imposes upon a local authority a duty to register suitable applicants for exhibiting performing animals. It was held that the district council could not validly exercise licensing powers so as to deny all material effect to their duties under the 1925 Act. Against that background the respondents' policy could not be a good reason for refusal and the petition was granted. It was also observed that the district council's decision was irrational since their policy was irreconcilable with an exception to their policy for displays by working animals such as sheep dog trials or police dog displays.

Although the authority of a decision-maker usually stems from statute, acting according to the statutory rules may not preclude a decision being found to be unreasonable. Over-rigid adherence to rules in circumstances where discretion should have been exercised may amount to unreasonableness. This was held to be so in the case of *McMillan v. Kyle and Carrick District Council*.[49] McMillan sought judicial review of a district council's decision to refuse her application for housing. Her application had been refused on the grounds that although she had a priority need, she did not have a local connection in terms of section 27(1) of the Housing (Scotland) Act 1987. McMillan was born in Ayr and had lived there until 1989 when she and her parents moved to Tyne and Wear. In 1994, following the birth of her daughter, McMillan had returned to Ayr and stayed with her sister. In her application she stated that she wished to return to Ayr because

---

[48]　1990 S.L.T. 235.
[49]　1995 S.C.L.R. 365.

she had grown up there. She wished to be near members of her family who had lived in the district all their lives. The council argued that in strict interpretation of the rules they were entitled to treat her as having no local connection. It was held that the council had not consciously exercised their discretion. They had made errors in interpreting the rules and had applied them too rigidly and it was unreasonable to hold that McMillan had no connection. The decision was reduced and declarator was granted that the council were bound in terms of section 31(2) to secure accommodation for McMillan.

A similar rigid application of rules was held to be unreasonable in the case of *Woods v. Secretary of State for Scotland.*[50] A student applied to the Scottish Education Department for a postgraduate student's allowance. The closing date for applications was December 31, 1988. There was no record of the form having been received by the department and the applicant received no acknowledgment. In May 1989 the non-payment of his fees was notified to the student by his university and he wrote to the department explaining that a grant application form had been sent. On July 26, 1989, the department determined to refuse payment. The applicant sought judicial review of that decision, contending that it was unreasonable for the closing date to be relied on where such a reliance merely produced a windfall profit to the department. It was held that in the circumstances the department were wrong to rely rigidly on a closing date which had no statutory force. The department had budgeted to pay the petitioner's fees and the decision to refuse payment was therefore unreasonable. The decision was reduced and an order to make payment pronounced.

It has been held that it is not necessarily unreasonable for a licensing board to refuse one application for a grant of a licence and then grant another application with regard to the same premises.[51] A company applied to a licensing board for the grant of a betting shop licence under the 1963 Act, to operate a betting shop in Stranraer. Operators of two of the existing betting shops in Stranraer objected to the application on the basis that existing facilities in the area were sufficient to serve the area adequately. The initial application having been refused by the board, the applicant appealed to the sheriff who directed the board to reconsider the application. At the subsequent board meeting the original application was heard together with a further application by the same applicants. The board refused the original application but granted the second application. The objectors raised a petition for judicial review seeking reduction of the board's decision to grant the second application on the grounds that the board, having refused the first application, had proceeded without additional information or further

10–63

---

[50] 1991 S.L.T. 197.
[51] *Ladbroke Racing (Strathclyde) v. William Hill (Scotland)*, 1995 S.L.T. 134.

discussion of the matter to grant the second application and must have acted in an irrational and unreasonable manner. It was held that as it was not competent to grant both applications, there was no inherent irrationality in the board electing to grant the second rather than the first of the two applications.

10–64   However, it has been held to be unreasonable for a second application for planning permission to be granted where the first application is the subject of an appeal. The case of *Trusthouse Forte (U.K.) v. Perth and Kinross District Council*[52] concerned an application for planning permission for change of use of a building from stores to a nightclub and discotheque. The petitioners, who were the owners of an adjacent hotel, objected to the application. The district council refused the application in March 1988. The refusal was appealed by the applicants to the Secretary of State, who appointed a reporter to consider and determine the appeal. Prior to the reporter issuing his decision, the applicants submitted a further identical application for planning permission to the district council. The petitioners also objected to that application. Prior to the reporter issuing his decision, the district council granted the second application. The petitioners sought judicial review of the decision to grant the further planning application, seeking declarator that the decision was *ultra vires* and of no effect. It was held that the appeal to the Secretary of State had reached such an advanced stage that it was unreasonable for the district council to grant the further application without having regard to the outcome of the appeal and a decree of declarator and suspension was granted.

10–65   The courts may be more willing to hold that a decision has been unreasonable where fundamental human rights or freedoms are at stake. The strict *Wednesbury* test, which provides that a decision will only be invalid if it was so unreasonable that a reasonable authority could never have come to it, seems to be less strictly applied in human rights cases. In *R. v. Secretary of State for the Home Department, ex parte Bugdaycay*,[53] a case concerned with the judicial review of a decision of the respondent on an application for asylum as a refugee, Lord Bridge of Harwich, referring to the court's power of review, said:

> "The Court must, I think, be entitled to subject an administrative decision to the more rigorous examination, to ensure that it is in no way flawed, according to the gravity of the issue which the decision determines. The most fundamental of all human rights is the individual's right to life and when an administrative decision under challenge is said to be one which may put the applicant's life at risk, the basis of the decision must surely call for the most anxious scrutiny."[54]

---

[52]   1990 S.L.T. 737.
[53]   [1987] A.C. 514; [1987] 1 All E.R. 940.
[54]   [1987] A.C. 514 at 531.

In the case of *R. v. Ministry of Defence, ex parte Smith*,[55] Sir Thomas
Bingham M.R. said:

> "The court cannot interfere with the exercise of an administrative discretion
> on substantive grounds save where the court is satisfied that the decision is
> unreasonable in the sense that is beyond the range of responses open to a
> reasonable decision-maker. But in judging whether the decision-maker has
> exceeded the margin of appreciation the human rights context is important.
> The more substantial the interference with human rights, the more the court
> will require by way of justification before it is satisfied that the decision is
> reasonable."

This approach by the courts is probably an indirect effect of the growing
impact of the European Convention on Human Rights in judicial review
cases.

PROPORTIONALITY

Proportionality is a principle found in European Community law and in 10–66
French, German and Canadian law that an action taken must be proportionate
to the intended result. It has been described as a way of approaching the
Wednesbury formula by deciding whether the act or decision complained
of was so much out of proportion to the needs of the situation as to be
unreasonable.[56] It has also been described as a situation where the courts
will quash exercises of discretionary powers in which there is not a
reasonable relationship between the objective which is sought to be achieved
and the means used to that end or where punishments imposed by
administrative bodies or inferior courts are wholly out of proportion to the
relevant misconduct.[57] An appropriate balance must be maintained between
the adverse effects an administrative authority's decision may have on the
rights, liberties or interests of the person concerned and the purpose which
the authority is seeking to pursue.

The principle of proportionality is well established in European law,
and will be applied by courts where European law is enforceable in the
domestic courts.[58] A restriction on a fundamental right cannot be regarded
as "necessary in a democratic society" unless, amongst other things, it is
proportionate to the legitimate aim pursued. The doctrine of proportionality
has not yet been accepted as an independent ground for judicial review in
the United Kingdom but, in cases involving infringement of basic human

---

[55] [1996] 1 All E.R. 257 at 263.
[56] *R. v. Secretary of State for Transport, ex p. Pegasus Holdings (London) Ltd* [1988] 1 W.L.R. 990.
[57] *Halsbury's Laws of England* (4th ed.), Vol. 1, reissue (1989), p. 144.
[58] *Dudgeon v. United Kingdom*, 4 E.H.R.R. 149.

rights, it may be used as a consideration in deciding whether a decision is unreasonable. In the case of *Council of Civil Service Unions v. Minister for Civil Service*[59] Lord Diplock discussed future developments in the grounds for judicial review and said: "I have in mind particularly the possible adoption in the future of the principle of proportionality which is recognised in the administrative law of several of our fellow members of the European Economic Community."

10–67   The case of *R. v. Secretary of State for the Home Department, ex parte Brind*[60] was a petition to challenge directives issued by the Home Secretary under the Broadcasting Act 1981 requiring both the BBC and the IBA to refrain from broadcasting certain matters by persons who represented terrorist organisations, such as the IRA. Persons representing such organisations could be filmed as long as their voices were not broadcast. The applicants sought judicial review. One of the grounds for challenge was that the directives were disproportionate to the end they sought to attain, the purpose of the directives being to deny such organisations the appearance of political legitimacy and to prevent intimidation. The House of Lords held that proportionality was not a separate ground of review but acceded that it could be relevant in establishing *Wednesbury* unreasonableness. Lord Bridge and Lord Roskill agreed that proportionality might, at some future time be incorporated into U.K. law but felt that there was a risk of this leading to the courts substituting their decisions for those of administrators as they would have to consider the merits of the decision. The application was dismissed.

    In the case of *R. v. Manchester Metropolitan University, ex parte Nolan*[61] it was observed that proportionality was potentially available as a discrete head of challenge in appropriate cases. That case was a challenge against a decision by a university to refuse to allow a student on a law course to resit examinations after he had been found to have notes in his possession during an examination. In the case of *National and Local Government Officers Association v. Secretary of State for the Environment,*[62] it was held that proportionality could be applied in U.K. courts when deciding a case concerning E. C. law or when deciding the appropriateness of a particular penalty or where the case involved the exercise of a judicial discretion. Following the *Brind* case, it was not open to a court to depart from the traditional grounds of *Wednesbury* unreasonableness when reviewing the exercise of ministerial discretion. It was observed that it would be desirable for all courts in the European Community to apply common standards in the field of administrative law.

---

[59] [1985] A.C. 374.
[60] [1991]1 A.C. 696.
[61] [1994] E.L.Rev. 380.
[62] (1992) T.L.R. 576.

The issue of the disproportionate effect of a decision was considered in 10–68
the case of *R. v. Secretary of State for Health, ex parte RP Scherer Ltd.*[63]
Scherer, a pharmaceutical company, sought judicial review of a decision
by the Secretary of State to place gel-filled Temazapam capsules on the list
of drugs which were not permitted to be prescribed to NHS patients. The
reason was to prevent drug abuse as the gel could be removed and used in
injections by drug abusers. Scherer were the only manufacturers of capsules
in the United Kingdom. The grounds of challenge included a claim that the
decision was disproportionately harmful to their business. The Secretary of
State had considered the expert evidence and his conclusion that the capsules
had to be banned to reduce the risk to drug abusers was held not to be
disproportionate. The harsh consequence of the decision on Scherer could
not provide a reason for setting aside the decision as the overriding
consideration was the Secretary of State's duties to protect health and safety.

The move towards the adoption of proportionality has not found universal
favour. It has been criticised as involving the court in a process of policy
evaluation which goes far beyond its constitutional role and invites
consideration of the merits of decisions as well as legality. Questions
involving compromises between competing interests should be resolved
by the legislature rather than the judiciary. Where the legislature has
conferred a decision-making power on an individual the courts should not
substitute its evaluation of the merits of a decision for the judgment of the
decision-maker.[64] However, a test of proportionality is more objective than
a test of reasonableness as it is focused on the consequences of a decision
rather than the state of mind of a decision-maker. For this reason it should
be an easier test for judges to apply consistently. This should result in a
greater degree of certainty in the law relating to challenges of unreasonable
ministerial decisions. Harmonisation with the laws of other European states
would also be facilitated by the use of a test of proportionality rather than a
test of reasonableness.

GROUNDS OF APPEAL THROUGH STATUTORY APPEAL
PROCEDURES

The scope of the court's powers is substantially the same under statutory 10–69
appeal procedures as it is when considering petitions for judicial review on
common law grounds. The grounds on which the courts can intervene
through statutory appeal procedures may, however, be slightly different
from the grounds for raising an action through ordinary judicial review
procedure. Two examples of areas where there are statutory rights of appeal
are planning and licensing. The statutory right of appeal in relation to

---

[63] Q.B.D., March 8, 1996.
[64] Lord Lester of Herne Hill, "The Impact of Human Rights Law" (1996) J.R. 21–28.

planning decisions allows appeal to be made on the grounds that the validity
of a decision, notice or order can be questioned where:

(1) the decision in question is not within the powers of the relevant statute
     or statutes, or
(2) there has been a failure to comply with a relevant statutory require-
     ment.

The first ground allows the court to decide whether the decision itself is
intra vires and the second grounds allows consideration of whether or not
proper procedures have been followed.[65]

10–70   A failure to follow proper procedures would include a failure to take
relevant considerations into account. The Town and Country Planning
(Scotland) Act 1997, s. 37(2), requires that in making planning decisions
all "material considerations" should be taken into account. As the term
"material considerations" is not defined in the Act it is still a matter for the
court to determine which considerations are material and which are not.
There are some instances, however, where a statute may be more specific,
e.g. in making planning decisions the provisions of any relevant development
plan must be taken into account.[66] Decisions must be taken in accordance
with such a plan unless material considerations indicate otherwise.[67] In the
case of *The Noble Organisation v. Falkirk District Council,*[68] it was held
that the planning authority had discretion to decide on the merits of an
application and that the court could not interfere with the decision of the
planning authority unless they had left out of account a material
consideration, taken a wrong consideration into account or had arrived at a
view that no reasonable planning authority could have reached. The Noble
Organisation appealed against a refusal of an application for judicial review
of the decision of a planning authority to refuse a second application which
they had made for premises for which an earlier application had been refused.
Section 26A of the Town and Country Planning (Scotland) Act 1972
provided that a planning authority could decline to determine an application
for planning permission for the development of any land if within two years
prior to the receipt of the application the Secretary of State had refused a
similar application and the authority considered that there had been no
significant change in the development plan so far as material to the
application, or any other material considerations. Since these conditions were
fulfilled the authority was acting *intra vires* and as none of the procedural
grounds were established, the decision at first instance was upheld.

---

[65] Town and Country Planning (Scotland) Act 1997, s. 239(1).
[66] *The Bath Society v. Secretary of State for the Environment* [1991] 1 W.L.R. 1303.
[67] Town and Country Planning (Scotland) Act 1997, s. 25.
[68] 1994 S.L.T. 100.

The Licensing (Scotland) Act 1976 gives a right of appeal to the sheriff 10–71 from the decisions of licensing boards and local authorities. In addition to ruling on whether decisions are *intra vires* in the narrow sense, the sheriff has power to review the decisions made in order to ascertain whether there has been a breach of natural justice or unreasonableness. These more limited grounds were considered in the case of *Latif v. Motherwell District Licensing Board*.[69] Section 39(4)(d) of the 1976 Act provides that a sheriff may uphold an appeal from a licensing board if he considers that the board "exercised its discretion in an unreasonable manner". Latif appealed against the refusal of an off-sale licence on the grounds that the grant of the application would result in over provision of licensing facilities in the locality. The sheriff held that the licensing board had exercised its discretion unreasonably in refusing the application and granted the licence. In an appeal by the licensing board it was held that a narrow interpretation should be given to the word "unreasonableness". The sheriff could interfere with the decision of the board on the ground in section 39(4)(d) only if he concluded that the course followed by the board was one that no reasonable board, having taken into account all the relevant circumstances, could have adopted. The sheriff had erred in substituting his own judgment for that of the board; and the appeal was allowed.

The fact that a decision has been made on the basis of irrelevant 10–72 consideration will also provide a ground for appeal against a licensing decision. In the case of *Macfarlane v. Glasgow Licensing Authority*,[70] the court considered which matters were relevant when considering the renewal of a betting office licence. The Betting, Gaming and Lotteries Act 1963 provided that a licensing authority might refuse to renew a betting office licence if "the premises have not been properly conducted under the licence". At a betting shop in Glasgow a dispute arose between a Mr Meiklejohn who had bet on a winning horse and the bookmaker, Macfarlane, who had lost the betting line and refused to pay Mr Meiklejohn his winnings. He did, however, pay later. Meiklejohn raised an objection to the renewal of Macfarlane's licence on the ground that there had been improper conduct in the running of the betting office and the licence was not renewed. The sheriff overruled the decision of the licensing authority and granted renewal of the licence. The licensing authority had considered matters which were not relevant. Proper conduct had to be determined on the basis of section 63 of the Act which was concerned with matters relating to quiet occupation of the premises and not to the operation of the business itself.

---

[69] 1994 S.L.T. 414.
[70] 1971 S.L.T. (Sh.Ct.) 9.

CHAPTER 11

GROUNDS FOR JUDICIAL CONTROL OF ADMINISTRATIVE DECISION-MAKING: PROCEDURAL IMPROPRIETY

INTRODUCTION

11–01 The procedures that are followed by administrative authorities are no less important than the substance of the decisions which they make. Good administrative practice requires that there should be openness and fairness in the procedures under which administrative authorities operate. When Parliament is conferring a power or imposing a duty on an official or an organisation it is not unusual for a set of procedures to be laid down for carrying out the operations necessary to fulfil that function. The purpose of such procedures may be, for example, to ensure that there have been appropriate consultations before a decision is made or to ensure that, once a decision is taken, individuals whose rights may be affected are informed of any rights which they have to appeal or object. In addition to the need to comply with procedural requirements laid down by Acts of Parliament, certain types of decisions are made subject to the common law requirement that the principles of natural justice should be followed. Procedural fairness is also becoming increasingly important as a ground of challenge, partly because of an increased concern for openness and fairness and partly because of European influence.

INCORRECT PROCEDURE

Where powers are delegated to a person or body by Parliament there will often be provision for the procedures to be followed in order to carry out the function concerned. Authorities must exercise their powers in accordance with the procedures laid down by statute or other enabling instrument. Some of the procedures which are laid down will simply be directions as to how the function is to be carried out, but others will be compulsory steps, which must be followed. If such compulsory procedures have been laid down and the correct procedures are not followed, the court may declare the action to be *ultra vires*.

MANDATORY OR DIRECTORY PROCEDURES

The extent to which compliance with every detail of a procedure is required 11–02
will depend on the overall intention of Parliament. Not every minor departure
from a proscribed procedure will render an action or decision invalid. The
validity of the decision will depend to some extent on whether the court
considers the procedures which were not followed to be mandatory (as
opposed to directory). Mandatory or imperative requirements specifying
procedures, which must be adhered to, are often expressed in terms such as
"shall" and "must". Procedures which are only directory or regulatory are
more usually expressed in words such as "may". A breach of a directory
procedural provision does not necessarily invalidate an action on the grounds
of breach of procedure. Deciding which failures to follow procedure
invalidate decisions is not entirely a simple matter of interpreting a statute
to ascertain the intention of Parliament. There are other factors, which need
to be considered, the most important of which is the consequence of the
failure to follow procedures. In the case of *London and Clydeside Estates
Ltd v. Aberdeen District Council,*[1] Lord Hailsham stressed the importance
of having regard to the nature and the consequences of each departure from
procedure in order to decide whether or not the failure to follow procedure
was sufficiently serious to justify declaring an action or decision invalid.
The case concerned a notice refusing to reclassify a certificate of alternative
development (a procedure whereby a higher value could be claimed for
some pieces of land about to be compulsorily purchased for educational
development) in which notice of the property owners right to appeal against
the decision was omitted. It was held that the certificate was invalid because
of the defect in procedure. Lord Hailsham said: "I find it impossible to
accept that a requirement by an instrument of statutory force designed for
the very purpose of compelling a public authority to inform the subject of
his legal rights can be treated as simply regulatory if the requirement is not
complied with."[2] Lord Hailsham discussed the difficulties of categorising
procedures as mandatory or regulatory and stressed the importance of the
courts being free to decide each case on its merits. He observed that: "The
jurisdiction is inherently discretionary and the court is frequently in the
presence of differences of degree which merge almost imperceptibly into
differences of kind." He warned against the risk of the terms such as
"mandatory" and "directory" leading towards rigid distinctions. Important
issues that the courts should consider are the extent of the non-compliance
with a procedural requirement and the effect that the non-compliance has
had on the person making the complaint. A failure to follow a procedure in
every small detail should not invalidate a decision if no harm has been

---

[1] 1980 S.C. (H.L.) 1.
[2] *ibid.* at 27.

caused as a result and if the important principles of the procedure were respected. Serious prejudicial effect to a citizen renders it more likely that the court will find that a failure to adhere to a procedure invalidates a decision or action.

MANDATORY PROCEDURES

11–03   A procedural defect which causes unfairness, such as a failure to notify a person of his right of appeal, will usually invalidate an action. In the case of *Moss Empires Ltd v. Assessor for Glasgow*,[3] an owner of property in Glasgow challenged the revised valuation for rates of his property on the basis that the proper procedures were not followed. The Valuation of Lands (Scotland) Act 1854 required that the assessor send every revised entry in the valuation roll to the owner of the property affected. The owner could then, if he so wished, appeal against the assessment to an appeals court. Section 30 of the Act provided that "No valuation roll ... shall be challengeable or be capable of being set aside ... by reason of any informality or of any want of compliance ... with this Act in the proceedings for making up such valuation roll." A Glasgow property, which had been valued at £950 per annum, was raised to £1,300 the following year but no notice was given to the owner. The owner was consequently not informed of his right of appeal against the revised valuation. He sought reduction of the new entry and substitution of the existing figure. The House of Lords held that the non-compliance with the terms of the statute, which required that notice be given to the property owner, was not protected by section 30. Failure to adhere to a mandatory procedure rendered the valuation *ultra vires*. The consequence of the failure to follow procedure was serious since it caused a person to be deprived of his right of appeal against the decision.

11–04   Similarly, in the case of *Ryrie (Blingery) Wick Ltd v. Secretary of State for Scotland*,[4] a procedural requirement was found to mandatory because the failure to follow the prescribed procedures caused the petitioner to suffer substantial prejudice. Section 29 (4) of the Agriculture Act 1970 provides that, before revoking an agricultural grant, the Secretary of State shall give the applicant for grant a written statement of reasons for the revocation and an opportunity of appearing before a person appointed by the Secretary of State. The Secretary of State shall consider the report by that person and supply a copy to the applicant. Applicants for a grant under the Agriculture and Horticulture Grants Scheme 1980 sought reduction of the Secretary of State's decision under section 29 (4) to revoke the grant paid. The Secretary of State considered that the applicants had given false or misleading

---

3   1917 S.C. (H.L.) 1.
4   1988 S.L.T. 806.

information in their application. Written reasons were given to the petitioners for the revocation and they were given an opportunity to be heard before a person appointed by the Secretary of State. However the Secretary of State did not supply the petitioners with a copy of the report, although a copy had been requested, before revoking the grant. The petitioners argued that this amounted to a failure to comply with a mandatory requirement of the 1970 Act and accordingly that the decision was invalid and should be reduced. The Secretary of State argued, first, that the requirement was directory and not mandatory and, secondly, in any event, there had been no prejudice to the petitioners since there was no provision for any further representations to be made on receipt of the report. He also argued that any representations from the petitioners would not have altered the decision. It was held, nevertheless, that the Secretary of State had failed to comply with a mandatory requirement and that the petitioners had thereby been deprived of the opportunity to make representations about the terms of the report and the decision was reduced.

In the case of *Stakis v. Boyd*,[5] a requirement that an order should be on 11–05 sworn information was held to be mandatory. Section 9 of the Food and Drugs (Scotland) Act 1956 set out the procedure by which the destruction of food unfit for human consumption could be ordered. Section. 9(3) provided that: "If it appears to a justice of the peace on sworn information in writing that any food … is unfit for human consumption, he shall condemn it and make an order in writing for it to be destroyed." An environmental health officer who informed the company that he was taking action under section 9 (3) of the 1956 Act appropriated food supplied by a company to a school. A hearing was arranged before a justice of the peace at which the company was represented. Oral and written information was submitted to the justice to the effect that the food was unfit for human consumption. The justice made an order condemning the food as unfit and ordering its destruction. The environmental health officer was not put on oath at the hearing. The company petitioned for judicial review of the order, arguing that the requirement for "sworn information in writing" was mandatory. It was held that it was not essential that the information should be in written form. It was essential, however, to the validity of an order made under section 9 (3) that it proceeded upon sworn information, whether it was sworn prior to or to at the hearing, and a decree of reduction was granted.[6]

---

[5] 1989 S.L.T. 333.

[6] See also *Arcari v. Dunbartonshire County Council,* 1948 S.C. 62 (failure by a local authority to adopt a resolution required by statute); *McDaid v. Clydebank District Council,* 1948 S.L.T. 162 (failure to serve on owner's proper notice of action affecting their property and failure to notify a right of appeal); *McDonald v. Lanarkshire Fire Brigade Joint Committee,* 1959 S.C.141 (failure to serve notice on an individual against whom occupational or disciplinary sanctions are envisaged); *Allied Breweries (U.K.) Ltd v. Glasgow District Licensing Board,* 1985 S.L.T. 302 (failure to make byelaws or other delegated legislation necessary for achieving a particular purpose).

DIRECTORY PROCEDURES

11–06 A procedural defect that causes no unfair consequences should not invalidate an action. The case of *Johnston v. Secretary of State for Scotland*[7] concerned a police constable who was convicted of assault. He was subsequently found guilty of an offence against discipline and required to resign forthwith by the chief constable as an alternative to dismissal. He appealed against the chief constable's decision. The statement and supporting documents required to be provided by the chief constable under rule 3(1) of the Police (Appeals) (Scotland) Rules 1969 were received by the Secretary of State three days late. The Secretary of State nevertheless considered the statement and supporting documents and dismissed the appeal. The constable brought a petition for judicial review, seeking reduction of the decision of the Secretary of State on the ground that he acted *ultra vires* in considering the statement and supporting documents. The Lord Ordinary dismissed the petition. The constable reclaimed. It was held that what mattered was not whether the rule was directory or mandatory but what were the consequences of failure to observe it. The rule was made to enable the Secretary of State to consider the parties' interests and the public interest in a quasi-judicial way. His right to receive the material embraced in rule 3 could not be lost simply because the chief constable delayed in the performance of his duty to provide it. As there was no suggestion of prejudice to the petitioner the reclaiming motion was refused.

An example of a procedural requirement that was regarded as directory rather than mandatory can be found in the case of *National Commercial Bank of Scotland v. Fife Assessor.*[8] Appeals against valuations for the valuation roll had to be lodged by September 15. The appellants had posted an appeal by registered post on September 14 but it had not arrived until September 15. The assessor contended that the appeal, not having been lodged timeously was incompetent and time-barred. It was held that the valuation committee had discretion, despite the failure in procedure to consider the appeal. Similarly in the case of *Tait v. Horsborough,*[9] which concerned an application to Glasgow Licensing Board for renewal of a liquor licence, an application was received by the clerk to the board on September 30 for submission to the board on October 3. The clerk returned the application, having refused to put it before the board. Tait raised a petition for judicial review on the basis that the clerk had erred in law in refusing Tait's application and failing to place it before the Board. It was held that the clerk exceeded his powers by rejecting the application on grounds of its lateness without giving Tait an opportunity to explain the reasons for the

---

[7]   1992 S.L.T. 387.
[8]   1963 S.C. 197.
[9]   1987 S.L.T. 340.

delay and seek a postponement. The 1976 Act does not impose an absolute exclusion of all applications that are out of time. Rigid adherence to a procedure, in circumstances when discretion should have been exercised may itself lead to unjust consequences for an individual.[10] An underlying appreciation of the intentions of Parliament, combined with a respect for principles of fairness to the individuals affected by decisions should be evident in administrative decision-making.

If procedural guidelines or rules do not define the procedures which must be followed in specific circumstances all that is required is that the decision-maker should act fairly. The methods used to reach a fair decision will depend on the nature and the context of the decision that was being made. In the case of *Saleh v. University of Dundee*[11] it was held that there was no requirement for examiners of a Ph.D. thesis to give reasons to support their decision that Saleh should not be allowed to resubmit his thesis. The internal and external examiners had disagreed about whether Saleh should be allowed to resubmit and the academic board had therefore consulted another independent examiner before making a decision that he could not resubmit. There was no unfairness and nothing to suggest that Saleh should have been granted a hearing. It was a matter of academic judgment and it was therefore inappropriate for the court to interfere.

11–07

UNAUTHORISED DELEGATION

In order to ensure accountability it is important that powers which are given to a particular authority should be exercised by that authority. Delegation is not allowed without express provision to that effect. There is a Latin maxim that applies to a broad range of relationships where a power, authority or duty has been delegated: *delegatus non potest delegare* — a delegate may not delegate. It is not always a straightforward matter to determine which powers need to be exercised by a person or body to whom a power has been delegated and which can be delegated further within an organisation. Confusion on the matter of delegation arose, for example, as a result of the establishment of a statutory scheme for the registration of dockworkers. There was some doubt about the extent to which the powers of the national board that had been delegated could be further delegated at local level. In the case of *Barnard v. National Docks Labour Board*[12] a challenge arose because the London Dock Board delegated its disciplinary function to the port manager, who suspended Barnard from work because of a breach of discipline. Barnard challenged the validity of the decision to suspend him

11–08

---

[10] *Indpine Ltd v. City of Dundee District Licensing Board,* 1992 S.L.T. 473; 1992 S.C.L.R. 353.
[11] Extra Div., June 8, 1994.
[12] [1953] 1 All E.R. 1113.

and it was held that the disciplinary powers of the local board could not be delegated lawfully to the dock manager. The decision to suspend Barnard from duty was held to be a legal nullity. Similarly, in the case of *Vine v. National Docks Labour Board*,[13] the dismissal of a dock worker by a disciplinary committee was held to be *ultra vires* as only the board itself had the power of dismissal.

Where an official carries out an action that falls outside his powers, the authority in whose name he acts is not bound. In the case of *Argyllshire County Council v. Local Government Board for Scotland*,[14] a medical officer had told the occupants of a house that they would have to leave the house as a guest staying there had smallpox. A local authority had power under section 47 of the Public Health (Scotland) Act 1897 to remove residents who were not sick from a house in which there was an infectious disease. The medical officer was not, however, authorised to issue such an order. It was held that the local authority had not used its power to remove the family and therefore was not obliged to provide alternative accommodation for them.

AUTHORITY TO DELEGATE

11–09 The extent to which delegation is possible depends on the relevant legislation, the nature of the decision-making body and the character of the function in question. In the case of *R. v. Commission for Racial Equality, ex parte Cottrell and Rathon*,[15] it was held that the Commission for Racial Equality could entrust its officers or a sub-committee with the investigation of a complaint while retaining the power to make the substantive decision. In *McCall v. Mitchell*[16] it was held that a byelaw regulating the use of a market may authorise the appointment of a market officer with delegated power to allocate stalls. However, decisions that have been entrusted to one body should not be delegated to another organisation. In the case of *R. v. Children's Hearing for the Borders Region*,[17] it was held that the children's hearing, which had specific responsibilities in relation to children at risk, could not delegate important decisions about such children. The children's hearing was required to review the supervision requirements imposed under section 44 of the Social Work (Scotland) Act 1968 in relation to a child whose brother (a battered baby) had already been adopted. The children's hearing varied the supervision order for the child, stating that the baby should be placed in a pre-adoptive home, which should be chosen by the

---

[13] [1957] A.C. 488.
[14] (1902) 9 S.L.T. 484.
[15] [1980] 3 All E.R. 265.
[16] 1911 S.C. (J.) 1.
[17] 1984 S.L.T. 65.

local authority. It was held that the children's hearing had acted *ultra vires* because they had not specified the "place" where the child was to reside. They could not delegate that discretion to the local authority.

DELEGATION OF POWERS WITHIN GOVERNMENT DEPARTMENTS

Where powers are conferred on a Minister, it is validly accepted that they 11–10 may be exercised by a civil servant in his department unless it appears from a statute that a personal decision is required.[18] A central government department is regarded as a single entity where civil servants take decisions on behalf of the Minister for which the Minister is legally responsible. This principle was the basis for the decision in the case of *Dalziell School Board v. Scottish Education Department.*[19] The school board had dismissed a teacher whom they considered to be unable to give religious instruction adequately following conversion to Roman Catholicism. The teacher appealed to the Scottish Education Department under the Education (Scotland) Act 1908 and its secretary wrote to the board stating that the department did not consider the dismissal to be justifiable and had decided that the board should pay three months' salary to the teacher. The board challenged this decision on the basis that the S.E.D. decision was not valid and not binding on it since the matter had been incorrectly delegated to the secretary. The Inner House held that there had been "tacit delegation" within the department and the decision was therefore *intra vires* and valid.

In the case of *Carltona Ltd v. Commissioner of Works,*[20] a challenge was made to the validity of a requisitioning order on grounds which included an argument that the commissioners never brought their minds to bear on the issues. It was held that the commissioners had validly entrusted such tasks to an official. This case was followed in *Air 2000 v. Secretary of State for Transport (No. 2).*[21] An airline company challenged regulations by the Secretary of State for Transport, which required that transatlantic flights from Edinburgh and Glasgow should stop at Prestwick. The company argued that the rules were invalid as the Secretary of State had not complied with section 31(4) of the Airports Act 1986 which required him to obtain advice from the Civil Aviation Authority before making any rules. Even if advice had been obtained, it had not been given to the Secretary of State but only to an interdepartmental working party. It was observed that where there was a requirement of receipt of advice by a Minister of the Crown it would be insufficient to show only that a letter had been delivered to the minister's department. It would, however, suffice if the letter had been received by an official with responsibility for the matter in question.

---

[18] *Local Government Board v. Arlidge* [1915] A.C. 120.
[19] 1915 S.C. 234.
[20] [1943] 2 All E.R. 560.
[21] 1990 S.L.T. 335.

11–11   Delegation to persons or bodies outwith the government department requires specific authorisation. In the case of *Allingham v. Minister of Agriculture and Fisheries*,[22] the Minister delegated his power to give directions as to the cultivation of land during wartime to local committees. A local committee made decisions in relation to part of Allingham's land but left the decision regarding the location of that part to an executive officer. Allingham was fined for non-compliance with the officer's direction. It was held that the direction by the executive officer was invalid, as he was not authorised to give directions. Specific statutory provision has now been made to preserve the principle that decisions are made on behalf of a Minister when functions are contracted out to a private person or body.[23] In the case of *Lavender v. Minister of Housing and Local Government*,[24] it was held that a Minister cannot delegate his authority to another Minister. The case concerned an application for planning permission for gravel extraction. The Minster of Housing stated that his policy was not to grant such permission with regard to agricultural land unless the Minister for Agriculture gave his permission. It was held that the decision to refuse planning permission was unlawful. The Minister of Housing had unlawfully delegated his discretion to another and had fettered his discretion. He had made the views of the Minister of Agriculture the only consideration on which he based his decision and had ignored other relevant considerations.

DELEGATION OF POWERS WITHIN LOCAL GOVERNMENT

11–12   Within local government there is a general power providing for the delegation of a local authority's functions.[25] Except for the raising of local taxes and borrowing powers, a council may arrange for the delegation of the performance of any of its functions to any committee, sub-committee, officer of the council or to any other local authority in Scotland insofar as there is no other statutory provision to the contrary. The delegation to committees, sub-committees or officers must be carried out by appropriate formal procedures. In England, in respect of a similar provision, in the case of *Western Fish Products v. Penwith District Council*,[26] it was held that delegation based on informal custom and the practice of councillors and officials is *ultra vires*. The council would not be bound by the acts of such councillors and officials.

    Usually, defects in the appointment of members of the body or an official do not render decisions made under delegated authority invalid. There are,

[22] [1948] 1 All E.R. 780.
[23] Deregulation and Contracting Out Act 1994, ss. 69–72.
[24] [1970] 1 W.L.R. 1231.
[25] Local Government (Scotland) Act 1973 (as amended by the Local Government and Planning (Scotland) Act 1982).
[26] [1981] 2 All E.R. 204.

however, instances where defects in the constitution of a body could render its decisions null and void, as in the case of *Cannon v. Secretary of State for Scotland*,[27] in which a consultative council intended to represent all teachers was declared a nullity because its members were all nominated by one union and the other unions were not represented.

PERSONAL BAR

It is possible that there may be circumstances in which an authority will be 11–13 personally barred from denying the validity of the acts of any of its officials. Personal bar may not, however, be used so as to enlarge the statutory powers of a public authority or to reduce duties that are binding on an authority. Although in general a public authority is not bound by unauthorised acts by its officials, an authority may commit an abuse of power if it acts without regard to a prior representation. Where, for example, an authority has provided information on the criteria on which it will make certain decisions it may be barred from departing from those criteria. In the case of *Pirie v. City of Aberdeen District Council*,[28] it was held that a local authority had acted *ultra vires* in taking into account behaviour of a tenant's wife in considering his application for housing. It was observed that the local authority's failure to list in the summary of their rules unsatisfactory behaviour of anyone other than an applicant as a ground for refusing an application barred the local authority from considering the behaviour of the applicant's wife.

Where an authority has given assurances about the future procedure that it will follow in dealing with a certain matter, the authority may be required to honour those assurances on grounds of fairness. Such a situation arose in the case of *Attorney-General of Hong Kong v. Ng Yuen Shui*.[29] The applicant was an illegal immigrant in Hong Kong. The immigration authorities announced that if such persons made themselves known to the authorities, each case would be dealt with on its own merits before any determination was made. Ng Yuen Shiu, who had been in Hong Kong for four years and had established a successful business, made himself known to the authorities who detained him whilst an order for his deportation was made. He challenged the deportation order on the ground that he had been given no opportunity to make representations to the authorities as to why he should not be deported. It was held that the public undertaking to consider each case on its merits created a right on the part of each illegal immigrant that would otherwise not have existed. Authorities should abide by such undertakings to the extent that they do not conflict with statutory duties.

---

[27] 1964 S.L.T. 91.
[28] 1993 S.L.T. 1155.
[29] [1983] 2 All E.R. 346.

11–14   It was held in *Chisholm v. Mackenzie*[30] that this same principle may not
         apply in relation to criminal law. There is no general defence in criminal
         law that an accused person acted in good faith on an assurance or advice
         from an official but there may be circumstances in which such assurance or
         advice is relevant to proof of an offence. In the case of *Bremner v. Morrison,*[31]
         a prosecution was brought for holding a public show (dog racing) without
         permission. This activity had gone on for four years and the magistrates
         had not previously objected. Although it was not necessary for the disposal
         of the case as the conviction was quashed for other reasons, there were
         dicta to the effect that there had been tacit consent. One of the most famous
         instances of assurances being given in relation to criminal proceedings arose
         in the case of *H.M. Advocate v. Waddell.*[32] On October 24, 1969 Patrick
         Meehan was convicted of the murder of Mrs Esther Ross. On May 19,
         1976 he was granted a royal pardon. The Lord Advocate had made public
         statements that prosecution of Ian Waddell for the same crime would not be
         justified. On August 6, 1976 Ian Waddell was charged with the crime. It
         was held that the statements by the Lord Advocate did not render the
         prosecution incompetent.

PRESUMPTION OF REGULARITY

11–15   The legal maxim *omnia praesumuntur rite esse acta* (presumption that all
         proper procedures have been followed) may be used as a defence against a
         challenge of incorrect procedure. The maxim does not apply if there is
         actual evidence that correct procedures have not been followed. The level
         of the presumption that all procedures were correctly followed increases
         with the lapse of time between the decision and any challenge that is made.
         In the case of *Scottish Milk Marketing Board v. Paris,*[33] a petition was
         brought for an interdict preventing milk being sold by Paris except through
         the milk marketing scheme. Paris alleged irregularities in the introduction
         of the scheme. Lord Morrison said: "It is sufficient to say that the scheme
         was approved by the majorities of the milk trade as required by law and it
         has been passed by Parliament. In these circumstances we have no discretion
         in regard to the enforcement of its provisions." The interdict was granted.

NATURAL JUSTICE

11–16   The principles of natural justice derive from the ordinary rules of civil and
         criminal procedure, which serve to ensure that every party to proceedings

---

[30] (1893) 20 R. (J.) 79.
[31] 1930 S.L.T. 738.
[32] 1976 S.L.T. (Notes) 61.
[33] 1935 S.C. 287.

in a court has the opportunity of knowing the case which he has to meet and of presenting his case before an impartial judge. Without the fundamental procedural requirements of natural justice there would be no fair judicial process. The superior courts in their supervisory role over tribunals and administrative agencies require natural justice to be observed by many bodies which are not courts but which exercise powers which involve consideration of facts and making decisions that directly affect the rights and interests of individuals. Breach of a rule of natural justice in which a body is required to act judicially will lead to its decisions being declared *ultra vires*. The rules do not apply to purely administrative functions although there is a perceptible tendency in recent years to require fairness and openness in administrative decision-making. Certain aspects of natural justice, such as the duty to give reasons and the recognition of legitimate expectations are increasingly required in administrative decision-making. These recent developments are partly the result of increased European influence and the English courts tend to be quicker than the Scottish courts to adopt the new principles. The Scottish courts pay a great deal of respect to the decisions of the English courts and so the law in Scotland on natural justice and fairness does not differ appreciably from the law in England.[34]

PRINCIPLES OF NATURAL JUSTICE

JUDICIAL FUNCTIONS

It may be difficult to decide whether a decision is being made in circumstances in which the principles of natural justice apply. It is a well-established principle that the rules of natural justice must be observed when a judicial function is being exercised. The Donoughmore Committee on Ministers' Powers in 1932 tried to analyse and differentiate between different types of functions carried out by way of government. They categorised decisions into three types: administrative, judicial and quasi-judicial. 11–17

Administrative decisions

An administrative decision puts no legal obligation upon the person charged with the duty of reaching the decision to consider and weigh submissions and arguments or to collate any evidence or to solve any issue. The grounds on which he acts and the means he takes to inform himself of the surrounding circumstances before acting are left entirely to his discretion.

---

[34] Bradley, "Administrative Law" in *Stair Memorial Encyclopaedia*, Vol. 1, p. 59 at 101.

Judicial decisions

A judicial decision is one reached on a dispute following presentation of the case by each party, including the taking of evidence, submission of legal argument and the application of law to the facts. It is clear that the rules of natural justice will apply to judicial decision-making according to this definition.

Quasi-judicial decisions

11–18   The committee also identified a type of decision-making which has judicial characteristics and which they called quasi-judicial. A quasi-judicial decision is one that resolves a dispute following a presentation of the case by each party, the adducing of evidence and the possible submission of legal argument. The consequence of the decision is administrative action based on Ministerial discretion.

The committee summed up the difference between quasi-judicial and judicial decision-making thus: "His ultimate decision is quasi-judicial and not judicial because it is governed not by a statutory direction to him to apply the law of the land to the facts and act accordingly, but by a statutory permission to use his discretion after he has ascertained the facts and to be guided by considerations of public policy." The committee recognised the similarity between administrative and quasi-judicial decisions, saying: "Indeed generally speaking a quasi-judicial decision is only an administrative decision, some stage or some element of which possessed judicial characteristics." Natural justice is an inherent part of this sort of decision-making. This was held to be so in the case of *McDonald v. Lanarkshire Fire Brigade Joint Committee*.[35] Thomas McDonald and other firemen brought an action against Lanarkshire Fire Brigade Joint Committee for a reduction of the decisions of their disciplinary tribunal and interdict to prevent the penalty of stoppages of pay occurring. McDonald had been charged with an offence under the schedule to the Fire Service (Discipline) (Scotland) Regulations 1953. He was charged on June 2 and 13. The regulations stated that a brigade member who had been charged would be informed in writing as soon as possible of the charge and receive other reports or written allegations on which the charge might be founded. McDonald received written notification of the charge and reports only days before his hearing on July 15. At the hearing McDonald complained that the regulations had not been complied with. He requested an adjournment due to the shortage of notice given. The Fire Brigade Joint Committee considered that the regulations had not been breached and the request for adjournment was rejected. McDonald brought a petition for judicial review.

---

[35]   1959 S.C. 141.

It was held that the decision of the joint committee should be reduced since it was a quasi-judicial body that should have adhered to the principles of natural justice. Lord Guthrie said:

> "I think that the Fire Service (Discipline) (Scotland) Act Regulations 1953 do provide for judicial or quasi-judicial proceedings. If that be so, then it is necessary that the defenders act in accordance with the procedure laid down by the regulations. If they do not comply with the regulations, their proceedings are null and void and a person who has been penalised is entitled to have a punishment imposed on him set aside without averment or prejudice."[36]

The term "quasi-judicial" is not really very helpful in describing situations where the functions that are being exercised are not judicial but there is nevertheless a duty to adhere to some extent to the principles of natural justice. What is clear is that the principles of natural justice are not confined solely to judicial decision-making. There is a general duty to act fairly in a wide range of administrative activities, although specific aspects such as a right to a hearing and a right to representation may not apply in every case. The flexibility and variety of procedural protection under the duty to act fairly represents an evolutionary advance in natural justice which is demonstrated by the ability of the requirements of fairness to alter according to the particular decision-making context.[37]

11–19

In the case of *McDonald v. Burns*,[38] it was held that the principles of natural justice should be observed where Church authorities are making decisions which affect individual rights and interests. Several nuns were dismissed from their convent in Edinburgh but refused to leave. An action was brought in the Court of Session for a decree for their removal. The sisters claimed that no charges had been made against them and that they had been given no right of reply, contrary to the rules for dismissing sisters. The Lord Ordinary allowed the decree for their removal and the sisters appealed. The Lord Ordinary's decree was recalled by the Inner House on the grounds that, although religious authorities have privative jurisdiction within their own sphere, the courts can entertain an action where the religious body has acted beyond its constitution in a manner calculated to affect the civil rights and patrimonial interests of any of its members. The fact that the principles of natural justice had not been adhered to meant that the decision was *ultra vires* and void.

---

[36] 1959 S.C. 141 at 147.
[37] Jabbari, "Critical Theory in Administrative Law" (1994) 4 *Oxford Journal of Legal Studies* 189–215.
[38] 1940 S.C. 376.

Justice Must be Seen to be Done

11–20   The two main principles of natural justice are: *audi alteram partem* (hear
the other side), known as the right to a hearing, and *nemo judex in causa
sua (potest)* (no one can be a judge in his own cause), known as the rule
against bias. Underlying these there is a third principle that justice must not
only be done but must manifestly be seen to be done. The case of *Barrs v.
British Wool Marketing Board*[39] related to circumstances where there had
probably been no unfairness but an opportunity had been created in which
unfairness could have taken place. The British Wool Marketing Scheme
1950 provided that wool delivered to the marketing board should be valued
by appraisers. A producer who was aggrieved by the valuation by the
appraisers had a right of appeal to a tribunal consisting of five members.
One producer, Barrs, whose wool was valued at 3d per pound below the
maximum price, appealed to the tribunal. The tribunal examined the wool
in the presence of a representative of the producer and the two appraisers
who had originally valued it. The tribunal then retired for consideration.
The representative of the producer was excluded at this stage but the two
appraisers retired with the tribunal members although they took no part in
the discussions. The tribunal dismissed the appeal and reduced the value of
the wool by another penny per pound. Barrs sought reduction of the tribunal's
decision on the ground that it had reached its decision in circumstances that
were contrary to natural justice. It was held that the tribunal was a body
that was required to act judicially. By creating a situation in which one side
may have had an opportunity to put forward arguments without giving an
equal opportunity to the other, they had transgressed the principles of natural
justice and the decree of reduction was granted. Lord Clyde said: "The test
is not, has an unjust result been reached? but, was there opportunity afforded
for injustice to be done? If so the decision cannot stand."[40]

11–21   This same principle applies where there has been a possibility that a
person making a judicial decision has been biased. Such were the
circumstances in the case of *Bradford v. McLeod*.[41] During a prolonged
national strike by coal miners a conversation took place at a social function
in Ayr in which the strike was discussed. A sheriff and a solicitor were both
present. At one point the sheriff made remarks to the effect that he "would
not grant legal aid to miners". Subsequently a miner represented by that
solicitor appeared before that same sheriff accused of breach of the peace
on a picket line. The solicitor moved that the sheriff should declare himself
disqualified from hearing the case because of the views that he had
expressed. The sheriff declined to disqualify himself. The miner was

---

[39]   1957 S.C. 72 .
[40]   at 157.
[41]   1986 S.L.T. 244.

convicted of the offence, as were 13 others in similar circumstances. They all sought to have their convictions and sentences suspended. It was held that there had been a miscarriage of justice. Although the sheriff himself might have been satisfied that he was not biased and would not act in a manner contrary to his judicial oath, circumstances existed which could create in the mind of a reasonable man a suspicion of the impartiality of the sheriff. It was not enough that justice was done, it must also be seen to be done. Lord Ross quoted from the judgment of Eve J. in *Law v. Chartered Institute of Patent Agents*[42]: "If there are circumstances so affecting a person acting in a judicial capacity as to be calculated to create in the mind of a reasonable man, a suspicion of that person's impartiality, those circumstances are themselves sufficient to disqualify although in fact no bias exists." Lord Ross said: "That dictum, also represents the law of Scotland upon this matter." He also said: "This case may serve as a reminder that the law of Scotland is jealous of its reputation for doing justice and for ensuring that justice is seen to be done; it may also serve to remind judges that if justice is not merely to be done but is to be visibly done, they like Caesar's wife, must be above suspicion."

Although there are few Scottish cases in which natural justice is mentioned prior to *Barrs v. British Wool Marketing Board*, that case made it clear that English developments in the case law of natural justice applied equally within Scotland. The House of Lords decision in the English case of *Ridge v. Baldwin*[43] marked a revival of interest in the principles of natural justice. This was followed in the judgment on the Scottish case of *Malloch v. Aberdeen Corporation.*[44] The principles of natural justice apply to a broader sphere of decision making than decisions made by public bodies. The right of an individual to be heard applies in principle to domestic tribunals such as the ruling bodies of sports.[45]

THE RULE AGAINST BIAS — *NEMO JUDEX IN CAUSA SUA*

The principles of natural justice confer a right to be judged by a person who is impartial. Erskine said: "It is a rule founded in nature itself that no man can be a judge in his own cause."[46] This fundamental principle applies to the whole system of legal adjudication as well as to judicial decision-making in the context of administrative law. The risk of bias may arise because of the identity of the decision-maker or because of his relationship with or knowledge of the parties. A risk of bias may also arise where the

11–22

---

[42] [1919] 2 Ch. 276 (at 289).
[43] [1964] A.C. 40.
[44] 1971 S.C. (H.L.) 85.
[45] *St Johnstone Football Club v. Scottish Football Association Ltd.,* 1965 S.L.T. 171.
[46] Erskine, *Institute*, I, 2–25.

interests of the decision-maker may be affected by the decision with which he is entrusted or because of the procedures that have been followed.

BIAS ARISING FROM THE STATUS OR IDENTITY OF THE DECISION-MAKER

A judge may not hear a case if he is related to one of the parties. The Declinature Acts 1594 and 1681[47] specified the prohibited degrees of relationship within which a judge should decline to hear a case. A judge may not sit in cases involving his father, son, brother, uncle, nephew or son-in-law. (This also included mother, daughter, etc.) Breach of these rules lead to the nullity of all proceedings whether or not any objections were raised to the judges at the time the case was heard. In the case of *Moncrieff v. Lord Moncrieff*[48] the Lord President declined to sit on the bench, as he was the brother-in-law of the appellant in the case. Where the relationship is between a decision-maker and a party to an action who is appearing in the capacity of a public official and not in a personal capacity there may not be a need for disqualification. In *McGilvray v. Oban Assessor*[49] it was held that such a distinction could be made as the interest rose through discharge of a public duty. The case was an appeal to the Lands Valuation Court against a decision by the Valuation Committee. One of the members of the committee was the brother-in-law of the assessor. It could not be supposed that he would be biased in favour of his brother-in-law when a decision to change the valuation decision would have no detrimental impact on him.

11–23   Bias may arise from a person's previous connection with one of the parties or because of a prejudgment of the case. In *Free Church of Scotland v. McRae*[50] it was held that a judge should be disqualified if he had previously acted as counsel for one of the parties. In the case of *McPherson v. Hamilton*[51] a sheriff fined the accused for contempt of court (non-attendance for a court appearance). In doing so he expressed the view that he did not believe the explanation for non-attendance. The actual case was called before the same sheriff later that day. It was decided that the sheriff should have declined to sit, as he had expressed a view as to the credibility of the accused, and this was an issue in the case. A judge should also decline to hear a case if he holds an extra-judicial public office, which may give rise to a conflict of interests. In the case of *Jex-Blake v. Edinburgh University Senatus*[52] Lord President Inglis declined to hear a case involving Edinburgh University

---

[47] Repealed by Court of Session Act 1988, Sched. 2.
[48] (1904) 12 S.L.T. 267.
[49] 1916 S.C. 665.
[50] (1905) 13 S.L.T. 77.
[51] 1991 S.L.T. 611.
[52] (1873) 11 M. 784.

because he was Chancellor of the university. Lord Justice-Clerk Moncrieff also declined to preside but his declinature was repelled because he was only a member of the university court and that was not such a direct connection.

Prior involvement with the matter to be decided may also give rise to a risk of bias. In the case of *London and Clydeside Estates v. Secretary of State for Scotland,*[53] the Secretary of State for Scotland had issued a direction in terms of the Town and Country Planning (Scotland) Act 1972 that he, rather than the reporter, would decide the appeal against a refusal of planning permission after a public local inquiry. Some time prior to these events the Secretary of State, as the local member of Parliament, had written letters supporting an objection to development of the site on behalf of one of his constituents. At the opening of the inquiry counsel for the developers drew attention to these letters and invited the reporter to adjourn the inquiry. He did so, but the Secretary of State instructed him to reopen the inquiry. The developers then presented a petition under the judicial review procedure for reduction of the direction that the Secretary of State should himself decide the appeal and reduction of the appointment of the reporter. The petitioners claimed that the previous involvement of the Secretary of State raised a suspicion in a reasonable man that he could not decide the appeal impartially. It was held that a Minister was not disqualified from exercising a quasi-judicial function merely because of previous support for a particular policy in relation to a particular development. It was possible, however, that such disqualification would occur where a Minister expressed such support so intransigently that a reasonable man might suspect that he would be unable to weigh up proven facts in a fair way. The nature of the Minister's previous support in this case was, however, not of that character and the evidence at the present inquiry was likely to differ from that of the previous inquiry. There was therefore no basis for suspicion that the Secretary of State would not consider the petitioner's application fairly; and the application was dismissed.[54] This case seems to reflect a move away from the idea that a person should not preside wherever there is a small risk that it might appear that there was prejudgment of the issues. It introduces a standard whereby a person only needs to refrain from making a decision if there is actual evidence that he has formed a prejudgment. In *Brown v. Executive Committee of Edinburgh Labour Party,*[55] interim interdict and suspension were granted where members of a disciplinary committee who were due to deal with a complaint against nine local labour party councillors

11–24

---

[53] 1987 S.L.T. 459.
[54] See also *Black v. Scott Lithgow Ltd,* 1990 S.L.T. 612 and *Anderson v. Hillary,* 1991 S.L.T. 521.
[55] 1995 S.L.T. 985.

had, in the course of a council meeting, voted to pass a motion critical of the conduct of the nine councillors. It was held that a risk of bias in the minds of some members of a body would invalidate a decision by the whole body. The likelihood of a prejudgment having been made was also very strong in the case of *Lockhart v. Irving*.[56] Lockhart and other police officers presented a petition for suspension and interdict against Irving, the chief constable, to prevent him investigating complaints in which he was personally concerned. Lockhart and others had made a report to the Coatbridge town clerk about the chief constable using the police patrol car for his personal use. They were then suspended from duty for offences against discipline. If they appealed an investigation would have been held by the chief constable. Interdict was granted. The case of *Harper of Oban Ltd. v. Henderson*[57] was a prosecution of a company for actions in contravention of certain statutes. The case was heard by a justice who had previously worked for the company and who had been dismissed. Although the company had submitted a plea of guilty to the offences, and taking into account that in a small community it would be a common occurrence for a justice to have a connection with at least one of the parties, it was held that it would be contrary to natural justice for this particular case to be heard by the justice, as there was a risk of bias arising from a personal grievance. The rule against bias has been held to apply to arbitration. An arbiter must carry out his duties impartially and fairly. It was held in the case of *Edinburgh Magistrates v. Lownie*,[58] that an arbiter may be disqualified if he accepts employment or has business dealings with one of the parties after his employment as arbiter.

BIAS ARISING FROM INTEREST

11–25   A judge should decline to hear a case if he has an interest in the outcome of the case. This applies to any case in which he has a pecuniary interest, which might be likely to influence him, or which others might think would influence him. In the English case of *Dimes v. Grand Junction Canal Company*,[59] a judgment of Lord Chancellor Cottenham was set aside, as he was a shareholder in the canal company. Lord Campbell said: "No one could suppose that Lord Cottenham could be … influenced by the interest that he had in this concern but … it is of the last importance that the decision that no man is to be a judge on his own case should be held sacred."[60] In the Scottish case of *Sellar v. Highland Railway Company*,[61] Lord Buckmaster said: "The importance of preserving the administration of justice from

---

[56]   1936 S.L.T. 567.
[57]   1989 S.L.T. 21.
[58]   (1903) 10 S.L.T. 752.
[59]   (1852) 3 H.L. 759.
[60]   A similar case in Scotland was *Caledonian Railway Company v. Ramsay* (1897) 4 S.L.T. 371.
[61]   1919 S.C. (H.L.) 19.

anything which can even by remote imagination infer a bias or interest in the judge upon whom falls the solemn duty of interpreting the law is so grave that any small inconvenience experienced in its preservation may be cheerfully endured." [62]

A direct and personal interest or holding in a company seeking a remedy or a license will always disqualify. In the case of *Ower v. Crichton*,[63] where licensing magistrates had taken part in a decision affecting premises in which they had a financial interest the court held that the decision was a nullity on the ground that there had been a breach of natural justice.[64] However, a less direct interest does not always lead to disqualification. In the case of *Houston v. Ker*,[65] it was held that a magistrate who was the owner of a public house in a burgh was not disqualified from deciding applications regarding other licensed premises in the burgh despite the interest which he might have in minimising competition. In *Gray v. Fowlie*,[66] a case concerning a parish's provision for paupers, it was held that a judge should not decline to hear a case merely because he owned property in the parish and may have to pay more through possible rate increases depending on the outcome of the case. In the case of *Hercules Insurance Company v. Hunter*,[67] six judges were disqualified from hearing a case because they held policies with the insurance company bringing the action. As this would mean that the case could not be heard, it was necessary to disregard the disqualifications. Similar problems arose in other cases and eventually the problem was resolved by the Court of Session Act 1868, s. 103, which stated that merely holding fire insurance or life insurance policy with a company, or holding stock in an unincorporated company merely as a trustee, was not to be ground for declinature by a judge. Direct personal interest such as holding shares in a personal capacity continued to be a ground for declining to hear a case.

The general rules relating to bias were explained in the judgment of Lord 11–26 Justice-Clerk Moncrieff in the case of *Wildridge v. Anderson*.[68] Wildridge was convicted of a charge of malicious mischief and fined 7s. 6d. It was alleged that he had damaged a cushion of the billiard room of the Moffat Library in Port Glasgow. Later Wildridge discovered that Niven, the magistrate who had convicted him, was one of the trustees of the library and therefore one of the proprietors of the damaged property. He sought suspension of his conviction and sentence before the High Court, claiming that Niven

---

[62]   1919 S.C. (H.L.) 19 at 20.
[63]   (1902) 10 S.L.T. 271.
[64]   See also *Blaik v. Anderson* (1900) 7 S.L.T. 299; *McDonald v. Findlay,* 1957 S.L.T. 81.
[65]   (1890) 28 S.L.R. 575.
[66]   (1847) 9 D. 811.
[67]   (1837) 15 S. 800.
[68]   (1897) 25 R. (J.) 27.

was disqualified because of interest from presiding at his trial. It was held that: "The general and salutary principle is that no man can be a judge in his own cause, and that rule within certain limits is vigorously applied. The reason of it is obvious, to ensure not merely that the administration of justice shall be free from bias but that it shall be beyond suspicion. It is subject however, to qualifications and exceptions." The result of the authorities, which were cited in the judgment, was summarised as follows:

> "(1) As a general rule a pecuniary interest, if direct and individual, will disqualify, however small it may be.
> (2) An interest although not pecuniary may also disqualify, but the interest in that case must be substantial.
> (3) Where the interest which is said to disqualify is not pecuniary, and is neither substantial nor calculated to cause bias in the mind of the judge, it will be disregarded, especially if to disqualify the judge would be productive of grave public inconvenience."

Lord Moncrieff decided, on applying these guidelines to the case, that the presiding magistrate had no pecuniary interest, and no appreciable personal interest in the outcome of the case. If he were disqualified, then so were all the other magistrates in Port Glasgow as they were all *ex officio* trustees of the Moffat Library. Having to bring in the sheriff from Greenock every time there was a case involving the library would be inconvenient. Therefore it was held that any breach of natural justice could be disregarded.

11–27   This doctrine of grave public inconvenience will apply in circumstances where all of the judges who would otherwise be available to hear a case would be disqualified.[69] It has also been recognised that in smaller jurisdictions, it is more likely that the judge will know some of the parties.[70] If disqualification were to result from every instance of a person making a judicial decision also holding a public office there would be interference with the operation of many of the functions of public offices, particularly at a local level. Disqualification will, however, always result where a person is personally or individually interested in the particular matter or question before him.[71]

An interest that is not pecuniary will not lead to disqualification unless it appears to create a risk of real bias. In *McGeehan v. Knox*,[72] McGeehan, who had held a licensing certificate for a number of years, was refused a licence one year by the licensing court in Airdrie. Knox, the chairman of the licensing court, was Chief Templar of the Independent Order of Good

---

[69] See also *Downie v. Fisherrow Harbour Commissioners* (1903) 11 S.L.T. 250; *Martin v. Nicholson* 1920 1 S.L.T. 67.

[70] *Harper of Oban (Engineering) v. Henderson,* 1989 S.L.T. 21.

[71] Court of Session Act 1988, s.4.

[72] (1913) S.C. 688.

Templars and had published a pamphlet on temperance. Three other members of the licensing court were also active members of temperance organisations. McGeehan sought reduction of the court's decision to refuse his licence on the ground that these members were disqualified through bias from sitting on the court. The Inner House held that there had been no breach of natural justice. It is not impossible for someone to administer faithfully a law of which he disapproves.

BIAS ARISING FROM IMPROPER PROCEDURE

The conduct of proceedings should be such as to ensure that there has been 11–28 an impartial consideration of the matter to be decided. In the case of *Macdougall v. Millar,*[73] it was held that a magistrate was not allowed to canvass other magistrates, urging them to oppose the grant of a licence. In the case of *Goodall v. Shaw,*[74] an apparently unfair procedure was held to be acceptable. In an area where there were too many licences in operation the licensing court adopted a policy of granting all of the unopposed licences before considering the licenses which had been opposed by temperance organisations. It was held that this was competent because the court exercised its discretion in each case and not all of the licences that had been opposed were withdrawn. It does seem though that this is an example of prejudging the applications in a way that gives an unfair advantage to objectors.

The need to balance the requirement for natural justice for the individual against practical convenience was a factor in the case of *Laughland v. Galloway.*[75] Laughland was convicted of theft in a J.P. court and sought to suspend the conviction on the ground that the clerk of that court and the procurator fiscal were also partners in the same firm of solicitors. The Court of Session held that their public official duties should be distinguished from their connection in the legal firm, holding that the test laid down in *Wildridge v. Anderson* should be applied in this case. There was therefore no breach of natural justice. In this case all of the proceedings were held in public, but in the case of *Low v. Kincardineshire District Licensing Court,*[76] where the solicitor of one party and the clerk to the court, his father, were partners in the same firm and the proceedings took place partly in private it was held that there had been a breach of natural justice.

Participation in an appeal or subsequent litigation by a person who was 11–29 involved in the making of the original decision probably also creates a real likelihood of bias. In *R. v. Sussex Justices,*[77] a man called McCarthy was

---

[73] (1900) 8 S.L.T. 284.
[74] 1913 S.C. 630.
[75] 1968 S.L.T. 272.
[76] 1974 S.L.T. (Sh.Ct.) 54.
[77] [1924] 1 K.B. 256.

summonsed for dangerous driving and was also the defendant in a civil action arising from the same incident. The acting clerk to the justices in the criminal case was a member of the firm of solicitors who were retained by the plaintiff in the civil action against McCarthy. The acting clerk retired with the justices and, although he was not consulted, McCarthy's conviction was quashed on the ground of a breach of natural justice.[78] In the case of *McDonnell, Petr.,*[79] an applicant for housing benefit from Cumbernauld Development Corporation appealed in terms of the Housing Benefits Regulations 1985 to the Cumbernauld Development Corporation review board. At the hearing the applicant's representatives left the room after the parties' submissions and the representatives of the corporation remained while the members deliberated. The applicant presented a petition for judicial review for the reduction of the decision of the review board on the ground that the presence of the corporation's representatives constituted a breach of natural justice. He did not claim that these representatives had taken any part in the deliberations. It was held that natural justice required that a tribunal exercising a quasi-judicial function must offer a fair and equal opportunity to the parties before it. The presence of one party alone during the deliberations of the tribunal was sufficient to invalidate the decision regardless of whether the party was present accidentally and took no part in the proceedings and the decision was reduced.

Scots law does not rely on a particular test to establish whether or not bias exists. It is a matter for consideration in the context of each case. The criteria for disqualification have been prioritised as follows: the factor most likely to lead to bias is a personal relationship, followed by shareholding, personal pecuniary interest, and prior involvement with the parties. Non-pecuniary interest is the least likely to lead to disqualification. This must be considered in the context of the nature of the function of the decision-maker and the remoteness of the interest.[80]

RIGHT TO BE HEARD — *AUDI ALTERAM PARTEM*

11–30 One of the five principles recommended by the Committee of Ministers of the Council of Europe is that a person concerned with an administrative act which is likely to affect directly and adversely his rights, liberties or interests should have a right to be heard. He should be informed of this right and be given the opportunity to put forward facts and arguments and (where appropriate) evidence. All this should be taken into account by the

---

[78] See also *Barrs v. British Wool Marketing Board,* 1957 S.C.72.

[79] 1987 S.L.T. 486.

[80] McMurtie, "The Principle of *Nemo Judex in Causa Sua* in Scots Law" (1996) 5 J. R. 304–320.

administrative authority before deciding.[81] There are two aspects to the principle that everyone is entitled to a right to a hearing. First, every party to judicial proceedings has the right to reasonable notice of the case against him and, secondly, every party is entitled to the opportunity to make submissions to the hearing and to bring evidence to it.

In the case of *Inland Revenue Commissioners v. Hood Barrs,*[82] Lord Reid said: "No tribunal, however informal, can be entitled to reach a decision against any person without giving to him some proper opportunity to put forward his case." Where a taxpayer and the Inland Revenue dispute the amount of income tax to be paid, the General Commissioners of Income Tax have the authority to settle the dispute. Appeal lies from them, on a point of law, to the Court of Session. Barrs, who owned a sawmill on the island of Mull, claimed that his business had suffered heavy losses and that he was, as a consequence, entitled to large refunds of income tax. The inspectors disputed his figures. When the Commissioners of Income Tax for Mull met to consider the amount of Barr's losses, without any further procedure and without holding any hearing, they issued loss certificates for £34,000. This was considerably more than the losses of £18,000, which Barr had claimed. The House of Lords held that the commissioners were performing a judicial function and therefore the principles of natural justice should have been followed. Their procedures had not allowed the tax inspectors a proper right to be heard and the decision to issue the loss certificates was reduced.

The principles have also been held to apply to the disciplinary procedures   11–31 of trade unions, as in the case of *Breen v. Amalgamated Engineering Union.*[83] A district committee of a trade union decided not to approve the election of Breen as a shop steward. Breen protested as he had not been informed of any reason for the withholding of approval and asked for the decision to be reconsidered. The committee affirmed its decision and asked the secretary to inform Breen of the reasons. One of these reasons related to an accusation of fraud in 1958 of which Breen had been acquitted. At first instance it was held that the decision should stand as there was no bias, malice or bad faith and, as this was not a judicial body, the rules of natural justice did not apply. Although the appeal failed on other grounds it was held that the committee was under a duty to act fairly according to the rules of natural justice. Lord Denning said that the right to be heard depended upon what was fair in the circumstances. Such a right was more likely to arise if a person's rights were being infringed.

---

[81] Committee of Ministers of the Council of Europe, Resolution (77) 31, "On the Protection of the Individual in relation to the Acts of Administrative Authorities".
[82] 1961 S.C. (H.L.) 22.
[83] [1971] 2 Q.B. 175.

A person should not be denied a hearing on the basis that the hearing would be futile unless it can be clearly demonstrated that such is the case. In the case of *Malloch v. Aberdeen Corporation*,[84] Malloch and other teachers appealed against a decision of the Court of Session in which it had been held that, although guidelines issued by the Secretary of State had been *ultra vires*, the decision by the local council to dismiss the teachers was not *ultra vires*. An education sub-committee had dismissed Malloch, and other teachers, upon the passing of a resolution on the ground that he was not a registered teacher as required by regulations made under statute. He claimed that his dismissal had been a breach of natural justice, as he had not been granted a hearing. It was held that the appellant had a general right to be heard before being dismissed. It had been argued that a hearing would be futile but the House of Lords decided that any such hearing would not necessarily be futile because the relevant legislation was sufficiently ambiguous for the appellant to make out a case.

11–32   Although *audi alteram partem* is referred to as the right to a hearing or the right to be heard, rights such as the right to call witnesses, the right to legal representation and the right to cross-examine witnesses are not inherent in the common law rule. Such rights may be conferred by an individual statute or regulation but if there is no such provision there is no right to insist on a particular type of procedure being followed. The principle is more concerned with fairness and ensuring that there is a procedure that affords an equal opportunity to both sides to put their case. In the case of *Board of Education v. Rice*,[85] it was held that a government department, in determining an appeal from the decision of a local authority must act in good faith and listen fairly to both sides. This is a duty that lay on everyone who decided anything. The department was not, however, required to treat such a question as a trial and was not required to follow the procedure of a court of law.

EXISTENCE OF RIGHT TO BE HEARD

11–33   The existence of a right to be heard will depend on the nature and context of the decision that is being made and the impact that it will have on the person or persons affected. The case of *Cooper v. Wandsworth Board of Works*[86] arose because the board, acting under statutory powers, had demolished a house which Cooper had started to build without giving the Board of Works seven days notice as required by the Act. The decision of the board to demolish the building was held to be *ultra vires* since Cooper had not been given a hearing

---

[84] [1971] 1 W.L.R. 1578, H.L.
[85] [1911] A.C. 179.
[86] (1863) 14 C.B.N.S. 180.

before it reached its decision. The case of *Ridge v. Baldwin*[87] followed the dismissal of the chief constable of Brighton, without a hearing, by the police authority after he had been acquitted on a charge of conspiracy. The decision to dismiss him was held to be void on interpretation of the provisions regulating the dismissal of constables. The Police (Appeals) Act 1943 provided that a constable dismissed by a police authority could appeal to the Home Secretary whose decision should be "final and binding on all the parties". The Home Secretary upheld the decision to dismiss the Chief Constable on appeal but it was held that the watch committee had based its decision on the evidence from the criminal trial. Ridge should have been informed of the charges against him and should have been given an opportunity to be heard

In the case of *Durayappah v. Fernando,*[88] Lord Upjohn stated that the right to a hearing depends on:

(1) The nature of the property, the office held, status enjoyed or services to be performed by the person complaining of injustice.
(2) The circumstances in which the person making the decision is entitled to intervene.
(3) The sanctions which the latter is entitled to impose.

Right to Notice

In the case of *Moss Empires Ltd v. Glasgow Assessor*[89] it was held that it is a breach of natural justice to fail to give proper notice of procedures, especially if this means that a right of appeal may be lost. In the case of *St Johnstone Football Club v. Scottish Football Association Ltd,*[90] a decision was held to be *ultra vires* because of a failure to notify a football club of proceedings being taken against it. The football club had arranged a benefit match for one of its players. The association wrote to the club criticising its arrangements for the match and informing it that the Executive and General Purposes Committee had decided to censure and fine St Johnstone. In a later letter it was stated that the decision of the Executive and General Purposes Committee had been confirmed by the association's council and that the club, if it was dissatisfied with this decision, should have challenged the decision at the meeting of the council. When the association pressed for payment of the fine, the club brought an action for declarator that the fine and censure were illegal and *ultra vires*. It was held that the council, acting as a judicial authority, should have observed the principles of natural justice. As it had acted contrary to natural justice declarator

11–34

---

[87] [1964] A.C. 40.
[88] [1967] 2 All E.R. 152.
[89] 1917 S.C. (H.L.) 1.
[90] 1965 S.L.T. 171.

that the decision was *ultra vires* was granted. The notice must be given in sufficient time to allow a person to prepare his answers to the case against him.[91]

11–35   If proceedings are to be conducted fairly it is important that a person who will be affected by a decision should be provided with an opportunity to make representations either before the decision is made or before it is implemented to his detriment. This right to submit argument need not always involve a right to be heard in person. It is important, however, that both parties are treated impartially and are given an opportunity to state their case in some form. In the case of *R. v. Army Board of the Defence Council, ex parte Anderson*,[92] a soldier sought judicial review of a decision by the Army Board rejecting his complaint of racial discrimination. It was held that the board should have made a specific finding as to discrimination in accordance with the Race Relations Act 1976. Also, given the importance of its function, the board should ensure that there is a high standard of fairness in its procedures. It should have considered whether to hold an oral hearing. Material should have been made available to the complainant and he should have been given an opportunity to respond.

The right to submit argument will not necessarily include a right to bring evidence in support of that argument or a right to bring evidence to refute the arguments of the other party. In the case of *J.A.E. (Glasgow) v. Glasgow District Licensing Board*,[93] J.A.E sought judicial review of the licensing board's refusal of its application for a regular extension of permitted hours to its entertainment licence. At the quarterly meeting of the licensing board the chief constable had objected to the application and read out a list based on information from police and civilian witnesses of incidents which had occurred in or around the premises. J.A.E did not accept that the list was fully accurate. The board refused J.A.E's motion that evidence should be heard. The board stated that they had preferred to accept the chief constable's submissions and that there were sufficient grounds to find that the extension was likely to cause undue public nuisance or to be a threat to public order or safety. J.A.E. argued that the board was bound as a matter of natural justice to hear evidence. It was held that, although the 1976 Act made no express provision for the hearing of evidence, it was intended that the board would have discretion to decide according to the circumstances what material they were prepared to entertain. The board's decision to proceed on one type of material and not another was not of itself a breach of natural justice.

---

[91]   *McDonald v. Lanarkshire Fire Brigade Joint Committee*, 1959 S.C. 141.
[92]   [1992] 1 Q.B. 169.
[93]   1994 S.L.T. 1164.

Natural justice required only that there was equality of treatment. In this case there had been equality of treatment since both parties had had the opportunity to make submissions in regard to the incidents. J.A.E. had no right to insist on being allowed to bring evidence. The reasons given by the board did not indicate that they had found as fact the entirety of the allegations by the chief constable, merely that there were sufficient grounds for refusing the application.

RIGHT TO KNOW EVIDENCE SUBMITTED BY OTHERS

The principles of openness and fairness require that each party should know   11–36
the case that he has to answer and the basis on which a decision is made. A
right of access to information is one of the five principles recommended by
the Committee of Ministers of the Council of Europe. The resolution states
that a person concerned, in order effectively to exercise his right to be heard,
should on request be given access, by appropriate means, to the relevant
factors on which the administrative act is intended to be based before the
act is taken.[94] If a decision of a judicial nature is being made in a forum
where the parties tender arguments on which a decision is made no other
considerations should be taken into account unless the parties know about
them and have an opportunity to comment. In *Freeland v. Glasgow District
Licensing Board*,[95] Freeland challenged the legality of the board's decision
to refuse to grant him a licence. One of the reasons for the board's decision
was that: "The Board drew on its own knowledge of the area in which the
premises are situated and had regard to information supplied by the police
about the general pattern of disorder in the vicinity of the premises." It was
held that the rules of natural justice are contravened if a board takes a
decision on the basis of its own previous knowledge without disclosure of
that fact or those facts to the party for his comments.[96] Another case which
illustrates that an implication of the *audi alteram partem* rule is that it is
not sufficient that a body places reliance on the record of previous
proceedings without allowing the party to answer that evidence is *General
Medical Council v. Spackman*.[97] Spackman had been cited as co-respondent
in a divorce action and was held to have committed adultery. The woman
concerned was a patient of Spackman and the General Medical Council
was considering whether to strike Spackman's name from the Medical
Register. Spackman made no written submission but tried to call fresh

---

[94] Committee of Ministers of the Council of Europe, Resolution (77) 31, "On the Protection of the Individual in relation to the Acts of Administrative Authorities".

[95] 1979 S.C. 226.

[96] See also *Tomkins v. City of Glasgow District Licensing Board*, 1994 S.L.T. 34; *William Hill v. Kyle and Carrick District Licensing Board*, 1991 S.L.T. 559.

[97] [1943] 2 All E.R. 337.

witnesses in rebuttal of the adultery charge. The General Medical Council refused to hear these witnesses and Spackman applied for certiorari (an order to quash a decision in English law). The House of Lords granted the order holding that the General Medical Council was under a statutory duty to make due inquiries before making a decision.

11–37   Although the principles of natural justice do not usually require that a person be given an opportunity to cross-examine witnesses there may be special circumstances where it would be unfair to refuse to allow cross-examination. One case in which special circumstances arose was that of *Errington v. Wilson*.[98] This was an appeal by a local food authority against a decision to grant Errington's petition for judicial review of a decision by a justice of the peace to order the destruction of 44 batches of Lanark Blue cheese. The batches of cheese had been seized by environmental health officials on the ground that they were unfit for human consumption. The Lord Ordinary had found that there had been a breach of natural justice in refusing to allow Errington to cross-examine the local food authority's witnesses. The appeal was refused. It was held that the justice was bound to act fairly. This included a duty to have regard to the principles of natural justice, which were designed to achieve fairness of procedure. There was an obvious risk of unfairness and of defects in the evidence lying undetected if there was a refusal to allow cross-examination. Errington had also been denied the opportunity of raising issues with the food authority's witnesses. Fairness also required that cross-examination should be allowed because the decision would have a serious effect on Errington's business and livelihood. It was not necessary for Errington to prove that he had suffered any prejudice, as the fact that proceedings had not been conducted in accordance with the principles of natural justice meant that his rights had been infringed.

11–38   Each case involving an allegation of a breach of natural justice needs to be considered in the light of all the surrounding circumstances. Where there is no statutory procedure laid down the person making the decision will usually have discretion as to how the proceedings are conducted as long as the proceedings are fair to all parties. In the case of *Stewart v. Secretary of State for Scotland*[99] a former sheriff sought judicial review of an order made by the Secretary of State removing him from office. Section 12(1) of the Sheriff Courts (Scotland) Act 1971 provides that an investigation into a sheriff's fitness for office may be undertaken by the Lord President and the Lord Justice-Clerk who may then report to the Secretary of State for Scotland. The Secretary of State may make an order removing a sheriff from office if the report is to the effect that the sheriff is unfit for office. An investigation had been undertaken at the request of the Secretary of State,

---

[98]   1995 S.C. 550; 1995 S.L.T. 1193.
[99]   1995 S.L.T. 895.

which took the form of a general investigation into the sheriff's conduct since 1980. Particular examples of the sheriff's conduct were identified and investigated in detail. Statements were taken from a number of persons with experience of his conduct. At the completion of their preliminary inquiries the senior judges provided the sheriff with a list of the cases relevant to his conduct which they were to investigate, together with short details of each case, and appended documentation where appropriate. He was invited to answer a number of questions and make observations. Following the sheriff's written response the senior judges interviewed a number of persons before interviewing the sheriff. Thereafter the senior judges submitted their report to the Secretary of State. The sheriff sought reduction of the order and the report on grounds which included an allegation that there had been a failure to comply with the requirements of natural justice. He argued that he should have been told who had spoken both for and against him, been informed what evidence had been rejected and for what reasons, been given copies of all the witnesses' statements, have had the opportunity to examine the relevant court processes, and been informed of the senior judges' preliminary conclusions. It was held that as no rules were laid down by statute as to the procedure to be followed, the senior judges were the masters of their own procedure subject only to the requirement to act fairly. They were not required as a matter of fairness to do more than they had done to give him notice of the case that he had to meet. The petition was dismissed. It was observed that the question whether the requirements of natural justice had been met by the procedure adopted in any given case had to depend to a great extent on the case's own facts and circumstances.

The right to a fair hearing and the right to know evidence submitted by 11–39 others must be balanced against issues of privilege and confidentiality. It will not be appropriate to reveal information that has been provided in confidence, such as personal references. In the case of *R. v. Joint Higher Committee on Surgical Training, ex parte Milner*,[1] it was held that, when considering an application for accreditation as a surgeon, the Joint Higher Committee on Surgical Training is not obliged to disclose the references it relied upon. Milner applied to the committee for accreditation as a surgeon. The committee rejected his application partly on the basis of references from his tutors, who were senior surgeons. Milner sought judicial review on the basis that he should have been informed of the gist of his references so that he could respond to them. It was held, refusing the application, that the applicant was not entitled to be told the content of the references. As the references were matters of opinion, not disputed facts, natural justice did not require the applicant to have an opportunity to challenge them. The rejection of the application for accreditation did not change the applicant's

---

[1] (1995) 7 Admin. L.R. 454.

status, nor was it a finding of wrongdoing, and so the interests of confidentiality of references outweighed the applicant's interest in disclosure.

11–40 Whether or not there is a right to be heard in person will depend on the context in which the decision is being made. This was discussed in the case of *Local Government Board v. Arlidge.*[2] Section 17 of the Housing, Town Planning, etc. Act 1909 authorised local authorities to make an order if a dwelling was unfit for human habitation. There was a right to appeal against such an order to the Local Government Board. In 1911 Hampstead Borough Council issued a closing order on Arlidge's house. He appealed to the Local Government Board, which appointed an inspector to hold a public local inquiry. The inspector visited the house and reported to the Local Government Board who confirmed the closing order. Arlidge appealed on the basis that:

(1) The notice of refusal of appeal did not show which officers of the Local Government Board had considered the appeal.

(2) Arlidge was entitled to be heard in person by the Local Government Board and he had not been invited to the inquiry.

(3) Arlidge had not seen the inspector's report.

It was held that:

(1) There was no procedural requirement to inform Arlidge who had heard the appeal.

(2) The rules of natural justice do not necessarily require that a party should be invited to be heard in person. Arlidge's written submission of evidence had been considered.

(3) Arlidge was not entitled to insist on seeing the inspector's report.

Viscount Haldane stated: " when the duty of deciding an appeal is imposed, those whose duty it is must act judicially. They must deal with the question referred to them without bias, and they must give to each of the parties the opportunity of adequately presenting the case made. But it does not follow that the procedure of every tribunal must be the same."

Procedures laid down by Parliament must, of course, be followed but due regard must also be given to administrative efficiency. Lord Shaw of Dunfermline said:

"when a central administrative board deals with an appeal from a local authority it must do its best to act justly, and to reach just ends by just means. If a statute prescribes the means it must employ them. If it is left without ex-

---

[2] [1915] A.C. 120, H.L.

press guidance it must still act honestly and by honest means. In regard to these certain ways and methods of judicial procedure may very likely be imitated; and lawyer-like methods may find especial favour from lawyers. But that the judiciary should presume to impose its own methods on administrative or executive officers is a usurpation. And the assumption that the methods of natural justice are ex necessitate those of courts of justice is wholly unfounded".

The matter had been determined in a judicial spirit in compliance with the principles of substantial justice and so the decision was held to be valid.

More recently, in *Malloch v. Aberdeen Corporation*,[3] the education   11–41 committee dismissed Malloch and 37 other teachers because they were unregistered in terms of the Schools (Scotland) Code 1956, as amended. By a letter of March 19, Malloch was given one month's notice of dismissal to take effect on April 24. Malloch sought reduction of the resolution of the education committee and the notices of dismissal on the ground that, contrary to natural justice, the committee refused to receive written representations or to afford Malloch the right to be heard in person before the resolution was passed. The House of Lords held by a majority of three to two that there had been a breach of natural justice. This case differed from *Arlidge* in that Malloch had been denied an opportunity to submit his arguments in any form, either in writing or in person at a hearing. In the case of *Young v. Criminal Injuries Compensation Board*,[4] Young challenged a decision by the Criminal Injuries Compensation Board to refuse compensation on the ground that his previous convictions showed that he had poor character. He had asked for an oral hearing but the CICB refused to grant such a hearing. Young argued that the refusal contravened the scheme and the provision of the scheme entitling the board to refuse an oral hearing was itself contrary to natural justice. It was held that as there was no dispute about the material facts on which the decision to refuse compensation was based, the applicant was not entitled to an oral hearing. There was a distinction between a right to a hearing and a right to be heard. In a scheme which was administrative and non-adversarial the refusal of a hearing was not contrary to natural justice where the applicant had the opportunity of presenting the board with all relevant information in writing.

Right to be Represented

The Committee of Ministers of the Council of Europe stated that it should   11–42 be possible for a person concerned to be assisted or represented in the administrative process. It is not clear whether they were recommending

---

[3]   1971 S.C. (H.L.) 85.
[4]   1997 S.L.T 297.

that legal representation should be allowed or whether less formal advice and representation was what they had in mind.[5] In the case of *Enderby Town Football Club v.. Football Association Ltd*[6] it was held that natural justice did not necessarily require that a person should be entitled to legal representation. However, although there is not always a right to legal representation, the broader principles of natural justice, that proceedings should be carried out fairly and that justice should be seen to be done, may require that representation be permitted. In the case of *R. v. Leicester City Justices, ex parte Barrow*,[7] Barrow challenged the refusal to allow him to have a friend to sit with him and give advice and assistance when he was prosecuted for non-payment of poll tax. It was held that the administration of justice had to be open and fair and had to be seen to be fair. Fairness required that a party conducting proceedings in person should be afforded all reasonable facilities to enable him to represent himself, including a friend to give advice, unless this would be contrary to the interests of justice. The conviction was therefore quashed. In the case of *Pett v. Greyhound Racing Association (No. 2)*,[8] a greyhound trainer who was the subject of an inquiry into the illegal use of drugs applied for a declaration that the association was acting *ultra vires* in refusing to allow legal representation at a hearing. His application was refused on the basis that natural justice related to the elementary principles of fairness, whereas legal representation was a sophisticated procedural matter. The right to legal representation will therefore only exist if such a right has been conferred by statute or if the matter in question is so serious that to deny legal representation would be unfair.

RIGHT TO FAIRLY CONDUCTED PROCEEDINGS

11–43   Even where there is no procedural requirement for specific provisions such as the right to be heard in person and the right to legal representation there is a general presumption that proceedings will be conducted fairly. There are also specific statutory requirements for fairly conducted proceedings in certain spheres of government activity. The Licensing (Scotland) Act 1976, s. 39(4)(c), and the Civic Government (Scotland) Act 1982, s. 4, require that licensing authorities observe the principles of natural justice in their hearings. This is particularly important because the granting, refusing or revoking of a licence has an impact on the ability of a citizen to carry on his business.

---

5   Committee of Ministers of the Council of Europe, Resolution (77) 31, "On the Protection of the Individual in relation to the Acts of Administrative Authorities".
6   [1970] 3 W.L.R. 1021.
7   [1991] 2 Q.B. 260.
8   [1970] 1 Q.B. 46.

The case of *Cigaro (Glasgow) Ltd v. Glasgow District Licensing Board*[9] was a challenge to the decision of a licensing board. A company applied to a licensing board for a gaming licence, in respect of premises in Bath Street, Glasgow. Among a number of objectors were three companies operating casinos in Glasgow. At the licensing hearing representations were made by counsel on behalf of the applicant and on behalf of the objectors. The licensing board refused the application on the ground that the demand for gambling was met by the existing facilities. The applicant appealed on the basis that there had been a breach of natural justice as the board had not required evidence to prove that the demand for gambling was met in full by existing facilities. It was held that, as the licensing authority had heard representations from all parties, it was not in breach of natural justice for failing to ask for evidence in support of the representations.[10]

It is important that fair procedures should be followed when disciplinary decisions are taken with regard to public sector employment. In *Palmer v. Inverness Hospitals Board*,[11] Dr Palmer was a house surgeon who was dismissed by the deputy medical superintendent of a hospital following a disagreement between Dr Palmer and a nursing sister. Palmer appealed against his dismissal, relying on a circular dealing with disciplinary procedures issued by the Department of Health for Scotland. The hospital board of management appointed a committee to hear the appeal and to produce a report. After listening to both Palmer and the medical superintendent, the committee unanimously reported that the dismissal was not justified. When the hospital board of management considered this report, the chairman allowed the medical superintendent, the deputy superintendent and the hospital's lawyer to be present, although neither Palmer nor his representative was present. The hospital's lawyer successfully argued that the report of the appeal committee should not be accepted. Palmer then brought an action for reduction of the resolution on the ground that it was contrary to natural justice. The Court of Session held that there had been a breach of natural justice in circumstances where the principles of natural justice should have been adhered to and reduction of the decision was granted.

The principles of fairness may require that competing commercial 11–44 interests should be given equal treatment with regard to matters such as the granting of licences or permissions. In the case of *Asda Stores Ltd v. Secretary of State for Scotland*,[12] Asda, a supermarket chain, sought judicial review of a decision by the Secretary of State of a decision not to call in an application for planning consent by a rival supermarket chain. Both Asda

---

[9] 1982 S.C.104.
[10] See also *Johnston v. Edinburgh District Licensing Board*, 1981 S.L.T. 257.
[11] 1963 S.C. 311.
[12] O.H., February 12, 1997, unreported.

and the other supermarket had submitted plans for overlapping sites and it was clear that the local development plan would only allow for one new supermarket in the area. It was argued that it was inconsistent and illogical not to treat both applications in the same way. In the absence of any statement of reasons why he was calling in one application and not the other, the court ought to draw the inference that the decision was either irrational or procedurally improper. The petition was granted and the decision reduced. The Secretary of State should have devised a procedure that was not unfairly prejudicial to the interests of Asda.

Fairness may require that sufficient information be provided to allow both sides a fair opportunity to make their case. In *R. v. Nature Conservancy Council, ex parte Bolton MBC*,[13] Bolton Council applied to quash the decision by the Nature Conservancy Council confirming notification of a site of special scientific interest under the Wildlife and Countryside Act 1981, s. 28. The Nature Conservancy Council had considered the site both on its current state and on its potential for restoration, whereas Bolton Council had only made representations on the latter. The Nature Conservancy Council had failed to correct Bolton Council's approach. It was held that there had been a breach of natural justice in that the Nature Conservancy Council had never made the basis for the notification sufficiently clear to enable Bolton Council to make a full objection and they ought to have known about the mistaken approach and corrected it. The decision was quashed. *Reilly v. University of Glasgow*[14] was a petition for judicial review brought by a young man of 17 who, in the summer of 1994, sat six Higher examinations in which he obtained passes at A grade. He applied to be admitted to study medicine at a number of universities including the University of Glasgow. He was called for interview and subsequently received a letter stating that his application for admission to the medical faculty at Glasgow had been rejected. He asked to be given reasons for the refusal and, after repeated requests, received a letter in which reasons were set out. The application for judicial review was on the ground that in refusing the application the university had "acted in a manner contrary to natural justice by failing to advise the petitioner, within the prospectus issued by them, that a pre-requisite of entry to the Faculty of Medicine was the requirement to make independent effort to acquaint himself with the way of life offered by a career in medicine by work shadowing in a general practice, hospital, or by voluntary work in a caring environment". Reilly claimed that the university was operating a policy of imposing a requirement for work experience of which he had not been informed. It was held, however, that there was no rigid adherence to such a policy. A significant

---

[13] [1995] Env. L.R. 237.
[14] O. H., August 22, 1995.

number of students were admitted who had not undertaken work experience. The reason for his rejection was that the interviewing panel did not consider that he had shown motivation and commitment to studying medicine and the petition was dismissed as there had been no unfairness in the procedures followed.

One issue, which arises from time to time, is whether or not a breach of 11–45 natural justice at first instance can be cured by a subsequent appeal procedure where the appeal procedure is fair and the principles of natural justice are adhered to. In *Calvin v. Carr*,[15] a case involving disciplinary proceedings under the Australian jockey Club Rules of Racing, Lord Wilberforce said: "no clear and absolute rule can be laid down on the question whether defects in natural justice appearing at an original hearing can be 'cured' through appeal proceedings. The situations in which this issue arises are too diverse, and the rules by which they are governed so various, that this must be so".[16] In *Calvin v. Carr* the appeal took the form of a re-hearing of all the issues and it was held that any defects in earlier proceedings were thereby cured, but in the case of *Brown v. Executive Committee of Edinburgh Labour Party*,[17] the court was asked to decide in advance that breaches of natural justice which had affected proceedings about to take place would be remedied by an appeal procedure. Lord Osborne said: " I know nothing of any appeal which might follow the determination of these proceedings… It appears to me therefore that I cannot, at this stage, reach any conclusion as to whether such an appeal might or might not 'cure' the apprehended defect in natural justice in the original contemplated hearing." It was held, therefore, that the breach of natural justice in the proceedings, which had already taken place, rendered a decision to discipline certain councillors *ultra vires*.

LEGITIMATE EXPECTATIONS

The phrase "legitimate expectation" has been increasingly used in judicial 11–46 review cases in recent years. The use of the expression has been more frequent in English cases but the concept of legitimate expectation is also developing in Scottish cases. It is generally accepted that legitimate expectation is a principle that is rooted in the concept of fairness.[18] Legitimate expectations may arise because of custom and practice, because of previous promises or undertakings or because of the principles of natural justice. The doctrine of legitimate expectations is part of a general principle that

[15] [1980] A.C. 574.
[16] *ibid.* at 592.
[17] 1995 S.L.T. 985.
[18] Singh, "Legitimate Expectation in 1996. Where Now?" [1996] J.R. 17–20.

those who are exercising powers, which affect individual rights and liberties, will act fairly. The meaning and scope of the principle of legitimate expectations is far from clear as it appears to have been used in different ways in the decided cases. Indeed, in *R. v. Devon County Council, ex parte Baker*,[19] Brown L.J. identified four different ways in which the term "legitimate expectation" has been used:

1. To refer to a substantive right or entitlement that the claimant asserts cannot be denied him.
2. To refer to the claimant's interest in some ultimate benefit he hopes to retain.
3. To refer to a right to a fair procedure.
4. To refer to a procedure to be applied because of a public body's promise or past practice.

LEGITIMATE EXPECTATION OF A SUBSTANTIVE RIGHT OR ENTITLEMENT

11–47   Whether the principle of legitimate expectations can provide protection for substantive as well as procedural rights is still in some doubt.[20] Although there is increasing acceptance of a principle of legitimate expectations that fair procedures would be followed it is not clear whether the courts should require public authorities to stand by their promises to confer a substantive right or privilege on an individual. However, in the case of *R. v. Secretary of State for the Home Department, ex parte Ruddock*,[21] it was held that a citizen has a legitimate expectation that his telephone calls will not be intercepted by government security agencies unless certain established criteria are met. (In that case the criteria had been met and the interception was held to be lawful.) Taylor J. considered that the principle of legitimate expectation could apply to substantive issues as well as to procedural requirements such as a right to be heard. He said:

> "The doctrine of legitimate expectation imposes a duty to act fairly: Whilst most of the cases… are concerned with a right to be heard, I do not think the doctrine is so confined. Indeed in a case where there is *ex hypothesi* no right to be heard, it may be thought even more important to fair dealing that a promise or undertaking given by a minister as to how he will proceed will be kept."[22]

It has been argued that it is no less unfair to frustrate a legitimate expectation that something will or will not be done by the decision-maker

---

[19] [1995] 1 All E.R. 73.
[20] Singh, *op. cit.,* n. 18, above.
[21] [1987] 1 W.L.R. 1482.
[22] See also *R. v. Inland Revenue Commissioners, ex p. Unilever plc.* [1994] S.T.C. 841; *R. v. Inland Revenue Commissioners, ex p. Matrix Securities* [1994] 1 W.L.R. 570.

than it is to frustrate a legitimate expectation that the applicant will be listened to before the decision-maker decides whether to take a particular step.[23]

The reluctance by the judiciary to rush to extend the principle of legitimate expectations to substantive as well as procedural issues stems from a concern that they should not overstep the bounds of the supervisory jurisdiction and review the merits rather than the legality of a decision. If the courts become over enthusiastic in protecting substantive expectations there is also a risk that the discretion which has been granted by Parliament to a particular decision-maker may be eroded.[24] This view was apparent in the opinion expressed by Laws J. in *R. v. Secretary of State for Transport, ex parte Richmond London Borough Council,*[25] that "such a doctrine could impose an obvious and unacceptable fetter upon the power of a responsible public authority to change its policy". However, where a promise has already been made or a practice has been firmly established, requiring a decision-maker to adhere to a promise should not involve a scrutiny by the courts of the merits of that policy or practice. The function that the courts would be fulfilling would be to prevent a decision-maker changing his policies in circumstances where it would be unfair to the person affected.

LEGITIMATE EXPECTATION OF THE CLAIMANT'S INTEREST IN SOME ULTIMATE BENEFIT HE HOPES TO RETAIN

An example of legitimate expectations in the sense of a benefit or interest   11–48 which the claimant hopes to retain arose in the case of *R. v. Board of Visitors to Hull Prison, ex parte St Germain (No. 2).*[26] It was held in that case that a prisoner was entitled to challenge, by judicial review, a decision by a prison board of visitors, awarding him loss of remission of sentence, although he had no legal right to remission, but only a reasonable expectation of receiving it. In the case of *O'Reilly v. Mackman,*[27] which also concerned a challenge to a decision to reduce a prisoner's period of remission, Lord Diplock said that the reduction of remission did not infringe any right derived from law. Remission is not awarded as a matter of legal right but of indulgence. However, a legitimate expectation that remission would be awarded if there had been no breach of discipline by the prisoner did give a prisoner sufficient interest to challenge the legality of any adverse disciplinary award made

---

[23] *R. v. Minister for Agriculture, Fisheries and Food, ex p. Hamble Fisheries* [1995] 2 All E.R. 714.
[24] Singh, *op. cit.,* n. 18, above, at 19.
[25] [1994] 1 W.L.R. 74.
[26] [1979] 1 W.L.R. 1041.
[27] [1983] 2 A.C. 237.

against him if the board had exceeded its powers or failed to observe the rules of natural justice.[28]

The case of *R. v. Commissioners of Inland Revenue, ex p. Unilever plc*[29] extended the doctrine of legitimate expectations and gave a higher priority to considerations of fairness to the individual rather than legal certainty. Unilever sought judicial review of the Inland Revenue's decision to refuse to allow it tax relief for trading losses incurred in the year ending December 31, 1988 because the claim was too late. A claim for tax relief for trading losses had to be made within two years but the Inland Revenue had power, under section 1 of the Taxes Management Act 1970, to extend this period. On 30 occasions over the previous 20 years the Inland Revenue had allowed late claims for loss relief to be paid although they had never made any assurances that late claims would be paid. It was held that, even though there had been no unambiguous representations by the Inland Revenue, their conduct had amounted to substantial acquiescence with regard to late claims. Unilever had been genuinely misled by this conduct and it would be an abuse of power for the Inland Revenue to rely on the time limits without giving notice that they would be followed. It was wholly unreasonable not to exercise its discretion to extend the time-limit. Brown L.J. stated that unfairness amounting to an abuse of power is unlawful not because it offends some equivalent private law principle but because it is illogical or immoral or both for a public authority to act with such conspicuous unfairness.

Legitimate Expectation of a Right to a Fair Procedure

11–49   There may be situations in which a person has a legitimate expectation that actions will be carried out or that decisions will be made in a certain way. The principle that a person may have a legitimate expectation that certain procedures should be followed before a decision is taken which amounts to an infringement of his rights appears to have gained a wide acceptance in recent years. Such legitimate expectations were held to exist in the case of *Matthew Rooney, Petitioner*,[30] in which it was held that a police constable had a legitimate expectation that a chief constable would act according to the procedures recommended in a procedures manual. Legitimate expectations that a person will be treated fairly may arise in circumstances where the decision that is being taken is not judicial in nature and the principles of natural justice would not ordinarily need to be followed. In the case of *Breen v. Amalgamated Engineering Union*,[31] Lord Denning said

---

[28]   See also *Rea v. Parole Board for Scotland*, 1993 S.L.T. 1074.
[29]   [1996] S.T.C. 681.
[30]   O. H., November 15, 1995; 1996 G.W.D. 39–2235.
[31]   [1971] 2 Q.B. 175.

in relation to the right to a hearing: "If he is a man who has some right or interest, or some legitimate expectation of which it would not be fair to deprive him without a hearing, or reasons give, then these should be afforded to him, according as the case may demand."[32]

LEGITIMATE EXPECTATION OF A PROCEDURE TO BE APPLIED BECAUSE OF A PUBLIC BODY'S PROMISE OR PAST PRACTICE

The courts will protect the legitimate expectations of parties that they will be consulted or otherwise involved in procedures once such expectations have been created by either the consistent past practice of an authority or its express promise. The case of the *Council of Civil Service Unions v. Minister for Civil Service*[33] involved legitimate expectations based on previous undertakings or promises. There was a legitimate expectation by civil service unions that they would be consulted before any change in conditions of service affecting their members. The interest of national security prevailed in this case, however, because of the strategic importance to the intelligence services of the particular place of employment (GCHQ). In the case of *McInnes v. Onslow Fane*,[34] the plaintiff had applied to the Western Area Council of the British Board of Boxing Control for a boxing manager's licence but his application was refused. He sought a declaration that the board had acted in breach of natural justice, in not informing him of the case against him and not giving him a hearing. It was held that the declaration would not be granted. The applicant merely had a right to have his application considered fairly which it had been. Megarry J. said that, in relation to the granting of licences, cases fell into three categories:

11–50

(1) cases of forfeiture, where an existing licence or other benefit is being withdrawn. In these cases there is a decision which takes away some existing right or position;

(2) cases of application where a licence or benefit is sought but there is no legitimate expectation that it will be granted. These are cases where the decision merely refuses to grant the applicant the right or position that he seeks;

(3) cases in an intermediate category where there is a "legitimate expectation" from what has already happened that the application will be granted. This includes cases where a licence holder applies for a renewal of his licence or a person already appointed seeks confirmation from some appointing authority.[35]

---

[32] [1971] 1 All E.R. 1148 at p. 1154.
[33] [1985] A.C. 374.
[34] [1978] 3 All E.R. 211.
[35] See *Breen v. Amalgamated Engineering Union* [1971] 2 Q.B. 175; *Schmidt v. Secretary of State for Home Affairs* [1969] 2 Ch. 149; *R. v. Barnsley Metropolitan Borough Council, ex p. Hook* [1976] 1 W.L.R. 1052.

There is a substantial distinction between the forfeiture cases and the application cases. There is a threat to take something away for some reason; and in such cases the right to an unbiased tribunal, the right to notice of the charges and the right to be heard in answer to the charges are important. In the application cases, on the other hand, nothing is being taken away, and in all normal circumstances there are no charges, and so no requirement of an opportunity of being heard in answer. Instead there is the far wider and less well-defined question of the general suitability of the applicant for the licence. In the intermediate category the legitimate expectation of the renewal of a licence is one which raises the question of what has happened to make the applicant unsuitable for the licence or membership for which he was previously thought suitable. The principles of natural justice apply in the first and third categories but not in the second category.[36] The concepts of natural justice and the duty to be fair must not be allowed to discredit themselves by making unreasonable requirements and imposing undue burdens on administrators.

11–51   In the case of *Attorney-General of Hong Kong v. Ng Yuen Shui*,[37] where immigration authorities had undertaken to consider the merits of the case of each illegal immigrant who made himself known it was held that the public undertaking to consider each case on its merits created a right on the part of each illegal immigrant that would otherwise not have existed. This case was an appeal to the privy council and Lord Fraser discussed the concept of "legitimate expectations" in his judgment. He recognised that the phrase "legitimate expectation" was lacking in precision but said that it meant more than "an entitlement or recognition by law".[38] Legitimate expectations mean reasonable expectations and so may include expectations that go beyond enforceable legal rights, provided they have some reasonable basis.[39] In the case of *R. v. Swale Borough Council and Medway Ports Authority, ex parte Royal Society for the Protection of Birds*,[40] it was held that, as the council had given the RSPB express undertakings that they would be consulted before certain planning decisions were taken, they had a legitimate expectation that they would be consulted. A failure to consult would be grounds for challenge to a decision.

11–52   In the case of *Perfect Leisure v. City of Edinburgh District Licensing Board*,[41] it was held that legitimate expectations may exist where it is reasonable to presume that existing procedures will be followed. The case

---

[36] See also *Nagle v. Feilden* [1966] 2 Q.B. 633; *R. v. Gaming Board for Great Britain, ex p. Benaim and Khaida* [1970] 2 Q.B. 417.
[37] [1983] 2 All E.R. 346.
[38] Distinguishing the judgment in *Salemi v. Mackellar (No. 2)* (1977) 137 C.L.R. 396.
[39] *R. v. Criminal Injuries Compensation Board, ex p. Lain* [1967] 2 Q.B. 864.
[40] (1990) 2 Admin. L.R. 790; (1991) J.E.R.L 135.
[41] 1996 S.L.T. 1267.

concerned the refusal of a grant for a liquor licence for extended hours. Section 47 of the Law Reform (Miscellaneous Provisions) (Scotland) Act 1990 provides that a licensing board: "shall not grant an application ... for an extension of permitted hours unless it is satisfied by the applicant ... (a) that there is a need in the locality ... for a regular extension of the permitted hours; and (b) that such an extension is likely to be of such benefit to the community as a whole as to outweigh any detriment to that locality". Licensees of a public house applied for a regular extension of the permitted hours from Monday to Saturday between 5.30 a.m. and 11.30 a.m. There were written objections to this application and so, immediately prior to the hearing of the application, it was amended to restrict the regular extension of permitted hours to between 8 a.m. and 11 a.m., a regular extension which the board had permitted in the previous five years. The residents' association maintained their objections. The board was addressed by the objectors and the solicitor for the licensees who made no submission in respect of "need in the locality" or "benefit to the community". The board refused the early morning regular extension, giving as one of its reasons that it was not satisfied that the early morning extension could have met a need in the locality or would have been of some benefit to the community. The licensees sought judicial review of the board's decision, arguing that the board's ordinary practice in dealing with application for existing extensions was to deal with contentious matters only. The board denied such a practice and argued that the onus was on the applicant to satisfy them as to need and benefit whenever an objection was made to an extension application. It was held, that it could not be right to require of applicants that they addressed every conceivable issue so as to ensure that there was nothing left uncovered which might form the basis for refusal of the application. In planning matters there was held to be legitimate expectation that competing applications would be treated fairly in the case of *Lakin v. Secretary of State for Scotland.*[42] Two planning applications for supermarkets had been submitted in circumstances in which only one would be allowed to proceed. It was held that, in considering the merits of the competing applications before deciding not to call in one of the applications, the Secretary of State had deprived the other developers of their legitimate expectation of having their appeal determined at a public local inquiry. He had prejudged that issue and pre-empted the appeal. The procedure adopted by the Secretary of State was improper and unfair.

Legitimate expectations cannot arise where the circumstances, which may 11–53 otherwise have given rise to legitimate expectations, have been created by the party claiming the legitimate expectation. The case *Mohammed Akbar Butt, Petitioner*[43] was a petition for judicial review of a decision to enforce a

[42] 1988 S.L.T. 780.
[43] O. H., March 15, 1995; 1995 G.W.D. 16–905.

deportation Order. Butt was detained under the Immigration Act 1971. He claimed that the decision to enforce the deportation order was made on the basis of an error in law and was unreasonable. The deportation order had been made some years earlier but had not been enforced. Meanwhile guidance had been issued by the Immigration Minister (Wardle) in 1992 "that in principle an application from a spouse for an entry clearance or for leave to remain should be allowed when it is accepted that the marriage is genuine and subsisting and either the couple have been married for at least five years or one or more children of the marriage have the right of abode in the United Kingdom." In 1994, Butt had married and a child of the marriage was due to be born in the United Kingdom in 1995. In December 1994 the petitioner's solicitors formally applied for leave to the petitioner to remain in the United Kingdom on an exceptional basis in the light of his marriage. The Secretary of State refused that application. On February 21, 1995 his wife gave birth to their son. The child had a right of abode in the United Kingdom. In the argument for the petitioner in support of the motion the central propositions were:

(1) that the petitioner qualified under the Wardle guidance and,
(2) that the guidance gave him a legitimate expectation that he would be allowed to remain in the United Kingdom.

At the date on which Butt's original application for leave to remain was submitted, he did not meet either of the qualifying conditions. He had not been married for five years and there was no child of the marriage. The guidance was announced in June 1992. At that time Butt was not one of those to whom it applied. Thereafter Butt himself brought about the circumstances which fell within the Wardle guidance, namely his marriage and the birth of the child. It was held that a petitioner cannot create his own expectation in this way: nor can he describe such an expectation as legitimate when he created it in the face of an existing deportation order.

11–54   In the case of *R. v. Secretary of State for the Home Department, ex parte Ruddock*,[44] it was held that a telephone subscriber had a legitimate expectation that the published criteria under the Interception of Communications Act 1985, on the interception of private telephone communications, would be complied with by the Home Secretary. However, guidelines and published information will not always be deemed to create legitimate expectations. In the case of *R. v. Secretary of State for the Home Department, ex parte Hargreaves*,[45] Hargreaves, a prisoner at Risley Prison,

44 [1987] 2 All E.R. 518.
45 [1997] 1 All E.R. 397; *Re Findlay*, [1985] 1 A.C. 318, followed. *R. v. Ministry of Agriculture, Fisheries and Food, ex p. Hamble (Offshore) Fisheries Ltd* [1995] 2 All E.R. 714, overruled to the extent that it required a court to conduct such an exercise.

appealed against the dismissal of his application for judicial review of a decision by the Secretary of State to amend the rules relating to eligibility for home leave. At the time Hargreaves commenced his sentence, the notice to prisoners, which was issued to him, provided that prisoners could apply for home leave after serving one-third of their sentence. However, under the Prison (Amendment) Rules 1995, which implemented changes, prisoners could not apply until they had served half their sentence. Hargreaves contended that the notice and inmate compact signed by prisoners at the start of their sentences created a legitimate expectation that home leave could be applied for after serving one-third of their sentence. It was held that, in the case of convicted prisoners, legitimate expectation, at its highest, merely required that each case be examined individually in light of whatever policy the Secretary of State saw fit to impose. The notice to prisoners and the compact, read together, were incapable of providing a legitimate expectation and the appeal was dismissed. Similarly, in the case of *Rea v. Parole Board for Scotland,*[46] a prisoner had been advised that his release on licence had been recommended by the Parole Board for a date later the same year, and that the Secretary of State had accepted that recommendation. He was transferred to an open prison to train for freedom. Prior to his release he was called before the prison governor in connection with matters involving suspected irregularities in the use of a visitor pass. Following adjudication, the prisoner was returned to a closed prison. He was invited to make representations against the transfer, and did so. Although further representations on his behalf were made to the Parole Board, the board withdrew its recommendation that he be released on licence. The prisoner sought reduction of the board's decision on grounds which included a claim that, once he had been informed of a release date, there had emerged a legitimate expectation that the intention to release would be implemented, and that there would be no deviation from that intention because of a change in the board's recommendation. It was held that the discretion conferred on the board and the Secretary of State should not be hampered so as to inhibit the continuous reassessment by the board of its recommendations. The petitioner had not established any grounds either by express promise or by implication, for the legitimate expectation with regard to the procedures to be followed and the application was refused.

The courts are reluctant to recognise expectations except in very clear 11–55 cases. There is concern that if legally protected expectations are created too easily, public authorities, afraid that their future decision-making powers will be hampered will become too cautious in holding discussions and consultations with individuals and groups.[47] However, even in situations

---

[46] 1993 S.L.T. 1074.
[47] Reid, "Judicial Review and the Environment" in *Judicial Review: a Thematic Approach* (Hadfield, ed., 1995).

where the principle of protecting legitimate expectations has not been accepted as a ground on which a decision can be challenged by way of judicial review, the legitimate expectations of those affected by a decision should be taken into account by a decision-maker. Failure to take legitimate expectations into account as a relevant consideration may provide a basis for judicial review on the ground of failure to consider a relevant consideration. Such an approach would give the decision-maker the right to exercise his discretion in the way which he considers appropriate but, if he has completely ignored the legitimate expectations of those affected by his decision, a challenge could be made on the ground that all relevant considerations have not been considered.

RIGHT TO KNOW REASONS

11–56 Those who exercise administrative authority should be ready to give an account of the criteria on which they operate. Where a discretion has been exercised and an individual wishes to challenge the legality of the decision which was reached the court often needs to consider the reasons for making the particular decision. Where no reasons have been given for administrative decisions it is very difficult for a person affected by the decision to find out whether the decision has been based on relevant considerations, whether irrelevant considerations have been taken into account or whether the decision was reached on the basis of an error in interpreting the law. Despite the importance of knowledge of reasons in order to inform the process of assessing the validity of decisions, there is no general common law duty on an administrator to give reasons for a decision.[48] There has, however, been a tendency in recent years for the courts to find that reasons should have been given in more and more circumstances. This is part of a perceptible trend towards insisting in greater openness and transparency in making administrative decisions. The Justice-All Souls review considered that reasons are needed for three reasons:

(1) to improve the quality of decision-making
(2) to satisfy the citizen's desire for just and fair treatment
(3) to enable him to decide whether the decision is open to challenge.[49]

One of the five principles of good administration recommended by the Committee of Ministers of the Council of Europe is that where an administrative act is of such a nature as adversely to affect the rights, liberties

---

[48] *Thomson, Petr.*, 1989 S.L.T. 343; *Purdon v. City of Glasgow Licensing Board,* 1989 S.L.T. 201.

[49] Report of the Justice-All Souls Review of Administrative Law, "Administrative Justice: Some Necessary Reforms" (1988).

or interests of the person concerned, it is essential (particularly in view of a possible appeal) that it should be reasoned. The reasons may be given at the time when the act is taken or, upon request, subsequently.[50]

In certain circumstances, the nature of a particular decision may entail giving reasons.[51] This would be the case if the right of appeal depended on the reasons for the decision as in the case of *Minister of National Revenue v. Wright's Canadian Ropes Ltd*.[52] Wright's Canadian Ropes Ltd complained that the Minister should have allowed claims for expenses to be set against tax. It was held that the Minister was not bound to disclose the reasons for his decisions but the company could not appeal unless the reasons were known. The court could therefore look at the facts which the Minister had considered and, if these were insufficient to support his decision, the court would deem that the decision must have been arbitrary.

Where the decision of an authority is challenged by judicial review it may 11–57 be essential for the reasons to be given if the decision is to be upheld. This point was discussed in *R. v. Secretary of State for Trade and Industry, ex parte Lonrho plc*.[53] The takeover of Harrods by the Al Fayeds resulted in a report by inspectors, under the Companies Act 1985, s. 432, and inquiries by the Serious Fraud Office. Lonrho urged the Trade Secretary to exercise his power to publish a report "if he thinks fit", and to make a reference to the Monopolies and Mergers Commission, under the Fair Trading Act 1973, s. 64(4)(b). The Minister announced his decision not to publish a report "for the time being" and declared that a reference to the Monopolies and Mergers Commission was "not appropriate". Lonrho sought judicial review of this decision. It was held that the application failed as the Minister had acted within his powers and irrationality had not been proved. Nevertheless Lord Keith said: "If all other facts and circumstances appear to point overwhelmingly in favour of a different decision, the decision-maker who has given no reasons cannot complain if the court draws inference that he has no rational reason for his decision."[54] One of the recommendations of the Justice-All Souls Committee was that there should be a general duty to give reasons for administrative decisions that involved the exercise of discretion.[55] There was some comment on the desirability of giving reasons for decisions in *Padfield v. Minister of Agriculture*[56] to the effect that if some reasons are given for a decision and they are all bad, the court may infer that there are no

[50] Committee of Ministers of the Council of Europe, Resolution (77) 31, "On the Protection of the Individual in relation to the Acts of Administrative Authorities".
[51] Craig, "The Common Law, Reasons and Administrative Justice" [1994] 53(2) C.L.J. 282; Munro, "The Duty to give Reasons for Decisions" 1995 S.L.T. (News) 5.
[52] [1947] A.C. 109.
[53] [1989] 1 W.L.R. 525.
[54] *ibid.* at 620.
[55] Justice-All Souls Committee, *op. cit.*, n. 49, above.
[56] [1968] A.C. 997.

good reasons for the decision. Where reasons are given for a decision they must be proper, adequate, and intelligible and must deal with the substantive issues raised.[57]

11–58   The existence of a duty to give reasons in limited circumstances was recognised in the case of *R. v. Secretary of State for the Home Department, ex parte Doody*.[58] Doody was a convicted murderer who had been sentenced to life imprisonment. The Home Secretary adopted a practice in relation to mandatory life sentences of consulting the trial judge and the Lord Chief Justice before setting the minimum period of custody. Doody had not been informed of the reasons for the Secretary of State's decision as to the period of time that he had to serve in prison. He applied for judicial review on the grounds that the Home Secretary was not entitled to depart from the judge's recommendations. Doody also claimed that the Secretary of State should have provided him with information on the judge's recommendations and comments, and should have given reasons for his decision to depart from those recommendations. Lord Mustill held that there was no general duty to give reasons but he found that there was a duty to give reasons in this case. One rationale for this was that the reasons would facilitate any challenge by way of judicial review by the prisoner, who might wish to argue that the Secretary of State had erred in departing from the sentence originally recommended by the judges. The giving of reasons was required by the "minimum standard of fairness". In explaining this minimum standard of fairness he said:

(1)   Where an Act of Parliament confers an administrative power there is a presumption that it will be exercised in a manner which is fair in all circumstances.

(2)   The standards of fairness are not immutable and change over time, both in general and in their application to particular cases.

(3)   Principles of fairness cannot be applied by rote, but depend on the context of the decision in question.

(4)   An essential feature of the context is the statute creating the discretion, in terms of the language and shape of the administrative system within which the decision is taken.

(5)   Fairness will often require that a person who may be adversely affected by the decision will have the opportunity to make representations, either before the decision to produce a favourable result or after the decision to ensure its modification, or both.

(6)   Since the person affected cannot usually make worthwhile representations without knowing what factors weigh against his interest, fairness will very often require that he is informed of the gist of the case he has to meet.

The decision in *Doody* did not create a general duty to give reasons but it did create a further exception to the rule that reasons do not have to be

---

[57]   *Re Poyser and Mills' Arbitration* [1964] 2 Q.B. 467.
[58]   [1993] 3 All E.R. 92.

provided. It has been suggested that this exception is an important step towards overturning the generality of the rule itself.[59] Lord Mustill commented on the general commitment to greater openness or transparency in the making of administrative decisions.

Where a judicial function is being exercised the principles of natural 11–59 justice may require that reasons for decisions are given as was held in the case of *R. v. Civil Service Appeal Board, ex parte Cunningham*,[60] in which a prison officer challenged an award of compensation for unfair dismissal. Lord Donaldson made it clear that there is no general duty to give reasons for decisions. He held, however, that there was a duty on the Civil Service Appeal Board to give reasons for awarding the applicant a much smaller sum by way of compensation for unfair dismissal than he would have received under the normal employment protection legislation. Lord Donaldson said: "Fairness requires a tribunal such as the board to give sufficient reasons for its decisions to enable the parties to know the issues to which it addressed its mind and that it acted lawfully." He also stated that the mere fact that Parliament had imposed a duty to provide reasons on some tribunals did not mean that the courts were forbidden from imposing a similar duty on other tribunals. The duty to give reasons was held to exist in this case because the Civil Service Appeal Board was exercising a judicial function. Therefore, the principles of natural justice should be followed and the Board should, on the grounds of fairness, be required to state its reasons in outline. Similarly, in *R. v. Parole Board, ex parte Wilson*,[61] where a 76-year-old prisoner serving life imprisonment sought judicial review of the Parole Board's failure to disclose reports which would be used in a forthcoming review. It was held that the applicant was entitled to know of the reasons why he was not being recommended for release, on the general ground of natural justice. Lord Mustill stated that failing to give reasons was not fair since the prisoner had a real interest in understanding how long the term of imprisonment would be and why the particular period was imposed.[62] There is now a statutory duty to provide reasons in these circumstances.[63] These principles were extended to victims of miscarriages of justice in *R. v. Home Secretary, ex parte Hickey (No. 2)*.[64] Where a convicted prisoner applies to the Home Secretary to refer his case to the Court of Appeal, the interests of fairness and informed decision-making

---

[59] Craig, "Reasons and Administrative Justice" [1994] 110 L.Q.R, 12–15.
[60] [1991] 4 All E.R. 310.
[61] [1992] 1 Q.B. 740.
[62] See also *R. v. Home Secretary, ex p. Georghiades* [1992] 5 Admin. LR. 457; *R. v. Home Secretary, ex p. Duggan* [1994] 3 All E.R. 277.
[63] Prisoners and Criminal Proceedings (Scotland) Act 1993, s. 20, and Criminal Justice Act 1991, s. 34.
[64] [1995] 1 W.L.R. 734.

now require that the petitioner be given sufficient disclosure to present his case effectively.

11–60 The duty to give reasons has been held to apply to decisions relating to housing benefit and homelessness. In *MacLeod v. Banff and Buchan District Housing Benefit Review Board*,[65] a tenant challenged decisions as to the level of benefit to be paid as statutory rent allowance in terms of the Housing Benefit Regulations 1985. The amount of the allowance depended on a comparison of the rent being paid with rents for similar accommodation. Not being satisfied with the authority's decision he applied for a review before the appropriate housing benefit review board. The review board upheld the decision of the local housing authority. The tenant sought judicial review of the review board's decision arguing that the board had not given a good reason for its conclusion that the rent actually being paid by the petitioner was unreasonably high by comparison with alternative accommodation in the area. It was held that the decision of the review board did not give satisfactory or sufficient reasons and that the review board had not had proper regard to the statutory tests imposed upon it. The decision of the review board was reduced and case remitted to it for reconsideration. Similarly, in *Malcolm v. Tweeddale District Housing Benefit Review Board*,[66] an applicant for housing benefit who lived in rented accommodation paying £40 per week challenged a decision to cap his housing benefit at £25 per week. The applicant referred the matter to the housing benefit review board who decided that it was reasonable for the authority to reduce the eligible rent to £25 and that there were no exceptional circumstances justifying an increase. The applicant sought judicial review. It was held that the board had failed to take into account the nature of any alternative accommodation and the facilities provided and had failed to explain their reasons for deciding that the alternative accommodation was suitable for the applicant. The question for the board was not whether £25 was reasonable rent, but whether £40 was unreasonably high, and the board had failed to explain why they held that the rent paid by the applicant was unreasonably high. The decision was reduced.[67] In the case of *Wilson v. Nithsdale District Council*,[68] it was observed that the absence of stated reasons made the basis of the decision more dubious. Although silence as to whether a code of guidance had been considered when reaching a decision did not suggest that it had not, the presumption that the authority had acted properly could readily be displaced by even slight indications to the contrary.

---

[65] 1988 S.L.T. 753.
[66] 1994 S.L.T. 1212.
[67] See also *R. v. Lambeth London Borough Council, ex p. Walters, The Times*, October 6, 1993 and *R. v. Islington London Borough Council, ex p. Trail* [1994] 2 F.C.R. 1261.
[68] 1992 S.L.T. 1131 (O.H).

Cases such as *Lawrie v. Commission for Local Authority Accounts in* 11–61
Scotland[69] show that there are still cases where fairness would seem to
indicate that reasons should be given for decisions but, because of the lack
of a general duty to give reasons, the courts have been reluctant to decide
that reasons should have been given. The Local Government (Scotland)
Act 1973, s. 103 (3), requires the Commission for Local Authority Accounts,
if they find that an irregularity has occurred, to recommend the Secretary
of State make an order requiring any person responsible to pay an amount
of money to the local authority. A local authority sustained a loss of around
£24 million as a result of certain financial transactions. The Commission
for Local Authority Accounts found that the losses had been largely the
result of the negligence of the director of finance and depute chief executive
but that some of the losses had been caused by the chief financial officer
and depute director of finance. The commission recommended that
the Secretary of State make an order requiring the officials each to pay to the
local authority "such amount as the Secretary of State considers appropriate".
The chief financial officer petitioned for judicial review of the commission's
findings. He argued that, even in the absence of a statutory duty to give
reasons, natural justice demanded that if the reasons for the commission's
findings were not self-evident they ought to be given. If no reasons were
given, then, if the facts did not seem to support the findings, the court was
entitled to infer irrationality. It was held that the commission was acting in
an administrative rather than a judicial capacity and in the absence of
uncertainty as to the issue or the facts to which they addressed themselves,
there was no duty to state reasons. In the case of *R. v. Lancashire County
Council, ex parte Huddleston,*[70] a university student sought judicial review
of a decision by a county council to refuse to award her a discretionary
grant. It was held that the council was under a duty to give reasons for its
decision only to the extent necessary to meet the grounds on which she
relied, but it was because she did not know why the grant had been refused
that she had applied for judicial review. Without knowing the reasons she
could not claim that, for example, the decision had been irrational or that
there had been an error in law.

STATUTORY DUTY TO GIVE REASONS

There are specific instances where reasons are required by statute. Under 11–62
the Tribunals and Inquiries Act 1992, s. 10, there is a duty to supply reasons
on request where decisions are made by a tribunal or following a public
inquiry. Specific statutes or regulations may require reasons to be given for

---

[69] 1994 S.L.T. 1185.
[70] [1986] 2 All E.R. 941.

certain decisions, such as the refusal of planning permission. Where there is a statutory duty to give reasons failure to give adequate reasons may render a decision invalid.[71] A statutory duty to give reasons applies to certain immigration decisions. In *Re EK v. The Secretary of State for the Home Department*[72] an appeal against deportation by a person who feared persecution in his home country, it was held that the tribunal had not applied the proper test in deciding whether a person was in fear of persecution. Even if the tribunal had considered and rejected the claims that a racial group was likely to be persecuted, they had given no reasons for rejecting that approach. Under rule 39 of the Procedure Rules they were under a duty to give reasons for their decision. It was held that: "The decision must, in short, leave the informed reader and the Court in no real and substantial doubt as to what the reasons for it were and what were the material considerations which were taken into account in reaching it."[73] In this case it was held that the tribunal's reasons were defective and that their decision should be reduced.

The reasons that are required are usually the reasons for the decision itself and not reasons relating to any ancillary matters such as the procedure to be followed.[74] Even where there is a statutory duty to give reasons there may not be a duty to provide reasons, as a matter of course, following every decision which is made. In the case of *Bass Taverns Ltd v. Clydebank District Licensing Board*,[75] it was held that the duty to provide reasons under section 18 of the Licensing (Scotland) Act 1976 is a duty to provide reasons on request. In the absence of any request, there was no obligation to provide detailed reasons for decisions and a failure to give reasons could not lead to an assumption that the decision had been irrational. The applicant who fails to exercise his entitlement to a statement of reasons therefore places himself in the same position as a person who never had any right to know reasons.

11–63   Where there is a duty to give reasons, proper adequate reasons must be given. Failure to give such reasons may cause the court to quash the decision or to remit the matter back to the decision-maker for reasons to be given.[76]

---

[71] *Di Ciacca v. Lorne Mid-Argyll, Kintyre and Islay Divisional Licensing Board,* 1994 S.L.T. 1150; *McLuskie v. Glasgow District Council,* 1993 S.C.L.R. 551; *Great Portland Estates v. Westminster City Council* [1984] 3 All E.R. 744.

[72] O. H., March 11, 1988.

[73] *Albyn Properties Ltd v. Knox,* 1977 S.C.198, *per* Lord President Emslie at 112, and *Wordie Property Co. Ltd v. The Secretary of State for Scotland,* 1984 S.L.T. 345, *per* Lord President Emslie at 348.

[74] *J.A.E. (Glasgow) v. Glasgow District Licensing Board,* 1994 S.L.T. 1164.

[75] 1994 S.C.L.R. 601.

[76] *Elder v. Ross and Cromarty District Licensing Board,* 1990 S.L.T. 307; *Brechin Golf and Squash Club v. Angus Licensing Board,* 1993 S.C.L.R. 191; *Zia v. Secretary of State for the Home Department,* 1994 S.L.T. 288; *Malcolm v. Tweeddale District Housing Benefit Review Board,* 1994 S.L.T. 1212; *Bass Taverns Ltd v. Clydebank District Licensing Board,* 1995 S.L.T. 1275.

The reasons need not be lengthy but they must leave the informed reader in no real and substantial doubt as to the reasons for the decision and the material considerations that were taken into account in reaching it.[77] In the case of *R. v. Immigration Appeal Tribunal, ex parte Iqbal (Iram),*[78] it was held that, in a case where entry into the United Kingdom has been refused because the primary purpose of a marriage was to gain entry, the immigration adjudicator must ensure that the reasons for his determination are clearly and rationally expressed in accordance with the principles set out in previous cases. Iqbal, the applicant for judicial review, intended to marry her only cousin under an arranged marriage. The cousin applied for entry clearance but it was refused. The adjudicator dismissed the appeal in April 1990 and in May the Immigration Appeal Tribunal refused to grant leave to appeal. Iqbal sought judicial review of that decision, arguing that the adjudicator had failed to decide issues of fact and that it was impossible to tell whether some questions of fact had been decided and if so how. It was held that in the context of immigration cases the principles governing the giving of reasons were that:

1. The reasons must bear upon the point at issue between the parties.
2. The reasons must indicate the basis of fact upon which the conclusions have been reached.
3. It is not necessary to isolate every piece of evidence.
4. Sufficient indication must be given that the adjudicator has taken factors into account by including them in his determination.
5. The adjudicator must show whether he has in mind any balancing factors in the motivation of the parties.[79]

In the case of *Brechin Golf and Squash Club v. Angus District Licensing Board,*[80] it was held that where reasons are given they must be sufficient to fulfil the purpose of informing the party affected by the decision of the grounds on which it was made. Section 18 of the Licensing (Scotland) Act 1976 provides that in certain circumstances a licensing board shall give written reasons for its decision. A golf and squash club presented an application to the licensing board for the grant of a regular extension of permitted hours on Sundays from 11 a.m. until 12.30 p.m. and from 2.30 p.m. to 6 p.m. Similar extensions to permitted hours had been granted for the 13 preceding years and operated without problems arising. There was no opposition from objectors or the police. The licensing board refused that part of the application relating to the period 11 a.m. until 12 noon. The club asked the licensing board to give a statement of the reasons for their

11–64

---

[77] *Wordie Property Co. Ltd v. Secretary of State for Scotland,* 1984 S.L.T. 345.
[78] [1993] Imm. A.R. 270.
[79] See also *Zia v. Secretary of State for the Home Department,* 1994 S.L.T. 288.
[80] 1993 S.L.T. 547.

decision. In a letter setting out the purported reasons for their decision the board maintained that they were not satisfied that:

> there was a need for golfers and squash players to be able to have a drink on Sundays between 11 a.m. and 12 noon;
> or that the number of persons participating in the club's activities justified a need for an extended hour of drinking time;
> or that the extension from 11 a.m. to 12 noon on Sundays would be of such benefit to the community as a whole as to outweigh any detriment which the permitted extension would have.

The club petitioned for judicial review of the board's decision on the ground *inter alia* that the purported statement of reasons for the decision was insufficient to fulfil their statutory responsibility under section 18. It was held that the reasons stated by the board failed to specify the circumstances they took into account and so were not sufficiently informative to comply with section 18. Although the reasons given for a decision need not be immaculately precise and exhaustive, the interested party who looked at the reasons should be left in no doubt as to why the licensing board had arrived at the relevant decision. A statement of reasons that was confused and ambiguous would afford the party who called for it no help whatsoever.[81] In the case of *McKinstry v. Law Society of Scotland*,[82] a case involving a disciplinary decision by the Law Society, it was observed, that, in dealing with decisions made by organs of the statutory body representing the solicitors' branch of the legal profession in Scotland, the court was entitled to look for clarity and coherence in the expression of those decisions. It was entirely reasonable to suppose that, in decisions relating to professional misconduct, express reference would be made to the criterion that had been applied.

11–65   Reasons will not necessarily be required where there has been a judgment that has been made on academic grounds. In the case of *R. v. Higher Education Funding Council, ex parte Institute of Dental Surgery*,[83] the institute sought judicial review of the decision by Higher Education Funding Council which rated the institute for research purposes at level two, lower than the level three rating that the institute believed it deserved. The institute sought to challenge the rating on the grounds that reasons had not been given and that the failure to give reasons was unfair. Sedley J. rejected the application on the ground that, where the decision was a matter of academic judgment, fairness did not require reasons to be given. In the judgment it was, however, accepted that there are circumstances where reasons should

---

[81]   See also *McLuskie v. City of Glasgow District Council*, 1993 S.L.T. 1102.
[82]   1996 S.C.L.R. 421.
[83]   [1994] 1 All E.R. 651.

be given where there are important interests at stake or where there is a legal obligation to give reasons. He summarised the law thus:

"1. There is no general duty to give reasons for a decision, but there are classes of case where there is such a duty.

2. One such case is where the subject matter is an interest so highly regarded by the law — for example personal liberty— that fairness requires that reasons, at least for particular decisions be given as of right.

3. ...Another such class is where the decision appears aberrant. Here fairness may require reasons so that the recipient may know whether the aberration is in the legal sense real (and so challengeable) or apparent. ... It follows that this class does not include decisions that are themselves challengeable by reference only to the reasons for them. A pure exercise of academic judgement is such a decision. ... Procedurally, the effectiveness of the challenge in such cases will depend upon prima facie evidence that something has gone wrong. The respondent may then seek to demonstrate that it is not so and that the decision is an unalloyed exercise of an intrinsically unchallengeable judgement. If the respondent fails, relief may take the form of an order ... to give reasons, or (if a justiciable flaw has been established) other appropriate relief."[84]

Lord Cameron, in *Wordie Property Co. Ltd v. Secretary of State for Scotland*,[85] said that it is important that the purposes of giving reasons are served but without the decisions "being subjected to hypercritical analysis or criticism". And, in the case of *Save Britain's Heritage v. Number 1 Poultry Ltd*,[86] Lord Bridge said: " I should be sorry to see excessive legalism turn this requirement (to give reasons) into a hazard for decision-makers in which it is their skill at draughtsmanship rather than the substance of their reasoning which is put to the test."[87] In the case of *Board of Management of Lauder College, Petitioners*,[88] a challenge was made to a decision not to transfer certain land to the management board of Lauder College when the college became independent of the local authority under the Further and Higher Education (Scotland) Act 1992. The local authority had bought two pieces of land for the use of Lauder College but they had never been used by the college and had been let out by the local authority on a seasonal basis. The management board argued that they had not been given adequate reasons for the decision and that reasons were required because the facts and circumstances pointed overwhelmingly in favour of a different decision. It was held that there was no evidence of any intention to develop the land for

---

[84] [1994] 1 All E.R. 651 at 671.
[85] 1984 S.L.T. 345 at 356.
[86] [1991] 1 W.L.R. 153.
[87] *ibid.* at 170.
[88] O. H., January 19, 1996.

use by the college at any time and in the circumstances the reasons given for the decision were adequate and intelligible and therefore sufficient.

11–66   One of the arguments against a general duty to give reasons is that such a duty would be impracticable and would impose too great a burden on the decision-making authorities. A lot of effort would be wasted and inevitably delays would be caused.[89] The difficulty is in achieving an appropriate balance between the efficacy of the decision-making process and the needs of those whose rights are affected by the decisions. Where there is a requirement to give reasons the reasons will not be regarded as adequate unless they fulfil the purpose that was intended by the imposition of the duty to give reasons. They must, for example, be sufficient to provide a person with an opportunity to answer a case against him or they may need to give enough information about the grounds on which a decision was made so that an appeal could be made against the decision if the grounds were unlawful. In the case of *Safeway Stores Ltd v. National Appeals Panel*,[90] it was held that where an appeal panel was reversing an earlier decision it must give sufficient reasons to show why it decided to depart from the earlier decision. A company had applied to a health board to be included in the board's pharmaceutical list for the provision of pharmaceutical services from supermarket premises. The board's pharmacy practices committee granted its application. A number of objectors appealed against this decision to the National Appeal Panel. The appeal was upheld and the panel wrote to the company, advising it of the panel's decision and that, having taken into account all the factors, including demand and supply in the area, the granting of the application was not justified at that time. It was held that where there was an obligation to give reasons, the reasons had to deal with the substantive questions in issue in an intelligible way, and therefore not leave the informed reader or the court in any real doubt as to what the reasons for the decision were, and what were the material considerations which were taken into account in reaching it. The amount of detail which the panel required to give would depend upon the circumstances, but where the panel was differing from the relevant committee, the panel had to indicate what material factors it considered in arriving at its decision and what conclusions it reached on these material factors. It was not sufficient simply to paraphrase the regulations. The case was remitted to the panel to provide a proper and adequate statement of the reasons for its decision.

11–67   There are some exceptions to the general development of a duty to give reasons. It was held in the case of *R. v. Secretary of State for Social Services, ex parte Connolly*,[91] that Social Security Commissioners are specifically

---

[89]   Reid, "An Expectation of Explanation", 1990 S.L.T. (News) 133–135.
[90]   1996 S.L.T. 235.
[91]   [1986] 1 W.L.R. 421.

exempted from the requirement to give reasons for their decisions. Accordingly, it is only if an applicant can show that the commissioner has acted on improper or insufficient reasons that his decision will be upset. Commissioners may give reasons if they think fit but there is no general principle that reasons should be given. An attendance allowance board did not consider that Connolly, who was severely mentally retarded, fulfilled the requirements for a night time attendance allowance. The Social Security Commissioner refused leave to appeal against that decision, but gave no reasons. It was held that the commissioner was specifically excluded from the usual requirement to give reasons for his decision and it would be improper to draw any adverse inferences from his failure so to do. An applicant must show that the commissioner had acted improperly or had had insufficient reasons for his decision. The court was entitled to assume that the commissioner had acted properly.

There is no requirement for the Secretary of State to give reasons for his decisions with regard to naturalisation applications although it was held in *R. v. Secretary of State for the Home Department, ex parte Fayed,*[92] that he is under a duty to act fairly. The Secretary of State refused Fayed's application for naturalisation under the British Nationality Act 1981. Section 44(2) of the Act stated that the Secretary of State was not obliged to provide reasons for decisions which were at his discretion, and that his decision was not to be subject to appeal or review in any court. Fayed appealed against the refusal of his application for judicial review. It was held that the Secretary of State was not obliged to give reasons for his decision, provided the duty of fairness had been discharged by giving the applicant sufficient information as to the nature of any possible objections to allow him to make any representations he felt necessary. Parliament did not intend that section 44 (2) exclude the need for notice of the objections against him to be given to the applicant. The duty to give notice was, however, limited to complex cases where the applicant would have difficulty making out his case without some indication of the nature of the objections to his application.

It is probable that E.C. law will have an effect on this aspect of administrative decision making. Article 190 of the Treaty of Rome imposes a duty to furnish reasons for decisions. All decisions, regulations and directives made and issued by the Council and Commission under E.C. law must comply with Article 190 which provides: "Regulations, directives and decisions of the Council and Commission shall state the reasons on which they are based and shall refer to any proposals or opinions which were required to be obtained pursuant to this Treaty." In the case of *Germany v. Commission* it was held that the giving of reasons is more than a mere

11-68

---

[92] Q.B.COF 96/0365/D; Q.B.COF 96/0422/D; *The Times,* November 18, 1996; *The Independent,* November 19, 1996.

formality. Article 190 "seeks to give an opportunity to the parties of defending their rights, to the Court of exercising its supervisory functions and to Member States and to all interested nationals of ascertaining the circumstances in which the Commission has applied the Treaty". The statement of reasons in that case, which was a challenge to a limit imposed on wine imports into Germany, was held to be vague, inadequate and inconsistent. The decision was annulled.[93] This duty to give reasons applies principally to Community Institutions but it is possible that it could apply to national authorities which are themselves applying relevant community norms. The extent of this duty will depend on the nature of the relevant Act and the context within which it was made. European law may also have a wider impact. Following a decision in the European Court of Human Rights in *Thynne, Wilson and Gunnel v. U.K.*,[94] a requirement to give reasons in respect of applications to the parole board by discretionary prisoners was recognised by statute.[95]

The development of the duty to give reasons has been increasingly apparent over recent years. Lord Woolf wrote in 1990: "if I were to be asked to identify the most beneficial improvement which could be made to … Administrative Law I would unhesitatingly reply that it would be the introduction of a general requirement that reasons should normally be available on request for all administrative actions".[96] The Code for Open Government includes reasons for administrative decisions as one of the types of information which government departments will supply.[97] It is probable that before long the weight of judicial decisions will lead to a reversal in the old rule: reasons will in general have to be given for decisions, unless there are special factors that make this inappropriate.[98] The courts have moved closer to the imposition of a general duty to give reasons, even though they continue to evoke the principle that no such general duty exists.[99] The current state of the law would appear to be that, in addition to cases where the fundamental liberties of a person affected are at stake the duty to give reasons applies in cases where there are circumstances which give rise to a particular need for an explanation of the decision under review.

---

[93] *Germany v. Commission* [1963] E.C.R. 63, 69.
[94] (1990) 13 E.H.R.R. 666.
[95] Prisoners and Criminal Proceedings (Scotland) Act 1993, s. 20, and Criminal Justice Act 1991, s. 34.
[96] Lord Woolf, "Protection of the Public" at 2, in Bradley, "Tell us Why" (1994) 138 S.J.
[97] Cm. 2290 (1993).
[98] Bradley, *op. cit.,* n. 96, above.
[99] Craig, "The Common Law, Reasons and Administrative Justice", *op. cit.,* n. 96, above; C.L J. (1994) 53(2) 282–302.

NATIONAL SECURITY AND PUBLIC INTEREST

It is always necessary to balance the rights of the individual against the wider issues of national security and public interest. The interests of national security may, for example, give rise to an exemption from a statutory duty to give reasons for a decision. Although there is a general duty for tribunals to give reasons for their decisions under the Tribunals and Inquiries Act, the tribunals, which investigate complaints under national security legislation, are protected from the requirement to give reasons.[1] Even where there are legitimate expectations that certain procedures will be followed, considerations of national security may exclude the principles of natural justice. In the case of *R. v. Secretary of State for the Home Department, ex parte Hosenball*,[2] it was held that an alien who was to be deported under the Immigration Act 1971 for reasons of national security had no right to be heard and no right to know the allegation against him. Similarly, in *R. v. Secretary of State for the Home Department, ex parte Cheblak*,[3] it was held that a decision to deport an alien on the ground of national security was a sufficient statement of reasons for the 1984 Regulations. In the absence of evidence of bad faith or of some irrelevant factor being taken into account or of some irrationality, such a decision could not be investigated on an application for judicial review. Cheblak was a Lebanese citizen who had indefinite leave to remain in the United Kingdom. He visited Iraq in 1979. After the outbreak of hostilities with Iraq he was arrested and served with a notice of the Home Secretary's intention to deport him on the grounds that such deportation "would be conducive to public good for reasons of national security". Cheblak was refused leave to apply for judicial review and he appealed on the ground that the reason given for his detention and deportation was not sufficient for the purposes of the Immigrations Appeals (Notices) Regulations 1984. It was held that in the absence of evidence of bad faith or some procedural defect which would render the decision *ultra vires* the court had to accept that the reasons for the decision were proper ones. The court would not require the Home Secretary to produce evidence to substantiate his reasons. This was a decision of the Court of Appeal during the Gulf War. The Home Secretary stated that further details could not be disclosed because it would be an unacceptable risk to national security to do so.[4] However, the Minister cannot always avoid a challenge by claiming that national security is at risk. In the case of *R. v. Secretary of State for the*

11–69

---

[1] Intelligence Services Act 1994; Interception of Communications Act 1985.
[2] [1977] 3 All E.R. 452.
[3] [1991] 2 All E.R. 319.
[4] See also *R. v. Secretary of State for Foreign and Commonwealth Affairs, ex p. Manelfi*, Q.B.D., October 25, 1996.

Home Department, ex parte Ruddock,[5] the court would not decline to exercise its supervisory jurisdiction over the Home Office merely because a claim of national security was raised in answer to a claim of telephone interception. The applicant claimed that his telephone calls had been intercepted under a warrant signed by the Home Secretary in August 1983. He applied for judicial review to quash the warrant claiming that it was unlawful as not complying with the published criteria governing such interceptions. The Secretary of State declined to confirm or deny the existence of a warrant but contended that the court ought to decline jurisdiction on the grounds of national security. It was held that evidence of risk to national security was required, either in open court or in camera, to justify any modification of the court's normal procedure.

11–70   Public interest issues may also limit the rights which would normally be protected under judicial review procedure. In the case of *R. v. Gaming Board for Great Britain, ex parte Benaim and Khaida,*[6] it was held that, although the principles of natural justice usually apply to an application for a gaming licence, this does not entitle applicants to be notified of any information held by the Gaming Board from which they could discover the identity of police informants or which might prejudice the public interest. Important matters of public interest such as public health concerns occasionally have to be weighed in the balance against commitments that may have been made by public officials. In the case of *R. v. Secretary of State for Health, ex parte United States Tobacco Inc,*[7] the tobacco company challenged regulations banning oral snuff in the United Kingdom. The company had, after discussion with the DTI and the Industry Department for Scotland, set up (with Government encouragement) a factory in Scotland for the production of oral snuff under the name of "Skoal Bandits". Subsequently, following publicity about the high risk of users of oral snuff developing cancers of the mouth and throat, the Secretary of State announced a proposal to make regulations banning oral snuff. The tobacco company challenged the regulations on grounds that included a claim that they had a legitimate expectation that they would be encouraged to continue to produce oral snuff in the United Kingdom. Lord Justice Taylor said that the applicants were understandably aggrieved that, after leading them on, the Government should then strike them a mortal blow by totally banning their product. However, he felt that if the Secretary of State concluded on rational grounds that a policy change was required that oral snuff should be banned in the public interest. His discretion could not be fettered by moral obligations to the applicants derived from his earlier favourable treatment of them. It would

[5]   [1987] 2 All E.R. 518.
[6]   [1970] 2 All E.R. 528.
[7]   [1992] 1 All E.R. 212.

be absurd to suggest that some moral commitment to a single company should prevail over the public interest.

Under European law the courts are required to consider evidence to establish that a rule or decision has been made in the interests of national security. In *Johnstone v. Chief Constable, Royal Ulster Constabulary*,[8] a woman from Northern Ireland challenged a rule of the RUC which discriminated between male and female police officers as being in breach of the Equal Treatment Directive. The Secretary of State certified that the rule was made for the purpose of safeguarding national security and protecting public safety. Under Northern Ireland statute law such a certificate was conclusive evidence of the matters stated therein. The European Court of Justice held that the statutory rule could not be upheld so as to exclude judicial review of the matter since this would deprive the court of effective judicial control of the decision to issue the certificate. Notwithstanding the certificate the court must examine whether the rule had been made for the purpose of safeguarding national security and protecting public safety.

The current position with regard to cases involving national security appears to be as follows: 11–71

1. If there has been an excess of power a decision made for reasons of national security can be challenged.
2. If there is evidence of bad faith a decision can be challenged, although it is difficult to perceive how evidence of bad faith would be available to the court.
3. If there is a challenge on the grounds that adequate reasons have not been given, the court may ask for further information but it may be a sufficient answer for the Secretary of State to state that further information would amount to an unacceptable risk to national security. The disclosure of confidential sources of information may be an unacceptable risk to national security.
4. A mere assertion that a decision was taken for reasons of national security is not sufficient. The courts will require some evidence as to the nature of the risk. The question of whether any decision or action was justified on the grounds of national security is a question of fact to be decided by the person to whom the authority to act or decide has been delegated.

In *Fox Campbell and Hartley v. United Kingdom*[9] the European Court 11–72 of Human Rights decided that the approach in the courts of the United Kingdom may fall short of the standard of judicial review now required under the European Convention on Human Rights. The court found that there had been a breach of Article 5 (1)(c) of the Convention which permits detention of persons "on reasonable suspicion of having committed an

---

[8] Case 222/84: [1986] E.C.R. 1651; [1987] Q.B. 129.
[9] (1990) 13 E.H.R.R. 157.

offence". Fox Campbell and Hartley had been arrested in Northern Ireland as suspected terrorists. It was held that there had been a violation of Article 5 (1)(c) because there was no disclosure of the reasons for suspecting the two people. In deportation cases currently before the European Court of Justice[10] the Advocate General expressed the view that it did not suffice for the national court to accept a deposition on behalf of the Home Secretary that the grounds for deportation existed. The court needs to be able to verify that Community rules have been complied with.

The nature of administrative decision-making is such that there will always be a conflict between a desire for complete openness to judicial review and the interests of national security. It may be the case that, under European influence, an approach will need to be found which provides for more effective judicial scrutiny while still protecting the interests of national security.

---

[10] *R. v. Home Secretary, ex p. Shingara and Radiom*, Cases C–65 and 111/95.

CHAPTER 12

JUDICIAL CONTROL OF ADMINISTRATIVE DECISION-MAKING: PROCEDURES FOR JUDICIAL CONTROL

INTRODUCTION

The courts will provide protection against the infringement of rights in 12–01 several ways. Where a statute confers a power on a public authority or official to make decisions, which may have an impact on the rights of persons or bodies, it is increasingly common for the statute to provide a procedure and a remedy to redress any grievances. Another way in which an administrative decision may be brought to the attention of the court is where the illegality of the exercise of a power to make a regulation is used as a defence by a person against whom legal action is taken for infringement of the regulation. The procedure of judicial review whereby the Court of Session exercises its supervisory jurisdiction over administrative decision-making provides a remedy where none is otherwise available.

STATUTORY APPEAL PROCEDURES

It is common for a statute which empowers an authority to infringe the 12–02 right of an individual to provide a right of appeal. This appeal may be to a Government Minister but, more commonly, the right of appeal will be to the sheriff court. This statutory right of appeal provides an alternative to judicial review. In 1977 the Committee of Ministers of the Council of Europe adopted Resolution (77) 31 entitled "On the Protection of The Individual in relation to the Acts of Administrative Authorities". This resolution recommended that the governments of Member States should be guided in their law and administrative practice by five principles set out in the annex to the resolution. Principle number five relates to indication of remedies and states that: "Where an administrative act in written form adversely affects the rights, liberties, or interests of the person concerned, it should indicate the normal remedies against it (including the applicable time limits)." The resolution deliberately abstained from indicating what sanction should be attached to a failure to comply with the principles and the matter was left to be dealt with by domestic rules.[1] The effect of this has been that there is an indication of both the procedure to be used and the remedy available in a wide and increasing range of statutes.

12–03   Applications to the court made by way of appeal or review, provided specifically under any enactment are expressly excluded from judicial review procedure.[2] This was contrary to the recommendation of Lord Dunpark's working party. The consequence is that citizens may be left with an inferior right under a statute rather than being able to use the judicial review procedure under Chapter 58 of Rules of Court 1985.[3] It is common, for example, for there to be a time-limit for seeking a redress under a statutory remedy. One example is an objection to a compulsory purchase order which has to be made by an aggrieved person within six weeks of the order.[4] The general rule is that where a statutory procedure exists it is the method of challenge which should be used. There may, however, be special circumstances which make the use of judicial review procedure appropriate, as in the case of *McDaid v. Clydebank District Council,*[5] where the time limit for using the statutory procedure had expired.

ILLEGALITY AS A DEFENCE

12–04 An alternative to instituting judicial proceedings to challenge an administrative decision or regulation which the citizen considers to be *ultra vires* is for the individual to wait until enforcement proceedings are taken against him and to use the illegality of the decision or recommendation as a defence. In civil proceedings any matter may be raised as a defence which would have afforded grounds for reduction of the regulation or order.[6] This applies to proceedings in both the Court of Session and the sheriff court.[7] Each court has a discretion to decide that the matter be decided in a separate action of reduction. Illegality has also been used as a defence in criminal cases. In the case of *Blair v. Smith*[8] an appeal was brought against the imposition of a fine on the basis that a licensing condition was *ultra vires.* Blair was a boat-hirer in Saltcoats who was convicted of hiring out a boat

---

[1]   Report of the Committee of the Justice-All Souls Review of Administrative Law in the United Kingdom,"Administrative Justice: Some Necessary Reforms" (1988), pp. 9-10.
[2]   Act of Sederunt (Rules of Court Amendment No. 2) (Judicial Review) 1985, rule 260B, para. 3 (now Chap. 58 of Act of Sederunt (Rules of the Court of Session) 1994 (S.I. 1994 No. 1443)).
[3]   Act of Sederunt (Rules of the Court of Session) 1994 (S.I. 1994 No. 1443).
[4]   Town and Country Planning Act 1990, ss. 289 and 290.
[5]   1984 S.L.T. 162.
[6]   *North British Rly. v. Steel Co. of Scotland,* 1921 S.C. 252.
[7]   Rules of the Court of Session, rule 174; Sheriff Courts (Scotland) Act 1907, Ist Sched, r. 50.
[8]   *Blair v. Smith,* 1924 J.C. 24.

on a Sunday in contravention of his licence. He was fined £5 but appealed on the ground that the condition against Sunday hiring contained in the licence was *ultra vires* the Burgh Police Act (Scotland) Act 1892 in that its purpose was to promote Sabbath day observance. The High Court of Justiciary held, however, that the Sunday veto was *intra vires* as it was necessary for reasons of safety as fewer rescue facilities were available on Sundays.

More recently in the case of *Colley (Procurator Fiscal, Banff) v. Michael*   12–05 *Duthie, Bawejem Ltd,*[9] it was apparent that a defence for a breach of a condition could be based on the ground that the decision to impose the condition was unlawful. Section 4 of the Sea Fish (Conservation) Act 1967, as substituted by section 3 of the Fishery Limits Act 1976, provides for the licensing of fishing boats. Section 4(5) provides that a licence may authorise fishing generally or may confer such authority limited by reference to the area within which fishing is authorised. Section 4(6) provides that a licence may authorise fishing "subject to such conditions as appear to the Minister granting the licence to be necessary or expedient for the regulation of sea fishing" and that a licence may contain conditions as to the landing of fish and the use to which fish taken may be put. Breach of a condition is an offence. The respondents were the master and owners of a vessel licensed under section 4 to fish in certain areas. It was a condition of the licence that the skipper of the vessel had to contact the authorities before the vessel crossed the 40 degrees west line in either direction. The respondents were charged with a breach of that condition. They challenged the competency of the complaint on the ground that the condition was *ultra vires* since it applied whether or not the vessel was engaged in fishing. The sheriff upheld that plea and held that the condition constituted a restriction on the free movement of the vessel. He acquitted the respondents and the procurator fiscal appealed to the High Court by stated case. It was accepted in the appeal that the condition did apply to the vessel while it was not engaged in fishing. It was held that the Minister was entitled to impose conditions for the regulation of sea fishing and that the condition could not be said to be *ultra vires* on the grounds that it applied to vessels whether or not they were fishing. The appeal was allowed and the case was remitted to the sheriff.

JUDICIAL REVIEW

HISTORICAL DEVELOPMENT OF JUDICIAL REVIEW IN SCOTLAND

Although the introduction of the term "judicial review" into Scots law is   12–06 relatively recent and the increase in importance and prominence of judicial

---

[9]   1994 S.L.T. 1172; 1993 S.C.C.R. 737.

review procedure has taken place mainly since 1985, the concept of control of the actions of administrators through judicial process is not new. Lord Hope of Craighead has said that: "Judicial Review, as it is known in Scotland today is not a new concept. The supervisory jurisdiction of the Court of Session was developed by the judges long ago, to enable them to provide a remedy which was not otherwise available."[10]

Although supervisory jurisdiction has been exercised over a span of several centuries, the principles of judicial review are complex and have not been developed as a coherent system. Prior to the abolition of the Scots Privy Council in 1708 it had exercised an equitable jurisdiction which differed from the ordinary jurisdiction of the courts of that time.[11] The Court of Session was bound by the strict doctrines of the law but the Privy Council could administer abstract justice and had a power to intervene if strict adherence to the rules of law would lead to injustice. When the Privy Council was abolished there was no formal transfer of this power to any other body. It was left to the Court of Session to develop its own jurisdiction to provide an equitable remedy where none was otherwise available.[12]

12–07   Actions for judicial review of administrative action under the supervisory powers of the Court of Session have been brought for several centuries. Early references can be found to the Court of Session having "superintending authority" and "supereminent jurisdiction". It is not clear, however, how close a correspondence there is between this early supervisory jurisdiction and the modern law of judicial review. In *Magistrates of Perth v. Trustees on the Road from Queensferry to Perth,*[13] it was held that a provision in a statute that the Trustees should "Finally determine" questions between the road trustees and other persons did not exclude the supreme jurisdiction of the Court of Session "to determine what it is that falls within their powers; but whatever matter is found to be within their power, this court cannot review their proceedings". In the case of *Countess of Loudon v. Trustees on the High Roads in Ayrshire,*[14] it was clear that a distinction was being made between review of the merits of a decision and review of the process of decision-making where a discretion had been entrusted to a public authority. There was no doubt that where there was an allegation of an excess or an abuse of power by a decision-maker, the Court of Session had the power to review. In *Ross v. Findlater,*[15] it was held that the Court of Session had jurisdiction to set aside a decree of a presbytery removing a schoolmaster,

---

[10] In the foreword to *Judicial Review in Scotland* by Mullen, Pick and Prosser (1996).
[11] Sheriff McNeill, "The Passing of the Scottish Privy Council" (1965) J.R. 263.
[12] *West v. Secretary of State for Scotland*, 1992 S.L.T. 636; 1992 S.C. 385 (*sub nom. West v. Scottish Prison Service*).
[13] (1756) Kilkerran's Notes, Brown's Supp., Vol. 5, 318. *Brown v. Hamilton District Council*, 1983 S.L.T. 397 at 414.
[14] (1793) Mor. 7398.
[15] (1826) 4 S. 514.

when they had failed to comply with the procedural requirements of a statute. Lord Justice-Clerk Boyle said: "the Supreme Civil Court is bound to … keep all inferior jurisdictions within the law. We are entitled to quash the proceedings of the presbytery but without interfering on the merits of the question."[16] In the case of *Campbell v. Brown,*[17] a schoolmaster who was dissatisfied with the proceedings for his dismissal argued that the Court of Session had a *jus supereminens* which entitled them to review the decision of the presbytery where there had been an informality in the proceedings, even though the presbytery held that decision to be final and without appeal to any court. This argument held in the Court of Session and the House of Lords. Lord Lyndhurst L.C. said: "a jurisdiction is given in this case to the Court of Session, not to review the argument on its merits, but to take care that the Court of Presbytery shall keep within the line of its duty, and conform to the provisions of the Act of Parliament."[18]

The *nobile officium* of the Court of Session, the power to grant a remedy where justice requires it but none is otherwise available, has been described a part of the supervisory jurisdiction of the court.[19] The extent to which the *nobile officium* and the supervisory jurisdiction have been co-extensive is unclear but the *nobile officium* is now a power which is exercised quite separately from judicial review proceedings. Action under the *nobile officium* is still possible in circumstances where judicial review procedure is not available.[20]   12–08

There is no doubt that, even before the introduction of a special judicial review procedure in 1985, the Court of Session, in addition to its ordinary functions, had a general power to review, by suspension or reduction, the judgments of inferior courts or persons vested with judicial or administrative authority, on the ground that they had exceeded the jurisdiction committed to them, had been guilty of an error in procedure so fundamental as to make their decision a nullity or had contravened the rules of natural justice.[21] It was made clear in the case of *Moss Empires v. Assessor for Glasgow,*[22] that the court has, at common law, inherent jurisdiction to grant redress in all cases where the rights of a subject have been infringed through any administrative body acting *ultra vires* of its statutory powers.

---

[16] See also *Countess of Loudon v. Trustees on the High Roads in Ayrshire* (1793) Mor. 7398; *Heritors of Corstorphine v. Ramsay,* March 10, 1812, F.C.; *Guthrie v. Miller* (1827) 5 S. 711; *Ashley v. Magistrates of Rothesay* (1873) 11 M.708; *Macfarlane v. Mochrum School Board* (1875) 3 R.88.

[17] (1829) 3 W. & S. 441.

[18] *ibid.* at 448.

[19] *per* Lord Inglis in *Forbes v. Underwood* (1886) 13 R. 465.

[20] *The Royal Bank of Scotland plc v. Clydebank District Council,* 1992 S.L.T. 356.

[21] Maxwell, *The Practice of the Court of Session* (1980).

[22] 1917 S.C. (H.L.) 1.

12–09   The conflicts which arise between the rights of the citizen and actions taken by administrators are similar throughout the United Kingdom and consequently the substantive law relating to grounds for judicial review is substantially the same in Scotland as it is in England and Wales.[23] However, the environment in which public law has developed in Scotland since the Treaty of Union in 1707 is different to that in England and Wales and there are therefore differences in the procedures for judicial review between the two jurisdictions.

DEVELOPMENT OF A SIMPLIFIED JUDICIAL REVIEW PROCEDURE IN SCOTLAND

12–10   In England and Wales a simplified judicial review procedure was introduced by Order 53 of the Rules of the Supreme Court.[24] There was a significant growth in the number of judicial review cases in England and Wales following the introduction of the new procedure. This growth in the number of cases was attributed to the existence of the new procedure which was relatively cheap and straightforward. Until 1985, however, there were usually only a few cases under the supervisory jurisdiction of the Court of Session in Scotland each year. It was therefore highly probable that the lack of such a procedure in Scotland was acting as a deterrent to citizens who might otherwise have instigated proceedings. The likelihood was, therefore, that there was an unfulfilled need in Scotland for a simple, effective and economical procedure for judicial review which would improve the access to justice at least to the same extent as that in England and Wales. The need for an equivalent procedure in Scotland was emphasised by Lord Fraser of Tullybelton in the course of pronouncing judgment in the case of *Brown v. Hamilton District Council*,[25] in which the decision of a housing authority was challenged. A housing authority decided that although an applicant was a homeless person with a priority need, he had become homeless intentionally within the meaning of section 17 of the Housing (Homeless Persons) Act 1977 and so was not entitled to priority housing. The unsuccessful applicant raised an action in the sheriff court seeking declarator that the purported decision of the housing authority was not a decision which they were entitled to reach. He also sought an order ordaining the housing authority to provide him with accommodation and that he should be awarded damages. The housing authority maintained that the action was incompetent and that the sheriff court had no jurisdiction to entertain it. The Second Division found that the action was competent, that the sheriff

---

[23]   *West v. Secretary of State for Scotland*, 1992 S.L.T. 636; 1992 S.C. 385 (*sub nom. West v. Scottish Prison Service*).

[24]   Supreme Court Act 1981, s. 31(6); R.S.C., Ord. 53, r. 4(1).

[25]   1983 S.L.T. 397.

had jurisdiction. The housing authority appealed to the House of Lords which held that, regardless of whether the decision of the housing authority was administrative or judicial in character, the sheriff had no jurisdiction to review it. The decision of the housing authority could not be effectively reviewed by a declaratory order and that since reduction was not a competent remedy in the sheriff court, the action was incompetent. There was a duty on the housing authority to make inquiry into the adequacy of the applicant's accommodation, but as he was, nevertheless, intentionally homeless, the appeal was allowed and the action dismissed. Lord Fraser proposed that there would be advantages in the adoption of a special procedure for judicial review in the Court of Session. The procedure should be a quick and cheap means of providing suitable remedies but it should also protect public authorities from unreasonable actions.

There was no criticism of the principles upon which judicial review is 12–11 founded, only an observation that the procedure for obtaining judicial review from the Court of Session was too slow and cumbersome and was in need of reform. In making this recommendation for procedural reform, Lord Fraser used expressions which were relied on in subsequent cases as defining the scope of judicial review. He said: "it is for consideration that there might not be advantages in developing special procedure in Scotland for dealing with questions in the public law area, comparable to the English prerogative orders".[26] Lord Fraser reiterated this opinion in the case of *Stevenson v. Midlothian District Council*[27]:

> "In the recent case of *Brown v. Hamilton District Council* I suggested there might be some advantages in developing or reviving a special procedure in Scotland, comparable to the procedure under Order 53 of the Rules of the Supreme Court of England, for obtaining judicial review of decision by public bodies. This appeal is a good example of a case where such a procedure might have been useful ... I hope that the question of procedure may receive some attention from the appropriate authorities."

A working party, chaired by Lord Dunpark, was established to consider such a procedure. The terms of reference were:

> "Having regard to the observations of Lord Fraser of Tullybelton in speeches in *Brown v. Hamilton District Council* and *Stevenson v. Midlothian District Council*, to devise and recommend for consideration a simple form of procedure, capable of being operated with reasonable expedition, for bringing before the court, for such relief as appropriate, complaints by aggrieved persons;
> (1) against acts or decisions of inferior courts, tribunals, public bodies, authorities or officers, in respect of which no right of appeal is available,

---

[26] 1983 S.L.T. 397 at 418.
[27] 1983 S.L.T. 433 at 437.

alleging that the acts are ultra vires, that they have been done or taken without compliance with particular statutory requirements; and

(2) of failure of any person to perform a statutory duty, which it or he could be compelled to perform in terms of s. 91 of the Court of Session Act 1868."

12–12   The working party recommended that a new form of application should be introduced which should give access to the "supervisory jurisdiction of the Court of Session in relation to acts or decisions of inferior courts, tribunals, public authorities, public bodies, or officers acting in a public capacity".[28] The working party made it clear that its recommendations with regard to public bodies and tribunals would be confined to acts done or decisions taken in the field of administrative law.[29] In the final form of the rule which was developed there was no reference to supervisory jurisdiction over tribunals or public bodies and there was no limit imposed as regards the authorities, bodies or officers or others to whose acts or decisions it was to apply.[30]

JUDICIAL REVIEW PROCEDURE

12–13   The reform of the judicial review procedure, which followed the report of the Dunpark Committee, enabled actions to be brought before the court quickly, simply and at minimum cost. This streamlined procedure is a major cause of the realisation of the full potential of judicial review in the modern context. Although judicial review has been a useful procedure for centuries its importance has grown over the last 11 years. This is due mainly to the availability of the modern judicial review procedure but an increased awareness of the availability of judicial review on the part of the public has also been a contributory factor. The view has also been expressed that a lack of confidence in political accountability through parliamentary procedures has also been a factor which has led to an increased reliance on judicial controls.[31]

The Dunpark Committee considered that the ends of justice would be best served by a procedure which was flexible and that flexibility would be enhanced if it is the judge who controls the procedure. The report stated that: "We have given the judge complete control of the procedure so that he may at every stage assess the amount of time likely to be required by the parties before the next stage is reached."[32] The procedure as implemented

---

[28]   Report to the Rt. Hon Lord Emslie, Lord President of the Court of Session, by the Working Party on Procedure for Judicial Review of Administrative Action (1984), para. 7.

[29]   *ibid.* para. 4.

[30]   *West v. Secretary of State for Scotland*, 1992 S.L.T. 636 at 645.

[31]   Deans, *Scots Public Law* (1995), p. 137.

[32]   Report to the Rt. Hon Lord Emslie, Lord President of the Court of Session, by the Working party on Procedure for Judicial Review of Administrative Action (1984), para. 5.

does indeed give the Lord Ordinary considerable discretion as to the regulation of proceedings. Access to the supervisory jurisdiction of the Court of Session by exclusive means of a judicial review procedure was introduced as Rule of Court 260B. This rule has now been subsumed into a consolidated new version of the rules of the Court of Session. Rule 58.3 requires that "an application to the supervisory jurisdiction of the court ... shall be made by petition for judicial review".[33]

The procedure is designed to minimise the time spent in face to face confrontations in court. The first stage is the submission of a petition.

Petition for judicial review

Applications for judicial review are commenced by way of a petition set out according to Form 58.6 of the Rules of Court. The form requires that not only the factual basis of the challenge but also the legal arguments with references to statutory and judicial authority must be listed. Relevant documents under the control of the petitioner must also be lodged. Other documents which are not in the petitioner's possession must be listed in a schedule of documents appended to the petition. The remedies sought must be listed in the petition. Remedies which can be sought include:

    (i)   reduction (quashing the act or decision complained of),
    (ii) declarator (declaring rights and duties of parties) and
    (iii) specific implement.

Interdict and interim interdict may be available against a public authority but not against the Crown directly.[34] Although it is competent to seek damages in judicial review cases these are awarded in restricted circumstances only, either where a statutory duty is expressed so as to give rise to liability in damages or where there is common law duty of care. In *Mallon v. Monklands District Council*[35] there appears to have been no dispute that where the duty was such as to give rise to liability in reparation, damages could be awarded in judicial review proceedings. The court has a wide discretion as to the remedies which it can grant. It can even make an order for a remedy which has not been sought in the application, although Lord Clyde, in *Mecca Leisure Ltd v. City of Glasgow District Council*,[36] observed that "the court should not compel a petitioner to accept a remedy not sought and not desired by him or her". The court may order the production of documents by any party at first hearing. This power is not often used. According to rule 58.6(4), affidavits are lodged where the decision complained of and the grounds on which it is alleged are not apparent from

12–14

---

[33] Act of Sederunt (Rules of the Court of Session) 1994 (S.I. 1994 No. 1443).
[34] *McDonald v. Secretary of State for Scotland*, 1994 S.L.T. 692.
[35] 1986 S.L.T. 347.
[36] 1987 S.L.T. 483 at 486.

the documents. Affidavits can be lodged by all parties, although it is unusual for the respondent to do so.

First order

12–15   The petition is brought before the court the day after lodging. This is for the first order to be pronounced. This authorises service of the petition and specifies the persons upon whom service should be made and which documents should be served. The first order may designate the date for the first hearing although the date is usually left blank. The first order will be granted without attendance of counsel unless an interim order is sought. If the respondent authority has lodged a caveat, they may be represented and then service will not be required. Lord Clyde, in *Sutherland District Council v. Secretary of State for Scotland*,[37] observed that where a case raises points of general interest, counsel should attend the application for first order in order to advise the court of the matter raised in the application and of the appropriate form of first order. Interim orders are not usually granted at this stage because there is a short period between this stage and first hearing but there are instances of interim orders being granted.[38] A petition for judicial review may, in exceptional circumstances, be refused at this stage.

12–16   The petition was refused at the first order stage in the case of *Mohammed Akbar Butt, Petitioner*.[39] This case was a petition for judicial review of a decision by the respondent to enforce a deportation order in respect of the petitioner. The petitioner was detained under the Immigration Act 1971, as he was classed as an overstayer in terms of section 3 (5)(a). This was the third petition for judicial review by the applicant who had been detained pending deportation in 1988 and, in a petition for judicial review, had been granted bail pending the outcome of his appeal against deportation. His appeal was unsuccessful and a deportation order was made in 1992. He sought judicial review of the deportation order and the petition at that time was refused on a first hearing. He was eventually detained pending deportation in March 1995 and again sought judicial review. It was held that the Court of Session may refuse an application for judicial review at the stage of the first order. Rule of Court 58.7 makes it clear that a first order is one which the Lord Ordinary "may" grant. The court has a discretion whether or not to grant an order and there is precedent for refusal at this stage.[40] Lord Gill said:

---

[37] 1988 G.W.D. 4–167.
[38] *Lord Advocate v. Strathclyde Regional Council*, 1990 S.L.T. 158 (interim interdict); *Lord Advocate v. Dumbarton District Council*, 1988 S.L.T. 546 (interim suspension).
[39] O. H., March 15, 1995; 1995 G.W.D. 16–905.
[40] *Sokha v. Secretary of State for the Home Department*, 1992 S.L.T. 1049.

"In the normal case the relevancy of the petition will fall to be decided at a first hearing because, in the majority of judicial review cases only the petitioner is represented at the hearing on a first order. Even if the respondent is represented at that hearing the court will usually be in no position to make a decision disposing of the petition: for example, because the petitioner may have to recover essential documents relating to the decision complained of, or may be ordered to serve specified documents on the respondent (RC 58.7 (a)(ii)); or because the respondent may wish to lodge answers to the petition and to have time to prepare his defence on the facts and on the law."

He suggested that it would certainly be appropriate for the court to consider, and if need be to refuse, the petition at a first order hearing in a case where:

(1)   the respondent is represented;
(2)   all necessary documents are to hand;
(3)   the respondent wishes to have the petition disposed of without resort to a first hearing and is in a position to present a fully prepared case; and
(4)   there is no dispute of a factual nature such as to prevent the court from making a properly informed decision at that stage.

All of these criteria were satisfied in this case and the petition was dismissed.

First hearing

The first hearing enables a judge to dismiss a hopeless case without further 12–17 ado or to grant relief if there is no substantial defence to a good claim. The first hearing is usually no earlier than seven days after expiry of any period specified for intimation and service. In practice this will be several weeks. This allows a person who has received intimation of the first hearing to lodge answers and any relative documents in advance of the first hearing. The court may also appoint a reporter at first hearing to inquire into factual circumstances. Again, this is a rare occurrence.[41] Petitions tend to be defended as it is usually a legal issue which is being considered. The first hearing allows an opportunity for argument between opposing counsel and the majority of petitions are disposed of at first hearing. In *Re EK v. Secretary of State for the Home Department*,[42] the petitioner sought reduction of a decision of the Immigration Appeal Tribunal. Answers to the petition were lodged by the respondent, who was the Secretary of State for the purposes of the Immigration Act 1971. Lord Cullen stated that it was matter of agreement that the matters at issue between the parties should be resolved at the first hearing. It is common to find statements such as this in judicial

---

[41]   Mullen, Pick, and Prosser,"Trends in Judicial Review in Scotland" 1995 *Public Law* 52–56.
[42]   O. H., March 11, 1988.

review cases. Where the judge does not determine the action at the first hearing, he is empowered to make such interim order or such order for further procedure as he thinks fit.

Second hearing

12–18 A second hearing may be ordered but this is rare. Rule 58.10(3) empowers the Lord Ordinary to put out petition for hearing on the by order roll for the purpose of obtaining such information from parties as he may consider necessary. The most likely reason for a second hearing will be to hold proof by parole evidence. The need for this is often pre-empted by the placing of affidavits before court so that factual disputes in the later stages are not common. However, there are still cases where parole evidence is required. In *Walker v. Strathclyde Regional Council (No. 2)*,[43] the judge commented that "affidavits may not be appropriate to deal with contentious issues of fact or opinion even although the affidavits may be amplified by ex parte statements relative to matters raised at the hearing by parties or by the court."

Reclaiming

A final interlocutor or determination by a judge may be reclaimed without leave but other interlocutors may be reclaimed only with permission.[44] A motion applying for leave of the judge must be made not later than seven days after the date of the order.

ADVANTAGES OF JUDICIAL REVIEW PROCEDURE

Judges

12–19 There is a special panel of nominated judges to consider judicial review cases although other judges may also preside. This has the advantage that their court time can be allocated to allow for hearing a judicial review case at relatively short notice. Several Court of Session judges have built up particular expertise in administrative law and this helps to promote consistency of decision-making. There is flexibility and efficiency as a petition can be heard by any single judge. The use of judges who are knowledgeable with regard to the principles of administrative law also has the advantage that counsel can confine their submissions to the application of the principles of judicial review to the particular circumstances of the case. This further contributes to the speedy disposal of cases.

---

[43] 1987 S.L.T. 81.
[44] Rule 38.4(4).

Speed

Speed is the keynote of judicial review procedure. Decisions of public   12–20
authorities which can affect the lives of many require to be challenged
promptly. The preliminary procedures are designed to bring cases to court
quickly. The effect of the new procedure was apparent very soon after it
was brought into operation. Research into judicial review applications in
Scotland which proceeded to final interlocutor between April 1985 and
April 1987 revealed that 49 per cent were disposed of within six weeks
and 68 per cent within two months of being raised.[45]

Information

The procedure is designed to facilitate the process of providing relevant
information for the court and the parties. The court may appoint a reporter
to investigate the facts and affidavits may be lodged by a petitioner where
the documents alone provide insufficient information. The court can also
take evidence from witnesses.

BODIES WHOSE ACTIONS ARE SUBJECT TO JUDICIAL REVIEW

Given the variety of bodies over which the court's powers may extend, it is   12–21
difficult and probably undesirable to attempt an exhaustive catalogue of
them, far less to identify any single characteristic which would encompass
the whole.[46] In *Brown v. Hamilton District Council*,[47] Lord Fraser proposed
that the supervisory jurisdiction of the Court of Session should cover
decisions of:

    (a)   inferior tribunals
    (b)   local authorities
    (c)   public bodies.

The Rule of Court is not prescriptive about the bodies, officers or others
to whose acts or decisions it applies but the following types of organisation
are representative of the types of organisation against which petitions for
judicial review may be sought.

(i) Inferior courts and tribunals, *i.e.* all lower civil courts and courts of   12–22
special jurisdiction, such as the Lands Valuation Appeal Court, Election
Court, Church Courts, Court of Lord Lyon. The Court of Session's
jurisdiction also extends to arbitration on grounds of bias by the arbiter,

---

[45] Page, *Judicial Review of Administrative Action: The Scottish Dimension* (1988).
[46] Lord Clyde,"The Nature of the Supervisory Jurisdiction and the Public/Private Distinction
in Scots Administrative Law" in Finnie, Himsworth and Walker, *Edinburgh Essays in Public
Law*, p. 286.
[47] 1983 S.L.T. 397.

procedural irregularity or where the terms of the reference have been disregarded. Although tribunals are within the jurisdiction of the Court of Session, petitions for judicial review are only competent when all other avenues of appeal have been exhausted. However, if hardship or injustice would result, the supervisory jurisdiction of the court may be invoked before all appeals have been exhausted.

(ii) Crown, Ministers' and their servants' actions authorised by statute are reviewable but Crown prerogative powers are not always reviewable. The remedies of interdict and specific implement are not available against the Crown to compel them to perform statutory duties conferred on them by Parliament.

(iii) Public industries and services: nationalised industries and public boards may have their activities reviewed.

12–23 (iv) Other statutory and non-statutory bodies. The list of other statutory and non-statutory bodies whose decisions may be the subject of judicial review is constantly expanding and evolving as new public bodies are created. The following are a few examples of the type of organisation whose actions may be reviewable but is by no means an exhaustive list:

(a) disciplinary tribunals, *e.g.* Law Society of Scotland, Faculty of Advocates;
(b) universities incorporated by the Universities (Scotland) Act 1858 are subject to judicial review as are universities incorporated by Royal Charter and financed by statute;
(c) broadcasting authorities such as the BBC and the IBA are subject to judicial review but it is unlikely that the independent broadcasting companies are subject to the procedure;
(d) other bodies, *e.g.* Parole Board, Scottish Homes, Scottish Arts Council, etc. are all subject to judicial review.

(v) Local authorities: All local authorities are regulated by the Local Government (Scotland) Act 1994 and are subject to judicial review.

12–24 Certain matters in relation to arbitration agreements, such as the appointment of an arbiter have been held to be amenable to judicial review[48] and certain decisions by the Parliamentary Commissioner for Administration may be subject to judicial review. The first petition for judicial review of a decision of the Parliamentary Commissioner for Administration was *R. v. Parliamentary Commissioner for Administration, ex parte Dyer*.[49] This was the first substantive application for judicial review of the PCA to be considered by the courts as an application for leave in an earlier case had been refused. The complainant's grievance was that her applications for benefits were mishandled by the Department of Social Security. The PCA

[48] *Haden Young Ltd v. William McCrindle & Son Ltd*, 1994 S.L.T. 221.
[49] [1994] 1 All E.R. 375.

investigated and found that there had been maladministration. The department apologised and sent her £500. She was dissatisfied with this outcome and claimed that the PCA had not investigated all of her complaints and had not let her comment on his draft report. It was claimed on behalf of the PCA that his exercise of jurisdiction is not susceptible to review by the courts because of the wide discretion conferred by the Parliamentary Commissioner Act 1967. This claim was rejected. The ombudsman's function is dependent on discretion, but unlike that of a politician it is investigative rather than policy-making. Except where constitutional conventions operate or where matters are not justiciable for reasons such as national security, the policies followed by public authorities are subject to review by the courts to ensure that their legal limits are not exceeded. It was held that the ombudsman is subject to judicial review but "it does not follow that this court will readily be persuaded to interfere with the exercise of the PCA's discretion. Quite the contrary".[50] To succeed, the complainant must attack not the desirability but the legality of what the ombudsman decided. In this case the complainant failed because "the PCA was entitled in the exercise of his discretion to limit the scope of his investigation, to be selective as to just which of Miss Dyer's many detailed complaints he addressed, to identify certain broad categories of complaint and investigate only those".[51]

In a more recent case, *R. v. Parliamentary Commissioner for Administration, ex parte Balchin*,[52] Balchin sought judicial review of a decision by the ombudsman. The ombudsman had investigated a complaint that the Secretary of State for Transport was guilty of maladministration in confirming a road order without seeking assurances as to the adequacy of compensation to Balchin from the local planning authority. Balchin claimed that the local authority should have exercised its powers under the Highways Act 1980, s. 246(2A), which came into force between the date of the inspector's report recommending the route and its confirmation by the Secretary of State, to award more generous compensation. Balchin's property was adjacent to the proposed route and its value was seriously affected by the proposal. Balchin submitted, *inter alia*, that the ombudsman's decision that maladministration had not occurred was tainted by his rejection of the contention that the Secretary of State's failure to draw the local authority's attention to its discretionary powers under section 246(2A) of the 1980 Act caused Balchin injustice. It was held that the ombudsman's acceptance that the power under the 1980 Act, s. 246(2A) had been overlooked should not have been dismissed on the basis that it was a foregone conclusion that the

12–25

---

[50] [1994] 1 All E.R. 375 at 381.
[51] *ibid.* at 383.
[52] [1996] E.G.C.S. 166; [1996] N.P.C. 147.

local authority would have rejected any such application. Although the ombudsman had no authority to consider the functions of the local planning authority, the refusal by the authority to contemplate its powers under section 246(2A) amounted to fettering of its discretion, and the ombudsman should have decided that the refusal was an unacceptable answer. The conscious omission of an evaluation of the authority's stance amounted to a failure to consider a relevant fact and meant that the ombudsman had omitted a potentially decisive element in determining whether the Department of Transport caused Balchin injustice by maladministration in its dealings with the local planning authority. The application was allowed.

SUMMARY OF CONDITIONS TO BE FULFILLED BEFORE JUDICIAL REVIEW PROCEDURE CAN BE USED.

12–26 The following conditions must normally be fulfilled before judicial review procedure can be used to challenge an administrative decision:

1. There are grounds for judicial review of acts complained of.
2. The person or body complained of is subject to judicial review
3. The type of act complained of can be the subject of judicial review
4. The person bringing action has both title and interest to sue.
5. The remedy sought is an appropriate remedy and is available against the person complained of.
6. There is no appeal procedure still open to aggrieved person (although, where there are exceptional circumstances, judicial review may be available despite the existence of appeal procedures).

The grounds on which a petition for judicial review may be brought, matters relating to title and interest and the remedies available are discussed in other chapters.[53]

COMPARISON WITH OTHER U.K. JURISDICTIONS

12–27 There are some notable differences between the judicial review procedure in Scotland and that in operation in England and Wales.

Time-limits

The English procedure is confined by a complex system of time-limits. Applications have to be made within a prescribed time of up to three months of the decision being made.[54] The difficulties caused by these extremely strict time-limits are compounded by uncertainty caused by poor drafting

---

[53] Grounds for judicial review, Chaps. 10 and 11; Title and interest, Chap. 13; Remedies, Chap. 14.
[54] Supreme Court Act 1981, s. 31 (6); R.S.C., Ord. 53, r. 4.(1).

of the relevant rules. An example of this is the case of *R. v. Dairy Produce Quota Tribunal for England and Wales, ex parte Caswell.*[55] The applicants were Welsh farmers who failed to qualify for a wholesale milk production quota and applied for a quota under the exceptional hardship scheme. The quota given meant that a herd of 70 cows could be milked. It was indicated to the appellants that should they wish to increase their herd size, they would be allocated an increase in their quota. It turned out that this was not so and the quota awarded could not be increased and the farmers were duly charged a superlevy for over production of milk. It was not until 1987 that they became aware that the quota decision by the Dairy Produce Quota Tribunal (DPQT) could be challenged by judicial review and they subsequently brought an application for judicial review. The Divisional Court held that the DPQT had erred in law by misconstruing the relevant regulations. The court dismissed the claim since there had been "undue delay" within the meaning of section 31(6) of the Supreme Court Act 1981 and R.S.C., Ord. 53, r. 4(1) and the court could not exercise its discretion to allow the appeal out of time. The appeal court also took the view that to allow the appeal would be detrimental to good administration and, if the appeal was allowed it may result in many applications from those in a similar position to the applicants. The House of Lords upheld the appeal court decision, with Lord Goff of Chieveley stating: "To me it is plain, as it was to the judge and to the Court of Appeal, that to grant the appellants the relief they sought in the present case, after such a lapse of time had occurred, would be detrimental to good administration."[56]

It appears that the needs of the administration are being given priority 12–28 over the right of the citizen of access to justice to redress a grievance caused by poor administration although, as Lord Woolf said: "Judicial review is all about balance: between the rights of the individual and his need to be treated fairly, and the rights of government at local and national level to do what it has been elected to do." The Law Commission has considered judicial review procedure and has recommended that the three-month time-limit for judicial review applications should be retained with an overriding requirement of promptness even within that period.[57]

The Dunpark Committee was of the opinion that the imposition of a time-limit in Scotland was not appropriate when the procedure was to be the only procedure giving access to judicial review. This does not mean that a citizen can be dilatory in bringing a challenge to the court. Delay in bringing an action may affect the willingness of the court to grant a remedy.

---

[55] [1990] 2 A.C. 738. See also *R. v. Independent Television Commission, ex p. TVNI Ltd* [1993] 2 FLR 866.
[56] *ibid.* at 750.
[57] Law Commission, *Administrative Law: Judicial Review and Statutory Appeals*, Law Com. No. 226 (H.C. 669).

In the case of *Hanlon v. Traffic Commissioner*,[58] a group of holders of taxi operator's licences in Glasgow failed to challenge a decision fixing a new scale of fees before the scale was implemented. There was a period of only three weeks for implementation but a large number of people had changed their circumstances on the basis of the changes. New microchips had been fitted in all taxi meters and operators had made arrangements to implement the changes. Later a group of operators applied for judicial review on the ground that a breach of natural justice had occurred. The court held that the applicants were barred from proceeding by reason of *mora*, taciturnity and acquiescence. It was held that their failure to act against the commissioner's decision before the introduction of the new fare scale inferred their acceptance of the decision. Delay itself will not usually suffice to produce bar. It was argued on behalf of the pursuers that there would also need to be conduct which indicated that a party had truly abandoned an objection open to him in law, that this had occurred when he was in knowledge of the full circumstances giving rise to his right to object; and that his conduct had been relied on and produced a material change of circumstances. Lord Prosser said, however, that: "it is clear that the requisite conduct for bar can consist in the negative conduct of standing by in silence, and that silence can indeed constitute an implied intimation that one is offering no opposition to the course of events".[59] He also expressed a view that the length of time before implications of acquiescence arise will be almost infinitely variable depending on circumstances.

12–29   In a contrasting case, *Perfect Swivel v. Dundee District Licensing Board (No. 2)*,[60] a delay of over six months from the date of the decision to refuse to grant a regular extension of opening hours was deemed to be insufficient to cause the petition to be barred by *mora*, taciturnity and acquiescence. For a period of delay to result in a bar it must be accompanied by a period of silence during which the petitioner had full knowledge of the circumstances giving rise to the right to object. The combination of the delay and the silence must have created an impression that the petitioner acquiesced in the decision. Delay on its own will not necessarily be a bar to an action but the absence of a strict time-limit for bringing a petition does not mean that the decisions of public authorities will be open to challenge until the 20-year prescriptive period has expired. In the case of *Carlton v. Glasgow Caledonian University*,[61] Elaine Carlton had been refused the award of an honours degree by Glasgow Polytechnic (now Glasgow Caledonian University) due to failure to satisfy the examiners. She appealed against this decision to the academic appeals committee which decided, as it was

---

[58]   1988 S.L.T. 802.
[59]   *ibid.* at 805.
[60]   1993 S.L.T. 112.
[61]   1994 S.L.T. 549.

empowered to do, there was prima facie no case and that her appeal should not proceed to the academic appeals committee. She sought judicial review of the decision on four grounds all of which were held to be irrelevant. Had they been relevant the petition would still have failed due to the delay in its presentation of almost two years after the decision. The petition was barred by *mora*, taciturnity and acquiescence on the part of the petitioner.

Despite the time-limits in England and Wales delay has become a problem. There is now a backlog of cases waiting to be heard with the consequence that the advantage of having a speedy procedure for such matters is being lost. One of the reasons for the build-up of cases is that two areas of administrative decision-making, housing and immigration are producing so many judicial review cases that, in addition to causing delays, the full potential for the use of judicial review proceedings in other spheres of administrative decision-making is not being realised.[62]

Granting of leave

The procedure in England and Wales also differs from Scottish judicial   12–30
review procedure in having a filtering stage. Leave must be obtained from the court before the action can progress to a full hearing. The leave procedure does have a practical advantage in that it empowers the court summarily to dispose of applications for review without needing to devote time to testing the evidence or the legal submissions of the parties. Lord Diplock, in *IRC v. National Federation of Self-employed and Small Businesses*,[63] said that the granting of leave stage exists: "to prevent the time of the court being wasted by busybodies with misguided or trivial complaints of administrative error, and to remove the uncertainty in which public officers and authorities might be left as to whether they could safely proceed with an action while proceedings for judicial review were actually pending even though misconceived". It appears, however, that this hurdle in judicial review proceedings makes it potentially more difficult to obtain justice against bodies exercising public functions than against other bodies.[64] Also, when the modern judicial review procedure was introduced in England and Wales there were inconsistencies in the judicial decision-making with regard to the granting of leave to proceed with the action. Evidence indicates that applications which are well founded may be being prematurely rejected at the leave to proceed stage.[65] Even the purpose of the leave requirement is

---

[62] Sunkin, Bridges, and Meszaros, "Judicial Review in Perspective", Public Law Project. (1993).
[63] [1982] A.C. 617 at 643
[64] Report of the Justice-All Souls Review of Administrative law, "Administrative Justice: Some Necessary Reforms" (1988), p. 157.
[65] Sunkin, Bridges, and Meszaros, *op. cit.*, n. 62, above.

Administrative Law

the subject of some doubt. It has been identified as being necessary to protect the court from an overwhelming burden of cases. Lord Donaldson in the case of *R. v. Panel on Take-overs and Mergers, ex parte Guinness plc,*[66] said: "given the constraints imposed by limited resources, this necessarily involved limiting the number of cases in which leave to apply should be given." A second purpose is to protect public authorities from challenges by filtering out unmeritorious applications. It has also been argued that the leave requirement benefits the applicant because it is a quick, cheap and easy way to test the view of the court on whether the application has any merit. The existence of these three potentially incompatible objectives for the requirement of leave adds to the confusion and uncertainty.

12–31   The fact that there is uncertainty with regard to the granting of leave to proceed may even be acting as a deterrent to potential petitioners. The Justice-All Souls Committee recommended abolition of the granting of leave to proceed stage from the procedure.[67] The Law Commission has proposed that the term "leave to appeal" should be removed. Instead there is to be a "preliminary consideration" stage which will usually be conducted on paper with the respondent being allowed, in the court's discretion, to advance reasons why the matter should not proceed further. Oral hearings will be preserved in exceptional cases where interim relief is sought or where an oral hearing is desirable in the interests of justice.[68] The Dunpark Committee rejected the requirement that leave be obtained before proceeding to judicial review in Scotland, preferring a procedure whereby the judge should have power to dismiss an action as incompetent or irrelevant at a preliminary diet. The procedures as implemented provide for petitions to be brought before a judge to deal with matters such as intimation and service and interim relief, if appropriate.[69] The court does have power to dismiss the case at this stage but, normally, the preliminary diet does not involve consideration of the merits of the action (except by agreement with the parties). In certain cases, *e.g.* immigration cases, the respondent may oppose the petition at the preliminary stage.[70]

Public/Private law

12–32 When judicial review procedure was introduced in England and Wales it was not the only procedure which could be used for challenges to administrative decision-making. Therefore, there were some situations when judicial review procedure would be appropriate and others where alternative

---

[66] [1990] Q.B. 146, 177–178.
[67] LeSueur and Sunkin, "Applications for Judicial Review: The Requirement of Leave" (1992) P. L. 102–129.
[68] Law Commission, *op. cit.*, n. 57, above.
[69] Rules of the Court of Session, rule 58.7.
[70] *Butt v. Secretary of State for the Home Department,* 1995 G.W.D. 16–905.

remedies could be used. In England and Wales a frequent reason for refusing leave in judicial review applications was that Order 53 was not available because there was an alternative remedy (*e.g.* an appeal) or the case raised no issue of "public law". Clarification was required as to the scope of judicial review and this was provided by the House of Lords in the case of *O'Reilly v. Mackman,*[71] in which it was held that it was obligatory to use judicial review procedure where a challenge was based on rights entitled to protection under "public law". The case related to a challenge by four prisoners at Hull prison to decisions regarding disciplinary awards of forfeiture of remission given after rioting at the prison in 1976. The decisions, made by the prison's Board of Visitors, were challenged on the grounds that they were in breach of the rules of natural justice. The prisoners issued writs and summonses against the board asking that the findings of the board and the subsequent penalties were declared null and void. The board applied to the court for the action to be struck down as an abuse of the process. The facts of the case were never in dispute, merely the procedure by which the prisoners sought relief. It was held that to allow the action to continue would be an abuse of the process and the correct way to proceed was by way of an application for judicial review under Order 53. Lord Diplock's judgment in the case has been referred to as an "outstanding feat of analysis and synthesis, ranging widely over the landmarks of administrative law".[72] First, he noted that the applicants had no private law rights. The distinction between what is private law and what is public law is a recent development in the English legal system, and is a consequence of the development in the prior 30 years of the procedures available for judicial control of administrative action, culminating in the new form of Order 53 as confirmed by section 31 of the Supreme Court Act 1981. He said:

> "it would in my view as a general rule be contrary to public policy, and as such an abuse of the process of the court, to permit a person seeking to establish that a decision of a public authority infringed rights to which he was entitled to protection under public law to proceed by way of an ordinary action and by this means to evade the provision of Ord. 53 for the protection of such authorities".[73]

Lord Diplock then went on to point out that there may be exceptions to this rule, and whilst identifying one or two of them, he noted that whether there should be other exceptions should at this stage in the development of procedural public law be left to be determined on a case-by-case basis.

A consequence of this was that it was only for these public law matters 12–33 that public authorities would benefit from the tight time-limits for challenges

---

[71] [1983] 2 A.C. 237.
[72] Wade and Forsyth, *Administrative Law* (7th ed., 1994), p. 683.
[73] [1983] 2 A.C. 237 at 285.

against them and the filtering process of the granting of leave stage in the procedure. The case law relating to public law rights and private law rights in relation to public authorities has become extremely complex. In the case of *Davy v. Spelthorne Borough Council,*[74] Lord Wilberforce said: "The expressions "private law" and "public law" have recently been imported into the law of England from countries which, unlike our own, have separate systems concerning public law and private law ... In this country they must be used with caution, for, typically English law fastens, not upon principles but upon remedies." A move away from the rigid classification of cases into those involving public law and those involving private law was evident in the case of *Roy v. Kensington and Chelsea and Westminster Family Practitioner Committee.*[75] Dr Roy was a G.P. and was on the list of doctors undertaking NHS work within the Family Practitioner Committee's area. The committee decided that, under NHS regulations, Dr Roy was not entitled to his full "basic practice allowance" since he had not fulfilled the requirement of devoting a "substantial amount of time to general practice under the NHS". The Family Practitioner Committee therefore reduced his allowance by 20 per cent. Under the regulations a person dissatisfied with the decision could make representations to the Secretary of State. Dr Roy instead issued a writ for damages and a declaration that the Family Practitioner Committee's decision was wrong. The committee applied to have the claim struck out on the basis that it was a public law decision and was only challengeable by judicial review, not through the private law, and that this was competent only after making representations of dissatisfaction with the decision to the Secretary of State. On appeal to the House of Lords it was held that the claim would not be struck out for several reasons including the fact that, as there was a contractual or statutory private law right to payment, private, rather than public law rights dominated the proceedings and that the action should be allowed to proceed unless it is plainly an abuse of the process. Lord Lowry noted that: "He has in my opinion a bundle of rights which should be regarded as his individual private law rights against the committee, arising from the statute and regulations and including the very important private law right to be paid for the work that he has done."[76] He went on to state:

> "Furthermore, even if one accepts the full rigour of O' Reilly v. Mackman, there is ample room to hold that this case comes within the exceptions allowed for by Lord Diplock ... the rule in O' Reilly v. Mackman, assuming it to be a rule of general application, is subject to many exceptions based on the nature of the claim and on the undesirability of erecting procedural barriers ... We have not yet reached the point at which mere characterisation of a

---

[74] [1984] A.C. 262 at 276.
[75] [1992] 1 A.C. 624.
[76] *ibid.* at 649.

claim as a claim in public law is sufficient to exclude it from consideration by the ordinary courts: to permit this would be to create a dual system of law with the rigidity and procedural hardship for plaintiffs ...".[77]

Judicial review has been used to challenge non-legal powers by non-statutory bodies in England and Wales in recent years.[78] It is becoming apparent that the distinction between public law and private law matters does not provide a definitive rule with which to assess the competency of judicial review procedure. Insisting on the use of judicial review for those cases which involve questions of public law has raised difficulties in England and Wales and, although clarification of the scope of judicial review in Scotland was provided by Lord Hope in *West v. Secretary of State for Scotland*, there is still some confusion in Scotland regarding the scope of judicial review in Scotland. The Justice-All Souls Committee[79] expressed the view that Scotland has wisely borrowed from England the best features of the application for judicial review and succeeded in avoiding two aspects which are subject to adverse criticism, namely the need for leave and the short time-limit. The committee recommended that the requirement for granting of leave under English law should be abandoned, that the term "public law" should cease to be used as the key to identifying those cases which should appropriately be dealt with by judicial review procedure and that strict time-limits should be replaced by a more general rule that cases should be allowed unless there has been undue delay.

12–34

IMPACT OF JUDICIAL REVIEW PROCEDURE

In *West v. Secretary of State for Scotland*,[80] Lord Hope observed that the most striking feature of the development of judicial review in Scotland is the consistency of approach over a period in excess of two centuries: "This approach was both simple and understandable, untroubled by disputes about the scope of remedies or distinctions between public and private law which in England have given rise to much difficulty."[81] A recent research project carried out in the School of Law of the University of Glasgow, which examined the operation of judicial review in Scotland, found that since the introduction of the simplified and accelerated procedure[82] there has been a significant increase in the number of applications for judicial review. The rate of increase in applications has risen as public awareness of the opportunity provided by judicial review procedure has increased.[83]

12–35

---

[77] [1992] 1 A.C. 624 at 650–654.
[78] *R. v. Panel on Take-overs and Mergers, ex p. Datafin* [1987] Q.B. 815.
[79] Justice-All Souls Report, *op. cit.*, n. 1, above.
[80] *sub nom. West v. Scottish Prison Service*, 1992 SC 385; 1992 S.L.T. 636.
[81] 1992 S.L.T. 636 at 644.
[82] Act of Sederunt (Rules of the Court of Session 1994) (S.I. 1994 No.1443).
[83] Mullen, Pick, and Prosser, *op. cit.*, n. 41, above.

The increasing number of judicial review proceedings throughout the United Kingdom has had an effect on the government itself. Since 1987 the Cabinet Office has made efforts to increase the awareness of civil servants to the nature and scope of judicial review by distributing a publication called "The Judge over your Shoulder".[84] The effect of the increased awareness of such matters as the grounds on which decisions may be challenged should have a beneficial effect on the quality of administrative decision-making within central government departments.

[84] The Treasury Solicitor's Department, "Judge over your Shoulder: Judicial Review: Balancing the Scales" (1994).

CHAPTER 13

JUDICIAL CONTROL OF ADMINISTRATIVE DECISION-MAKING: TITLE AND INTEREST TO SUE AND STATUTORY EXCLUSION OF JUDICIAL CONTROL

INTRODUCTION

One limitation on the efficacy of court action as a method of ensuring   13–01
that administrative decision-makers stay within the bounds of the powers
which have been delegated to them is that the courts can only exercise
their supervisory jurisdiction over administrative decision-making when
an action has been raised by an appropriate person. In order to qualify as an
appropriate person to bring an action an individual or organisation must
establish that he has *locus standi*, or standing. Cases cannot be brought
by persons whose rights and interests have not been affected by the
decision which is being challenged. Judges tend to be reluctant to relax
the rules about standing as the administrative system could be brought to
a halt if challenges were to be allowed by busybodies and bystanders.
There has, however, been a trend in England and Wales in recent years to
relax the rules to a certain extent and so, for example, certain pressure
groups have been able to petition for judicial review on behalf of the
interests of the people they represent.[1] In Scotland the rules with regard
to standing have not been relaxed to the same extent and the restrictive
and confused nature of the law related to standing (title and interest to
sue) is seen as a problem which might limit the utility of the judicial
review procedure in Scotland. There is, however, some evidence of a
broader approach being adopted in some cases.[2]

---

[1]   *R. v. Secretary of State for the Environment , ex p. Friends of the Earth* [1994] 2 C.M.L.R.
   760; *R. v. Secretary of State for Foreign and Commonwealth Affairs, ex p. World
   Development Movement Ltd* [1995] 1 W.L.R. 386; [1995] 1 All E.R. 611; *R. v. HM
   Inspectorate of Pollution, ex p. Greenpeace* [1994] 1 W.L.R. 570; [1994] 4 All E.R. 321.
[2]   Mullen, Pick, and Prosser, *Judicial Review in Scotland* (1996), p. 52.

TITLE AND INTEREST TO SUE

13–02 In order to seek protection of a right from infringement a party needs to demonstrate that he has both title and interest.[3] He must be the proper person to instigate the proceedings, thus having title, and he must also be able to show that he has a real interest in the result of the proceedings. Similarly, an applicant who has interest but cannot establish that there is a relationship that gives him title has no standing to bring an action. In the case of *A.B. v. C.D*[4] a law agent had wilfully concealed from his clients an offer made by the petitioner for a lease of certain premises. The petitioner suffered a financial loss and therefore sought to bring an action to have the law agent removed from the rolls of the Law Agents Society. It was held that he had no title to bring a petition although he did have interest as a person who had suffered a loss. In practice it is often difficult to separate title and interest and in some circumstances judges may simply state that a person has or has not "title and interest" rather than deliberating separately on the qualifying title and interest.[5]

TITLE

13–03 A person will only be regarded as the proper person to bring an action if he has title to sue. A definition of "title" was given in the judgment of Lord Dunedin in the case of *D. and J. Nicol v. Dundee Harbour Trustees*.[6] The harbour trustees were authorised to operate ferry services on the river Tay. They proposed to use the ferries for pleasure cruises at times when they were not in operation as ferries. D. and J. Nicol, who were local shipowners, sought suspension and interdict with regard to the pleasure cruises. The House of Lords held that such usage was *ultra vires* since the use of the ships for pleasure cruises could not be interpreted as being reasonably incidental to the authorised purpose of running a ferry service. An interesting aspect of the case was that the motive of D. and J. Nicol in challenging the operation of the ferries as pleasure boats was probably because their pleasure cruises would have fewer customers but their title to sue did not arise from their status as business competitors. Their title to sue was rather on the basis that they resided in, and carried on business in Dundee. Lord Dunedin stated that: "For a person to have title he must be a party (using the word in

---

[3] *D. and J. Nicol v. Dundee Harbour Trustees*, 1915 S.C. (H.L.) 7.

[4] (1899) 2 F. 67.

[5] *Cockenzie and Port Seton Community Council v. East Lothian District Council*, 1996 S.C.L.R. 209; *Lennox v. Scottish Branch of the British Show Jumping Association*, 1996 S.L.T. 105.

[6] 1915 S.C. (H.L.) 7.

its widest sense) to some legal relation which gives him some right which the person against whom he raises the action either infringes or denies."

It has been held that the recipient of a State benefit may have title to sue with regard to a decision taken by a Secretary of State which affects that individual's entitlement to payment. In a case where a bankrupt recipient of income support benefits challenged the right of the Secretary of State for Social Security to deduct money she owed as repayment for a social fund loan paid to her before sequestration from income support benefits paid to her after sequestration, it was argued that she had no title or interest to sue. It was held, however, that she satisfied the requirement for title as she was a party to a legal relation which gave her some right which the Secretary of State for Social Security had infringed.[7] Similarly, a holder of a licence will have title to sue with regard to decisions which affect him as a recipient of that licence. It has been held, in the case of *Tait v. City of Glasgow District Licensing Board*,[8] that an applicant for a licence, who has submitted an application is also party to a relationship which gives him title to sue. An applicant for renewal of a public house licence had his application returned by the clerk to the licensing board on the ground that it was too late. The lateness of the application arose from confused circumstances in which the applicant believed that the licence had already been transferred into his name. The applicant sought judicial review of the clerk's decision to reject the application for renewal, arguing that the board had discretionary power to consider the late application under section 13(2) of the Licensing (Scotland) Act 1976. The clerk and the board argued that the applicant had no title because he was not the holder of a licence. It was held that, as applicant for a licence, the petitioner had entered into a relationship which gave him title to seek judicial review of the clerk's actings.

If a statutory duty is owed to a class of persons, a member of that class   13–04
of persons may have title if there has been a breach of that statutory duty. In the case of *Docherty v. Burgh of Monifieth*,[9] the burgh claimed that Docherty had no title to sue, but the Court of Session having recognised that Docherty had interest as a person affected by a decision of the burgh not to lay sewers up the boundary of his land, found that he would also have title to sue if he could show that the decision was in breach of the burgh's statutory duty, which was owed to him, to provide drains and sewers.

Although it will usually be an individual who has title it has been held that a community council has title to represent members of the community because the statutory purpose of such organisations includes a power to represent the interests of the community. In the case of *Cockenzie and Port*

---

[7] *Mulvey v. Secretary of State for Social Security*, 1995 S.C.L.R. 102.
[8] 1987 S.L.T. 340.
[9] 1971 S.L.T. 13.

Seton Community Council v. East Lothian District Council,[10] a local community council sought to challenge a decision by the district council to demolish a swimming pond and other buildings and sell the land. The council maintained that the community council had no title or interest to sue. However, community councils were established under section 51 of the Local Government (Scotland) Act 1973 and subsection (2) of that section provides that: "In addition to any other purpose which a community council may pursue, the general purpose of a community council shall be to ascertain, co-ordinate and express to the local authorities for its area, and to public authorities, the views of the community which it represents, in relation to matters for which those authorities are responsible, and to take such action in the interests of that community as appears to it to be expedient and practicable." It was held to follow from the statutory purpose of the community council that they were in a close legal relationship with the respondents. This was the kind of legal relationship referred to in Lord Dunedin's observations in *D. and J. Nicol v. Dundee Harbour Trustees* and so the community council had title to sue. It was also held that this was a case where title and interest very much run into each other and that the petitioners possessed an interest to protect the rights of members of the community which they represented. It was held, however, that the actions of the district council were *intra vires* and the petition was dismissed.[11]

13–05   A trade union has been held to have title and interest to sue as an organisation representing its members in the case of *Educational Institute of Scotland v. Robert Gordon University*.[12] The EIS, a trade union, sought judicial review of the university's decision to apply new conditions of service to teaching staff appointments made after February 1, 1996. The EIS claimed that the decision was inconsistent with a centrally negotiated agreement and sought declarator that the university was acting *ultra vires*, and reduction of the university's decision. The university argued that the EIS had no title to make the application concerned as it should have been at the instance of the individuals affected by the decision. It was held that the EIS had title to sue as a representative body and it was unrealistic to presume that any new staff would accept an offer of employment and then seek to challenge the university's decision. The EIS had power to sue where the university made an unlawful decision in breach of statutory requirements. Lord Milligan said:

> "in the particular circumstances of this case, the petitioners clearly have a title to raise the present proceedings. This indeed, seems to me a particularly strong case for a representative body having a title to make application for

---

[10] 1996 S.C.L.R. 209.
[11] See also *East Lothian District Council v. National Coal Board*, 1982 S.L.T. 460; *Kirkcaldy District Council v. Burntisland Community Council*, 1993 S.L.T. 753.
[12] O. H,. May 29, 1996; *The Times*, July 1, 1996.

judicial review of a decision which, at the time of lodging the petition, has not yet actually affected a member of the petitioners, so far at least as they are aware. Where, as here, a trade union is able to allege that amongst its membership are persons who are likely to be adversely affected by an *ultra vires* decision of the respondents and that it is unrealistic for such members individually, both on timetabling and prospect of acceptance grounds, to challenge the decision individually, it seems to me that trade union has not only an interest to challenge the decision but also title to do so. The governors of the respondents have a duty to comply with statutory requirements for conditions of service of persons employed by them and in my opinion the petitioners are amongst those having a title to see that that duty is performed and to challenge a decision contravening these requirements. In my opinion the circumstances disclose a relationship between the petitioners and the respondents which gives the petitioners a title to sue the respondents in respect of what they allege to be an unlawful decision in breach of statutory requirements".

This decision recognises the efficacy of allowing representative organisations to sue on behalf of their members, thus avoiding the need for separate actions by each individual affected by the decision. The circumstances were unusual as the people who would be affected were potential applicants for posts at the university who were not immediately affected by the decision and who would be unlikely to risk jeapordising their career prospects by challenging the university's policy.

INTEREST

Even if a person qualifies as having title to raise an issue, the court must 13–06 also be satisfied that he or she has an interest to do so. This requires that the particular issue is of real concern to the party and not an academic issue or merely something which is being raised as matter of general public-spirited concern.[13] In order to qualify an interest the pursuer "must show that he will be prejudiced in status, patrimony or otherwise if his claim is rejected".[14] In the case of *Docherty v. Burgh of Monifieth*[15] the Court of Session held that since Docherty was affected by the decision of the burgh not to provide sewers to link drains and sewers from the boundary of Docherty's land to the main drains and sewers he had interest. The interest arose from the fact that, if the sewers were not provided by the burgh, they would have to be laid by Docherty at his own expense.

Although a holder of a licence or an applicant for a licence has title to sue, he will only have interest if he has a right to occupy the premises to which the licence relates. A case in which it was held that the petitioner

---

[13] *Scottish Old People's Welfare Council, Petrs.*, 1987 S.L.T. 179.
[14] Walker, *The Law of Civil Remedies in Scotland* (1974), p. 10.
[15] 1971 S.L.T. 13.

lacked interest was *Barrett (Edward) v. City of Dundee District Licensing Board*.[16] A company which held a betting office licence for certain premises vacated the premises before the term of the licence had expired. Subsequently, and while the licence remained in force, an individual made application to the licensing board for a similar licence for the same premises which he had leased. The licensing board granted that application over the objections of the original company. The company raised a petition for judicial review seeking reduction of the board's decision. It was held that the company's licence ceased to have effect on their ceasing to have any right to occupy the premises; consequently the company lacked title and interest and the petition was dismissed.

Sufficiency of interest

13–07   The courts used to require that a person's legal or financial interests would be affected by the court's decision in order for the person to be qualified to bring an action, however the attitude of the courts to the nature of the interest required has relaxed over the years. The interest need no longer be a formal legal or property interest. Historically, the standing of a person or body to bring an action in the Court of Session depended upon his being able to establish that he had a pecuniary interest.[17] In the case of *Strang v. Stewart*,[18] Lord Inglis said: "if there be a pecuniary or a patrimonial interest, however small, depending on the determination of the question, the parties have the right to involve the aid of a court of law to resolve their difference". The court however has moved away from an insistence in every case on the presence of a pecuniary interest.[19] The interest need be neither pecuniary nor large provided that there is also title. In the case of *St Johnstone Football Club Ltd v. Scottish Football Association Ltd*,[20] it was held that, where the procedure of a tribunal has been marked by gross irregularity, the court has jurisdiction whether or not there has been interference with the civil rights and patrimonial interests of its members. In the case of *Gunstone v. Scottish Women's Amateur Athletic Association*,[21] the sufficiency of interest which was required was said to be a matter of circumstances in which considerations of patrimonial or pecuniary or proprietal interest are not regarded as definitive tests. In relation to voluntary organisations this development of the law appears to be furthering the important principle

---

[16] 1992 S.L.T. 963.
[17] Lord Kames, *Historical Law Tracts* (4th ed., 1778) as cited in *West v. Secretary of State for Scotland,* 1992 S.L.T. 636.
[18] (1864) 2 M. 1015.
[19] Lord Clyde "The nature of the supervisory Jurisdiction and the Public/Private Distinction in Scots Administrative Law".in Finnie, Himsworth and Walker, *Edinburgh Essays in Public Law* (1991).
[20] 1965 S.L.T. 171.
[21] 1987 S.L.T. 611.

that every wrong should have a remedy and fulfilling the Dunpark recommendations that access to justice should be a feature of judicial review procedure. This development has occurred despite the fact that neither modern judicial review procedure nor statutory reforms have altered the old rules of title and interest to sue. The Dunpark Committee, which was established in 1983 to recommend a simple form of procedure for judicial review considered the rules relating to title and interest to sue in Scotland and was inclined to favour the extension of the rules by adopting a test which would ensure that all people affected by a decision would have the right to challenge it. They proposed a test of "sufficient interest" arguing that there was: "a strong case for the extension by the legislature of our common law rules of title to sue to enable every person who is directly or indirectly affected by alleged unlawful acts or decisions competently to challenge them".[22] The reason that this proposal was not implemented was that the Dunpark Report was intended to bring about a speedy change to the procedural rules of the Court of Session. In order to avoid the need to wait for parliamentary legislation the changes to the procedures were implemented by an Act of Sederunt. The rules relating to title and interest to sue are rules of substantive law and consequently could not be changed without parliamentary legislation. No legislation to reform the substantive law has yet taken place. There has, however, been a tendency for the courts in Scotland to give a more liberal construction to the rules of title and interest to sue, although this is not a consistent trend and cases can be divided into those where a broad approach was taken and those which epitomise a narrower approach. The broad approach is based on the premise that priority should be given to access to justice and that individuals should be able to challenge all unlawful acts. The narrow approach, on the other hand, is more concerned that the rules should not be relaxed to the extent that people who have no interest can interfere with the efficient despatch of administrative matters.

Narrow approach

The narrow approach requires that the complainant's rights, as an individual, have been infringed. The rights of an owner of neighbouring property may not necessarily create sufficient interest. In the case of *Simpson v. Edinburgh Corporation and the University of Edinburgh*,[23] Simpson, the owner of a house in George Square in Edinburgh, objected that the character of the square would be destroyed when the university obtained planning permission from the corporation for the erection of modern buildings. He sought declarator that the grants of planning consent were *ultra vires* as contrary

13–08

---

[22] Report to the Rt. Hon. Lord Emslie, Lord President of the Court of Session, by the Working Party on Procedure for Judicial Review of Administrative Action (1984), para. 8.

[23] 1960 S.C. 31.

to the Edinburgh development plan, reduction of the grants, and interdict against the University to prevent it proceeding with the building programme. The plea of no title to sue made by both defenders was accepted by the court in interpretation of the Town and Country Planning (Scotland) Act 1947. Lord Guest said: "I have no doubt that, in certain circumstances, ownership of property may give a party an interest, but he must in my view, in the present case qualify a patrimonial interest in the sense that some right of his, conferred by the Act of 1947 is being contravened."[24] He went on to say that he could not find any indication in the 1947 Act that the pursuer had title to enforce planning control. In the case of *North British Railway Co. v. Birrell's Trustees*,[25] the company obtained a declarator that the trustees, who owned neighbouring land, had no right or title to object to the company granting a lease of its surplus land for mining purposes and in the case *Khan v. City of Glasgow District Licensing Board*,[26] Abdul Khan sought a reduction of a decision of Glasgow District Council Licensing Board to make a provisional grant of a public house licence for a new bandstand complex in Kelvingrove Park. It was held that he did not have interest as the amenity value of his property, which did not adjoin Kelvingrove Park, was not affected. In the case of *Wilson v. Grampian Regional Council*,[27] Ronald Wilson and others, as community charge payers, sought judicial review of a decision by Grampian Regional Council to purchase a house to provide accommodation for adults with learning difficulties. It was doubted whether a community charge payer would have a sufficient interest, based upon amenity concerns, to challenge the illegal actings of his local authority.

13–09   The case which is regarded as the current leading authority in relation to title and interest is that of *Scottish Old People's Welfare Council, Petitioners*.[28] The Scottish Old People's Welfare Council (commonly known as Age Concern Scotland) raised a petition for judicial review challenging the legality of a circular issued by the chief adjudication officer appointed by the Secretary of State for Social Security. The circular purported to give guidance on the application of regulation 26 of the Supplementary Benefit (Single Payments) Regulations 1981, which related to extra payments for severe weather conditions. The petitioners argued that, for the purposes of making single payments in terms of the regulation, the standards by which severe weather should be judged and normal consumption of fuel assessed ought to be national, based on circumstances prevailing throughout the whole of the United Kingdom. They argued that instructions in the circular, which advocated a local standard, were erroneous in law and *ultra vires*. The chief

---

[24] 1960 S.C. 311 at 317.
[25] 1918 S.C. (H.L.) 33.
[26] 1995 S.L.T. 332.
[27] 1993 S.L.T. 588.
[28] 1987 S.L.T. 179.

adjudication officer argued that the petitioner had no title and interest to raise the petition. In relation to the issue of title it was held that that:

(1) *locus standi* was logically prior to and conceptually distinct from the merits of the case;

(2) that the introduction of judicial review procedure did not introduce any changes in the substantive law nor in the law of *locus standi*;

(3) that any member of the public had a title to sue, and accordingly there was no reason in principle why members of the public should be deprived of that title simply because they combined together into an association;

(4) that, except in the special case of *actio popularis*, a voluntary association which sued did not generally act in any representative capacity on behalf of the general public.

It was held, however, that the interest of the petitioners was too remote to give them a right to challenge the validity of the circular. This was because there were too many contingencies to make it certain that they would ever benefit directly from the challenge. An important factor was that Age Concern was an organisation whose purpose was to further the interests of elderly people. Its own membership did not necessarily include elderly people who would be in a position to benefit from a favourable decision.

Age Concern Scotland was held therefore to have title but no interest to 13–10 challenge the official guidance that limited the making of supplementary payment to old people during severe weather conditions. However, Lord Clyde said:

"The phrase 'his pecuniary rights and status' should perhaps in the light of Wilson[29] be not regarded as an exhaustive or complete description of what may comprise an interest ... The interest must be such as to be seen as material or sufficient. The pursuit of an academic issue would not suffice nor would an attempt to seek a general pronouncement of law on facts which were hypothetical. There must be a real issue. But the existence of a sufficient interest is essentially a matter depending upon the circumstances of the particular case. The variety of adjectives which are employed to describe the quality of interest required by the law reflects the difficulty of defining any single criterion."[30]

More recently, in the case *Mulvey v. Secretary of State for Social* 13–11 *Security*,[31] it was argued by the respondent that there were too many contingencies to overcome before the petitioner, who had had repayments for a social fund loan prior to sequestration deducted from her post-sequestration benefit payments, could qualify an interest which was material or sufficient and that there was no live issue between the parties in relation

---

[29] *Wilson v. Independent Broadcasting Authority*, 1979 S.C. 351.

[30] 1987 S.L.T. 179 at 317.

[31] 1995 S.C.L.R. 102.

to the deductions from income support made by the Secretary of State. This argument was based on the premise that she would not have had direct control of any income surplus to her needs as it would have been managed entirely for the benefit of her creditors. It was held, however, that if the deductions had not been made, the full amount of the income support would have been paid to the petitioner and some of it might have been retained by her. It was held, therefore, that the petitioner qualified a material and sufficient interest and that there was a live issue between the parties in relation to the deductions.[32] In certain cases the applicant may be able to achieve some practical result by bringing the grievance into court and thus obtaining publicity even if the application itself is dismissed. *The Scottish Old People's Welfare Council, Petitioners* case[33] was unsuccessful as a legal challenge but it did result in raised public awareness of the hardship caused by the implementation of the rules relating to cold weather benefit payments in Scotland.

Broad approach

13–12   The broad approach is more objective. Once the court has determined that the individual is within the class entitled to enjoy a public right, it is concerned thereafter with whether the acts are lawful. Using this approach an *actio popularis* may be recognised. In the case of *Wilson v. Independent Broadcasting Authority*,[34] three members of a group campaigning in the period leading up to the referendum on devolution of political power to Scotland were held to have title and interest to sue for an interdict to restrain the showing of certain political broadcasts by the Independent Broadcasting Authority. The broadcasts did not maintain a proper balance between opposing views. Lord Ross could see "no reason in principle why an individual should not sue in order to prevent a breach by a public body of a duty owed by that public body to the public".

13–13   Involvement in proceedings as an objector may transform a person from a mere bystander or busybody into a legally interested party, and therefore, for example, in *Patmor Ltd v. City of Edinburgh District Licensing Board*,[35] competitors of an applicant for a grant of a licence were held to be entitled to challenge the grant of a licence. It was held that although holders of a gaming licence who feared increased competition if a new licence was granted had no title in that capacity to challenge the grant of a licence to another company for similar premises

---

[32]   The case was appealed to the Inner House and the House of Lords where it was held that the post-sequestration deductions were not inconsistent with the provisions of bankruptcy law.

[33]   1987 S.L.T. 179.

[34]   1979 S.C. 351.

[35]   1988 S.L.T. 850.

in the same area as their own premises they did, however, have title as objectors to the new planning application as they had submitted formal written representations when the application was first advertised. Lord Jauncey said: "the petitioners have no title, by reason alone of their holding a gaming licence, to take action to protect the value of the benefits flowing from that licence, for example, by limiting competition. They do, however, as objectors to County's application have the right to see that their objection, and hence County's application are dealt with in accordance with the relevant paragraphs of Sched. 2" (of the Gaming Act 1968). In the case of *Matchett v. Dunfermline District Council*,[36] it was held that participation as an objector did not, however, give title and interest where there was no statutory right to object. Two individuals applied to Dunfermline District Council for a permit in respect of gaming machines under the Gaming Act 1968. A business rival objected to the application. A licensing sub-committee met and heard representations from the objector. The application was refused and the applicants appealed to the sheriff. The sub-committee held another hearing to consider the application afresh and a permit was granted. The appeal to the sheriff was later dismissed. The business rival of the applicants sought judicial review of the sub-committee's second decision. It was held that there was no title and interest to sue. The fact that the council had allowed the objector to be heard in support of an objection which he had no statutory right to make was not sufficient to give him title to petition. In the case of *Lakin v. Secretary of State for Scotland*,[37] it was held that the petitioners had a title to sue by virtue of their legal relation with the Secretary of State occasioned by their pending appeal against a refusal of planning consent and in the case of *Lothian Regional Council v. Lord Advocate*,[38] it was held that council employees who had been criticised by a sheriff in a fatal accident inquiry had title and interest to challenge his decision.

As involvement in proceedings as an objector may give a person title and interest to sue it follows that failure to object in the early stages of a licensing or planning application can lead to a situation in which a petitioner finds himself without title or interest to sue. The case of *Hollywood Bowl (Scotland) v. Horsburgh*[39] involved the granting of entertainment and liquor licences. Section 33 of the Licensing (Scotland) Act 1976 provides for the grant of an occasional licence to the holder of a licence authorising the sale of alcoholic liquor in the course of catering for an event taking place outwith his licensed premises. A company applied for an entertainment licence in respect of premises which it intended to operate as a bowling alley. This 13–14

---

[36] 1993 S.L.T. 537.
[37] 1988 S.L.T. 780.
[38] 1993 S.L.T. 40.
[39] 1993 S.L.T. 241.

application was granted by the licensing board despite objections to the application. The objectors appealed to the sheriff court. Prior to the hearing of the appeal, the applicant company applied for an occasional licence, in terms of section 33(1) of the Act, for permission to sell alcoholic liquor at the bowling alley in the course of catering for "an event" at the premises, namely a bowling competition. (The application was made by the company as licence-holders in respect of other licensed premises). The objectors to the original application did not lodge an objection to this application for an occasional licence. The occasional licence application was granted and the objectors then presented a petition for judicial review. They argued that the grant effectively enabled the applicants to operate the premises as if an entertainment licence was in full force and effect. It was held that the failure to object to the occasional licence application precluded the objectors from having the necessary *locus standi*, which would otherwise have been conferred upon them by reason of their objection to the grant of the entertainment licence, and so the objectors had no title to sue.

13–15   In order to establish that he has *locus standi* it is necessary for an applicant to show that the interest in any decision or act challenged is sufficient. If the interest of the applicant is too remote the application may be dismissed, although in some cases questions of title and interest are so tied into the merits of the case that the issues of title and interest are only decided after the Court has had a hearing on the merits. The case of *Lennox v. Scottish Branch of the British Show Jumping Association*[40] was such a case. Lennox stood for re-election to the council of the British Show Jumping Association but he was advised that he was not eligible because he owed money to the branch. His nomination was rejected without warning and without any opportunity to make representations. He was later informed that he had been removed from office as a judge. He claimed that the actions of the council were contrary to natural justice and *ultra vires* and sought reduction of the election for Glasgow South council and reduction of the decision to remove him from office as a judge. The case was dismissed on the ground that it should have been brought against the British Show Jumping Association rather than its Scottish branch but Lord Abernethy expressed his views on other aspects of the case including the defenders claim that Lennox did not have sufficient interest to sue. He decided, on the authority of *Wilson v. Independent Broadcasting Authority*,[41] that the pursuer did have an interest: "Furthermore, insofar as the case was based upon breach of natural justice that was sufficient itself to qualify an interest ... In earlier days it was considered necessary for this purpose for the pursuer to aver that the question at issue involved his pecuniary rights or his status. But in

---

[40]   1996 S.L.T. 105.
[41]   1979 S.C. 351.

my opinion the test now is not so restricted."[42] In *Hardie v. North East Fife District Licensing Board*,[43] it was held that an owner of neighbouring property had sufficient title and interest to challenge a decision by a licensing board to grant permission for a tent to be erected in the garden of a public house for two months to host a beer and jazz festival. (He had, however, delayed too long in bringing the matter to court.)

Future interests may be sufficient if they are sufficiently likely to occur 13–16 and are not hypothetical or academic. Title and interest to sue has been held to exist where a company has an intention to apply for a licence. In the case of *Air 2000 v. Secretary of State for Transport (No. 2)*,[44] a company which held a licence to operate chartered air flights from Glasgow to Orlando, Florida, and which was "contemplating the possibility of operating charter flights from Edinburgh to Orlando" during the following year, presented a petition for judicial review seeking to challenge the validity of two sets of regulations made by the Secretary of State for Transport which forced transatlantic flights from Glasgow and Edinburgh airports to stop at Prestwick airport. The Secretary of State argued that Air 2000 had no title or interest to sue since they had not yet made an application for a licence to fly from Edinburgh airport. It was held that Air 2000, as an established operator already using Glasgow airport and contemplating the possibility of using Edinburgh, had a title to challenge the rules. The issue of the validity of both sets of rules was a matter of "immediate and real concern" to the petitioners sufficient to give them an interest to sue. The additional cost to the petitioners in having to land aircraft at Prestwick in accordance with the rule was a live issue in relation to which the petitioners had a reasonable concern.[45] However, in the case of *Shaw v. Strathclyde Regional Council*,[46] the future interests were held not to be sufficiently "live". In May 1986 a parent challenged the policy of Strathclyde Regional Council in relation to clothing grants for her children under the Education (Scotland) Act 1980, s. 54. The applicant's children had already received a grant for the school year 1985–86 and she was concerned that any further application which she made for a clothing grant would be refused since the policy statement of the council allowed only one automatic clothing grant in each school year. The council claimed that she had no interest to challenge the policy since she did not have an interest in a live issue. It was held that where there is a live issue in which the applicant had a reasonable concern it might be sufficient to be a potential applicant but that there was no live issue in the *Shaw* case. Lord Cullen said:

---

[42] See also *McDonald v. Burns*, 1940 S.C. 376; *St Johnstone Football Club v. SFA*, 1965 S.L.T. 171.

[43] 1996 G.W.D. 29–1757.

[44] 1990 S.L.T. 335.

[45] *Shaw v. Strathclyde Regional Council*, 1988 S.L.T. 313, commented on.

[46] 1988 S.L.T. 313.

"What amounts to sufficient interest depends essentially upon the circumstances of the particular case. The question arises here as a matter of relevancy. It does not seem to me that it would always be necessary for a person to have made an application before he or she could be regarded as having sufficient interest to litigate in regard to a matter which was pertinent to an application. If there was a live issue in which a person had a reasonable concern, it might be sufficient if he or she was a potential applicant."[47]

It was held, however, in this case, that the petitioner's apprehensions about the fate of a further application during the current school year raised a hypothetical or future issue and the petitioner lacked sufficient interest.

13–17   In the case of *Moriarty v. City of Edinburgh District Licensing Board*,[48] it was held that the petitioner had no interest to sue because the petition was directed at the decision of a clerk not to receive a licence application for consideration at a meeting of the licensing board and the date of the meeting had passed. No purpose could be served in relation to the interests of the applicant. Moriarty argued that he did have an interest because future applications by him may be affected, but it was held that, if a future application by him was rejected he could challenge the decision at the time. The petition related to a particular decision taken at a specified date and circumstances might well have changed before another application was considered at a future date.

Enforcement of public rights

13–18   The broader interpretation of the rules of title and interest to sue in Scotland may allow an individual to sue directly to enforce a public right as an *actio popularis*. In the case of *Ogston v. Aberdeen Tramways Company*,[49] a tramway company which had a statutory right to use certain streets in a town during periods of heavy snow, ploughed the snow from the tramlines to the sides of the street. The piles of snow at the side of the streets caused an obstruction to pedestrians. A member of the public sought suspension and interdict to stop the tram company continuing the practice. It was held that the tram company did not have statutory authority to create a nuisance in this way and the member of the public had title to sue. The Lord Chancellor, Lord Halsbury, observed:

"If the question had arisen in England, I think some doubt might be entertained whether the obstruction as proved was such that a private person could sue without further proof of peculiar damage to himself; but that question does not arise according to the law of Scotland. Mr Ogston is entitled to sue

[47]   1988 S.L.T. 313 at 316.
[48]   1995 S.L.T. 40.
[49]   (1896) 24 R. 8.

in respect of an interference with the highway, which is applicable to him in common with the rest of Her Majesty's subjects."[50]

An interdict was granted to prevent the tram company creating obstructions of the highway.

The ability of pressure groups to bring actions has not yet been recognised   13–19 in Scotland in the same way as in England. Consequently, members of a body such as a conservation group are unlikely to have a legally recognised interest in all matters which are of concern to them, but if they can show a genuine and lasting concern with regard to a particular subject or a local site they may be able to argue successfully that they have an interest to accompany their title as members of the public. It is more likely that the parties will be deemed to have sufficient interest if they have invested money, time or effort in the location or in the campaign. In the case of *Glasgow for People Ltd v. Secretary of State for Scotland*,[51] a local pressure group challenged as unreasonable a proposal to build additional bridges over the river Clyde. Glasgow for People was an amenity group which represented the local community and was concerned with the impact of the new bridges on the communities on either side of the river. They campaigned to preserve the physical and social environment of the communities. The action failed on the ground that the decision was not unreasonable. In *Kincardine and Deeside District Council v. Forestry Commissioners*,[52] it was held that a local authority had the necessary interest to challenge a decision to award a grant to extend Glen Dye forest. The council had a reasonable concern with the payment of the grant because it was more likely that the planting would go ahead if the grant was awarded. An extension of the forest might affect the economy or amenity of the area generally. Accordingly, they had a material or sufficient interest as there was a reasonable connection between the decision to award the grant and the matters in which the council was interested.

The case of *R. v. Secretary of State for Scotland, ex parte Greenpeace*,[53]   13–20 provides a useful comparison between the laws of England and Scotland on the issue of the title and interest of a pressure group. Although the case was a challenge to a decision by the Secretary of State for Scotland and related to the dumping at sea of a buoy containing radioactive material in Scottish waters, the case was brought in England as the petitioners claimed that they would not have title and interest in the Scottish courts. If the Scottish courts did not have jurisdiction the case could properly be dealt with in an English court. It was held that the Scottish courts would have

---

[50]   At 10.
[51]   1991 S.C.L.R. 775.
[52]   1992 S.L.T. 1180.
[53]   Q.B.D. CO/1485/95, May 24, 1995.

jurisdiction. On the issue of standing it was observed that in English courts, although Greenpeace, in appropriate cases, does have standing, this does not mean that in every case in which Greenpeace makes an application it necessarily has an interest. Mr Mitchell, Q.C., one of two Scottish advocates whose opinions were sought by the court, said that he had little doubt that Greenpeace would have title to sue in Scotland but it was less certain that they would be able to establish that they had interest. He thought it unlikely that Greenpeace had an interest in the North Sea of a kind which a court would be prepared to recognise. Mr Davidson, Q.C. said that the usual practice in Scotland would be to find a relevant individual who could qualify an interest. "In practice what now happens where challenge is sought to be made to a decision affecting a sector of the population which a pressure group claims to represent is that the judicial review proceeds in the name of an individual who claims to be affected by the decision." One example of a public interest group challenging an official decision in this way was the case of *McColl v. Strathclyde Regional Council*,[54] in which a challenge was made by an individual, against the decision of a regional council to add fluoride to the water supply.

Title and interest as a threshold qualification

13–21 One question which arises in relation to title and interest to sue is whether the requirement for title and interest is a threshold qualification which should be settled in advance of a hearing or whether it is an issue which should be considered in the context of the hearing itself. There have been cases in which questions of title to sue and the merits of the case have been held to be inseparable[55] however in *Scottish Old People's Welfare Council, Petitioners*[56] Lord Clyde said: "In my view, the matter of *locus standi* is logically prior to and conceptually distinct from the merits of the case. It is properly of a preliminary character even although there may be cases where it cannot be resolved without inquiry into the merits." In *Matchett v. Dunfermline District Council*,[57] it was observed that, as a general rule in Scotland a favourable or adverse decision on the merits, should not determine the existence or absence of *locus standi*.[58] The question of title and interest should therefore be a threshold qualification for the right to bring an action.[59]

In England and Wales there is a filtering stage in judicial review procedure whereby an applicant has to apply for leave to proceed to a formal judicial

---

[54] 1983 S.L.T. 616. For further discussion of this case, see McManus, *Environmental Health Law in Scotland* (1989).
[55] *Gordon v. Kirkcaldy District Council*, 1989 S.L.T. 507.
[56] 1987 S.L.T. 179 at 184.
[57] 1993 S.L.T. 537.
[58] Lord Kirkwood at 540.
[59] This view was supported in the case of *Paisley Taxi Owners' Association Ltd*, O.H., October 17, 1996.

review hearing. There have been very few cases where failure to show a sufficient interest in the matter to which the application related was cited as a reason for refusing leave. And there appear to have been even fewer cases where the absence of standing was the only ground for refusing leave. In *IRC v. National Federation of Self-employed and Small Businesses*[60] the House of Lords stated that only in "simple cases" can the question of standing be determined at the leave stage. In other cases the issue could only be decided when the legal and factual context was examined in detail at the substantive hearing.

Approach in England and Wales — Sufficient interest

In England and Wales there has been some progress towards widening and simplifying the rules relating to standing since the introduction of the judicial review procedure under Order 53 in 1977.[61] The English Order referred to the need to show a "sufficient interest", and this has been interpreted liberally, although the trend has not always been consistent and there are some decisions which depart from the general trend of liberal interpretation of the rules. One such case was *R. v. Environment Secretary, ex parte Rose Theatre Trust Company*.[62] Developers of land in Southwark had found the remains of the Rose Theatre, where some of Shakespeare's plays had been performed for the first time. A trust company was set up to preserve the remains of the theatre and to make them accessible to the public. Under the Ancient Monuments and Archaeological Areas Act 1979, s. 1, the Secretary of State may list any monument which appears to him to be of national importance. A consultation procedure must be followed before this is done. The trust company requested the minister to list the site. He agreed that it was an important historical site but declined to list it. The trust company applied for judicial review but it was held that the trust company lacked standing. (It is likely that the issue of title and interest would have been decided differently in Scotland if the broad approach adopted in the case of *Wilson v. Independent Broadcasting Authority* had been followed). The reluctance of the courts to grant standing to pressure groups is probably because the function of such bodies is essentially that of lobbying for political change and to allow them to litigate their concerns would risk transforming judicial review into a mode of redress for political rather than legal grievances.[64]

13–22

---

[60] [1982] A.C. 617.
[61] R.S.C., Ord. 53, r. 4(1).
[62] [1990] 1 Q.B. 504.
[63] 1979 S.L.T. 279.
[64] Hare, "Due Process — Thorp, Sellafield and Greenpeace" (1995) 54 C.L.J. 1–3.

13–23   The case of *Inland Revenue Commissioners v. National Federation of Small Businesses*[65] is the leading English case on standing. It is known as the "Fleet Street Casuals" case. The Inland Revenue granted a tax amnesty to some Fleet Street workers who had been using false names to avoid paying tax. The National Federation of Small Businesses challenged the legality of this amnesty as their members had not been granted a similar amnesty for recent tax avoidance. On appeal it was held that the National Federation of Small Businesses had standing to challenge the tax amnesty as illegal but in the House of Lords it was held that there will be cases where the issue of *locus* (standing) should be resolved together with the legal and factual context of the case, rather than as a threshold condition as to whether or not the case should be heard. This was such a case but, nevertheless, the National Federation of Small Businesses did not have sufficient interest to ask the court to investigate the tax affairs of another taxpayer or to complain that the latter had been over or under assessed. Lord Fraser stated:

> "All are agreed that a direct financial or legal interest is not now required ... There is also general agreement that a mere busybody does not have a sufficient interest. The difficulty is, in between those two extremes to distinguish between the desire of the busybody to interfere in other affairs and the interest of the person affected by or having a reasonable concern with the matter to which the application relates ... The correct approach is to look at the statute under which the duty arises and to see whether it gives any express or implied legal right to persons in the position of the applicant to complain of the alleged unlawful act or omission."[66]

13–24   The liberal interpretation given to the test of sufficient interest has lead to the question of standing being viewed as a matter to be considered as part of the broader consideration of the factual and legal circumstances of the case rather than as a threshold test to be satisfied before a case will be heard. A "sufficient interest" requirement has been included in the Supreme Court Act 1981, s. 31(6), and recent case law has indicated a more liberal approach to applications by pressure groups. In *R. v. H.M. Inspectorate of Pollution, ex parte Greenpeace (No. 1)*,[67] it was held that Greenpeace, an environmental pressure group, had standing to challenge variations to existing authorisation to permit testing of the thermal oxide reprocessing plant (THORP) at Sellafield. Otton J. said that the issue of standing should be considered both at the threshold stage of instigating proceedings and during the hearing when the court was deciding whether it was appropriate

---

[65] [1982] A.C. 617.
[66] *ibid.* at 646.
[67] [1994] 1 W.L.R. 570.

to grant a remedy in the particular circumstances. One important factor in this case was that Greenpeace had around 2,500 supporters in the local area in Cumbria who were concerned about the dangers to their health. The issues raised were serious ones worthy of determination by a court. Allowing Greenpeace to have standing also had a practical advantage. It provided an effective way of dealing with the issue in one case rather than a series of cases brought by individual litigants. The judgment in the Greenpeace case is an affirmation of the advantages of allowing pressure groups to contribute their expertise to the review process. Otton J. emphasised that Greenpeace: "with its particular experience in environmental matters, its access to experts in the relevant realms of science and technology (not to mention the law), is able to mount a carefully selected, focused, relevant and well-argued challenge".

In the case of *R. v. Secretary of State for Foreign and Commonwealth* 13–25 *Affairs, ex parte World Development Movement Ltd,*[68] it was held that a pressure group had standing to challenge the legality of spending overseas development funds on the Pergau dam in Malaysia, a project which was economically unsound. In July 1991 the Foreign Secretary, under section 1(1) of the Overseas Development and Co-operation Act 1980, approved aid and trade provision for a dam and hydroelectric power station in Malaysia. This was against the advice of the Overseas Development Administration who had held the project to be economically unsound. The World Development Movement, a pressure group who campaign against the abuses of overseas aid, sought an assurance from the Foreign Secretary in April 1994 that he would withhold the outstanding payments for the scheme. He refused to do so and the applicants sought to challenge the legality of the original 1991 decision to grant aid and the subsequent decision not to withhold payment. The Foreign Secretary contended that the applicant had no *locus standi* to challenge his decisions and that he was entitled to take wider political and economical considerations, such as the formal offer of financial support for the scheme which the British Government had given to the Malaysian Government, into account when deciding to make a grant. It was held that the applicants did indeed have *locus standi*. Rose L.J. stated:[69] "If there is public law error, it is difficult to see how else it could be challenged and corrected except by such an applicant." Contributing factors to the decision were the extreme importance of the issue raised, the absence of any other responsible challenger and the fact that the applicants had a major role in giving advice and assistance in such matters.

The Law Commission recommended that a test be adopted of asking 13–26 whether the applicant has been or would be adversely affected, or,

[68] [1995] 1 All E.R. 611.
[69] *ibid.* at 618.

alternatively, whether it is in the public interest for the applicant to make the application.[70] If there is no individual who has sufficient interest there is a possibility that the Attorney-General may be persuaded to instigate proceedings by way of a relator action, although such actions are not common. In the case of *R. v. Poole Borough Council, ex parte Beebee*,[71] representatives of the Worldwide Fund for Nature and the British Herpetological Society sought to challenge a grant of planning permission affecting a site of special scientific interest on lowland heath which was an important habitat for lizards. It was held that the Society did have standing to challenge this decision because it had a long connection with the site. It had carried out surveys of lizard populations and other research and had made a significant financial input to the site. The Society also had an express connection with the planning permission since it contained a condition that the society should be given the opportunity to catch and relocate lizards from the site before the development commenced. The Worldwide Fund for Nature did not have any close connections with the site and would not have had standing on its own.[72] In the case of *Twyford Parish Council v. Secretary of State for Transport*,[73] (known as the *Twyford Down* case) the decision of the Secretary of State to allow the building of a motorway through Twyford Down, a scenic area near Winchester, was challenged by two parish councils and three individuals from the local area. Standing was assumed to exist and the question of standing was not discussed in the judgment. This in itself raises a question about whether or not standing has to be established to the satisfaction of the court in each case or whether it is a matter which need only be asserted if standing is challenged by the other party.

TITLE AND INTEREST IN STATUTORY APPEAL PROCEDURES

13–27 Where a right of statutory appeal is being exercised, the right to challenge a decision is normally granted to a "person aggrieved" by the decision and this may set a test for standing which differs from the normal rules of title and interest. The Town and Country Planning (Scotland) Act 1997, s. 239(5), provides that where an authority has failed to follow the prescribed procedure in making a decision, the court should only intervene if the applicant has been "substantially prejudiced" by a failure to comply with any of the procedural requirements. In order to establish substantial prejudice it is not

---

[70] Law Commission, "Administrative Law: Judicial Review and Statutory Appeals", Law Com. No. 226 (1993 H.C. 669), para. 5.22.

[71] (1991) 3 J.E.R.L. 293.

[72] See also *R. v. Swale Borough Council and Medway Ports Authority* (1990) 2 Admin. L.R. 790; (1991) J.E.R.L. 135.

[73] (1992) 4 J.E.R.L. 273.

necessary to prove that the outcome would have been different if procedural requirements had been adhered to. The fact that a person has been deprived of the exercise of a right is sufficient alone to amount to substantial prejudice. In *Wordie Property v. Secretary of State for Scotland*,[74] Lord Cameron said that: "where an applicant has been deprived of the exercise of a right conferred on him by Parliament, that fact alone would appear ... to indicate that he has suffered substantial prejudice".

If there are procedural irregularities in decision-making and a person has made no objection at the time, any attempt at a later date to claim that there has been substantial prejudice will be less likely to succeed.[75] However, in the case of *Cumming v. Secretary of State for Scotland*,[76] the right to apply to the court was extended to a potential objector to a planning decision who had not in fact participated in the inquiries prior to the grant of planning permission. The reason for this was that the advertisement did not make it clear that an application for consent for a "roadside petrol station and service area" was actually an application for two petrol stations, one at each side of the road, two restaurants and a motel. The court recognised that the public should be properly informed and given appropriate opportunity to make representations if they consider that they are adversely affected by a decision. The court held that the appellant qualified as a person aggrieved. The requirement to establish that the interests of the applicant have been substantially prejudiced does not apply where the decision in question is outside the powers of the relevant statute. All that is required in such a case is that the person should qualify as a person aggrieved.

STATUTORY EXCLUSION OF JUDICIAL CONTROL

Parliament has often sought to exclude or restrict the supervisory role of the courts by incorporating ouster or privative clauses in statutes but Erskine said: 13–28

> "the privilege of appeal to the supreme court not being expressly prohibited, an exclusion of jurisdiction is not to be presumed ... Even when a final and conclusive jurisdiction is conferred in the broadest terms, still if the inferior court exceed its powers, or refuse to act, or otherwise proceed in a way inconsistent with and not recognised by the statute, the Court of Session may competently review the proceedings and give redress ... Upon the same principle, where a particular jurisdiction is appointed under a canal, or road, or other local act, to determine all questions that may arise in carrying such act into execution; it the statutory trustees do not follow the terms of the act, or exceed the powers thereby given, the party aggrieved is not limited to the

---

[74] 1984 S.L.T. 345.
[75] *Midlothian District Council v. Secretary of State for Scotland*, 1980 S.C. 210.
[76] 1993 S.L.T. 228.

statutory or local jurisdiction, but may at once apply for his redress in the Court of Session".[77]

There is therefore a strong presumption that the legislature does not really intend that access to the courts should be denied, but it is appropriate that, for instance, where Parliament has appointed a specific tribunal for the enforcement of new rights and duties any recourse will need to be through that tribunal at first instance. In *Guthrie v. Miller*,[78] it was held that the court could not interfere with the exercise of the discretionary powers vested in commissioners of police under a local Police Act except in cases of excess of power or deviation from the statute. Lord Alloway stated that when the court has previous jurisdiction, it requires express terms to exclude the jurisdiction. When there is no previous jurisdiction and a new jurisdiction is created by statute the court cannot interfere unless there is an excess of the power created by the statute.[79] Although the jurisdiction of the court to consider the merits of a decision may be excluded the court nevertheless has authority to see that the decision-taking body keeps within the limits of their duty and does not exceed the authority which has been granted to them.

13–29　　Where statutes contain words which appear to oust the jurisdiction of the courts the judges will endeavour to interpret them so as to leave the supervisory jurisdiction of the courts intact. In *Magistrates of Perth v. Trustees on the Road from Queensferry to Perth*,[80] it was held that a provision in a statute that the trustees should "finally determine" questions between the road trustees and other persons did not exclude the supreme jurisdiction of the Court of Session "to determine what it is that falls within their powers; but whatever matter is found to be within their power, this court cannot review their proceedings". In the case of *Countess of Loudon v. Trustees on the High Roads in Ayrshire*,[81] it was held that the right of the Court of Session to review the legality of decisions was essential in order to prevent the smallest excess of power. The trustees had been authorised by statute to close any by-road which they considered not to be of importance to the public. There was a right of appeal from their judgment to the next meeting of the quarter sessions whose order and sentence was to be final and conclusive. Some members of the public objected to the closure of a road and presented a bill of advocation to the Court of Session as well as an appeal to the quarter sessions. The Court of Session held that, although the judgment of the quarter sessions was final on matters such as the fixing of

---

[77] Erskine's *Institute of the Law of Scotland* (Nicholson's Edition) (1871), I.ii, 7, Ivory's fn. 15.

[78] (1827) 5 S. 711.

[79] *ibid*. at 713.

[80] (1756) Kilkerran's Notes, Brown's Supp., Vol. 5, 318.

[81] (1793) Mor. 7398.

the line of a road or the position of toll bars, which were discretionary in nature, and in the exercise of powers which had been entrusted to the trustees alone, the Court of Session nevertheless had the right to review the decisions in order to ensure that there was no excess of power.

Statutory provisions which state that a particular decision "shall be final" have been made from time to time for many years. In *Heritors of Corstorphine v. Ramsay*,[82] it was held that the Court of Session had jurisdiction to review a judgment by a presbytery, with regard to the employment of a schoolmaster, although the decision of the presbytery was held by statute to be final. The Court of Session could review a decision which was an excess of power or where there was a failure to act. "It is very true that (the statute) gave the exclusive jurisdiction as to schoolmasters to presbyteries alone. But that jurisdiction is exclusive only where they act in matters committed to them. But if they refuse to act at all, or go beyond their powers, they may be controlled by this court."[83] This judgment recognised the distinction between a privative jurisdiction entrusted to the decision-maker, whereby the court cannot interfere with the merits of the decisions, and control by the court when the decision-maker exceeds the powers which have been entrusted to him or refuses to act. Similarly, in the case of *Young v. Milne*,[84] it was held that the jurisdiction to review a decision could not be excluded where the decision amounted to an excess of power. This case was a challenge to the decision of a jury established to fix the compensation payable to landowners whose land was acquired by compulsory purchase for road building. There was a term in the enabling act that "the jury's decision shall be final and cannot be removed or questioned by any other court whatsoever". It was held that this did not exclude the supervisory jurisdiction with regard to an *ultra vires* decision which, legally, was not a decision at all.

In a well-known case about the opening and closing hours of inns and public houses in Rothesay[85] it was also held that the role of the Court of Session in ensuring that inferior bodies act within their jurisdiction cannot be excluded. The magistrates of Rothesay had power to vary the opening and closing hours for public houses and inns for any area within their jurisdiction. They made a resolution, which applied to the area wherein all inns and public houses were situated, that all inns and public houses were to close at 10 p.m. instead of 11 p.m. Ashley and other hotel-keepers brought an action to the Court of Session for reduction of the licensing certificates and declarator that the resolution was *ultra vires*. The defenders pleaded

13–30

13–31

---

[82] March 10, 1812, F.C..
[83] *ibid.* at 459 and 550.
[84] June 23, 1814, F.C.
[85] *Ashley v. Magistrates of Rothesay* (1873) 11 M. 708.

that the action was incompetent because review by the court had been
excluded by statute. It was held that when an inferior court exceeds its
power, the Court of Session may reduce its decree, even though that decree
is made under an Act which excludes reduction. Lord President Inglis
explained:

> "the answer to the objection founded upon in this section is that the present
> is not a process of review, nor is it in a proper sense a stay of execution. It is
> a proceeding brought in the Court for the purpose of setting aside as incom-
> petent and illegal the proceedings of an inferior court and the jurisdiction of
> this court to entertain such an action cannot be doubted, notwithstanding the
> entire prohibition of review of any kind. This is not review, as I said before,
> but it is the interference of the Supreme Court for the purpose of keeping
> inferior courts within the bounds of their jurisdiction. The magistrates have
> exceeded their powers under statute, their order, whatever it may be — or
> decision — is liable to be set aside".[86]

(The use of the word "review" was referring to a review of the merits of
the decision not to the exercise of a supervisory jurisdiction.)

13–32   This role of the court in ensuring that a power conferred by statute is
only exercised within the limits prescribed by Parliament was an important
factor in the case of *Macfarlane v. Mochrum School Board*.[87] A schoolmaster
raised an action of reduction of a decision of a school board to remove him
and reduction of the decision of the board of education which had confirmed
the decision to dismiss him. One of the grounds was that statutory procedures
had not been followed. It was held that the court had jurisdiction in the
action to consider whether there had been deviations from the statutory
procedure. It had no power to review the decision on its merits. Lord
President Inglis stated that:

> "The school board and Board of Education are both creatures of statute.
> They can do nothing except under statutory authority. They can exercise no
> power whatever, except that which is given to them by the statute: and if
> they do not conform to the conditions by which the statute authorises them
> to exercise that power then they are no longer acting under the statute, and
> their proceedings would be liable not to be reviewed but to be set aside as
> incompetent."[88]

Once again the term review was used to indicate a consideration of the
merits of the decision as opposed to the legality of the exercise of power.
In *McDonald v. Burns*,[89] sisters brought an action challenging their
expulsion from a convent in Edinburgh on the basis that the procedures

---

[86] *Ashley v. Magistrates of Rothesay* (1873) 11 M. 708 at 716.
[87] (1875) 3 R. 88.
[88] *ibid.* at 98.
[89] 1940 S.C. 376; 1940 S.L.T. 325.

were not in conformity with the laws and constitution of the Roman Catholic Church. It was recognised that religious bodies in Scotland have exclusive jurisdiction and that their own decisions within their own sphere are final and binding upon their members and not open to review. Nevertheless, as Lord Justice-Clerk Aitchison explained, the court will entertain actions arising out of the judgment of ecclesiastical bodies where a body has acted beyond its own constitution in a manner calculated to affect the civil rights and patrimonial interests of any of its members and where, although acting within its own constitution, its procedure has been marked by the sort of gross irregularity which would, in the case of an ordinary civil tribunal, be sufficient to render the proceedings *ultra vires* and void. In the English case of *Ridge v. Baldwin*,[90] (a challenge to the decision to dismiss a chief constable). The Police (Appeals) Act 1943 provided that a constable dismissed by a police authority could appeal to the Home Secretary whose decision should be "final and binding on all the parties". The Home Secretary upheld the decision to dismiss the chief constable on appeal but it was held that this did not preclude the jurisdiction of the court to review the decision as it was *ultra vires*, being contrary to natural justice.

It is common for it to be stated that where a statutory order is made it 13–33
shall have effect as if it was enacted in the Act which authorised it. However, the courts may hold such an order to be invalid if it conflicts with the provisions of the Act.[91] When including such a clause in an Act it must have been the intention of Parliament that the clause would only apply to orders which themselves conform to the Act since they are the only orders which the Act contemplates. Despite the strict interpretation which is given to ouster clauses by both the courts in Scotland and the courts in England and Wales, there is a view that a clause which is expressed by an exceptionally strong formula may deprive a court of its supervisory jurisdiction. The British Nationality Act 1981, ss. 6(1) and 44(2) and Sched. 1, for example, states that the Home Secretary may, if he thinks fit, grant naturalisation to an alien who satisfies certain conditions. Even if these conditions are satisfied naturalisation may be refused. The Home Secretary is not required to assign any reason for refusal and his decision is not subject to appeal or review in any court.

One of the reasons why courts are unwilling to interpret statutory provision as effectively ousting the jurisdiction of the courts is a concern that a person whose rights have been infringed should not be left without a legal remedy. There is therefore a relaxation of the strict interpretation given to such ouster clauses where a remedy is provided by a procedure laid down by the statute itself. This willingness for the courts to accept a clause

---

[90] [1964] A.C. 40.
[91] *Minister of Health v. R., ex p. Yaffe* [1931] A.C. 494.

excluding jurisdiction where a statutory remedy for challenge exists was shown in the case of <u>Smith v. East Elloe Rural District Council</u>.[92] The plaintiff, whose land had been taken compulsorily for the building of council houses nearly six years previously, alleged that the making of the order had been caused by wrongful action and bad faith on the part of the council and its clerk. She submitted that the exclusion clause in the relevant statute did not exclude the court's power in cases of fraud or bad faith. The Acquisition of Land (Authorisation Procedure) Act 1946, Sched. 1, para. 16 provided that a compulsory purchase order made under the Act should not, except for statutory recourse provided in the legislation, "be questioned in any legal proceedings whatsoever". On this preliminary point of law, the House of Lords held, by a bare majority, that the effect of the Act was to protect compulsory purchase orders from judicial review except by statutory challenge during the specified six-week period.

13–34   A different attitude is shown in the more recent House of Lords case of <u>Anisminic Ltd v. Foreign Compensation Commission</u>,[93] where the court was more reluctant to accept that Parliament intended to oust the jurisdiction of the courts. The Foreign Compensation Act 1950, s. 4(4), provided that the determination by the commission of any application under the Act "shall not be called in question in any court of law". The commission was responsible for distributing funds supplied by foreign governments as compensation to British subjects. It rejected a claim by Anisminic for a reason which the company claimed was an error in law. It was held that section 4(4) did not debar a court from inquiring whether the commission had made a correct decision in law on the question of eligibility to claim. "Determination meant real determination not a purported determination." By taking into account an irrelevant consideration the commission's decision became a legal nullity. Lord Wilberforce said: "What would be the purpose of defining by statute the limit of a tribunal's powers, if by means of a clause inserted in the instrument of definition, those limits could safely be passed?" In other words, the court was not calling a determination into question but was investigating whether or not there was in fact a determination.

This case led to a revision of the legislation in order to allow for questions of law and challenges on the basis of a breach of natural justice to be referred to the courts. However, section 3 of the Foreign Compensation Act 1969 extended the protection from challenge in the courts to "anything which purports to be a determination". The approach in *Anisminic* and in the earlier Scottish cases allows the court to exercise its powers of judicial review without restriction as the supervisory jurisdiction is concerned only with the validity and not with the merits of a decision.

[92]   [1956] A.C. 736.
[93]   [1969] 2 A.C. 147.

TRIBUNALS AND INQUIRIES ACT 1992

The statutory protection against clauses which may be interpreted as ousting 13–35
the jurisdiction of the court to review the decisions of tribunals is currently
provided in the Tribunals and Inquiries Act 1992, s. 12 of which provides
that:

"(2) as respects Scotland:
(a) any provision in an Act passed before 1 August 1958 that any order or
determination shall not be called into question in any court, or
(b) any provision in such an Act which by similar words excludes any
jurisdiction which the Court of Session would otherwise have to entertain an application for reduction or suspension of any order or determination, or otherwise to consider the validity of any order or
determination, shall not have effect so as to prevent the exercise of
any jurisdiction."

There is corresponding provision for the High Court in England and Wales.

Exceptions

There are some exceptions as follows: 13–36

(a) an order or determination of a court of law,
(b) where an Act makes special provision for application to the court within
a specified time, (such as the six-week period for challenge to compulsory purchase orders).

The First Schedule lists the tribunals which come under the scope of the
Act. They are all concerned with disputes affecting the rights of
the individual. This provision allows for exclusion of the jurisdiction of the
courts at common law but only where there is an alternative provision for
the redress of grievances provided in the statute itself. Lord Denning held
(in relation to an earlier provision along the same lines) in the case of *R. v.
Secretary of State for the Environment, ex parte Ostler*,[94] that where a statute
allows for challenge to the validity of the decision but thereafter seeks to
exclude recourse to the courts, the courts will accept the statutory provision
as a limitation on the right to challenge, but where there is a provision
which purports to totally exclude the jurisdiction of the courts, the courts
will not accept that all decisions and purported decisions are immune from
challenge.

In the case of *McDaid v. Clydebank District Council*,[95] it was held that 13–37
the existence of a statutory appeal procedure will not always prevent recourse

---

[94] [1977] Q.B. 122.
[95] 1984 S.L.T. 162.

to the Court of Session after the expiry of the six-week period provided for appeal. The existence of special circumstances may make it unfair to deny a remedy to an applicant. In that case the council, acting under section 84 of the Town and Country Planning (Scotland) Act 1972, served three enforcement notices on the occupier of a yard and of a garage, requiring him to cease to use the yard as a scrap metal business and to remove all scrap metal and machinery. He was also required to restore the garage to its prior dimensions as there had been a breach of a planning condition imposed when it was extended. No notice of the enforcement notices was served on the owner of the yard although section 84(5) requires that enforcement notices should also be served on the owner in addition to the occupier. The occupier failed to appeal timeously against the enforcement notices and the owners did not become aware of the existence of the notices until a considerable time after the expiry of the period for lodging an appeal to the Secretary of State. The owners petitioned for suspension of the enforcement notices and interdict of the respondents from relying on the notices. The Lord Ordinary refused the petition on the ground that the effect of section 85(10) was that the validity of an enforcement notice could not be questioned in any proceedings whatsoever except by way of an appeal under the statutory appeal procedure. The petitioners reclaimed against this decision and the Inner House held that the jurisdiction of the Court of Session was not excluded by section 85(10) of the Town and Country Planning (Scotland) Act 1972 in cases in which, for reasons beyond the control of the persons seeking to challenge the planning authority's action, the procedure provided by the statute could not be used. As the enforcement notice was not properly served in terms of section 84(5) of the Town and Country Planning (Scotland) Act 1972, it was a nullity.[96]

This decision was not followed in cases in England based on similar legislation such as *R. v. Greenwich London Borough Council, ex parte Patel*,[97] in which it was held that, although the required enforcement notices had not been served, the jurisdiction of the courts to determine challenges to decisions was ousted by section 243 of the Town and Country Planning Act 1971.[98] In *Martin v. Bearsden and Milngavie District Council*,[99] it was held that, since the relevant Act was clear, any challenge, even on the basis of lack of service had to be taken within the six-week period. The case concerned the compulsory purchase of an area of ground in Milngavie. The ground belonged to the Roman Catholic Archdiocese of Glasgow and no notice in terms of the Acquisition of Land (Authorisation Procedure) (Scotland) Act 1947 had been served on the owners. The archdiocese,

---

[96] See also *Tarmac Econowaste v. Assessor for Lothian Region*, 1991 S.L.T. 77.
[97] (1986) L.G.R. 241.
[98] See also *R. v. Collett* [1994] Crim. L.R. 607.
[99] 1987 S.C. 80; 1987 S.L.T. 300; 1987 S.C.L.R. 267.

unaware of the compulsory purchase order, subsequently sold land which included the area of land subject to the compulsory purchase order to Martin. He petitioned to reduce the compulsory purchase order but it was held that any challenge outside the six-week period laid down by the Act was incompetent.

In the case of *Pollock v. Secretary of State for Scotland*,[1] the contrasting 13–38 approaches in *Martin v. Bearsden and Milngavie District Council* and *McDaid v. Clydebank District Council* were considered. Pollock sought declarator that a decision of the Secretary of State extending planning permission for tipping of waste at a disused quarry on land adjoining that owned by Pollock, was *ultra vires*, and reduction of that decision. Pollock had not been notified of the application and had also not been notified of the inquiry held by the Secretary of State into the application. He had therefore been deprived of his right to make representations and to raise objections. The requirements of notice were mandatory and failure to comply with them rendered any subsequent act *ultra vires* and void. The Secretary of State challenged the competency of the petition since Pollock had not exercised his rights of appeal under the 1972 Act and any subsequent challenge was excluded by sections 231 and 233. Pollock argued that the irregularity was of such a nature that a common law remedy should remain open notwithstanding the existence of a statutory appeal. The court should not exclude a party from the common law remedy where there were special circumstances which prevented use of the prescribed statutory means of review and a miscarriage of justice might occur. It was held that the words: "the validity of … any such action … shall not be questioned in any legal proceedings whatsoever", as used in section 231(1) of the Town and Country Planning (Scotland) Act 1972, were clear in their meaning. As an appeal had been before the Secretary of State and he had been acting within his powers and there was no question of bad faith, the words of the subsection served to bar any challenge to the decision, from whatever source and on whatever grounds it might come, after the expiry of six weeks from the taking of the decision and the petition was dismissed as incompetent.

The provisions of the Tribunals and Inquiries Act did not mark the end 13–39 of any attempts by parliamentary draftsmen to include provisions in legislation which attempt to oust the jurisdiction of the courts. Under the Interception of Communications Act 1985 a tribunal was established for hearing complaints of breaches of the Act's provisions. Section 7(8) provides that the decisions of the tribunal (including any decisions as to their jurisdiction) shall not be subject to appeal or liable to be questioned in any court. The inclusion of the reference to decisions as to jurisdiction appears to exclude the jurisdiction of the courts even where a decision is *ultra vires*.[2]

---

[1] 1993 S.L.T. 1173; 1992 S.C.L.R. 972.
[2] See also Security Service Act 1989 and Intelligence Services Act 1994.

The exclusion of judicial review is more strictly controlled in E.C. law. In the case of *Johnston v. Chief Constable of the RUC*,[3] a sex discrimination case, it was held that clauses enacted at any date that seek to exclude judicial review on matters affecting directly effective rights in Community law are not effective in excluding jurisdiction.

13–40   The approach taken by the courts to clauses which exclude jurisdiction attempts to strike a balance between the competing interests of the desire for certainty and finality on the part of administrators and those benefiting from their decisions and the need to avoid injustice to a person or body with a right to challenge a decision.[4] However, the period available for statutory appeals against administrative decisions is usually only six weeks which is a very short period in which to initiate a legal challenge. In many cases, a six-week time limit is not reasonable. The same time-limit has been set in different types of statute relating to different activities. A six-week time-limit may be appropriate for some purposes but it is a very short period in which to prepare a challenge to a decision such as a planning decision which may have been made under complex procedural rules. The comment has been made that too many time-limits have been enacted in too severe terms and with too little attention to the right overall policy.[5] The Justice-All Souls Review[6] considered the six-week period for statutory challenge and concluded that challenges after the six-week period should still be permitted provided that they were prompt and that decisions would be set aside only if no innocent third party would suffer.

---

[3]   [1987] Q.B. 129.
[4]   Reid, "Judicial Review and the Environment" in *Judicial Review: a Thematic Approach*, (Hadfield, ed., 1995).
[5]   Wade, and Forsyth, *Administrative Law* (7th ed., 1994), p. 748.
[6]   Report of the Justice-All Souls Review of Administrative law, "Administrative Justice: Some Necessary Reforms" (1988).

CHAPTER 14

JUDICIAL REMEDIES

INTRODUCTION

There would be little use in having a system of substantive law providing 14–01
grounds for an individual to challenge actions of the state and efficient
procedures for challenge unless there is a also range of remedies to
redress the grievances of any individual or body whose rights have been
infringed. There are therefore three essential elements for adequate
protection of the rights of the individual in relation to administrative
decision-making:

1. Principles of substantive law which establish the grounds on which administrative decisions can be challenged.
2. Procedures which are straightforward and flexible so as to provide access to justice.
3. Remedies which can be granted to redress any grievances, provide compensation for any loss or injury suffered and prevent the continuation or
   repetition of the conduct which has caused the loss or injury or has
   infringed the rights of the individual.

An important and long recognised legal maxim is *ubi jus ibi remedium* 14–02
(wherever there is a right there is a remedy). It is of fundamental importance
that there should be appropriate remedies available both to redress any wrong
which a person may have suffered and to prevent any continuing
infringement of his rights. In cases where a decision is held to be *ultra vires*
on the ground, for example, that it is unreasonable or is made on the basis
of an error in law or possibly that it is disproportionate to the purpose
intended the remedies provided may result in the decision being reduced
and not repeated. There are also remedies which are specifically aimed at
enforcing public authorities to fulfil their statutory duties, for example a
local authority may be ordered to fulfil its statutory duty to provide home
care services for a disabled person.[1] In judicial review proceedings, however,
success in court and the granting of appropriate remedies does not always
guarantee that the pursuer will benefit from a decision which is more

---

[1] *R. v. Bexley London Borough Council, ex p. B,* July 31, 1995, unreported.

favourable to him. A successful petition for judicial review may result in the reduction of a decision which was wrongly made and declarator that the official responsible for making the decision was acting unlawfully, but where the defect is due to a failure to follow correct procedures it is possible that the decision will be returned to the administrator who made the original unlawful decision. The administrator may then make his decision again, taking due account of the legal constraints surrounding the making of the decision and following all prescribed procedures. There are instances where the administrator may then make a lawful decision which is no more favourable than the original unlawful one. The success of such an action can only be measured by the fact that the decision-maker has been prevented from implementing an *ultra vires* decision.

REMEDIES IN JUDICIAL REVIEW PROCEEDINGS

14–03   In Scotland, apart from statutory remedies which apply both in England and Scotland, the remedies available in judicial review proceedings are remedies which could be described as ordinary remedies. In other words, they are the same remedies which would be available in any litigation between private individuals in the Court of Session. Civil remedies in Scotland can be classified according to their purpose and include the following:

1. declaratory judgments (declaring that particular rights do or do not exist);
2. reduction (reducing or setting aside as invalid a contract, will, decree or other writing);
3. prevention (stopping a threatened legal wrong, or the continuance or perpetration of a legal wrong by an order of interdict);
4. enforced performance (ordering the doing of what should have been done);
5. damages (pecuniary compensation, for loss caused or injury suffered by the failure to implement some legal duty); and
6. remedies competent under particular statutes in particular cases.[2]

These are all remedies which serve a variety of purposes in Scots law. The fact that such a broad range of remedies is available when the Court of Session is acting under its supervisory jurisdiction is one of the reasons for the increasing popularity of judicial review proceedings. When a petition has been made for judicial review the court may make such order as it thinks fit, whether or not such order was sought in the application. The court may make an order for reduction, suspension, declarator, interdict, implement, restitution or payment (whether of damages or otherwise). A

---

[2]   Walker, *The Scottish Legal System* (1997).

combination of suitable remedies may be awarded. The court also has power to make an interim order if this is necessary to preserve the rights or interests of the parties until the date of the hearing.[3] There is a great advantage in vesting the discretion to award the most suitable remedies in the court as an action cannot fail simply because the litigant has sought the wrong remedy or has failed to seek all of the remedies available to him. The Dunpark Committee considered that flexibility was of fundamental importance in judicial review proceedings and that flexibility would be enhanced by maximising control by the judge. It was said in the report that: "the judge must have power to grant any decree or make any order which he considers necessary in the interests of justice ... every possible remedy should be made available in this process so that no ancillary litigation should be necessary".[4]

DECLARATOR

The purpose of seeking the remedy of declarator is to have the existence of a right declared by the court. Declarator is a remedy which has been available from early times and which can provide a solution to a wide range of legal problems, including, of course, those arising from official acts and omissions. Unless it relates to personal status, in which case jurisdiction is reserved for the Court of Session, declarator may be granted by either the Court of Session or the sheriff court.

14–04

The remedy of declarator may be available for any kind of legal right. It was described by Stair as a remedy which was available for "instructing and clearing any kind of right relating to liberty, dominion or obligation",[5] and by Bell as a form of action by which some right of property or of servitude or of status, or some inferior right or interest is sought to be judicially declared.[6] No new right is created but rather an existing right is authoritatively declared. Declarator on its own therefore does not undo any decisions which have been made. It simply declares when a decision or action has been unlawful. In order to redress the wrongs which have been suffered, the remedy of declarator is often sought along with other remedies such as reduction, interdict or damages. In combination with other remedies declarator can be used to good effect to prevent public bodies exceeding their powers. It is a remedy which has been granted in relation to administrative decision-making for several centuries. In the case of *Tait v. Lauderdale*,[7] tenants and merchants in Lauder sought reduction and

---

[3] Act of Sederunt (Rules of the Court of Session) 1994 (S.I. 1994 No. 1443), Chap. 58.
[4] Report to the Rt. Hon Lord Emslie, Lord President of the Court of Session, by the Working Party on Procedure for Judicial Review of Administrative Action (1984), para. 5.
[5] Stair, IV.3.47.
[6] Watson, *Bell's Dictionary and Digest of the Laws of Scotland* (1889), p. 291.
[7] (1827) 5 S. 330.

declarator against the Earl of Lauderdale who had obtained a decree from the justices of the peace closing a road near his castle, and in the case of *Tennent v. Partick Magistrates*,[8] a licensee obtained a declarator that the licensing jurisdiction of the county justices of the peace, by whom he had been licensed, had not been transferred to the burgh magistrate under the Burgh Police (Scotland) Act 1892.

14–05   An advantage of declarator as a remedy is that it can be sought before the adverse effects of a decision cause harm to an individual. The efficacy of this use of the remedy of declarator was apparent in the case of *Rossi v. Edinburgh Magistrates*,[9] where an icecream vendor obtained a declarator that conditions which the magistrates proposed to attach to his statutory licence for selling ice cream were *ultra vires*. In the House of Lords, Lord Robertson considered that it would have been unfortunate if the question of *vires* could not have been settled until Rossi's lawful trade had been interrupted by a prosecution for breach of those conditions. He said: " It seems to me that the action of declarator, which is peculiar to the Scottish system, exactly meets the case." In the case of *Stirling C.C. v. Falkirk Borough,*[10] ratepayers who had paid their annual assessment of rates obtained a declarator that the defenders had no right to levy additional rates to pay for the expenses of an unsuccessful promotion of a provisional order seeking a burgh extension.

Although a declarator is no more than a declaration of the rights of the parties it has the effect that actions of public bodies may be halted or at least delayed while a lawful means is sought to achieve the result intended. In the case of *Ayr Magistrates v. Lord Advocate*,[11] a police authority obtained a declarator that a public inquiry into a proposed police reorganisation was irregular, *ultra vires* and not in accordance with substantial justice and in the case of *Adams v. Secretary of State for Scotland*[12] declarator was sought that the Secretary of State was bound to try to secure that a woman was appointed to a particular post.

14–06   A recent example of the use of the remedy of declarator in combination with other remedies is the case of *Highland Regional Council v. British Railways Board.*[13] Highland Regional Council, in a petition for judicial review, sought:

> 1.   declarator that the British Railway Board's proposal to withdraw the Fort William to London sleeper service constituted a proposal to discontinue all passenger services on three sections of a line;

8   (1894) 21 R. 735.
9   (1904) 7 F. (H.L.) 85.
10   1912 S.C. 1282.
11   1950 S.C. 102.
12   1958 S.C. 279.
13   1996 S.L.T. 274.

2. reduction of the decision to discontinue the service; and
3. interdict against the board from withdrawing the service until the closure procedure under section 37 of the Railways Act 1993 had been instituted and a final decision reached.

British Railways Board had attempted to avoid the need to carry out proper consultations before discontinuing the Fort William to London sleeper service by running "ghost trains" on a section of track during the night. The petition was granted, preventing the closure of the sleeper service until the required consultations had taken place.

It may also be possible to use declarator as a means of declaring that an objection to an action is unlawful and thus establishing a right in the pursuer to follow a certain course of action without fear of legal restraint, as in the case of *North British Rly. v. Birrell's Trustees,*[14] where the company obtained a declarator that the trustees, who owned neighbouring land, had no right or title to object to the company granting a lease of its surplus land for mining purposes.

Declarator is potentially a very valuable remedy because it can be used 14–07 to establish a legal principle which will then be followed in subsequent decisions or resolutions by a tribunal or public body. The use of declarator to restrain future decision-making has not, however, been encouraged by the courts and therefore declarator will not be granted where there is an alternative remedy which the court considers should be exhausted before declarator is sought. In the case of *Dante v. Assessor for Ayr,*[15] a pursuer brought an action in the Court of Session seeking declarator that he was not the tenant or occupier, for the purpose of the Valuation Acts, of certain land in the Low Green at Ayr which he leased from the town council, and that he was therefore not liable to be rated or assessed in respect thereof. He had appealed to the Valuation Committee but only against the value of the subjects and not against the entry of his name on the valuation roll as tenant or occupier. The action was held to be incompetent because he had failed to exhaust his available remedies. There may nevertheless be circumstances in which a declarator is granted even though the subject matter may be within the scope of a statutory remedy or procedure.[16] In the case of *Edinburgh and Glasgow Railway Co. v. Meek,*[17] the majority of judges held that it was competent to make a declarator which would lay down the mode of assessment of a railway which was to be adopted by 23 poor law authorities who were parties to the action. It was more convenient to grant

---

[14] 1918 S.C. (H.L.) 33.
[15] 1922 S.C. 109.
[16] *Edinburgh and Glasgow Rly. Co. v. Meek* (1849) 12 D. 153; *Hogg v. Parochial Board of Auchtermuchty* (1880) 7 R. 986; *Glasgow District Rly. v. Glasgow Magistrates* (1884) 11 R. 1110; *West Highland Rly. Co. v. Inverness C.C.* (1904) 6 F. 1052.
[17] (1849) 12 D. 153.

one declarator in advance rather than wait for 23 separate actions of reduction to reduce any unlawful assessments.

Declarator will be more readily granted where the issue in dispute is not one which could be resolved by a statutory procedure, as in the case of *Hope v. Corporation of Edinburgh*,[18] where the statutory remedy was not appropriate to the circumstances of the case. In that case an action of declarator and interdict was entertained where it was claimed that property for which a rating assessment had been made was outwith the city boundary. No appeal to the magistrates of Edinburgh under the Valuation Acts had been taken. It was held that an appeal to the magistrates would have been contrary to the fundamental principles of justice because the magistrates would, in effect, be judges in a cause to which they were parties. It could also be argued that the magistrates had no jurisdiction since the subjects were outwith the city boundary. Therefore, the pursuer had no statutory remedy and so the action was competent. Declarator was granted and the defenders were interdicted from assessing land outside the city boundary.

14–08   Declarator will not be granted in respect of abstract, academic or hypothetical questions. According to Bell's *Principles*, "It is not competent to ask the court to declare a fact or a right in the abstract without pointing out the consequent right to the party who concludes for such declarator."[19] Lord Neave declared: " It is not every fact that can be declared or negatived by declarator. It must be something of a practical kind leading to patrimonial conclusions that is sought to be established."[20] A question may be regarded as hypothetical if the action has been raised too far in advance of a proposed course of action, as in the case of *Ayr Magistrates v. Secretary of State for Scotland*,[21] where, in an action brought by a local authority against the Secretary of State for Scotland and a reporter appointed by him to hold a local inquiry into a reservoir scheme the pursuers sought declarator that an order which the Secretary of State proposed to make under the Water Act 1946 was *ultra vires*, and declarator that it was the duty of the Secretary of State for Scotland to refrain from causing a local inquiry to be held into the order and for declarator *ad interim* as interim relief to preserve the status quo until the final hearing. (Interim interdict was not available as interdict is not available against the Crown or Crown servants.) It was not necessary for the disposal of the case but Lord Fraser considered the competency of interim declarator and pointed to the problem which could be created if a declaration in relation to a legal question is given before the case is decided by a full hearing. He refused the motion for declarator *ad interim* as it would have amounted to a preliminary ruling on the question. It is extremely

---

[18] (1897) 5. S.L.T. 195 (*sub nom. Hope v. Edinburgh Magistrates*).
[19] *Gifford v. Traill* (1829) 7 S. 854.
[20] *Offices of State v. Alexander* (1866) 4 M. 741 at 753; *Morton v. Gardner* (1871) 9 M. 548.
[21] 1966 S.L.T. 16.

doubtful that there could be any circumstances in which an interim declarator would be available.

The courts will not grant declarator if there is no dispute which that 14–09 declarator would resolve.[22] A declarator will not, therefore, be available to establish the meaning of an Act of Parliament unless a ruling on the interpretation of a statutory provision is necessary in the course of resolving issues relating to the rights and interests of persons immediately affected by the Act.[23] It is, however, possible to obtain declarator to establish the application of a statute to a particular set of facts.[24] The general principle, therefore, is that declarator may be granted to resolve a particular dispute, be it based on common law or statute but it may not be used to declare an abstract principle of law which has no immediate effect on the parties to the action.[25] Although a declarator requires nothing to be done by the defender, if subsequent actions are raised between the same parties the content of the prior declarator will be *res judicata* and a declarator on a matter of public right may bind other members of the public. For this reason declarator can be sought or granted as the sole remedy in a judicial review petition.

REDUCTION

The remedy of reduction involves undoing a decision or a resolution. It 14–10 enables the Court of Session to exercise its supervisory jurisdiction over a broad range of official acts. There are two types of reduction: first, ordinary reduction, which can be used to rescind or quash any deed, contract or other instrument; and second, reduction of decrees, which is used to enable the court to review its own decrees or the decrees of inferior courts. Ordinary reduction can be used for documents created by public bodies such as local authority byelaws and decisions or directions from government ministers or other officials. According to Bell's *Principles*, the object of this class of actions, "is to reduce and set aside deeds, decrees, and rights whether heritable or moveable."[26] Stair said that this remedy is "peculiar to this nation, and is a more absolute security of men's rights than any form of process in Roman Law or in any neighbouring nation."[27] The effect of reduction may merely be to declare that a document is invalid or illegal or it may set aside

---

[22] *Morton v. Gardner* (1871) 9 M. 548; *Callender's Cable Co. v. Glasgow Corporation* (1900) 2 F. 397.

[23] *Todd & Higginbotham v. Burnet* (1854) 16 D. 794; *Orr v. Alston,* 1912 1 S.L.T. 95.

[24] *Leith Police Commissioners v. Campbell* (1886) 5 M. 247; *West Highland Rly. Co. v. Inverness C.C.* (1904) 6 F. 1052.

[25] *Griffin v. Lord Advocate,* 1950 S.C. 448.

[26] Watson, *op. cit.,* n. 6, above.

[27] Stair, IV. 20. 8. From Scot. Law Com. Memo., "Remedies in Administrative Law" (No. 14, 1971).

a document which would otherwise have legal effect.[28] Reduction is always concerned with a decision which has already been made or with a document which is already in existence. Reduction has been sought in a wide variety of circumstances. Such as:

1. A decision of a licensing authority, as in *Macbeth v. Ashley,*[29] where hotel-keepers successfully sought reduction of a resolution of the magistrates and the licensing certificates which had been issued.
2. A direction from a government minister; as in the case of *Ettrick and Lauderdale District Council v. Secretary of State,*[30] where Ettrick and Lauderdale District Council were granted reduction of a direction issued by the Secretary of State that the council had awarded work to the district services organisation without adequate reason.
3. Dismissal from public service.[31]
4. Decision of a valuation tribunal on the value of wool[32];
5. Rating valuation; in the case of *Moss Empires v. Assessor for Glasgow,*[33] where reduction of the new entry in the valuation role was granted because the assessor had not complied with the statutory requirements regarding notice to proprietors of increased assessments for rates.[34]

Reduction should not be sought where a lesser remedy would suffice.[35] In the case of *British Oxygen Co. v. South-West Scotland Electricity Board,*[36] British Oxygen Company sought reduction of various tariffs imposed by the Electricity Board and declarator that the tariffs were in excess of the Board's powers. In his judgment, Lord Keith indicated that the case would be best resolved by way of interdict or an action to recover overpayment.

14–11   Reduction will not be granted if there will be no effect on the position of the parties by virtue of the action. In *Shetland Line v. Secretary of State for Scotland,*[37] the petitioner, a shipping company, sought reduction of certain

---

[28] *Edinburgh & Glasgow Rly. v. Meek* (1849) 12 D. 153.

[29] (1874) 1 R. (H.L.) 14.

[30] 1995 S.L.T. 996.

[31] *Malloch v. Aberdeen Corporation,* 1971 S.C. (H.L.) 85. *Palmer v. Inverness Hospitals Board,* 1963 S.C. 311.

[32] *Barrs v. British Wool Marketing Board,* 1957 S.C. 72.

[33] 1917 S.C. (H.L.) 1.

[34] See also *Scott v. Glasgow Corporation* (1899) 1 F. (H.L.) 51; *De Prato v. Partick Magistrates,* 1907 S.C. (H.L.) 1. *Caledonian Rly Co. v. Glasgow Corporation* (1905) 7 F. 1020 (register of street widths); *McDonald v. Lanarkshire Fire Brigade Committee,* 1959 S.C. 141 (disciplinary action within public service); *Glasgow Corporation v. Glasgow Churches Council,* 1944 S.C. 97 (refusal by a sheriff to confirm byelaws). *Kerr v. Hood,* 1907 S.C. 895 (school board elections); *Brown v. Hamilton D.C.,* 1983 S.L.T. 397 (a local authority decision that a person was intentionally homeless).

[35] Thomson and Middleton, *Manual of Court of Session Procedure* (1837) p. 141.

[36] 1956 S.C. (H.L.) 112.

[37] 1996 S.L.T. 653.

decisions of the Secretary of State for Scotland relating to subsidies for shipping lines carrying freight to islands. Lord Johnston said: "the substance of the petitioner's claim for a remedy was that of reduction of the relevant decisions in circumstances where it was perfectly apparent that in all four cases the decisions had both been made and implemented ... the remedy of reduction is inappropriate in this case because the decisions are spent".

Partial reduction

There have been cases where a reduction of part of a document or parts of 14–12 a decision have been possible. Partial reduction will be considered only where the parts impugned can be readily severed from the remainder of the document or decision.[38] In the case of *Smith v. Lord Advocate*,[39] two general practitioners sought judicial review of a sheriff's determination after holding a fatal accident inquiry into the death of a patient in a nursing home. The two doctors had visited the patient on separate occasions. The sheriff found that they had failed to provide a proactive system of care for the patient. One of the general practitioners argued that he was not responsible for nursing care in the home and had not been involved until a later stage and had relied on the notes made by his colleague. It was held that part of the sheriff's determination was reduced in so far as it considered the two doctors together where they should have been treated separately. The remainder of the determination would stand. Similarly, in the case of *Lothian Regional Council v. Lord Advocate*,[40] the determination of a sheriff in a fatal accident inquiry under the Fatal Accidents and Sudden Deaths Inquiry (Scotland) Act 1976 (c. 14), s. 6, was partially reduced in so far as it purported to determine that a road accident had been caused by Lothian Regional Council blocking a roadway.

Reduction is a remedy which can be granted only by the Court of Session 14–13 and not by the sheriff court.[41] In 1967, the Grant Committee on the sheriff court recommended against extending the jurisdiction of the sheriff court to include reduction. Applications for reduction were said to "raise questions of great legal difficulty and importance which ought to be handled by the Court of Session".[42] The sheriff court does have jurisdiction to hear certain statutory appeals and to confirm certain local administrative matters and it could be argued that it would be appropriate for the same court to be able to

---

[38] *Islay Estates Ltd v. McCormick*, 1937 S.N 28; *Moss Empires v. Assessor for Glasgow*, 1917 S.C. (H.L.) 1; *Mitchell v. Cable* (1848) 10. D. 1297; *Miller v. Oliver and Boyd* (1903) 6 F. 77; *McEwen's Trustees v. Church of Scotland General Trustees*, 1940 S.L.T 357; *Adams v. Great North of Scotland Rly.* (1899) 16 R. 843.

[39] 1994 S.L.T. 1161.

[40] 1993 S.L.T. 40.

[41] Sheriff Courts (Scotland) Act 1907, s. 5.

[42] Cmnd. 3248, paras. 119 - 120.

reduce local administrative decisions. When the Sheriff Court is used to enforce a decision by a local authority the court may need to make decisions on whether or not there may be grounds for reduction of a decision if this is raised by a defender. Therefore, the Sheriff Court may already be considering these "questions of great legal difficulty" and it could be argued that the need to use the Court of Session may be a barrier to the challenge of less important decisions.[43] The equivalent remedy in English law is the writ of certiorari which can be obtained by a more summary remedy than ordinary civil procedure. In some statutory provisions, a remedy with the same effect as reduction is available in the Sheriff Court, for example, a Sheriff has power to set aside the award of an arbiter appointed to determine sheep values if he has failed to comply with statutory procedures.[44] There is a strong argument, therefore, for making reduction available as a summary remedy in Scotland.

Reduction is a negative remedy. The effect of reduction is therefore to quash an official decision. The court has no power to change the official decision or to substitute a lawful decision for an unlawful one. A court may, however, have the power to direct that the administrative body, inferior court or tribunal deal with the matter lawfully. This was done in the case of *Macbeth v. Ashley*,[45] where an order was made requiring the magistrates clerk to amend and re-issue licensing certificates which had been reduced as being invalid, having been issued in order to achieve an improper purpose.

INTERDICT

14–14 An interdict is an order prohibiting the implementation of a decision or the continuance of an action. It can be use to prevent anticipated wrongs or to stop wrongful activites in progress. Interdict has been defined as "an order of the Court of Session, or of an inferior court, pronounced on case shown, for stopping any act or proceedings complained of as illegal or wrongful".[46] The remedy can be used to prevent *ultra vires* acts by local authorities if those acts would directly infringe an individual's rights. In *Campbell's Trustees v. Police Commissioners of Leith*,[47] interdict was sought to restrain a statutory body from acting in excess of its powers. Lord Hatherley, L.C. said: "In all matters regarding their jurisdiction they (statutory authorities) are, of course, allowed to exercise those powers according to their judgement and discretion; but when they exceed those powers, they are immediately arrested by interdict or by injunction".[48]

---

[43] Scot. Law Com. Memo. *op. cit.,* n. 27, above.
[44] Agricultural Holdings (Scotland) Act 1991 (c. 55) s. 68(4).
[45] (1874) 1 R. (H.L.) 14.
[46] Watson, *op. cit.,* n. 6, above, p. 575.
[47] (1870) 1 R. 2 H.L. S.C. 1.
[48] *ibid.* at 3.

Interdict will not be granted where the actings complained of are in the course of carrying out a statutory duty or are empowered by statute. Consequently, in the case of *Central Regional Council v. Clackmannan District Council*,[49] interim interdict against the issue of a stop notice following a valid enforcement order under the Town and Country Planning (Scotland) Act 1972, s. 84 (1), was refused. An interdict may, however, be granted if actings authorised by statute have been carried out in a biased way[50] or without taking reasonable precautions to avoid harm.[51]

Interdict has frequently been granted to restrain the *ultra vires* acts of a variety of public bodies. Examples include: *Hope v. Edinburgh Magistrates*,[52] where the defenders were interdicted from assessing land outside the city boundary; *Distillers Co v. Fife County Council*,[53] where interdict was granted against the issue of unlawful rate demands; *Innes v. Royal Burgh of Kirkcaldy*,[54] where interdict was sought against a town council proposal to reduce local rates by 25 per cent; *McColl v. Strathclyde Regional Council*,[55] where interdict was sought to prevent fluoride being added to the water supply; *D. & J. Nicol v. Dundee Harbour Trustees*,[56] where interdict was granted on an action by shipowners to prevent the Dundee Harbour Trustees operating of pleasure cruises and *Adams v. Secretary of State for Scotland and South-Eastern Regional Hospital Board*,[57] where interdict was granted to prevent the offering of a post in a women's hospital to male consultants until it had been advertised as open to women doctors only.

Interdict will only be granted if there is evidence that a wrong is taking place or grounds of reasonable apprehensions that such a violation is intended. In *Hay's Trustees v. Young*,[58] Lord Ormidale defined interdict as: "a remedy by decree of court, either against a wrong in course of being done, or against an apprehended violation of a party's rights, only to be awarded on evidence of the wrong, or on reasonable grounds of apprehension that such violation is intended." In the case of *Malloch v. Henry*,[59] the pursuer sought an interdict against a community charge registration officer from enforcing fines due from the pursuer for non-registration. The court held

14–15

---

[49] 1983 S.L.T. 666.
[50] *Wilson v. IBA*, 1979 S.L.T. 279.
[51] *Gillespie v. Lucas & Aird* (1893) 20 R. 1035.
[52] (1897) 5 S.L.T 195.
[53] 1925 S.C. (H.L.) 15.
[54] 1963 S.L.T. 325.
[55] 1983 S.L.T. 616.
[56] 1915 S.C. (H.L.) 7.
[57] 1958 S.C. 279.
[58] (1877) 4 R. 398 at 401.
[59] 1989 G.W.D. 16-705.

that interdict was only available to remedy a legal wrong and not for something unpleasant but legally authorised.

The remedy of interdict is not granted as a matter of right but only in the exercise of sound judicial discretion.[60] It can be considered therefore as an equitable remedy but the court's discretion to refuse it is strictly limited.[61] In the case of *Ferguson v. Tenant*,[62] Lord Wheatley said that, apart from some understandable exceptions: "the general rule is that when operations have been found to be illegal by a final judgement of the Court, the petitioner has a definite right to interdict, unaffected by questions such as balance of convenience or loss".

14–16   An interdict will usually be a positive order to an individual or body to refrain from certain acts. As a general rule an interdict cannot be negative, as an order not to refrain from acting would be the same as an order of specific implement, but there are instances of interdicts being granted to stop authorities from ceasing to offer a service. In the case of *Deane v. Lothian Regional Council*,[63] the Inner House granted interim interdict against the local authority preventing it from carrying out the statutory procedure for closing a denominational school. However, in the case of *Edinburgh Property Management Association v. Edinburgh District Council*,[64] the pursuers sought to interdict the local authority from stopping payment of housing benefits to landlords. The Lord Ordinary held that the pursuers were seeking a negative interdict which was incompetent. In the case of *Highland Regional Council v. British Railways Board*,[65] interdict was granted against the British Railways Board from withdrawing a railway service until the closure procedure had been instituted and a final decision reached. An interdict may not be used to compel a public authority to exercise a discretionary power in a particular way. In the case of *Fleming v. Liddesdale District Committee*,[66] it was held that an interdict could not be granted so as to direct the committee's choice between two different methods of street lighting. If, however, a discretion is exercised *ultra vires* or in bad faith interdict may be appropriate.[67]

Interdict will not be granted where there is an available statutory remedy which has not been exhausted[68] or if it would be premature[69] or

---

[60]   *Kelso School Board v. Hunter* (1874) 2 R. 228, *per* Lord Deas at 232.
[61]   *Ferguson v. Tenant,* 1978 S.C. (H.L.) 19 at 47; *Webster v. Lord Advocate,* 1984 S.L.T. 13; 1985 S.L.T. 361.
[62]   1978 S.C. (H.L). 19.
[63]   1986 S.L.T. 22.
[64]   1987 G.W.D. 38–1348.
[65]   1996 S.L.T. 274.
[66]   (1897) 24 R. 281.
[67]   *Pollok School v. Glasgow Town Clerk,* 1946 S.C. 373.
[68]   *Cumming v. Inverness Magistrates,* 1953 S.C. 1(applied in *Stornoway Town Council v. Macdonald,* 1971 S.C. 78); *Hamilton v. Lanarkshire County Council,* 1971 S.L.T. (Notes) 12.
[69]   *Hamilton v. Lanarkshire C.C.,* 1971 S.L.T. (Notes) 12.

ineffectual.[70] In the case of *Ayr Magistrates v. Secretary of State for Scotland*,[71] an action brought by a local authority against the Secretary of State for Scotland and a reporter appointed by him to hold a local inquiry into a reservoir scheme, the pursuers sought interdict against the individual reporter from holding the inquiry and for interim interdict. It was held that an interim interdict against the individual reporter would be of little use as the Secretary of State could simply appoint another reporter to replace him.

Interim interdict

Interdicts may be permanent, applying without limit of time, or interim, 14–17 designed to preserve the status quo or prevent temporary or imminent wrong. The Court of Session Act 1988, s. 47 provides a statutory authority for the Inner House or the Lord Ordinary to grant interim interdict. The circumstances in which interim interdict will be granted include: restraining a public authority or body from doing some act which is *ultra vires* or a manifest abuse of power and which is likely to cause immediate and irreparable harm to any person[72]; preventing a public authority from doing any act which is prima facie a breach of its statutory authority[73]; and simply for the purpose of preserving the status quo. Interim interdict may be sought at any stage of a process for permanent interdict, either alone or with other legal remedies such as declarator and damages. Interim interdict is decided on the basis of the pleadings and it may be granted without the respondent being present. It is a discretionary remedy, the basic requirements for which are title and interest to sue, a prima facie case and a favourable balance of convenience.[74] An interim interdict was granted, in the case of *Meek v. Lothian Regional Council*,[75] against a local authority preventing it from supporting a publication known as the *Lothian Clarion* during a local election campaign. The interdict sought must be precise in its nature and wording and so framed that the party against whom it is granted may

[70] *Butler v. Registrar-General for Scotland*, 1962 S.L.T. (Notes) 12; *Ayr Magistrates v. Secretary of State for Scotland*, 1965 S.C. 394.
[71] 1965 S.C. 395.
[72] *Deane v. Lothian Regional Council*, 1986 S.L.T 22; *Meek v. Lothian Regional Council*, 1980 S.L.T. (Notes) 61; *Sleigh v. City of Edinburgh District Council*, 1989 S.C.L.R. 563; *Gordon v. Kirkcaldy District Council*, 1989 S.C.L.R. 90; *British Medical Association v. Greater Glasgow Health Board*, 1989 S.L.T. 493.
[73] *Wilson v. IBA*, 1979 S.L.T. 279; *J. Aitken & Sons v. Edinburgh District Council*, 1990 S.L.T. 241;*Pollok School v. Glasgow Town Clerk*, 1946 S.C. 373; *Innes v. Royal Burgh of Kirkcaldy*, 1963 S.L.T. 325: *McColl v. Strathclyde Regional Council*, 1983 S.L.T. 616.
[74] *Innes v. Royal Burgh of Kirkcaldy*, 1963 S.L.T. 325; *Brown v. Executive Committee of the Edinburgh District Labour Party*, 1995 S.L.T. 985.
[75] 1983 S.L.T. 494.

understand his rights and the restrictions placed upon him.[76] Lord Emslie stated that: "Where interdict is granted by the Court, the terms of the interdict must be no wider than is necessary to curb the illegal actings complained of and so precise and clear that the person interdicted is left in no doubt what he is forbidden to do."[77]

14–18   When interim interdict is granted it is done *periculo petentio*: that is, the party who has obtained the interim interdict will be liable in damages to the other party if, at the final determination of the case, the court holds him not entitled to interdict and the other party has suffered loss by reason of being temporarily prevented from carrying on the acts complained of.[78] In the case of *Bonnes v. West Lothian District Council*,[79] Bonnes sought interim interdict and suspension of planning permission granted by the local planning authority to the owner of an adjoining property, for a two-storey extension to his house. Bonnes claimed that he had not received a neighbour notification of the neighbour's application before permission was granted and had therefore been denied the opportunity to object. The extension would have a serious effect on Bonnes' amenity by blocking light. However, the neighbour had already purchased materials and building had begun. It was held that interim interdict should be granted. It was clear that Bonnes had a prima facie case in that he had not been given opportunity to object. The balance of convenience was in Bonnes' favour. If building works were allowed to proceed the existence of a fully constructed extension would be bound to affect the decision on a second application. The neighbour would have a remedy of damages for wrongful interdict if Bonnes' claims were found to be wrong.

Despite the speed of judicial review procedure in the Court of Session, circumstances may still arise where petitioners seek interim interdict pending the outcome of the petition for reduction if that is the only way to preserve the petitioner's rights. Interdict may be refused or recalled in the public interest,[80] or on an undertaking by the respondent which is acceptable to the court.[81] The interim interdict will, of course, be recalled if the respondent successfully challenges the petitioner's case in the subsequent hearing. Breach of interdict constitutes a challenge to the authority and supremacy of the court and is punishable by admonition, fine or imprisonment.[82] It is unclear what sanction is available when it is a public body such as a local authority which is in breach of interdict. It is, of course, assumed that public

[76] *Kelso School Board v. Hunter* (1874) 2 R. 228, *per* Lord Deas at 232.
[77] *Murdoch v. Murdoch,* 1973 S.L.T. (Notes) 13.
[78] *Stair Memorial Encyclopaedia*, Vol. 13, para. 19.
[79] 1994 G.W.D. 31-1888.
[80] *Alexander v. Traffic Commissioners for Southern Scotland*, 1936 S.N. 38.
[81] *Campbell v. Edinburgh and Glasgow Rly.* (1855) 17 D. 790.
[82] *Johnson v. Grant,* 1923 S.C. 789; *Macleay v. Mcdonald,* 1928 S.C. 776.

bodies would never intend wilfully to act in breach of interdict and therefore the more serious sanctions would not be required.

Interdict against the Crown

Interdict is not available against the Crown in Scotland. Prior to the Crown 14–19 Proceedings Act 1947 it was competent in Scotland to seek the remedy of interdict against the Crown and when an officer of the Crown was sued in that capacity this was regarded as being an action against the Crown.[83] Section 21 of the Crown Proceedings Act 1947 provides that: "Where in any proceedings against the Crown any such relief is sought as might in proceedings between subjects be granted by way of injunction or specific performance, the court shall not grant an injunction or make an order for specific performance, but may in lieu thereof make an order declaratory of the rights of the parties." In the case of *Mcdonald v. Secretary of State for Scotland*,[84] the Inner House confirmed that the effect of the Crown Proceedings Act 1947, s. 21 in Scotland, is that interdict cannot be obtained against the Crown or a minister of the Crown. In circumstances where, but for the fact that the defender is the Crown, an interdict would have been granted, the court may instead make an order declaring the rights between the parties.[85]

SUSPENSION

Suspension is a summary procedure at common law to stay or arrest some 14–20 single act or proceeding complained of, and to preserve the *status quo* pending a final decision. Suspension differs from interdict in that it does not have any effect in relation to repetition of an act and for that purpose interdict is the necessary remedy. Suspension is therefore often used in conjunction with interdict to prevent infringement of a right. In the case of *Sharp v. Latheron Parochial Board*,[86] the remedy of suspension was granted where subjects were entered twice in the valuation roll without the knowledge of the proprietor. The assessor had failed to send him copies of the entries as required by statutory procedure. Suspension and interdict may be appropriate where the proceedings of a lower court or a tribunal are shown to be outside its statutory powers. It has been held that suspension may not be sought if advantage has not been taken of other opportunities

---

[83] *Somerville v. Lord Advocate* (1893) 20 R. 105; *Smith v. Lord Advocate,* 1932 S.L.T. 374; *Wilson v. 1st Edinburgh City Royal Garrison Artillery Volunteers* (1904) 12 S.L.T. 488; (1904) 7 F. 168.
[84] 1994 S.L.T. 692.
[85] Crown Proceedings Act 1947, ss. 21(a) and 23(a) as applied to Scotland by s. 43(a).
[86] (1883) 10 R. 1163.

for review.[87] Although suspension is mentioned specifically in Rule of Court 58.3 in relation to judicial review it is unlikely to be used frequently.[88] There is little recent case law to suggest that use is common. Interdict in modern practice is taken as the generally available remedy for the prevention of a wrong, of whatever nature, being done.

Interim suspension may be awarded as a remedy in combination with interim interdict. In *Brown v. Executive Committee of Edinburgh Labour Party*,[89] interim interdict and suspension were granted in respect of disciplinary proceedings against nine Labour councillors by a District Labour Party when there was evidence of an apparent bias caused by pre-judgment of the issues by some of the members of the disciplinary committee. It was held that interim interdict and suspension can be granted only if two requirements are satisfied. First, there should exist a prima facie case for such remedies, and secondly, the balance of convenience must favour a grant. The conditions were fulfilled in that case as there was prima facie evidence of a breach of natural justice and the balance of convenience was in favour of granting the remedies, as otherwise the councillors would have to await the outcome of appeal procedures and, meanwhile, being excluded from the political party, could lose the opportunity to stand for election in the local elections.

IMPLEMENT

14–21 Implement is an order of the court to do or perform some act which the defender or respondent should have done in the course of fulfilling a legal duty incumbent on him. This is an aspect of the role of the Court of Session in the performance of its supereminent jurisdiction as the supreme civil court of the country. In the case of *Forbes v. Underwood*,[90] it was held that the Court of Session, and only the Court of Session, has power to compel a person to fulfil a duty. The case related to the appointment of an arbiter and Lord President Inglis said:

> "The position of an arbiter is very much like that of a Judge in many respects, and there is no doubt whatever that whenever an inferior judge, no matter what kind, fails to perform his statutory duty, either by going beyond his jurisdiction, or by failing to exercise his jurisdiction when called upon to do so by a party entitled to come before him, there is a remedy in this Court and the inferior judge ... may be ordered by this Court to go on and perform his duty, and if he fails to do so he will be liable to imprisonment as on a decree ad factum praestandum."[91]

---

[87] *West Highland Rly v. Grant* (1902)10 S.L.T. 413.
[88] Act of Sederunt (Rules of the Court of Session) 1994 (S.I. 1994 No. 1443), Chap. 58.
[89] 1995 S.L.T. 985.
[90] (1886) 13 R. 465.
[91] *ibid.* at 467.

In addition to the power of implement at common law, a general power of implement is laid down in the Court of Session Act 1988, s. 45(b).[92] which provides that the court, upon application by summary petition, may order the specific performance of any statutory duty under such conditions and penalties (including fine and imprisonment where consistent with the statute) in the event of the order not being implemented as to the court shall seem proper. The remedy can be sought where a clear, definite duty is laid by statute (whether expressly or by necessary implication) upon some definite body or individual on whom the court can lay its hand and order the specific performance of the duty. It must be clear that the statute is imposing a duty, not merely conferring a power. The allusion in the statute to fines and even imprisonment for disobedience to the order "where consistent with the statute" relates to circumstances where a duty is imposed in the public interest upon private individuals rather than public bodies or public officials in their official capacity. Where the respondent is a local authority the court may make a finding as to its statutory duty. This occurred in the case of *Docherty v. Burgh of Monifieth*,[93] where the local authority was ordained to perform their statutory duty under the Burgh Police (Scotland) Act 1892 to construct sewers to the borders of land owned by Docherty.

An additional power is conferred by the Court of Session Act 1988, s. 46, which provides that where a respondent in proceedings has done an act which the court may have prohibited by interdict, the court may order the respondent to perform any act necessary to reinstate the complainer in a possessory right or to grant specific relief against the illegal act in question.

DAMAGES

Although it is competent to seek damages in judicial review cases these are awarded in restricted circumstances only, either where a statutory duty is expressed so as to give rise to liability in damages or where there is common law duty of care. The Scottish Law Commission memorandum on remedies in administrative law observed that liability for breach of statutory duty in relation to unlawful action by administrative authorities has tended to be restricted to circumstances in which there may be liability at common law for physical injury caused by negligence but public authorities and officials who fail to perform a statutory duty may be liable in damages.[94] Whether a particular statute can be enforced this way is a matter for judicial interpretation and may depend, *inter alia*, on whether the statute provides a

14–22

---

[92] Formerly Court of Session Act 1868, s. 91.
[93] 1970 S.C. 200.
[94] Scot. Law Com. Memo. *op. cit.,* n. 27, above p. 42.

Administrative Law

particular means of enforcing the duty.[95] The duty must be a ministerial one, which means that it must involve an administrative, rather than a judicial function. Although not every administrative function will give rise to liability for breach of statutory duty,[96] breach of the duty imposed on housing authorities to house the homeless under acts such as the Housing (Homeless Persons) Act 1977 has been held to give rise to liability in damages.[97] The liability of the Crown for the delictual acts of Crown servants under section 2 (1) of the Crown Proceedings Act 1947 is the same as that of a private person of full age and capacity. Public authorities can be held liable for negligent advice or for the negligent discharge of their functions. In the case of *Ministry of Housing v. Sharp*,[98] it was held that an individual who relied to his detriment on inaccurate statements made to him by a public official in the course of his duties had a remedy in damages against both the official and his employing authority.

STATUTORY REMEDIES

14–23 Where there is a statutory provision for a right of appeal the statute, in addition to indicating the procedure for the appeal, will indicate the remedies available. A right of appeal under a statute is usually to the sheriff court but appeal may lie to a Government Minister. In 1977 the Committee of Ministers of the Council of Europe adopted Resolution (77) 31 entitled "On the Protection of The Individual in relation to the Acts of Administrative Authorities". This resolution recommended that the Governments of Member States should be guided in their law and administrative practice by five principles set out in the annex to the resolution. Principle number five relates to indication of remedies and states that: " Where an administrative act in written form adversely affects the rights, liberties, or interests of the person concerned, it should indicate the normal remedies against it (including the applicable time limits)." The use of the word "remedies" in the resolution includes the procedures by which the remedy is sought as well as the remedy which is provided as the outcome of any proceedings. The resolution deliberately abstained from indicating what sanction should be attached to a failure to comply with the principles and the matter was left to be dealt with by domestic rules.[99] The effect of this has been that there is an indication of both the procedure to be used and the

---

[95] Report of the Committee of the Justice-All Souls Review of Administrative Law in the United Kingdom, "Administrative Justice: Some Necessary Reforms" (1988), p. 335.

[96] *X v. Bedfordshire C.C.* [1994] 2 W.L.R. 554.

[97] *Mallon v. Monklands D.C.*, 1986 S.L.T. 347; *Thornton v. Kirklees MBC* [1979] Q.B. 626; *Kelly v. Monklands D.C.*, 1986 S.L.T. 169.

[98] [1970] 2 Q.B. 223.

[99] Report of the Committee of the Justice-All Souls Review, *op. cit.*, above, n. 95, pp. 9–10.

remedy available in a wide and increasing range of statutes. The statutory remedy may consist simply of a power to quash an order or decision. There is, for example, a statutory appeal against certain decisions in relation to town and country planning.[1] The court may make an interim order to suspend the operation of the order either generally or only so far as it will affect the applicant's property. The court will take into account the same factors which it would take into account in granting an interim interdict. If the application is successful the court may quash the order or decision, either in whole or in so far as it affects the property of the applicant. Other remedies, such as declarator and damages are not available under the statutory appeal procedure.

A right of appeal to the sheriff court is provided in several statutory provisions relating to local government functions, inlcuding matters relating to licensing.[2] The extent of the jurisdiction of the sheriff court will depend on the individual statute but there are instances where, as the sheriff court is exercising an appellate jurisdiction, it may consider the merits of the case and may substitute a fresh decision in place of the one which has been challenged.[3] The remedy of reduction is not available in the sheriff court, but depending on the relevant statutory provision, all of the other ordinary remedies may be available.

REMEDIES IN ENGLISH LAW

The most important remedies which are available at common law in English 14–24 administrative law are the remedies known as prerogative remedies. They are called "prerogative remedies" because they were originally available only to the Crown and not the citizen. The Crown could use orders of certiorari, mandamus or prohibition to ensure that public authorities carried out their duties and did not exceed their powers. These remedies are now available to the subject in addition to private law remedies such as declaration, damages and injunction which may be suitable for the resolution of some administrative disputes. Certiorari and prohibition are remedies used to control powers of public authorities and mandamus is a remedy for enforcing public duties.[4] Until 1977 there was a strict division between the procedures for the granting of prerogative and ordinary remedies which caused unnecessary complications in procedural rules and caused gaps and anomalies. Although this division has been removed and there is now a judicial review procedure, the dichotomy between the principles of public and private law in English law still causes procedural problems.

---

[1] Town and Country Planning (Scotland) Act 1997.
[2] Civic Government (Scotland) Act 1982; Licensing (Scotland) Act 1976.
[3] Grant Committee, Report of the Committee on the Sheriff Court, Cmnd. 3248 (1967).
[4] For further reading, see Wade and Forsyth, *Administrative Law* (7th ed., 1994), Chaps. 16 and 17.

The existence of special remedies for public law disputes may have advantages but the fact that the remedies for judicial review in Scots law are the ordinary private law remedies, all available under the same procedure, provides a simple system which provides a judge with sufficient flexibility to give the best remedy in each individual case before him.

CHAPTER 15

LIABILITY OF THE CROWN AND PUBLIC AUTHORITIES

INTRODUCTION

In the course of carrying out its functions the Government enters into a   15–01
range of contracts. It owns land, it employs staff, it purchases equipment
and enters into contracts of sale. Public authorities operating under statutory
authority have a diverse range of functions which involve entering into
legal relationships with other public authorities, commercial and non-
commercial organisations and with individual citizens. According to the
doctrine of the rule of law, public authorities should be subject to the same
rules of liability in contract and delict as private individuals and companies.
In explaining this concept of equality before the law Dicey said: "With us
every official, from the Prime Minister down to a constable or a collector
of taxes, is under the same responsibility for every act done without legal
justification as any other citizen."[1] It is unfair for a person who has entered
into a contract with a government organisation to be denied the access to
justice and redress that he would have enjoyed had his contract been with a
private individual. A person who is injured or who suffers loss because of
the fault of another should not be denied compensation simply because the
person or body at fault is part of the Government. It is all the more important
that the Government should be subject to the ordinary law because in the
United Kingdom there is no separate law of administrative liability for
wrongful acts by public bodies and no special provision of administrative
courts such as the Droit Administratif in France.

Despite the requirement that, in order to maintain a just and equitable
society, a person who suffers an infringement of rights because of a wrongful
exercise of power should have access to a remedy, the extent to which the
Crown will be liable for a breach of contract is not necessarily the same as
in the case of a private individual. Although the powers given to public
authorities in order to carry out their functions often enable them to infringe
the private rights of others, there are exceptions to the liability of public
authorities and the Crown in delict.

---

[1]   Dicey, *The Law of the Constitution* (Wade ed.) (10th ed., 1995), p.193.

LIABILITY OF THE CROWN IN CONTRACT

15–02   Historically, there were differences between the laws of Scotland and England with regard to the amenability of the Crown to litigation for breach of contract. In Scotland it has always been possible to sue the Crown for breach of contract or in respect of contract in the Court of Session. The common law principle that the Crown could sue and be sued in the courts was given statutory force by the Crown Suits (Scotland) Act 1857, described in its preamble as "An Act to regulate the Institution of Suits at the Instance of the Crown and the Public Departments in the Courts of Scotland". Section 1 of the Act provided: "Every action, suit or proceeding to be instituted in Scotland on behalf of or against her Majesty or in the interest of the Crown, or on behalf of or against any public department, may be lawfully raised in the name of and at the instance of or directed against Her Majesty's Advocate for the time being acting under this Act." It is not necessary for the individual office-holder to be named in the action as section 5 provides: "Nothing in this Act contained shall affect the instance or defence of any action, suit or proceeding instituted or that may be instituted in conformity with law existing at the date of passing of this Act; and no action, suit, or proceeding raised or to be raised at the instance of or against Her Majesty's Advocate for the time being shall abate or be affected by any change in the person holding the office of Her Majesty's Advocate." In the case of *Lord Advocate v. Black*,[2] a challenge was raised to the competency of an action by the Lord Advocate as representing Her Majesty's Commissioners of Customs and Excise because the name of the Lord Advocate had not been included. The individual against whom the action had been raised argued that the action was incompetent in that the Lord Advocate had no legal persona and could not competently sue him. It was held the action was competent since, as section 5 of the Crown Suits Act demonstrated, the identity of the Lord Advocate was not of the essence. It had long been established practice not to name the individual in cases where he was suing as a representative of the Crown covered by the Crown Suits (Scotland) Act 1857. The Lord Advocate would, however, require to be named if he was suing in any other capacity.

PETITION OF RIGHT

15–03   In contrast to the position in Scotland, in England, prior to 1947, an action against the Crown for breach of contract was only possible by means of a petition of right. A direct action against the Crown in England was not possible because of the presumption that "the King can do no wrong". In order to allow certain actions to be taken against the Crown a device had to be used whereby the Crown consented to allow action to be taken against

---

[2]   1995 S.L.T. 540.

it. This was a petition to the Crown by the subject for his just rights, which was voluntarily referred by the Crown to the courts for a decision. The person concerned had, first of all, to obtain the consent of the Crown. The case was then tried by the courts in the normal way except that the judgment took the form of a declaration of the rights of the individual. There was no way of enforcing this legally but, in practice, the Crown always respected such a decision. There was no remedy if the Crown refused to give consent but in practice consent was given whenever a subject had a possible claim.

CROWN PROCEEDINGS ACT 1947

The purpose of the Crown Proceedings Act 1947 was to provide for redress   15–04
against the Crown through ordinary litigation where it had not previously been available. Section 1 of the Crown Proceedings Act 1947 (which does not apply to Scotland) provides that any person having a claim against the Crown which previously might have been enforced by petition of right may now proceed directly against the Crown. This does not, however, render the Crown liable for breach of contract in the same way in which a private person would be liable. In the case of *Commissioners of Crown Lands v. Page*,[3] a tenant of land sought relief from the obligation to pay rent when he could not occupy the land. Page occupied the land under lease from the Crown. The land was requisitioned by a Government department and Page withheld payment of rent, claiming that he had been evicted. He was found liable to continue to make payments under the terms of the lease as the Crown is not liable under a contract with a private person for actions taken by the Government in the national interest. Devlin L.J. observed: "When the Crown, in dealing with one of its subjects, is dealing as if it too were a private person, and is granting leases or buying and selling as ordinary persons do, it is absurd to suppose that it is making any promise about the way in which it will conduct the affairs of the nation."

Although the Crown Proceedings Act did not alter the liability of the   15–05
Crown under contract law in Scotland it does have relevance to some issues of contract law in Scotland. Section 50(2)(d), for example, provides that a Government department cannot set debts owed to another Government department against a claim made against the department without the consent of the court. In the case of *Smith v. Lord Advocate*,[4] the liquidator of Upper Clyde Shipbuilders Ltd raised an action against the Lord Advocate, as representing the Ministry of Defence, for payment of £1,353,369 due to Upper Clyde Shipbuilders by the Ministry. The Lord Advocate admitted that that sum was owed to the pursuer but sought leave under section 50(2)(d)

---

[3]   [1960] 2 Q.B. 274.
[4]   1980 S.C. 227; 1981 S.L.T. 19.

of the Crown Proceedings Act 1947 to set off against that sum four debts owed by Upper Clyde Shipbuilders to other Government departments. The Lord Ordinary refused to grant leave to the Lord Advocate who appealed against his decision. It was held that there were no circumstances which could properly justify a refusal to grant the leave sought by the Crown under section 50 of the Crown Proceedings Act 1947; and that the appeal should be allowed and leave should be granted to the Crown to set off the liabilities. It was observed that in common law and practice the Crown is regarded as an indivisible entity, the source and repository of the powers and duties of Government, and that the Lord Advocate is the representative of the Crown.

LIABILITY IN DELICT

LIABILITY OF INDIVIDUAL PUBLIC SERVANTS

15–06 Every individual is liable for his own wrongful acts and omissions. Therefore, any person who is not protected by statutory immunity can be sued for damages for negligence or breach of statutory duty. The most famous instance of this is the case of *Entick v. Carrington.*[5] King's messengers had broken into Entick's house and seized papers. They pleaded as a defence that they were acting under a warrant from the Secretary of State. It was held that this was no defence as the Secretary of State had no authority to issue the warrant. Superior orders will therefore not be a defence to an individual unless he is:

(a) Acting under the authority of a court acting within its jurisdiction, or
(b) Protected by statutory immunity whilst acting bona fide in the course of his duties.

Although a person who has suffered a loss because of the wrongful actions of a public official will usually prefer to sue the employing authority as being vicariously liable for the wrongful acts and omissions of its employee, there are some situations where an officer of central or local Government has an independent statutory authority by virtue of his office, because a statute imposes a duty on him as a designated officer rather than on the public authority which appoints him.[6] It was held in the case of *Stanbury v. Exeter Corporation*[7] that a local authority was not vicariously liable when their inspector of animals had seized sheep which he had believed were diseased. The inspector was acting under a statutory duty which was conferred on him by reason of his office and not on the authority which

---

[5]	(1765) 19 St. Tr. 1030.
[6]	Wade and Forsyth, *Administrative Law* (7th ed., 1994), p. 764.
[7]	[1905] 2 K.B. 838.

employed him. This was a case where the duty was carried out by one official but if the duty is one which is delegated to the employees of a local authority other than the designated official then the local authority may be liable for wrongful acts of omissions. In the case of *Ministry of Housing and Local Government v. Sharp*[8], it was held that an authority was liable where an employee had negligently certified that there were no local land charges registered against land which was being sold. The statutory duty of issuing certificates was imposed on the clerk to the local authority as registrar but, as it was a function which was in practice delegated to other employees, the local authority was vicariously liable.

ACTS AND DECISIONS GIVING RISE TO LIABILITY IN DELICT

Liability will arise only if there has been an act which amounts to a legal   15–07
wrong. In the case of *Malone v. Metropolitan Police Commissioner*,[9] it was held that no damages could be awarded at common law for the interception of telephone calls, which was held not to be a delict.[10]

DISTINCTION BETWEEN POLICY AND OPERATIONS

The formulation of a policy which may cause harm to others will not   15–08
necessarily lead to a liability on the part of the Crown to pay compensation, unless of course the decision to formulate that policy is *ultra vires*. However, the negligent operation of activities authorised by that policy may give rise to liability in negligence. In the case of *Dorset Yacht Company v. Home Office*,[11] it was held that a duty of care was owed by Borstal officers to neighbouring property owners. The Home Office was sued for the value of a yacht which had been damaged when seven borstal boys absconded at night from a borstal summer camp on an island in Poole Harbour. The plaintiffs, the owners of a yacht, claimed that the borstal officers had been negligent. The Home Office argued that the system of open borstals was authorised and would be jeopardised if liability was imposed on the Government for the wrongful acts of those who absconded. It was held that the Home Secretary could not be held liable for the policy which set up the regime in operation at the borstal. The borstal officers, however, owed a duty of care to the plaintiff to exercise proper supervision of the borstal boys in their care since it was reasonably foreseeable that damage to the plaintiff's property (a yacht in Poole Harbour) would be likely to occur if

---

[8]   [1970] 2 Q.B. 223.
[9]   [1980] Q.B. 49.
[10]   Compensation for wrongful telephone tapping may now be payable under the Interception of Communications Act 1985.
[11]   [1970] A.C. 1004.

the officers failed to exercise proper control or supervision. Lord Reid said that there would be no liability for the way in which a statutory power was exercised unless the person exercising the power had departed so far from its terms as to be outside it altogether. In other words it would need to be proved that they were not only acting negligently but also *ultra vires*. It was held that the Home Office was liable for the negligence of the officers. There was no ground in public policy for granting immunity to the Home office or its officers and damages were awarded. They owed a duty of care to the yacht owners, the damage to the yacht being a reasonable foreseeable consequence of a failure to take reasonable care.

15–09   In considering the differences between liabilities for the formulation of policy and liability for their operation Lord Diplock said that, in exercising his rule-making power, it would be inconsistent with what are now recognised principles of law to suggest that the Home Secretary owed a duty of care capable of giving rise to any liability in civil law to avoid making a rule the observance of which was likely to result in damage to a private citizen. For a careless exercise of his rule-making power he is responsible to Parliament alone. The only limitation on this power which courts of law have jurisdiction to enforce depends not on the civil law concept of negligence but on the public concept of *ultra vires*.

In accordance with this principle, in the case of *Bonthrone v. Secretary of State for Scotland*,[12] it was held that, where the exercise of a statutory power confers a discretion as to the manner in which it is to be exercised, then if the discretion is exercised within the ambit of the power, and in good faith, a person who suffers a loss as a result of the exercise of the power will not have an action of damages against the authority which exercised it. Lord Grieve said that the duty of care in exercising a statutory power "does not arise until the discretionary stage of its exercise has ceased and the executive stage has begun".

15–10   This approach to Crown liability was also evident in *Shetland Line v. Secretary of State for Scotland*.[13] The case related to subsidies paid to shippers of freight to the Northern Isles. The Secretary of State had power, under the Highlands and Islands Shipping Services Act 1960, to operate a discretionary scheme of subsidies. Applicant companies submitted freight projections for each financial year from which the Secretary of State calculated the rate of subsidy. Two shipping companies submitted projections for three financial years which were understated due to their being based on wrong information provided by the Scottish Office. Other companies had submitted projections which had been made on the correct basis, and this resulted in the two companies' subsidies under the scheme being less than if their projections had been correctly submitted. The two companies

---

[12]   1987 S.L.T. 34. See also *Ross v. Secretary of State for Scotland*, 1990 S.L.T. 13.
[13]   1996 S.L.T. 653.

brought a petition for judicial review in which they sought reduction of the decisions of the Secretary of State fixing the rates for the relevant three years. It was not suggested that the Secretary of State had acted in bad faith. It was argued that, if the court decided that the decisions were spent and so could not be reduced, the petition should be continued so that remedies of declarator and damages for negligence could be sought. It was held that damages could not be awarded in respect of the consequences of a decision of a Minister of the Crown in the absence of misfeasance or an abuse of power amounting to bad faith, although a duty of care might arise in respect of the manner in which a power was exercised. Lord Johnston said that:

> "The concept of a duty of care being owed by a Minister to a potential recipi-
> ent of a decision in making that decision the breach of which will admit, if it
> on the facts can be said to be negligent, a claim for damages by the latter is
> novel to the current law of Scotland. In so far as text books may refer to
> negligence being actionable, in my opinion they are looking at situations
> where the way in which the power in question is being exercised amount to
> a breach of duty of care which it can be said to be owed by reason of the
> relationship between the parties or the context in which the public body or
> Minister is operating. There is to my mind a clear distinction between the
> manner in which a particular power may be exercised particularly when physi-
> cal consequences may occur, *i.e.* personal injury and the way in which a
> Minister sets about making a decision and informing himself of the basic
> facts that relate to that. The former may in itself create a situation which
> could be categorised as negligence and give rise to a duty of care, the latter
> as I understand the present law does not do so."

VICARIOUS LIABILITY OF PUBLIC AUTHORITIES

Unless they are acting within their powers public officials are liable in the   15–11
same way as any other person for delicts such as nuisance, negligence and
defamation. Actions against individual officials serve little purpose and a
better prospect of adequate damages is provided by suing the relevant
employer who will be regarded as vicariously liable. It was established in
England in 1866 that the vicarious liability of a public body whose servants
are negligent in the course of carrying out their duties is the same as the
liability of any private organisation. In the case of *Mersey Docks and
Harbour Board Trustees v. Gibb*,[14] damages were claimed from the Harbour
Board Trustees. A ship and its cargo were damaged because a mud bank
had been left negligently at the entrance to a dock. The trustees had been
held liable but appealed to the House of Lords as they were not a commercial
organisation making profits. The House of Lords held that the trustees were

---

[14]   (1866) L.R. 1 (H.L.) 93.

nevertheless under a duty of care to ensure that safe navigation of the docks was possible. Historically, the approach by the courts in Scotland was more open to delictual actions against public bodies, including the Crown. There were some nineteenth-century differences in the House of Lords in relation to cases brought against non-Crown authorities but these were eventually resolved in favour of holding them liable in reparation.

In the case of *Cassidy v. Minister of Health*,[15] it was held that a hospital authority is liable for the negligent acts of doctors employed by the authority in the performance of their professional duties. In the case of *Allen v. Bloomsbury Health Authority*,[16] a negligence claim succeeded against the health authority for failing to diagnose that a patient was pregnant at the time of her sterilisation operation. Damages were awarded for economic loss based on the anticipated costs of the child's upbringing.[17] There are also specific statutory provisions confirming that a public body is vicariously liable for the wrongful acts or omissions of those carrying out operations, for example, the Police (Scotland) Act 1967, s. 39, provides that a chief constable is vicariously liable for the acts committed by police officers in the performance of their functions.

Liability for negligence

15–12　When actions are being carried out by or on behalf of a public authority or official under statutory authority there is a presumption that the actions are to be carried out lawfully. There can never be a presumption that Parliament intended to authorise activities to be carried out in a negligent manner. Persons working under statutory authority are under a duty to exercise the standard of care which would be expected of a reasonably competent member of their trade or profession. In the case of *Geddis v. Proprietors of Bann Reservoir*,[18] a reservoir company was held to be liable for a negligent failure to clean a stream. The stream had become blocked causing flooding to neighbouring property. Lord Blackburn said: "it is now thoroughly well established that no action will lie for doing that which the legislature has authorised, if it be done without negligence, although it does occasion damage to anyone; but an action does lie for doing what the legislature has authorised, if it be done negligently".[19]

In an action against the fire brigade which failed because of lack of proof of negligence, it was held that the fire brigade is under a duty of care to owners of property. The claim for damages in the case of *Duff v. Highland*

---

[15]　[1951] 2 K.B. 343.
[16]　[1993] 1 All E.R. 651.
[17]　The Scottish courts have refused to follow this case holding that the benefit of having a child outweighs any costs which may result.
[18]　[1873] 3 A.C. 430.
[19]　*ibid.* at 455.

and Islands Fire Board[20] arose because a fire in a chimney was attended to by the fire brigade but restarted after they had left, causing the destruction of the house. It had been argued on behalf of the fire brigade that considerations of public policy prevented there being any duty of care owed by the brigade towards owners of property. In any event the only loss which could be recovered would be loss beyond the loss which would have been sustained had the fire brigade never attended at all. It was held, however, distinguishing the position of fire-fighters from that of the police, that fire-fighters did owe a duty of care as there was a statutory duty imposed on fire authorities to make provision for fire fighting purposes; and that damages for breach of the duty extended to all the loss resulting from the negligence.[21]

Where the activities which give rise to liability for negligence comprise the provision of services such as roads, drains or sewers it is easy to establish the nature of the duty of care and the persons to whom that duty is owed. Matters are not so straightforward when the claim of negligence arises from the discretionary role of inspection or regulation carried out by a public authority. For some years there was an extension of the law in England which rendered a public authority liable for negligence in the performance of a regulatory function. It was held that, where local building inspectors failed to inspect, and then failed to inspect properly, the foundations of a new building, negligence by the council officials rendered the council liable for the cost of repairing the building. A block of flats developed cracks because it had been built on inadequate foundations. The council had a discretion whether or not to carry out inspections but once they exercised the discretion to carry out inspections, they were liable for any negligence in their operations.[22] The House of Lords held that negligence by council officials rendered the council liable for the cost of repairing the building. Lord Wilberforce drew a distinction between the actions of a public authority which could be described as the adoption of a discretionary policy and those which could be described as operational. Operational actions involve "practical execution of policy decisions". Where an authority is acting in the area of discretionary policy, it will not be liable for negligence unless it can be proved that it was acting not only negligently but also *ultra vires*. In operational matters the duty of care is easier to establish. 15–13

In Scotland, although the decision in *Anns v. Merton Council* had some influence it was more cautiously accepted than in other parts of the United Kingdom. The reasoning in *Anns* was very logical but, as *Anns* was followed by a series of decisions which attempted to limit the wide duties of care which it established, the consequence was uncertainty as to the principles to be applied and a dependence on judicial discretion. Public authorities 15–14

---

20 1995 S.L.T. 1362.
21 See also *East Suffolk Rivers Catchment Board v. Kent* [1941] A.C. 74.
22 *Anns v. London Borough of Merton* [1978] A.C. 728.

have been protected from liability, either by categorising actions of public authorities as "policy" and so not giving rise to liability,[23] or by finding that a duty of care has not been established[24] or by finding that liability will only arise if a statutory power has been exercised improperly. In the Scottish case of *Hallett v. Nicholson*,[25] it was held that where there is statutory authority there will be no liability on the part of the organisation for damages for acts or omissions committed in the proper exercise of its statutory duties or powers. However, liability would arise in respect of an act or omission committed in the course of an improper exercise of the authority's statutory powers. A statutory power or duty would be regarded as having been exercised improperly where it was not exercised in good faith in the interests of the public within the limits of any statutory discretion, or where it was not exercised in accordance with the statute. A failure to exercise a statutory power in accordance with the statute would include performing an authorised act in an unauthorised manner, which might include a negligent manner. The case arose following a fire in an Oban hotel in which a husband and wife had died. The hoteliers were sued by the children on the grounds that they had failed to take reasonable care for the safety of the guests by providing adequate fire precautions. The hoteliers claimed that, under the terms of the Fire Precautions Act 1971, s. 5(3) the fire authority was bound to carry out an inspection of the hotel in order to award a fire certificate. They would, therefore, have been aware of the extent of the fire risk and should have advised the hoteliers not to reopen. The fire authority averred that only if the inspection was in response to a request for advice would they have been under a duty to advise the hotel of fire risks. The same duty did not apply to inspections for fire certificates. It was held that the local authority was not liable.

15–15   A statutory duty or power is regarded as exercised improperly where it is not exercised bona fide in the interests of the public, within the limits of any statutory discretion, or where it is not exercised in accordance with the statute or if actings authorised by statute have been carried out in a biased way[26] or without taking reasonable precautions to avoid harm.[27] The case of *Rowling v. Takaro Properties Ltd*[28] was a decision of the Judicial Committee of the Privy Council. The plaintiff owned a tourist lodge in New Zealand. After several years' unsuccessful trading he drew up a financial rescue package which included the sale of some shares to a Japanese company. This required the consent of the Minister of Finance

---

[23] *Ross v. Secretary of State for Scotland*, 1990 S.L.T. 13.
[24] *Gibson v. Strathclyde Regional Council*, 1992 S.C.L.R. 902.
[25] 1979 S.C. 1.
[26] Wilson v. IBA, 1979 S.L.T. 279.
[27] *Gillespie v. Lucas & Aird* (1893) 20 R. 1035.
[28] [1988] A.C. 473.

who refused to give his consent. An action for judicial review had been allowed on the basis that the Minister's refusal had been motivated by an irrelevant consideration of putting the land back into native New Zealand ownership. The Privy Council case was an appeal against an award of damages for breach of duty as the rescue package could no longer be implemented because of the delay. It was held that the distinction between policy and operations does not itself provide a touchstone of liability. The question is whether or not the case is suitable for judicial resolution, as in cases concerning the discretionary allocation of scarce resources or distribution of risks. Arguably, the only private law action which should have been allowed to succeed in these circumstances was an action for malicious abuse of power.

In 1991, a case similar to *Anns v. Merton Council* arose; that of *Murphy v.*   15–16
Brentwood Council,[29] and the House of Lords held that the *Anns* case had been wrongly decided. The defendant council owed no duty of care to the plaintiff when it approved the plans for defective foundations for his house. The decision in *Murphy* was apparently influenced by a reluctance to award damages for pure economic loss and by the view that a local authority with a responsibility to ensure compliance with building regulations should not be held to owe a common law duty of care to avoid losses of the type suffered by the plaintiff. The court is not willing for councils to take on a role as insurers for those who suffer losses where the primary fault is with a third party (in this case the builder). Economic loss will not in general be recoverable unless, either it is the result of negligent misstatement, and then only in limited circumstances,[30] or it is consequential on injury or property damage, although this will depend on the interpretation of the relevant statute in each case. It was not decided whether negligence in adMinistering building regulations might give rise to liability in the case of personal injury or damage to other property.

In the case of *Stovin v. Wise and Norfolk County Council*,[31] which related to an alleged breach of a common law duty of care owed by a local authority by failing to take reasonable measures to reduce the dangers to road users at a road junction, Lord Hoffman said that the distinction between policy and operations is an inadequate tool with which to discover whether it is appropriate to impose a duty of care or not. Even if the distinction is clear cut, leaving no element of discretion in the sense that it would be irrational for the public authority not to exercise its power it does not follow that the law should superimpose a common law duty of care. He stated:

---

[29] [1991] 1 A.C. 398.
[30] See *Hedley Byrne & Co. v. Heller & Partners Ltd* [1964] A.C. 465.
[31] [1996] A.C. 923; [1996] 3 All E.R. 801.

"This can be seen if one looks at cases in which a public authority has been under a statutory or common law duty to provide a service or other benefit for the public or a section of the public. In such cases there is no discretion but the courts have nevertheless been willing to hold that a member of the public who has suffered loss because the service was not provided to him should necessarily have a cause of action, either for breach of statutory duty or for negligence at common law."

Whether a statutory duty gives rise to a private cause of action depends on construction of the relevant statute. It requires an examination of the policy of the statute to decide whether it was intended to confer a right to compensation for breach.

Duty of care

15–17 Liability for negligence will only arise where it can be proved that the person at fault owed a duty of care to the person who suffered the loss or injury. A duty of care is not owed to the world at large but only to those to whom it is reasonably foreseeable that harm could be caused by a failure to take care. In the case of *Forbes v. City of Dundee District Council*,[32] damages were claimed from the local council for injuries sustained when Mrs Forbes fell down a flight of stairs. She claimed that the local authority was at fault for failing in its duty to take reasonable care to ensure that the stairs were built to comply with building regulations. It was observed that the council was not being sued as the designers, builders, owners or occupiers of the stairway. The persons who fell into those categories, and who might be regarded as responsible for the physical condition of the stairway were not parties to the action. It was held that Parliament did not intend any civil liability to arise from the Building (Scotland) Act 1959, the purpose of which was to enable a local authority to regulate building works. In order to establish that there is a duty of care it is necessary to show that there is a sufficiently determinate class of persons to whom a duty of care could be said to be owed. This class must be smaller that the public at large. It was held that in this case there was no such class to whom a duty of care could arise. It was observed that: "Given that a local authority has finite resources, and must exercise their discretion, in the public interest, as to how best to use those resources, I would regard it as a form of interference which would tend adversely to affect the sound exercise of this discretion if the local authority felt it necessary to protect itself against claims for civil liability in this way."

---

[32] O. H., February 12, 1997.

Need for a relationship of sufficient proximity

In addition to the principle that a duty of care is only owed to those to 15–18
whom it is reasonably foreseeable that harm would occur in the event of a
breach of duty it is necessary to establish that there is some relationship
between the person who has suffered the loss and the person who is under
the duty. In the case of *Yuen Kun Yeu v. Attorney-General*,[33] Lord Keith
referred to the judgment of Lord Wilberforce in *Anns v. Merton London
Borough Council*,[34] where Lord Wilberforce had said that duty of care in
delict would arise only where there was a relationship between the plaintiff
and the public authority of sufficient proximity. Lord Keith said that this
meant that, not only was there a test of reasonable foreseeability of harm,
but also that it was necessary to show a relationship between the plaintiff
and the public authority. Reasonable foreseeability of harm is not enough
on its own to establish a duty of care. The question to be considered was —
taking into account the nature and extent of relevant statutory powers, did
there exist between the public authority and the plaintiff such close and
direct relationship as to place the authority under a duty of care to the
plaintiff? The case of *Hill v. Chief Constable of West Yorkshire*[35] established
that the police are not liable for failure to apprehend an unknown criminal
before he committed further crimes. There needed to be proximity of
relationship in order for a duty of care to arise. The case was an action for
damages raised by the parent of one of the later victims of the serial killer
Peter Sutcliffe, known as the Yorkshire Ripper. It was alleged that the police
had been negligent in not apprehending the killer earlier in the investigation.
It was held, dismissing the plaintiff's appeal, that, in the absence of any
special relationship between the police and a criminal arising out of the
fact that the criminal was in police custody or had escaped from it,
the general duty owed by the police to suppress crime did not give rise to a
duty owed to individual members of the public in respect of damage caused
to them by a criminal whom the police had failed to apprehend where it had
been possible to do so. There was no special relationship between the police
and Sutcliffe since he had neither been in police custody nor escaped from
it. It was also held that, even if such a duty existed, it would be impossible
to define the class of persons at risk and in any event the harm committed
was too remote to constitute a breach of duty.

Even where it has been established that a statute was intended to create 15–19
a statutory duty which would give rise to a liability in damages, that liability
only extends to those who fall within the class of persons which the act was

---

[33] [1988] A.C. 175.
[34] [1978] A.C. 728.
[35] [1988] 2 All E.R. 238.

intended to protect or benefit. An individual who receives a benefit in consequence of the operation of a statute rather than as an intended recipient of a benefit or protection will not be entitled to damages. In the case of *X. v. Bedfordshire County Council*,[36] a claim for damages was brought against a local authority for breach of its duties under child care legislation. Abused children claimed that the authority was in breach of its duty to protect them from harm. The court concluded that the childcare legislation did not give rise to liability for breach of statutory duty. The purpose of the legislation was to establish an administrative system designed to promote the social welfare of the community. In such a context it would require exceptionally clear statutory language to show a parliamentary intention that there should be liability for breach of statutory duty.[37] In the case of *T. v. Surrey County Council*,[38] damages were claimed from a local authority for injuries inflicted on a child by a childminder. The local authority had failed to maintain its register of childminders and was therefore in breach of the Nurseries and Childminders Regulation Act 1948. The name of the childminder should have been removed from the register as she had been implicated in a previous case involving injury to a child in her care. However, it was held that the statutory duty in question did not give rise to a right of action at the instance of the injured party.

15–20   Similarly, in the case of *Armstrong v. Moore*[39] it was held that a building authority's regulatory function of ensuring compliance with building regulations did not create a duty of care to owners of neighbouring properties. The owners of properties within a tenement raised an action of damages against the builders of an adjoining building for losses caused by rainwater running off the gutter of the adjoining building on to the roof of the pursuers' tenement and making the tenement damp and uninhabitable. They also raised an action against the local building authority on the ground that the building authority had a duty not to issue a completion certificate in respect of buildings which would cause damage to neighbouring property. They also claimed that the authority had a duty to take reasonable care to ensure that the new tenement did not cause damage to the pursuers' property. It was held that the purpose of the building standards regulations was to secure the health and safety of those inhabiting the new building. There was no provision in the Building (Scotland) Act 1959 to indicate an intention to create a duty of care on the part of the authority towards the owners of other properties. There was no liability to make reparation even where the

---

[36]   [1994] 2 W.L.R. 554.
[37]   *M. v. Newham London Borough Council; X. v. Bedfordshire County Council* [1994] 2 W.L.R. 554.
[38]   [1994] 4 All E.R. 577.
[39]   1996 S.L.T. 690.

authority should have been aware that damage to the pursuers' property or health was foreseeable.

In the case of *R. v. Legal Aid Board, ex parte Amoo-Gottfried*,[40] Amoo-Gottfried claimed damages for breach of statutory duty by the Legal Aid Board which had failed to reinstate her on the duty solicitor scheme for a period following a decision that she had been unlawfully suspended. It was held that there was a breach of duty but that did not automatically entitle the injured party to damages. The breach of a statutory duty might give rise to a private law remedy if it could be shown in the legislation that Parliament intended to protect a limited class of the public and there was no other remedy stated in the legislation. The Legal Aid Board Duty Solicitor Arrangements 1992, however, were designed to benefit those who required assistance, not those who provided it, and no damages could be awarded.

Liability for breach of statutory duty

If a public authority fails to fulfil a statutory duty an action may be brought 15–21 under section 45 of the Court of Session Act 1988 to enforce performance of the duty. A public authority may also incur liability for injury or loss caused by the non-performance of the statutory duty. This principle was stated by the House of Lords in the case of *Ferguson v. Earl of Kinnoul*,[41] in which it was held that a presbytery was liable in damages for refusal to accept a presentee to a church. Lord Lyndhurst said: "When a person has an important duty to perform, he is bound to perform that duty; and if he neglects or refuses to do so, and an individual in consequence sustains injury, that lays the foundation for an action to recover damages by way of compensation for the injury that he has so sustained."[42]

Proof of negligence is not always necessary to establish a claim for breach of statutory duty. A statute may provide for stricter liability than common law. This will depend on the interpretation of the statutory provision which applies. In the case of *Mallon v. Monklands District Council*,[43] damages were awarded for psychiatric illness following a failure by a local authority to provide accommodation for a homeless person with a priority need and in *R. v. Lambeth London Borough Council, ex parte Barnes*,[44] it was held that the continued failure of a local authority to house an applicant for accommodation under Part 3 of the Housing Act 1985 was a breach of statutory duty which gave rise to liability in damages. Barnes had applied as a homeless person to her local authority who had accepted a duty to

[40] June 20, 1996; *The Independent*, July 29, 1996.
[41] (1842) 9 Cl. & F. 251.
[42] *ibid.* at 280.
[43] 1986 S.L.T. 347.
[44] (1992) 25 H.L.R. 140.

house her but failed to fulfil the duty. It was held that she was entitled to recover damages for the breach of statutory duty and also for the authority's negligence in failing to respond to correspondence for eight months.

15–22   Shortage of the resources which are required to fulfil statutory duties imposed on local authorities creates difficult problems. Local authorities have many statutory duties and are often placed in a position where they have to ration the services which they provide and even reduce the level of provision which they make in performing statutory duties. If they fail to fulfil a duty they may incur liability in delict where those duties are owed to identifiable individuals. Specific provision for remedies may be made in a statute but, if this is not the case then an action for damages at common law may be appropriate. The duties which may be enforceable by individuals include the duty to make adequate provision for disabled persons. In deciding whether there will be liability for a breach of statutory duty one approach is for the court to consider whether the legislation was passed primarily to protect a particular class of individuals. In the case of *R. v. Bexley London Borough Council, ex parte B.*,[45] Bexley, a severely disabled boy with quadriplegic cerebral palsy and deafness, applied for judicial review of the council's decision to reduce the number of care-hours provided for him each week. The court held that authorities are under an obligation to make provision under the Chronically Sick and Disabled Persons Act 1970 whenever they are satisfied that the relevant conditions have been met. The application failed for other reasons but the court observed that the duty laid upon authorities by section 2(1) of the 1970 Act was a duty, owed to a specific individual, breach of which is capable of giving rise to a remedy in tort. The very specific nature of the duties themselves means that they would readily be capable of evaluation in money terms

15–23   The House of Lords has considered the problems which face local authorities when there is a shortage of resources in the case of *R. v. Gloucestershire County Council and the Secretary of State for Health, ex parte Barry.*[46] The case was also related to the statutory duty to disabled persons under the Chronically Sick and Disabled Persons Act 1970. Section 2 of the Act provides that where a local authority is satisfied that a disabled person needs special arrangements, then the local authority is under a duty to make those arrangements. Mr Barry's needs were assessed and arrangements were made for home care, cleaning and laundry services and meals-on-wheels. In 1994 the council informed Mr Barry that it would no longer be able to provide him

---

[45] July 31, 1995.
[46] Conjoined appeals of *R. v. Gloucestershire County Council and the Secretary of State for Health, ex p. Barry* and *R. v. Gloucestershire County Council and Another, ex p. Barry*, House of Lords, March 20, 1997, unreported.

with his full needs as assessed. The reason was that the money allocated to the council by central Government had been reduced by £2.5 million. In a petition for judicial review it was held that the local authority was right to take account of resources, both when assessing needs and when deciding on the arrangements which it will make to meet those needs, but the Court of Appeal allowed an appeal by Mr Barry holding that:

> "1. By withdrawing the said services without the council being satisfied that the applicant's previously assessed needs had diminished, the respondent is in breach of its continuing duty under section 2 of the Chronically Sick and Disabled Persons Act 1970;
> 2. That in assessing or re-assessing whether it is necessary to make arrangements to meet them, a local authority is not entitled to take account of the resources available to such local authority."

The House of Lords allowed an appeal from this decision, holding that cost is a relevant factor in assessing a person's needs for services. In deciding how much weight is to be attached to cost some evaluation has to be made about the impact which cost will have upon the authority. If the authority's financial resources are limited it may need to change the criteria for providing certain services with the consequence that fewer people may be eligible to receive assistance. The level of service provided may also have to be reduced. This does not mean that a local authority has a complete discretion over whether or not to allocate resources to fulfil a statutory duty. The local authority must carry out its functions in a reasonable fashion. In the event of a local authority acting with *Wednesbury* unreasonableness, a disabled person would have a remedy.

Not every act which is carried out by a public authority can be attributed to a statutory duty. In the case of *Paterson v. Humberside County Council*,[47] Paterson claimed damages in nuisance and negligence against the local council for cracks in his house resulting from trees, which had caused subsidence to the property by drying out the soil. It was held that the council's knowledge about the type of soil in the locality meant that the risk of damage caused by tree roots was foreseeable and therefore the council, which was responsible for the trees in question, could be held liable in nuisance and negligence and damages were awarded. Paterson's claim for breach of statutory duty was, however, denied because the trees had not been planted pursuant to statutory powers.   15–24

Breach of statutory duty under E. C. Law

It is no longer the case that the duties of public authorities are all based on legislation from the Westminster Parliament. The Treaty of Rome and other   15–25

---

[47] *The Times*, April 19, 1995.

Community legislation impose many duties on member states and on the public authorities within Member States. Under the European Communities Act 1972, such duties are given legal effect in the United Kingdom and are enforced by courts within the United Kingdom. The extent to which duties under E.C. law are enforceable will depend on the nature of any particular duty and interpretation of the individual instrument by which that duty was imposed.

In the case of *Garden Cottage Foods Ltd. v. Milk Marketing Board*,[48] the House of Lords held that the duty imposed by Article 86, not to abuse a dominant position, is to be regarded as a statutory duty. The majority of the judges expressed a view that damages would be awarded for breach of such a duty.[49] In the contrasting case of *Bourgoin S.A. v. Ministry of Agriculture, Fisheries and Foods*,[50] it was held that the implementation by a national Government of measures which amount to a breach of Article 30 of the EEC Treaty does not of itself give a right to damages. Bourgoin was engaged in the business of importing turkeys from France. In 1981 the Government of the United Kingdom introduced a policy of preventing imports of turkeys from countries where disease was controlled by vaccination rather than slaughter. The ban prevented imports from France and caused Bourgoin to lose business. The European Court held that the new rules were in breach of Article 30 and Bourgoin was able to resume importing turkeys from France in November 1982. In an action before the U.K. courts he claimed damages for the loss of business in the intervening period, on the ground that the Ministry of Agriculture, Fisheries and Food was in breach of the statutory duty imposed by Article 30. It was held that a breach of Article 30 gave rise to a right to judicial review, by anyone with a sufficient interest but there was no right to damages unless there had been an abuse of power. The purpose of Article 30 was not to protect individual traders but rather to protect the public at large. The measures implemented by the U.K. Government were a simple excess of power and not a breach of statutory duty and no damages were due.

15–26   The conflict between these two cases leaves some uncertainty as to the position in relation to breach of statutory duty under E.C. law. An underlying principle of E.C. law is that national courts should enforce rights under the E.C. Treaty by remedies which are not less favourable than those available for similar rights under domestic law. As there is no overriding principle which establishes when liability for breach of statutory duty arises under national law then it is logical to presume that a remedy which is not less

---

[48]   [1984] A.C. 130.
[49]   See also *An Bord Bainne v. Milk Marketing Board* [1984] 2 C.M.L.R. 584.
[50]   [1986] Q.B. 716.

favourable in relation to E.C. law is provided by following the same principle that liability will depend on the interpretation of the individual legislative instrument in each case.

Liability for negligent misstatement.

The principle of liability for negligent misstatements was recognised by 15–27 the House of Lords in the case of *Hedley Byrne & Co. v. Heller & Partners Ltd,*[51] in which it was established that liability may arise if a person is under a duty to take care that his statements are accurate and he fails to fulfil that duty.[52] In the case of *T. (A Minor) v. Surrey County Council,*[53] it was held that a failure by the local authority to meet its implied obligations under the Nurseries and Childminders Regulation Act 1948 to suspend a childminder's registration did not confer a private law right of action for statutory breach of duty on a child who had been injured while in the care of the childminder. A child suffered a serious non-accidental injury while in the care of a registered childminder. The mother of the child, prior to engaging the childminder, had contacted the local authority's nursery and childminding adviser, who confirmed that the childminder was registered as a childminder under the 1948 Act and that there was no reason why a child could not safely be left in her care. In fact the adviser was aware that, less than three months earlier, another child in the care of the same childminder had been seriously injured, probably through violent shaking, although it had not been established that the childminder had caused the injury. As a result of his injuries T claimed damages for personal injuries against the local authority for breach of statutory duty in failing to cancel the childminder's registration under the 1948 Act, breach of a common law duty of care in failing to cancel the registration and negligent misstatement. It was held that although there was no liability to the child for breach of statutory duty, as the local authority knew that there was a significant risk in placing a child in the care of a particular childminder, yet still informed a parent that there was no reason why a child should not be placed in that person's care the local authority was liable for negligent misstatement. The local authority had failed to tell the mother the full facts, and if she had been aware that there were unresolved concerns about a child injured whilst in the childminder's care, she would never have placed the child with the childminder. Damages were awarded because the injury could be attributed to reliance on the negligent misstatement.

---

[51] [1964] A.C. 465.
[52] See also *Ministry of Housing and Local Government v. Sharp* [1970] Q.B. 223.
[53] [1994] 4 All E.R. 577.

Vicarious liability for misfeasance in public office

15–28   Misfeasance in public office is fortunately a very rare occurrence. It is the wrongful use of a power by a public official with the intention of causing harm to an individual or organisation. The concept of a delict of misfeasance in public office is relatively new to Scots law but in the case of *Micosta v. Shetland Islands Council*,[54] Lord Ross expressed the opinion that Scots law is sufficiently flexible to accommodate a delict under such a description. The tort has a longer history under English law. In the early case of *Ashby v. White*,[55] the plaintiff was an elector who was wrongly prevented from voting in the Aylesbury election. He sued the borough constables in charge of the poll for damages of £200 on the grounds of fraud and malicious intent. The House of Lords held that damages were due to the plaintiff. The most famous instance of misfeasance in public office occurred in the Canadian case, *Roncarelli v. Duplessis*,[56] in which damages were awarded against the Prime Minister of Quebec in person. He had directed the cancellation of a liquor licence for a restaurant because the owner of the restaurant had, on many occasions, provided bail for fellow members of the religious sect of Jehovah's Witnesses, which was then in conflict with the authorities. Damages of $33,123 were awarded. The cancellation of the liquor licence was an abuse of discretion based on irrelevant and illegal grounds. The Prime Minister had no legal authority to interfere with the jurisdiction of the liquor commission, which nevertheless followed his instruction to cancel the licence. Rand J. said: "Malice in the proper sense is simply acting for a reason and purpose knowingly foreign to the administration, to which was added here the element of intentional punishment by what was virtually outlawry."[57]

15–29   The question of vicarious liability for misfeasance by employees arose in the case of *Racz v. Home Office*.[58] Racz claimed to have been mistreated by prison officers whilst being held on remand. The mistreatment included unjustified strip searching and throwing his food onto the floor of his cell. He brought an action claiming damages for assault battery, negligence and misfeasance. The purpose of adding the allegation of misfeasance was that it might provide the courts with the basis for making an exemplary award of damages under English law. The Home Office applied successfully to have the claim of misfeasance struck out on the ground that it could not be held vicariously liable for such actions, a ruling upheld by the Court of Appeal. The plaintiff appealed to the House of Lords and it was held that

---

[54] 1986 S.L.T. 193.
[55] (1703) 2 Ld Raym. 938, 3 Ld Raym. 320; Wade and Forsyth, *op. cit.*, n. 6, above, p. 790.
[56] [1952] 1 D.L.R. 680.
[57] *ibid.* at 706.
[58] [1994] 2 W.L.R. 23, H.L..

the appeal would be allowed. The Home Office had argued that they could not be vicariously liable for the acts complained of since, if the prison officers had committed these acts they were acting in contravention of the rules and therefore outside the scope of their employment. Lord Jauncey held that this argument could only be justified if the unauthorised acts of the prison officers were so unconnected with their authorised duties as to be quite independent and outside those duties. It was also possible that the prison officers were engaged in a misguided and unauthorised method of performing their authorised duties. The claim for misfeasance should therefore be dealt with at the trial.

In the case of *Bennett v. Commissioner of Police of the Metropolis*,[59] it 15–30 was held that intent to injure the plaintiff is an essential ingredient in the tort of misfeasance in public office and must be pleaded in a statement of claim. Bennett, a citizen of New Zealand, had been arrested in South Africa and was placed on a flight to New Zealand. The flight stopped off in London where Bennett was wanted on criminal charges. He was arrested and committed for trial. He applied for judicial review claiming that he had been detained in England as a result of an avoidance of the South African extradition procedure. Bennett had originally been refused access to documents but subsequently was held to be entitled to discovery of the documents as they were essential for his case. He then brought a claim for damages against, amongst others, the Secretary of State for the Home Department. He argued that, in not considering whether the public interest in non-disclosure was outweighed by the public interest in proper administration of justice, the Secretary of State had been negligent and committed an act of misfeasance. It was held that intent to injure was an essential ingredient of the tort of misfeasance in public office, and that as no such intent had been pleaded, the statement of claim contained no cause of action.[60]

In *Bourgoin S.A. v. Ministry of Agriculture, Fisheries and Food*,[61] Bourgoin claimed damages for the disruption of his business (importing turkeys from France) caused by a ban on the import of turkeys from France which had been wrongfully introduced in the United Kingdom. It was held that a mere breach of the treaty article did not give rise to a right to damages. However, if it could be shown that, in implementing the measures, there had been an abuse of power then damages could be claimed for the commission of the tort of misfeasance in public office. The proof of malice upon the part of the officer concerned was not necessary but it must be proved that the officer knew that he had no power to act as he did and that he knew his act would injure the plaintiffs. Damages were not awarded in

---

[59] [1995] 1 W.L.R. 488.
[60] See also *Dunlop v. Woollahra Municipal Council* [1982] A.C. 158.
[61] [1985] 3 All E.R. 585.

Bourgoin's case because the actions of the U.K. Government were deemed to be a simple excess of power.

15–31   In Scotland, although the term misfeasance in public office was not always used, there have been cases in which liability in damages for the wrongful use of a power has been held to exist. In the case of *B. v. Forsey*,[62] a mental patient who had been unlawfully detained in circumstances whereby the hospital authorities were aware that the detention was unlawful was awarded damages. The use of the term misfeasance in public office has now been recognised in Scotland. In the case of *Micosta v. Shetland Islands Council*,[63] damages were claimed against a harbour authority on the basis that the harbourmaster had used his powers in an improper way in the knowledge that he could not lawfully do so. A bulk carrier which was held off shore at Sullom Voe awaiting berthing instructions had discharged dirty ballast into the sea. This was a breach of the conditions of charter. The harbour authority said that they would issue a special direction preventing the ship from loading cargo. The charterparty was then cancelled on the grounds that the contract of charter was frustrated. The owners of the ship sought damages on the grounds that their loss of the profit from the remaining term of the charter arose from deliberate misuse of the authority's statutory powers. It was held that there is a remedy in Scots law for a third party loss which is a result of a deliberate misuse of statutory powers provided that there is proof of malice, or proof that the statutory body knew that it did not have the power which it purported to exercise. In this case it was held that the harbour master's intention in issuing the direction was to prevent further discharge. His actings were in good faith and the action was dismissed.

15–32   The elements which have to be proved in order to establish misfeasance in public office are therefore:

1.   The defender knows that he has no legal authority to act in a particular way.
2.   The defender nevertheless does act in that manner either;
       (a) in order to injure the pursuer, or
       (b) in order to benefit a third party in the knowledge that by so doing, injury will inevitably accrue to the pursuer.[64]

Malice, in the sense of a specific intention to cause harm to an individual as the primary purpose of the action or decision is not always required but there must be a conscious abuse of power in the knowledge that harm may occur.

---

[62]   1988 S.L.T. 572.
[63]   1986 S.L.T. 193.
[64]   McManus, "Misfeasance in Public Office" in McManus, Bisacre, Russell *et al.*, *Delict* (1997).

LIABILITY OF THE CROWN IN DELICT

Under the law of delict a person will be liable in damages for a wrongful 15–33
act or omission which causes harm to another person. Public authorities,
including Ministers of the Crown have no exemption from the ordinary
law of delict unless the exemption has been provided by statute. In Scotland
there was no legal barrier to an action against the Crown for a civil wrong
until the case of *McGregor v. Lord Advocate.*[65] McGregor was knocked
down by an army car, the driver being employed by the War Department
and acting in the course of his employment. McGregor tried to sue the War
Department but the action was held to be incompetent as the War Office
represented the Crown. In England, before the Crown Proceedings Act 1947,
the Crown was, in strict law, immune from proceedings. The monarch was
subject to the law but there was no means of enforcing the law against a
monarch as the King could not be sued in his own courts. Since writs were
issued in the name of the King, they could not be issued against him.

Nominated Defenders

Action had, therefore, to be taken against the individual Crown servant. 15–34
The Crown accepted its moral responsibility whenever a Crown servant
was held to be liable and, in practice, the department concerned paid the
compensation. This developed into the practice of using a nominated
defender. The Crown would nominate an official to defend the action and
would not use as a defence the fact that there was no evidence that he was
personally liable. Where this was done the idea of an action against an
individual servant of the Crown was a mere fiction and in 1946 the House
of Lords condemned this practice in the case of *Adams v. Naylor.*[66] A local
commander of the Royal Engineers had been nominated to defend an action
when two children were injured in a minefield. The House of Lords pointed
out that whether or not the Crown stood behind the individual defendant,
so as to make the trial really a matter of suit against the Crown, the reality
was that judgment could only be given for the plaintiff if it could be shown
that the individual defendant was himself liable.

The use of a nominated defender had not provided a universal solution
for actions in delict against the Crown. It could not be used in cases where
the only possible defender was the Crown itself, such as cases against the
Crown as occupier of land or as an employer. It became obvious that a
reform of the law to provide a right of action against the Crown was
necessary and the Crown Proceedings Act was passed in 1947. Following

---

[65] 1921 S.C. 847.
[66] [1946] A.C. 543.

the 1947 Act, petitions of right were abolished and the use of nominated defenders was no longer required. Section 17 of the Act requires the Treasury to publish a list of the authorised Government departments and the names of the person against whom proceedings should be taken. If there is no appropriate department proceedings may be taken against: the Attorney-General in England; the Lord Advocate, in the case of an action against a British department in Scotland; the Secretary of State for Scotland in the case of an action in Scotland against a Scottish department.

Crown Proceedings Act 1947

15–35 Section 2 of the Crown Proceedings Act provides that, with exceptions, the Crown is subject to the same liabilities in tort/delict as if it were a private person of full age and capacity in respect of:

> 2(1)(a) torts/delicts committed by its servants or agents.
>> (b) duties which an employer, at common law, owes to his servants or agents.
>> (c) breach of the common law duties attaching to the ownership, occupation, possession, or control of property.
> 2(2)(d) breaches of statutory duty, provided that the statute is one which binds the Crown as well as private persons.

By section 2(6) vicarious liability for torts/delicts of crown officers is restricted to an officer appointed directly or indirectly by the Crown and paid out of the Consolidated Fund, moneys provided by Parliament or a fund certified by the Treasury. In order to protect the independence of the judiciary section 2(5) provides that there is no vicarious liability for acts done by officers acting in a judicial capacity or in execution of judicial process. Section 43(b) defines the meaning of tort in its application to Scotland as "Any wrongful or negligent act or omission giving rise to liability in reparation".

15–36 In the case of *Hughes v. Lord Advocate*,[67] the Crown was held to be vicariously liable for injuries incurred by two boys as a result of Crown servants having left a manhole unguarded with a naked light inside. This was an instance of ordinary liability for personal injury arising from negligent acts or omissions. The Act does not authorise proceedings against the sovereign in her personal capacity (section 40(1)). There is also an exception where death or injury is caused by a member of the armed forces of the Crown to another serviceman in the execution of his duties where the Minister certifies that the accident is attributable to the service for the purposes of a pension award. (section 10.) This exception is made on the grounds that compensation is already provided for in the pension award. The section would, however, have been better expressed if it had made the

---

[67] 1963 S.C. (H.L.) 31.

exception only in cases where the pursuer stood to benefit from a pension, thus avoiding the effect that the section had in the case of *Adams v. War Office*[68] wherein it was held that no action will lie whenever the Minister issues a certificate that the accident is attributable to the service for the purposes of a pension award, even although no award is made. Adams Jnr. was a reservist, serving in a territorial unit, who was killed by shell burst on a military exercise. His father alleged negligence on the part of the serviceman who allowed a live shell to be fired on an exercise. The War office relied on section 10 of the Crown Proceedings Act 1947 as a defence as the Minister of pensions had certified that the accident would give entitlement to pension. In fact, no pension was awarded as Adams Jnr. was dead and his parents did not qualify as dependants. Section 10 was eventually put into suspension by the Crown Proceedings (Armed Forces) Act 1987. It may be revived if it appears to the Secretary of State necessary or expedient so to do. This may occur in the event of war. Until section 10 is revived, members of the armed forces (and, in the event of death, their dependants) may sue fellow members and the Crown for damages for death or injury arising from their service.

STATUTORY AUTHORITY AS A DEFENCE

Where Parliament expressly authorises something to be done, to do it in accordance with that authority cannot be wrongful. A public authority cannot therefore be held liable in delict where the loss or injury is the inevitable result of activities authorised by Parliament. The effectiveness of statutory authority as a defence will depend on interpretation of the specific legislation in order to ascertain whether an infringement of private rights is authorised. There may be provision in the legislation for compensation for authorised infringement of private rights.

15–37

It is assumed that, when discretionary power is given to a public body, there is no intention to interfere with private rights, unless the power is expressed in such a way as to make such interference inevitable. In the case of *Metropolitan Asylum District v. Hill*,[69] hospital trustees were empowered by statute to build hospitals in London. A smallpox hospital was built at Hampstead in such a way as to create a nuisance at common law. It was held that the building of the hospital in such a place was unlawful because there were no express words or necessary implication in the statute authorising the commission of a nuisance. The Act gave no compulsory powers, it made no provision for compensation, and the inference was that it was not intended to permit interference with private rights. Lord Watson

---

[68] [1955] 1 W.L.R. 1116.
[69] (1881) 6 A.C. 193.

observed: "Where the terms of a statute are not imperative, but permissive … the fair inference is that the legislature intended that discretion be exercised in strict conformity with private rights and did not confer licence to commit nuisance."[70] If the exercise of a statutory duty or power inevitably involves injury to private rights there is no remedy unless the statute itself makes provision for compensation. In the case of *Allen v. Gulf Refining Company Ltd*,[71] the House of Lords held that a local Act which envisaged the building of an oil refinery at Milford Haven, though it did not give express power to construct the refinery or define the site, did give authority by necessary implication, for its construction and use. Such authority protected the company against liability for nuisance caused to neighbouring owners which was the inevitable result of the building of the refinery. The Act made no provision for compensation and so neighbours who complained of excessive smell, vibration and noise had no remedy.

15–38   Liability for negligence in the operation of a function, however, may not be taken away by statutory authority where, as in the case of *Dorset Yacht Company v. Home Office*,[72] the negligent actings of officials rendered their actions *ultra vires* the statutory authority. In the case of *Bell v. McGlennan*,[73] it was held that whilst there would be no liability for actions taken in accordance with the statutory authority there may be liability for any actions which amounted to an excess of power. Acting under authority of a warrant from the sheriff under section 15(1) of the Wireless Telegraphy Act 1949, an officer of the radio investigation service of the Department of Trade and Industry searched premises and seized equipment which appeared to have been used in connection with an alleged offence under the Act. No criminal proceedings were raised within six months after which time proceedings were incompetent and in terms of section 83(1) of the Telecommunications Act 1984 the property should have been returned to the owner. After a further six weeks the property was returned but it was damaged. The owner of the property brought an action for damages against the procurator fiscal. He argued that the procurator fiscal was vicariously responsible for the actings of the investigation officer. The defender argued that, by virtue of section 456 of the Criminal Procedure (Scotland) Act 1975, he had immunity from damages in respect of acts done under Part 3 of the Act. There was doubt as to whether there was immunity under Criminal Procedure (Scotland) Act 1975 because the acts of the investigation officer might have been done under the 1949 Act, in which case section 456 of the 1975 Act would not apply. It was probable that the negligent handling of

---

[70] See also *Manchester Corporation v. Farnworth* [1930] A.C. 171; *Tate & Lyle Ltd v. Greater London Council* [1983] 2 A.C. 509.

[71] [1981] A.C. 1001.

[72] [1970] A.C. 1004.

[73] 1992 S.L.T. 237.

property was not authorised by statute and proof was accordingly necessary on that question. As the warrant was lawful, statutory authority would preclude the award of damages for deprivation of the equipment seized during the authorised period of six months. Damages may be due for loss arising from detention of the property in respect of the period after the defender's statutory authority to hold it had expired.

Where a public authority can achieve an objective by exercising powers 15–39 under more than one statute, each of which prescribes the procedures to be followed and the remedies which may be available to individuals affected, the authority may choose which statute to follow and will not be called to account for failing to follow the course of action which is most advantageous to individuals who may be affected. An individual will not be able to claim compensation on the ground that the authority chose to follow procedures under one statute when alternative procedures would have provided for more generous compensation to individuals affected.[74] General powers under one Act may not however be used to achieve a regulatory goal which is authorised expressly in another Act.[75] In the case of *Westminster Bank Ltd v. Minister of Housing and Local Government*,[76] the House of Lords held that an authority's choice of action may be restricted by special circumstances.[77]

STATUTES NOT APPLYING TO THE CROWN

It has long been established that the Crown is not bound or restricted by 15–40 any statutory provision unless it is expressly stated or necessarily implied that it applies to the Crown. The application of statutes to the Crown was considered in the case of *Lord Advocate v. Strathclyde Regional Council*.[78] The Property Services Agency was carrying out work on the perimeter fence at Faslane. A temporary fence and works on part of the A814, a public road, caused an obstruction of the highway for which no permission had been sought from either the roads authority, Strathclyde Regional Council, or the planning authority, Dumbarton District Council. Both authorities took action to have the road cleared. The Lord Advocate, on behalf of the Ministry, sought judicial review of these acts, including declarators that the notices were *ultra vires* and that those provisions had no application to uses of land carried out by the Crown in the exercise of the prerogative. The Crown

---

[74] *Montgomerie & Co. v. Haddington Corporation*, 1908 S.C. 127; 15 S.L.T. 474 (affirmed by the House of Lords, 1908 S.C. (H.L.) 6; 1908 15 S.L.T. 910); *Hawick Orange Lodge v. Roxburgh District Council*, 1980 S.C. 141; 1981 S.L.T. 33.
[75] *British Airports Authority v. Secretary of State for Scotland*, 1979 S.C. 200; 1979 S.L.T. 197.
[76] [1971] A.C. 508; [1970] 1 All E.R. 734.
[77] Bradley, "Administrative Law", *Stair Memorial Encyclopaedia*, Vol. 1.
[78] 1990 S.L.T. 158.

argued that it was not subject to the restrictions in the roads and planning legislation. There was no specific statutory exemption in this case, however, as the work was not on Crown land. The Lord Ordinary, however, held that the Crown was not bound by statute unless named expressly or by necessary implication, declared the orders null and pronounced interdict. In an appeal to the House of Lords, Strathclyde Regional Council and Dumbarton District Council argued that in modern circumstances the rule that statutes do not apply to the Crown unless there was express provision to that effect was limited to provisions which would affect prejudicially the property rights, interests and privileges of the Crown.[79] The House of Lords held that the Crown was not bound by any statutory provision unless there could be gathered from the relevant Act an intention to that effect. The Crown would be bound only by express words or necessary implication.

INTERDICT AGAINST THE CROWN

15–41   Interdicts were available against Ministers of the Crown in the Scottish courts until the Crown Proceedings Act 1947 came into force in 1948.[80] The Act transformed the procedure by which actions could be brought against the Crown in England but made no changes to the procedure in Scotland. In Scotland, accordingly, the procedure continues to be governed by common law, the Crown Suits (Scotland) Act 1857 and, in relation to the Secretary of State, the Reorganisation of Offices (Scotland) Act 1939. Prior to the Crown Proceedings Act 1947 it was competent in Scotland to seek the remedy of interdict against the Crown and when an officer of the Crown was sued in that capacity this was regarded as an action against the Crown.[81] In *Somerville v. Lord Advocate*[82] Lord MacLaren stated:

> "I do not think that it ever was doubted in Scotland that the Crown might be called as a defender in a proper action, either through the Officers of State collectively, or through the King's Advocate or other officer representing the Crown in the matter of the action ... His Highness, or His advocate as representing the King, may be convened in the Court of Session in actions and pleas at the instance of any private person."

Section 21 of the Crown Proceedings Act 1947 provides that:

> "(1) In any civil proceedings by or against the Crown the court shall, subject to the provisions of this Act, have power to make all such orders as it has

---

[79]   See also *Somerville v. Lord Advocate* (1893) 20 R. 1050 and *Magistrates of Edinburgh v. Lord Advocate*, 1912 2 S.L.T. 133.

[80]   *Russell v. Magistrates of Hamilton* (1897) 25 R. 350; *Bell v. Secretary of State for Scotland*, 1933 S.L.T. 519.

[81]   *Somerville v. Lord Advocate* (1893) 20 R. 105; *Smith v. Lord Advocate*, 1932 S.L.T. 374; *Wilson v. 1st Edinburgh City Royal Garrison Artillery Volunteers* (1904) 12 S.L.T. 488; (1904) 7 F. 168.

[82]   (1893) 20 R. 105.

power to make in proceedings between subjects, and otherwise to give such appropriate relief as the case may require: Provided that:— where in any proceedings against the Crown any such relief is sought as might in proceedings between subjects be granted by way of injunction or specific performance, the court shall not grant an injunction or make an order for specific performance, but may in lieu thereof make an order declaratory of the rights of the parties.

(2) The court shall not in any civil proceedings grant any injunction or make any order against an officer of the Crown if the effect of granting the injunction or making the order would be to give any relief against the Crown which could not have been obtained in proceedings against the Crown."

Section 38(2) provides *inter alia*: that " 'Civil proceedings' includes 15–42 proceedings in the High Court or the county court for the recovery of fines and penalties, but does not include proceedings on the Crown side of the King's Bench Division." Part 5 of the Act deals with the application of the Act to Scotland and provides that although Part 2 (which includes section 21) does not apply to Scotland. There is an express exception in relation to section 21 with the result that section 21 does apply to Scotland. Section 43 of the Act of 1947 provides interpretation for the purposes of the application to Scotland and provides *inter alia* that for any reference to the High Court there shall be substituted a reference to the Court of Session, that the expression "plaintiff" means "pursuer", and that the expression "injunction" means "interdict".

Section 21 therefore has had the effect of changing the law of Scotland by exempting the Crown from interdict. It has been said that: "In one respect, contrary to the general policy of the Act, the rights of the subject against the Crown are restricted; by section 21(1)(a) (as applied to Scotland by sections 42 and 43) it is provided that the court shall not in future grant an interdict against the Crown."[83] The purpose of section 21(2) is to prevent avoidance of the Act by raising actions against officers of the Crown as individuals, and not against the Crown itself.[84] In the case of *British Medical Association v. Greater Glasgow Health Board*,[85] Lord Jauncey, in considering what was meant by the expression 'proceedings against the Crown' in section 21(1), said:

"Historically the position of the private litigant vis-a-vis the Crown differed in Scotland and England. While actions founded in tort and delict could be brought against the Crown in neither country, other actions could be brought as of right in Scotland, whereas in England it was necessary to proceed by petition of right. Indeed, interdict was available against the Crown in Scotland although such a remedy was, I understand, inconceivable in England. It

[83] Fraser, *An Outline of Constitutional Law* (2nd ed., 1948), p. 165.
[84] Mitchell, *Constitutional Law* (2nd ed., 1968) p. 309.
[85] 1988 S.L.T. 538, 1989 S.L.T. 493.

could be said that Scots law took a more robust view of the individual's rights against the Crown than did the law of England."[86]

15–43   In circumstances where, but for the fact that the defender is the Crown, an interdict would have been granted, the court may instead make an order declaring the rights between the parties.[87] Lord Fraser said: "Presumably it will be possible in future to obtain an interim declaratory order, corresponding to an interim interdict, for these purposes, but the point is not altogether clear from the terms of the Act."[88] Judges including Lord Fraser himself have proved to be reluctant to pronounce interim declaratory orders. In *Robertson v. Lord Advocate, as representing the Central Land Board*,[89] Lord Strachan declined to make an interim declaratory order on the ground that he could not make such an order without prejudging the merits of the case and in *Ayr Magistrates v. Secretary of State for Scotland*,[90] Lord Fraser followed the decision in *Robertson v. Lord Advocate*. He expressed a view that an interim declaratory order would be a prejudgment on the rights of the parties and that that was something which he was not entitled to do.

15–44   Where the Crown and an individual are both called as defenders, a declarator may be sought against the Crown and an interdict against the individual. In *Prince v. Secretary of State for Scotland*,[91] voters in the elections to the European Assembly sought declarator of their right to a system of proportional representation against the Secretary of State and interdict against the returning officer from conducting the election. The basis of the claim was that the existing system was *ultra vires* and contrary to the European Communities Act, s. 2. The interim interdict was refused because it had not been established that the election system was *ultra vires*. It is doubtful now whether a remedy will be granted against an individual Crown servant in circumstances where the action is really against the Crown. An official or a public body may, however, be classed as part of the Crown for some purposes but this does not necessarily mean that they will be regarded as part of the Crown for all purposes. In the case of *British Medical Association v. Greater Glasgow Health Board*,[92] the pursuers sought interdict to prevent action which was not in compliance with agreed procedures for the resolution of disputes by the Health Board. The defenders argued that this was incompetent in terms of section 21 of the Crown Proceedings Act 1947. They argued that the action was really an action against the Crown as

---

[86] 1989 S.L.T. 493 at 497.
[87] Crown Proceedings Act 1947, ss. 21(a) and 23(a) as applied to Scotland by s. 43(a).
[88] Fraser, *op. cit.*, n. 83, above, p. 166.
[89] 1950 S.L.T. (Notes) 22.
[90] 1966 S.L.T. 16; 1965 S.C. 394.
[91] 1985 S.L.T. 74.
[92] 1988 S.L.T. 538; 1989 S.L.T. 493; 1989 S.C.L.R. 478; 1989 S.C. (H.L.) 65.

the Health Board was part of the Crown. Their case was supported by an earlier decision of the House of Lords that the use of drugs by the National Health Service was, for the purpose of the Patents Act 1949, for the services of the Crown. The House of Lords held that the proceedings in this case were not proceedings against the Crown. The fact that a body may enjoy one Crown privilege does not necessarily mean that it will enjoy Crown privilege in a different context. When section 2 (8) of the National Health Service (Scotland) Act 1978 and sections 17(3) and 21 of the Crown Proceedings Act 1947 were read together, the inference was that a health board was not intended to be regarded as part of the Crown. Another important consideration in the case was that the general purpose of the 1947 Act was to make it easier rather than more difficult for a subject to sue the Crown and the appeal was dismissed.

In the case of *Mcdonald v. Secretary of State for Scotland*,[93] the Inner   15–45 House confirmed that the effect of the Crown Proceedings Act 1947, s. 21, in Scotland, is that interdict cannot be obtained against the Crown or a Minister of the Crown. The *Mcdonald* case was not a petition for judicial review but was an ordinary action for reparation totalling £300,000 for approximately 3,000 searches which the pursuer claimed were carried out wrongfully. Macdonald was a convicted prisoner serving his sentence in a Scottish prison. He sought interdict against the Secretary of State restraining him, or anyone acting on his behalf, from subjecting Macdonald to illegal searches. It was held that the effect of section 21 is that interdict is not available against the Crown in any civil proceedings. Lord Ross also said, with regard to section 21, that:

> "its purpose appears to be to prevent circumvention of the Act by raising actions against officers of the Crown as individuals and not against the Crown itself... I am quite satisfied that the granting of interdict or interim interdict is prohibited by virtue of the provisions of section 21(1) of the Act of 1947. The action which the pursuer has raised plainly constitutes civil proceedings. Moreover, these clearly are civil proceedings against the Crown since directing the proceedings against the Secretary of State for Scotland is one method by which civil proceedings can be instituted against the Crown".[94]

Lord Sutherland stated that "the construction of section 21 which prevents an individual from obtaining relief by way of interdict against the Crown is a restriction on the remedies available prior to 1947, which may seem strange in legislation designed to expand the remedies available against the Crown, but the wording of the section is such that there can be no doubt that this was the intention of Parliament".[95]

---

[93] 1994 S.L.T. 692.
[94] *ibid.* at 699.
[95] *ibid.* at 701.

15–46   This case has clarified the scope of the Crown Proceedings Act 1947 so
far as it relates to Scottish actions of interdict. It is now clear that one effect
of the 1947 Act is that a court in Scotland cannot grant interdict against the
Crown in ordinary civil proceedings. As the purpose of the 1947 Act was to
facilitate actions against the Crown it is ironic that its effect in Scotland has
been to take away a remedy which had previously been available against
the Crown. It is even more ironic when it has been held in England by the
House of Lords in the case of *M. v. Home Office*,[96] that the court has
jurisdiction in judicial review proceedings to grant an order such as an
injunction against a Minister of the Crown acting in his official capacity.
That decision appears to have been made mainly on the basis that judicial
review under section 31 of the Supreme Court Act 1981 does not fall within
the definition of civil proceedings against the Crown under section 23(2)
of the 1947 Act. Prerogative orders were exempted from the definition of
civil proceedings under the 1947 Act and the current judicial review
procedure in the provisions of section 31 of the Supreme Court Act 1981
and Order 53 of the Rules of the Supreme Court is therefore also excluded
from the definition of civil proceedings. The House of Lords held that the
court had jurisdiction on applications for judicial review to grant injunctions,
including interim injunctions, against Ministers and other officers of the
Crown.

15–47   In *Mcdonald v. Secretary of State for Scotland*[97] opinion was reserved as
to whether the term "civil proceedings" includes judicial review proceedings
in Scotland. The court considered whether there was an argument that if
the pursuer had applied to the Court of Session for judicial review, then it
might have been open to him to seek interim interdict upon the ground that
an application to the supervisory jurisdiction of the Court of Session did
not come under the definition of civil proceedings against the Crown within
the meaning of section 21(1) of the Crown Proceedings Act 1947. Modern
judicial review procedure in England falls outside the definition of civil
proceedings in section 38(2) but the supervisory jurisdiction of the Court
of Session was not expressly excluded by the terms of section 38(2). It was
suggested that it might be argued that the intention of section 38(2)
was also to exclude the supervisory jurisdiction of the Court of Session. It was
suggested that Parliament, by exempting prerogative writs in England, had
shown an intention that "civil proceedings" should not include proceedings
in which courts would consider whether the Crown had exceeded its
authority or actions for judicial review. Prior to 1947 the Crown and officers
of the Crown had been regarded as susceptible to the jurisdiction of the
Court of Session and liable to having interdict pronounced against them.

---

[96]   [1992] Q.B. 270; [1993] 3 All E.R. 537.
[97]   1994 S.L.T. 692.

However, Lord Sutherland noted that the supervisory jurisdiction of the Court of Session existed prior to 1947 even though it was not exercised by the present judicial review procedure. In the definition section of the 1947 Act, Parliament made it clear that proceedings by way of prerogative writs did not fall within civil proceedings but made no such provision in relation to the supervisory jurisdiction of the Court of Session. Since Parliament made specific provision for the exemption of the English prerogative writs but did not provide similarly for the supervisory jurisdiction in Scotland the rules of statutory interpretation (*expressio unius est exclusio alterius*) lead to the presumption that the intention of Parliament was to exclude prerogative writs but not to exclude the supervisory jurisdiction. It would, accordingly, seem very difficult to see how judicial review should not be regarded as civil proceedings within the meaning of the Act.

As it was not necessary for the disposal of the case, opinion was reserved 15–48 but it seems probable that judicial review proceedings will be held to come within the definition of civil proceedings for the purpose of the 1947 Act and interdict would not, therefore, be available against the Crown in judicial review proceedings. This leaves a situation where there is now a striking disparity between the remedies available to a litigant depending on whether the action is brought in England or Scotland. This is unfortunate since, when the Crown Proceedings Act was passed only certain of its provisions applied to Scotland. In an article in the *Canadian Bar Review* by Sir Thomas Barnes it was said that only those provisions of the Act were applied to Scotland which "are necessary to bring the position of the Crown as a litigant in Scotland into line with the position of the Crown as a litigant under the Act in England".[98] If this was indeed an intention behind the Act then the decision in *Mcdonald v. Secretary of State for Scotland* appears to be in conflict with the purpose of the Act. This is one respect in which the law of Scotland now provides inferior access to justice in comparison with the law in England and Wales and there is now a need for reform of the law as it applies to Scotland.

The current law in Scotland is therefore that an interdict will not be granted against the Crown[99] unless it relates to an area where European law impinges upon national law and the operation of the Crown Proceedings Act 1947, ss. 21(a) and 23(a), would prevent a pursuer obtaining an interdict against the Crown and its Ministers. It was held in *R. v. Secretary of State for Transport, ex parte Factortame (No. 2)*[1] that, in such cases, European law must prevail and the immunity of the Crown is removed.

---

[98] Barnes, "The Crown Proceedings Act 1947" (1948) Can. B. R. 387 at 397.
[99] Crown Proceedings Act 1947, s. 21; *Ayr Magistrates v. Lord Advocate,* 1950 S.C. 102.
[1] [1991] 1 All E.R. 70.

LIABILITY OF THE CROWN FOR BREACH OF E.C. LAW

15–49 Membership of the European Community has introduced new levels of regulatory activity. The effect of E.C. law in this area is likely to extend the scope of public authorities' liabilities. Community obligations may arise both directly from the E.C. Treaty and also from regulations, directives and decisions. Treaty provisions and regulations may have direct effect and therefore may confer rights enforceable in national courts.[2] Treaty provisions tend to be phrased in too general a way to confer personal rights or even to create definite obligations on the Government,[3] but regulations may be passed which are designed to have direct effect in Member States. This means that no change in national law is required to bring them into force in each State. Directives could be described as instructions to the Government of Member States to implement a change in national law to bring it into line with European policies. Each Member State may choose how to bring the directive into effect. The Member States do not always implement directives with alacrity and do not always legislate in a way which achieves the full purposes of directives and so the European Court has now developed a doctrine that a directive may have direct effect, without national legislation. One consequence of this is that an action may be raised against the Government or an emanation of the State which is failing to implement the directive.[4] Direct effect is only possible where the European provisions, whether in a treaty or a directive, are clear and precise and render it certain exactly what rights and obligations should exist without leaving discretion to the Member States in implementing the measures.

15–50 In the case of *Marshall v. Southampton and South West Hampshire Health Authority (Teaching) (No. 2)*,[5] Miss Marshall, having established in a claim for wrongful dismissal that her compulsory retirement at the age of 60 constituted a sex discrimination contrary to an E.C. directive, was awarded the meagre statutory maximum damages under national employment law and no interest. She appealed on the ground that the statutory upper limit for compensation and the exclusion of interest payments were contrary to E.C. law. The European Court of Justice ruled that the directive required an effective remedy and that since the limit to compensation and the rule that no interest would be paid were obstacles to adequate compensation they

---

[2] E.C. Treaty, Art 189; *Van Gend en Loos* case [1963] C.M.L.R.. 105.

[3] Reid, "Judicial Review and the Environment" in *Judicial Review: a Thematic Approach* (Hadfield, ed., 1995).

[4] *Van Duyn v. Home Office* [1975] Ch. 358 (E.C.J.); *Marshall v. Southampton and South West Hampshire Health Authority* [1986] Q.B. 401 (E.C.J.): *Marshall v. Southampton and South West Hampshire Health Authority* (No. 2) [1993] 3 W.L.R. 1054 (E.C.J.).

[5] [1993] 3 W.L.R. 1054 (E.C.J.).

were contrary to E.C. law. In the case of *R. v. Secretary of State for the Health Department, ex parte Richardson,*[6] Richardson, aged 64, contended, in an application for judicial review, that, as a result of regulation 6(1) of the National Health Service (Charges for Drugs and Appliances) Regulations 1989, he had suffered discrimination contrary to Council Directive 79/7. The regulations provided for differences in the charges for men and women between the ages of 60 and 65 years. The Secretary of State argued that prescription charges did not fall within the scope of the directive and the Queen's Bench Divisional Court sought a preliminary ruling from the European Court of Justice. It was held that as prescription charges were part of a statutory scheme to provide protection against the risk of sickness, regulation 6(1) fell within the scope of Directive 79/7. Discrimination was permitted where it was necessarily and objectively linked to the difference in retirement age set by a Member State for the purpose of granting retirement pensions, but the discrimination underlying regulation 6(1) was not a necessary consequence of different ages for retirement. The European Court of Justice also ruled that the direct effect of the directive could be relied upon to support claims for damages for periods prior to the date of the judgment.[7]

Directives which are directly effective are enforceable only against the national Government and not against other individuals or bodies. They are described as having vertical but not horizontal effect. A failure to comply with a directive cannot give rise to an action against private individuals so the *Marshall* case was only competent as it was a case against a public authority as an employer and not a private employer. An alternative form of redress may be sought through an action for damages against the Government itself. A European directive normally contains a time-limit within which it must be implemented by each Member State. If a Member State fails to implement a directive within the time limit indicated it may render itself liable to pay compensation to any individual who suffers damage as a direct consequence of this failure to implement in time. This liability will only arise if it was the intention of the directive to confer rights on individuals and that the content of those rights is identifiable from the directive itself. In the case of *Francovich v. Italy,*[8] the Court of Justice ruled that a Member State might be liable in damages in respect of the loss and damage suffered by a private individual which was directly caused by the State's failure to implement a directive which conferred directly enforceable rights. The case concerned the failure by the Italian Government to give effect to a directive requiring state guarantees for wages owed to employees by bankrupt employers. The employers were a private firm, and so the

15–51

---

[6]   [1995] 2 All E.R. 865.
[7]   See also *Thomas v. Chief Adjudication Officer* [1993] I E.C.R. 1247.
[8]   [1992] IRLR. 85; Case 6/90 [1991] I E.C.R. 5357.

claims of the employees could not be enforced directly. It was immaterial whether or not the directive had direct effect since the liability was for failure to translate the directive into national law. The court also ruled that the individual's entitlement to damages must be determined in accordance with national procedural rules, which must not be less favourable than those relating to similar domestic claims and must not be framed so as to make it virtually impossible or excessively difficult to obtain compensation. Some of the remarks made in the judgment of the European Court of Justice in this case support a wider principle that a Member State is liable to indemnify any individual injured under these conditions by any breach by the State of E.C. law and not merely where the breach consists of non-implementation of a directive.

15–52   The case established that a Government could incur liability to an individual for failure to implement a directive if the following three conditions were met:

1. the result prescribed by the directive entails the grant of rights to individuals;
2. the content of those rights is identifiable on the basis of the provisions of the directive; and
3. a causal link exists between the breach of the State's obligation and the loss or damage suffered by the injured parties.

Liability for failure to implement a directive may be strict. The case of *Wagner Miret v. Fondo de Garantia Salarial*,[9] arose because Spain had taken no action to implement a particular directive since it considered that the national law of Spain was adequate for this purpose. This view was held to be incorrect but there was no discussion in the judgment as to whether the argument put forward by Spain was a reasonable one. It appears therefore that liability is strict and does not depend on a deliberate or culpable failure to implement the directive in question. This was confirmed in two linked cases, *Brasserie du Pêcheur* and *Factortame III*,[10] wherein it was held that reparation for loss or damage cannot be made conditional upon fault (intentional or negligent) on the part of the organ of State responsible for the breach, going beyond that of a sufficiently serious breach of Community law. In *Brasserie du Pêcheur* and *Factortame* the court held that individuals who have suffered damage have a right to reparation where three conditions are met:

1. the rule of law infringed must have been intended to confer rights on individuals;
2. the breach must be sufficiently serious; and

[9]   Case C–334/92: [1993] I E.C.R. 6911.
[10]   [1996] 1 C.M.L.R. 889.

3.   there must be a direct causal link between the breach of the obligation resting on the State and the damage sustained by the injured parties.

These three conditions differ from those laid down in the *Francovich* case as there was no express reference in the *Francovich* case to the need for the breach to be serious. The need for the breach to be serious was, however apparent from the circumstances of that case.[11]

The judgment in the *Brasserie du Pêcheur* and *Factortame* cases is likely   15–53 to determine the court's approach to questions of liability of both Member States and the European Union in the foreseeable future. The European Court of Justice has recognised a general principle common to the legal systems of the Member States that unlawful conduct gives rise to an obligation to make good the damage caused. Breach of a directly effective treaty provision by a Member State or its failure to correctly transpose a directive into national law gives rise to liability where a manifest and serious breach is present. A breach of Community law is sufficiently serious if a Community institution or a Member State, in the exercise of its rule-making powers, manifestly and gravely disregards the limits on those powers.[12] It has subsequently been held that failure to take any measures to transpose a directive in order to achieve the result it prescribes within the period laid down for that purpose constitutes *per se* a serious breach of Community law and consequently gives rise to a right of reparation for individuals suffering injury if the result prescribed by the directive entails the grant to individuals of rights whose content is identifiable and a causal link exists between the breach of the State's obligation and the loss and damage suffered.[13]

The case of *R. v. H.M. Treasury, ex parte British Telecommunications*,[14] established that the clarity and precision of the rule which has been breached will be a factor in determining whether or not a breach is sufficiently serious to give rise to liability to make reparation. British Telecom brought proceedings for damages, claiming that the United Kingdom had incorrectly implemented Council Directive 90/531 on procurement procedures for entities operating in the telecommunications sector by the Utilities, Supply and Works Contracts Regulations 1992. The court held that the United Kingdom was in breach of Article 8(1)of the directive but the breach of Community law was not sufficiently serious as Article 8(1) was imprecisely worded and reasonably capable of bearing the interpretation given to it by the United Kingdom in good faith. No guidance had been available from

---

[11]   Judgment of October 8,1996. Joined cases C178, 188 & 190/94.
[12]   *Brasserie Du Pêcheur III* [1996] 1 C.M.L.R. 889; *R. v. HM Treasury, ex p. British Telecommunications* [1996] 2 C.M.L.R. 217.
[13]   *Dillenkofer v. Germany* [1996]All E.R. (E.C.) 917; [1996] 3 C.M.L.R. 469.
[14]   [1996] 2 C.M.L.R. 217.

case law as to the interpretation of the provision, and the Commission had not raised the matter when the 1992 Regulations were adopted. It was held therefore that the United Kingdom was not liable in this case to compensate British Telecom.

15–54　　　In *R. v. Ministry of Agriculture, Fisheries and Food, ex parte Hedley Lomas*,[15] it was stated that if, at the time when it committed the infringement, the Member State in question was not called upon to make any legislative choices and had only considerably reduced, or even no, discretion, the mere infringement of Community law may be sufficient to establish the existence of a sufficiently serious breach. The case related to a refusal by the Ministry to issue licences for the export of live sheep to Spain. The refusal to grant the licences was on the ground that their treatment in Spanish slaughterhouses was contrary to Council Directive 74/577 of November 18 on stunning of animals before slaughter. The directive had been implemented in Spanish law but the Ministry considered that it was not being complied with in some Spanish slaughterhouses. It was held that the U.K. Government had little discretion at the time when it committed the infringement. It was obliged to comply with the directive. Failure to do so constituted a sufficiently serious breach to give rise to liability to an individual who suffered a loss. It was observed that the United Kingdom was not even in a position to produce any proof of non-compliance with the directive by the slaughterhouse to which the animals for which the export licence was sought were destined.

Member States may claim that the period allowed for the implementation of a directive is too short but it has been established that a Member State may not rely on provisions and practices within its own legal system to justify a failure to observe a time-limit for implementation.[16] If the period allowed for implementation is too short, the only step available to a Member State is to take appropriate initiatives within the Community in order to have the competent Community institution grant the necessary extension of the period.[17]

15–55　　　In *Brasserie du Pêcheur* and *Factortame III*,[18] it was held that reparation for loss or damage caused to individuals as a result of breaches of Community law must be commensurate with the loss or damage sustained. In the absence of relevant Community provisions, it is for the domestic legal system of each Member State to set the criteria for determining the extent of reparation. The criteria must be no less favourable than those applying to similar claims based on domestic law and must not be such as

[15]　(C5/94) [1996] All E.R. (EC) 493.
[16]　*Commission v. Belgium* [1988] E.C.R. 3271, para. 7.
[17]　*Commission v. Italy* [1976] E.C.R. 277, para. 12.
[18]　[1996] 1 C.M.L.R. 889.

in practice to make it impossible or excessively difficult to obtain reparation. The injured party must show reasonable diligence in limiting the extent of the loss or damage. A State may not exclude liability for loss of profit in the case of a breach of Community law. It was also held that, in circumstances where an award of exemplary damages may be awarded in a similar action under domestic law they must also be awarded in an action based on Community law.

LIABILITY OF THE CROWN FOR BREACHES OF THE EUROPEAN CONVENTION ON HUMAN RIGHTS

The U.K. Government is a party to the European Convention on Human 15–56 Rights which guarantees that certain rights freedoms and privileges will be enjoyed by individuals within states which adhere to the Convention. The Convention has not yet been incorporated into U.K. law, as successive Governments have claimed that the required standards are already met by the existing laws of the jurisdictions within the United Kingdom. The United Nations Human Rights committee is not convinced by these arguments. It has noted that the legal system of the United Kingdom does not ensure that an effective remedy is provided for all victims of violations of the rights contained in the Covenant. Concern has been expressed regarding the extent to which the implementation of the Covenant in the United Kingdom is impeded by non-incorporation into U.K. law.[19]

After exhausting any effective and sufficient domestic remedies, individuals may raise actions for compensation in the European Court of Human Rights in Strasbourg. Claims by both states and individuals go first to the European Commission on Human Rights, which is a body of independent experts. The Commission decides whether the application should be admitted for consideration on the merits. If it is admitted, the commission examines the facts and the legal arguments and, if a friendly settlement is not possible, adopts a report indicating its findings of fact and its opinion as to whether the defendant state has infringed the Convention. Following the adoption of the report, which is not legally binding, the case may be referred by the Commission or a party with a recognised interest in it to the European Court of Human Rights. If it is not so referred the case will be decided by the Committee of Ministers of the Council of Europe, which is composed of government representatives of all the Member States. In either case, the outcome is a decision that is binding in international law.

One of the grounds on which an application may be made is breach of 15–57 Article 6(1) which provides that there should be access to justice. In the case of *Fayeds v. United Kingdom*,[20] it was held that Article 6(1) had not

---

[19] CCPR/C/79/ Add. 55, July 27, 1995.
[20] Judgment of September 21, 1994, Series A, No 294B.

been breached as judicial review procedures had not been used. Judicial review would provide an effective remedy if there had been unfairness. Similarly, in the case of *Air Canada v. United Kingdom*,[21] a case involving the seizure of an aircraft by Customs and Excise officials who refused to return it unless a penalty was paid, it was held by a majority that Article 6(1) had not been breached because Air Canada could have petitioned for judicial review which was a procedure capable of providing effective remedies. In the cases of *Boner v. United Kingdom* and *Maxwell v. United Kingdom*,[22] it was held that there had been a violation of the right to a fair trial, specifically the right to legal aid. Boner and Maxwell were both convicted in separate trials of offences of violence and given sentences of eight years and five years respectively. Despite the fact that both persons were having difficulty finding counsel who were willing to represent them it was held that the failure to award legal aid was a violation of the Convention.

In *Lithgow v. United Kingdom*,[23] the court held that the shareholders in shipbuilding companies nationalised by the Aircraft and Shipbuilding Industries Act 1977 were entitled to rely on Article 6(1) in questioning the provision made by the Act for assessing compensation, since the right to compensation derived from owning shares was undoubtedly a civil right. However, the court held that Article 6(1) did not guarantee shareholders an absolute right to a court for the determination of the right to compensation: the Arbitration tribunal set up by the 1977 Act met the requirements of Article 6(1).

15–58	In *W v. United Kingdom*,[24] it was held that the question of a right of access by parents to their children who had been taken into the care of a public authority involved matters of civil right and obligation. The court considered that this was a domain where despite the difficult discretionary decisions to be made by the authorities, there was a great need for protection against arbitrary interference with parental rights. The decision-making process must ensure that the views and interests of parents were made known and taken into account by the local authorities. This was not a situation in which it was sufficient for an aggrieved parent to institute judicial review proceedings since the reviewing court would not be able to examine the merits of the local authority's decision on parental access. What was required by Article 6(1) in relation to the rights in question was that parents must be able to have the decision taken by a local authority with regard to access reviewed by a tribunal with jurisdiction to examine the merits of the matter. The powers of the courts in the United Kingdom did not extend to this and a breach of Article 6(1) had occurred.

---

[21]	Judgment of May 5, 1995, Series A, No. 316.
[22]	Judgments of October 28, 1994.
[23]	(1986) 8 E.H.R.R. 329.
[24]	(1987) 10 E.H.R.R. 29.

A Bill was proposed in the Queen's Speech on May 14, 1997 which will incorporate the European Convention on Human Rights into the domestic law of the United Kingdom. Where U.K. law appears to be in direct conflict with the Convention, cases will still need to be taken to the European Court of Justice but the frequency with which resort to the European Court of Justice is required should diminish.

CHAPTER 16

CROWN PRIVILEGE OR PUBLIC INTEREST
IMMUNITY

16–01 In any legal action, there is a general principle that all relevant evidence is admissible and must be presented to the court.[1] Parties to a case may require the production of documents held by the other party. The procedure in civil actions for obtaining documents from the other party is called "discovery". The party seeking discovery makes a list of documents they wish to see and which are material to the dispute. If the other party refuses, the court may be asked to intervene to resolve the matter.

In actions against the Crown or public bodies, it can be difficult to obtain confidential documents which are required for one party's case. The public body may refuse to divulge these, citing that it is not in the public interest to do so, and thus claiming Crown privilege or public interest immunity to protect the documents. Crown privilege or public interest immunity is a common law rule which has been developed over the years by the courts; it is found most often in civil cases, but has been increasingly used in criminal cases, where it has caused considerable controversy. "Public interest immunity is needed because of the potential conflict between two important public interests: the clear public interest in the administration of justice, in a criminal case the fair trial of an accused, and what is sometimes also the clear public interest in the confidentiality of certain documents or information."[2]

16–02 The name of the rule has changed over the years. Originally, in both Scotland and England it was called "Crown privilege". The term persists in Scotland although it appears now to be more commonly known as "public interest privilege".[3] However, in England and Wales the term "Crown privilege" was felt to be inappropriate by Lord Reid in *Rogers v. Secretary of State for Home Department*[4] and it was changed to "public interest immunity".

---

[1] For general discussion, Zuckerman, "Public Interest Immunity — A Matter of Prime Judicial Responsibility" (1994) 57 M.L.R. 703.
[2] Lord Chancellor, Lord MacKay of Clashfern, *Hansard,* H.L., col. 1507 (December 18, 1996).
[3] McShane, "Crown Privilege in Scotland — The Demerits of Disharmony" (1992) 3 J.R. 256.
[4] [1972] 2 All E.R. 1057. See also *Alfred Crompton Amusement Machines Ltd v. Customs and Excise Commissioners (No. 2)* [1974] A.C. 405; [1973] 2 All E.R. 1169.

Lord Reid remarked that the expression "Crown privilege" was "wrong and may be misleading. There is no question of any privilege in the ordinary sense of the word".[5] Garner contends that the term was inappropriate because the decision as to public interest is made by the courts, not by the Executive.[6] Since about 1993, however, the expression "gagging order" has been used, particularly by the popular press in response to the events after the Matrix Churchill trial.

The law relating to public interest immunity has been undoubtedly confused and difficult in England and Wales but has not encountered the same difficulties in Scotland. "It is a rule of substantive law, a constitutional principle, and as a nation we would ignore it at our peril."[7] The development of the rule has taken a different path in Scotland as compared to England and Wales and in this chapter we will first discuss the position in Scotland, which is relatively straightforward, and then the position in England and Wales, where the rule is more complex.

THE DOCTRINE IN SCOTLAND

The common law rule was that discovery of documents could not be ordered   16–03
against the Crown where it was a party to the action. This rule was abolished by the Crown Proceedings Act 1947, s. 47, which applies only to Scotland, and s. 28 which applies to England and Wales. Both sections allow the courts to require the Crown to produce documents for inspection. Section 47 has two provisos:

> "(i) this subsection shall be without prejudice to any rule of law which au-
> thorises or requires the withholding of any document on the ground that its
> disclosure would be injurious to the public interest:
> (ii) the existence of a document shall not be disclosed if, in the opinion of a
> Minister of the Crown it would be injurious to the public interest to disclose
> the existence thereof."

Section 28 makes similar provisions for England and Wales.

According to McShane[8] the first proviso to section 47 leaves the common law of Crown privilege in Scotland untouched and thus has allowed it to be developed further. The discovery of documents in Scottish actions is further mentioned in the Administration of Justice (Scotland) Act 1972, s. 1(1), where the powers of the Court of Session and sheriff court were extended to allow "inspection, photographing, preservation, custody and detention of documents and other property". Section 1(4) extended the effect of section

---

[5]   [1972] All E.R. 1057 at 1060.
[6]   Jones and Thompson, *Garner's Administrative Law* (8th ed., 1996) p. 348.
[7]   Rt. Hon. Simon Brown L.J., "Public interest immunity" (1994) P.L. 579.
[8]   McShane, *op. cit.*, n. 3, above.

47 of the 1947 Act by allowing applications for the recovery of "other property" as well as documents.[9]

16–04   In Scotland, it appears that only the Crown may make objections to the production of evidence, using the public interest grounds. In England and Wales, the courts have recognised that other public bodies may be able to use public interest immunity[10] but the Scottish courts have not accepted that view.

> "There has been no case in Scotland ... in which public interest privilege has been extended beyond departments of national government or the Lord Advocate... Whatever may be the position in England I would respectfully adopt what was said by Lord Avonside in *Higgins*[11]... that public interest privilege in the strict sense is confined to the privilege of the Crown and the Lord Advocate."[12]

The Scottish courts have long exercised the right to challenge the Crown's plea of Crown privilege. In *Donald v. Hart*[13] the Inner House of the Court of Session refused to allow the production of a precognition relating to the pursuer's alleged wrongful imprisonment but went on to declare *per* Lord Hope, "I am not prepared to say, that there is no case in which the court would not, when it was necessary for the ends of justice ... order production of a precognition."[14] Crown counsel also recognised that Crown documents could not be withheld where "some great and overwhelming necessity was made out".[15]

16–05   Lord Normand in *Glasgow Corporation v. Central Land Board*[16] referred to the *Donald* case, stating that it had been the basis of a line of authority which recognised the power of the courts to order that Crown documents be produced in the public interest. There are a number of cases in this line of authority, expressing the court's inherent powers in this area, but not always exercising that power.[17] The Lord President in *Dowgray v. Gilmour*[18] asserted the court's right to order production but stated that "it would require very strong circumstances to induce the court to order the Lord Advocate to produce a document which he said it was against the public interest to produce".

---

[9] *P. Cannon (Garages) Ltd v. Lord Advocate,* 1983 S.L.T (Sh.Ct.) 50.
[10] For instance *D v. NSPCC* [1978] A.C. 710.
[11] *Higgins v. Burton*, 1968 S.L.T. (Notes) 52.
[12] *Parks v. Tayside Regional Council*, 1989 S.L.T. 345, *per* Lord Sutherland at 347I–348A.
[13] (1844) 6 D. 1255.
[14] *ibid.* at 1255–1256.
[15] See *Halcross v. Shearer* (1892) 20 R. 216; *Arthur v. Lindsay* (1895) 22 R. 417.
[16] 1956 S.C. (H.L.) 1.
[17] For instance, *Carmichael v. Scottish Co-operative and Welfare Society*, 1934 S.L.T. 158; *Rogers v. Orr*, 1939 S.C. 492.
[18] 1907 S.C. 715 at 720.

The courts also during this period recognised that the Crown had discretion in deciding whether or not a public interest objection should be made. This was affirmed in *Admiralty v. Aberdeen Steam Trawling and Fishing Co.*[19] The courts also recognised that the Crown should determine what constitutes the public interest and accepted that the courts could not therefore examine documents for which the claim had been made.[20]

After the *Duncan v. Cammell Laird* case[21] the Scottish courts found   16–06
themselves in some difficulty. Scottish authority stated that the Crown was the sole arbiter of what constituted public interest and *Rogers v. Orr* stated that such documents could not be inspected by the courts. The *Duncan* case, however, inferred that the courts would have to inspect documents to decide whether the Crown's objections were valid. The Scottish judges were reluctant to accept *Duncan* as binding authority and indeed it was not until the *Glasgow Corporation* case that the Inner House accepted that a validly stated objection by the Crown was conclusive. The House of Lords, however, took a different view, saying that *Duncan* did not represent the law of Scotland. The Lords held that the Scottish courts possessed an inherent power to disregard a claim of Crown privilege.

There have been no further pronouncements on this matter by the House of Lords in a Scottish case[22] and accordingly the case has to be taken as binding authority. The principles regarding the doctrine in Scotland can therefore be summarised as follows: first, only the Crown may raise a public interest objection; secondly, the court has an inherent power to reject such an objection; and thirdly, the court is not able to examine the document which is the subject of the claim for privilege. As will be seen below, these principles are at variance with the development of the doctrine in England and Wales, and some commentators have indicated that the English authorities will prevail in Scotland or at least will have a persuasive influence.[23]

With regard to who may be able to raise a public interest objection, the   16–07
position in England is that a public body may be able to object to the production of documents using public interest immunity. This was clearly stated by the House of Lords in *R v. Lewes Justices, ex parte Home Secretary*[24] where Lord Reid said "In my view, it must always be open to any person interested to raise the question (of privilege) and … the trial judge should himself raise the question if no-one else has done so…".[25]

---

[19]   1909 S.C. 335.
[20]   *Rogers v. Orr*, 1939 S.C. 492.
[21]   [1942] A.C. 624 discussed below.
[22]   McShane, *op. cit.*, n. 3, above, at 273.
[23]   See Field, *The Law of Evidence in Scotland* (1988), para. 11–12.
[24]   [1973] A.C. 388.
[25]   *ibid.* at 412.

The position in Scotland is difficult; binding authorities,[26] which have not been overruled, indicate that only the Crown itself may raise a public interest objection. Viscount Simonds observed: "The objection that was taken was one that could only be taken by or on behalf of the Crown."[27] In *Higgins v. Burton*[28] Lord Avonside confirmed that the public interest could only be put forward by a minister or by the Lord Advocate. This view was reaffirmed in *Parks v. Tayside Regional Council*[29] where Lord Sutherland added: "In my view, decisions of courts in England in this field have to be treated with some caution."[30]

16–08   The doctrine of Crown privilege in Scotland has developed differently from the doctrine in England and Wales but although the Scottish doctrine appears stricter it must be said that the Scottish courts have not appeared to have had the same problems as their English counterparts. The existence of different principles in an area of constitutional import is perhaps unfortunate. The undesirability of the situation between the two jurisdictions was referred to in *Lord Advocate v. Dumbarton District Council*.[31] The two jurisdictions could be brought into line by means of a judgment of the House of Lords in a Scottish case (it is doubtful that given the extent of litigation in England that they would change their authorities) or by legislation.

THE DOCTRINE IN ENGLAND

16–09   The Crown Proceedings Act 1947, s. 28 governs the discovery of documents in England and Wales. This section abolished the common law rule that discovery of documents could not be ordered against the Crown where it was a party to the action. Where the Crown was not a party, the rule was set out in *Duncan v. Cammell Laird*,[32] the House of Lords holding that regardless of whether the Crown was a party in a case, documents relevant and liable to production should not be produced if the public interest required that they be withheld. In this case, the dependants of men killed when a new submarine, the *Thetis*, sank during her sea trials sued the shipbuilders. The Admiralty objected to the release of the plans of the submarine.

The court held that a document could be withheld in two circumstances: first, where disclosure of the *contents* would be damaging to the public interest, for instance, it would endanger public security or prejudice diplomatic documents; an example would be the plans of the submarine

---

[26] Including *Admiralty v. Aberdeen Steam Trawling and Fishing Co.*, 1909 S.C. 335; *Rogers v. Orr*, 1939 S.C. 492; *Glasgow Corporation v. Central Land Board*, 1956 S.C. (H.L.) 1.
[27] 1956 S.C. (H.L.) 1.
[28] 1968 S.L.T. (Notes) 52.
[29] 1989 S.L.T. 345.
[30] *ibid.* at 348.
[31] [1990] 1 All E.R. 1, *per* Lord Keith at 7H–8A.
[32] [1942] A.C. 624.

Thetis. Secondly, the document belonged to a *class of documents* which the public interest required to be withheld from production to safeguard the "proper functioning of the public service". Examples would be civil service memoranda and minutes. The House of Lords also indicated that a certificate signed by a Minister objecting to the disclosure would be conclusive. In Scotland, the courts were not minded to follow this principle and indeed the House of Lords itself in 1956 decided that the Ministerial certificate was not conclusive and a Scottish judge could overrule it if he believed that best served the interests of justice.[33]

In *Duncan*, the House of Lords had unanimously agreed that a court 16–10 could never question a claim of Crown privilege made in the proper form regardless of the nature of the documents to which it referred. This applied to the contents of documents and to classes of documents. The effect of this ruling was to allow Ministers to be the sole arbiters of the public interest and if the Minister objected to the disclosure of a document after personal scrutiny by him or by the permanent head of the department in the Minister's absence, his certificate or affidavit had to be accepted by the court as conclusive. The circumstances of this case are worth noting; the case was heard at the height of the Second World War and this undoubtedly had an effect upon the outcome. The judges in *Conway v. Rimmer*,[34] while overturning the reasoning for the decision, nonetheless agreed with the final decision.

The consequences of the *Duncan* case in English law were profound. 16–11 These were noted by Lord Pearce in *Conway v. Rimmer*.[35] He said that departments quite naturally would wish their documents to remain confidential and unseen by the outside world and the claim for protection on the ground of candour was understandable. He quoted from Wade's *Administrative Law*[36]: "It is not surprising that the Crown, having been given a blank cheque, yielded to the temptation to overdraw." There was no weighing of injury done to litigants, and thus to the public at large, by the resulting denial of justice. He said that the court was unable to weigh the balance between a consideration of the public interest on the one hand in keeping the document confidential or the public interest on the other hand in ensuring justice was done. Wade remarked that the case gave the Crown the right to "override the rights of litigants not only in cases of genuine necessity but in any case where a government department thought fit".[37]

---

[33] *Glasgow Corporation v. Central Land Board*, 1956 S.C. (H.L.) 1; see *McKie v. SMT Co. Ltd*, 1952 S.C. 206; *Whitehall v. Whitehall*, 1957 S.C. 30; *Friel, Petr.*, 1981 S.L.T. 113.
[34] [1968] A.C. 910.
[35] *ibid.*
[36] (2nd ed., 1967) at p. 285.
[37] Wade and Forsyth, *Administrative Law* (1994), p. 847.

By the 1960s, there was considerable judicial pressure to reconsider *Duncan* and judges showed their disquiet with the situation. For instance, in *Re Grosvenor Hotel (London) Ltd (No. 2)*,[38] the Court of Appeal insisted on the Crown making it clear why immunity was being sought.

16–12   The claim that the contents of a particular document should not be released because of national security or some other valid reason was generally accepted as justifiable. However, the class claim was always more difficult to justify.[39] Certainly it was apparent that there was a public interest in ensuring that the public service was able to function properly but there was a fear that a blanket ban on certain classes of documents would in fact prevent justice being done in some cases. The government contended that if a class of document could be held to be immune from disclosure in one case and then released in another, this would prevent officials giving advice freely and with candour, since they would never know when that advice would be made public.

16–13   In 1956, the Lord Chancellor (Lord Kilmuir) made a statement in the House of Lords regarding the rule.

> "The reason why the law sanctions the claiming of Crown privilege on the 'class' ground is the need to secure freedom and candour of communications with and within the public service, so that Government decisions can be taken on the best advice and with the fullest information. In order to secure this, it is necessary that the class of documents to which privilege applies should be clearly settled, so that the person giving advice or information should know that he is doing so in confidence. Any system whereby a document falling within the class might, as a result of a later decision, be required to produce in evidence, would destroy that confidence and undermine the whole basis of class privilege, because there would be no certainty at the time of writing that the document would not be disclosed."[40]

To try to allay the fears of judges that the privilege was being claimed too readily, the Lord Chancellor said that privilege would not be claimed in certain areas, for instance reports of witnesses of accidents on roads or government premises or involving government employees; medical reports for civilian employees; medical reports where the Crown was being sued for negligence; materials required for defence against a criminal charge and witness statements to the police.

The House of Lords finally departed from its own precedent in *Conway v. Rimmer* and held that a Minister's certificate was not conclusive and the court would decide where the balance of public interest lay. In Scotland,

---

[38] [1965] Ch. 1210.
[39] See *Ellis v. Home Office* [1953] 2 Q.B. 135; [1953] 2 All E.R. 149.
[40] *Hansard*, H.L., Vol. 197, col. 742–743 (June 6, 1956).

the principle, giving the court discretion, had already been established in
Glasgow Corporation v. Central Land Board.[41]

Lord Reid gave the leading judgment in *Conway*. The full judgment is 16–14
worth reading but a short extract will serve here to indicate the depth and
clarity of Lord Reid's judgment.

> "It is universally recognised that there are two kinds of public interest which
> may clash. There is the public interest that harm shall not be done to the
> nation or the public service by disclosure of certain documents, and there
> is the public interest that the administration of justice shall not be frustrated
> by the withholding of documents which must be produced if justice is to be
> done. There are many cases where the nature of the injury which would or
> might be done to the nation or the public service is of so grave a character
> that no other interest, public or private, can be allowed to prevail over it.
> With regard to such cases it would be proper to say, as Lord Simon did, that
> to order production of the document in question would be to put the interest
> of the state in jeopardy. But there are many other cases where the possible
> injury to the public service, is much less and there one would think that it
> would be proper to balance the public interests involved. I do not believe
> that Lord Simon really meant that the smallest probability of injury to the
> public service must always outweigh the gravest frustration of the adminis-
> tration of justice."

Where a claim that a document should be withheld is made on the ground
that disclosure of its *contents* would be injurious to the public interest, the
position can be summarised as follows:

> "In those rare instances when a Minister claims that it would be contrary to
> the public interest to reveal a document on the ground that revelation of its
> contents would prejudice the public interest in, for example, national secu-
> rity or diplomatic relations, a court should be very reluctant to go behind the
> Executive's judgment or even to inspect the document itself. In the absence
> of abuse of authority, or manifest error of law or fact, a certificate covering
> these areas may well be conclusive."[42]

CLASS CLAIMS

On the *class* of documents, Lord Reid[43] described the kinds of documents 16–15
he thought would be exempt from discovery. He included Cabinet minutes
and documents not because disclosure would prevent Cabinet members
speaking candidly but because disclosure would "create or fan ill-formed
or captious public or political criticism". Thus, he also included policy papers

---

[41] 1956 S.C. (H.L.) 1.
[42] De Smith, Woolf and Jowell, *Judicial Review of Administrative Action* (1995), p. 75.
[43] [1968] A.C. 910 at 952–953.

within departments, and minutes of meetings and correspondence with outside bodies. Lord Widgery in *Attorney-General v. Jonathan Cape Ltd*[44] agreed with the idea that Cabinet papers be immune: "It is quite clear that no court will compel the production of Cabinet papers in the course of discovery in an action."

16–16   In *Air Canada v. Secretary of State for Trade (No. 2)*,[45] however, Lord Fraser considered that Cabinet papers had a high, but not complete, degree of protection. The applicants, however, failed in their case because they had not made out a sufficient case for inspection. The courts would not allow a 'fishing expedition'; the applicants had to show that there was a high probability that the documents contained material supportive to their case and that without those documents their case would be seriously damaged. The severity of this test was modified in *Re HIV Haemophiliac Litigation*[46] where 962 haemophiliacs who had been exposed to the risk of HIV infection through infected blood imports sought discovery of various documents from the Department of Health, including ministerial briefings on blood products and documents relating to the allocation of resources. The Court of Appeal adopted a two-stage approach; first considering whether the claim of public interest immunity was made out generally and secondly whether the claim could be overridden by the greater public interest in ensuring justice. The first approach required the applicant to show that the documents would very likely contain material of assistance to their claim but Ralph Gibson L.J. stated: "The test must, of course, be understood and applied with regard to the fact that the party seeking disclosure, and the court, know only the class of documents as described and do not know what is in them." The application for discovery, therefore, does not require to be as specific as appeared to be the case after *Air Canada*.

Routine documents would not normally be included in the immunity and here the courts would balance the interests of justice in disclosure against the interests of the public service in non-disclosure. Simon Brown L.J. referred to the class claim thus: "What documents in the class attract is more than a prima facie immunity from disclosure, an immunity dependent on there being no weightier public interest requiring their disclosure."[47]

16–17   Class claims now appear to rest not on arguments of candour in the public service, but on aspects of national interest such as international relations, police operations or national security. Simon Brown L.J. goes on to doubt whether class claims actually exist, or whether immunity is sought

---

[44] [1976] Q.B. 752.
[45] [1983] 2 A.C. 394; [1983] 1 All E.R. 910.
[46] 1990 New L.J. 1349.
[47] *R. v. Horseferry Road Magistrates' Court, ex p. Bennett (No. 2)* [1994] 1 All E.R. 289 at 293.

for the contents of the documents, rather than the class of document to which they belong.[48]

The position now seems to be that no class of document is immune automatically from disclosure. In *Burmah Oil Co v. Bank of England,*[49] Lord Wilberforce said that even if a claim for immunity was based on a level of public interest of the highest importance, that fact by itself was not necessarily conclusive, and the public interest might on occasion prevail against it. In 1974, the company was in financial difficulties and entered into talks with the Bank of England and the Government to try to prevent its liquidation. On the Government's instructions, the bank offered to buy certain shares held by the company. The bank considered that Burmah should receive a share of any profits realised from the sale of the shares but the Government did not agree. Within a year, the value of the shares had doubled and Burmah brought an action to try to have the sale set aside on the grounds that it was unconscionable, unreasonable and at an undervalue. On the bank's list of documents, papers relating to the involvement of the Government were included and, on the instructions of the Government, the bank objected to their discovery. The Minister signed a public interest immunity certificate on the grounds that disclosure would be injurious to the public interest. The documents fell into three categories. Category A related to the formulation of government policy; category B related to communications between the bank and the Government on the policies referred to in category A. The documents in category C related to minutes of meetings between representatives of other oil companies and the Government. These notes recorded information given in confidence and it was argued that these should be withheld to preserve confidentiality and ensure such information would be given in future.

While Lord Reid had referred to documents such as Cabinet minutes being exempt from discovery, thus protecting the inner workings of government,[50] Lord Keith in this case said:

16–18

> "The courts are … concerned with the consideration that it is in the public interest that justice should be done and should be publicly recognised as having been done. This may demand, though no doubt only in a very limited number of cases, that the inner workings of government should be exposed to public gaze, and there may be some who would regard this as likely to lead, not to captious or ill-informed criticism, but to criticism calculated to improve the nature of that working as affecting the individual citizen."[51]

---

[48] *R. v. Horseferry Road Magistrates' Court, ex p. Bennett (No. 2)* [1994] 1 All E.R. 289 at 298.
[49] [1980] A.C. 1090.
[50] [1968] A.C. 910.
[51] [1980] A.C. 1090 at 1134.

Lord Scarman was also doubtful about the Government keeping documents secret where they did not relate to national security. He did not think that such secrets would justify injustice in the courts.

However, it should be noted that once an actual or potential risk to national security is identified in a Ministerial certificate the courts will not inspect the documents.[52] The implications of the words "national security" thus have some import, although there is a fear that a Minister could improperly or incorrectly certify that a document should be withheld on this ground and the courts would accept this without question.[53] The court is required to balance the interest of protecting the function of the public service and the interests of securing the administration of justice.[54]

16–19   The position of documents and statements made in the course of police complaint investigations has been considered on a number of occasions. They were held by the Court of Appeal to belong to a class of document which should not be disclosed on public interest grounds.[55] However, in *R. v. Chief Constable of West Midlands, ex parte Wiley*,[56] the House of Lords overruled these previous decisions concerning statements obtained during investigations under the Police and Criminal Evidence Act 1984. A class claim did not attach generally to all documents made during the course of an investigation under the 1984 Act, because there was no clear and compelling evidence that a class-based public interest immunity was necessary. The court observed that a contents claim might be available. The case did not, however, address the question of whether a public interest immunity claim could be made in respect of the report of an investigating officer into a complaint of police misconduct. The Court of Appeal resolved this by saying that such reports were of a class which could be covered by the immunity.[57] The reason given was that such officers needed to be free to report on professional colleagues or members of the public without being concerned that their opinions would become known to such persons. However, it appears that the question of public interest immunity attaching

---

[52] *Balfour v. Foreign and Commonwealth Office* [1994] 2 All E.R. 588; this case confirmed the *Duncan v. Cammell Laird* position as regards national security implications.

[53] For instance as occurred in the *Matrix Churchill* case discussed below; note that in the U.S. the courts have retained jurisdiction to judge claims of privilege on grounds of national security — *United States v. Reynolds* 345 U.S. 1(1953).

[54] See *AB v. Glasgow and West of Scotland Blood Transfusion Service*, 1993 S.L.T. 36, where it was held that a plea of public interest privilege in a certificate signed by a Minister should be overridden only if it was patently unreasonable or was expressed on an erroneous basis.

[55] For instance *Neilson v. Laugharne* [1981] Q.B. 736; [1981] 1All E.R. 829; *Makanjuola v. Metropolitan Police Commissioner* [1992] 3 All E.R. 617, C.A.; *Halford v. Sharples* [1992] 1 W.L.R. 736.

[56] [1994] 3 All E.R. 420.

[57] *Taylor v. Chief Constable of Greater Manchester* [1995] 2 All E.R. 420.

to such documents depends on not the class, but on the contents, of the specific documents.

The question of confidentiality has raised difficulties. In *Rogers v. Home Secretary* [58] Rogers had been refused a licence under the Gaming Acts on the strength of a letter from the chief constable to the Gaming Board. Rogers then raised an action of criminal libel against the Chief Constable alleging that the libel was in the letter written by him. The House of Lords held that the letter from the chief constable should not be produced because it belonged to a class of document which should be protected. The board could not properly carry out its investigative duties regarding applicants for licences unless it could preserve the confidentiality of communications to it.

TYPE OF BODY WHICH MAY CLAIM PUBLIC INTEREST IMMUNITY

It is obvious that government departments will claim public interest immunity most often, but over the years, the English courts have allowed a number of other bodies to claim public interest immunity. The courts have however adopted a case-by-case approach. As well as the Gaming Board in *Rogers* the courts have included other bodies. 16–20

In *D v. NSPCC*,[59] the House of Lords said that public interest immunity extended to bodies who could bring care proceedings under statute, particularly where the confidentiality of information was important. In this case, an informant told the NSPCC that D was abusing her child. The allegations were unfounded and D tried to take civil action against the informant. The NSPCC however refused to divulge the name of the informant and the House of Lords agreed that disclosing such information might prevent others from giving information about suspected child abuse. "The private promise of confidentiality must yield to the general public interest that in the administration of justice truth will out, unless by reason of the character of the information or the relationship of the recipient of the information to the informant, a more important public interest is served by protecting the information or the identity of the informant from disclosure in a court of law."[60] The status of the public body was held not to be sufficient reason in itself to justify a claim for public interest immunity.[61]

---

[58] [1973] A.C. 388; [1972] 2 All E.R. 1057.
[59] [1978] A.C. 171; [1977] 1 All E.R. 589.
[60] *ibid., per* Lord Diplock.
[61] *Science Research Council v. Nasse* [1980] A.C. 1028; *Leyland Cars Ltd v. Vyas* [1980] A.C. 1028; [1979] 3 All E.R. 673, H.L.

THE CANDOUR ARGUMENT

16–21   The candour argument has been put forward by the government as a means of preventing discovery. The argument is that if an official gives advice, whether in writing or during the course of a meeting, then he will be inhibited from giving full and frank advice if there is a possibility that the advice will be disclosed at some future date. To ensure that officials speak with candour, public interest immunity should be claimed. Lord Keith of Kinkel doubted whether the candour argument had any validity. "The notion that any competent and conscientious public servant would be inhibited at all in the candour of his writings by consideration of the off-chance that they might have to be produced in a litigation is in my opinion grotesque."[62]

Confidentiality is not of itself a separate ground for withholding evidence. This was established in *Alfred Crompton Amusement Machines Ltd v. Customs and Excise Commissioners (No. 2),*[63] where the court held that confidentiality was not of itself a reason for non-disclosure but could be a material consideration when privilege was claimed on the ground of public interest. Another leading case in this area is *D. v. NSPCC.*[64]

16–22   The court will consider: the significance of the documents in relation to the likely effect on the decision in the case; whether their absence results in a partial or complete denial of justice to one or both parties, and the importance of the litigation to the parties and the public. This was illustrated in *Peach v. Commissioner of Police of the Metropolis,*[65] where the balance of justice in knowing how a man died outweighed the confidentiality of evidence collected from informers. The court will normally only order production of documents obtained under compulsory powers where the administration of justice outweighs the public interest in the confidentiality of the documents.[66] In *Norwich Pharmacal Co. v. Customs and Excise Commissioners*[67] information was given in confidence and under statutory duty. The House of Lords said that there was no statutory provision to prevent the court ordering disclosure if the public interest in the administration of justice so required it and disclosure was ordered.

CATEGORIES OF CLASSES WHICH MAY ATTRACT IMMUNITY

16–23   (a) Police informers. There are limits here if the interests of justice outweigh the interests of non-identification of informants.

---

[62] *Burmah Oil Co. v. Bank of England* [1980] A.C. 1090 at 1133.
[63] [1974] A.C. 405.
[64] [1978] A.C. 171; [1977] 1 All E.R. 589.
[65] [1986] Q.B. 1064.
[66] *Lonrho plc v. Fayed (No. 4)* [1994] 1 All E.R. 870.
[67] [1974] A.C. 133; [1973] 2 All E.R. 943.

(b) Proceedings regarding the welfare of children. The decision in *D v. NSPCC*[68] was upheld in a later case where the proper functioning of a child care service was held to require that confidential reports remain undisclosed.[69] However, where a teacher had been assaulted by a violent pupil and sought damages, it was held that the teacher would be denied justice if the reports of psychologists on the pupil's nature were not disclosed.[70]

(c) Journalists' sources. The courts have generally rejected attempts by journalists to claim public interest immunity. For instance in *British Steel v. Granada TV*[71] the corporation tried to obtain a list of names of people who had supplied the television company with British Steel documents, these being used by Granada in a programme about British Steel. The House of Lords upheld the decision to grant the order for discovery. However, the Contempt of Court Act 1981, s. 10, says that there is no requirement to disclose sources except where the court considers it necessary in the interests of justice or national security or for the prevention of disorder or crime.

(d) Communications between police forces may be a class claim although they have been made available in judicial review proceedings.[72]

PROBLEMS

One of the most difficult problems to be overcome by a party who wants to see a document which may attract PII is knowing whether the document exists, and then whether its contents have any relevance to his case. A party wanting disclosure has to show that the document will have a central bearing on the case, but he may not be able to prove this if he does not know what is in the document — Catch 22! The party wanting disclosure will also have to provide a reasonably accurate description of the document so that it can be identified; the courts will not allow vague descriptions. In other words, the court will not allow a "fishing expedition". The applicant has to show that the document is necessary for the fair disposal of the case or for saving costs. In *Air Canada v. Secretary of State for Trade (No. 2)*[73] Lord Keith of Kinkel took the view that the test should be that of reasonable probability. If the claim for disclosure shows relevance, the judge may then examine the documents and will decide whether they may be released to the party requesting disclosure.

16–24

[68] [1978] A.C. 171.
[69] *Gaskin v. Liverpool City Council* [1980] 1 W.L.R. 1549.
[70] *Campbell v. Tameside Metropolitan Borough Council* [1982] Q.B. 1065; [1982] 2 All E.R. 791.
[71] [1981] A.C. 1096.
[72] *R v. Horseferry Road Magistrates' Court, ex p. Bennett (No. 2)* [1994] 1 All E.R. 289.
[73] [1983] 2 A.C. 394.

CRIMINAL CASES

16–25   There are fewer cases of public interest immunity in criminal actions, largely because the individual's life or liberty is involved and the courts have thus taken a tougher line with the Executive. The balance of interest in criminal trials will be different to that in civil proceedings and Mann L.J. observed that the privilege of public interest immunity could not "prevail if the evidence is necessary for the prevention of a miscarriage of justice. No balance is called for. If admission is necessary to prevent miscarriage of justice, balance does not arise".[74] The 1956 statement by the Lord Chancellor outlined the Government's policy on the use of public interest immunity in criminal cases. "We also propose that if medical documents, or indeed other documents are relevant to the defence in criminal proceedings, Crown privilege should not be claimed. At present many of these documents are made available only in the case of the more serious crimes, such as murder, manslaughter and rape." [75] Lord Reid in *Conway* noted that documents might be made available for a criminal case and then PII claimed for those same documents in a subsequent civil case. This was to protect the *writer* from civil suit, not to protect the documents. In *Neilson v. Laugharne*[76] Oliver L.J. said: "If public policy prevents disclosure, it prevents it, in my judgment, in all circumstances except to establish innocence in criminal proceedings."

16–26   In 1981, the Attorney-General issued "Guidelines for the disclosure of unused material to the defence in cases to be tried on indictment".[77] These rules have largely been superseded by decisions of the courts. The Criminal Procedure and Investigations Act 1996 has now replaced the common law rules regarding disclosure.

The prosecution's duty to disclose "unused material" to the defence was established in *R. v. Bryant and Dickson*[78] and extended in *Dallison v. Caffery*.[79] In *R. v. Hennessey (Timothy)*,[80] the courts held that those who prepare and conduct prosecutions owe a duty to the courts to ensure that all relevant evidence of help to the accused is either led by them or made available. The 1981 guidelines, however, said that in certain cases there was a discretion not to disclose material until counsel has advised on the matter. These cases would be where there was an issue of national security, or the material disclosed the identity of an informer which would put him

---

[74] *R. v. Governor of Brixton Prison, ex p. Osman* [1992] 1 All E.R. 108 at 118.

[75] *Hansard*, H.L., Vol. 197, col. 742–743 (June 6, 1956).

[76] [1981] 1 Q.B. 736 at 753.

[77] [1982] 74 Cr. App. R. 302; Practice Note [1982] 1 All E.R. 743.

[78] [1946] 31 Cr. App. R. 146.

[79] [1965] 1 Q.B. 348.

[80] [1978] 68 Cr. App. R. 419.

in danger, or it discloses evidence by a witness who might be intimidated, or the details would facilitate another offence, or it was supplied on a confidential basis, or it contains details of private "delicacy" which might lead to domestic strife. Note that the guidelines were advisory only and they did not form part of the law.

Case law in fact superseded the guidelines. In *R. v. Saunders et al*[81] the definition of "unused material" was widened; the defence were entitled to material "that has, or might have, some bearing on the offences charged", including preparatory notes and tape recordings which led to the making of the witness statements. In *R. v. Ward*[82] the court quashed a conviction for murder and causing explosions in an IRA bombing campaign of the 1970s. The Court of Appeal further extended the prosecution's duty of disclosure; it was for the court, not the prosecution, to judge whether the material may be properly withheld from the defence on the ground of public interest immunity. The court also stated that if the prosecution were unwilling to have the issue of public interest immunity determined by the court, then the prosecution must be abandoned. This decision put the defence in a better position since it made the courts the final arbiters of the claim of public interest immunity, rather than the prosecution, thus increasing the chances of the prosecution not proceeding.[83]

16–27

The *Ward* approach was qualified in *R. v. Davis, Johnson & Rowe*[84]; where public interest immunity is relied on to justify non-disclosure the prosecution should give notice to the defence that an application is being made for a ruling by the court, indicating the category of the material. If indicating the category would reveal something which should be revealed, then the prosecution should simply inform the defence that an application is being made and the case should then proceed *ex parte*. Thereafter, if the public interest immunity application is allowed, the court should continue to monitor the position and if necessary change its view. If this occurs, the prosecution should be asked to reconsider their case. However, this means that Ministers could make a claim in secret, the court could uphold the claim and the defence would be left in the position of having no knowledge of the claim and no opportunity to comment on it. In such a situation, the role of the court in ensuring the rights of the defence become crucial.

In 1994, the Court of Appeal commented on how to determine whether material the Crown wished to withhold might be of assistance to the defence.[85] The prosecution should put before the court those documents it regards as material but wishes to withhold. The judge will then balance the

16–28

---

[81] Unreported, September 29, 1990.
[82] [1993] 2 All E.R. 577.
[83] Smith, "Public interest immunity and Sensitive Material" (1993) 52 C.L.J. 357.
[84] [1993] 1 W.L.R. 613.
[85] *R. v. Keane* [1994] 2 All E.R. 478.

public interest in non-disclosure as against the interests of justice and fairness to the defence. The prosecution is now obliged to disclose any material which might undermine the prosecution case.[86] In *R. v. Brown*[87] the Court of Appeal gave four propositions. First, it is for the court to rule on the question of immunity and so the court has to study the material for which immunity is claimed. Secondly, the judge has to perform the balancing exercise. Thirdly, the balancing exercise has to be reconciled with the defendant's fundamental right to a fair trial; if the disputed material may prove the defendant's innocence or avoid a miscarriage of justice, the balance "comes down resoundingly" in favour of disclosure. Finally, even if the trial judge comes down initially in favour of public interest immunity, he is under a duty to keep that decision under review during the trial.

Note that the Criminal Procedure and Investigations Act 1996, s. 3(1), places the prime responsibility for disclosure upon the prosecutor, not the court.

16–29   The number of criminal cases involving public interest immunity is very small; in the 10 years from 1986 to 1995, only 18 applications were made by the Crown Prosecution Service in England and Wales. In *R. v. Governor of Brixton Prison, ex parte Osman*[88] Mann L.J. observed that there were few cases giving authority and suggested that the explanation perhaps was that prosecutions were not brought where sensitive material was involved.

It has been argued, however, that the application of public interest immunity principles to criminal cases should not be made since they apply essentially to civil matters under section 28 of the 1947 Act. Sir Richard Scott maintained that public interest immunity claims might be made in criminal cases but that specific principles should be devised for criminal cases, rather than use those which have been developed for civil cases.[89] "In a criminal trial the balance must always come down in favour of disclosure if there is any real possibility that the withholding of the documents may cause or contribute to a miscarriage of justice. The public interest factors underlying the public interest immunity claim cannot ever, I suggest, have a weight sufficient to outweigh that possibility." He went on to state that the judge in a criminal trial cannot perform the balancing exercise which is appropriate in civil trials, since the scales should never be allowed to tip in favour of public interest factors at the expense of justice. In criminal cases "The only question is, or should be, whether the documents in question may assist the defendant in proving his innocence."

---

[86] 1996 Act, s. 3.
[87] [1994] 1 W.L.R. 1599.
[88] [1992] 1 All E.R. 108.
[89] Scott, "The use of public interest immunity claims in criminal cases" (1996) 3 Web Journal of Current Legal Issues, Pt. 1.

CRIMINAL PROCEDURE AND INVESTIGATIONS ACT 1996

Part 1 of this Act applies to the rules on disclosure in criminal cases and   16–30
replaces in the main the common law provisions with statutory requirements.
Part 1 applies only to England and Wales. The common law rules on non-
disclosure in the public interest, that is public interest immunity, remain.
Non-disclosure in the public interest is specifically allowed and third parties
who are originators of sensitive material may still request non-disclosure,
for instance in child welfare cases.

VOLUNTARY DISCLOSURE

Voluntary disclosure of material which would normally attract public interest   16–31
immunity is permissible with the express approval of the Treasury Solicitor,
who would then consult with other departments and decide whether the
balance of interest was in favour of disclosure.[90] Bingham L.J. defined it
thus: "Public interest immunity is not a trump card vouchsafed to certain
privileged players, to play when and as they wish. It is an exclusionary
rule, imposed on parties in certain circumstances, even where it is to their
disadvantage in litigation."[91]

There is some evidence that the prosecution have made documents,
normally covered by public interest immunity, available to the court where
these documents are helpful to the prosecution case. For instance, in the
Ponting trial, highly secret documents known as "The Crown Jewels" were
admitted in evidence although the court had to go *in camera* and the jury
members were vetted. In the trial of Randle and Pottle for helping George
Blake to escape, Special Branch documents were put before the court —
these had not previously been acknowledged and no public interest immunity
was claimed. In *M v. Home Office*[92] the notes of a meeting between the
Home Secretary, Kenneth Baker, and his officials were released to the court,
although such notes would normally have been immune. The view was
taken that the greater public interest lay in the court hearing a full account
of the facts.

DUTY TO ASSERT PUBLIC INTEREST IMMUNITY AND MATRIX CHURCHILL CASE

The *Matrix Churchill* case has become something of a cause célèbre.[93] Three   16–32
directors of the Matrix Churchill company were prosecuted for allegedly

---

[90] *R v. Horseferry Road Magistrates' Court, ex p. Bennett (No. 2)* [1994] 1 All E.R. 289.
[91] *Makanjuola v. Commissioner of Police for the Metropolis* [1992] 3 All E.R. 617 at 623.
[92] [1992] 2 W.L.R. 73.
[93] See, for instance, Ganz, "Matrix Churchill and Public interest immunity" (1993) 109 M.L.R. 564; Tomkins, "Public interest immunity after Matrix Churchill" (1993) 109 P.L. 530.

breaching the Government's guidelines on exports to Iraq of materials which could be used for military purposes. The accused contended that the Government had known of their activities and sought discovery of documents which support their assertions. Four Government Ministers signed public interest immunity certificates stating that the documents belonged to a class which should not be released. The prosecution collapsed after a former Government Minister, Alan Clarke, revealed in evidence that the Government had been aware of the company's activities. There was much public disquiet over the case, since it appeared that the Government, and in particular the four Ministers, had been conspiring to send innocent men to prison. The Government was forced to set up the Inquiry into the Export of Defence Equipment and Dual-Use Goods to Iraq and Related Prosecutions, otherwise known as the Scott Inquiry.[94]

The Scott Inquiry addressed a number of issues with regard to the use of public interest immunity in criminal cases. It accepted that public interest immunity was available in criminal cases but stated that it should not succeed if the document contained material of use to the defence.[95] Scott also felt that class claims should not be available in criminal trials. He was concerned that the Government could prevent a document, which was prima facie disclosable and the contents of which did not justify a contents claim, from being disclosed by using a class claim.[96]

16–33   During the case and in the inquiry and debates held in its wake, the Attorney-General asserted that the Ministers involved in signing the public interest immunity certificates had no choice but to sign, indeed he said that they had a duty to do so. On November 10, 1992, the Attorney-General made a statement to the House of Commons in which he said that the courts had indicated that Ministers have a duty to claim public interest immunity for either specific documents or recognised classes of documents.

He also claimed that the duty could not be waived, basing this assertion apparently on two cases. In *Rogers v. Secretary of State for the Home Department*, Lord Simon said "'Crown privilege' is not a privilege which may be waived — by the Crown — or by anyone else." Lord Scarman in *Air Canada v. Secretary of State for Trade (No. 2)*[97] said:

> "The Crown, when it puts forward a public interest immunity objection, is not claiming a privilege but is discharging a duty. The duty arises whether the document assists or damages the Crown's case or, if, as in a case to which the Crown is not a party, it neither helps not injures the Crown. It is not for the Crown but for the court to determine whether the document should be produced."

---

[94] (1995–96 H.C. 115).
[95] *ibid*. para. G10.10.
[96] *ibid*. para. K6.25.
[97] [1983] 1 All E.R. 910.

In the *Wiley* case, the court discussed the duty to assert public interest   16–34
immunity and voluntary disclosure. Lord Templeman said that if a document
is known to be relevant and material, the holder of it should voluntarily
disclose it unless he is satisfied it will cause substantial harm. If he is in
doubt he should refer the matter to the court. "A rubber stamp approach to
public interest immunity by the holder of a document is neither necessary
nor appropriate."[98]

Of course, the *Wiley* decision was made after the *Matrix Churchill* case
but the point regarding the duty or otherwise of ministers to sign public
interest immunity certificates was debated in the House of Commons and
discussed at length in the Scott Report.

In his report, Sir Richard Scott observed:

> "None of the submissions to the respective Ministers made the Ministers
> aware that in criminal trials public interest immunity class claims for Cat-
> egory B documents were certainly unusual and had not been underwritten by
> judicial *dicta*. The Ministers were not made aware that neither of the decided
> cases to which reference was made, namely *Conway v. Rimmer* and
> *Makanjuola*, was a criminal case."

Scott also felt that the view expressed by the Attorney-General that a   16–35
minister is under a duty to claim public interest immunity was based on a
fundamental misconception of the principles of public interest immunity
law. He asserted that the minister should be satisfied that the production of
the documents would cause damage to the public interest. The approach of
Lord Templeman in *Wiley* above was regarded by Scott as sensible and
practical. Scott's view appears to be borne out by a letter from the former
Prime Minister Lord Callaghan in which he stated: "I was never advised by
law officers or civil servants that a class of documents existed which placed
a binding duty upon a minister to sign a public interest immunity certificate
irrespective of its contents."[99]

In the *Matrix Churchill* case, it appears that one of the Ministers who
was required by the Attorney-General to sign a certificate was under the
impression that the judge would see the documents and make a decision as
to their relevancy. "I would not have acted in the way I did unless I had
been absolutely satisfied that the judge would make available those
documents or those parts of a document which he considered necessary for
the proper conduct of the case."[1] However, it appears that in this case, the
prosecution told the judge that the documents contained nothing of assistance
to the defence. It was not until the counsel for Henderson, one of the accused,
brought out his links with MI6 (against the advice of the counsel for the

---

[98] [1994] 3 All E.R. 420 at 424.
[99] *The Times*, February 24, 1994.
[1] Michael Heseltine, in House of Commons debate, November 23, 1992.

other two) that the judge then ordered disclosure of documents on the security services. It appears that the judge had to be persuaded to order disclosure.

16–36   The Scott Report recommended *inter alia* that public interest immunity claims should only be made in criminal trials in relation to documents which might be of assistance to the defence if, in the opinion of the person putting forward the claim, disclosure would cause substantial harm; and if the judge is asked to rule on the claim he should be asked to decide whether the documents might be of assistance to the defence, and if a document satisfies that test, it ought not to be withheld on public interest grounds.

After publication of the Scott Report, the Government promised to consider the recommendations and consult with interested parties. Accordingly on December 18, 1996, the Attorney-General and the Lord Chancellor made statements to the House of Commons and the House of Lords respectively regarding the future of public interest immunity in relation to government documents as it operates in England and Wales.[2]

The Attorney-General referred to the *ex parte Wiley* case, stating that Ministers now had the general discretion to disclose documents without the prior approval of the court if they felt this was in the public interest. The new approach of the Government is that a Minister will focus directly on the damage that disclosure would cause and that class claims will no longer be made. A Minister will claim public interest immunity only when he is convinced that the disclosure of a document would cause real damage or harm to the public interest. The Attorney-General gave examples of when he thought damage might occur, for instance, in relation to the safety of an individual, or damage to international relations by disclosure of confidential diplomatic communications. He stated that, in all cases where public interest immunity is claimed, the nature of the harm will be explained. He went on to state that Ministers will not in future claim public interest immunity "to protect either internal advice or national security material merely by pointing to the general nature of the document".[3]

The new guidelines apply only to claims made by the Government. They will not apply to other organisations such as the police, where the expectation was that the existing practices would continue.

16–37   The Lord Chancellor was asked during his statement whether the new guidelines would apply to Scotland. He stated that since the difficulties had arisen in England and Wales only and there had been no such difficulties in Scotland, the statement did not apply to Scotland. He acknowledged that while the principles in the two jurisdictions were the same, the development of law and practice was different as was the administration of justice.

---

[2]   *Hansard*, H.C. 287 col. 949 (December 18, 1996); 576 col. 1507 (December 18, 1986).
[3]   *Hansard*, H.C. 287 col. 950.

BIBLIOGRAPHY

BOOKS

Bradley, A.W., "Administrative Law" in *Stair Memorial Encyclopaedia on the Laws of Scotland*, Vol. 1, (1987), The Law Society of Scotland/ Butterworths.
Bradley, A.W. and Ewing, K.D. Wade and Bradley, *Constitutional Law and Administrative Law* (1993) Longmans

Cane, P., *An Introduction to Administrative Law* (2nd ed., 1992) Clarendon Press
Clyde, (Lord) "The nature of the Supervisory Jurisdiction and the Public/ Private Distinction in Scots Administrative Law" in Finnie W., Himsworth C.M.G. and N. Walker, *Edinburgh Essays in Public Law* (1991) Edinburgh University Press
Craig P.P., *Administrative Law* (3rd ed., 1994) Sweet & Maxwell

Deans, M., *Scots Public Law* (1995) T&T Clark,
Dicey, A.V. (ECS Wade, ed.), *The Law of the Constitution* (10th ed., 1959) Macmillan

Edwards, D, "Administrative Law in Scotland: The Public Law/ Private Law Distinction revisited" in Cuffin, D. and O'Keefe, D. (eds.) *Constitutional Adjudication on EC and National Law: Essays for the Hon. Mr Justice T. F O'Higgins* (1992) Butterworths

Fenwick, H. and Phillipson, G., S*ource Book on Public Law* (1996) Cavendish Publishing Ltd
Foulkes, D., *Administrative Law* (8th ed., 1995) Butterworths

Ganz, G., *Quasi-Legislation: Recent Developments in Secondary Legislation* (1994) Sweet & Maxwell
Ganz G., *Understanding Public Law* (2nd ed., 1994) Fontana
Genn, H., "Tribunal Review of Administrative Decision-making", in Richardson G. and Genn H., *Administrative Law and Government Action* (1994) Clarendon Press
Gillis, R., "Information Law, Policy and Ethics: Canadian Federal Government Experience" in Thomas R., *Teaching Ethics* (1993) Centre for Business and Public Sector Ethics
Graham C. (1994) "Self-Regulation", in Richardson, G. and Genn, H. *Administrative Law and Government Action* (1994) Clarendon Press

Greer, P., *Transforming Central Government: The Next Steps Initiative* (1994) Open University Press

Halsbury's Laws of England (4th ed., vol. 1 (reissue) 1989), Butterworths
Harden, I., *The Contracting State* (1992) Open University Press
Harlow, C. and Rawlings R., *Law and Administration* (1984) Weidenfeld & Nicolson
Helm, D. (ed.), *British Utility Regulation:Principles, Experience and Reform* (1995) Oxera Press
Hewart (Lord), *The New Despotism* (1929)
Himsworth, C.M.G., "Judicial Review in Scotland," in *Judicial Review a Thematic Approach*, Hadfield, B. (ed.) (1995) Gill & Macmillan
Himsworth, C.M.G., *Local Government Law in Scotland* (1995) T&T Clark,
Hogwood B., "The Growth of Quangos: Evidence and Explanations", in Ridley F. and Wilson D., *The Quango Debate* (1995) Oxford University Press
Hutton N., *Lay Participation in a Public Local Inquiry* (1986) Gower Publishing

Jennings I., *The Laws of the Constitution*, (5th ed., 1959) University of London Press
Jones B. and Thompson K., *Garner's Administrative Law* (8th ed., 1996) Butterworths
Jowell, J. and Oliver D. (eds.), *New Directions in Judicial Review* (1988) Stevens
Jowell J. and Oliver D., *The Changing Constitution* (1994) Clarendon Press
Jowell, J. and Birkenshaw, P., "On the Convergence of the Administrative Laws of the EU Member States" in Schwarze, J. (ed.), *Administrative Law under European Influence* (1996) Sweet & Maxwell

Kames Lord, *Historical Law Tracts* (5th ed.)

McAllister, A. and McMaster, R., *Scottish Planning Law* (1994) Butterworths
McAuslan, P. and McEldowney, J., *Law, Legitimacy and the Constitution* (1985) Sweet & Maxwell
McEldowney, J., *Public Law* (1994) Sweet & Maxwell
Maloney, A., "The Ombudsman as Mediator, Reformer and Fighter", in Caidon, G., *International Handbook of the Ombudsman* (1983) Greenwood Press
Maxwell, D., *The Practice of the Court of Session* (1980) Scottish Courts Administration
Miers, D. and Page, A., *Legislation* (1990) Sweet & Maxwell
Mitchell, J. *Constitutional Law* (2nd ed., 1968) W. Green

Natzler, D. and Silk, P., "Departmental Select Committees and the Next Steps programme", in Drewry, G. and Giddings, P., *Parliament and executive agencies* (1994)

O'Toole, B. and Chapman, R., "Parliamentary Accountability", in O'Toole, B. and Jordan, G., *Next Steps: Improving Management in Government* (1994) Dartmouth Publishing
Oliver, D., *Government in the UK: The Search for Accountability, Efficiency and Citizenship* (1994) Open University Press
Osborne, D. and Gaebler, T., *Reinventing Government* (1992) Addison Wesley

Ponting, C., *Secrecy in Britain* (1990) Blackwell Press
Prosser, T., *Nationalised Industries and Public Control: Legal, Constitutional and Political Issues* (1994) Blackwell
Prosser, T., "Regulation, Markets and Legitimacy", in Jowell, J. and Oliver, D., *The Changing Constitution* (1994) Clarendon Press
Puttick, K., *Challenging Delegated Legislation* (1988) Waterlow
Pyper, R. and Robins, L., *Governing the UK in the 1990s* (1995) MacMillan

Reid, C.T., "Judicial Review and the Environment" in *Judicial Review a Thematic Approach* Hadfield, B. (ed.) (1995) Gill & Macmillan
Richardson, G. and Genn, H., *Administrative Law and Government Action* (1994) Clarendon Press
Richardson, G. and Genn, H. (eds), *Sovereignty, Accountability and the Reform of Administrative Law in Administrative Law and Government Action* (1994)
Ridley, F. and Wilson, D., *The Quango Debate* (1995) Oxford University Press
Robinson, S.S. *The Law of Interdict* (2nd ed., 1994), Butterworths / Law Society of Scotland
Roper, M. "Access to Public Records", in Chapman, R. and Hunt, M. *Open Government* (1987) Routledge
Rush, M., "Parliamentary Scrutiny", in Pyper, R. and Robins, L., *Governing the UK in the 1990s* (1995) MacMillan

Seneviratne, M., *Ombudsmen in the Public Sector* (1994) Open University Press
Schwarze, J., *European Administrative Law* (1992) Sweet & Maxwell
St. Clair, J. and Davidson, N.F., *Judicial Review in Scotland* (1986) W. Green
Steele, J., *Public Access to Information* (1995) Policy Studies Institute/ Department of Environment
Street, H., *Justice in the Welfare State* (1975) Stevens
Sunkin, M., Bridges, L. and Meszaros, *Judicial Review in Perspective Public Law Project* (2nd ed, 1996) Cavendish

Thomas, R., *Teaching Ethics* (1993) Centre for Business and Public Sector Ethics
Turpin, C., *British Government and the Constitution* (3rd ed., 1975) Butterworths

Wade, H.W.R. and Forsyth, C., *Administrative Law* (7th ed., 1994) Clarendon Press,
Waldegrave, W., *The reality of reform and accountability in today's public service* (1993) Public Finance Foundation
Watson, G.A., *Bell's Dictionary and Digest of the Laws of Scotland* (1889) Bell and Bradfute
Weir, S., "Questions of Democratic Accountability", in Ridley, F. and Wilson, D., *The Quango Debate* (1995) Oxford University Press
Wilson, D., "Quangos in the Skeletal State", in Ridley, F. and Wilson, D., *The Quango Debate* (1995) Oxford University Press
Winetrobe, B., "Next Steps and Parliamentary Scrutiny", in Drewry, G. and Giddings, P., *Parliament and executive agencies* (1994)
Wolffe W.J., "Crown and Prerogative in Scots Law," in Finnie W., C.M.G. Himsworth C.M.G. and Walker N. (eds.), *Edinburgh Essays in Public Law* (1991) Edinburgh University Press
Woodhouse, D., *Ministers and Parliament* (1994) Clarendon Press
Wraith, R. and Hutcheson, P., *Administrative Tribunals* (1973)
Wraith, R. and Lamb, G., *Public Inquiries as an Instrument of Government* (1971) Allen and Unwin

Zander, M., *The Law-Making Process* (4th ed., 1994) Butterworths
Zifcak, S., *New Managerialism: Administrative reform in Whitehall and Canberra* (1994) Open University Press

ARTICLES

Alder, J., "Hunting the Chimera — the End of O'Reilly v. Mackman" (1993) 13 L.S.

Boyle, A.E., "Administrative Justice, Judicial Review and the Right to a Fair Hearing under the European Convention on Human Rights" [1984] P.L. 89

Collar, N., "Judicial Review: The Significance of an Alternative Remedy", (1991) 36 J.L.S.S. 299
Craig, P.P. "The Common Law, Reasons and Administrative Justice" [1994] 53 C.L.J. 282

Dickinson, I.S. "Still no Interdicts against the Crown", 1994 S.L.T. (News) 217
Drewry, G. and Harlow, C. "A Cutting Edge? The Parliamentary Commissioner and MPs" [1990] 53 M.L.R. 745

Feldman, D., "Presumption against Retrospective Legislation" (1995) 111 L.Q.R. 33

Finnie, W., "Triangles as Touchstones of Review", 1993 S.L.T. (News) 51

Foulkes, D., "The Council on Tribunals: visits policy and practice" [1994] P.L. 564

Freedland, M., "Civil Service (Management Functions) Act 1992" (1994) 23 I.L.J. 32

Freedland, M., "Government by Contract and Public Law" [1994] P.L. 86

Freedland, M., "Rule against delegation and the Carltona doctrine in an agency context" [1996] P.L. 19

Gamble, A., "Privatisation, Thatcherisms and the British State" (1989) 16 J. Law of Soc. 1

Ganz, G., "Matrix Churchill and public interest immunity" [1993] 56 M.L.R. 564

Genn, H. "Tribunals and Informal Justice" [1993] 56 M.L.R. 393

Giddings, P. "Select Committees and Parliamentary Scrutiny: Plus ca change?", 47 Parl. Aff. 669

Gordon, R and Ward, I., "The Billowing Fog" (1996) 146 N.L.J. 1663

Gray, A. and Jenkins, W. with Flynn, A. and Rutherford, B. "The Management of Change in Whitehall: the Experience of the FMI" [1991] 69 Pub. Admin. 41

Hadfield, B. and Weaver, E., "Trends in Judicial Review in Northern Ireland", [1993] P.L. 12

Harden, I., White, F. and Hollingsworth, F. "Value for Money and Administrative Law" [1996] P.L. 661

Hare, I. "Due Process — Thorp, Sellafield and Greenpeace" [1995] 54 C.L.J. 1

Hare, I "Military bases and Military Biases" [1996] 55 C.L.J. 179

Hayhurst, J. and Wallington, P., "Parliamentary Scrutiny of Delegated Legislation" [1988] P.L. 547

Hazell, R., "Freedom of Information in Australia, Canada and New Zealand" [1989] 67 Pub. Admin. 189

Hazell, R., "Freedom of Information: Implications for the Ombudsman" [1995] 73 Pub. Admin. 264

Himsworth, C.M.G., "Public Employment, the Supervisory Jurisdiction and Points West", 1992 S.L.T. (News) 257

Himsworth, C.M.G., "Delegated Powers Scrutiny Committee" [1995] P.L. 34

Himsworth, C.M.G., "Further West? More Geometry of Judicial Review", 1995 S.L.T. (News)127

Hood, C., "A Public Management for All Seasons ?" [1991] 69 Pub. Admin. 3

Hunt, D., "Worthwhile Bodies" 48 Parl. Aff. 192

Jabbari, D., "Critical Theory in Administrative Law" (1994) 4 O.J.L.S. 189
Jowett, M., "UK Tribunals — Observations of a Legal Chairman" 17 I.L.P. 4
Junor, G., "Judicial Review and the Intricacies of the Tripartite Relationship" (1995) 226 SCOLAG

Leigh, I., "The Prerogative, Legislative Power and the Democratic Deficit: the Fire Brigade Union Case", 3 Web Journal of Current Legal Issues — http:/// webjcli.ncl.ac.uk
Leopold, P., "Letters to and from 'Next Steps' Agency Chief Executives" [1994] P.L. 214
Lester of Herne Hill (Lord), "The Impact of Human Rights Law", 1996 J.R. 21
LeSueur, A. and Sunkin, M., "Applications for Judicial Review: The Requirement of Leave" [1992] P.L. 102
Lewis, N., "The Citizen's Charter and Next Steps: A New Way of Governing?" 1993 Political Quarterly 316

McHarg, A., "The Competition and Services (Utilities) Act 1992: Utility Regulation and the Charter" [1992] P.L. 385
McNeill, "The Passing of the Scottish Privy Council" 1965 J.R. 263
McPherson, G.I., "Judicial Review in Employment" (1992) 37 O.L.S.S. 314
McShane, F., "Crown Privilege in Scotland — Demerits of Disharmony", J.R., Vol. 3, 256, Vol.4, 41
Marsh, D., "The Extent and Depth of Judicial Review decisions of PCA" [1994] P.L. 347
Marshall, G., "The Evolving Practice of Parliamentary Accountability: Writing down the Rules" 44 Parl. Aff. 460
Mays, R., "Twenty-five Years of the Ombudsman" (1992) 195 SCOLAG 185
Morris, P., "The Revenue Adjudicator — the First Two Years" [1996] P.L. 309
Mowbray, A., "A Right to Official Advice: The Parliamentary Commissioner's Perspective" [1990] P.L. 68
Munro, C.R., "The Duty to give Reasons for Decisions", 1995 S.L.T. (News) 5

Oliver, D. "Parliament, Ministers and the Law" 47 Parl. Aff. 630

Palmer, S., "Tightening Secrecy Law: the Official Secrets Act 1989" [1990] P.L.
Partington, M., "The Future of Tribunals", May 1993 Legal Action 9
Preston, M., "Openness and the EU Institutions" (1996) 4 *European Access*

Prosser, T., "Poverty, Ideology and Legality: Supplementary Benefit Appeal tribunals and their predecessors", 1977 *British Journal of Law and Society* 44

Prosser, T., "Privatisation, Regulation and Public Services", 1994 J.R. 3

Rawlings, R., "The MPs Complaints Service" [1990] 53 M.L.R. 22 and 149

Raz, J., "The Rule of Law and its Virtue" (1977) 93 L.Q.R. 195

Reid, C.T., "An Expectation of Explanation" 1990 S.L.T. (News) 133

Richards, S. and Rodrigues, J., "Strategies for Management in the Civil Service: Change of Direction", April–June 1993 *Public Money and Management* 33

Ridley, F., "Reinventing British Government", 48 Parl. Aff. 387

Samuels, A., "Codes of Practice and Legislation" [1986] S.L.R. 29

Schick, A., "Budgeting for results: Adaptation to fiscal stress in industrial democracies", 50 *Public Administration Review* 26

Scott, R., "Procedures at Inquiries — the Duty to be Fair" (1995) 111 L.Q.R. 596

Scott, R., "The Use of Public interest immunity claims in criminal cases", Vol. 3 Web Journal of Current Legal Issues, Part 1

Singh, R., "Legitimate Expectation in 1996. Where Now?", 1996 J.R. 17

Smith, A., "Public interest immunity and Sensitive Material" [1993] 52 C.L.S. 357

Stewart, R. B., "Reformation of American Administrative Law", 88 *Harvard Law Review* 1669

Sunkin, M., Bridges, L. and Meszaros, G. "Trends in Judicial Review" [1993] P.L. 443

Sunkin, M. "What is Happening to Applications for Judicial Review?" [1987] 50 M.L.R. 432

Tant, A. "The Campaign for Freedom of Information: A Participatory Challenge to Elitist British Government" [1990] 68 Pub. Admin. 477

Teubner, G., "Substantive and Reflexive Elements in Modern Law, Politics and Social Theory" [1984] 47 M.L.R. 603

Tomkins, A., "Public interest immunity after Matrix Churchill" [1993] P.L. 560

Ward, I., "The Anomolous, The Wrong and the Unhappy: UK Administrative Law in a European Perspective" [1994] 45 N.I.L.Q. 46

Wass, D., "Scott and Whitehall" [1996] P.L. 467

Wikeley, N. and Young, R., "The Administration of Benefits in Britain: Adjudication Officers and the influence of Social Security Appeal Tribunals" [1992] P.L. 238

Wilkinson, H., "Complaining to the Ombudsman" (1992) 142 N.L.J. 1348
Williams, D., "Unfettered Ministerial Discretion" [1989] 48 C.L.J. 161
Winetrobe, B., "Governing Scotland (1994)", 39 J.L.S.S. 459
Woodhouse, D., "Ministerial Responsibility in the 1990s: When Do Ministers Resign?", 46 Parl. Aff. 277

Zuckerman, A., "Public Interest Immunity — A matter of Prime Judicial Responsibility" [1994] 57 M.L.R. 703

MISCELLANEOUS

Cameron, G. with Johnston, R., *Personal Injury Litigation in the Scottish Courts; A Descriptive Analysis* (Scottish Office Central Research Unit, 1995)
Civil Service Code: http://www.open.gov.uk/co/cscode.htm, January 15, 1997
Code of Practice on Access to Information: http://www.open.gov.uk/m-of-g/code.htm

Dunpark report: *Report to the Rt. Hon. Lord Emslie, Lord President of the Court of Session, by the Working party on Procedure for Judicial Review of Administrative Action* (1983) HMSO

Efficiency Unit, *Making the Most of Next Steps: the Management of Ministers' Departments and Executive Agencies* (1991) HMSO
Efficiency Unit, *The Government's Guide to Market Testing* (1993) HMSO
Efficiency Unit, *Competing for Quality Policy Review* (1993) HMSO

Government's Response to the Defence Committee's Fourth Report, 1985–86, Cmnd 9916, HMSO
Government reply to Eighth Report of the Treasury and Civil Service Committee (H.C. 494 I) Cm 524, (1988) HMSO
Government, *Response to comments on the Green Paper government.direct*: http://www.open.gov.uk/citu/gdirect/govresp.htm, March 5, 1997

Hall, W. and Weir, S., *EGO-Trip: Extra-governmental organisations and their accountability* (1994), Democratic Audit Paper no. 2, University of Essex
HM Treasury, *Competing for Quality: Buying Better Public Services*, Cm 1730 (1991) HMSO
HM Treasury, *Executive agencies: a guide to setting targets and measuring performance*, Cm 2175 (1992) HMSO
HMSO, *Annual Report of Scottish Legal Services Ombudsman 1992*, Cm 661 (1993) HMSO

HMSO, *Annual Report of Scottish Legal Services Ombudsman 1994*, Cm 377 (1995) HMSO

HMSO, *The Functions of the Council on Tribunals: Special Report* Cmnd 7805 (1980), HMSO

Hogwood, B., *The Uneven Staircase: Measuring up to Next Steps, Strathclyde Papers on Government and Politics*, no.92 (1993) University of Strathclyde

Home Affairs Select Committee, *Third Report: Next Steps* (1990–91) H.C. 177

Home Office, *Reform of Section 2 of the Official Secrets Act 1911*, Cmnd 7285 (1978) HMSO

House of Commons, *Report of the Committee on Administrative Tribunals and Enquiries*, Cmnd 218 (1957)

House of Commons, *First Report of Select Committee on PCA* (1970–71 H.C. 240 (1971)

House of Commons, *Fourth Report of Select Committee on PCA* (1979–80, H.C. 595) (1980)

House of Commons, *Second Report of the Select Committee on PCA: The Implications of the Citizen's Charter for the Work of the PCA*, (1991–92, H.C. 158) (1991)

House of Commons, *First Report of Select Committee on Parliamentary Commissioner for Administration, Vol. I : The Powers, Work and Jurisdiction of the Ombudsman* (1993–94, H.C. 33) (1993)

House of Commons, *Report of Select Committee on PCA, Minutes of Evidence*, (1992–93, H.C. 650i) (1993)

House of Commons, *Fifth Report of Select Committee of PCA* (1993–94, H.C. 619) (1994)

House of Commons, *Annual Report of PCA* (1994, H.C. 307) (1995)

House of Commons, *Sixth Report of PCA, Access to Official Information*, (1995–96, H.C. 593) (1996)

House of Commons, *Report by Lord Clyde of the Inquiry into the removal of children from Orkney in February 1991*, (1991–92, H.C. 195) (1992)

House of Lords Select Committee on the Scrutiny of Delegated Powers, First Report, (1992–93 H.L. Paper 57)

House Report 102–146, 102nd Congress, 1991 http://www.open.gov.uk/ocpa/leaflet.htm January 15, 1997

Jenkins, K. Caines, K. and Jackson, A., *Improving Management in Government: the Next Steps: Report to the Minister* (1988) HMSO

Jordan, G., *Next Steps Agencies: from management by command to management by contract*, Aberdeen Papers in Accountancy, Finance and Management, W6 (1992)

Justice Report *The Citizen and the Administration: Redress of Grievances*, (1961) Justice

Justice *Our Fettered Ombudsman*, (1977) Justice

Justice-All Souls, *Report of the Justice-All Souls Review of Administrative*

Law, Administrative Justice: Some Necessary Reforms (1988)

Law Commission, *Administrative Law: Judicial Review and Statutory Appeals,* (1993, H.C. 669) Law Comm. No. 226

Littlechild, S., *Regulation of British Telecommunications' Profitability,* (1984) Department of Industry

Member of European Parliament considering openness and transparency: http://www.europarl.eu.int/dg7/bonde/en/bonden07.htm 5 February 1997

Michael *Freedom of Information comes to the EU* (1996) 31

National Consumer Council, S*elf Regulation* (1986) National Consumer Council

NHS Executive, *Code of Practice on Openness in the NHS (1995)*

Office of Commissioner for Public Appointments leaflet :

Page, A., "Judicial Review in the Court of Session" in *Socio-Legal research in the Scottish Courts,* Vol. 2, Scottish Office Central Research Unit Papers

Price Waterhouse, *Regulated Industries: UK Framework, Regulatory Brief 2,* (1992) Centre for Study of Regulated Industries

Public Service Committee, *First Special Report: Government response to the Second report from the Committee (Session 1995–96) on Ministerial Accountability and Responsibility,* (1996–97, H.C. 67), The Stationery Office (1996)

Public Service Committee, *Second Report Ministerial Accountability and Responsibility,* (1995–96, H.C. 313–I), (1996) HMSO

HMSO *Reform of Section 2 of the Official Secrets Act 1911, White Paper* (1988) Cm 408

Report and Evidence of the Committee on Section 2 of the Official Secrets Act 1911 (Franks Committee) (1972) Cmnd 5104, HMSO

Report of Committee on Civil Service (Fulton Committee) (1968) Cmnd 3638, HMSO

Report of Committee on Ministers' Powers (Donoughmore Committee) (1932) Cmd 4060, HMSO

Report of the Inquiry into the Export of Defence Equipment and Dual-Use Goods to Iraq and Related Prosecutions, (Scott Inquiry) (1995–96, H.C. 115) HMSO

Report of the Inquiry into the King's Cross Underground Fire, HC 499 (1987–88, H.C. 499) HMSO

Report of the Inquiry into the Shootings at Dunblane Primary School on 13 March 1996 (Cullen Report)(1996) Cm 3386, HMSO

Report of the Joint Committee on Delegated Legislation, (1971–72, H.L. 184, H.C. 475)

Report of the Royal Commission on Tribunals of Inquiry (the Salmon Report), Cmnd 3121, 1966

Report of the Wilson Committee (1981) Modern Public Records, Cmnd 8204, HMSO

Report on Non-Departmental Public Bodies (1980) Cmnd 7797, HMSO

Scottish Law Commission, *27th Annual Report,* 1992 S.L.C. No. 139

Scottish Law Commission, *Memorandum no. 14. Remedies in Administrative Law* (1971)

Swedish Government, *Swedish Working Document concerning Access to documents in the European Institutions*, European Access, No. 4 August, page 12

The Treasury, Solicitors Department, *Judge over your Shoulder: Judicial Review: Balancing the Scales* (1994) Cabinet Office Development Division

Treasury, *Government Accounting* (1989) HMSO

Treasury and Civil Service Committee, *Seventh Report: Civil servants and Ministers: Duties and Responsibilities*, (1985–86, H.C. 92) (1986) HMSO

Treasury and Civil Service Committee, *Seventh Report: Next Steps Initiative*, (1990–91, H.C. 496) (1991) HMSO

Treasury and Civil Service Select Committee, *Fifth Report*, (1993–94, H.C. 27) (1993) HMSO

Treasury and Civil Service Select Committee, *Sixth Report: The Role of the Civil Service, Interim Report*, (1992–93, H.C. 390) (1993)

Waldegrave, W., *Speech to the Institute of Directors*, (1992) Office of Public Service and Science Press Release, 18/92

Woolf (Lord), *Access to Justice — Draft Civil Proceedings Rules*, HMSO,

Woolf (Lord), Lord Chancellor's Department. Access to Justice — Final Report, HMSO

INDEX

Franks Report 8.10–12
judicial functions 2.07
law reports 8.20
one-person tribunals 8.06
reasons for existence 8.02
status 8.07
Twyford Down case, *locus standi* 13.26

ultra vires **doctrine**
application to statutory bodies and
government departments 10.16
distinction between merits and legality
of decisions 10.17–19
judicial review 10.12–25
meaning 10.12
principles of good administration 10.13
scope 10.13–16
United States
access to information 6.15, 6.18, 6.31,
6.38, 6.39
appeal machinery 6.41
constitution 2.04
Espionage Act 6.37
executive orders 6.37
Privacy Act 6.36
universities
fair proceedings, supply of information
11.44
judicial control 9.38–39
procedural propriety 11.07
refusal of discretionary grants, right to
know reasons 11.61
unlawful detention, damages 15.31

valuation
method of challenge 9.23, 9.24
rights of appeal
notices 11.03
time-limits 11.06

valuation appeal committees, judicial
review, unreasonable procedure
10.59
Valuation Appeal Tribunal, status 8.07
vicarious liability of public authorities
15.06, 15.11–32
breach of statutory duties 15.21–26
duty of care *see* **duty of care**
misfeasance in public office 15.28–32
negligence 15.12–16
negligent mis-statements 15.27
prison service 4.75
procurator fiscal, actings of
investigation officers 15.38

Waldegrave, William 3.15, 3.12n21,
4.48, 4.85n13
war crimes 2.18
water authorities, powers 10.33
welfare state 1.02
philosophical basis 1.03
West, Fred 3.14
Westland Affair 3.17, 3.21, 4.18,
4.19n39
whistle blowing, public interest 6.12
Whitemoor Prison, break-out 3.14,
4.50n22
Widdicombe, Ann 3.14n27
Wilson Committee 6.08
Wireless Telegraphy Tribunal 8.09
words and phrases
aggrieved persons 8.38, 13.27
civil proceedings 15.42, 15.47
exceptional circumstances 9.23
maladministration 7.18–20
point of law 8.25
reasonable cause 3.22
tort 15.35
Wright, Peter 6.10